The Raven Chronicles
In Our Own Words

Stories by Forward Air Controllers
From the Secret War in Laos

Editors John H. Fuller and Helen Murphy

Copyright

ISBN 978-0-692-56612-1

Published by the Chronicles Project, Inc.

Cover: Raven Craig Morrison returning to Long Tieng
Photograph by Raven Jerry Greven
Cover Design by Helen Murphy
Back Cover Design by John Fuller

"The Raven forward air controllers were one of the success stories of the war. They built a legend of efficiency and daring in their control of RLAF and USAF strikes in support of Laotian ground units. Additionally, they helped solidify the backing of the Lao Government by sometimes skeptical natives."

THE AIR FORCE IN SOUTHEAST ASIA
FAC OPERATIONS, 1965-1970
Office of Air Force History, May 1975

"The Raven FACs at Long Tieng are nothing but a ragged band of Mexican bandits."

Comment attributed to:
Major General Robert L. Petit,
Deputy Commander Seventh Air Force/Thirteenth Air Force, December 1969

A <u>lot</u> of details about this operation were never made clear to me, but then I was but a lowly lieutenant. There was never anything resembling a formal orientation briefing. Nobody ever showed me "THE BIG PICTURE" and nobody ever introduced me to "THE REGULAR CREW CHIEF."

1st Lt. Bob McCollough, Butterfly 44

It was exciting…. listening to three radios at the same time, four sets of fighters overhead all running out of fuel, troops on the ground crying for help and confused as to where the enemy is located, and the distraction of ground fire aimed at putting you out of commission.

Captain Art Cornelius, Raven 48

A short vesper, quietly uttered each evening after completion of my final Intel debrief of the day… "I came home to supper tonight. My enemy did not." That's how you can tell if you had a good day at the war.

Major Chuck Hines, Raven 20

The Hmong had fought for years just to be left in peace, and by the time I was there they had lost all their brave young men resisting the most brutal of invaders. As a Raven you felt you could really make a difference with the weapons we could bring to bear. And it is heartbreaking to realize that we never had a chance in hell of success.

1st Lt. Smoky Greene, Raven 42

Contents

The Raven Chronicles

Raven FACs - USAF History DECLASSIFIED

Political Foundations: A Very Brief History by Jerry Klingaman

Section One
The Combat Controllers "First There"

Section Two
MR I Luang Prabang The Royal Capital

Section Three
MR II Long Tieng General Vang Pao's War

Section Four
MR III, IV, V Savannakhet, Pakse, Vientiane War in the South

Foreword

My Raven friend, John Fuller, asked if I would like to write the foreword to this book and I jumped at the opportunity. I spent a total of 6 ½ years in Laos with Air America and Continental Air Services, most of that time flying and surviving over the same terrain and in the same weather as the Ravens. In those days we monitored each other's activities routinely and we relied on each other as fellow aviators in a very hostile environment.

I first became aware of U.S. air operations in Laos during the summer of 1961 while stationed in Fairbanks, Alaska as a smokejumper. Several friends got jobs as "kickers," flying as crewmembers with Air America. I later found out they were rigging specialty loads for airdrops, the only method for resupplying CIA supported forces in remote areas of the country. I tucked the name Air America into my memory bank. I applied for one of those jobs, and, in January 1964, being "young, broke and invincible," off I went to Laos to seek fame and fortune. My ultimate goal was to be a pilot and figured if I could get my foot in the door, I would wrangle a pilot job, but that was not to be. I had over 700 hours, commercial and instrument tickets, but that didn't cut it with the Chief Pilot.

With no chance of moving into the pilot ranks, I headed to New Zealand where I landed my first flying job as a crop duster. I returned to Oregon and flew a season as a fire recon pilot, obtained my Air Transport Pilot rating and flew for the Bureau of Land Management in Fairbanks as a bush pilot in the summer of 1966.

Air America contacted me and offered me a pilot position. I quickly accepted and reported to Saigon in September, 1966, and started flying for them as a Caribou co-pilot for several months, and then transferred to Vientiane. After sitting in the right seat for 18 months, I decided to move across the ramp and was hired by Continental Air Services, which was a better fit for me, and I quickly upgraded to the left seat.

At that time the United States Air Force (USAF) was using combat controllers to direct the increasing number of U.S. Navy and Air Force airstrikes in-country. I knew about these Butterfly forward air guides but never flew with them. I did, however, know Continental Pilatus Porter pilots who had flown with them and had formed a special bond. They jerry-rigged equipment and tactics successfully to support an ever-increasing number of airstrikes around the country.

Later, after transferring to the Porter, I started seeing Raven forward air controllers at different Lima Sites around the country. They had replaced the Butterflies in 1967. My first direct support to the Ravens was in 1968, while flying out of Savannakhet, Laos. The Raven intel officer, Tom Lee, came to air ops and requested a flight to the east as they had just received a message that Raven 30, Hoss McBride, might have gone down due to enemy fire. We immediately launched and we soon spotted Hoss's O-1 in the river, near the shore, with no sign of life. Hoss and his backseater were killed in the crash. I remember seeing Hoss in the club prior to this. He was a bit older than the rest of the Ravens, wore his customary "bib overalls" and projected his "good old boy, Southern charm"—another character in the Raven ranks. Hoss was the fourth Raven to be killed in action; sadly, there would be more to follow.

One incident with the Ravens, near the northwest edge of the Plaine des Jarres (PDJ), was not unusual for Continental and Air America pilots. I was attempting to do an aerial resupply drop to a Hmong outpost, the NVA (North Vietnamese Army) were lobbing mortars into the outpost in an attempt to hit me as I was overhead. I had enough of the nonsense so I called a Raven. Within minutes, a Raven arrived with Hmong-flown T-28s and circled overhead as I made my air drops. No mortars came in. I guess you could say, a Raven got my "chestnuts" out of the fire on that one.

I met Lieutenant Fuller at Pakse Site 38, a small dirt airstrip on the Bolavens Plateau in southern Laos. He had been dropped off by a USAF OV-10 that was flying a local mission with a Lao backseater and then going on to Udorn, Royal Thai Airbase. John was on his way to his Raven assignment; we flew a local flight, then he moved on to Long Tieng, Lima Site 20 Alternate. Sometime later, I would see "Mr. Fuller" now and again at LS-20A and we would chat. After another month went by, I didn't see him and asked where he was. Seems John had been shot down over the PDJ in a T-28 and bailed out. Fortunately, he was picked up by an Air America helicopter, but was shipped home due to his injuries. It wasn't until 40 years later that we met again.

The Air America helicopter pilot guys hung it out all the time and when the "MAY DAY" call came in from a downed American pilot, they would drop whatever they were doing and go immediately to the rescue. A number of the rescues described herein were by these pilots. They were always nearby, they were the first rescue asset contacted by the Ravens, and could get in and out before the bad guys got their act together. The Ravens knew better than anyone that time was of the essence and a few minutes' delay could cost the downed airman his life or capture.

I flew on several search and rescue missions, some described in the following collection of stories. On my missions, however, we sadly never found the missing Ravens. It's been my privilege to have known a number of them during the war, and to this day I remain in contact with some of those who made it home. In my opinion, Ravens are the best of the best, they were an elite group of USAF pilots that flew in very dangerous conditions. Many, however, paid the ultimate price in what has been called the Secret War.

Lee Gossett

Editor's Note: *Lee has had a long career in civilian aviation. He has flown over 70 types of aircraft, for over 60 years, for a wide variety of customers, including the US intelligence community. He was inducted into the Oregon Aviation Hall of Honor in 2011 and remains an active flyer in his Piper Super Cub. He can be found exploring the backwoods of Idaho every summer with his wife Mary.*

Preface

This book introduces new personal stories by Ravens, United States Air Force (USAF) forward air controllers who lived in Laos and flew secret combat missions during the American war in Southeast Asia. They are first-person accounts, in the participants' own words.

The seminal book on this subject is *The Ravens - The Men Who Flew in America's Secret War in Laos* by Christopher Robbins, published in 1987. Robbins solicited inputs from every Raven and provided context, a running account, and an epilogue for what was called the Steve Canyon Program. Not all Ravens responded, and many responses could not be included. His account, however, is highly respected by those of us who were there. The book is not a perfect history— few are—but it is still the best starting point for anyone interested in this unique aspect of combat operations in Southeast Asia.

Since that first book, much has happened. Some Ravens have written books and articles about their experiences. Information has been declassified. Professional authors have prepared excellent accounts of the war, many of which include aspects of Raven operations.

Craig Duehring and Ed Gunter, Ravens who have been active in the Edgar Allen Poe Literary Society since we all came home, observed that there were still stories out there that should be told before any more Ravens "flew west." They put out a call to all Ravens, and we had more than 25 respond with contributions to this book.

The **INTRODUCTION** contains a report, initially classified by the United States Air Force, giving an "official version" of how the Raven program came to be, and how it functioned. The real world, as described by these writers, wasn't nearly as neat and tidy. In addition, "Political Foundations: A Very Brief History" was prepared by Jerry Klingaman, an Air Operations Center commander and a Raven. It provides orientation on what, to most Westerners, was a very disorienting government and culture, especially to those of us who fought there. Historical information is also embedded throughout the book, in other chapters, by other writers.

SECTION ONE, COMBAT CONTROLLERS, contains stories by the men who preceded the Ravens into Laos, starting in 1965. "First There" was the motto of the Air Commando combat controllers. USAF combat controllers continue a tradition of quiet excellence to this day. I have been privileged to work with them in many settings.

SECTIONS TWO, THREE, AND FOUR are arranged geographically, and then chronologically within the section. While this provides some structure to the narrative, the reader should be aware that many Ravens moved to different Military Regions (MR) during their tours. Call signs can be confusing. They were assigned to individuals, but may have been changed based on primary operating location. Beginning in 1970, the first digit designated the Military Region. For example, in Military Region 1, Luang Prabang, Ravens call signs began with 1; in MR 2, Long Tieng, Ravens call signs began with 2, etc. Some stories describe the same incidents, but from the writers' own perspectives, in their own words. There are differences. *Caveat emptor.*

Mary Browning, Senior Technical Editor, retired from Microsoft, significantly improved readability by suggesting edits for all writers to meet best practices for punctuation, capitalization, and grammar without affecting the writers' content, style, or voice. Her husband, Dural (Dave) Browning, LCDR, USN (Ret.), former Technical Programmer/Writer and Documentation Manager at Microsoft, assisted Mary by reviewing the edited material and providing comments and suggestions.

Helen Murphy, Co-Editor, is founder and director of the T-28 Trojan Foundation along with maintaining its excellent associated website. She has worked with other writers and aided immeasurably in the development and production of this book.

The profits from this book go to a nonprofit, 501(c)(3) organization, the Chronicles Project, Inc., formed to manage publication and distribution of funds. All profits go to charities designated by the writers and editors. The primary recipient, the Edgar Allen Poe Literary Society Scholarship Fund, assists families of those we fought with in Laos.

A large collection of related contemporaneous interviews, combat footage, declassified reports and other related documents may be found at: theravenchronicles.com.

John H Fuller
Editor
Col. (Ret.), USAF, Raven 28

Introduction

Raven FACs - USAF History DECLASSIFIED

THE AIR FORCE IN SOUTHEAST ASIA

FAC OPERATIONS

1965 - 1970

by

Lt. Col. Ralph A. Rowley

OFFICE OF AIR FORCE HISTORY

May 1975

The Raven FAC Program in Laos

(S) (U) In 1966 Ambassador Sullivan told the State Department he needed more people to assist in the Lao Government's war against the communist Pathet Lao and North Vietnamese. The United States, however, didn't want to draw attention by formally adding more advisors to the U.S. Embassy in Laos. Consequently, JCS Project 404 became the instrument in early 1966 for adding 117 officer and enlisted spaces to Army/Air Force Attache staffs in Vientiane. They were assigned for administration to the Deputy Chief, Joint United States Military Advisory Group (JUSMAG), Thailand, with duty stations in Laos. Personnel filling the extra 42 USAF slots performed operational, intelligence, and administrative duties. Three forward air controllers* assisted Butterfly** FAC teams in controlling airstrikes for Laotian ground forces.[78]

(S)(U) Borrowing aircraft wherever they could, the three controller (using call sign Butterfly) commenced flying cover for Lao forces in Barrel Roll and Steel Tiger. By December 1966 they had the go-ahead to put radios and marker rocket tubes in a Royal Laotian Air Force (RLAF) O-1. This plane, flying out of the airfield at Savannakhet, supported special Lao Army operations.

> * Officers occupied three FAC positions on 90-day TDY tours.
> ** The Butterfly call sign identified different but related FAC activities—ALO/FAC teams, intelligence officers flying recce out of the Air Attache office, and Cricket controllers in Barrel Roll (Enlisted forward air guides were phased out in the spring of 1967).

A little later, the controllers secured two single-engine aircraft on loan through the Air Attache office—a U-6 and a Continental Air Services Helio-Porter.[79]

(S)(U) Three more TDY FAC's were on board as of August 1967. Since the Air Attache office had no position vacancies for them, they were attached to Detachment 1, 606th Air Commando Squadron (later the 56 SOW) at Udorn, Thailand. From there these new arrivals operated covertly in Laos, alongside the three Project 404 controllers.[80]

(S)(U) The use of borrowed aircraft for FAC work proved unsatisfactory. The Air Attache therefore asked Seventh/Thirteenth Air Force to furnish unmarked O-1E/F's. switched to permanent change of station. First action and hint of an expanded program came in September with the change of the FAC call sign to Raven. Then in October, three aircraft arrived. The number of temporary duty Raven FAC's was boosted to eight in November, and the requested change to PCS status was granted.[81]

Recruiting the Raven FAC's

(S)(U) To qualify for the Raven FAC program, a pilot needed a minimum of 4 months combat duty—at least 60 days of it as a forward air controller or fighter pilot in Southeast Asia. He further required 100 hours as a controller or fighter pilot and no fewer than 750 total flying hours. He also had to have 6 to 8 months left on his SEA duty tour.[82]

(S) The keen interest in the Raven program let highly skilled forward air controllers be picked.* The new FAC, assigned to the 56th Special Operation Wing's Detachment 1 at Udorn, received a rundown on the Raven mission. He was then placed on TDY with the Air Attache office at Vientiane, ostensibly as a member of the U.S, Agency for International Development (USAID). Furnished Embassy identification and a Laotian driver's license, the Raven wore civilian clothes on FAC missions, but took along his military identification card (ID) and cap (with grade insignia).** As a cover story—if he was shot down, he was on a "rescue mission out of Thailand."*[83]

* In South Vietnam the program was known as Steve Canyon.
** The Ravens stored all military uniforms and personal effects at Detachment 1. He kept his ID at the forward operating location when not carrying it during a mission.

===

(S) The Ravens staged out of five forward operating locations, one in each of the five military regions (MR's)—Luang Prabang (MR I), Long Tieng (MR II), Savannakhet (MR III), Pakse (MR IV), and Wattay Airfield at Vientiane (MR V).(See Figure 28).The commander of the air operations center at each location reported to the Air Attache and coordinated operations with his ALO and Daddy Raven- -the senior Raven ALO, stationed at Vientiane.[84]

(S) The quickening tempo at Laotian ground combat imposed greater demands on the Raven forward air controllers.** Their number gradually grew from 12 in November 1968 to 15 in March 1969*** On the other hand, the program had only eight O-1's as of December 1968, due to FAC aircraft demands in other parts of SEA. This impelled Ambassador Sullivan to point out to CINCPAC that 12 working O-1's were necessary, plus another 4 to permit proper maintenance and to take care of attrition. Thus, in a few weeks, the Ravens received 6 aircraft which expanded the total O-1 force to 14.[85]

(S) At first the Raven program put no mechanics in the field. All aircraft went back to Udorn for periodic maintenance checks. Since on-the-spot repairs fell to the pilots or untrained Lao mechanics, maintenance malfunctions soared. Following a record of 14 engine failures during September-December 1968, all O-1s rotated to Udorn to have their fuel tanks removed and cleaned, (Some had gone 18 years without it.) Mud and sludge from the dirt airfields encrusted most tanks. Moreover, the O-1's higher power setting—a must for takeoff from short strips- -helped shorten engine life to 400 hours.[86] In December the Embassy requested that TDY mechanics (one for each two O-1's) be brought in and by May 1968 they were on the job. Air America mechanic's had bridged the gap between September and May. [87]

* Cover stories ceased in October 1970, after the United States admitted there were military personnel at the Embassy in Laos.
** The bulk of the Ravens worked out of Long Tieng (MR II) and supported Gen. Vang Pao's Meo tribesman in and around the strategic Plain of Jars.
*** There was never a dearth of applications.Raven duty appealed to "the young flamboyant officer" willing to take chances to prove his capabilities.[Interview with Lt Col Robert E Drawbaugh, Dir/Ops, Proj 404 (Chief Raven, Jun 1970-Jan 1971), Jun 72].

RAVEN FAC OPERATING LOCATIONS & MILITARY REGIONS OF LAOS

Figure 28 (S)

(S) As the sharper, more frequent Communist thrusts strained Raven support, the Air Attache in July 1969 secured six additional FAC spaces. Plenty of pilots applied for the extra slots but some of them failed to muster the required flying hours. Those coming nearest to doing so were selected. To provide ample aircraft for the bigger Raven force, the 56th SOW chose some FAC's for checkout in the T-28. However, out-and-out necessity governed use of this plane in combat.[88]

Forward Air Guide and Roadwatch Team Support

(S) Dovetailed with Raven air support was the network of native forward air guides and the CAS-supported roadwatch teams. The FAG's trained by Detachment1, 56th SOW * operated around the clock reporting enemy movements by radio to ABCCC's, Raven FAC's, or to Gen. Vang Pao's headquarters.[89]

(S) Lao observers picked for the FAG program were the cream of the crop. All held the grade of company commander or higher and could speak and read English. The new FAG's underwent an intensive 4-day (30-hour) course at Udorn to master the elements of map and compass reading, FAG methods, basic fighter strike tactics, as well as the rudiments of aircraft ordnance and radio procedures. They further took two helicopter rides, flew on two T-28 sorties, and went as passengers on an AC-47 mission to observe air-ground tactics. They also learned how to identify/mark targets and to report bomb damage assessment.[90]

(S) An excellent intelligence source, the forward air guides frequently snapped pictures of enemy targets. Moreover, they approved the targets to be hit. However, due to their working chiefly with Vang Pao's troops in MR II, the FAG's were not as far-ranging as the roadwatch teams.[91]

(S) Controlled American Sources deployed more than 200 10-man roadwatch teams in areas where the members had grown up. Most activity happened to be in southern Laos with Cricket and Raven forward air controllers. Sticking close to roads and trails the roadwatch team could relay findings instantly to the FAC.** If the latter could spot the team's position, airstrikes on nearby targets came within minutes.[92]

> * The first FAG's were trained by Detachment 1 in 1964.
> ** The team could use a "keyed" radio to encode the information.

===

(S)The men of the roadwatch teams were a special breed. Constant operation in enemy-controlled areas where discovery meant certain death steeled their courage and loyalty. Often within earshot of trail users, they moved softly and surely to gather much-needed information.[93]

Raven FAC Procedures

(S) Raven techniques for visual reconnaissance, target marking, and strike control resembled those used by other forward air controllers. Conditions did dictate minor variations. The Raven, for example, carried a Lao or Meo observer in the backseat who knew the operational area and assured the right targets were struck. Again, strike control left little time for VR, so the Raven turned to the roadwatch teams and forward air guides for the latest intelligence.[94]

(S) Each new Raven took orientation/reorientation training (Phases I/II) at Wattay airport outside Vientiane. He got the rest of his training at the forward operating location. It included no fewer than 12 extra hours of supervised flying that stressed home base traffic patterns, takeoffs and landings at forward staging areas, and specifics of known enemy positions and defenses.[95]

(S) The Raven drew his daily assignment the day before or early on the day of the mission. After preflight briefing, he went over current situation maps and studied the latest ABCCC log. Airborne usually by 0600, the controller contacted friendly ground troops for fresh information. He touched down at the forward staging area to pick up his Lao/Meo observer who furnished him intelligence gleaned from FAG's and roadwatch teams. The Raven and observer were sometimes briefed by the staging area commander before continuing on their way.*[96]

(S) To enhance rescue chances should a Raven be downed, flight following was mandatory on all missions.** After takeoff from home base, the Raven checked in with the ABCC and gave

> * At times the observer boarded the aircraft at home base (the FOL). If so the Raven stopped at the staffing area for a briefing.
> ** The Command Operations Center in South Vietnam also kept track of each Raven's position.

===

point of departure and time, intended working area, and radio frequencies. From then on, he contacted the ABCCC every 20 minutes , each time he changed operating areas, or when going in or out of an airfield. If he had to land at an alternate airstrip he called in an explained. The missing of a single call triggered search procedures.[97]

(S) In November 1969, 11 of the 21 Ravens in Laos worked in MR II, engaged mostly in close air support of Vang Pao's troops. These FACs consequently developed a close rapport with the General, dining with him and receiving first hand intelligence. He and his roadwatch teams similarly briefed the Meo/Lao observers. A general coordination meeting to place each evening at 2030.[98]

(S) Raven operations varied slightly in other regions. In MR I, the FAC's kept busy controlling USAF/RFAF strikes against enemy moving towards the Plain of Jars. The controllers and FAG's of MR III supported the Lao Army, using tac air as an extension of artillery. MR IV's Ravens handled mostly interdiction—their instructions flowing from CAS/USAF intelligence sources. Only the Chief Raven at Vientiane operated in MR V, the activity there being more political than military.[99]

(S) Many times the FAC's flew two sorties a day. When without specific instructions, they were free to carry out VR in their areas. If "reconning" for Vang Pao, they commonly worked a box area whose size varied with the deployment of the friendlies and the extant of the operation.[100] Search procedures were a lot like those of the Cricket FAC's in the Laotian panhandle. The Ravens never flew the same path twice and stuck closely to set strike guidelines.

(S) A mission now and then demanded four crewmembers—the contract pilot of a larger aircraft, Raven FAC, Thai translator, and Lao observer. Strike instructions funneled from the translator and observer to the RLAF fighter pilot.[101]

Turning the Raven Program Over to the Lao FAC's

(S) During 1970 the number of Raven controller spaces stood at 24.* Qualifications needed to be relaxed, however, in light of inexperienced volunteers coming to Southeast Asia. It also grew harder to get seasoned O-1 FAC's because of the Bird Dog's withdrawal from the USAF SEA inventory. Hence, training courses were set up to qualify the volunteers as O-1 Raven forward air controllers.[102]

(S) The RLAF FAC training program got underway in November 1971 with two students. They and later volunteers were lead qualified T-28 pilots having over 3,000 combat flying hours. With six RLAF controllers doing Raven duty by May 1971, the USAF program began to foldup.[103]

(S) The Raven forward air controllers were one of the success stories of the war. They built a legend of efficiency and daring in their control of RLAF and USAF strikes in support of Laotian ground units. Additionally, they helped solidify the backing of the Lao Government by sometimes skeptical natives.

* The number peaked at 27 in 1971 then dwindled.

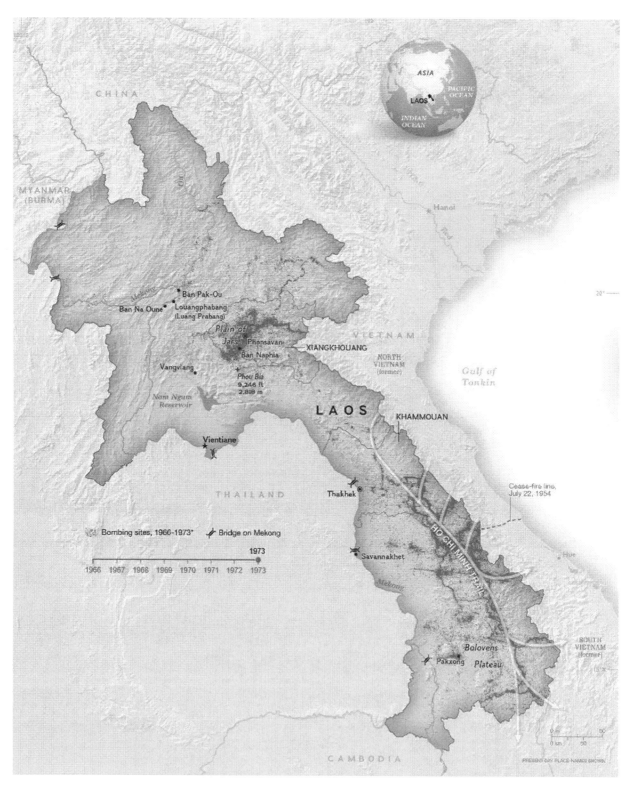

Interactive Map and National Geographic article: "Laos Finds New Life After Bombs"
http://ngm.nationalgeographic.com/2015/08/laos/bombs-map

Political Foundations: A Very Brief History

By Jerry Klingaman
AOC Commander, Vientiane, Sep 1966 – Feb 1967
AOC Commander/ Raven 50, Pakse, Oct 1968 – Apr 1969

What follows here is an irresponsibly-abbreviated distillation of the historical literature on the conflict in Laos. In fact, there is a book by that name (*Conflict in Laos* by Arthur J. Dommen). Most of the following is based on ancient lecture notes, which are, in turn, based on books like *Conflict in Laos*. There are, of course, other books on the history of Laos, and the reader is encouraged to look to them for more detailed guidance. So, very briefly:

As an overview, two major, interlocking agendas underpin this incredibly complex conflict. First, there was a resistance movement within Laos that began during the second phase of French colonialism following the Second World War. Second, there was ever-increasing North Vietnamese support of that resistance, which was eventually linked to their plans to reunify Viet Nam and politically dominate Indochina. Initially, the Viet Minh organized, within Laos, a Vietnamese resistance against the French. The anti-French resistance later brought in Lao insurgents, and eventually turned against the Royal Lao Government (RLG) and its military. The Lao resistance operated under the title *Neo Lao Hak Sat*; i.e., the Pathet Lao (PL).

Vietnamese forces invaded Laos in 1953 and defeated the French in 1954. This is the point where events established the political context for covert actions by the United States in Laos. To stabilize the situation, and I suspect to prevent a Vietnamese occupation of the country, certain Geneva Accords were drawn up in 1954 establishing the neutrality of Laos. So far, so good (at least if you're not French), but the Pathet Lao--in violation of the Accords--remained a separate force, both politically and militarily.

Coalition efforts to unify the Royalist and Communist factions failed, and in 1957, the two parties reengaged in civil war. The Viet Minh provided material and advisory support to the Pathet Lao, and the United States provided the Forces Army Royale (FAR) with equipment and advisory personnel in civilian clothes. This may have been more of an attempt to reduce our profile and visibility in Laos than to actually go covert, but one can see a tendency to go in this direction that far back.

As if this wasn't complicated enough, there was also a Neutralist faction in Laos led by a General Kong Lee, but he joined the Pathet Lao after an unsuccessful coup attempt against the Royal Lao Government (RLG) in 1959. That association eventually came apart on the Plain of Jars (PDJ) a few years later, but that is another story and beyond the scope of this paper.

Geneva Accords were again drawn up in 1962 reaffirming the neutrality of Laos. These accords also required the removal of all foreign forces from Laos with the exception of a very small French training contingent, presumably to prevent the RLG from becoming completely impotent militarily. The Accords also established a tripartite government in Vientiane—Royalists, Neutralists, and the Pathet Lao. That was why you could find military personnel of all three factions roaming the streets of Vientiane throughout the war, even though the tripartite government had dissolved earlier.

During my 1966-67 AOC tour at Vientiane, I was told that there was a hands-off policy good out to six kilometers from town. Beyond that, you were fair game. Why six kilometers? Supposedly, it was because a school for the children of international families was located six kilometers out from town. In fact, the school was called "Klick Six." One was probably OK out beyond that for a few kilometers, but who knows how far? Who knew even then? That was bizarre stuff, to say the least.

The Vietnamese ignored the neutrality stipulation and continued moving people and supplies down the Ho Chi Minh trail through eastern Laos. That was crucial to them for a victory in South Viet Nam, so they chose to not see it as a violation of the 1962 Accords. The United States saw it as a clear violation, and this is when our military support to the RLG entered the covert realm. We wanted to continue supporting the rightist faction, but we also wanted plausible deniability. Our initial action in 1962 was to move in with a military aid mission called the Requirements Office (RO). One could say that the RO, a logistics enterprise, was not technically a violation of the Geneva Accords, as it was made up of retired U.S. military personnel, but the intent was obvious and transparent.

I am covering these events in leaps and bounds, but to do otherwise is impossible in this short space. A lot happened between 1962 and 1964, so I am going to summarize, relying greatly on Arthur J. Dommen's book *Conflict in Laos: Keystone of Indochina*:

In 1963, the Coalition Foreign Minister is assassinated, the Pathet Lao move out of Vientiane in a huff, and the tripartite government caves in. As a result, the Prime Minister, Souvanna Phouma, threatens to resign. The rightist military faction stages a coup and arrests the Prime Minister. The coup fails and the Prime Minister regains power through the help of the U.S. Ambassador, who offers all kinds of military assistance. Now, Souvanna Phouma moves even closer to the right.

In 1964, we moved in with vastly increased military assistance and advisory support, and we did it covertly. From all available accounts, 1964 was the year AOC operations began at Wattay. The AOC and the B-Team were created by the CIA and the office of the air attaché (AIRA), Vientiane. The air attaché at that time was Colonel Robert L .F. Tyrrell. The B-Team was created primarily to support General Vang Pao's Hmong army that the Agency had trained and equipped in Military Region 2 (MR 2).

A quick word on my use of the term *Hmong*: During the 1960s we knew both the indigenous and immigrant hill-tribe people of Laos by their specific names; e.g., Miao (or the Thai corruption-- Meo), Yao, Akha, Lisu, Kha, etc. For very controversial, complicated, (and political) reasons, ethnologists have now subsumed the entire ethnic community of these tribal groups under the term *Hmong*. I seriously doubt that tribal groups in the half-wild interior of Laos even know about this.

You may ask why we were at such pains to maintain the appearance of compliance with the Geneva Accords by remaining covert when the North Vietnamese were using the trail for logistics into South Viet Nam and maneuvering thousands of armed personnel around various parts of eastern and northern Laos. What was not transparent at the time, and what few people understand even today, is that Laos was an area of understanding between the United States and Russia; i.e., the United States would not confront Russia with an open violation of the 1962 Geneva Accords, and Russia would not have to intervene in Laos to maintain credibility with Hanoi.

I don't have hard evidence for this understanding between the two countries, but an account of it is given in Arthur Dommen's book, above. Whether the story is true or not, it is likely that we were also loath to press-to-test the Geneva Accords. Another problem was revealing to the American public, and even the Congress, that we were involved in a conflict much bigger than Viet Nam.

Nevertheless, the secrecy attached to our operations in Laos had regretful consequences. We might have made a good case for supporting the RLG against a foreign aggressor, but our "understanding" with Russia precluded it. The secrecy also gave the U.S. Congress cause for saying we were involved in an illegitimate war. Perhaps more significant than anything, the secrecy prevented us from attending scheduled talks with China over Laos. We might have learned, as Ambassador Sullivan learned from discussions with the Chinese after the war, that China would not have intervened if we had moved into Laos overtly in a much bigger way to blunt North Vietnamese aggression. It came out in those same discussions that the Chinese had the same sentiments towards North Viet Nam. That made sense: China did not relish having a powerful North Vietnamese Army on their southern border. I heard Ambassador Sullivan say just that after his tour as U.S. Ambassador to the Philippines.

Whatever options we might have surrendered by operating covertly, winning outright in Laos and ensuring its survival as a non-Communist entity was not a centerpiece of U.S. strategic thinking in Southeast Asia. The main goal was successfully concluding the war in South Viet Nam. The strategy in Laos was to "maintain the status quo without provoking a stiff Chinese response," thus buying time to reach our goal in South Viet Nam. The survival of Laos might have followed from that, but who knows?

We can speculate all we want on what we might have done differently, but there is no escaping the reality that we did not want to widen the war in Laos. Again, the game was maintaining the status quo. After all, we did not know back then what form a "stiff Chinese response" might take, or how we would counter it. Accordingly, covert options on our part were more than merely convenient, and we *did* go to great pains to maintain compliance, even if it was a sham.

That's how some of us wound up in-country with no identification or Geneva Convention cards, wearing Lao flying suits or blue jeans, and trying to hide on U.S. Agency for International Development (USAID) manning rosters. We even had odd code names that were used for radio communications (mine was *Eve*).

There was a mechanism in place to monitor compliance with the Geneva Accords and possibly compromise our identities. An International Control Commission (ICC), composed primarily of representatives from Canada, India, and Poland (in 1966), was in Laos to do the monitoring. They were headquartered in Laos at Vientiane. They had their own aircraft, both helicopters and an ancient civilian round-nose variant of the Boeing B-17. They flew around Laos, taking photographs and making visual observations everywhere they could. The Soviet bloc representatives (Poland) were always looking for ways to expose U.S. violations.

The Pathet Lao (PL) did not allow inspections by the ICC, thus making it easier for the North Vietnamese to operate with PL forces and to use the trail network in eastern Laos. The United States, of course, was subject to constant observation by the ICC, particularly from the air around Vientiane. At the same time, we wanted access to the trail for bombing North Vietnamese truck convoys.

With the tripartite government dissolved and the Royalist faction now representing the RLG and shifted to the right, our vastly increased assistance to the military essentially bought their acquiescence (a sanction of sorts) to bomb targets on the trail.

Hopefully, the discussion above will make it easier to understand why we proceeded as we did during Project 404.

Section One

The Combat Controllers "First There"

Chapter 1
Ron Wishart, Eagle Control
Nov 1965 – Apr 1966

This is a brief account of my experience with the 1st Air Commando Wing (ACW) in Laos, and a summary of my career following that assignment.

November 1965 – April 1966

I received a 179-day temporary duty (TDY) assignment to Detachment 6, 1st ACW (Water Pump) at Udorn Royal Thai Air Force Base. Almost all of that time was in Laos where I relieved Capt. Jack Teague, who flew missions with me as a forward air guide for a week. He and I had gone through the Air Traffic Control course together at Keesler AFB. I was introduced to Dean Perrin, a boss at Air America (AA) in Vientiane. Many of my flights were in AA and Continental Air Services, Inc. (CASI) aircraft. I was introduced to "Svede" Svenson and Ken Alnwick (U.S. Air Force Academy '60) at the air attaché (AIRA) office. Col Pettigrew was the air attaché. I stayed at AIRA Ice House 2 when in Vientiane and stored some of my gear there.

We passed through Lima Site (LS) 20A, where I was introduced to Pop Buell, and then proceeded to Na Khang, LS 36. I met Gen. Vang Pao, who was often there for meals, many of which I was invited to. There was a Thai Army unit there and I usually flew in their O-1E, which was still called an L-19 back then. I had written the names Captain Sa-Wad and Lt San and Khan. They may have been the names of the Thai pilots. Air Force Jolly Green Giants rescue choppers were on the other side of the strip much of the time.

I also controlled a lot of missions at Muong Soui, LS 108, on the west side of the Plaine des Jarres (PDJ) where the Neutralists had their headquarters. Most of those missions were from the ground. Gen. Kong Le came to observe some of the missions from the hilltop OP (observation post) that I usually directed from. There were a few uniformed U.S. Army personnel there that I stayed with.

During those six months I flew 63 forward air control (FAC) sorties as a non-pilot forward air guide with the call sign Eagle Control. I flew in the Thai L-19 and Air America or CAS Pilatus Porters and Helio Couriers. I also flew one in an A-1E with a USAF pilot over the PDJ as I guided his flight on a bombing mission. I also flew 19 visual recce sorties, including three search and rescue. I controlled about 120 flights from the air and another 40 flights from the ground for a total of about 600 aircraft sorties. My aircraft was fired at about 20 times and hit three times by small arms fire, but sustained no significant damage. Aircraft that I was controlling reported six hits with no aircraft lost and no pilots wounded that I am aware of. There were almost as many flights that I was in radio contact with but who couldn't arrive on target due to weather or diversion to other targets. Many of my flights came to me because of weather or other diversions from targets in North Vietnam. I controlled mostly USAF flights of F-105s and F-4s from Thailand, but I had almost anything in the inventory including Navy aircraft, A-1Es, and T-28s. Many of the call signs were names of cars.

May 1966 – August 1967

I was with the 1ACW Combat Control Team, England AFB, LA, where the 1st ACW had moved while I was in Laos.

August 1967 – August 1970

I transferred to the U.S. Army. I had expected to return to Laos after 30 days back at the 1st ACW, but the mission was taken over by Ravens. So I put in paperwork to transfer to the Army. It took a year. I went to Ranger School, then to Vietnam with an infantry battalion that formed up at Ft Lewis (McChord AFB), got a Purple Heart (minor wounds from a hand grenade), and came back to Ft Bragg (Pope AFB) in the 82nd Airborne Division. I got out in August 1970.

August 1970 – June 1992

I joined the New Jersey National Guard in infantry units; and then ultimately retired out of the Army Reserve as a lieutenant colonel in 1992.

Other Life Events

I got married in Japan in November 1968, on R&R from South Vietnam, to a stewardess I had met at Ft Lewis. We moved to New Jersey when I left active duty. I worked at the New York Daily News, retired, and we moved to Arlington, Virginia in 2007.

Chapter 2

Bob McCollough, Butterfly 44
Long Tieng, Mar 1966 – Sep 1966

BUTTERFLY MEMOIRS

I graduated from the Air Force Academy in June of 1965. Not being pilot qualified, I had requested, and received, an assignment as a Combat Control Officer with the 1st Air Commando Wing (ACW), then stationed at Hurlburt Field (Eglin AFB Auxiliary Field # 9), Fort Walton Beach, Florida.

After a couple of months of leave, and four months of Air Traffic Control Officer training at Keesler AFB, Mississippi, I joined the Commandos, who had, in the meantime, been moved to England AFB, Louisiana.

[*Note: in the fall of 1965, the 1st Air Commando Wing at Hurlburt was split into two wings. The so-called "operational wing" retained the 1st ACW designation and moved to England AFB, LA; the "training wing" remained at Hurlburt as the 4410th Combat Crew Training Wing.*]

So in December 1966, I became part of the advance party of the 1st Air Commando Wing at England AFB. The place had just been vacated by a tactical fighter wing (F-100s) who were pulled out and shipped to Viet Nam in a unit movement.

[*Note: The fighter jocks and their support troops were mostly all gone. Their wives remained, however, having been granted some months to relocate from base housing. So you had all these super-macho Air Commandos, whose wives were still back in Florida...and you had all those unattended fighter-wing wives, whose husbands were all overseas for the next year...Let me tell you - it was PARTY TIME in the clubs at England Air Force Base. Someone could probably write a book about all that. Maybe they have by now.*]

In March of 1966, with maybe three months of on-the-job training (OJT) as a Combat Control Team Officer under my belt, I received temporary duty (TDY) orders for 179 days, to proceed to the Royal Thai Air Force Base (RTAFB) at Nakhon Phanom (NKP), Thailand, on Operation Lucky Tiger. This operation was to provide an advance party for the establishment of the 606th Air Commando Squadron (later, the 56th Air Commando Wing) at that base in the northwest part of the country. The Air Force must have considered that I had some natural gift for this "advance party" business.

In addition to the 30 or 40 officers and enlisted troops from the 1st ACW, I was accompanied on this TDY by two enlisted combat controllers, Staff Sgt. Jim Stanford and Airman 1st Class Andy Guillet. Jim and I later became Butterfly forward air controllers (FACs). Andy, sadly, became missing in action, as I will mention below.

Operating out of Nakhon Phanom (NKP) when we arrived was the 23rd Tactical Air Support Squadron (TASS), an O-1 outfit who flew FAC missions over Laos and Viet Nam using the call sign "Gombey."

[Note: Nobody there could explain just what a "gombey" was. The dictionary defines it as a word used in Bermuda for a form of local African-American music related to calypso. That seems rather esoteric for an Air Force call sign, but who knows?]

Permission was soon granted for we three CCT guys to fly along as observers with the Gombey's. I never knew whose idea that was. It was probably Jim Stanford who told me about it. Maybe there was a plan all along for us to go north and become Butterflies. If so, nobody bothered to tell the second lieutenant. Nonetheless, we began making these flights, and the experience proved invaluable for Jim and me, because we learned the procedures and techniques for the conduct of FAC missions. We were thus able to immediately become effective when we did go north.

In May of 1966, we lost Andy Guillet and his pilot, Captain Lee Harley, on one of those missions. Their bodies were never recovered, and they remain on the MIA list. After that, we were no longer allowed to fly along with the Gombey's. I think I had accumulated 19 missions with them by then. Shortly after Andy's regrettable loss, the permanent change of station (PCS) Combat Controllers, seven or eight of them, all enlisted men, showed up at NKP. Among them were Staff Sgt. John Webb, Airman 1st Class Donald Carlyle, and Airman 1st Class Ronald Kosh. All of these three became Butterfly FACs after Jim Stanford and I finished our tours in September of 1966.

In June of 1966, I became a first lieutenant, as the phase point for that promotion had shortly before been lowered to 12 months.

In July, I left NKP and travelled north to Laos. There were no written orders. I simply got a phone call, from whom I can't remember, that basically said, "There's an airplane leaving for Udorn this afternoon. Pack your gear and be on it." All my gear amounted to a B-4 bag and a footlocker, so it wasn't hard to do. Nobody bothered to ask me if I wanted to volunteer for what lay ahead, although I would have done so gladly. The Commandos were an all-volunteer outfit, so I guess it was assumed that we had all pre-volunteered for pretty much anything.

At Udorn RTAFB, the 1st ACW had for several years been running Operation Water Pump, the purpose of which was to train Lao and Thai pilots to fly T-28's. I knew of this operation, and had flown there from NKP to visit the Water Pump detachment on several occasions prior to this. When I reported in, I was told to take off my uniform and change into civvies. Lt. Col. "Spider" Ramsey, the Water Pump commanding officer, helped me rip the name tape off of my B-4 bag, and he and I obliterated the name, rank, and serial number on my footlocker with a can of gray spray paint. *[Note: I still have that footlocker with the gray paint on it.]*

I then met up with Tech. Sgt. Charlie Jones, who I knew from the CCT at England AFB, and who was there to escort me to Laos, Vientiane, and then Long Tieng. I had heard that he and Capt. Bob Farmer, both from the 1st ACW CCT, had deployed on Water Pump, but I had had no contact with them, and thus had no idea what they were doing. Charlie and I spent the night partying in the city, and caught a hop to the Laotian capital the next morning.

In Vientiane, we went to the air attaché office at the embassy, where I turned in my Air Force ID card and my Geneva Conventions card, and was issued a card that said I worked for the United States Agency for International Development (USAID). I was also given a Lao driver's license.

Then Charlie and I, and the B-4, and the footlocker, went to the airport and boarded an Air America Caribou that took us to Sam Tong, LS 20. There, we got into a Turbo Porter and made the short hop over the hill to Long Tieng, LS 20A. On this short hop we were accompanied by another passenger, an older guy who seemed either half-drunk or all hung over, and who looked like he'd been sleeping in his clothes. He slept all the way over to 20A, deplaned, and I never saw him again. Charlie informed me that this was the renowned Tony Poe. The name meant nothing to me at the time.

At Long Tieng, we met up with Bob Farmer, and I finally learned what he and Charlie had been up to, and what I would soon be doing as well.

[*Note: In this same time frame, Jim Stanford also went north and became a Butterfly. I don't remember if he went upcountry before me, or after, but we didn't go on the same day. Jim wound up operating out of a number of sites as Butterfly 22, but I only operated out of 20A as Butterfly 44. Lots of times, the pilot and I would spend the entire day landing and taking off from another site, or sites, to control the various fighter flights that would be sent to us during the course of the day, but we always returned to Long Tieng at sundown.*]

I was checked out in the FAC operation by Bob Farmer and Charlie Jones. However, shortly after I was deemed sufficiently oriented, Bob was called down to Vientiane to run the operations center there, and Charlie and I remained to handle the FAC missions.

The established routine was that each day, one of us would go out a-FACing, and the other would remain at the base, and monitor the radio link to Vientiane. For this ground-to-ground link, we used a PRC-47 HF radio, which was a standard piece of CCT gear at the time. A man-portable PRC-41 UHF, another standard CCT radio, was carried by the FAC aircraft, as will be described below, for air-to-air communication with the strike aircraft. Both of these radios were powered by wet-cell batteries. A battery charger was kept in our operations room, and the radio monitor would also tend to the charging of the spare batteries.

After breakfast in the rudimentary mess hall, the FAC du jour would gather up his gear (i.e., weapons, in my case an AR-15 and a .38 caliber pistol), shoulder the 40-pound PRC-41, load into a jeep, and ride down the hill about a quarter mile to the little pierced steel planking (PSP) pad at the north end of the runway. Whichever one of us (Charlie or I) wasn't the FAC that day would drive. There we'd meet the aircraft and pilot who had been detailed to fly the FAC missions that day. These missions were flown in aircraft from Air America and Continental Air Services (CAS), civilian companies under contract to provide aerial delivery services in Laos. Just who they were under contract to was never made clear to me.

[*Note: A lot of details about this operation were never made clear to me, but then I was but a lowly lieutenant. There was never anything resembling a formal orientation briefing. Nobody ever showed me "THE BIG PICTURE," and nobody ever introduced me to "THE REGULAR CREW CHIEF."*]

Many things, I was too dumb to ask about. And many times when I would ask what seemed like a reasonable question, I would get brushed off with some smartass non-answer like:

6

"You don't need to know that."
"What makes you think I'd know that?"
"Who told you to ask me that?"
"Who do you really work for, anyway?"

The CIA guys were particularly bad about that. Charlie and Bob would give me a straight answer, if they knew one, but damned few other folks would. After a short while, I stopped asking. Not that I really cared. I was over there to kill communists and make the world safe for democracy. As long as the airplanes showed up, and the radios worked, and there was ice for the scotch at the end of the day, the rest of it was just details.

But I digress. In the (embarrassingly short) time frame in which I operated, only CAS Pilatus Turbo Porters showed up for the FAC missions. Consequently, those were the only aircraft that I FACed out of. Other Butterflies flew missions, from time to time, in all manner of oddball aircraft, even helicopters, but I was never presented with that opportunity; only Porters, and only from CAS.

When we loaded up the Porter, we'd strap the PRC-41 to the back of the co-pilot's seat, and connect it to an external antenna with a short piece of coaxial cable. The FAC would sit in the right front seat. The pilot, naturally, would sit at the left front. Usually, we would be met at the aircraft by an English-speaking interpreter. When all was in readiness, we'd take off for whatever Lima site was the scene of the day's action.

During my brief tenure, most of the missions were flown out of Ban-Ban. Some were out of Muong Soui, some out of Luang Prabang, some out of other places whose names I can't recall, if indeed I ever knew them. Upon landing, we'd be met by a Laotian soldier who knew where the target was. He would be carrying a walkie-talkie with which to communicate with the ground forces. The mode of operation was for the guy with the walkie-talkie to speak to the ground troops, who would tell him where the bad guys were. He would then feed the info to the interpreter, who would, in turn, tell the FAC. The FAC would then direct the pilot to the target area.

Every day there were two flights of two F-105s, call sign "Bango Whiplash," scheduled for our operation, one in the morning and one in the afternoon. Other flights could be diverted to us by the airborne command post if they became available for whatever reason. Usually these were flights which had been "weathered out" at their primary targets. Sometimes they were A-1s, call sign "Firefly," who flew armed reconnaissance missions. If the Fireflies hadn't been able to find any targets on their own, they were always more than happy to come help us out. The majority of the airstrikes I controlled were by F-105s.

When it was nearly time to meet the strike aircraft, we'd take off, and the Lao guys would show me and the pilot where the target was. Then we would contact the fighters and call in the strike. Controlling airstrikes from a civilian aircraft was challenging, to say the least. We had no way to mark the targets. Civilian aircraft did not carry ordnance. Therefore, we had no white phosphorus rockets. Our civilian pilots were under instructions from their chain of command to not go below 3,000 feet on these missions. From that altitude, smoke grenades burned themselves out before they reached the ground. All we could do was to try to paint a word picture for the fighters, using whatever landmarks and descriptive terminology we could come up with. When the flight leader finally thought he saw what we were taking about, he'd roll in and drop a bomb. That first bomb amounted to a spotting charge. It was rarely very close to the target, but we could make corrections from the smoke plume.

Now it's time for me to talk about all my hairy scary missions. Bummer. There weren't any. Besides dumb luck, there are reasons for that. We didn't go into areas where there was known to be anti-aircraft artillery (AAA). The Plaines des Jarres (PDJ) was full of it. It was serious bad guy country. Consequently, if we needed to get to the other side of the PDJ, we went around. We never overflew the place. Well, okay. One time. Which I will talk about later.

Not that we didn't get shot at. It wasn't unusual for the Lao interpreter to inform me that the friendly troops on the ground were telling us that the enemy were shooting at our airplane. My usual response was, "No shit? Where?" I always looked, but I never saw a muzzle flash. It's hard to hit an aircraft with a shoulder weapon, especially when the airplane is at 3,000 feet. Not that it can't be done. The "golden BB" phenomenon definitely exists. But even if you're well trained, and if you have an understanding of ballistics and windage and lead times, it's damned tough. Judging our adversaries to be deficient in these areas, I didn't worry about it. Maybe I should have, but what does a dumbass lieutenant know? The phrase "fool's paradise" comes to mind.

My most memorable mission was one where we had troops in contact. There was a fortified position on top of a ridge south of the PDJ. It was typical of what we'd see in the area - a cluster of huts surrounded by zig-zag trenches and bunkers. The bad guys were holding the position, and the good guys were trying to capture it. Or maybe recapture it. Those places seemed to change hands regularly. We were able to contact a couple of Fireflies (A-1s) who were looking for a place to put their ordnance. I briefed the Fireflies on the situation, and cleared them for a couple of bomb runs. Then, in concert with the Fireflies and the friendly ground troops, I asked the A-1s to start alternating dry runs with live fire runs. I would tell the friendly troops, through the interpreter, when the Sky Raiders were going to make a dry run, so that they could move up the ridge while the bad guys were keeping their heads down, expecting to take more bombs. Then we'd make another hot run, then more dry runs. In this way, the friendlies were able to work their way up the ridge and eventually, to capture the position. A week or two later, the CIA man at 20A told me that when they finally got into that compound, the friendlies found about a dozen enemy troops killed by the air strikes, and they could hear another estimated 20 or 30 out in the jungle, screaming in pain from their wounds. They wisely didn't go out to check on those guys. I assume the screaming eventually subsided. Of all the air strikes I controlled, maybe 50 or 60, during my two months or so as a Butterfly, that was the only one that I ever got any feedback from.

My most dangerous mission, or maybe the dumbest, happened late one afternoon when we had put several strikes in on a target east of the PDJ, but had no more fighter flights available. We started for home, 20A, which required us to fly around the south edge of the PDJ and then north. We were west of the enemy territory when the airborne command post called and told us there was a flight available, but they had only a limited amount of flying time left. I wanted to put them on the target we had just left, but the only way to get there in time was to fly directly across the PDJ (lots of AAA guns, remember?). I talked it over with the pilot, and we decided to go for it. So I gave the coordinates to the command post and told them to send the fighters. Fortunately, it was a day with a lot of towering cumulus clouds. The pilot took the Porter up to near-oxygen altitude, and we went picking our way from cloud bank to cloud bank across the PDJ. We got there in time to rendezvous with the fighters, and put another load onto the target. So that qualified, in those days, as doing something hairy.

In September of 1966, the 179 days on my original TDY orders ran out. I requested to be extended, because I liked the job and I felt like we were doing some good. Headquarters in Vientiane, and the 606th Air Commando Squadron at NKP, endorsed the request, but HQ 1st Air Commando Wing wouldn't buy off on it. "You should fill this requirement with a PCS resource" was the way they put it. So I went home, and Staff Sgt. John Webb became a Butterfly.

Chapter 3

Bob Farmer, Butterfly 44
Long Tieng, Apr 1966 – Oct 1966

The Origin of Butterfly 44

At the end of April 1966, as a fairly new captain, I was deployed from the 1st Air Commando Wing Combat Control Team, England Air Force Base, Louisiana to Southeast Asia for a six-month tour in support of Operation Waterpump. I was accompanied by MSgt Charlie Jones, also a member of the 1ACW Combat Control Team. We knew that it was Top Secret and that we would be directing air strikes, and we knew it was in Laos. Beyond that, we knew little else.

On arrival in Udorn, at Waterpump Headquarters, we were briefed and given instructions on the clandestine nature of the operation. From there we continued on to the American Embassy in Vientiane, Laos. There we were given an embassy I.D. card and a Lao driver's license before being sent on north to Long Tieng, the classified site known as 20 Alternate, usually abbreviated as 20A. On arrival at Site 20A, we met Captain John Garrity, an Air Force Intelligence Officer who completed our education on the mission.

Captain Garrity was at the time engaged in directing air strikes. In fact, my first mission was an orientation by him which involved watching and listening to him direct an air strike. He left to go south shortly after, and we were on our own with the exception of a Major Peerson, who was a "legal" embassy officer and spent a lot of his time at Alternate, but did not get involved in the operational business of FACing during my time there. We soon fell into a routine of alternating days flying the combat mission with days of HF radio watch, connecting the sites with the embassy Air Attache office (AIRA) in Vientiane.

I have been asked many times where the call sign Butterfly came from. I believe it was possibly devised by John Garrity. When I first arrived, I remember seeing a piece of paper at 20A with different Butterfly call signs for different regions. It seemed that the region I operated in most was labelled 44; others were 22, 33, 99, etc. I used the others a time or two, but decided to stick with 44 to simplify matters and avoid confusion, so it was Butterfly 44 for the rest of my time. The others followed suit, and 44 became the default call sign unless there were two or more FACs up simultaneously.

At this distance of time the following months dissolve into a blur of days. Misty memories remain of flying in Pilatus Porters over ruggedly beautiful mountainous jungle terrain, with waterfalls and river valleys, and makeshift airstrips that were merely small bald patches on the sloping sides of mountains. In spite of the stunning beauty of the forest and mountains, however, you could never quite forget the mortal danger that lurked in all that arboreal beauty.

Patchy memories also include: lunches with Hmong tribesmen in mountain huts, and evening's end on the porch by the hooch at 20A, drinking with whomever happened to be around. Impressions also remain with me of the impact on the skin of the Porter of the pressure wave from an exploding bomb, and the often startling bang of the Porter's leading edge slats dropping to their full extent on landing, often a tense situation in those mountains. Secondary target explosions, the bang of a bullet tearing through aluminum. The friendly smiling Hmong, and a Basi at Vang Pao's "club" drinking White Horse scotch and eating roasted piglet. Some memories linger as fragments that would be incomprehensible alone and out of context. Those will remain untold, but from the aforementioned "blur of days" a few memories remain as stand-alone entities...complete and sharp. Some of these I tell in the following stories.

About two-thirds through my tour, I was called to Vientiane by AIRA because, I was told, the personnel serving there knew nothing of the operations in the north. I objected, but on arrival, I soon understood the problem, and did what I could to make a smoother-running operation. I was upcountry again for about a week to instruct the Army personnel at Site 108 in FAC procedures and techniques, but otherwise worked in the AIRA command post to the end of my tour. It was an entirely different world.

I would like to extend my thanks to comrades in arms and long-time friends, Robert B. McCollough and Jerome Klingaman for their assistance in editing, and helping me to rescue slowly fading memories from an aging brain. Without their help, the retelling of these stories would have been far more difficult.

The Orientation Flight

Upon arrival at Udorn, Thailand, it was suggested to me that Charlie Jones and myself should take an orientation ride in an armed recce flight in the north of Laos, to help us familiarize ourselves with the terrain in which we were going to operate. As best I can remember, it was to be along a route leading into North Viet Nam.

On the day we were scheduled, I was eagerly looking forward to the experience. The aircraft were A1-Es, which added a whiff of WWII flavor to the mission. My pilot, a major whose name I sadly do not remember, was an experienced and no-nonsense professional. Up and over the Thai/ Laos border we went as a flight of two, on a partly cloudy day that promised much excitement---too much as I was soon to discover.

The further north we went, the more cloud cover we encountered, which began to obscure much of the terrain. In any event, I was enjoying every minute of it. Observing the many fires of the tribal inhabitants' slash-and-burn method of farming was an interesting diversion while we swooped and rolled over and through the mountainous terrain. Dropping out of a cloud base, I noticed what I thought was a farmer's fire close to our starboard side. I glanced away, but when I looked again, we were closer, and it suddenly became apparent to me that this was no slash-and-burn site, but the muzzle flashes of a quad .50---four .50 caliber machine guns in a frame, mounted on a carriage--- furiously banging away at us. I quickly grabbed the pilot's arm and when he followed my gaze to the right, his eyes snapped wide open. I then looked back out, and we were close enough that I could make out an individual standing beside the gun wearing one of those iconic pith helmets and seeming to point to the sky in the general direction of our flight. By this time we were rolling hard to the left, and I could just make out our wingman with Charlie on board sliding off to the right.

We were almost immediately back in the safety of the cloud base. The pilot then, half to himself, said, "Should I go back and get that gun?" I knew I should have shouted, "Yes...let's go back and get that SOB," but the words somehow didn't come out. In the next instant, the pilot said "I've got less than thirty days to go, somebody else can get that gun." It was about then that I realized that I had probably been holding my breath.

We were so close, I still don't know why that gun crew didn't nail us. I can only imagine that our speed and sudden appearance out of the cloud gave them little time to traverse the gun and get a bead on us. Or perhaps an overzealous supervisor in a pith helmet had been issuing confusing directions---who knows.

It was a sobering beginning to my tour, and a firm reminder that I was no hero, and this was no flying club.

The CIA Storeroom

One day at 20A, while browsing around in the CIA storage room---a real Aladdin's cave of interesting and unusual items, with everything from crew-served weapons to propaganda leaflets, I came across a large box of U.S. Army bugles in regulation issue pouches. Whatever could these be for, I asked the CIA agents there.

I was told that there was a site far up north that had been the scene of a fierce battle between the French and the Japanese during WWII. There had been many dead, and the bodies had been buried on the site. I remembered the site, and I also remembered the small shrine there that been destroyed by a string of cluster bomb unit (CBU) bomblets.

In the recent past, widespread sickness had occurred among the Hmong living there. The villagers had decided that this sickness was being caused by the restless spirits of the dead soldiers buried on the site. The solution decided upon was to obtain a bugle and have the French version of "Taps" played around the graves. This, the Hmong thought, would put these souls to rest, and put an end to their wandering the night and causing the sickness plaguing the village.

The CIA immediately put in an order for a bugle. When the box arrived, they were a bit perplexed that it contained what must have originally been at least twenty bugles. They just shrugged and ruefully said "typical." One trumpet was taken to the site, and the bugle call duly played. I don't remember if the desired result occurred, but as I had played trumpet in high school, I took one back to my room in our building. I still have it, and can still play it.

Also during one of my rummages, I discovered boxes of propaganda leaflets. Most depicted grisly pictures of dead North Vietnamese Army (NVA) soldiers pictured where they fell with captions like, "If you are wondering where Private _____ is, this is where we last saw him." Others showed cartoons of women and children sitting on porches of thatched houses, with captions asking if soldiers knew how their families back home were faring. One I particularly liked was simply the depiction of the Lao flag.

These various leaflets I would take along on strike missions. If we had some time over the target before the fighters checked in I would instruct the pilot to fly a pattern upwind of the target area and I'd climb into the back to toss them out the back window. Ostensibly the ones depicting the flag were meant to be safe-conduct passes, that when presented to Lao forces, would ensure safe passage to join the Lao National Forces. I'm not sure if any were ever used, but at least it did give one a sense of doing something constructive while waiting for the strike aircraft to arrive.

Vang Pao's Medical Treatment

One morning on entering the CIA shack at 20A, I noticed that everyone was bustling about and hurrying out in the direction of General Vang Pao's buildings. When I asked the head CIA man what all the fuss was about, he informed me that Vang Pao was going to have the bullet fragment that had shattered his arm some months ago removed by a shaman.

"Wow I'd like to see that," I exclaimed.

"Then come along," he replied.

When we entered Vang Pao's house, the general was seated, shirtless, on a stool, looking relaxed and chatting with his staff. After a short time, a spindly looking man dressed in a tattered green uniform entered with his "medical instruments." These consisted of a shallow metal bowl and a rattle about the shape and size of a doughnut.

The man, a shaman of some description, approached Vang Pao making bowing motions, as was the custom. He then squatted beside the general, and they chatted briefly. The shaman then suddenly seized Vang Pao's wounded arm and began sucking vigorously...almost violently at the now-healed bullet wound. After a few seconds he stopped and picked up his rattle, and began making circular motions around the location of the wound and peering through the "doughnut" hole to the wound, occasionally shaking it, and mumbling unintelligible words...well unintelligible to me anyway.

The routine of sucking, alternating with the rattle application went on for several minutes. The general tolerated it stoically, only occasionally wincing. Finally, and without warning, the shaman spit into the bowl, and there was a loud metallic "tink" as what looked like the chopped-off tip of an old and dirty AK-47 round rolled around in the dish.

A great sigh went up from the assembled staff, followed by applause. Vang Pao then made a short speech declaring that if this was true, this man would be made surgeon general of his entire army. The shaman appeared elated.
After the assembled crowd shuffled out, I turned to the CIA man and said in a lowered voice, "So, what now? We both know this was a trick of some sort."

He turned to me with a wry smile and said, "Now we put him on a chopper to Udorn so he can get x-rayed and have the operation to remove the bullet fragment."

"So why did he do it?" I asked." He surely doesn't believe in that mumbo jumbo."

"True," replied the CIA man, "but a surprising number of his staff do, so he has to do it for them."

I have often wondered how the shaman dealt with the disappointment of not being appointed surgeon general of Vang Pao's army.

Napalm

While operating out of 20A, I began getting requests from our liaison at the Udorn command post concerning bomb damage assessment (BDA). Pilots we were directing on targets were complaining that they never got reports on the results of these strikes. I approached General Vang Pao about this, hoping to get this information from members of his units. Unfortunately, I think there was a breakdown in communication, and he misunderstood what I was requesting. I sincerely believe that he thought I was insinuating that the targets his troops were supplying were not as important or vital as they could be. This was to result in a memorable walk in the jungle for me.

General Vang Pao's forces were in the process of retaking a site, I believe it was 48. We were assigned to the mission of attacking troop positions surrounding it. Vang Pao was flying with us and pointing out the positions himself from a back seat. As we approached the site he became excited about a location near a river valley, and directed our attention to a small wooded hill that bordered a small stream. Across from the stream was a flat expanse of rice paddies. I could see nothing, but assumed the general knew what he was talking about. He made it clear that our target was to be the paddy side of that wooded hill. I soon contacted a flight of two F-4s, and confirmed their load was napalm. Weather and communications made describing the target difficult, but eventually the F-4s acquired it. When the lead aircraft released, his cans flew long, and they passed over the hill, landing in the next valley. I was able to provide a correction to number two before he released, and his cans landed right in the middle of the wood. The napalm roiled through the trees in black and red plumes. With their ordnance expended the F-4s departed. I was then able to bring two A-1Es on to the scene that I had been in contact with during the F-4 strike. By this time, Vang Pao was pointing excitedly and calling to us loudly. I followed his pointing finger and saw there were figures running though the rice paddies. I directed the A-1Es on to the target, and they began strafing the rice paddies with 20mm high-explosive rounds. High clouds had moved in and the skies had darkened by this time and the impacting explosive rounds sparkled across the paddies like fireworks. After a few passes, they reported that they could not see any more movement in the paddies. I then directed them to put the rest of their ordnance into the tree line. When their ordnance load was expended, we ended our attack on the wooded hill.

Sometime after the site was retaken, and we were again in the area, Vang Pao invited me on a walk to the site to observe the bomb damage where I had directed the strike. I must presume the intention was to assuage what he thought were Air Force concerns about target validity. After a walk through the jungle of maybe twenty to thirty minutes or more, we came upon a camp, located at the site of our attack on the wooded hill. The napalm and 20mm had done their work, and the camp area was well burned off, but had been cleared by the enemy after the strike. What remained was well furnished, with a small rustic platform extending a short way into the shallow water, presumably for bathing (invisible from the air), and earthen cooking stoves. One of the napalm cans was wrapped completely around the berm surrounding one of the foxholes near the center of the camp. This cannot have been a pleasant death for an occupant. We crossed the small stream to the rice paddy, where I found a shoe with the side burnt out of it as if with a blowtorch, and a blue smock with a Made in Hanoi label in French attached to the collar. It was apparent that Vang Pao had been deadly accurate in his knowledge of the terrain and the location of the enemy troops---as he almost always was. It occurred to me that probably not many FACs had witnessed their handiwork this close.

Years later, while talking to an Air Force ordnance officer, I was told that napalm had been discontinued. I was astonished, as the only time I saw the enemy break, expose themselves, and run, during my time in theater was following its use. He told me that it was ineffective because it burned off in the treetops, and gave other various official reasons for its being discontinued. I wondered if he might like to explain that to the poor soldiers in that wood in Laos.

The New Pilot

A new Continental pilot arrived at 20-A. I remember him well, but I won't use his real name. I'll give him a pseudonym---Ken will do.

As a rule, the pilots who flew for Continental Air Services or Air America were military veterans, or were seasoned fliers with years of solid experience in civil aviation. These guys were pretty serious about their job, and were constantly aware of the inherent dangers we faced every day. Ken was younger than most of the other pilots, and it showed. He appeared sublimely casual about the whole affair. For example, whereas the other pilots would conscientiously call in their positions and altitudes when pushing through clouds on the normally travelled flight paths between sites, Ken seemed to think that frivolous. This was good practice; not only did it lessen the chance of a mid-air collision, it narrowed the search area in case you were to suddenly go down. He couldn't be bothered. There were other examples, and on the few missions I flew with him, I thought him dangerous---and I was a young, bold, twenty-six years of age. Now I liked a little excitement as much as the next guy, but in such a hostile environment, I felt Ken unnecessarily pushed our luck.

One evening Charlie Jones and I decided to drive over the mountain to have dinner at Sam Tong, the openly known site LS-20, using our "cover" of being aid workers. Returning at dusk, we drove down the valley approach to 20A. Entering the village, we noticed a portion of an aircraft's wing leaned against the porch of the civilian pilots' lodge. One of the civilian pilots was seated in a chair on the porch, so we laughingly called out that someone had been very careless about losing part of their airplane.

The pilot soberly replied that Ken had crashed and been killed a couple of hours ago. He had flown down the valley approaching 20A at treetop level, and had hit a radio antenna that only recently had been erected by the Thais. The antenna sheared off about six feet of his wing, which fell not far from where it now rested. The Porter had then rolled over and crashed off the far end of the runway.

Shortly after our return, Ken's body was brought from the crash site. He was burned all over, with both hands and one foot missing. The remaining foot that had gone through the windshield was unburnt, and still wore the jodhpurs boot that I recognized as his. We wrapped the body in two

15

ponchos, and placed it in a crate that had previously been used for farming equipment. The makeshift coffin was placed on the porch of the CIA building to await transport to Vientiane the next day.

The next morning, one of the CIA men and I were sitting on the porch rail talking, when we became aware of one of the Hmong dogs on the porch licking and eating something from the porch floor. Suddenly he exclaimed that the dog was eating parts of Ken. Sure enough, some crumbly bits had fallen on the porch floor and the dog had found them. We both looked up at one another and nervously laughed, retreating into the cold gritty comfort of a soldier's dark humor. I wondered whose bits the dog might be eating next.

The Flying Lesson

During most of my time at 20A I tried to fly with Mike Lepai, a pilot for Continental. Mike was a generally quiet and super-nice guy, and we seemed to get on well during the many hours we shared in the confines of the Pilatus Porter aircraft that was our platform for directing air strikes in northern Laos.

A lot of time was spent waiting for fighter aircraft, or delivering food and ammo to upcountry sites between strikes. Wishing to use this time productively, I asked Mike to teach me to fly the Porter. Mike agreed and we spent many hours drilling holes through the Laotian skies with me practicing my nascent skills.

One day after we took off from 20A on a flight to the Laotian capital, Vientiane, I asked Mike if I could pilot the plane. Mike agreed and immediately took out his log and began filling out the extensions that he had not completed. We soon encountered a cloud layer, and I asked Mike if he wanted to go over it or under it. He glanced up and said "whatever you want to do," and immediately went back to completing his log. I elected to go under.

We would normally follow a river valley until we were clear of the mountains, and then cross a broad plain to the capital, Vientiane. I followed this route on this occasion, but slowly the cloud base began to get lower and lower. I must admit, I was quite enjoying this, and simply maneuvered the aircraft lower to stay beneath the cloud.

Eventually, however, even I began to be a bit "concerned," as we were getting fairly close to the water, and the angles of bank I had to make in order to stay out of the trees were starting to look a bit steep, even to me.

After one particularly ungraceful bank Mike looked up and his eyes flashed open wide---I think in disbelief. "I've got it Bob," he shouted, tossing his log book into the side pocket. With that he began a steep climb into the clouds, and with luck we came out on top without being plastered on any of those mountains. By that time, I have to say, I was actually glad to let go of that stick. The last thing we needed was for me to make flying in that region more hazardous than it already was. The rest of the flight was, thankfully, uneventful.

Mike continued to teach me to fly the Porter, but I don't think he forgot that day--- I sure didn't. How does the saying go? "I learned about flying from that."

In little over a year, Mike was dead, taking a bullet between the eyes while landing alone upcountry. I will always remember him.

The Dead Neutralist

General Vang Pao's men had recently retaken a vital site that had been occupied by the Neutralists, then captured and destroyed by the NVA. Shortly after, on a FACing mission, I arrived on a Porter bringing supplies and two Lao soldiers from Vientiane in formal dress---sent on a very special mission and dressed for the occasion.

From the airstrip, we made our way to the recaptured site. The village was littered with bodies, body parts, and the debris of war---a grisly sight, but otherwise, a more idyllic setting you could not imagine. It occupied a level sandy position on a gentle bend of a small river with a sandy beach, and was overlooked by three hills. Lying on the ground, I found a square portion of what looked to be a skull with a gilded image of the Buddha carved on it. I was told by the Hmong with us that it was a human skull, and something in which they did not believe.

The site and hills had been occupied by Neutralist soldiers, but I was told by the Hmong that the Neutralists rarely patrolled, and had little awareness of, or concern with, what transpired beyond their perimeter. Largely because of this laissez-faire attitude, they were easily overrun by the Communist forces. The site had been commanded by a Neutralist lieutenant colonel, who was, if memory serves me right, a nephew of the prime minister or other high official.

We found the lieutenant colonel, the site commander, at the entrance to his damaged hut. His trousers were halfway up as if he had been in the process of dressing while exiting the hut. We were told by a Hmong who had been there during the attack, but had escaped, that a rocket-propelled grenade (RPG) had struck a post at the entrance to the hut and a shrapnel fragment had killed him instantly. There was a large hole in the side of his head, and the interior had been cleaned out by scavenging animals during the weeks that he had lain there where he fell.

Due to his lofty connections he was to be returned to Vientiane and not buried on site. The two soldiers, who had been brought along specifically for the job, wrapped him in fabric from parachute flares and escorted him back to the airstrip, where he was loaded into the back of our Porter. The soldiers climbed in and we took off for Muong Soui, Lima Site 108, where the body was to be transferred to a different aircraft for transport back to the Lao capital. The smell was appalling in the confines of the small aircraft. Fortunately the pilot had a can of aerosol disinfectant spray on board, but it was completely exhausted long before we reached Site 108.

That was not a very long flight...but it was an unforgettable one.

17

The Grenade Bomber

We were flying out of 20 Alternate, and we were over a potential target area in eastern Laos, in marginal weather. Jim Stanford and the Air America pilot were seated up front in the Air America Pilatus Porter. I was in the back seat, from where I intended to monitor Jim as he controlled his first air strikes. He had just recently come in-country as a new Butterfly FAC, and this was to be his check ride. The mission that day was, as usual, to support a unit of General Vang Pao's Hmong forces. The general was deeply concerned about a threatening enemy troop position on a ridge near one of his sites, and he had requested air support to deal with them.

Our operation out of 20A was allocated two flights of fighters per day, one in the morning and one in the afternoon, by the 7/13th Air Force. Via radio contact with the airborne command post, Hillsborough, other flights could be obtained from among the many who, for whatever reason, usually weather, were not able to hit their original targets. But on this day, we were the ones turning flights away. When our first scheduled flight of fighters checked in with us, we weren't able to put them on the target because of the weather, so we released them back to Hillsborough and returned to 20 Alternate to refuel and to prepare for the scheduled afternoon strikes.

During the break, we decided that if the afternoon weather was still bad, we would do whatever we could to help General Vang Pao and his beleaguered Hmong soldiers. I had some grenades, so while the Porter was being refueled, I collected four of them from my room.

Jim and I bent the grenade handles outward, and very lightly taped them with a small strand of masking tape so that after the pins were pulled, they wouldn't go off until they hit the ground. This technique was probably never condoned by serious explosive ordnance professionals, but it works.

On our second trip to the target area, the weather hadn't improved, so the afternoon airstrike was also aborted. At that point, we determined we'd use what we had, so we flew back over the target, at as low an altitude as our civilian pilot dared. I opened the back window, and as we passed along the enemy-occupied ridge, I began pulling the pins and tossing the grenades out the window.

Just as the fourth and last grenade left my hand, there was a loud bang in the back of the aircraft. Jim and the pilot looked back sharply. Four eyes fixed on me, thinking perhaps that I had dropped one of the grenades in the aircraft, or possibly that one had gone off near the plane. I quickly assured them that everything was OK with me, and the pilot immediately banked hard left away from the ridge.

As we circled around, and as the pilot's control checks indicated no problems with the aircraft, we decided to press the attack. I loaded my M-16 and prepared to fire it out the right rear window. I'm not sure how many passes we made, but I managed to empty four magazines into the enemy position before we decided we were pushing our luck and started back.

When we got on the ground at Long Tieng (20 Alternate), I crawled under the aircraft and discovered a bullet hole directly under my seat. Looking down the top of the rear fuselage, I found the exit hole. I knew Jim had his camera with him, so I stuck my finger in the exit hole and asked him to take a picture.

We never found out how much, if any, damage we were able to inflict but that photograph reminds me of a near miss.

AIRA in Vientiane

In August 1966, as an additional Butterfly FAC, Robert McCollough, had been posted to 20A and checked out, I was reassigned to the embassy at Vientiane in response to complaints that "the folks in AIRA (the office of the Air Attache) didn't have a clue what was going on upcountry." My charge was to get the air combat operations function there better informed and better organized.

Upon reporting for this new task, I discovered that the entire air war in Laos was (ostensibly) being run/monitored from a "command post" in an enclosed room not much bigger than a closet, in the AIRA offices. A bank of radios covered one wall and a large-scale map of Southeast Asia another. It was, to say the least, claustrophobic. Probably for that reason, it was only intermittently staffed.

Since no one seemed formally on duty, any occasional passer-by might stop and answer a radio call from a flight of fighters requesting permission to hit a target. Usually these fighters had been diverted from their primary objectives in North Viet Nam because of weather, and were requesting permission to bomb some likely looking potential target they had seen in the north of Laos. With a completely casual air, the passer-by would routinely approve these requests, without even the slightest reference to the map, let alone a call to 20A, or even the airborne command post, Hillsborough.

I quickly put a stop to this potential for a friendly fire disaster by insisting that no permissions be given without clearance from me or, in my absence, clearance from 20A or at the very least a call to Hillsborough, the airborne command post with a possible connection to an airborne Butterfly. Although the command post personnel didn't officially work for me, I attempted to organize a schedule that would guarantee a body in the command post at least when strikes were in progress in Laos or North Viet Nam.

Not Now, Goddammit!

Not long after I arrived for my new duties in Vientiane, I began hearing complaints from the fighter commands about the FACs at Lima Site 108, a classified site overlooking the hotly contested Plain of Jars. Five U.S. Army personnel were stationed there, ostensibly to provide gunnery training in 4.2 mortars to the Laotian Army. Additionally, the detachment had been provided with a Lao pilot and aircraft for forward observation and to direct air strikes on the Plain of Jars when any were allocated to them. The Army guys may have used the call sign Butterfly 99.

One day, in the command post, I listened to transmissions between the airborne Site 108 FAC and a flight of fighters (Whiplash, F-105s). After a brief description of the target, the FAC confirmed that a 4.2 white phosphorus mortar round would mark the target. The radio exchange went something like the following:

Butterfly 99: "Whiplash we will mark the target with a WP [white phosphorous] round."

A long period of silence followed.

Whiplash Lead: "Hey, Butterfly, how's that marker round coming?"

More long silence....

Butterfly 99: "It's coming."

More long silence....

Whiplash: "Hey Butterfly, I think I know what you are describing. We're getting a little short on fuel, so we're going to go on in." With that the fighter then began his dive on the target.

More long silence....

Butterfly 99: "Ok, round's on the way."

Whiplash: "Not now, Goddamit!"

Shortly after hearing this exchange, which could have possibly put a fighter and a 4.2 mortar round over the target at the same instant, I volunteered to go up to 108 and instruct the detachment in the finer points of forward air control.

The Hat

On the day I selected to fly up to Site 108, I caught a ride on an Air America chopper. Also on the chopper was a U.S. Army lieutenant colonel who was the embassy assistant Army attaché. He was dressed in fatigues so starched you could have bounced a tennis ball off of them. And, believe it or not, he carried a swagger stick.

A real martinet---I was amused, but respectful.

On the way up to the site, the lieutenant colonel entertained me with tales of how the detachment personnel at 108 lived. Not sparing any descriptive detail, he finished with exclaiming that they "live like pigs."

On arrival, I was astonished to see him stride into the bamboo shack where the five Army artillerymen lived, and exchange his ball cap for (unbelievable for a combat zone), a campaign hat of the type commonly associated with training instructors and Smokey the Bear. The hat had its own reserved hook on the wall. Thus adorned, he strode briskly and importantly around the compound on his inspection tour, using his swagger stick to point out their many shortcomings until it was time for him to catch the chopper back to Vientiane...and safety.

Before leaving, he placed the hat back on its reserved wall hook. There it hung: a large ominous presence, as if observing all the activities that transpired in the shack with its baleful, disapproving eye.

That evening, after a meal, and it has to be said, a few drinks, the entire detachment launched into an intense discourse about their superior. I wasn't surprised by their feelings, but their intensity was remarkable. After weighing up whether I should speak, I decided to tell them the story of my flight with the lieutenant colonel, and inform them of his views on their lifestyle.

After a second's silence, the eyes of one of the officers fell on the hat, and with a great roar he jumped up, grabbed the hat, and ran out the door. He slammed the hat onto a branch stub on a nearby tree, then immediately pulled out a .45 automatic and began firing at it. He was joined by his companions who also opened up, with an amazing array of fire power: Thompson submachine guns, carbines, whatever fell to hand. Keeping with the spirit of the occasion, and in a companionable act, I pulled out my Walther P-38, and I too emptied a magazine into the offending vestige of dictatorial tyranny.

The hail of gunfire was over in seconds, and as the last bullet casing fell to the ground and the smoke cleared, the group stared sullenly at their handiwork. The now-riddled hat was thrown to the ground, doused with barbecue lighter fluid, and set ablaze. It burned brightly while the group stood and watched it burn in smug satisfaction.

I last saw "the hat" as a smoldering, unrecognizable mass, lying in the clearing near the tree.

I have often speculated as to what explanation might have been offered for its absence at the next inspection visit.

I still have a treasured certificate from my Army comrades at Site 108 citing me for, among other things, assisting in ridding them of "the vile abomination and curse of the hat."

Communist Aerial Resupply of the PDJ

I spent nearly a week teaching FACing to the five U.S. Army personnel at Muong Soui, Lima Site 108. They were unfamiliar with Air Force phraseology, and they had little understanding of what Air Force pilots needed and expected to hear.

During one instructional session, the subject of Communist flights into the Plaine des Jarres (PDJ) came up. The captain who was the primary (read, most interested) FAC then informed me that there was a cargo-type aircraft that flew into the PDJ periodically to bring supplies to the Communist troops there.

I was flabbergasted, and could not understand why this had not been reported. Before my return to Vientiane I made him promise to call me in the command post the next time this happened.

On my return to Vientiane, I contacted our link in the Udorn command post (a lieutenant colonel whose name I cannot recall) and told him the story. He was very enthusiastic, and urged me to let him know the next time any aircraft was spotted. I promised I would.

Within a fairly short time, I received a radio call in the command post from my friend at Muong Soui that simply said, "He's here." I immediately called the Udorn command post, got the lieutenant colonel on the line and briefed him. He began scouring the area for resources and came up with a couple of A1-E's that could be diverted. These were perfect for the mission. I told him the coordinates of the approximate area the aircraft was in, and he was able to direct them to the target area.

Either the Communist aircraft had finished its turnaround or it had gotten warning of the approaching U.S. aircraft, but the Army troops at Muong Soui saw it lift off into clouds, and it had disappeared by the time the A-1's arrived.

All was not lost however; the trucks bearing the offloaded supplies were still on the airstrip, and the A1-E's set upon them with gusto. When they finished, the trucks were ablaze, and I must presume the area thoroughly strafed.

Meanwhile, my contact in Udorn, still trying to round up resources, had scrambled a flight of two F-102's. These were directed to the area most likely to be the route of the escaping aircraft. The weather was not helpful however, and sad to say, he escaped.

I must say, it was a hectic two hours in that closet of a command post. Unfortunately, there were no further reported sightings and we were never able to get that aircraft during my time left in Laos. The Communists got away clean with their mission.

General Thao Ma

As I recall, General Thao Ma was once the commander of the entire Lao Air Force, but had been removed from command of the transport aircraft by the commander-in-chief. I had heard that this was because Ma objected to the use of these aircraft in the smuggling of drugs rather than in the support of Lao troops in the ground war. Thao Ma was a real patriot, and a dedicated fighter pilot who pursued his duty with a remarkable zeal. It was our understanding that his pilots loved him.

One day near the end of my tour, I was in the AIRA command post when Ma came in and wanted to make a radio call to General Vang Pao at 20 Alternate. I tuned up the KWM-2 radio and requested the operator on the other end to summon Vang Pao to the radio. After a short time, Vang Pao came on the air, and they talked away in their native tongue. Ma became quite heated and animated during the course of the conversation, which went on for several minutes. When he finished and turned to go, as a throwaway remark, I asked him if General Vang Pao knew what was going on. He looked at me sharply, and said curtly, "he knows," and walked briskly out. I didn't have a clue what I was talking about--- just a shot in the dark, really. Probably a bit brash for a young captain, but I suppose I was in those days.

As the end of the 179 days on my TDY orders approached, I had forgotten about my casual remark. On the day of our intended departure, I was packing in the bedroom of the embassy villa where we were staying when suddenly I heard a plane overhead. This seemed unusual to me so I went to the window to see what it was. There, overhead, was a T-28 just beginning to roll over into a dive. I watched in amazement as it released a bomb that impacted less than two blocks from our villa. My immediate reaction was that in such a political climate as existed in Laos, this could be any sort of action. And while I did not know if it was Ma in the aircraft, I did know that Ma was extremely volatile, and it was unlikely that anybody else would attack Vientiane. Perhaps he had decided to rid Laos of Americans---who knew what was going on, or what the next target would be.

I looked down and saw the guards cowering in the courtyard trying to get cover from the low walls that surrounded it. The next thing I saw was Charlie Jones exiting the villa and scurrying around the courtyard trying to cram a Browning nine millimeter into his waistband, and shouting something about needing to find somewhere to shelter.

After a few more minutes I reasoned that Ma wasn't after Americans after all, and climbed the villa's water tower with my camera. The attack continued for a few more minutes, during which time I saw Ma come in low and flat on a strafing run against a building that I later discovered housed a French information office of some sort. Ma always did hate the French. I later heard that the French personnel had been lying flat behind desks and any cover they could find while Ma's bullets ricocheted around the building. We also heard that miraculously, none of them were seriously hurt.

We finished packing, and drove our car over to the AIRA office in the embassy compound. When we arrived, I went immediately to the command post. Shortly after I entered the command post, Colonel "Pappy" Pettigrew, the air attaché, entered the building, rushed to his office, and grabbed his phone. His face was flushed and sweat covered, and there were grass stains down the front of his khaki uniform. I later learned that the colonel had received a call from Ma prior to the launch of the raid, and he had rushed over to the target to warn them, arriving just prior to the strike. The grass stains were the result of their hasty exit from the house, and a long skid down the house lawn, diving for cover.

I believe Ma landed in Thailand after the raid, and sought asylum there.

Later in the day, after the excitement had died down, we caught a plane to Udorn RTAFB to begin our journey home, leaving that tragic little country forever. Sometime later I heard that Ma had been assassinated. A sad end to a sad story.

An additional misfortune was that my camera had not had the correct settings and none of the pictures of the raid turned out.

My close friend Jerry Klingaman, a senior captain at the time, who ran the Thai T-28 fighter operations at Wattay Airport, remained behind after my departure. He will cover the eyewitness accounts and implications of the attack much more thoroughly in his own narrative.

Section Two

MR I   Luang Prabang   The Royal Capital

Aerial View of Luang Prabang, Laos (L-54) Looking South. 1970 Photograph by Ernie Anderson, Raven 11

Chapter 4

Jack Drummond, Raven 25
Vientiane, Pakse, Savannakhet
Jan 1968 – Jun 1968

First Week in Laos

I did not arrive in Laos in the conventional Raven way of being assigned as a forward air controller (FAC) in South Vietnam, then getting selected for the Steve Canyon Program, then going to Laos. Mine happened much differently.

I was flying AT-28s from Nakhon Phanom (NKP), hunting trucks on the Ho Chi Minh Trail, and thought I was about to get into a great deal of trouble. Background: After a couple of folks had to bail out of the bird because of engine problems, the REMFs (Rear Echelon Mother F……rs) decided that we could not hunt for trucks in areas with guns. It did not take a psychic to figure out that the reason there were no guns in some areas was that there were no trucks in those areas. On my fateful night, Alleycat the Airborne Command and Control Center (ABCCC) reported numerous trucks at XYZ and I headed to the location. Sure enough, trucks were everywhere and I went to work. Soon a B-57 Yellowbird showed up. He worked high and I took the low road. We were flared by a Blind Bat C-130. We had just a good old time, destroying about 20 trucks between the three of us. Of course we received 37 mm, 14.5 mm, and 12.7 mm on each and every pass.

The Blind Bat crew was just ecstatic on the radio, saying over and over again that we were shit hot. After the strike, the navigator on Blind Bat gave us the bomb damage assessment (BDA), including the exact location of our strike. Now I had known since the Alleycat call that XYZ was right in the middle of a hot area of known guns. After all of the excitement, I became fearful of ignoring the edicts against flying in a known gun area, and I knew the number of trucks killed would highlight the mission in morning briefings at both 7ᵗʰ Air Force and NKP, but I decided to wait to see if I could slide by. But fate was not kind. After the Blind Bat crew got back to their base, they submitted Silver Star nominations for both the Yellowbird crew and myself. Of course the paperwork emphasized the known gun area and the quantity and quality of the antiaircraft artillery (AAA) received during the strike. I figured my goose was cooked.

What to do? The previous wing commander, Heinie Aderholt, had told me on his last night at NKP that if the occasion arose that I might want to do something else, I should call the Autovon phone number he gave me and tell Gus that Heinie said I should come to work for him. After spending several hours in the bar worried about my future in the USAF, I called about sunup. Col. Gus Sonnenburg told me that Heinie had told him to be on the lookout for my call. He further told me to be at NKP Base Ops at one that afternoon and I would be picked up. And, he added, don't bring any military stuff. I was at Base Ops and at one o'clock, a C-47 landed and told the tower that they were not going to shut down, just going to pick me up. The bird taxied in front of the tower, the door opened, a ladder was extended, and I loaded up, finding no one else on board but the crew. I took a seat. They taxied out and promptly departed. I had no idea where we were headed.

We turned west from NKP and flew over Udorn, then turned north. This was the first time I knew where we were going. After landing in Vientiane, the C-47 crew introduced themselves and told me to join them on the ride to the embassy. There I met Col. Sonnenburg, the assistant air attaché, and his staff. I was briefed on the Royal Lao Air Force (RLAF) and the embassy's concerns over aircraft losses, especially from the Savannakhet and Pakse locations. They told me that I was going to be the air ops commander in Savannakhet and Pakse and that my primary objective was to assist the RLAF to operate so as to lower the aircraft losses. I was further told that I could not fly operational missions – that I was restricted to maintenance test hops and ferrying aircraft back and forth to the overhaul facility at Udorn.

This was all fine and good, but I was very concerned that the folks at NKP would report me AWOL. The colonel assured me that the situation was covered, that I would be receiving temporary duty (TDY) orders shortly, that my Date Eligible for Return from Overseas (DEROS) remained unchanged, some 5½ months away, and that my next assignment was going to be to the Air Commandos at Hurlburt Field in Florida. I thought to myself that they really got things done in a hurry up there. I did not know my follow-on assignment before then.

Then Col. Sonnenburg told me that before I was to go down south, I had a special mission. He instructed that I go to the Air America (AA) terminal early the next morning and catch such-and-such flight. I would be visiting with a CIA guy who would give me some targets he wanted destroyed. Then I would go to Ban Houay Xay and work with Thai pilots to destroy the targets. Thai pilots? One of my additional duties at NKP was as liaison to the RTAF squadron on base, so I knew a lot about the RTAF. I flew with them at least once a week. Never once had any of them mentioned flying in Laos. So I queried the colonel. He was in a hurry to leave but quickly told me about a group of Thai pilots paid by the CIA that flew under the umbrella of the Royal Lao Air Force (RLAF). And he explained that the part of Laos where I was going did not normally have T-28 support so they periodically sent the Thais up there to support the CIA.

27

After spending a short night in the Ice House, I took my duffle bag, holding all of my worldly goods, to AA Ops, told them who I was, and they pointed to my ride, a Beech Baron being preflighted by two pilots. At the aircraft, I threw in my bag and off we went. I was in the back seat as this was the first flight in Laos for one of the pilots. He was getting his initial area introduction. But it was good for me as I listened in and got my initial area introduction also. I had only been in country for about 18 hours and did not know anything, so this was a great help. Our first stop was 20A. The old head told the new guy all about the approach, one-way traffic, etc. After we landed, we taxied up to the tower, shut down the right engine, and handed a package to a guy who drove up in a jeep. As I started to get out, the old head told me that this was not my stop; I was not getting off until the next stop. I was glad he knew where I was going because I was completely in the dark. The door was shut, the right engine restarted, and off we went, heading northwest.

We were in a part of Laos that I had never flown over. Where, I wondered, were we going? On the way, the old head pointed out Luang Prabang, the Royal Capital. I remembered from the briefing that the RLAF had a squadron at the location also. But on we flew. Ban Houay Xay was pointed out during the slow descent but we just kept going north. We finally landed on a dirt strip with a village on the east side of the runway. The pilots shut down the right engine, helped me with my bag, and bid me goodbye. In a few minutes, a young American guy picked me up in a jeep and took me to the largest house in the village. It was on the highest ground and it had a great view of the village and the surrounding area.

My host showed me a room in the house and offered me a beer. He said that "Tony" was out on business but should be back in an hour or so. I relaxed with my beer on the veranda and noted that I had been in country exactly 24 hours. Shortly thereafter, a very pretty tribal girl brought me something to eat and I also managed a nap.

Just before sundown, a Pilatus Turbo-Porter landed and the pilot was brought to the house. Then a UH-1 landed and the pilot was also deposited at the house. Over beers, I asked about who was the CIA guy I was supposed to meet. They took the opportunity to tell me about Tony Poe. He had been in the Office of Strategic Services (OSS) in WWII and had never left. He was the CIA guy for northwestern Laos and kept his eyes on what was happening in Burma, Southern China, and NW Laos. Quite a character was the summary.

Mr. Poe finally wandered in just as the evening meal was being served. He was very affable and began telling war stories. I kept very quiet. Was I still in Laos? All of his stories were about surrounding countries. As we got ready to hit the sack, he told me that we would be flying in the Pilatus Turbo-Porter the next morning and we needed to leave at sunup.

Next morning at the aircraft, he informed me that we would be looking at the locations he wanted the Thais to strike over the next few days. I asked him if he had a map, as I sure didn't. He looked at me very skeptically and forcefully told me that we didn't need a map – that he knew his way around. I had the opportunity to ask the Air America pilot if he had an extra map and he handed me a 1:250,000 scale that had few details on it.

So off we went, Tony and I in the back of the bird. The noise level in the back of the Turbo-Porter was very loud and Tony was talking continually. Listening to him, watching our flight heading over the pilot's shoulder, and trying to relate the terrain to the map was very difficult. After a bit, Tony pointed down to a mountain and told me to destroy everything on top of it. And then he took three glass jars containing hand grenades out of his briefcase. Scared me to death! Then he told the Air America pilot to fly low over the target he had pointed out to me and opened a door in the floor of the aircraft. The pilot started a dive towards the target and hollered "Now" when the time was right. Tony threw the glass jars out of the hole and closed the door. We headed back to Tony's home but he told me that I would be getting off at Ban Houay Xay on the way back. So I took my map and my duffle bag after we landed at what I thought was the middle of nowhere.

After Tony departed, I found that I was standing next to a small shack that had a fuel truck sitting outside. I went inside and met a young Filipino man in an Air America shirt. After we said hello, he asked was I the American that was going to be working with the T-28s. I told him yes. He then began to tell me the schedule of when the ordnance was coming in, when the T-28s would arrive, where to stay downtown, etc. – all of the stuff I should have been smart enough to ask the downtowners the afternoon and evening I was in Vientiane. Upon inquiry as to how I was going to get downtown to his recommended respite, he casually told me not to worry, so-and-so would be bringing my jeep soon.

Sure enough, my wheels soon arrived but they made me think that I was still in the ozone. In Laos, the proper side of the road to drive on is the right-hand side, but the jeep had the steering wheel on the right side, meaning it was designed to drive on the left side of the road. It was in the wrong country. Or was I?

I motored to downtown Ban Houay Xay. It reminded me of a town in an American western cinema – the downtown area was about three blocks long and all of the buildings had false fronts on them. Anyway, I found my hotel and it was nice enough. I walked back downtown to get something to eat. Found a nice-looking open-front restaurant and went inside. The owner/cook/waiter came over and asked me in English what I would like. I told him that whatever he felt like cooking would be fine with me. He brought me a warm coke and began to cook. He toiled and sweated over his fire and wok and then served me, over rice, the best meal I could have envisioned. Since no one else was in the place, we struck up a conversation. I asked how he knew English so well. Turns out that his father was French and insisted that he learn English as a boy. He had learned to cook from his mother, who had worked as a cook for the King in Luang Prabang. Of course, I did not know if any of it was true, but I thought to myself that I had come a long way from our farm in Jones County, Texas.

Next morning at the appointed time, an Air America Caribou landed, taxied to the far end of the runway, turned around, rolled two pallets out of the back of the airplane onto the runway, and took off. I drove up there (the runway was much higher on one end than the other) and found that my ordnance had begun to arrive. My problem was I did not know how I was going to get it off the runway. About that time, I saw a C-123 on downwind for landing. I took off in my jeep to ask the AA Filipino guy if he had radio contact with it. He did and I asked him to tell the C-123 to please not dump ordnance pallets on the runway. The pilot's answer was short – Where do you want them? I hurriedly drove back up the hill and found a location that would be close to where the T-28s were going to be parking but OFF the runway. By this time the C-123 had landed and taxied to my location. I pointed to my new bomb dump area and he rolled three pallets of bombs, rockets, and gun ammo out the back of the bird. And then, to my everlasting gratitude, off walked three young civilians with toolboxes. They had to be GIs, given their haircuts. I introduced myself and learned that they were from Detachment 1 at Udorn and were going to work with the Thais when they arrived. Two of them were ordnance experts and the other was a T-28 crew chief. This was their first time in country also and they had the same look on their faces that I was sure I still had.

We received two more C-123s in the afternoon and our ordnance stock was complete. The problem was that two pallets were still on the runway. Getting the bombs off the runway was not going to be easy. Each of the two pallets had six 250-pound bombs on it and weighed about 2,000 pounds. About this time, a 6X6 military truck came driving down the runway like it was a road, but it had to stop because of the stuff in the middle of the runway. The guy driving did not have on a shirt but his pants looked like they had a military origin – and he spoke more English than I did Lao. He asked how we were going to get the stuff off the runway and I had to tell him I did not have a clue. Well, it turned out he had some nylon straps in the back of his truck that we tied to the pallets, and he pulled them next to the rest of the stuff. I thanked him and he left.

One of the ordnance guys had thought to bring a crowbar with him and they commenced to pry the packing off the ordnance, exposing the bombs, fuses, rockets, and the 50-caliber ammo. The four of us worked the rest of the afternoon and finished the unpacking. Everything was lying on the ground but at least it was exposed so it could be worked with. All four of us were exhausted and almost dehydrated because we did not have any water. The decision was made to call it a day, so we went to the hotel and checked the guys in. After a cold beer or two, all three decided to go see downtown. I went back to the same restaurant as the night before and asked the owner if there was any place in town to get ice and drinkable water. He said he would have a can for me the next morning before we went to the airport.

The next morning, the beginning of my fifth day in Laos, we got our water and went to our ordnance. We discussed how we were going to load this stuff. We had no machinery and 250-pound bombs. We mutually decided that we would try to fly twice per day – with bombs in the morning and rockets in the afternoon. The bombs could be lifted and hung on the T-28s while it was cool and rockets would be hung for the afternoon flights. Fuses and arming wires would be put on the bombs after they were hung on the aircraft. Rockets were much lighter and could be easily loaded after the pods that held the rockets were put on the T-28s.

Shortly after noon, I heard the sweet sound of a T-28's 1820 engine and looked up to see it in the landing pattern. Soon we had six of them parked next to the ordnance. After the pilots got out of their planes, I walked over and introduced myself. The leader, a captain, was shocked to find out that an American was to be involved. It seemed it had not worked that way previously. We agreed that we would talk over a beer that night. Our gun plumbers decided to put bombs on the aircraft that afternoon, just to see if it would work as we had discussed. It did.

That evening the Thai flight lead and I met to talk about the following day's missions. He almost had a shit fit when I pulled out my large-scale map to talk about the targets. He insinuated that I must not understand much about targeting if that was the map I used. He further said that he did not think they could fly with such inaccurate info. The Thai captain did not know some of the things that I knew: first, a Thai had been in my pilot training class and he was now the T-28 squadron commander at Korat Air Base in Thailand; second, my trusty duffle bag contained my parachute and helmet; and third, I was not going to take any crap off of him. I told him I would lead the first flight to the inaccurately marked target and then they could accurately mark it on their maps.

He immediately told me that the airplanes belonged to the Thai Air Force and that I was not authorized to fly them. I got in his face and told him that I was going to call my old pilot training classmate and let him know that the pilots that had been sent were not professional. Further, I told him that the CIA had authorized me to dispense their flight pay the next pay period (not true but sounded good). He left in a huff.

Next morning, my sixth day in Laos, I briefed the flight under the wing of an aircraft without a word from the Thai captain. We flew it as briefed and dropped on Tony's mountaintop. That afternoon we went back to the target area and shot rockets at some North Vietnamese Army/Pathet Lao (NVA/PL) encampments that the bombs had uncovered. That evening, an Air America helo flew me back up to Tony's place and I briefed him on what we had accomplished during the day. He gave me another target for the next day, our last at Ban Houay Xay. And he asked me if I would be accompanying the next Thai deployment to his location. I had to tell him I did not have a clue.

The next day, I did not fly and pointedly encouraged the Thai captain to brief both morning and afternoon flights. The afternoon flight was returning to Udorn after their mission so after all the birds were gone, we cleaned up our work area as best we could and waited for our C-123 to take us back to Udorn. But we soon heard the sound of T-28s and two landed and taxied to the parking area. The Thai captain came over and told me that one of the two aircraft had experienced a loss of electrical generator so they were leaving it at Ban Houay Xay, and that both of the pilots would be returning to Udorn in the other aircraft – and they left.

The crew chief and I discussed the difficulties in repairing the aircraft at Ban Houay Xay. We also discussed the possible outcomes of flying it with an inoperative generator, including the dead generator catching on fire and no communications if the battery ran down. I finally decided that if it would start, I would take off, turn off the battery switch to conserve the battery, and turn it on to land at Udorn. I put my duffle bag in the T-28 baggage compartment, strapped in, turned on the battery switch, and started the engine. I took off towards Udorn and turned off the battery. Turned it on, landed at Udorn, taxied to the Det. 1 parking ramp, and shut down. Thus ended my first week in Laos!

A Weekend in Bangkok

I was the air ops commander for the RLAF squadrons in both Savannakhet and Pakse during my time in Laos, so I frequently flew back and forth between the two locations. One of our T-28s at Savannakhet was a real old D model that did not have all of the latest upgrades of radios and its tactical air navigation (TACAN) was completely inoperable. It also had the old 500-round gun pods on it, so it was a little slower than the later versions. And it must have had bad pi because the RLAF would not fly it. Anyway, by default it became my ride back and forth between the two sites.

It was not uncommon that I somehow would wind up in Pakse on Friday afternoons after flying had ceased. Since you could almost see the bright lights of Bangkok from Pakse (after all, it was only 300 nautical miles), about once a month I would go to Bangkok for the weekend and return to Savannakhet early on Monday.

Well, it was Friday afternoon late and I was at Pakse. As I was loading my trusty duffle bag into the luggage compartment of my ride, one of the Pakse Ravens drove up and asked where I was going. I told him Bangkok and asked him if he wanted to go. He assured me that he did and would be back shortly with his bag. He was back within the hour and we strapped in for the flight.

One of the reasons the Lao wouldn't fly this particular aircraft was due to the radio setup. The standard Tango had a UHF, VHF, and FM radio but this tired old D only had UHF. Plus, it was a crappy radio. Its normal range was about half that of others and it had a lot of static.

Full of anticipation for the weekend, we launched off towards Bangkok. After crossing the Mekong I called the USAF radar site at Ubon to file a visual flight rules (VFR) flight plan. I noticed that the radio was really bad and I had a lot of trouble understanding the radar site, but was sure that they had gotten my info.

It was also the "rice field burning season" in Thailand and the in-flight visibility was under a mile until we topped out of the smoke at about 10 grand. We were making good time but guard channel was really active. Even though radio reception was full of static, I could tell that the RTAF F-86L interceptors were really looking for someone. I wondered who it could be.

Time out for some background: For some unknown reason, the REMFs had decided that Bangkok was a probable target for someone (but no one knew who), so a detachment of USAF F-102s was based at Don Mueang with a standing alert commitment. Back to our story.

As we passed the northern border of Cambodia and Thailand, we made a slight left turn to Bangkok. We were making really good time.

As we rolled out of the turn, I noticed movement out to the left of our aircraft and, lo and behold, an F-102 came sliding into position about 100 yards off my left wing. I quickly checked my six and there was another one – in about a one-mile trail. I quickly pointed out both of the Deuces to my Raven passenger and told him that perhaps we should be concerned.

Then we received a radio transmission, "T-28 on heading of XXX, this is so-and-so on guard, state your intentions!" My first thought was about how clear the damn radio was now! Then I quickly answered him that I was an American and my intentions were to have a nice weekend in Bangkok. No answer. No answer for long enough that I began to get sort of nervous. What were they doing? Who were they communicating with? Stuff like that.

Then he transmitted, "What are the markings on your aircraft?" And it struck me – I had forgotten to remove the plates on each side of the aircraft that had the Lao three-headed elephant on them. I carried three sets of markings with me and had intended to replace the Lao markings with the USAF side panels I carried but had just overlooked that little chore in anticipation of going to Bangkok. I immediately informed him that I was an American and the side panels were Lao, a friendly country to both the Thais and the USAF.

Then he transmitted, "Why are you armed?" I politely asked him what he was talking about, I was not armed. The F-102 driver then said, "I can see your bombs from here." I realized that he was talking about the aforementioned 500-round gun pods that this D model was carrying. I then tried to explain to him that this model of T-28 had these external gun pods – they were not bombs.

After a short period of silence, the escorting F-102 instructed me to begin a descent to Don Mueang AB—that I would be accompanied by the two interceptors until landing. Now, several factors came together: One, the F-102 had slowed to about his stalling speed to maintain formation with us; two, we had gotten very close to our landing airfield during all of these conversations; and three, we were only about 500 feet above the smoke layer.

I pulled back the power and began a descent. The last time I saw the F-102 was as he pulled ahead of me because he could not slow up without stalling. After diving to hit the point to turn on initial for the pitch out, I called Don Mueang tower and requested landing instructions. The tower promptly approved a left-hand break for landing and to call turning base. The tower then said, "Bulldog (my call sign), you have 102 with you?" No, I replied, I did have but I had not seen them for a few minutes. "They look everywhere for you." was the tower's understated response.

I began my turn to base and reported gear and flaps down. Tower cleared me to land. Then I noticed that the runway was lined with blue USAF vehicles, many of them with flashing lights. I could not believe that the USAF had that many vehicles at Don Mueang. Touchdown was nice and we turned off at the first intersection. Two MP trucks blocked the taxiway. MPs exited the vehicles and were armed with AR-15s. Holy shit! For the first time, I realized I had really stepped on my dick and I might not get out of this situation unscathed.

A follow-me pickup emerged from the parking lot of blue vehicles and beckoned me to follow – which I did. They escorted us to a deserted taxiway and motioned me to shut down. After completing my cockpit checks, we exited to meet the oncoming hoard.

More background: My personal appearance was not USAF-like. We were encouraged to get away from the military look in our jobs in Laos and I had maybe gone just a little over even that line. First of all, I was wearing matching black top and pants with no markings. Next, my mustache had not been touched in four months. Last, my hair was a little longer that the USAF allowed but it only reached my collar. Back to the story.

Upon reaching the ground, I was accosted by a full colonel who was really pissed. He wanted to know who I was, who gave me permission to be on his airfield, and some other stuff I don't recall right now. Being in full CYA mode by this time, and having had four months of CIA exposure in Laos, I told the colonel that his security clearance was not high enough for me to answer those questions and I demanded to be taken to the U.S. ambassador.

During this exchange, I noticed that my Raven passenger had been able to work his way to the back of the pack of folks standing around, and was quietly walking towards the taxi line over at the passenger terminal. Good for him was my thought.

About this time, one of the MPs opened the door on the side of one of the 500 round gun pods and hollered, "These guns are armed!" The number of folks standing around quickly decreased by 75 percent. "No they are not," I replied, "I just haul ammo around in the pods in case I want to feed it through the breech for use on a strike." For some reason, my word did not seem to satisfy the colonel and I had to take the ammo out of each pod to show him. He directed an MP to take the bullets for evidence. The situation was about to get out of hand.

About this time an RTAF jeep pulled up and a Thai Air Force lieutenant colonel stepped out. I could hardly believe that the person was a pilot training classmate of mine. Last time I had seen him, he was a major and commanding the RTAF T-28 squadron at Korat, and now he was here in my time of need. He walked over, ignoring the USAF colonel, put his arm around my shoulders, pulled me to the side, and asked what was going on. I quickly explained the string of circumstances we had faced that afternoon and told him that I might be in a world of deep shit unless we could bullshit our way out of this. He nodded.

The Thai lieutenant colonel then walked over to the USAF colonel and told him that he would be taking responsibility for me. The USAF colonel turned a shade of very deep red, causing me some concern that he might be about to have a heart attack, and exploded at the Thai officer that he was the base commander and that no lieutenant colonel was going to take his prisoner. My pilot training classmate very professionally explained that Don Mueang was not a USAF base, it was a Thai AF base, and that he was the weekend duty officer with the responsibility for all operations. He assured the USAF colonel that if any more assistance was required he would let him know. Turning to me, he said, "Mr. Drummond, get in the jeep." I quickly complied and we drove away. He took me to the Thai AF HQ and asked could I join him and his family for dinner that night. "Sure," I said.

I saw the Raven at the bar in the military hotel later that evening and he mentioned that he probably would find another ride back to Pakse. So, just before dawn on Monday morning, I preflighted my bird and took off for Savannakhet for the morning Air Operations Center (AOC) meeting, concluding my weekend in Bangkok.

I learned several lessons from this experience:

1. Preflight your aircraft properly – ensuring that the markings on it are suitable for your destination.
2. Remove all ammo from your guns if going to a REMF destination.
3. Ensure your aircraft has a functioning radio.
4. Keep up and be friendly with all pilot training classmates from the country where you are currently living.

A Bridge Just Right

I had the best possible job back in the war in Southeast Asia (SEA). I was an air operations commander with the Royal Lao Air Force in southern Laos and was able to work and fly with a great bunch of jocks. The RLAF flew an armed version of the T-28, the T-28D-5. This version had six weapons carriage pylons and two 50-caliber machine guns. It was a real pleasure to fly. Furthermore, they were accurate.

The Ravens allowed me to fly their O-1s when I needed a break from working with the RLAF. One morning about daybreak, I was doing some O-1 visual reconnaissance in an area that I suspected the bad guys were using to sneak trucks past the well-known Ho Chi Minh Trail. Luckily I was able to find a small bridge that the enemy trucks were using. Putting a call in to the USAF airborne command post, I requested air to put in a strike on the bridge.

This was early in the war and the F-4C had just begun to be introduced into the war over North Vietnam. The F-4C units used strikes in Laos as training missions for their inexperienced aircrews to get them up to speed for the big stuff up north. My air from ABCCC was a flight of two F-4Cs.

Our target was a brown wooden bridge, about 20 feet by 30 feet, over a brown-colored dry streambed. It was difficult to see from the perspective of the F-4s at 12,000 feet and I had a lot of difficulty getting their eyes on the right area. My white phosphorous marking rocket went under the bridge and the white smoke rose up through the bridge. The F-4 pilots affirmed that they saw my smoke and began their strikes. After dropping a total of twenty-four 500-pound bombs towards the target, it emerged unscratched! I could not believe it.

I was really upset that the bridge still existed and starting hustling my O-1 back to base. After getting there, I jumped into a Tango (our term for the T-28) with four 500-pound bombs and two pylons of cluster bombs containing incendiary and antipersonnel bomblets. One of the Ravens came over to ask me where I was going and he elected to get into an O-1 to go out and look over the area with me.

Back to the bridge we went. I rolled into a dive-bomb pass and dropped one 500-pounder. After the dust settled, we could see that the bridge was in the dry streambed. The Raven asked me what I was going to do with the rest of my ordnance. He suggested that we try to find the trucks that had made the tracks. He began following the tracks in one direction and I went the other. In a few minutes he called that he had found where several trucks were parked under some trees. After pointing them out to me, we began to bend and break them with my bombs, CBUs, and guns.

During the strikes, we were able to open up the foliage and could see more trucks under the trees. After depleting my ordnance, I started back to base and called for the RLAF to quickly prepare four T-28s with suitable ordnance for the trucks. The Raven stayed there to ensure that the bad guys did not try to move the trucks. After returning to base, three of the most experienced RLAF pilots and myself fired up our 1820s and returned to the location of the truck park. We proceeded to destroy or damage upwards of 20 trucks.

Another great day in the best job in the war. And they even paid me for it! Another bonus.

Chapter 5

Ed Gunter, Raven 72
Luang Prabang, Jul 1969 – Feb 1970

Ed Gunter, Houei Sai, Laos

Author's Note: *Back in 2009, I pulled out all my old log books, BDA books, maps, photos, notes, orders, TDY vouchers, etc. in preparation for oral interviews covering my time in the Southeast Asia Conflict. I spent about 7 ½ hours on the phone with historians in the Vietnam Archive Oral History Project at Texas Tech University. I feel it was a very comprehensive, honest dialog about my time in the war. The recorded portion is available through their website. The final transcript (129 pages) is still being processed for completion and addition to the website (http://www.vietnam.ttu.edu/virtualarchive/items.php?item=OH0697).*

As I feel that was a very complete history, I will not try to replicate it. I will say that my boss and good friend, Don Moody has put on paper some details of a couple of my missions and for that, I thank Don. They are available in Episode 3 of "The Adventures of Bob and Don" (http://www.ravenfac.com/ravens/Adventures/Episode0003.htm).

Ed Gunter and Don Moody, Mexican Banditos

I won't be saying I won the war. I was just a young pilot, hungry to do something for my country and find some excitement. I did my job and did it well, I think. Like all of the Ravens.

I just wanted to add a couple of short stories that I feel captured some moments of my tour.

WHY WOULD I WANT TO DO THAT??

I had just arrived in Viet Nam as a young, inexperienced first lieutenant O-1 Bird Dog forward air controller (FAC) five months out of USAF pilot training. One of the first places I went was to the 504th Tactical Air Support Group for in-processing, briefings, and squadron assignment. At my initial in-brief, I was told the policy was that at the six-month point, if we were doing our job well, they'd let us volunteer for another assignment/site. The guys who were tired of the fight could go to staff, command post, make admin runs, etc. Guys who wanted more excitement could volunteer for hotter areas; and if you really want some excitement, there is the Steve Canyon program, but we can't tell you anything about it. Not even where it is. The Steve Canyon program had a requirement of six months SEA (Southeast Asia) FAC experience before you could get into it. You also had to accept tour extensions if needed to give you six months retainability.

At about the 3-4 month point, I had made my wishes known that I wanted to go to a hotter war. I even had an assignment to a hot province on the Cambodian border. About this same time, I was getting more than a little sick of the bureaucracy and overly restrictive Rules of Engagement (ROE).

The ROE were a crock. It was deadly for us to let the enemy stockpile guns, bombs, rockets, and ammo across some imaginary line, knowing we couldn't attack it. If I had a hot target and was taking ground fire, I still had to get approval from several levels before I could legally return fire.

37

We were fighting with one hand tied behind our backs. Target validation was a long, bureaucratic process and the bad guys usually knew a target was approved before we did. (Shades of the current war—target approval in the White House.) As far as the bureaucracy, I felt we were really silly with all the emphasis on grooming and uniform standards. I thought majors and lieutenant colonels should have something better to do than fly around looking for FACs flying below 1500 feet and harassing me about a mustache in a combat zone.

Several things happened about that time that convinced me that I wanted to go fight a different war.

First, I was covering an insertion of troops into a hot LZ (landing zone). They met intense resistance and were in a heavy firefight, so I called for air support—fighter bombers. Air was on the way, but the province chief refused authorization to expend, as "I have troops in that area." Hell, I knew he had troops there; I was talking to the US advisor and watching them get hosed.

Next, my roommate went down in a smoking hole. As I flew over the site, directing ground forces (Aussies) to the crash site to retrieve remains, I started taking ground fire. I called for air, but some REMF at a higher level decided that my getting shot at wasn't as important as some pre-planned tree-buster, so I couldn't get any fighters. Another day as a target.

Then one of my classmates, Dan Davis, came back through III Corps after a couple of months in Steve Canyon. (Dan was run over by a Thud over the PDJ later that year.) I dragged him to the bar, filled him up with Pabst beer and Jim Beam, but he still wouldn't give any details. He did say it was a hot war; they got to check out in the AT-28 with bombs, nape, CBU (cluster bomb units), armed guns, etc.; they wore civilian clothes; and there weren't many field graders and visiting brass up there. That's all I needed to hear. I knew what I wanted—ASAP. I let my boss know.

A couple of days later, I was in the colonel's office as he told me that it was a very hot area, lots of chances to screw up, and don't go up there and start smuggling drugs, yadda-yadda. About that time, Raven losses were mounting, so they waived the requirement for me needing six months in SEA.

A few days later, I was on an airplane to someplace, but nobody could tell me where I was going. As a lieutenant, it was kinda neat to be the only passenger on a Scatback jet to Udorn. Little did I know what adventures lay ahead of me.

I processed in at Udorn, Det 1 of the 56th Special Operations Wing, where I was officially assigned. I went through the usual in-processing drill. A couple of things were different though—all they could say was that I was going on TDY (temporary duty) orders "upcountry." I should have looked at a map. They also assigned me a locker, and told me to put all my uniform items in it and forget them until I was headed home or on R&R (rest and relaxation). Then they pointed me to a tailor right off base to have some "walking suits" made.

They also gave me a mailing address and said I could tell my family, friends, etc. ONLY that I was still flying, but no details. All mail was to be addressed to Mr. Ed Gunter. I probably wouldn't get to see anything addressed to Lt. Gunter.

I met up with two other lieutenants who were headed the same direction. One was a USAFA and pilot training classmate—Smoky Greene—and John White. Smoky and I finished our tours in one piece. John was airlifted home after a bad O-1 crash.

Ed Gunter and Smoky Greene upon arrival in Vientiane, Kingdom of Laos.
Two lieutenants lost and bewildered without their uniforms

They then told us to be on the Air America ramp bright and early the next morning for transportation to somewhere.

First Raven Flight

Here I was—a fresh-faced young lieutenant. Four and a half months' experience as a FAC in III Corps, South Viet Nam had made me an old head. I had just arrived at a whole 'nother war. No idea where it was.

After landing at Udorn, RTAB (Royal Thai Air Base) in Thailand, I found my way to Det 1 of the 56th Special Operations Wing. Most of that time was a blur, but I do remember them assigning me a locker with instructions to put my uniforms in there and forget them until my tour was over. They also said to go to the Air America ramp the next morning for transport to my unknown destination.

I dutifully complied, and found myself along with two other young lieutenants/civilians—headed deeper into the unknown. I had a picture of the three of us—looking lost and forlorn as I pondered the words of one of Gen. Custer's troops: "What am I doin' here??"

After in-processing, briefings, etc. in the air attaché office at Vientiane, Laos, they had us draw straws for our final destination. I was odd man out, but the name of the site I was going to meant little to me. Once again, I was told to be at a passenger terminal on a strange field in a strange country. I asked who I was supposed to meet there and they replied: "Oh, you'll know him…" and grinned.

I was on time, and after a short wait, I knew who I was meeting—dude came in with long muttonchop sideburns, a black outfit and black boots, a sidearm, and carrying a large brown paper sack. He must have recognized my lost look as he came over to me and said, "C'mon, Gunter, let's get out of here." I had met my new roommate and mentor as a Raven—Fred "Magnet Ass" Platt. I was to learn a lot from Fred.

We walked out to the ramp, to an airplane I had never been in before—a U-17 with just a tiny tail number, eight rocket tubes, and a red stripe on top of the wing. No other markings. Without the formality of a walk-around, he said: "Get in and take me to L-54." I asked where that was… thinking "where the hell is that??"

I settled into the left seat, and finally found a tattered old checklist in the map case. I was religiously going through each item, trying to find the various switches, knobs, dials, etc. in a new air machine. After a few minutes, Fred grabbed the checklist, threw it in the far rear baggage compartment, and said, "Get this thing started and let's get out of here." I did and we did. My only direction was to head north. I guess taxi-out, take-off, and climb were pretty uneventful as the next thing I remember was leveling off. As I tried to figure out what I might need to set for cruise flight and navigation, I noticed Fred was reaching into the back seat and getting out his brown bag. I was pretty occupied exploring the new airplane. When I looked over his way again, he was reaching into the bag. He pulled out a can of beer, popped the top, and handed it to me. Oh, Lord…. This was really going to be an interesting assignment…. Lest the reader be unduly concerned, that was one of only two times I flew during or after a drink. The other was one of those Silver Star vs. court-martial situations. Another story at another time.

We did get to L-54, and after a couple of landings, I was declared competent to fly the U-17. I guess the beer relaxed me just enough. The next day, I rode in Fred's back seat for 3.2 hours in an O-1 as he gave me a tour of the area and put in five flights of fighters. That was about what I'd do in a month back in Viet Nam.

Over the next two days, I flew over seven hours, getting to know the area and putting in airstrikes. I must have been doing something right, as I got 51 confirmed enemy soldiers killed by airstrikes I directed on my third day on the job.

Spin the wheel: Silver Star or court-martial?

6 January, 1970; about a month to DEROS (date of return from overseas) and two days before my birthday! It was a sloppy day—had worked a short day due to weather, got back to the field well before dark, helped refuel and rearm the U-17, and rode back to the house for a family-style dinner. After dinner, was sipping on Jim Beam as we watched one of the movies (on 16 mm reels) that were provided by the attaché. Our favorites were the Clint Eastwood movies—for a rating system, we'd count the dead bodies on each reel.

At some time during the movie, our radio operator was summoned to his station. Soon after, he came out and said that a friendly outpost was under heavy attack and they had to have a FAC and an interpreter (who had just arrived at the house) ASAP. There was one FAC who hadn't been drinking and it wasn't me. He said he didn't want to fly at night, in questionable weather in the mountains. After listening to several minutes of why it couldn't be done, I said, "There are people dying out there as we argue," grabbed the interpreter, and headed for the field.

We got airborne and I headed toward the outpost. The clouds were very patchy. I got above a thin broken layer and had the interpreter contact the troops on the ground. While en route, I contacted a "Spooky" gunship that was also airborne. Due to darkness and clouds, we could not see the outpost, but by flying over, they let us know when we were directly overhead and let us know where the bad guys were. Using that general guidance, I had the "Spooky" drop log flares, which provided a solid, steady reference point on the ground. That bright light showed nicely through the clouds below us. Using that as a reference, the "Spooky" was able to shoot enough to break off the attack.

Having relieved the immediate threat to the men on the ground, I headed back to L-54. We had one instrument approach there—an NDB (non-directional beacon) approach that had an MDA (minimum descent altitude) of 5,000 feet above the field due to mountains in the area. I knew that wasn't going to get me home, so I made one attempt at our home-grown instrument approach. I flew directly over the NDB. When I got station passage, I chopped the throttle, dumped the nose, and went into a steep turn, trying to keep the needle off the left wing. You'd descend until you puckered the seat cushion up your ass and if you didn't see the field at that point, add full power and climb back up. Well, that night, it didn't take much more puckering to convince me it was time to go somewhere else. So I called our control, told them I was diverting to Vientiane, 100 miles away, and headed south. Thank god I was in the U-17 with increased range. After 3.2 hours of night time, to include .4 of night instruments in the mountains, we were met by one of the strap hangers from downtown. The frown on his face made it obvious he could still detect the Jim Beam on my breath.

At any rate, it was apparently discussed in depth at pay grades far above mine. Bottom line was that I didn't get my Silver Star and didn't get a court-martial. I was quite happy to add my 17th oak leaf cluster to the Air Medal and know that I had saved some friendly lives.

I have the citation to my 18th Air Medal as proof of this exploit—except for the Jim Beam part. To protect the guilty, that was left out.

Lao Barbecue Party

Got Religion?

The Laotians were very religious and devout Buddhists. Buddhist monks were highly revered and seemed to be everywhere.

When a new Raven got upcountry, the first few weeks were a "wait and see" trial period. You'd be watched from a distance to see if you were a good guy, not a loose cannon or flaming assh…, good pilot and FAC, etc. If all went well, you would be presented with a Buddha or two to protect you for the remainder of your tour. The standard line was that Buddha would protect you from any and all harm. After a couple of weeks, I was presented three Buddhas that I wore for my whole time in Laos. I still wear them for the banquet at our reunions.

Most of our missions were solo, but some were with an interpreter to talk to the troops on the ground. Sometimes, we would drop packages to the troops on the ground (I never wanted to know what was in those securely wrapped packages. The colonel at 504th had told me not to run drugs…). Mostly, the interpreter would be talking to the troops on the ground to coordinate their position and locations of enemy troops. He would relay that information to me, I'd clarify any questions through him, and then I could effectively direct airstrikes.

One of these interpreters/air guides was a lieutenant named Sy. Sy was unique for a couple of reasons. First, he stood head and shoulders above most Laotians, who were physically small people. Secondly, he had made his way through the ranks, having started as an army private. He was now a lieutenant and obviously plenty gung-ho.

This particular mission was flown near the confluence of the Mekong River and the Beng valley. We had been talking to the troops on the ground and located some bad guys. We had put in 2-3 sets of fighters on the troop concentrations. There was time between flights, so I decided to drop down and get the BDA (bomb damage assessment), a report of what the strikes had damaged, destroyed, etc. As I made a low pass over one ridge line, it suddenly sounded like the 4th of July. Several 12.7 mm (.51 caliber) machine guns opened up at once. They were close and well-aimed for us to hear them so loud above engine and wind noise, headsets, etc. I continued jinking and headed for the next ridge line. As I crossed it, I dropped down into the valley, hoping to get out of sight of those guns and get far enough away to climb back to a safe altitude. As I did, I started climbing back up and took a deep breath. I looked over at Sy and his eyes were as big as saucers. I asked him if he was OK but got no response. I asked again, and still staring straight ahead, he said: "Mr. Gunter, I think we go home now." I tried to explain the importance of the target, that we had more fighters waiting for direction, and we needed to complete the mission. Sy continued staring straight ahead and said again, "I think we go home now." Digging deep into my bag of persuasion, I held out the two Buddhas on a chain and said: "No sweat, Sy; we have Buddhas. Buddha protect us." Sy finally looked at me and calmly stated, "Mr. Gunter, I think maybe Buddha take holiday today. We go home now."

Buddhas

Chapter 6

Words for Frank Birk

Frank T. Birk, Raven 12/45
Luang Prabang, 1970 – 71, Pakse, 1971

Stories about Frank Birk from the personal notes of Larry "Pepsi" Ratts

The best pilot among all the Ravens with whom I flew was Frank Birk. I checked him out in the Luang Prabang area using the U-17. By the second flight I knew that I was in the company of a natural airman. If Frank had a fault with his flying, it was disregard for his personal safety. I remember looking over an O-1 that he had flown back to Pakse one day that was so thoroughly ventilated that it was unbelievable that any human could have survived inside. It reminded me of those magic shows where someone is placed inside a box and so many swords are pushed through that there is no conceivable way that the "victim" inside would not be skewered. Both Frank and his Lao backseater had been aboard, and we could walk about the aircraft trying to line up the entry and exit bullet holes in the cabin. No matter how we tried to sight through the holes in the aircraft, there was no way we could see that either man could have avoided being struck in torso, head, leg, hip, and every other body part. Yet neither was injured. The only explanation was that just like Frank had been jinking, diving, and bobbing his aircraft around to try to escape the volley of shots, their bodies must likewise have been jinking and diving inside the aircraft so that as bullets flew through the space where their heads should have been, they must have ducked in a different direction. The arms, too, but there was no way we could figure how they squirmed their legs and hips out of the line of bullets streaming through the cramped space in an O-1. The Air Force did not like for pilots to take excessive risk, so all bullet holes were coved with gray Mylar tape to match the aircraft color before being turned in for maintenance. Ravens typically just shrugged when asked about the bullet holes. How could they know? But all this was not why I want to write about Frank Birk.

Frank was a hero and an adventurer, but, as is common with Ravens, he had heart that escaped notice of others. While flying at Luang Prabang in 1970, one of Frank's Lao back seat interpreters took a grievous hit to the abdomen. He survived after an emergency flight to Udorn for surgery that left him with a permanent colostomy. This soldier had to be fitted with a permanent, but prone to leak, latex pouch held in place by straps, unlike most virtually leak-proof replaceable appliances for colostomies that are now used stateside. He returned to his village and family with that one appliance that had to last him the rest of his life. He had no sources or means to ever replace his one and only colostomy pouch. Frank could not abandon his comrade and friend and until 1974, he took responsibility for the financial support of not only his flying partner but also his partner's wife and children.

In 1974, while on leave from USAF active duty, Frank disregarded regulations specifically prohibiting active duty personnel from entering Laos, and acquired a Lao visa and visited Luang Prabang. Frank knew that I had managed to do the same while still in the Air Force in 1972 and 1973. I was no longer in the Air Force in 1974 and Frank surprised me with his visit. He had come specifically to hunt for his backseater who with his family had moved far away from Luang Prabang. Frank and I were unable to reestablish contact with him and this was greatly distressing to Frank. But there was another family near Luang Prabang with nine children minus a father who had perished flying with Ravens. I had been trying to help them, but I was limited in funds to do so. Frank made a substantial and anonymous gift to support those nine kids. After the war, there was no veteran benefit program for those local combatants who had been our allies and who suffered casualties of injury or death.

A son and a daughter of that family eventually made it out of Communist Laos into the Nong Khai refugee camp. The son became a Christian while in the camp and served as a youth pastor to the Lao. He immigrated to Canada before moving to Australia. The daughter came to the states, lives in Portland, Oregon, and I am still in contact with her.

Frank did well in the Air Force and earned high rank. His flying acumen was recognized and he became a test pilot. But I am sure that none of his family or colleagues knew of his heartfelt obligation and generosity to the Lao who flew with him.

Recollections of Frank Birk by Ernie Anderson

On the surface, Frank Birk was a self-confident, laid-back, smooth-talking individual. However, once he climbed into an O-1E, Frank became a very different person. Flying is risky and very unforgiving. Each pilot tolerates risk differently. Frank Birk seemed to have a very high tolerance for risk. Frank always looked the enemy in the eye – eyeball to eyeball. At the time, after flying with Frank once or twice, and getting to know his methodology, I determined that Frank Birk was one of the luckiest men alive. He skillfully flew his aircraft on the ragged edge of disaster and always walked away from some very bad situations. I was told Frank once had a backseat observer killed sitting directly behind him (2 feet) in the O-1E. Frank was untouched. On another occasion, Frank got a Purple Heart when a round hit the O-1E's battery and a fragment of the battery struck his body.

One of Frank's more memorable missions comes to mind to indicate what a "true hero" he really was. As the L-54 Awards and Decorations Officer, I wrote Frank up for a Silver Star for a mission he flew late one afternoon in Northern Laos. This could have been, and possibly should have been, an award of the Air Force Cross. There is always a judgment call as to what the facts really are and which award they merit. Frank had flown a 4-hour mission and had just landed late in the afternoon. The U-17 was on almost on empty. Frank got a call that a helicopter had been shot down with casualties on the ground in the far northern reaches of our area. Frank called me before landing and asked me to get a fuel truck ready for him. After landing, Frank personally reloaded rockets on the U-17. After loading the rockets, I asked him if he was going to refuel and he said "No, I don't have time." He then took off without refueling. I thought I would never see him alive again since he did not have enough fuel to fly the mission that far north and back again.

When Frank got to the crash site, nobody could be seen. Frank, disregarding his personal safety, flew at treetop level, looking for crewmembers. He found several wounded crewmembers hiding in the tree line. He could see blood on several of the crewmember's clothing. In spite of small arms fire, Frank then directed a rescue helicopter to the exact location of the wounded crewmembers while firing marking rockets for cover. The crewmembers were then able to be successfully picked up. There was an active 23 mm gun and small arms in the area. After the rescue, Frank flew the long trip back to Luang Prabang, on empty, and in the dark. If he had ran out of gas, he would have gone down in the mountains, in triple-canopy jungle, at night without much hope for rescue. He risked his life, but he made it home in one piece – which I considered a miracle. I only knew Frank for several weeks before he was reassigned to a new operating area. However, in that short period of time, I determined that Frank Birk was indeed a "true hero." That's how I will always remember him.

Frank Birk from the personal notes of Craig W. Duehring

I made several trips to and from Luang Prabang (LP) during the winter of 1970-71. I seemed to be the replacement of choice to relieve other FACs who needed to depart the area for leave or something similar. On February 11, 1971, my log book tells me that I checked out Ernie Anderson at LP. That day I remember as two new FACs had just reported in to LP and needed to be checked out. On that day, Frank Birk, who I will discuss later, took Bill Blaesing up in the U-17 while I took Ernie Anderson in the Bird Dog. Frank flew as he usually did, low across the tree tops, while I climbed up high for a better view and more safety. After all, this was to be an area orientation. Ernie is a big guy – tall and large – so our little airplane had to work a bit. We cruised up and down the rivers for an hour or two when we heard a distress call coming from the other aircraft. Actually, the call may have been relayed through the operations center or Cricket as we often did not have radio contact with each other. It seems that Frank knew where some bad guys were working and raced over, only to be met with heavy AK-47 fire. As it happened, one round came up through the radio panel between Frank and Bill (side-by-side seating in the U-17) which immediately got their attention. Since they didn't know what else may have been hit, they promptly headed for home. Ernie was listening to this with extreme interest. After all, it was his first ride in country. He really, really didn't like ground fire so he made it a point to fly extra high for the remainder of his tour. As a result, the guys as LP nicknamed him "Astro FAC." I got to know both Ernie and Bill in a later life in the Air Force and we retold the story of that day over and over again.

The city of Luang Prabang is a beautiful city in the mountains with the Mekong River running by on its way to Vientiane. When my wife and I returned there for a visit in 1994, we learned that the city had 33 operating Buddhist temples which produced long lines of saffron-robed monks venturing out to receive the offerings of everyday people in their rice bowls. I learned quickly that the monks were not begging, they were allowing the people to make a sincere offering on behalf of Buddha. I never tired of watching that peaceful, graceful, and magical ritual early in the blue-grey morning with the smell in the still air of countless wood fires cooking wonderful things to eat and drink. There were the cries of waking babies and the calls of parents to their children – all woven into a great tapestry of soft colors. I have no quarrel with people trying to live peaceful lives.

In the center of town, on a small mountain top, stands the famous temple of Wat Chom Si. The "shirt-sized" Buddha pins that came from here were considered to be especially lucky, so I wore one on my shirt constantly, but also wore my Sacred Heart medal, a gift from my godparents, on a silver chain under my shirt. I wore the Buddha out of respect for our Laotian friends. The steps up to the temple climb a long way and, like so much in Southeast Asia, the gardens along the way were in need of attention. But, there was a war on.

It might be good to mention here the custom of wearing the Buddha. All of the Hmong and Lao pilots wore a Buddha (although the Hmong were more animist than Buddhist). It was generally believed that the Buddha pin itself had charms in that it brought you either good luck, bad luck or something in between. You never bought a Buddha for yourself but accepted one as a gift from a friend. Then, you live your life with great care for the next few days trying to determine if the Buddha would bring good or bad luck. If you did not get hurt, you could return to normal life. I asked one time what would happen if a pilot was shot down (bad luck) but rescued (good luck) and the response was that you should get another Buddha, just in case.

Frank, like Chuck Engle, was fearless and a great pilot. But, he flew low and took a lot of chances – and a lot of hits from ground fire. I heard that, after he moved to either Pakse or Savannakhet, his Bird Dog was hit over 40 times by ground fire – 19 times on one mission. The resulting damage included blowing out the windows, destroying the radios, blowing up the fire extinguisher (which hung on the back of the pilot's seat) in the backseater's face and causing an explosion in one of the wing fuel tanks that ripped the wing out of the fuselage by at least three inches and sweeping the wing back on one side only. Nonetheless, Frank flew the crippled O-1 back to base with the injured backseater and crash-landed it on the runway. It was irreparable.

Tall and lanky, he often wore printed T-shirts and jeans and was a confident, no-nonsense kind of guy. That isn't to say he wasn't friendly. He certainly was loyal to his friends but his motto might have been "Lead, follow or get out of the way." He earned a Silver Star for a mission that, as I heard it retold, might easily have qualified him for the Air Force Cross. On that day, an Air America aircraft disappeared beyond the dreaded Chinese Road. The Chinese Road was a series of roads that the Chinese continued to build throughout the war in Southeast Asia, simply because they had the power to do so. It ran from various points in China into the country of Laos and pointed southwards, towards Burma and beyond. Eventually, the road complex provided them with trade routes into Laos, Burma and, especially, Thailand. But, at that time, no one (especially the Thai's) was certain that it wasn't simply an invasion route. It could be used for either purpose.

Frank flew towards the Chinese Road in a U-17, dropped to the deck and raced as fast as he could northward. Two separate sets of 37 mm (5 guns each) opened up at him but he was gone in a few seconds. Amazingly, he made radio contact with the survivors and ascertained their position. He tried to contact Cricket but he was too far away from Cricket's orbit to be heard. Then, he flew back south across the road and was hosed again. He eventually landed at Luang Prabang and personally rounded up some Air America helicopters to go back and pick up the survivors before daylight faded. The little team headed north and followed him across the dreaded road and picked up the people on the ground. Finally, he led the team back across the road for the last time and brought everyone to safety at LP. I don't recall if he or any of the aircraft were shot up but this was an incredibly gutsy move.

Frank returned to the U.S. and was assigned to Military Airlift Command somewhere on the west coast. He was flying C-141's but hated it and did not fit in well with such a laid-back group of pilots. One evening, he attended the wing dining-in and the big event of the evening was a ceremony where crew members were awarded their single Air Medals for flying supplies in and out of Vietnam. It took them many months to earn just one Air Medal while we earned them every few weeks. Obviously, for a proven warrior like Frank, this event was painful. At one point, another aircrew member of some sort approached him and commented that he had never seen so many medals on the mess dress of an officer as young as Frank was. He wanted to know how he could have earned them all. Frank replied that he had spent two tours in Southeast Asia. The other guy responded, probably without thinking, "Two tours! How could anyone be so stupid as to volunteer to go back for another tour?" Frank cold-cocked him on the spot.

The next day in the wing commander's office, Frank unloaded his frustrations and said that he wanted to leave the Air Force. In this case, the wing commander was smart enough to realize the potential that Frank brought to the table and asked him to wait a few days. Later, the wing commander called Frank back and told him that there was an opening in test pilot school at Edwards that required a pilot with large aircraft experience. He offered the assignment to Frank and Frank accepted. Frank·was an Air Force Academy graduate with an engineering degree so he knew what he was getting into. Frank graduated from the training and began his work in earnest – and never looked back. He became the chief test pilot for the B-1 and one of the chief test pilots for the B-2. I recall one reunion at Randolph where Frank flew an F-16 in from Edwards just for the weekend. He was qualified in many aircraft. At that reunion, Frank treated us all to the first unclassified video about the new B-2 and he was featured in it twice. I was impressed and asked if I could get a copy. Frank simply handed the video to me and I still have it. It has been very useful over the years when I want to motivate some young person who wants to be an Air Force pilot. It has both raw footage and scenes set to music. It is fabulous. Eventually, Frank became the test wing commander and retired, having never left Edwards in all that time.

In early August, 1993, I came to work at the U.S. Embassy in Jakarta, approached the front door and showed my credentials to the Marine on duty. As I was cleared through, he said, "Colonel Duehring, I have a message for you," and handed me a slip of paper, possibly a fax. On it, one of my fellow Ravens informed me that Frank, who had recently retired from the Air Force, died as a result of a plane crash in Europe. At the time of the accident, Frank was flying a European trainer jet that they hoped to enter into competition as a replacement for the aging T-37. On short final, something unexpectedly deployed from the aircraft and it crashed. Frank lived in agony for several hours before he died. He is buried at the U.S. Air Force Academy, along with several other Ravens. I stood in stunned silence until I heard the Marine say, "I'm sorry, sir," I nodded silently and walked to my office. There was nothing to say.

Chapter 7

Ernie Anderson, Raven 11
Luang Prabang, Feb 1971 – Aug 1971

Most war stories have a way of getting better with age. My war stories are based on recollections of 43 years ago, and hopefully I've gotten most of the details right. I have changed a lot in the last 43 years, and I am praying it has mostly been for the better. This is my attempt to document a few of my more "family-friendly" Raven experiences – if there ever could be such a thing. The "family-unfriendly" stories, of which there are many, will be left for another time and place. Since most Raven stories typically involve heavy drinking, cussing, carousing, killing, fighting, arguing, singing, and frolicking, I will have to leave out about 98% of my Raven experiences.

Viet Nam Duty

I arrived in Viet Nam on 10 May 1970. Unfortunately, upon my arrival, many O-1E aircraft were grounded due to brake problems. This delayed my checkout in the O-1E for about four months. To gain combat experience, I flew night missions in the right seat of an O-2 as a SPAT Forward Air Controller (FAC). I was stationed at Binh Thuy flying over the Mekong Delta at night. After about four months in the O-2, I was checked out in the O-1E and stationed at Tay Ninh, Republic of Viet Nam (RVN) as a Sundog FAC (Figure 1). Most of my time at Tay Ninh was spent flying over Cambodia in the O-1E conducting visual reconnaissance (Figure 2) and airstrikes (Figure 3). After a few months, we were told the war was coming to an end and we were all being sent home early. But I wasn't ready to go home just yet. Hell, I was just getting started due to a delay because of the O-1's brake problems. Somehow I was informed about the covert Steve Canyon program and thought this assignment might fill my lust for adventure. Needless to say, there was plenty of lust and adventure being a Raven FAC.

Lt. Ernest B. Anderson, Jr. - USAF - O-1E Forward Air Controller (FAC) - Call Sign "Sundog"
Tay Ninh Airfield, Viet Nam Sep 1970
Figure 1. Ernie Anderson, Sundog FAC, at Tay Ninh, RVN

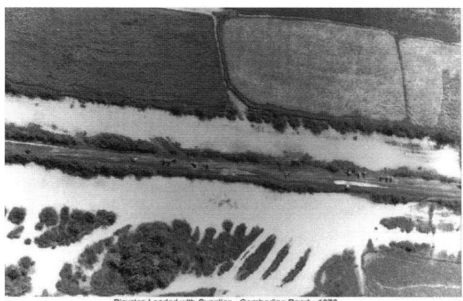

Bicycles Loaded with Supplies - Cambodian Road - 1970
Photo Taken by USAF Forward Air Controller (FAC) Lt. Ernest B. Anderson, Jr. - 1970
Figure 2. Infiltration Route on Cambodian Road

CBU Airstrike in Cambodia. O-1E Sundog Fac. Photo taken by Lt. Ernie Anderson Dec 1970.

Figure 3. Airstrike Delivering CBU in Cambodia

As a side note, in 2012, Lt Col Les Roodzant wrote his book *A History of Sundog FACS* and he included several of my Tay Ninh and Cambodia photos in it (Figure 4).

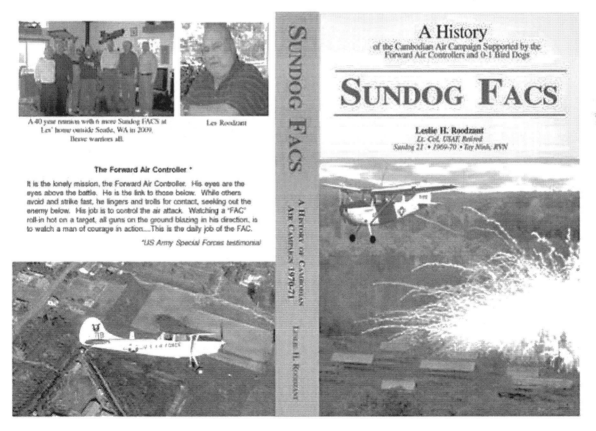

Figure 4. Les Roodzant Book - A History of Sundog FACS

I was selected for the Raven program in January 1971. On my way to Laos, the trip from Binh Hoa Air Base (AB), RVN to Tan Son Nhut AB, RVN was a most eventful and dramatic learning experience. I had packed everything I had, including all my orders, into one very heavy B-4 bag. The road was extremely bumpy, and I didn't want to sit in the back of the truck watching my luggage because of the really rough ride. That was a big mistake. Somewhere along the way, my B-4 bag was stolen from the back of the truck. The guy that lifted my B-4 bag must have gotten a hernia because it was extremely heavy to lift out over the tailgate of the truck. I was utterly amazed because we stopped only one time for about 30 seconds during a 45 minute trip, and "poof," it was gone. I lost everything I had except the clothes on my back. Thank goodness I was travelling with Bill Blaesing as he had an extra set of our orders with my name on them.

Laos Duty

I was officially assigned to Detachment 1, 56th Special Operations Wing (SOW), Udorn Air Force Base (AFB), Thailand during 1971. I was a Raven FAC from 4 Feb 1971 to 24 Aug 1971 (Figure 5). I spent five months flying out of Luang Prabang and one month flying out of Vientiane. My call sign was Raven 11.

Ernest B. Anderson, Jr. (Age 24) - O-1E Forward Air Controller - "Raven 11" - Luang Prabang, Laos - 1971
Figure 5. Ernie Anderson, Raven 11, Luang Prabang, Laos

Luang Prabang was a sleepy little town on the Mekong River in northern Laos. It was the royal capital of Laos, and the King resided there in a stately palace (Figure 7). Upon my arrival, I was briefed by the embassy that Luang Prabang was surrounded by two battalions of Pathet Lao. It was interesting to see the Pathet Lao soldiers hard at work for Laotian money given to me

King's Palace - Luang Prabang, Laos. Photo taken by Ernie Anderson April 1971

Figure 7. Royal Palace, Luang Prabang, Laos

Pathet Lao Money - Luang Prabang, Laos - July, 1971

Figure 8. Pathet Lao money

The Raven mission was to keep Luang Prabang from falling into enemy hands. We succeeded while I was there. I was assigned with fellow Raven FACs Bill Blaesing, Jim Roper, and for a short time, Frank Birk. My Area Operations Commanders were Ed Bender and Ed Troxel. We somehow all worked together in an amicable, sober manner (during the day) with three FAC pilots sharing two aircraft – an O-1E and a U-17. When I was assigned to Vientiane for a month, I flew with Bob Kain.

The Raven job at Luang Prabang required flying O-1Es and U-17s over some very dangerous mountainous terrain known as 'karst' (Figure 9). Flying a small single-engine observation aircraft in, around, over, and through karst is a scary proposition. It becomes readily apparent that clouds, mountains, and O-1E's don't mix very well. Flying on instruments in the O-1E was designated an emergency procedure. The only navigation aid was an Automatic Direction Finder (ADF), which was not reliable near a thunderstorm. Low-hanging clouds were a frequent problem. Once I flew over a mountain peak just below the cloud bottoms and, then, in a valley, found my way forward blocked with more clouds. When I tried to go back, I found my exit blocked by clouds that had moved in. Fortunately for me, after circling around in the valley for 10 to 15 minutes, I was able to sneak out of the valley when a break in the clouds came over a mountain top, allowing me to retreat by flying over the treetops (Figure 10). Otherwise, I was going to land somewhere in the valley – if that was even possible.

Nam Ou River in mountainous Northern Laos, north of Luang Prabang. Photo taken by O-1E Raven Fac Ernie Anderson July 1971.

Figure 9. Rugged mountains along the Nam Ou River

Raven Fac Mission - Clouds in Mountainous Terrain - O-1E - Northern Laos - Photo taken by Ernie Anderson May 1971

Figure 10. Clouds in the mountains of northern Laos

When the weather wasn't cloudy and rainy, it was extremely hazy. Flying in the very limited visibility of haze was always challenging as it was difficult to see other aircraft flying in your vicinity. Also, haze was really a problem when looking through it into the sun.

We directed T-28 and F-4 airstrikes on selected enemy targets. In addition to supporting indigenous troops, most of our targets were bunkers, caves, and boats along the Nam Ou River (Figure 11). The jungle was very dense so it was always hard to observe enemy troops. Jim Roper can give many of the more intimate details about the targets in our operating area. A squadron of Royal Laotian Air Force T-28's was based with us in the revetments at the Luang Prabang airfield (Figure 12). Our bombing activity, although limited, seemed to keep the enemy at bay since they never really seriously attacked Luang Prabang (Figure 13). Perhaps the Pathet Lao knew they could take the city whenever they wanted, so they were just waiting for the right opportunity. Or, perhaps it was politically expedient to wait until the time was right. Or, maybe we caused them to pay a very heavy price when they appeared on our horizon.

Bomb craters along the Nam Ou River in Northern Laos. O-1E aerial photo taken by Ernie Anderson June 1971

Figure 11. Bomb craters on the Nam Ou River

A tragic event occurred in August, 1971, the last month of my tour at L-54. It involved the T-28 accident of Maj. Ed Troxel and his backseater, Sgt. Walter "Andy" Capps. I will refer to these men by their rank; however, everyone always dressed in civilian clothes, so we referred to one another using first names, or used the title "Mr." This accident occurred near sunset at the L-54 airfield. I was getting ready for the evening communal meal when, all of a sudden, people started running from the back of the building yelling that "Troxel just went in at the airfield." Hell, I didn't even know he was flying the T-28. I didn't know he had a passenger. I really didn't know his reported condition. I roomed with "Doc," our medic, so I was not always "in the know" about what was going on at L-54. Blaesing and Roper roomed together at our compound, so they were up to speed on all the operations and grapevine info. Since I was a lieutenant, most times I just did what I was told to do, or, when necessary, I made a judgment call to do what I considered best under the circumstances. In this instance, I ran for a Jeep and raced to the airfield.

When I got to the airfield, the locals who had witnessed the crash were just standing around. I saw a group of men standing next to Major Troxel. I could barely feel a pulse on Major Troxel. I did not know of a hospital in Luang Prabang (there was none), but I knew there was a Swiss medical team compound in downtown Luang Prabang. I had Major Troxel loaded into the back of an ambulance, shoved the ambulance driver to the right seat, and I jumped into the driver's seat and headed for the living quarters of the Swiss medical team. The road was really rough and crowded, so I could not go as fast as I wanted. I even used the siren a couple of times during the trip. I arrived there in about 15 minutes, in the dark, unannounced. I performed cardiopulmonary resuscitation (CPR) on Major Troxel until the Swiss surgeons took over. The Swiss surgeons tried to resuscitate him but he was too far gone from the impact of the crash. Shortly after I arrived, another group of individuals arrived with the backseater, Sergeant Capps. At the time, I was shocked to learn there were two people onboard the T-28 when the accident happened. Unfortunately, Troxel and Capps did not make it. We did everything humanly possible to save their lives in very primitive medical conditions. Both of these men were very fine individuals that I greatly admired. I especially liked Capps for his easy-going manner. For me, it was a significant emotional event that you tend never to forget. Years later, I was able to visit the Vietnam Memorial in Washington, DC and pay my respects to Troxel, Capps, and another very fine individual from my pilot training class – Raven FAC Charles Russell.

Ordnance for Laotian T-28's at Luang Prabang Airfield, Laos. Photo taken by Ernie Anderson June 1971

Figure 12. Laotian T-28's in revetments

Downtown Luang Prabang, Laos. Photo taken by Ernie Anderson April 1971
Figure 13. Downtown Luang Prabang, Laos

Summary

This has been an overview of my six months as a Raven FAC in Luang Prabang, Laos. The assignment at L-54 was very challenging. Flying dramatically changed from one day to the next. The cloudy weather, rain, haze, mountains, and ground fire made it an art to survive flying the O-1 in a combat environment. I feel I was indeed fortunate to survive the extreme operating environment of L-54.

All the Ravens did amazing things as Forward Air Controllers. Ravens are true heroes and many gave their lives out of a sense of dedication to cause, loyalty, and patriotism. I salute all those that volunteered for the Steve Canyon program.

Following my Raven assignment, I was assigned as a T-38 Instructor Pilot and then as an A-10 Tactical Fighter Pilot. Personally, I will always be grateful that the United States Air Force gave me the opportunity to fly and provided me with many opportunities for adventure in places like Luang Prabang, Laos.

Chapter 8

Lloyd Van Zee, Raven 10
Luang Prabang, Mar 1972 – Oct 1972

Lloyd Van Zee's Rocket Raven Tale

The time has come, the Walrus said, to speak of many things.
Of Forward Air Controllers and rocket pods and wings.

If you didn't tell anybody, it didn't happen.

This story is about my first three days as a Raven FAC. I will tell you how I got the nickname "Rocket Raven."

I decided to volunteer for the Raven program after Dick Christie was shot down and killed in February 1972. He was the first Sundog FAC to die while I was at the 21st Tactical Air Support Squadron (TASS) at Tan Son Nhut. His loss affected me a lot. I wanted to do more than fly in Cambodia at 1500 feet. I heard from a lieutenant colonel in 7th Air Force Headquarters that there was a need for a volunteer for the Ravens, so I volunteered. I was selected because they needed a captain with a little more rank to replace Bob Abbott at Lima 54. He was overdue to rotate back to the States, and they needed someone right away. Little did I know the next few days would change my life forever.

Within a couple of days, I left Saigon on March 15th, 1972 in a C-130 for Udorn Royal Thai Air Force Base in northern Thailand. It was a normal intertheater airplane passenger service for the Air Force. All the new Ravens were in-briefed first. I went into the Air America compound at Udorn Air Force Base in the fenced off area that regular Air Force people couldn't go in because that was where Air America did maintenance on their airplanes. But it was right on Udorn Air Force Base.

I reported in to Detachment 1, 56th Special Operations Wing. They had me put all my uniforms in a duffel bag and told me it would be stored in a house in Udorn. I had bought some shirts, blue jeans, and polo shirts at the Base Exchange (BX) in Saigon, so that's what I wore. Later on, I had some camouflage shirts made that I wore while flying. The Det. 1 folks were in a big hurry to get me to Vientiane that same day, so I just did what they told me. I was issued a CAR-15, and I got on a C-47 about 2 PM for the trip north. When I arrived at Vientiane I got in a jeep and went to the embassy compound and got in-briefed—I think. It's all a blur to me now and I don't remember the details. I do remember that a former friend and Sundog, Spike Milam, met me after that and took me to the Raven house in town. That evening he showed me several of the local watering holes and lots of Air America and CIA people at the bars. I do remember Madame Lulu's establishment, but none of the others. I was a bit out of it by that time, since I had left Saigon that morning. That was a long day.

On March 16th, the next morning, I didn't feel very good, but Max Hottell met me at breakfast and told me he would check me out in the O-1 today. He was the one that checked out new Ravens that had never flown the O-1 or a taildragger. We flew a few patterns and got used to the O-1 and

58

landing a taildragger for the first time. We flew out over some bamboo and Max had me shoot one rocket to see if I could hit something, which I did the first time. No problem as I'd shot lots of rockets in the O-2. I thought he was going to give me a check ride later, but after we landed he went into the flight shack and had me sign the Form 8 check ride that I'd just passed! We had lunch and he said to take the plane and go north about 20 miles to an airfield and shoot landings all afternoon. I did for a couple of hours, and had a lot of fun learning to fly the O-1 solo, doing whatever I wanted with the airplane. I thought that I was really going to like this life.

Max told me to be at the field early the next morning to go to Luang Prabang (Lima 54). A mechanic was going to need a ride to Lima 54 also, so I was to meet him at 8. I think we partied again that night but don't remember where or who with.

On March 17th I managed to get someone to give me a map and the tower frequencies for L-54 the next morning at breakfast, and I went out to the airport. The first thing I noticed is that there weren't any O-1s sitting on the ramp. I thought, *well it must be in the hangar*. The doors to the buildings are all locked. *Must be a holiday or something*, I thought. Pretty soon another jeep drove up and an American hopped out. He introduced himself as Jim, the L-54 mechanic. He said, "Let's go if you are ready."

I said, "There's not an O-1 to go in."

He said, "We're supposed to bring our U-bird back home. They did a periodic check and it's our U-17 that goes to Luang Prabang."

Not wanting to seem cowardly, I said, "Okay, but I've never flown a U-17 before."

He said, "You are a Raven, aren't you?"

"Yes, I'm supposed to replace Bob Abbott as senior Raven there."

We threw our bags in the back and got in the plane. *Looks simple enough,* I think. *Can't be much different than the T-41 I flew in pilot training.*

Jim pulled the chocks and got back in.

I tried to start the engine, and it just wouldn't fire up. I gave it lots of throttle, but still no start. Smelled flooded. Battery was about done by this time, so I said, "Do you know how to start this thing?"

He said, "No, I only know T-28's."

I got out, thinking the engine might clear out after some time. More people were coming to work by now, so I asked who could get me a battery.

A little guy in a blue work uniform said, "You flooded it, didn't you?" Turns out he was an Air America mechanic, and he showed me how to start it. Not a lot of throttle, it has fuel injection, you know.

It cranked up right away, and it looked like we were all set. We took off and I headed about 345 degrees, which I calculated would be straight-line to Luang Prabang. The sky was partly cloudy with puffy small cumulonimbus about and beautiful green mountains and jungle below. *Great to be going to my next real good flying job,* I thought. I climbed to about 9000 feet, which cleared all the karsts according to the map. The clouds got a little thicker, so I kept my heading and went "tactical VFR" in the clouds. I was high enough, so no sweat. Thor thought I was getting too cocky I guess, and he unleashed some thunder and hail for my punishment. A quick 180 bat-turn and a bumpy five minutes got me back out of there. I knew the Mekong went through Luang Prabang, so I decided to follow the river under the clouds. It was longer that way, but we got there in about an hour and a half with no further problems.

Upon arrival we were greeted by Catfish (Major Fisher), the AOC commander. The FACs were Bob Abbott, Gene Hamner, and Mike Kelly. Gene was leaving real soon, and Mike was in Australia recovering from broken arms after crashing his O-1. Bill Tombes was the intel NCO, and Jim was the T-28 mechanic/advisor. We also had a radio operator. Since I was replacing Bob, I could see it was going to be a lonely little outpost. The T-28 squadron commander was a Lao, Lt. La. He also flew as a FAC, so I at least had some help.

Bob Abbott met us at the house, and we had lunch while he briefed me about what was going on. He was well past his time to leave, as the system had not replaced him in a timely manner. His plan was to fly with me twice that afternoon and once in the morning. He was then going to leave for Udorn and the USA that next afternoon. Pretty quick checkout for me, I thought.

Bob and I climbed in an O-1 and headed west where Bob showed me the Lima sites near the Burma border. We went to three strips, L-69 (Xienglom), L-25 (Ban Huoeisay), and another one up by L-25. We talked to the CIA case officers out there and got back about dark. It was another long day. However, the cook had saved us some dinner, and we ate on white tablecloths and had real silverware. I figured this was not going to be so bad after all.

The next morning we were going to look for boats on the Mekong and Nam Ou rivers at dawn, hoping to catch them early in the morning at sunrise. Then Bob was to head home to the USA.

We got going early, grabbed a coffee from the kitchen, and drove down to the airfield. It was dark, with nobody on the ramp except the night security. We looked the airplane (O-1) over and hopped in. The revetment where the aircraft was parked sat 90 degrees to the exit from the ramp, so I added power, pushed on the left rudder and brake to turn left, and pulled back on the stick with my forearm to keep the tail wheel down in any wind gusts.

After about 80 degrees of turn, I was shocked by a flash of light, whooshing noises, and smoke everywhere. Sure enough, eight 2.75-inch rockets fired simultaneously. The rocket tubes are not designed to do this, so things got tangled up as they all fired at once. Time slowed down to a crawl as I watched rockets bouncing off the ground and hitting each other. Two of the rockets managed to fly straight somehow, and they cleared the roof of the brand new hangar that was being built 50 yards in front of me. A couple more banged through the side of the hangar. The rest were sliding on the ground bouncing off things. The rockets that hit the hangar and the ones on the ground did not detonate. It took 22 g's for one second to arm the white phosphorus (WP) warhead, so they didn't have enough acceleration time to arm. However, the rockets that cleared the roof did have time, and I thought, *Uh-oh, that's bad.* They were headed toward the city of Luang Prabang, and worse, the King's palace sat in that direction.

I had a bad feeling in my stomach as I looked up to the arming circuit breakers, and yes, they were all pushed in (armed), and there was no safety pin in the trigger on the stick. Usually you pushed them in one at a time to fire a single rocket. I had not checked that panel in the dark, and the ground crew had missed it the night before in the dark also.

Bob Abbott in the back seat was not happy. He had planned to go to Udorn and out-process that afternoon. We told Catfish, the AOC commander, what had happened, and he said, "Let's go to the house and call the embassy." He had come down to the airfield after finding out that a smoke rocket had hit the Mekong by the King's palace and the smoke charge had gone off. After telling the story to the embassy and waiting an hour, they told Bob to fly the airplane to Vientiane for a stray voltage check, as that must have caused the rockets to all fire at once.

I saw my career as a Raven FAC waving good-bye. Nobody would forgive such a stupid mistake. I just wondered what desk in Vietnam I would be sitting at for the next six months.

Bob got all his belongings together and took off in that O-1 for Vientiane. I never saw Bob Abbott again. Years later at a Raven reunion I met Judy Abbott, Bob's widow, and found out he had died in an RF-4 accident at Red Flag. She said he had never told her why he was a week late.

We now had as FACs Gene Hamner, who was due to leave real soon, and Mike Kelly, who was in recovery for his broken arms. And of course there was me, who was probably grounded for a long time. I thought to myself, *at least I told the truth, and I was ready for my punishment. Maybe it would not ruin my next assignment, and I could fly again.*

Catfish seemed to think it would turn out OK, but I was not so sure. The next day, he told me to get a good breakfast, because I had to fly that day. He smiled and said I was forgiven and I'd better get to work. I never found out at what level I had been cleared, but I felt grateful to say the least. Gene left, and Mike Kelly also went home a few weeks later. That left only one American FAC at L-54, me, "Rocket" Raven, Raven 10. I flew about 300 missions in the next six months, and never forgot how lucky I was to be able to contribute to the lonely unknown and still largely untold war way up north at L-54.

Nevermore,
Rocket Raven

Section Three

MR II   Long Tieng   General Vang Pao's War

Long Tieng, Laos 1970 (William E. Platt Collection)

Chapter 9

The covert war in Laos was the biggest clandestine operation ever run by the CIA. Even though U.S. aid had been flowing into Laos since 1954, the year French forces fell at Dien Bien Phu, most Americans first began to hear about Laos in 1960 at a time when that country's neighbor to the east, Vietnam, was equally unknown. As the North Vietnamese increased their pressure on South Vietnam they also expanded their support for the Communist Pathet Lao in Laos. At the request of the Lao government the United States provided limited military support to counter North Vietnamese aggression.

A quiet and unassuming CIA agent named Bill Lair had organized and during the early 1960s continued to advise a Thai military organization known as the Police Aerial Reinforcement Units (PARU), which was very successful in fighting Communist infiltration in the remote villages and mountains of Thailand. The PARU quickly learned that the source of the infiltration into Thailand was the North Vietnamese-controlled areas of northern Laos, and started providing logistical assistance and training to the Lao army units fighting in the Lao provinces adjacent to North Vietnam. When the CIA heard about a Royal Lao Army Captain named Vang Pao and the success his Hmong guerrillas were having against the Communist Pathet Lao (PL) and their North Vietnamese Army (NVA) patrons, they wanted to establish contact with him. Bill Lair flew up into the Plaines des Jarres (PDJ) with one of the PARU, found Vang Pao, and the two men agreed that Vang Pao would fight the enemy with U.S. support in weapons and training.

The Geneva Accords of 1962 neutralized Laos and prohibited more than a tiny number of foreign military personnel in Laos. By 1965 the North Vietnamese had more than 15,000 army personnel in northern Laos and many more along the Ho Chi Minh Trail in eastern Laos. Something had to be done or Laos would be lost to North Vietnam and the Pathet Lao. To overcome the Geneva Accords limitation the U.S. used ex-military personnel for key support jobs in Laos. There were some tasks, however, that were better accomplished by current military personnel, so it was decided to covertly involve military people by requiring them to wear civilian clothes and assume a false status, often as a member of the U.S. Agency for International Development (USAID). Participants in this program called this process "sheep dipping." From the beginning of his service as Ambassador to Laos in 1964, William Sullivan kept a tight hold on actions by any U.S. personnel in the country. He wanted to maintain the fiction of United States observance of the Geneva Accords, even with the massive North Vietnamese violation, and prevent the capture of any covert U.S. personnel. Escalation continued on both sides and by 1966 the U.S. Air Force and Navy, which were bombing the infiltration routes into South Vietnam in eastern Laos, were providing support to Lao units fighting the North Vietnamese and Pathet Lao in northern Laos.

Early efforts to use air power in support of the commando-style operations in northern Laos had limited success. "There was a need to somehow mesh the U.S. Air Force, with its supersonic jets, with these iron age tribesmen on the ground," says Roger Warner, an author who has studied Laos and the CIA's involvement there. "The way to do it was through the Air Commandos, who had a long-standing connection to the CIA in Laos and elsewhere." Initially, Combat Control Teams from Air Commando units sent "sheep-dipped" NCOs into Laos to control airstrikes from Air

Commando, Air America, or Continental Air Services aircraft. Two of the first were MSgt Charlie Jones and TSgt Jim Stanford, and despite the difficulties inherent in this task they did an excellent job, dropping smoke grenades to mark targets and talking the strike aircraft onto the target. When General William Momyer, Commander of 7th Air Force, learned that his fighters were being controlled in Laos by non-rated NCOs, he directed that future airstrikes in Laos be controlled by rated Forward Air Controllers (FACs). That resulted in Truman (TR) Young and I being sent to Laos in May 1967.

Truman and I were stationed at Nakhom Phanom (NKP) when we were invited to join this new program. Our squadron commander made it clear it would be a hazardous assignment and gave us the option of refusing. He couldn't tell us much about where we were going but he did say that the requirement for FACs had been established and that there was a pipeline that would begin delivering FACs straight from the U.S. in the late fall. He mentioned we would be joining "Project 404" and asked us if we had heard of it. We had not. He also said he selected us for this because of the good job we had done while deployed to Khe Sahn in the spring of '67. That experience had included several hundred hours FACing for Marine reconnaissance teams, interdicting truck traffic on the Ho Chi Minh Trail, and numerous missions supporting road-watch teams in central Laos. He also said he was selecting us because we were bachelors (oh-oh).

On arrival at Udorn we received our initial briefings on Project 404, the covert American support to the Lao government, and why the large North Vietnamese presence in Laos made this necessary. Our Air Force uniforms and identification were put in storage and we were instructed to have suitable clothing tailored in Udorn. I had shirts and pants made of a tough, gray material that I thought would work satisfactorily in an escape and evasion situation. One problem I had was shoes. I was willing to wear the available smooth-soled shoes in town but I hid my USAF-issue canvas jungle boots in my pack when I left Udorn. If I had to walk out of a Laotian jungle it was going to be in those boots, not some flimsy city shoes.

When TR and I arrived at the Air Attaché (AIRA) in Vientiane in mid-June '67 there was a discussion underway about the call sign. They had received permission from 7/13 AF to use the Raven call sign and they asked TR and me if we thought it would be usable. We agreed it would do the job and became the first two FACs to fly with the Raven call sign.

Prior to our arrival Air Commandos were helping the Lao troops including General Vang Pao's Hmong guerilla units in northeast Laos. Initially the Air Commandos were ideal for the assignment that included supplying remote sites, personnel movement, and limited medical assistance as well as controlling air strikes. By 1967, however, the job had become exclusively airborne forward air control as Air America took over the complete transportation effort and USAID provided other needed support and services. The de Havilland Beaver used by the Air Commandos was a good STOL (short takeoff and landing) aircraft but not very good for the FAC mission since it did not have marking rockets. Target marking was done by hand-dropped flares, a tough proposition because it was inaccurate and required flying very close to the target. When the Air Commandos in Laos did FAC they used the call sign Butterfly that was easily confused with Firefly, the call sign of the A-1s flying out of NKP on attack missions when they were not on the SAR mission as Sandy. The call sign confusion was the reason AIRA had asked for and received the new call sign -- Raven.

TR and I were given almost new U-17As, the military version of the Cessna 185. It was a great airplane except for the communications; there was no UHF radio so we had to use a backpack radio tied into the back seat. Most of the time it worked okay. The plane had plenty of power (265 hp), and most importantly, it had eight rocket pods. The four-to-six-passenger U-17 compared favorably with the O-1Es and O-1Fs I had flown at NKP and Khe Sahn. I frequently put 100 hours on that airplane in 10 days. The planes had no marking but did have a bracket on the side where we could place insignia if desired. We were given metal flags from Laos, Thailand, South Vietnam, and the U.S. that would fit in the bracket. I seldom used any flags or markings at all. I flew with a side arm on one hip and a Philippine machete tied on to the other leg. I always had an AK-47 with plenty of ammo in the aircraft.

In the summer of 1967 there were only two of us flying FAC missions as Ravens. AIRA decided to split the country in half and gave TR everything southeast of Vientiane and me everything north of Vientiane. TR worked out of Pakse and several other locations in the south and I worked out of Long Tieng with short trips to Luang Prabang, Muong Soui, and Na Khang. My assigned call sign was Raven 41 and TR was Raven 21.

When I arrived in Long Tieng it quickly became apparent that the friendly effort in northern Laos was run by General Vang Pao (VP) and that my job was to serve as his FAC. At each evening meal, attended by about 50 of Vang Pao's men, the general would assign me a job supporting one of his commanders. The next morning I would fly to the assigned location where I would pick up a passenger/sidekick who could talk via radio to the Hmong ground troops. Since my sidekick usually did not speak English the languages we used were Lao/Thai and French. It worked surprisingly well and we had many successful missions. I found the side-by-side seating in the U-17 beneficial because we could look, point, and mark on the same map.

My first assignment from VP was to investigate a road the North Vietnamese were trying to cut through the forest about 15 km east of Long Tieng in an effort to connect the North Vietnamese-controlled PDJ south to the Mekong River. My Hmong lieutenant sidekick and I quickly found the road construction and called the Airborne Command and Control Center (ABCCC) for attack aircraft. With the help of two A-1s from NKP and four Lao T-28's working under a low overcast we accounted for one bulldozer and three trucks in two hours and ended any road building in that area. Finding and destroying that much equipment in one afternoon seemed to be a big deal in Long Tieng and there was a celebration when we returned. That evening at dinner with Vang Pao I was a minor hero and was awarded a Hmong delicacy for the day's best performance. The fried pig's ear was a very gristly, hard-to-chew prize.

Over the next seven months I provided FAC support over and around the PDJ west to Luang Prabang and northeast to the border of North Vietnam. Many of those missions were flown in support of mountain positions on the south side of the PDJ near Xieng Khouang Ville. VP's forces had a series of hilltop redoubts dotted along the south side of the Plain and these sites were frequently attacked by the North Vietnamese. As one of these positions came under attack we would use air strikes as the primary defense. Occasionally weather would prevent air strikes for several days and the Vietnamese could concentrate on one position with enough strength to force the guerilla forces to slip away and abandon the position. As soon as the weather cleared, the tables turned and we could concentrate enough air strikes to drive the enemy off the peak. Both forces dug deep defenses. The friendlies were defending against enemy artillery, and the enemy was defending against our air strikes. The Lao Air Force, including some Hmong pilots, flew T-28's out of Vientiane and Udorn and was ideal for this task. When on the defense, VP's guerilla army was good at pinpointing enemy troops and artillery. The very accurate bombs from the Lao aircraft and occasionally American A-1's and T-28's from NKP were effective in destroying and disrupting enemy concentrations. When on the offense the T-28's were frequently able to stuff a bomb directly into the defensive holes at the top of the rugged, hilltop targets. Frequently the dive angle was above 70 degrees and the pull-off altitude was below the top of the peak. The steep approach and low release allowed the T-28's to fly the bomb very close to the target and achieve excellent accuracy. They were very good pilots. Some of them had over 1000 combat missions before the war ended.

In addition to the U-17 we had a Helio Courier at Long Tieng. I didn't like to fly it because it had no rocket pods. I got that airplane shot up several times while trying to mark targets south of Xieng Khouang Ville. On one mission flying the Helio (U-10) I had Vang Pao aboard because he wanted a closer look at the North Vietnamese troops south of the PDJ. We took several bullet holes in the wings, and the CIA men helping the general would never let him fly with me again. VP was too important to risk on the judgment of a young lieutenant.

A major part of the effort while I was at Long Tieng involved support of the war raging around Lima Site 36 (Na Khang) about 140 km northeast of Long Tieng and 60 km north of the PDJ. LS-36 was the Lao government stronghold in the far northeastern part of the country and was very near the Pathet Lao/North Vietnamese headquarters at Sam Neua. Over the years there were many attacks on Na Khang. During the time I was in northern Laos there were a couple of sapper attacks but no major effort by the communists to drive the government forces from this strong position. An important reason for that was the very effective Hmong commander at LS-36. Major U Va Lee kept his reconnaissance forces well dispersed around the Sam Neua area, and we had excellent information about troop locations and early evidence of any major troop movement. The CIA men supporting Vang Pao called U Va Lee "The Indian" because he had the distinctive features of the North American Plains Indians. I had many interesting and mercurial sidekicks but The Indian was best by far. I'd pick him up at LS-36 by 0800 and we'd spend three hours in the morning and three hours in the afternoon flying over northeastern Laos checking in with his ground troops, getting the latest reports on troop movements, and putting in air strikes. The Indian was relentless. He was the only sidekick I had during my time in Laos who showed absolutely no fear no matter how intense the ground fire became.

A short story will illustrate the values and attitudes in north Laos in those days. One day with his M-16 in hand The Indian jumped out of my aircraft at 20 mph as I was landing at Long Tieng. He saw a bulldozer operator scraping the land where his first wife was interred and shot the driver right out of the seat -- yes, dead. I saw him that night at dinner with the general. He acted like nothing had happened. The only evidence of the event was a torn pants leg from his impact with the rocky runway. I don't know how they explained it to the Thai construction men who were working the project but there were no repercussions as far as I could tell.

One of our major weapons in the far northeastern corner of Laos was the frequent diversion of the Alpha Strike Force targeted in the Hanoi area. When weather forced the strike package to divert from their primary targets I was able to provide them worthwhile targets in northern Laos. I discovered this wonderful resource by accident one day early in my tour in Laos when I was asking ABCCC for strike aircraft to hit a truck on Route 6 southwest of Sam Neua. They offered me 16 F-105's each carrying six 750-pound bombs. The problem was that they were out of gas and had to be on and off target in four minutes. I took them and put them on a truck park and bivouac area nearby. I put a marking rocket into the middle of the area and had each F-105 pilot adjust slightly from the smoke he could see at roll-in. Sixteen aircraft with 96 bombs put on an amazing show. They wiped out an area half a mile square that had been interwoven with truck roads and storage revetments hidden under a jungle canopy. It would have taken us a month to do that much damage using two aircraft at a time.

Of course most of the time the Alpha Strike Force of 16 or 32 F-105's hit their targets in North Vietnam and were not available to us. But about 20% of the time they were weathered out and arrived in northern Laos out of gas and wanting to expend their bombs since they could not land with bombs aboard. All I had to do was be available about 0930 and 1430 each day and they were mine. From then on The Indian and I always had a good area target available for this remarkable resource and the North Vietnamese troop concentrations in the Sam Neua area became a lot smaller and less centralized.

Other strike resources were provided by ABCCC (Hillsborough). They frequently included F-4's from Ubon and Udorn and A-1's from NKP. Occasionally we received Navy carrier aircraft all the way from the Gulf of Tonkin. The Lao T-28's didn't have the range to support our effort north of the PDJ while they were flying out of Vientiane. After I left Laos they were stationed in Long Tieng and were able to work north of the PDJ.

Lima Site 85, a ten-minute flight northeast of Na Khang, was also known as Phou Pha Thi and Battleship Kharst. About 25 km west of Sam Neua and 12 km from the North Vietnamese border, Phou Pha Thi was the site of Channel 97, the American TACAN air navigation station closest to Hanoi. It was also the site selected for a secret AF radar facility that could direct fairly accurate bombs onto targets in the Hanoi area 24 hours a day and under all weather conditions. Once the North Vietnamese understood the capability of the all-weather bombing system, it became an important target for them. In October The Indian and I saw the North Vietnamese expanding their road network west of Sam Neua toward Phou Pha Thi. We spent a lot of our time in October, November, and December of 1967 targeting that well-defended road construction. Our success was mixed. In good weather we could slow it substantially, but during bad weather and at night it continued to push steadily west.

On 12 January 1968 one of the most bizarre incidents of the Southeast Asia war took place in an area I had been frequenting the previous three months. The North Vietnamese launched four Russian-built AN-2 Colt biplanes to try to take out the radar site at Phou Pha Thi. Unfortunately, my U-17 was at Udorn for maintenance that day or The Indian and I could have ended up right in the middle of this incident. As the four aircraft passed Sam Neua two of them broke off to watch as two of the aircraft proceeded straight for the American installation. An Air America Bell 212 helicopter, the civilian version of the Huey, was on the ground unloading supplies. Seeing the attack, the pilot, Ted Moore, and his kicker, Glenn Woods, jumped in their bird and chased down the slow biplanes. Glenn shot down one aircraft with his AK-47. Since the first shoot down took all their ammo, Moore flew the chopper directly over the wings of the second plane. The downwash resulted in the second biplane stalling and crashing in the jungle. The other two Colts fled back to North Vietnam. No damage was inflicted on the Phou Pha Thi radar or TACAN equipment. Many times over the intervening years I've pictured how I would have used the forward firing rockets and the superior speed of the U-17 to shoot down several or perhaps all those attack biplanes. Much has been written about the 12 January 1968 air attack on Phou Pha Thi and the 11 March 1968 ground attack that resulted in the loss of the site with the death of 13 of the 18 Americans manning those facilities. For more information read Air Force Magazine April 2006 and One Day Too Long, a book written by Timothy N. Castle.

In November '67 Fred Roth and Jim Cain, two FACs trained in the pipeline mentioned above, arrived in Long Tieng. Fred, an AF major, wanted the Raven 41 call sign. Jim Cain, a captain, became Raven 42. As a lieutenant I took Raven 49 for my last two months. That was my little protest about losing the Raven 41 call sign that I thought had a good reputation by then. The fighters wanted to work with 41 because I always had good targets thanks to my great sidekicks including The Indian.

It was a unique experience being a young lieutenant, temporarily removed from the Air Force, equipped with items I bought off the street in Udorn, and given a cover story that sounded like something out of a far-fetched movie plot. This combat tour was the most memorable of my four combat tours in SEA, including two combat tours in the F-105. As I reflect on my experiences in Laos, I recall visits with Captain Joe Bush at the Neutralist enclave of Muong Soui, the vital USAID effort run by Pop Buell, my mechanic Jim Casey, and the outstanding CIA personnel including Bag, Hog, Kayak, Burr, John, and many more whose names escape me now. Most of all there was General Vang Pao, who was a fascinating and talented man in a remarkable situation. In October 1967 the general gave me the pistol taken from a North Vietnamese officer who was captured south of the PDJ. It is my most treasured SEA war memento.

The visual images of northern Laos will always remain with me. Among other memories I can clearly recall the small, colorful town of Luang Prabang, missions flown up river from LP where the dramatic karst formations erupt out of the water, the startlingly beautiful countryside, the ancient burial jars that give the Plain of Jars its name, the market in Long Tieng where bricks of opium were openly for sale, and the Raven hooch that closely resembled the bar scene from Star Wars.

I left Long Tieng in late January 1968. During my seven months in Laos, I witnessed many victories and a number of difficult defeats. We lost some very good Hmong soldiers and we inflicted some important damage on the NVA stationed in northern Laos. The emotional attachment the Ravens established with the outgunned, outnumbered Hmong during their battle with the North Vietnamese is an important part of this history. They were the only people in Southeast Asia who, with our assistance, could stand up to the powerful North Vietnamese Army. I feel I speak for all the Ravens in expressing my deep admiration and respect for the Hmong people and the difficult struggle they endured during and after this war.

Chapter 10

Art Cornelius, Raven 48
Long Tieng, Feb 1968 - Sep 1968

When Jim Cain arrived at Long Tieng in 1967, General Vang Pao (VP) had two Jims working the area. In order to tell them apart, he began calling Jim Lemon "Little Jim" and Jim Cain "Big Jim." Jim Lemon is not particularly little but Jim Cain is truly a big man. He enlisted in the USAF as a teenager, married his high school sweetheart Amy, and served four years enlisted in the Air Force. Upon discharge, he went to the University of Alabama on the GI Bill, was in the Air Force ROTC, and played tackle on Bear Bryant's football team. Jim is a big guy, even though his family calls him "Tiny." Upon graduation, he went to pilot training and was assigned to Strategic Air Command (SAC) in the B-52 until selected, like Fred Roth, for a FAC assignment. Jim and Fred came through F-100 training while I was a gunnery instructor at Luke AFB, albeit in a different squadron, and I didn't interface with them while at Luke. The first time we met was at Long Tieng.

Jim Cain at Vientiane market

When Jim Lemon and Truman (TR) Young neared the end of their rotations, 19th Tactical Air Support Squadron (TASS) at Bien Hoa was tasked to send three FACs to the Air Attaché (AIRA) to take their place. The squadron commander decided he would send the three he could most easily afford to lose, which turned out to be two sector FACs (not cleared to work troops in contact) and Tom Richards, who was then with the Australians at Vung Tao. Within a week the two sector FACs were back. Tom, on the other hand, had been sent to work with Vang Pao at Long Tieng, and the General found his work excellent. Now, however, the Tactical Air Support Group (TASGp) was required to send two other, more qualified FACs to AIRA.

Just a little bit of information about Tom Richards may be in order. His father was an Army General Officer and of course Tom was raised as an Army brat. He was an enlisted member of the 11th Airborne Division in Japan on 25 June 1950 when the North Koreans invaded South Korea, so he was in Korea shortly thereafter. He spent nearly two years on the peninsula, was captured and escaped by killing his captor, was awarded two Purple Hearts, and finished his enlistment as a platoon sergeant. Returning to the U.S., he attended Virginia Polytechnic Institute and was commissioned as a Distinguished Graduate of the AFROTC program. Upon graduation he delayed reporting for a year to play football with the Baltimore Colts. After pilot training he went to SAC where he served as an aircraft commander on B-47 and B-52 aircraft. Chosen to be trained as a FAC, he was also sent through the short F-100 course at Luke while I was there. Tom's biography is worth googling.

Tom Richards on R&R north of Chang Mai, August 1968

Despite the fact that I had recently returned from a combat rotation to Bien Hoa in F-100's, because I was a rated parachutist I got my orders to report to the 2nd Brigade, 101st Airborne Division at Fort Campbell, Kentucky about the same time Tom did. After he went down to Fort Benning for a refresher course in parachuting, we deployed to Vietnam together. Assigned to the 19th Tactical Air Support Squadron (TASS) at Bien Hoa, the 101st was seen to have a plentitude of FAC talent, so many of us were pulled off and sent to other units, U.S. and allied, in South Vietnam. Tom was sent to the Australians. I was supposed to go to the Army of the Republic of Viet Nam (ARVN) 25th Division, but I told my boss, "I was sent over here with the 101st, and with the 101st I will stay." I was accommodated.

The 2nd Brigade FACs worked initially with the U.S. 25th Infantry Division out of Cu Chi as part of our area seasoning, but I moved up to Song Be with the 1st Brigade of the 101st in December 1967. On 25 January 1968 the TASGp commander, Colonel "Red" Herman, went out to find those two "more qualified" FACs. I had known Colonel Herman when he was an F-100 squadron commander at Cannon and his squadron relieved ours at Kunsan, Korea. He flew up to Song Be, about 55 miles north of Bien Hoa, and watched me control a strike, then told me over the radio to come down and see him, which of course I did. When I got there, the operations officer asked me if I was interested in an assignment in which I could make a lot more money. Since I knew I was going to separate from the Air Force after that tour, and planned to go to work for an airline which paid notoriously poor wages in the first year, I wanted to accumulate as much as I could in my savings account. I said I was interested. That's about all he knew, so he sent me to talk to an officer in Personnel who didn't know much more, except that I was to go to Udorn Air Base in Thailand to continue the interview process. I was scheduled to catch the Scatback, a T-39 Sabreliner, to Bangkok on 31 January and then take the C-130 support airplane on its trip around the American bases in Thailand and get off at Udorn. Unfortunately, the night before I was to leave, the Viet Cong (VC) and North Vietnamese Army (NVA) set off the Tet Offensive, so I was delayed about four days.

During that fight I captured a crew-served weapon and an AK-50 which, knowing I was to go somewhere unknown, I kept. In early February 1968, I finally got on the Scatback and reported to Detachment One, 56th Air Commando Wing for further questioning and information. I was quartered at a hotel in the town of Udon Thani. Each person who interviewed me would tell a little more (all he knew), and if I expressed interest, I would be passed along to the next person, who would tell me a little more. Had I expressed reservations, or been judged inadequate for their needs, I would have returned to my former assignment. I learned that the enterprise I was to support was called "Project 404" and that we were to be responsible to the Ambassador to Laos. We were to advise the CIA-supported Lao on the use of air support, coordinate airstrikes with the CIA and their paramilitary operations, and control airstrikes from aircraft assigned to us and/or from Air America or Continental Air Services aircraft for which we had priority. Active foreign military personnel were strictly limited by treaty and since all Ravens were excess to this limitation, I was given a State Department ID card and briefed on a cover story entailing working for the U.S. Agency for International Development (USAID) as an agricultural advisor. I was also told to have some civilian clothes made, including footwear, suitable for flying as a FAC since military clothing or accouterments of any kind were forbidden. I was being "sheep-dipped." I patronized the tailors and cobblers in Udorn and had several sets of flight-optimized garments made, along with a pair of elephant-hide boots. It was at Udorn that I met Lt. Col. Irv Hoyt, who was to also go to Project 404, which had not yet been tagged with the "Steve Canyon" nickname. I believe that the nickname was coined when Tom Richards became Raven 01. If anybody looked and acted like Steve Canyon, it was Tom.

Leaving my military gear in a CONEX (shipping container) at Udorn, I next caught a flight on the Lao Embassy C-47 up to Vientiane, Laos, a very short flight across the Mekong, and spent a couple of days at the Embassy getting more briefings. There I learned that all the Project 404 FACs used the call sign "Raven." In addition to working with Vang Pao and the Meo (Hmong) guerrillas from Long Tieng, Ravens also operated out of the Royal Capitol of Luang Prabang (LP) in the hills near the headwaters of the Mekong, and at Savannakhet and Pakse on the lower Mekong, supporting the Royal Lao Army. By far and away, as I was to discover, the most action was with Vang Pao.

Even though I was a couple of weeks late, I was replacing Jim Lemon. Tom Richards went down to Pakse to replace Truman Young, and Hoyt was sent to replace Tom at Long Tieng, designated Lima Site 98 (LS-98). Since Long Tieng was a secret location we were told to refer to it as LS-20 Alternate, LS-20A, or Alternate. LS-20 was Sam Thong, a legal USAID hospital location about 10 miles north of Long Tieng across Skyline Ridge. Hoyt was to be the senior FAC and air advisor to Vang Pao. VP was shortly to be promoted to Major General and it was felt that he should have a more senior air advisor, hence the assignment of Hoyt. I was given a lift out to the south side of the Vientiane Airport where the Air America passenger terminal was located, and checked in with them for a ride to Long Tieng. Hoyt would follow the next day. I was directed to an unpainted C-46 Curtiss Commando, an airplane about 25 years old at that time, and told that it would take me to Long Tieng. There were two other passengers. One was a young Lao Army soldier in khakis and red beret, and the other was a young Hmong woman dressed in her traditional costume of black pajamas, interlocked fluorescent pink and chartreuse sashes, maroon turban, and heavy silver necklace and bracelets.

I had never even seen a C-46 before, much less ridden on one, and this plane was really a new side of aviation to me. Both the passenger door and the freight door had been removed from this huge twin-engine transport, leaving at least an eight-foot hole at the left rear of the fuselage. Down the middle of the cabin were rollers which made a bend and ended at the doorway. It was obvious that if one fell on the rollers, one was going out the door. There were troop seats along the sides of the cabin where passengers were to sit. While waiting to board, I observed two ancient aviators (probably mid-50s) who had obviously been rode hard and put up wet more than once, dressed in blue-gray Air America uniforms (sans hat), stroll out to the airplane and prepare to take this large chunk of aluminum into the sky. Not without reservations, I boarded, and those two old guys worked together to get that great big machine off the runway and heading north. We climbed up through the overcast and flew for about an hour, then let down into the cloud again. Breaking out underneath, all I could see in every direction were jungle-covered mountains…BIG mountains. Then, down in a valley, I could see what looked like sparkle that a giant hand had flung across the valley floor. There were a half-dozen karsts (vertical outcroppings of limestone, the top edges of which appeared sharp as a razor) sticking up out of the jungle, and a single, narrow runway with a ridgeline at one end and karsts at the other end. As we got lower and lined up for an approach through a saddle in the ridge at the southeast end of the runway, I realized that the sparkle was water from the last rain, caught in the corrugated roofs of close to a hundred hooches around the runway.

We landed, and I thought that Shangri-La must have looked like this. The mountains surrounded the airstrip and went up to nearly 10,000 feet. The only pavement was the asphalt of the runway. All other paths, trails, and roads were dirt. There were small people everywhere, none much over five feet tall, There were soldiers dressed in fatigues, some with red or maroon berets and some with fatigue caps, some with boots of leather or canvas, others with shower shoes, others barefoot. There was a multitude of native people, dressed in a variety of traditional costumes, and there were helicopters, Porters, Helios, C-46s, C-47s, and C-123s constantly flying in, loading, and flying out. It was a beehive of activity, and I had no idea where to go. Asking the Air America agent for directions, I was told how to get to the Raven hooch. Carrying my footlocker, pack, and the AK-50, I hiked up the road and found the hooch. As I passed the karst at the northeast end of the airstrip, I noticed the remains of an Air America C-123 at the base, a souvenir of an attempted go-around. The only people at the Raven hooch were Fred Roth, Jim Casey who was a mechanic, and Red Roberts, the radio man. Also living at the hooch were several weather observers who would come and go. The other FAC, Jim Cain, was on R&R so I took the other bunk in his room. That's where I lived for the next seven months.

The next day I met John Randall, the head Sky (CIA) guy at Long Tieng, Burr (Mr. Clean) Smith who was the operations officer and one of the original World War II, Easy Company, Band of Brothers, Jerry (Hog) Daniels, and Howie Freeman, a former Special Forces soldier. Irv Hoyt and I went out on an orientation flight in 854, the U-17, the military version of the Cessna 185. Because we landed so often to pick up locals, the frequent starting load would deplete the standard Cessna battery, so a battery from a T-28 was installed. In order to remain within center of gravity (CG) limitations, the third row of seats was removed and the battery moved up to behind the second row of seats. The U-17 had long-range tanks (84 gallons) and eight rocket tubes, mounted four under each wing. It was powered by an IO-470, the fuel-injected version of

the engine in the O-1 Bird Dog I had been flying in Vietnam. It had a funky push-pull knob for a throttle, a vernier mixture control, and, God help me, a wheel instead of a control stick. Hoyt had a lot of experience in different reciprocating-engine aircraft, so his insight was valuable. Red Roberts had installed an antenna and connection for a PRC-41 back-pack UHF radio so we were able to control fighters as long as the battery didn't run out.

Art Cornelius and Red Roberts

The elevation at LS-98 is 3200 feet and the runway was about 4000 feet long, although the south 1000 feet was virtually unusable due to the ridgeline on the approach. We always landed to the northeast, toward the karst (known as the vertical speedbrake) and took off to the southwest. The following day Fred took me to Nha Khang, Lima Site 36 (elevation over 3,600 feet, length a little over 3,000 feet) and up to Phou Pha Thi, LS-85 (elevation over 3,000 feet, length less than 1,000 feet) for an area checkout. LS-85 was a critical piece of the Air Force campaign against the North because of the tactical air navigation (TACAN) station (North Station, Channel 97) and the TSQ-81 radar located atop the towering massif. There was also a TACAN station atop Skyline Ridge, north of LS-20A, known as South Station, Channel 79. Air America pilots got six months of orientation. I got these two days but now I was cleared to confront the enemy unsupervised, except for the local who would have to fly with me. I was taken down to General Vang Pao's home for dinner that night and met VP while being indoctrinated into the daily routine of discussing the day's operations and planning the next day with representatives of VP's staff, Sky, and Police Aerial Reinforcement Units (PARU). Oh, and with White Horse scotch.

The two TACAN stations in northern Laos weren't of any direct benefit to us since none of our airplanes except borrowed T-28s had a TACAN installed. They could, and were, used to effect rendezvous with strike aircraft. I drew TACAN azimuth and distance measuring equipment (DME) arcs on my maps, which worked just fine.

Fred Roth had no experience as a FAC outside of Laos, and most of his work had been done from Air America or Continental Air Services Porters using smoke grenades to mark and relaying instructions to jets through A-1 Fireflies. The Air America and Continental Air Services aircraft had only VHF radios and the fighters had only UHF. I went out on a limb and told Fred that I thought the U-17 was good if you had to carry more than just one other person, and it did have enough fuel to stay up for nearly six hours, but that it had limitations that reduced its utility in many instances. The U-17 was somewhat faster than an O-1, but to get into and out of many of the airstrips we would be working, the O-1 which would be much better in terms of agility and visibility.

Roth soon moved down to work at the Embassy in Vientiane, assuming the call sign Raven 01. From there he contacted Richard Secord at our logistics supply facility (Water Pump) at Udorn and we shortly got some O-1As that had been rescued from the Army and painted new. They had 1950s vintage crystal VHF radios and the only navigational aid was an RDF radio about which I had read but had never before seen. They did have FM and UHF radios, which was a big improvement over the back-pack PRC-41 radio we used in the U-17. Another advantage of these airplanes was that they were very light and had climb propellers.

I worked up there for about a week before "Big Jim" (Killer) Cain returned from R&R, and he and I developed a lasting friendship in the nearly six months before he finished his tour and went back to SAC. Irv Hoyt was in the job about ten days, but at 43 years old and a veteran of the closing days of World War II, was reluctant to take any risks or to be very effective. Vang Pao told the CIA to get rid of him, and he went back to his previous assignment in Vietnam. Big Jim Cain inherited command, even though he was junior to me, and that was appropriate. I was green and he was experienced, having survived losing one airplane at that time, and I took command when he left. Command is probably a misnomer, since we were all working hard and there was not a real military chain of command. Everyone just did his job as well as he could and tried to stay alive.

Vang Chou and Art Cornelius

The first time I went out to run airstrikes I was given a stocky, tall (for a Hmong) observer/translator named Vang Chou. I later learned that Chou's mother was Vang Pao's sister. Off we went in the U-17, which VP and Chou called "the Cessna," to cover an Air America H-34 helicopter extraction of wounded from a position on a hilltop overlooking the southern edge of the Plaines des Jarres (PDJ). We had some Thai mercenary T-28s called the B-team to work with us. We watched the helicopter come in and land, and he wasn't on the ground more than 20 seconds. He had barely lifted off when a mortar round hit right where he had been. The helicopter made it out OK, but I was so furious about not knowing from whence had come the mortar that I just growled and launched a white phosphorus (WP, or Willie Pete) rocket out into the Plain and we were immediately surrounded by 37 mm shells going off. I was very lucky not to have been hit and was still really mad. I guess Chou reported to VP that the new guy was OK, because that night at dinner he was all smiles. Vang Chou and I later flew over a hundred sorties together and even though we had close calls, neither of us was hurt.

As I began to work airstrikes, they ranged from south of the southern edge of the PDJ as far north as LS-85. It was obvious that the NVA were building a road from Sam Neua toward Phou Pha Thi, and I took pictures of it and brought them to Burr Smith. He and John Randall were very concerned about that road and what it portended for the site and the TSQ radar atop the rock, which was doing significant damage to the North. They brought their concerns to VP, but he was not worried. He believed that the enemy, which he called Viet Minh, could not reach the site.

Phou Pha Thi Lima Site 85

I had been at Long Tieng about a month when on the night of 10 March I was awakened by Burr Smith and told that LS-85 was under attack. That did it for sleep that night, and we made plans for me to get to Pha Thi at first light. It was about a good hour's flight time from Alternate in the U-17, so I decided to take it. That would give me more time on station as well. Burr assigned Roshen, a PARU NCO, to go with me so at about 0400 we got airborne from Alternate. It was as dark as the inside of a cow and of course we were not supposed to fly at night. All the Americans who discussed the problem felt that we could justify flying at night in this situation, but I never heard what the Ambassador had to say about it.

We arrived at LS-85 at about 0500, right at first light, but by that time the damage was done. I had met several of the technicians working at the TSQ radar site just days before, and I was furious that they had been lost. In any case, we dropped low over the rock looking for targets and controlled many F-105 and A-1 strikes harassing the retreating NVA before I had to break it off for rockets and fuel. After topping off at LS-36, we headed back up for another session, although an enlisted commando Forward Air Guide was working strikes from the ground. He did wonderful work that day and I heard later that he had been awarded the Silver Star. He deserved it.

77

We decided to try to evacuate the Thai and Hmong troops who had been protecting the site, and there were two armored and armed Super Jolly Green Giants (HH-53) circling to the south. Unarmed single-pilot Air America Hueys were going in and out, pulling people off, but they had limited capacity, particularly at that altitude. I got frustrated, as did the crews of the Jollys, at the refusal of their headquarters to allow them to come in. Finally, one of them came in and made a touch-and-go to the helipad to see if they would draw fire, which they did not. Then they both came in sequentially and pulled the troops out. My frustration was just boiling over by that time, but I had to again go refuel, this time at Alternate since LS-36 was saturated. I landed and took an O-1 that time and went back to LS-85, and by that time we had been instructed to destroy the radar and the TACAN, which we did. By the time I got back to Alternate I had flown over 12 hours and it was about 2030 and again dark. The guys on the ground drove two jeeps down to the strip and shined the lights of one across the end of the strip and the other down the longitudinal axis of the strip. I landed exhausted, but still fuming.

In March and April two more FACs came over from Vietnam to join us at Alternate. Tom Shera, who had been an AC-47 pilot, and Sam Deichelmann, who had flown Blind Bat C-130s and O-1s, integrated with us and we were glad to have the help. When Sam came trudging up the road to the hooch, I was sitting next to the windows doing paperwork and I watched him approach. He was about six feet tall, slim, with longish (for 1968) bright blonde hair, wearing jeans and a T-shirt with a logo from a Waikiki surf shop. He was carrying a beat-up alligator-skin bag with a tennis racket sticking out of it, and I thought, "What have they sent us?" Sam's father was an Air Force General Officer who had been Commandant of the AFROTC, stationed at Maxwell AFB, Alabama. I learned that he had told Sam as he approached high school graduation in Montgomery that he was going to the Air Force Academy. Sam didn't want to, so following his graduation in 1957 he took off and wound up in Havana, Cuba. There he met a guy who was sailing his sloop to New Zealand, through the Panama Canal, and he asked Sam if he wanted to go along. Sam agreed, and off they went. They stopped in Honolulu, and Sam decided he wanted to stay there and go to college at the University, so his mother supported him while he took his degree in Philosophy. Commissioned through the AFROTC at University of Hawaii, he went to pilot training and flew C-130s in France, then went into the Blind Bat program, flying C-130s with starlight scopes looking for traffic on the Ho Chi Minh Trail. Deciding he wanted to be a FAC, he extended, used his leave to go to the FAC school at Phan Rang and became a FAC in South Vietnam. When able, he volunteered for the Raven program.

An attack at LS-36 was foiled in April, and in May VP decided to begin an offensive northwest of Nha Khang near a village called Muong Xon. Toward the second week of this fight, Chou and I found an actual barracks complex northeast of Muong Xon, hidden beneath the jungle canopy, and struck it. That night VP said we had killed "a thousand enemee." I'm not sure that was accurate, but we did put a dent in the Vietnamese ability to have a presence in that piece of real estate. By 15 May I had logged 100 hours and 50 sorties for the month. I was physically whipped, so I took off for California and my son's fourth birthday, leaving the fight to the Jims, Tom, and Sam. There was plenty of work for everybody.

L-36

I got back to Long Tieng about 3 June and wasn't there more than a week or two when we got word that Sam and Chou had found a huge convoy of trucks on Route 4 over near the North Vietnamese border, east of the PDJ. They were in the U-17 and started putting in air on them. Soon the column of smoke was so high Sam didn't have to mark any more. Now the night before, Sam had been up late and was "tired," so as the strike flights began to sort out their own sequence, he had Chou fly the airplane while he reclined his seat for some rest. Chou decided he wanted to see what was under a tree line just west of the road and took the Cessna down low for a look. As he did so, a 12.7 mm machine gun opened up and stitched the side of the cockpit. One bullet hit Chou in the right upper arm, went through and into his chest, went through and barely missed Sam's reclined head. Sam immediately sat up, took the airplane and started climbing and running west across the PDJ to Sam Thong. When he could, he tried to apply a battle dressing to Chou's sucking chest wound but the dressing was too small. As he got to within radio range of Long Tieng he told us what had happened. The cockpit was covered with blood and neither Sam nor Chou was sure that Chou would survive. Landing at Sam Thong, Chou was rushed into the hospital and a call went out for blood donors.

All the Ravens, mechanics, radio techs, and weathermen got up to Sam Thong and held out their arms, but to no avail. Chou is blood type O-negative, the universal donor, but he has to have O-negative blood. Somehow, the word got out to the Sky guys all over Laos and pretty soon a dozen showed up to donate blood for Chou. Today he probably has more American than Lao blood in him. I accused Burr of hiring his people on the basis of blood type so they could all donate to one another. Chou obviously survived, but at the time none of us were sure that he would. He's one tough Hmong, but when I left in September he was still looking mighty puny. At that time he had three children with Mai, his wife. He now has five, so I guess that part was OK.

One morning in early June, Tom Shera and I were working targets near LS-36, me in the U-17 and Tom in an O-1. After the morning strikes we landed at Nha Khang, refueled, rearmed, and had a

79

lunch of C-rations. The U-17 had more time on it than the O-1 since their last maintenance visit to Udorn, but they were both approaching the mandatory 100-hour service. I didn't want both aircraft gone at the same time, so we decided to switch airplanes. Tom would control the small number of airstrikes in the afternoon, then take the airplane back to Alternate. I would stay at LS-36 and build up some rockets to replenish our supply, then fly the O-1 straight home. Tom, a Thai mercenary FAC and a Forward Air Guide, call sign Blue Boy, got in the airplane, started and taxied up the hill to the north end of the runway. As they began their takeoff roll, I was paying attention to the rockets I was building until I heard a collective moan from the fifty or so Hmong lining the runway and watching. As I looked up for Tom, I saw the airplane cartwheel into the swampy area just southeast of the strip. That swamp had mines in it that were laid by the French in the '40s, the Japanese also in the '40s, and the French again in the '50s, and by Sky in the '60s. Nobody knew where the other guys' mines were located. There were a few trails through the swamp, and you were OK if you stayed on those trails. Once in a while, one of the Hmong would get drunk, wander off the trails, and we'd find another mine.

U-17 at L-36

The U-17, as it cartwheeled, tore both wings off outboard of the struts, bent the tail around the fuselage, and came to rest with the nose buried in the muck. It hit no mines. One of the Sky operators was sighting in his Swedish-K off the south end of the runway when all of this occurred and his first impulse was to run out there to help. About ten steps into the minefield he remembered where he was and stopped dead, balanced on one foot, then backed out putting each foot exactly where it had landed on the way out. An Air America Huey was preparing to lift off at the top of the strip, and he kicked off his cargo and flew out to hover over the wreck. In the meantime, the Thai FAC, Blue Boy, and Tom exited the airplane, in that order, through Tom's window. They were afraid the airplane was going to burn and explode, and the smell of fuel permeated the air. By the time Tom got out he had boot marks up his back. He and the Thai had some bruises and minor cuts on their foreheads, but Blue Boy had a broken collar bone. He had not been strapped in. They climbed up on the skid of the Huey and into the cabin, then were all flown down to the hospital at Sam Thong for repairs. 854 was now just junk. Contaminated fuel caused the loss of power and we started filtering our fuel through a chamois.

We figured Tom deserved a day off, but the next time he flew he was in a Helio looking over an airstrip just southwest of Nha Khang when they took a bullet through the magnetos and the engine quit. Dead-sticking the airplane onto the (unoccupied) airstrip that had recently been the object of their attention, they were OK. Air America flew in a squad of Hmong for security and a mechanic to fix the mags, and they flew the airplane out. Now we gave Tom two weeks off. He went down to Bangkok and relaxed, and when he came back it was decided, after much thought, to send him up to LP to replace Marlin Siegwalt, who was nearing the end of his tour. Nothing ever happened at LP so we figured Tom deserved a little less pressure. Unfortunately, on his last orientation flight out of LP with Marlin, Tom was in the back seat of an O-1 with the stick removed and stowed on the sidewall and the rudder pedals folded down out of the way. While looking over one of the roads in the area, Marlin was shot in the chest and immediately incapacitated. Tom kept the airplane in the air with elevator trim until he could get the rudder pedals up and the stick in its socket, then flew Marlin to a hospital for medical attention. By the time they arrived, Marlin had bled out. The decision was made for Tom to complete his tour at the Embassy where his experience would be put to good use working with Tom Richards.

We tended to wear airplanes out, so we started getting O-1s that had been used in South Vietnam to augment and replace the ones we lost. In mid-August I had the opportunity to go down to Bien Hoa along with a FAC from another location, George Willams. It was an enjoyable trip during which I got to see old friends at Bien Hoa, Phan Rang, and Tuy Hoa. We brought the two airplanes into Udorn to have them configured for Raven duty. In September, Sam Deichelmann volunteered to make the run to Bien Hoa to pick up another Bird Dog and to see his brother who was flying A-37s there. On his flight back to Udorn, Sam disappeared and has never been found. Sam and I had become particularly close, especially after Jim Cain rotated, and his loss affected me greatly. I was moved to write a poem about my feelings and I gave a copy of it to Craig Morrison at the 1978 Raven reunion in Tucson. It became a tradition to read the poem at the annual Raven reunion, toast our absent comrades, and then fling our wine glasses into a mock fireplace. When Chris Robbins wrote "The Ravens" he included that poem in his narrative describing the reunions of the Edgar Allan Poe Literary Society. This is the Raven organization started in the 1970s and is intended to last until the sole surviving Raven drinks the bottle of Lau Lao rice whiskey saved all these years for that purpose.

About midway through my time in Laos I had checked out in the T-28D, used as a fighter-bomber by the Royal Lao Air Force. This airplane gave us a much quicker reaction time out of L-98 due to its much higher speed, and we could carry some ordnance in addition to our marking rockets. We also had two .50-caliber machine guns which would allow us to get defenders heads down when we marked. We weren't supposed to fly the T-28 because if we were shot down it would undermine the posture that the U.S. was scrupulously observing the provisions of the Geneva Accords. One day in early September at about midday we got a call for air to support an outpost under attack north of the PDJ and I grabbed a T-28 to go out and run the airstrike. The Lao pilot went with me in the back seat and it's a good thing he did. VP planned to include me in a Basi he was throwing for a visiting Thai general that night before I was to go down to Vientiane to out-process. Tom Richards and several of the staff at the Embassy were coming up and I didn't want to put Tom on the spot by landing a T-28 at Long Tieng with him there. Instead I landed up at Muong Soui after calling an Air America Porter to come and land there to pick me up and take me back to Long Tieng. It worked out and we all had a partly sober evening. I was concluding my second combat tour and leaving active duty. I had been <u>very</u> lucky.

When I wrote up my end-of-tour report I made several recommendations, some of which were observed and some of which were not. The OV-10 was coming into service in South Vietnam and was being flown by FACs out of NKP in northeastern Thailand. That airplane was designed to operate from unimproved airstrips (like Lima Sites), had the capability to carry more marking rockets, had improved range and loiter time, and had some 7.62 mm machine guns to at least enable us to get enemy heads down when marking. I recommended that we get some. We never did. Also we either had to prepare our meals or go to Sky's mess hall across the street. We were really a bit busy to take the time to prepare nutritious meals, so could they send us a cook. They eventually did. The A-1s were great at close air support but most of the F-4 and F-105 crews with whom we worked were used to the environment in North Vietnam. They would pull off quite high in the "One pass, haul ass" mode and as a consequence were much less accurate than needed. We were reluctant to use them very close to friendlies. The F-100 pilots from the South Vietnam bases were extremely proficient at close air support, and so should be fragged to Ravens, even if it meant they would have to refuel in-flight. That was also done, though rarely.

Leaving Laos closed a significant chapter in my life and I had bittersweet feelings about it. I left active duty, which I loved, but I had a job offer from an airline and I would get to participate in my marriage and in the raising of my children. Over the time I was there we had another half-dozen FACs cycle in and out, and I was the only one of my peer group who finished his tour without losing an airplane or being wounded or killed. Maybe Hoyt knew something I didn't. Vang Chou had been grievously wounded and the Hmong continued to suffer too many losses. After 1975 when the Hmong fled to Thailand, Chou and his family were resettled in the San Joaquin Valley in California. We still stay in touch and enjoy periodic joyful reunions. In subsequent years I was fortunate to have a wonderful career in the airline industry and in the Air National Guard, my children have adult children of their own, and I get to spend the days with my best friend, my wife. The surviving Ravens continue to gather annually at Randolph Air Force Base, and we stay in touch by email. My call sign was Raven 48, and Mike Cavanaugh and Moose Carroll, the other Raven 48's, and I are watching each other to see who gets to drink the Lau Lao.

Chapter 11

Mike Cavanaugh, Raven 48
Long Tieng, Apr 1969 – Oct 1969

Square Trees

Being a forward air controller (FAC) was an art form. It was exciting to say the least, listening to three radios at the same time, four sets of fighters overhead all running out of fuel, troops on the ground crying for help and confused as to where the enemy is located, and the distraction of ground fire aimed at putting you out of commission. The art of finding the bad guys took some imagination, observation, and persistence. I have to admit that it took a few months before I really could see clearly and pick out clues as to where the little bastards were hiding and their equipment stores.

I remember my first real FAC art job like it was yesterday. In my area of operations (AO) in the delta in Vietnam there was a graveyard located along a river bank, complete with a black iron gate and fence. There were about 16 graves, and half were empty and the other half had slabs covering the graves. After seeing it day after day all of a sudden I noticed a difference. I made a sketch of the graveyard and which graves were open and which were covered. Sure enough the next day several graves were covered that were empty the day before. So it was not a holy resting place after all, but a supply transshipment spot. I got a flight of two A-37s (Call Sign Rap) to hit my find and the reward was a tremendous secondary explosion from the crypt.

There were many such "finds" as time went on. I equipped myself with a set of binoculars with a zoom feature and I could let the aircraft fly itself while I studied the ground below looking for signs of what didn't fit nature's pattern. The bad guys would use foliage to camouflage their equipment and ammo, but if it wasn't fresh you could see the difference in color and the leaves dull side up instead of the natural shiny side.

Being a Raven FAC was close to heaven. You really could use creativity and the experience of a tour in Vietnam to do an excellent job of engaging the enemy and survive. It was no secret that trucks were moving supplies at night along the many routes through Laos to feed the war in South Vietnam. What the secret was where they hid during the day when the Ravens did their flying.

In 1969 I had the good fortune of being the first Raven to check out in the T-28D and fly FAC missions out of Lima Site 20A. The bad news for the North Vietnamese Army (NVA) was we could now reach them quicker and earlier in the T-28. The first early morning take-off "Dawn Patrol" in the O-1 Bird Dog was at least one and a half hours away from the NVA. In the T-28 "Dawn Patrol" it was only 30 minutes to show time. When I first started flying the T-28 I was able to surprise the NVA in early morning before they could secure their trucks and get their morning rice.

The roads all looked like the surface of the moon from all the bomb craters, but the enemy used native slave crews to patch the roads and the trucks kept on coming from north to south every night. I noticed one crossing point on Route 7 coming out of Ban Ban Valley and tried a trick that worked once. I hit the mushy road crossing with two sets of fighters at dusk. The next morning I flew the Dawn Patrol in the T-28 and what a wonderful sight! The road crews were still working on the damage and 17 trucks were all lined up on the mountain road waiting to cross and hide for the day. I knocked out the first and last truck with strafe. The truck drivers all bailed out from the festivities and we had the entire day to destroy the 17 trucks.

Another great mission was finding square trees in the Plaine des Jarres (PDJ) on a regular FAC flight with Moonface, my Lao backseater. I spotted a poor camouflage job and decided to hit it with an air strike. Moonface could not figure out what I was up and questioned my judgment. I told him, "Trees not square." with a visual to make him understand. The first set of bombs missed but it blew the brush back to reveal crates stacked six feet high. The second pass scored a direct hit and the rockets headed for Saigon blew sky high with a fireball about 1,000 feet in size. It was absolutely beautiful.

So, every day when I picked up Moonface to go fly, I would ask him, "What we do today?" He would say, "Many many enemy. Maybe we find square tree too OK?"

Mike Cavanaugh, Vang Pao and Burr Smith

How to Make a Combat Cook . . . Cook

Thanks to my good lifelong friend, Ronnie O. Rinehart (aka Papa Fox), we also had a combat cook at 20A. Previous to my arrival in April 1969 the Ravens had to cook for themselves until Papa Fox obtained/kidnapped a USAF cook from Nakhon Phanom (NKP) Royal Thai Air Base.

USAF Staff Sgt. Manual Espinosa (aka Espi) was a welcome addition to the Raven house and a decent cook. He enjoyed the camaraderie of the pilots and since we had no rank or uniforms we were all on first-name basis. Espi had a great personality and would often refer to his one-eyed friend in his pants as "Wally." Espi was never responsible for anything that went wrong on R&R

visits to Thailand…it was always Wally's fault. Wally got sick on occasion from meeting up with bad company in Udorn.

So one morning at 5 AM I was getting ready for Dawn Patrol and there was no cook. I went into Espi's room and kicked his bunk and told him I had a long combat day ahead and needed some breakfast. The reply from under the blankets was, "Mike, go fix breakfast yourself." I jerked our combat cook out of the sack. "Put on your boots, Espi, I am going to show you exactly why I need breakfast. You are going flying." There was much protesting of course, but my angry 220 pounds outmuscled this little insubordinate twerp. I threw Espi in the back seat with a USAF headset and fired up the T-28. He tried to get out but I closed the canopy and locked us both in for the ride. I flew up to Ban Ban Valley and got some F-4s to join me for an NVA greeting party and found some stragglers just off Route 7. I would look in my mirror to check on Espi when I could grab a moment and most of the time I could not see him. He ducked down inside the cockpit out of sight. I made sure I pulled a lot of Gs to keep him nailed to the seat cushion. When he did take a peek I would slam his head into the canopy by doing a wingover. I was hungry and evil.

I decided to show Espi some ground fire after we put in some air strikes. There was a three-level gunner by Arrowhead Lake that was attempting to earn a green card because his 37 mm shots were way off the mark but good for demonstration purposes. I got Espi to look as the gunner fired his five rounds in our general direction and it freaked Espi out. "We could get killed!" screamed Espi. At this point I guessed that Espi was fully combat oriented.

I opened the canopy during the landing so Espi would get plenty of fresh 160-knot air. I parked the T-28 and went to help Espi out of the back. To his credit he did not puke during the mission but I could see Espi was a different person. He was a bit shaky until his feet were on the tarmac. He put both hands on the wing and said, "You are the pilot and you do the flying." Then he put both hands on his chest and said, "I am the cook and I do the cooking." I said, "Espi, I think we understand each other."

The next morning at 5 AM I could smell bacon and coffee coming from the kitchen. Espi had his Air Force whites on and said, "How do you want your eggs, Baby, how do you want your eggs?"

Intel

In military terminology we refer to the intelligence function as "intel" for short and the folks that work in the intelligence field as "intel pukes"—sort of a term of endearment. intel can be excellent and it also can kill you as a pilot. Intel is not always very intelligent. Photo intel is hard evidence of a target but an agent report is suspect, so as a combat pilot you learn what to trust and when to be careful. As a class, intel pukes are arrogant and act like they have all the information in the world, and they will only give you what "you need to know." In Vietnam I would get a weather briefing, also suspect, and an intel briefing, mostly useless. I learned to generate my own intel with my own two eyes during the course of a combat mission. As a Raven flying in Laos it was so much better. No time-consuming briefings. We had our own intel from our activities.

In Laos there was a cluster of intel pukes in the embassy and they stayed out of our rice bowl for the most part and collected reports from us when we had time to send them. They had tea parties, trips to Bangkok, and important stuff to do anyway. However, there was a notable exception. The intel pukes identified the location of the Pathet Lao Communist radio, which was broadcasting anti-American propaganda to the entire countryside. It had to be silenced was the directive from downtown Vientiane. Unfortunately, the radio was transmitting from a building which was in a restricted circle we were not allowed to touch. It was a Chinese mission located right next to Arrowhead Lake in the Plaine des Jarres. We all knew that the "mission" was bogus but so were a lot of rules we were supposed to follow. There were nine buildings inside the circle and all of the two-story wooden structures were in poor repair, and I never saw a human being anywhere near or in this circle. Somehow the intel pukes got permission to hit this building inside the forbidden circle on a one-time-good deal.

The intel had eight-digit coordinates on the radio station. Normally we worked with six-digit coordinates and that was good enough, but eight digits gets down to a few feet, like the southwest corner of this particular building.

So the mission was given to a flight of F-4s from Ubon Royal Thai Air Base with one 2,000 pound laser-guided (LGB) smart bomb. The laser business was fairly new in 1969, especially in Laos. I was sent to FAC the mission but the F-4 guys basically told me to stay out of the way and that they had photos and the exact coordinates. In fact, I could not even see them because they were at such a high altitude. One aircraft was the laser designator and one was the bomber. It took some time for them to get the laser designation and the bomber in the proper geometry but they did. I was watching the target building through my binoculars as the 2,000 pound bomb obliterated the entire building…gone forever. Mission accomplished, I reported to Vientiane.

The next morning I got this nasty message that my report was incorrect and the target was NOT hit. I fired back a response that told them the eight-digit target they gave me was no longer part of this planet...it was a very deep hole and it was the intel that was faulty. That set off a word storm from a very hurt intel puke. I got a free lecture on their professionalism and dedication. Give me a break! The whole operation had to cost over a million dollars. For all I know that radio is still in operation today. They never did find the thing on my watch.

So every day I open my computer and there is a sticker on my computer, and yours too most probably, that says "Intel Inside." I smile and say, "Yeah, right!"

The Rescue of Raven 48

On June 25, 1969 I had been a Raven FAC for only two months in Laos, but during that short time I saw more combat than the entire year in Vietnam. I flew 10 hours of combat every day which is about one weeks flying at the end of my first tour. On this particular day flying the mighty O-1 Bird Dog, I was on my third mission of the day in the late afternoon. I was three hours into my four-hour gas tank and the ABCCC, call sign "Cricket," kept sending me fighters to strike targets on the Ho Chi Minh Trail. I looked at my Lao backseater, Moonface, who was half asleep. His job was to communicate with the Lao forces on the ground but on this type mission there were no ground forces involved so he had nothing to do. Moonface looked at his watch and said "We go home now?" Good idea my friend but I had fighters stacked up waiting for clearance to strike. I called Cricket and inquired as to my Raven replacement since I had just enough fuel to make it home. Cricket informed me that I had no replacement. 20A was socked in. The Ravens were weathered in. What??

I had been too busy flying to notice the black weather front making its way from south to north. The rainy season was just starting. A cold chill ran down my spine. I had no place to go. There was no friendly airfield within an hour of flight time and I had less than one hour of gas. I called Cricket and said, "Do you guys realize that if the Ravens are weathered in that I am weathered out?" Silence. The next transmission was a demand. "I want Zorro 50 and 51 to join me over the PDJ ASAP." I knew the first two night A-1 Skyraiders out of NKP would be taking off about this time. Our friendly forces had lost all of the PDJ and our forward operating base, Muong Soui, had been overrun two days prior. In fact we had to put several air strikes into Muong Soui to destroy all the military equipment we left behind. Landing in the PDJ was sure crash and capture. There were no good options. My first plan was to press through the weather front.

Cricket informed me that my request for Zorro 50 and 51 was honored. At least I would have company. With all the venom I could muster I told Cricket, "I am declaring a search and rescue at this time." The reply came back, "Who's down?" My answer, "ME, you idiots, you left me high and dry without a place to land. I will be down in less than 30 minutes, out of fuel, and there is not one friendly location within one hour of my present position. If I survive this I will be crawling up your flight deck and break your coffee cups into pieces and stuff them up your left nostril." Silence.

I had been heading south toward the PDJ ever since I realized how much trouble I was in. I hit the weather front with some sort of a loose plan to land at my home base even without radar or an instrument approach. The black wall of the storm was very unkind and spit me out immediately. There was no way my little Bird Dog was getting through this mess. The good news was the raspy voice of Dale Brink, Zorro 50, from his Skyraider. "Hey Raven 48 what's up?" I explained my dilemma with Plan B, which was suggesting a Bernie Fisher (Medal of Honor) A-1 rescue with me crashing the Bird Dog and one of them landing and picking me and Moonface up. Bad idea, I was told as Zorro 51, Rich Rose, joined the planning session. They told me that the night before the PDJ was ablaze with new guns and we would not survive a landing, much less a complicated pickup under fire. Scratch Plan B.

I started Plan C, which was to land at Muong Soui even though it was no longer under our control. At least there was a runway so we wouldn't have to crash-land. Also there was a secret stash of CIA gas in a bunker just off the runway. Maybe there was a chance it was still there. A lot of maybes came out in conversation. The Zorros could protect me on the landing and cover me while I worked out Plans D & E on the ground. Both tanks showed near empty at this point so I wasn't going any further in any case. We met up with Zorro 51, Rich Rose, over Muong Soui. Zorro 50 went on to help some of the Lao troops being overrun on a mountaintop position further north. I was not the only one in deep trouble. My life was pretty much over considering the pickle I was in.

Rich Rose laid down a field of fire on the north side of the runway for me. There was nothing but open space to the south so all the enemy were in bunkers and structures on the north side. So I put the O-1 down mid-runway where we used to refuel when we owned the location three days ago. It was quiet at first but soon bullets were whizzing overhead and I knew we were dead. There was no way out...the airplane was empty...nowhere to run...we were dead. I saw movement that caught my eye from the small hill at the end of the runway on the north side. This hill was about as high as a control tower might be, 300 feet. It was a gunner with his anti-aircraft gun already in place. I could see the gunner clearly! All he had to do was march down the hill with a rifle and kill us. He was busy trying to reset his gun to shoot down on us, but his problem was that the gun was entrenched to shoot up at aircraft airborne and not on the ground. The gun had fired on Zorro 51 prior to my landing and that gave up his location to the world's best fighter pilot, Rich Rose. The gunner's pride in his new gun cost him. Rich put a 500 pound bomb right into his bunker. It was close enough I could feel the concussion of the explosion in my chest and dirt came raining down on us along with real rain from the storm that was also hitting us from the south. The gun came rolling down the hill so that threat was eliminated.

Now the next problem was fuel. A warm feeling came over me as I knew I was about to die, but I decided I would keep doing stuff until it happened...keep busy! I left Moonface with the aircraft and sought out the CIA stash of aviation gas. The bunker was untouched and the gate was still chain-locked with two 55 gallon barrels of go juice. Unbelievable. If there was no gas, capture was inevitable. Rather than deal with the lock and chain, I broke the wooden gate off at the hinges. Surprising how strong you get when your life is on the line. I rolled a full 55 gallon barrel uphill to the O-1 and Moonface was nowhere to be seen. Oh God, the bad guys got him. As soon as I grabbed the old yellow hand pump still on the ground next to all the empty barrels, Moonface magically reappeared.

OK now how do we get the barrel open? I had no tools to open the machine-tight cap to get the fuel out. Here is where I believe in angels. I had no training to do what I did but fear is great for inventions. I took my trusty .38 caliber pistol out of my cowboy holster. Moonface panicked and thought I was going to try to shoot the cap off. "No! No!" came squeaking out of Moonface. Instead I took the butt of the pistol and wedged the wooden handles into the cap until all the wood broke away, and the metal part of the pistol grip fit perfectly into the cap! There was an angel or two helping me because I had no clue this would work. I unscrewed the cap and took the old yellow hand pump and stuck it in the barrel. It was bent but worth a try.

I got up on the wing and opened the aircraft fuel receptacle and told Moonface to pump. He did with more energy than I had ever seen from him. This definitely is a two-man operation...without Moonface I would be dead today. The bullets kept coming our way but it was getting dark and the storm was upon us, and besides Zorro 51 was overhead to protect us. I had to use two hands to steady the fuel pump but the cool aviation gas was a wonderful feeling. It seemed to take forever and Moonface cried "Enough??" Here is a Lao guy who only knew about 10 words in English...*enough* was not one of them. "Keep pumping Moonface, we are going to Bangkok if we get out of here!"

It was raining pretty hard by then, so I needed to fly out very soon or I would be weathered in right there in a North Vietnamese-owned airfield. I looked at the starter switch and said a prayer. "Dear God, please let this engine start one more time and I will be good for the rest of my life. I will become a priest!" Thank you God the engine did fire up. It was pitch dark and storming but that was good cover for us instead of a liability.

The next challenge was the takeoff. Where was the runway? No lights and no markings as to a solid takeoff surface. One of Rich Rose's napalm cans was still burning close to where the gun position was. That gave me a focus point so at least I wouldn't make any turns on the imaginary runway. I rolled down what was thought to be a runway until the aircraft felt like it wanted to fly. Once airborne, my ground problems over, I was surrounded by mountains on three sides. I turned to what my internal radar said was south. I climbed up waiting for the sound of a mountain in our path but we popped up over the storm clouds at 2,000 feet. I thought something was radically wrong with the bird because there was a horrible smell that was so strong my fear level cranked up again. Moonface had messed his flying suit. Solution…open the window.

A CIA bird was above the clouds waiting for me and joined up on my wing. Call sign "Jack" led me northwest to Luang Prabang (LP) where there was a Raven location and a good hard runway. Zorro 51 had been gone a long time thinking I was lost.

I had only put fuel in one side and the needle was not far off empty. Our pumping operation was interrupted before we could make a meaningful refueling. The folks at LP had been alerted we were coming in. The Raven operation was not a night one so they had to send a jeep out to the airfield to light up the end of the runway. I had never landed at LP before so I had no idea what the field looked like or how the runway was oriented. The jeep was in place and I lined up with the headlights. What I didn't know was they had a party in progress and the guy they sent out did not line up with the runway...he just went to the end and parked sideways! As I got close to the ground I saw nothing but the moon shining off a river of water. I was lined up with the river, not the runway. My saga was not over yet. I prayed there was enough gas to go around one more time and by then there was enough moonlight to see where the runway really was. I was mad, tired, but happy to be alive and that emotion trumped the other feelings. Don Moody, the LP site commander, was there to greet me. The Lao guys took Moonface off for cleanup. Instead of being good for the rest of my life like I promised God if he saved me, I went to the Raven house and had a drink or twelve. I had a hard time sleeping because the adrenaline had been pumping for a long time.

I had Zorro 51 and Moonface to thank for being alive and my own people to credit with trying to kill me. I had an angel or two by my side telling me things I didn't know normally.

The war was heating up and back to work the next day for Raven 48.

Footnotes

Dale Brink, Zorro 50, has passed but Zorro 51, Rich Rose, is alive and well in Tucson, Arizona with his wife Janice. He survived a bout with bone cancer and lost an ear but is OK. We saw each other several times in Hawaii and had a nice visit at his house in 2010.

Moonface probably lost his life in the war or the loss of Laos in 1975. His real name was so long I never could pronounce it; thus the nickname. His perfectly round face earned him the Moonface title. He was OK with it.

I never got revenge on Cricket because the war raged on without time for justice. I was awarded the Silver Star for this mission but the citation was classified.

Epilogue: How Not to Drown a Demon

After all the combat is over the warrior can't rest until the mission is complete and the battle won. We lost and ran back to the safety of the USA. For us Ravens the tours may be over but the mission is still in our minds and hearts. Walking away like we did is not good for a true warrior. Leaving our allies blowing in the wind and all our comrades who died for a mission unfinished eats away your brain. The only Rx I could find for my post-traumatic stress disorder (PTSD) and mental anguish was alcohol. It was legal and relatively cheap. No prescription needed. Alcohol could give me the oblivion I sought. It would drown my demons but they kept coming back. Eventually the alcohol became the new demon that almost killed me instead of an AAA gun in the PDJ.

I found out much too late that alcohol wouldn't cure my PTSD. It may put it on hold for a while but sooner or later either the alcoholism will kill you or, if you are lucky like myself, you will find sobriety. In order to get sober you need to admit total defeat…again! A bitter pill to swallow. You need help but trust no one. Alcohol was my mistress and she turned on me big time and left me broken and sick. So you are at a turning point, quit or die. But you can't quit because your new demon has a thirst like no other.

The Air Force was a drinking club during my time and I joined right in. Who deserved a drink more than a pilot who just got shot at for 10 hours straight? The social portion of our lives was always centered on a bar. Being able to drink large quantities of booze seemed to me to be the stripe of a real combat pilot. Little did I realize it was sign of impending alcoholism. I don't know exactly when I crossed the line from "social drinker" into a drunk, but it was somewhere in the combat zone. I drank every day after the guns were silenced even though I had lost my excuse. I didn't get into trouble every time I drank, but when I did get into a jam I had been drinking.

Finally my 29-year career came to a close because of my drinking. I left behind a star promised to me if I could quit and I was left to fight a war that was already lost. I knew I was an alcoholic by then and I didn't care. I was burnt out literally in every sense of the word. When the VA evaluated me for PTSD, I maxed their chart. I kept drinking and, as is the case for most alcoholics, I hit bottom. Sometimes that bottom could be death, jail, or a mental ward. I had a DUI and a car accident that inspired my soon-to-be ex-wife to force me into a treatment center as part of a pre-divorce decree. I was trapped like a rat and had to comply. I had to stop fighting everyone and everything. I surrendered and found sobriety with a lot of help. So I went through the process of giving up, owning up, cleaning up, and growing up. Lucky for me, a year into my sobriety the VA had a program for PTSD guys like me. It would not have worked if I was still drinking, but it cleaned out the demons of my combat past and set me free. I started my life over again without alcohol as a crutch. I would be dead if I had kept going but now I have enjoyed the best 22 years of my life beyond description.

After about 10 years of sobriety, I decided to revisit the combat zone. I was able to retrieve the parts of my soul that I had left behind in Laos and Vietnam. I found a new peace and forgiveness for my enemies and myself, the biggest foe of all. I finally conquered myself and became a true victor. I was not guilty of losing the war or for the loss of life of my friends. The war was, in fact, over at last. I felt more at home in Southeast Asia than I did anywhere in the USA. The PTSD cure, in part, was to live here in Thailand for 10 years now. I still jump at explosions, have war-fighting dreams, and scream in my sleep occasionally. I know a drink won't help any of that and one is never enough. I will always be an alcoholic and will always have PTSD, but that's reality and I am OK with the truth. So I live a great life without alcohol and help other alcoholics achieve sobriety. Finally a mission I can complete successfully!

Chapter 12

Smoky Greene, Raven 42
Long Tieng, Jul 1969 – Feb 1970

A RAVEN CHRONICLE: TALES FROM NEVERLAND
The experiences of 1st Lt Smoky Greene, USAF, as Raven 42 in Northern Laos

Author's Note: *Some have read my account and offered alternative wording or factual corrections. I have considered all these comments carefully and incorporated changes where I judged them to improve accuracy. But absent convincing evidence, I have not allowed my own memory to be trumped by someone else's memory. Thus some may judge my story inaccurate – but this is the way I remember these events.*

Preface

As I write this at the tail end of 2013, many of my memories of my time in Laos 43 years ago have faded, though a few remain sharp and colorful as if they happened yesterday. Having retired some years ago, with spare time to spread 70 years out on the table and assess my life to date (a potentially depressing exercise), I can't help but envy the young aviation adventurer I once was. When people ask me if I miss flying, I have lately begun to reply that I miss being 25.

In 1970 I had just completed my Raven tour and embarked on a single-seat fighter career that would span another 25 years and thousands of flying hours in the venerable F-100, the A-7D, the RAF Harrier, and the A-10. By any measure I enjoyed quite an enviable flying career, but on reflection my six months in Laos as 24-year-old Raven 42 trumps all the rest in ways difficult to understand myself much less explain to others. I wish now I had paid more attention to the people and events around me. I desperately wish now I'd kept a journal as some apparently did. I also wish I'd spent a fraction of my pay buying 18 ct gold bracelets at Villy Phuong's rather than investing in $100-a-glass whiskey. But in those strange days it was logical and natural to do things that seem bizarre to me now.

Fortunately, as I prepare to write, I do not have to rely completely on my fading memories of those long-ago days. I kept my small green Government Issue BDA (bomb damage assessment) book listing details of each strike I controlled. I also found some hand-scribbled notes from the early 80s when I briefly considered writing and apparently abandoned the idea.

Looking back, I suppose I held my peace about my Raven experiences for a number of reasons. After Laos I found myself pretty busy helping win the Cold War. (Yet another one we may not have really won.) Also, I've always valued my privacy and it doesn't come easy to share my memories publicly. Another reason old warriors tend to keep mum about their combat experiences is that people who haven't been there don't really understand what we are talking about. On top of all this there was the lingering concern that even though our escapades in Laos seemed to be widely known, the fact that we were in-country was for many years officially classified. And finally I suppose I felt that old demons are best left in the box. But my earlier reluctance to share my memories has been overcome recently as I have enjoyed reading the memories of other Ravens who have put pen to paper. Another motivation is that time may be short to leave a record of my part in those interesting times for interested readers – perhaps my grandkids.

In my experience the reflections of old soldiers tend to come across as self-centered and self-serving. Perhaps that is to be expected – especially in the case of the FAC (forward air controller) who was essentially a solitary warrior. We did not fly our missions in formations of witnesses to return from battle and sing our praises – or to rib us for our mistakes. Of course this was not the case with Raven escapades between missions, for which there were often far too many witnesses only too happy to share. As I write I'll try to resist embarrassing my former colleagues, living and otherwise.

From the anecdotes to follow I think the reader will find my experiences were in some ways similar but in other ways distinctive from those I have heard and read about from other Ravens and from Chris Robbins' book, *The Ravens*. I dedicate my amateur writing effort to my fellow Ravens – especially those who sacrificed their lives to consecrate our worthy mission – and to the Hmong people whose survival was the real objective of our mission.

Month-by-Month Raven Tour Overview

July 1969 – My last O-1G flight in Vietnam was on 19 July. My first flight from 20A was on 29 July. I logged an O-1E and a T-28 flight which I presume were my local orientation rides. I recall the weather was pretty gloomy and the clouds clung ominously to the hilltops.

August 1969 – I begin earning my combat pay flying 40 sorties and 128 hours in the O-1E and F. My BDA book shows I put in 120 sets of fighters around the periphery of the Plaines des Jarres (PDJ). Pretty much every day flying except for a break 18-21 Aug – maybe due to monsoon rain. VP's (General Vang Pao's) "About Face" offensive officially started 15 August. I note that most of my August strikes were in the low hills just north of the PDJ working around to the eastern edge as the month progressed. This matches up with the general expansion of friendly control into the PDJ and beyond to the north and east as "About Face" began to have success.

September – I flew 134.7 hours and 46 sorties in the O-1A/E/F. Between 1-21 September I put in 109 airstrikes concentrated around the PDJ especially to the south side of Phou Nok Kok (PNK) as "About Face" offensive continued. Flight records show I had long break from 22 Sept till I flew again on 10 Oct. Seems quite a long time. Maybe this was when I went to the States to visit family. I returned to learn I was AWOL according to 56th Special Operations Wing (SOW). (Who the hell are they?).

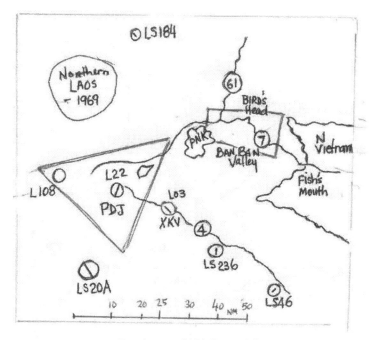

Rough map of 20A Raven AO

October – Back in saddle on 10 Oct and flew 140.5 hours in 47 sorties. I put in 150 airstrikes, generally concentrated just north of the PDJ and south of PNK in support of Lulu and Black Lion (radio call signs of indigenous FAGs (forward air guides)). Also a number of strikes 10 miles north of LS-236 or 20 miles south of Ban Ban.

November – T-28 checkout at Water Pump 31 Oct - 2 Nov. My November flying was 60 hours / 21 sorties in the O-1 and 52 hours / 25 sorties in the T-28. I put in 81 sets of fighters. Strikes tended to be concentrated just west of Phu Nok Kok near Ban Ban in support of Black Lion, in the Ban Ban Valley and 20 miles south of Ban Ban attacking rice harvest.

December – I was at the site all month flying 24.5 hours / 8 sorties in the O-1 and 90.5 hours / 40 sorties in the T-28, including three sorties for 7.5 hours on Christmas Day. I put in 82 airstrikes on troops, bunkers, storage, mortar positions, AA guns, and trucks. Strikes were concentrated south of PNK and LS-10 at Ban Ban. Several strikes along Route 7 from Bird's Head to the Fish's Mouth. Made several forays to Sam Neua. Lulu, Black Lion, and Rocket Mobile were under increasing enemy pressure and heavily supported with strikes.

January 1970 – I flew 15 sorties / 40.5 hours in the Bird Dog and 48 sorties / 101 hours in the T-28. I did not realize until researching for this piece that most of my most interesting memories occurred in this final month of my tour. I put in 72 airstrikes. Most were in support of sites under threat of attack, particularly Rainbow at LS-184 and Black Lion on PNK. Weather was bad much of the month. Flew my final Raven sortie on 29 Jan.

The Road to "Neverland" (In Vietnam we sometimes referred to Laos as "Neverland.")

O-1 FAC to SEA (Southeast Asia) was my first assignment out of pilot training. I got my wings after a year and some 240 hours of undergraduate training at Laughlin AFB, Del Rio, Texas in September 1968. I was very fortunate that my instructor pilot (IP) in the T-38 was Maj. Roy Ripley (or "Loy Lipley" as the Tahkli O'Club waitresses christened him). He wore a 100 Mission F-105 patch on the shoulder of his flying suit. He taught the same syllabus as every other IP but I knew I was getting my introduction to flying from a guy who had earned a special credibility in the profession I aspired to join. I wanted to be a fighter pilot since 7th grade. It was really the primary reason I wanted to go to the Air Force Academy. Assignments out of flying school were based on merit – order of graduation determined order of selection for the available aircraft assignments. Fighter assignments available to our class were one F-100, one Skyraider, one RF-4, a number of backseat F-4s. I graduated number 7 of about 50. The F-100, A-1, and RF-4 pretty much went 1-2-3. So I figured I would take a backseat F-4. But Roy took me aside and suggested I look at the other aircraft on the list. Down at the bottom were several O-1 Bird Dogs. He argued that the FAC was a key player in SEA. I would learn a lot about tactical ops and have a good chance at a fighter as a follow-on assignment. He thought I would have more opportunities as a FAC than as an F-4 backseater. At first I was somewhat astonished at his advice, but I had a lot of faith in Roy's judgment and selected the O-1.

It did not take long to get through the requisite O-1 training at Hurlburt (Holly Field) and survival schools at Fairchild and Clark before I found myself in Vietnam in early February 1969. I spent the first six months of my first SEA tour as the province FAC in Tuy Hoa province, Republic of Viet Nam (RVN). For the most part I was the only pilot for a single O-1E flying from a small tin strip across the river from the huge and busy Tuy Hoa Air Base, home of a wing of F-100s. It was generally a low-threat combat environment with plenty of O-1E flying, a few airstrikes, minimal supervision, and lots of off-duty fun. Being unsure of statute of limitations I won't go into too many specifics. I was 23 years old on my first operational assignment with essentially no immediate boss. Vietnam under those circumstances was a wonderful playground. As a FAC I had an airplane and a jeep. The only other guy with his own personal vehicle was the Tuy Hoa Air Base wing commander. The local Army nurses apparently thought this was a pretty big deal. I liked to hit the Tuy Hoa Officer's Club and rub elbows with the F-100 pilots over a beer or two. I was especially impressed with the Albuquerque Guard (call sign Taco) who all had big personalities on the ground and were very professional when I worked with them in the air. I recall we had some fabulous beach parties.

I lived in the Military Assistance Command Vietnam (MACV) compound on the edge of Tuy Hoa City just off the beach until there was a misunderstanding between myself and the US Army commander, who asked me to find somewhere else to bunk. I plead the fifth on what the precise nature of the problem was and where I went to live subsequently. Suffice to say I had more fun in Vietnam than the US Army felt was appropriate.

After I had been in-country maybe five months a tall guy in a plain black flight suit came through on a visit. I had not previously known Karl Polifka. We sat in a private office and talked about cabbages and kings for a bit, and that apparently started the ball rolling that led me to be called down to Bien Hoa for a meeting with another mysterious guy, and fairly quickly I was out of the hot tub of Vietnam and into the blast furnace of Laos. I was an adventure-seeking bachelor first lieutenant with just over 400 hours and 300 combat sorties in the O-1E. I had inherited my nickname "Smoky" and my spirit of adventure from my adventurous father who had been one of the early Montana smokejumpers. I was about to get all the adventure I could wish for.

Mr. Greene, Forest Ranger

I recall vaguely the process at Udorn and Vientiane that other Ravens have described about the conversion from Air Force officer to civilian flying forest ranger (a weak cover story unlikely to protect us if captured by the Pathet Lao (PL) or North Vietnamese). They collected up my meager possessions and issued me a US Embassy identity card and sent me downtown to shop for the stylish flying or two-piece "walking suits" as they were called. I recall thinking that I hoped to do as little walking in Laos as possible and I initially opted for several one-piece flying suits in various muted colors. Within a day or two I mounted the ramp of a silver C-123 with two other young pilots (including Air Force Academy and Del Rio pilot training classmate Ed Gunter) and we were soon letting down through scattered clouds into the crater that contained the storied CIA base at Long Tieng or Lima Site 20 Alternate (I usually abbreviate as "20A"). Most Raven accounts talk about their first magic impressions arriving in Laos featuring the limestone karst formations rising out of the ground accented with green foliage. When I saw the movie "Avatar" last year the scenes of the floating mountains reminded me of this moment of arrival.

The layout of 20A has been exhaustively documented so I won't repeat that here, but suffice to say first impression of this secret mountain airstrip is indeed something out of "Terry and the

Pirates" or "Steve Canyon" comic book tales just as many have said. Ravens were not CIA employees, but the Agency apparently funded the operation in Laos with black program money to maintain the illusion the US was complying with the 1962 Geneva Accords provision that there were to be no foreign combat troops in *neutral* Laos. We were there because apparently the North Vietnamese did not get that memo. CIA employees like Burr Smith (call sign "Yellow Dog") constituted the local US leadership at 20A during my time, coordinating US military support to Major General Vang Pao's (often simply "VP") Hmong army, the indigenous force opposing the Communist Pathet Lao and North Vietnamese Army in Northern Laos (Military Region II.)

CIA (euphemistically, Controlled American Source or CAS) employees (case officers) constituted the ground advisors in the field with their indigenous counterparts while Air America and Continental Air Service contracted to provide airlift with a large fleet of various helicopters, short takeoff and landing (STOL) aircraft such as the Helio-Courier and Swiss-built turbine-powered Pilatus Porter, and larger cargo planes such as Caribous, C-46s, and C-130s. These highly experienced aircrews typified by pilots like Al Adolph were consummate professionals who made very complex air missions look easy. They could take a C-130 in and out of mountain strips barely suitable for the O-1! I saw examples of this with my own disbelieving eyes.

The Ravens, though in civilian clothes, remained USAF officers and as experienced FACs were needed to coordinate the substantial US airpower flying out of bases in Thailand dedicated to opposing the Communist takeover of Laos. As serving military officers there was a fundamental difference between us and the CIA personnel. Although some became acquaintances and friends eventually, generally it seemed to me an unwritten rule to avoid being overly familiar or curious when dealing with these guys. But now I really wish I had made more of an effort to get to know some of these dedicated and impressive people.

Besides the relatively large group at 20A (generally about 10 Ravens), smaller detachments of Ravens flew from the royal capital, Luang Prabang, the political capital, Vientiane, and in southern Laos from Pakse and Savannakhet. The Air Force code-named operations in the northern region of Laos "Barrel Roll" to distinguish from operations along the Ho Chi Minh Trail in southern Laos, code-named "Steel Tiger." I think the North Vietnamese main priority in Laos was to keep the supplies flowing south along the Ho Chi Minh Trail. But they also wanted a communist Laos for a neighbor, hence their massive military effort in northern Laos where most of the population and traditional political capitals were. The US was essentially trying to prevent the fall of another "domino." Regrettably, America tired of the war before the Communists and another domino fell.

I Begin Operations as Raven 42

Given the time to move in and get checked out I calculate I must have arrived at 20A around 25 July 1969 because Air Force flight records indicate I flew a three-hour O-1A flight on 29 July and another on the 30th. I think at least one of these was with new Chief FAC Bill Yenke. I also flew a one-hour T-28 ride on the 30th - in Mike Cavanaugh's back seat. These were my in-country orientation flights with "old heads" who had arrived a few months before me.

My little green BDA book shows I directed my first strike as a Raven on 31 July 1969. Hobo 10 flight was two A-1s out of Nakhon Phanom (NKP) loaded with 10xMk82, 4xCBU14, 2xCBU24,

2xLAU32, 2xLAU59, and 200 rds 20mm. (Skyraiders were great for this close air support war – lots of time on target and lots of varied weapons on an accurate and rugged platform.) Target UTM (Universal Transverse Mercator coordinates) was UG 0044 4549, which plots out on the northern edge of the PDJ. Target type was not specified. Result of the strike was "NFSF" (nothing further [seen due to] smoke and foliage). There would be a lot of that in the next six months. Later when I began to put in a lot of strikes I would no longer take time to record the ordnance load in the BDA book. In fact I left out a lot of things I wish now I had recorded and our intel officer, Joe Bauer, would berate me for the paucity of my BDA reports. For example, leaving me a note on 30 Aug, "How's about telling me what is in the flight, hero?" (That is, he wanted me to specify the number and type of fighters.) My reply next to his note: "NOT A CHANCE!" But I liked the long-suffering Joe and I started trying harder to record the data he needed for his reports.

When I first arrived the friendly ground forces (Gen. Vang Pao's Hmong tribesmen supplemented with Lao and Thai government troops and some mercenaries) were in a defensive position after the winter and spring advances of the opposing Neutralist and Pathet Lao forces. I had assumed that this was a seasonal seesaw battle that had gone on since the 1960 coup that marked the beginning of this struggle for control of the Kingdom of Laos. But my research for this piece reveals that large force-on-force battles that would characterize 1969 were something new. Roger Warner's book, *Shooting at the Moon*, describes VP's "About Face" operation to take and hold the PDJ as something unprecedented for the guerrilla leader to aspire to. The pitched battle of Muong Soui (L-108) on the northwestern edge of the PDJ in June was fresh in memory of the 20A Ravens. When I arrived and began flying in late July friendly forces controlled only Skyline Ridge surrounding Vang Pao's HQ at 20A and strategic hilltops around the Plain of Jars, thanks to airdrop resupply by CIA contract air support and airstrikes directed by Ravens on nearby enemy forces. (Another Raven recently told me some of the more remote sites such as LS-46 and LS-236 were also manned during this time).

So the initial pattern of our Raven flying was to patrol within about 30 miles of base – generally to the north and east within and around the periphery of the PDJ. We would make contact with the various forward air guides (FAGs) at each friendly location and receive updates on the situation and satisfy their requests for airstrikes if we could. Ravens checked in with ABCCC (Airborne Battlefield Command and Control Center, an EC-130, call sign "Cricket" during the day in our area) and received information such as altimeter setting and any enemy situation or weather that had been relayed to ABCCC by other aircraft. The ABCCC senior controller was the on-scene representative of the 7/13 Air Force commander responsible for operations of air forces based in Thailand – primarily the USAF A-1, F-4, and F-105 fighter bombers supporting our operations in northern Laos. We would notify Cricket of our position and request for fighters and controllers aboard Cricket would direct available fighters to our rendezvous. There would typically be two to four Ravens airborne and linked on FM so if one of us had a good target or troops in trouble we would tell Cricket to redirect the fighters where most needed. There were times when there were few fighters available depending what was going on in other parts of the AO (area of operations) or theater, but during most of my tour Ravens seemed to have plenty of priority and plenty of fighters came our way. Our challenge was to find them worthwhile targets. This was a little difficult at first but in the last three months of my tour there were plenty of lucrative targets as the NVA mounted a major effort to reverse gains of Vang Pao's successful "About Face" offensive.

Normally, especially when a Raven was new, we flew with a specially trained FAG (called Robins) in the back seat who spoke reasonable English, was trained to use air-ground communications, and understood how to interpret the ground situation and assist his Raven to effectively support the ground forces. Like pilots, some backseaters were better at the job than others. We had our favorite backseaters and no doubt they had their favorite Ravens – as well as those they refused to fly with. My early introduction to flying in Laos was a "Welcome to the NFL, Rookie" experience the first week in August with "the ideal backseater." (At the Raven reunion in October 2014 I met two Hmong who escaped Laos after the war and settled in the States. It was fascinating to learn they were operating in MRII during my tour – one recalls flying in my back seat when he was a brand-new Robin and the other was a ground FAG I probably talked to often during my tour. More detail about Robins and ground FAGs later).

The Ideal Backseater

The O-1 was a tandem two-seater and we carried an indigenous forward air guide (Robin) with access to the FM radio to help coordinate our strikes with indigenous ground forces. I would find that these little guys varied in attitude, experience, and competence but were certainly a big help to a brand-new Raven. I had to admire their courage being willing to climb in the back with the likes of me experiencing my early missions in unfamiliar and unforgiving terrain and weather, to say nothing of hostile fire. I discovered these guys were keen students of their Raven pilots, and just as the backseaters developed reputations among the Ravens, the Ravens developed reputations among the backseaters. When you went down to the flight line your reputation determined if a backseater was available to fly with you or not. I guess I fell in the middle of the pack because during my six-month tour I flew about half my missions with a backseater. Upon reflection, the few times I got into serious trouble I was alone. It seems to me I seldom had a backseater when I flew the T-28 and later in my tour I was less likely to carry a backseater.

At any rate, as a brand-new Raven whoever was running things tried to take care of me with an experienced backseater. I regret I could not recall his proper name when I first drafted this but we called him Marshall Ky (I'll abbreviate as "MK") because he could have been the twin brother of the famous and handsome commander of the South Vietnamese Air Force at the time. (At the recent Raven reunion one of the Hmong told me MK's name was Yang Bee and he is apparently still alive somewhere in the US). I recall clearly being told this guy had long experience as a backseater, was very familiar with the local area, had phenomenal eyesight, and very importantly to me, was considered to be cautious to the point of cowardly. The perfect backseater, right? So we were patrolling at a conservative altitude just north of the PDJ on a relatively clear morning. My BDA book does not indicate the date but it was one of my first flights as a Raven. I've told this story so many times I remember the details fairly well.

I recall his words over the intercom: "Laven 42 – you fly to the low!" Hmmm. Well, why not? I maneuvered down to try to see what he was talking about. He continued to urge me to go lower and we ended up almost treetop level flying along a small road on the edge of a patch of forest. As usual my windows were latched open both for ventilation and to hear ground fire. MK had pulled my .30 caliber carbine from behind the seat and was firing at something out the left side of the aircraft – we were heading roughly west paralleling the road so he was firing north across the road into the trees.

Break, break. At this point my Raven buddies are asking themselves ".30 cal carbine? Are you serious?" Yeah well, as they know, part of our in-processing at 20A was to go through the extensive CIA "lending library" and choose personal weapons. I passed over AK-47s, Swedish Ks, CAR-15s, etc. and selected the lowly .30 cal carbine and a Colt .45 automatic pistol. I honestly did not expect it to make much difference if I ended up on the ground. Having said that, our weapons were not just for show – I recall a number of occasions when a group of us would walk over to the nearby firing range and burn through a few clips with our various hardware. While we are on subject of weapons, the tiny sleeping hooch I shared with Bob Passman and later Bob Dunbar was fitted out with a ready-to-fire Browning Automatic Rifle (BAR) sitting on the floor pointing at the door. This huge weapon barely fit in the confined space between our beds and the door. Also we each had half a dozen frag grenades taped under the rails of our bunks. Our personal weapons were hung on the bedpost ready to hand. We were told there was some risk of hostile intruders so most Ravens were well-armed on the ground as well as in the air. This would factor into a later story.

Back to that morning in early August 1969 on the northern edge of the PDJ. I recall making several low passes at MK's urging while he plinked out the back window and I strained to see what the hell he was shooting at. Then I saw it. I could hardly miss it. Under the trees beside the road facing us, the biggest PT-76 ever built. About 75 yards range – at eye level. I'll carry to my grave the sight of the leather-helmeted chap manning the 12.7mm machine gun on the turret. I "calmly" (yeah, right) selected full afterburner (jammed my throttle full forward) and began to throw the airplane around the sky like a madman, which I technically was at that point. We accelerated rapidly from 60 to 63 knots (can you detect the mild sarcasm?). The language accompanying this action cannot be repeated in print and may well have been heard by the PT-76 crew. I instantly regretted that I would have to meet St. Peter so shortly after such an un-Christian outburst. But on reflection I think he would have understood. I had just gotten to Laos and I was going to end up in a flaming pile right here 40 miles north of my new home. At least the stupid bastard in the back seat was going to die with me. So we sat there in the sights of this PT-76 commander for what seemed like an hour as the airspeed crept up toward 65 knots and I could see him hammering away. We didn't get a scratch. I guess he was so excited to see this enormous O-1 in front of him he couldn't shoot straight. Anyway I now worked to get my heartbeat down into the low 200s and had a few choice words for MK as I turned south for home. But this red-letter day wasn't over.

20A sat in a kind of bowl or crater with a couple cuts through the high terrain encircling the site. We could use these cuts to sneak in under the frequent low cloud deck that sat ominously on the tops of the surrounding hills of Skyline Ridge. It was very important to know how to put your airplane into a low cut that would lead into the airfield. On advice from the experienced Ravens checking me out, I had selected what I thought was a distinctive tree stump as my guidepost to home in low weather. I intended to practice the low entry on good weather days but my opportunities so far had been limited. After the near disaster with the PT-76 I was bringing MK home. In keeping with the way this day was going I found the clouds were indeed onto the tops of the hills surrounding home base. I found what I thought was my tree stump and began to climb up the little valley. My faith in MK had taken a beating, but I still hoped he was familiar with the local terrain and would help me get us home. I talked on the intercom and turned to observe his features as we climbed closer to the clouds. I could not determine if he was happy or uneasy about the path we were on. I myself was very under confident and as the O-1 entered clouds, I pulled into a tight 180, again spicing up the atmosphere with some choice words, and descended out of cloud and back down to the base of the valley. Let's look around a little more while working on that thundering heartbeat. I soon found another tree stump that looked much more familiar and fortunately led me safely under the clouds and into the crater containing the welcome airstrip.

I do not recall what I did next. I guess I did not beat the hell out of MK. I think we even flew together again but I was never again so naïve as to follow his advice. I am very surprised to find no mention at all in my BDA book of a live and firing PT-76. I certainly would have reported it right after changing my underwear. On the other hand, I would not have made a big deal of it with the other guys. I was a brand-new guy and the incident had a lot of potential for embarrassment unless I passed it off casually. That's huge for a 23-year-old trying to play with the big boys like Mike Cavanaugh, who had taken me under his wing and who I had quickly recognized as the unofficial leader of a group that seemed to naturally reject leadership.

I had in the space of about an hour literally dodged a (lot of) bullet(s) and escaped deadly weather. This day was my first attention-getting experience with the variety of dangers that lurked close by. I realized this was way different than my experience in Vietnam. Six months of this kind of day would make for a very long tour. As it turned out there were not so many such days and I got better at managing the risks. Nevertheless, I was not to escape Laos scot-free. I doubt any of us did.

The 20A Ravens (July 69 – Feb 70)

I took a few notes about 25 years ago trying to list the Ravens who were at 20A when I arrived (late July 69) and when I left (early Feb 70). Don't know if I recall them accurately but here's my list with my best-guess dates:

July 1969
Joe Potter (Site Commander) Jul – Dec 69
Bill Yenke (Chief FAC) Jul – Sep 69
Mike Cavanaugh May – Oct 69
Karl Polifka Mar – Dec 69
Ed Lauffer Jun – Nov 69
Bob Passman Mar – Aug 69
Mike Byers Jun – Dec 69
Jerry Greven Aug 69 – Feb 70
Jerry Furch (Raven 71) flew with us when we were short-handed

Jan 1970 when I left:
Jerry Rhein (Site Commander) Dec 69 –?
Tom Palmer (Chief FAC) Sep 69 –?
Bob Dunbar Aug 69 – Dec 70
Henry Allen Oct 69 – Mar 70 (KIA after 20A was attacked)
"Moose" Carroll Oct 69 – Mar 70
Tom Harris Oct 69 – Apr 70
Bill Kozma Sep 69 – Apr 70

Will "Tiny" Platt Dec 69 –?
Al Daines ? – Dec 69
Craig Morrison ? – Dec 69

My notes and memories can't place Craig Morrison or Al Daines there at 20A during my tour. However, Karl Polifka recalls Daines and Dunbar shared his farewell party and left with him in December, so I assume his recollections about that are accurate. But I am very surprised I don't recall my Academy classmate Al Daines being at 20A for most of my tour. I suppose we were on different operations and break cycles.

Daily Life at 20A

Several Ravens have described our daily life from their perspectives. I'll give a few of my impressions while trying to avoid repetition.

When I got there the Ravens lived in a rather large old wooden house – I think single-story with some large common rooms and a kitchen and a communications room with secure teletype used to send our reports and receive information and orders from headquarters at Victor (Vientiane). My BDA book reminds me that USAIRA (the US air Attache) at Victor was code-named Sydney or Geneva over the shortwave comm link used for admin and logistics. 20A was code-named Athens and Luang Prabang (LP) was Dover. Udorn was Cairo. This did not mean much to us as pilots – we never used these designations in the air. I just include it here because I thought it was a neat piece of trivia. (Karl Polifka recalled these differently – but this is what was written in my BDA book – and who cares, really?).

Our cook was an Air Force sergeant named Espinosa (Espi). We sorely missed him when he DEROS'd in September without replacement. More later on that. Suffice to say it is not only armies that travel on their stomachs.

Our living quarters were small rooms with bunk beds connected to the main part of the house by a long elevated covered wooden catwalk that ran outside along the back of the house. Because of (probably unfounded) security concerns, if you were on the catwalk after dark you were supposed to whistle or sing a typically American song until safely in your hooch. A bit later I'll tell a story about this. The rooms were small and sparsely furnished but we mostly just slept there for a few hours each night. I believe my first roommate was Bob Passman and later Bob Dunbar. As I previously mentioned, our tiny room was armed like a small battleship and we almost hoped some poor unsuspecting PL would try to breech our layered defenses. In November or December, the Ravens would move into a new multistory cinder block house nearby with private bedrooms.

During my early months at 20A we would get up in the morning – I do not recall a particular get-up time but most of us were anxious to get out there and get to an airplane. We would eat breakfast – at least while Espi was there – and head for the flight line, usually in a utility or jeep-type vehicle as it was about 1/4 mile from the house. We would often be gone flying all day, typically logging about 8-10 hours in three sorties. Once we got back home we would toss our little green BDA memo books on the intel officer's desk and head for the fridge and liquid refreshment. If a big operation was in progress, there would be more formalized comparing of notes and planning for tomorrow's operations – but usually with a beer in hand.

I recall walking the short distance down the hill to VP's residence and HQ for dinner fairly often although others have said this was a rare event. I recall very well the sticky rice we rolled up and dipped into some pretty spicy juice. I became practically addicted to that rice so I think I went over to VP's for dinner fairly often and I had the impression Ravens were always welcome. The image I recall of these evenings was of dozens of people, Hmong and round eyes, sitting together on the floor around the huge tables covered with plates of exotic food and huge bowls of rice. Only VP got white rice – the rest of us got sticky rice – which was fine with me. Women would keep the plates and glasses full throughout the evening. Once in a while there would be a special occasion such as a farewell for one of the guys and the White Horse scotch and Lao Lao would flow as string bracelets were tied to the honoree's wrist for good luck. I actually like scotch and I did my duty when the bottle came my way, but I think White Horse is an acquired taste that I never acquired. The gatherings at VP's have been well described by others so I'll just say they were always fun and I liked the native food and drink. More importantly, these evenings made me feel more empathy with the people we were supporting and more like an integral part of VP's team.

Many nights after flying a long day we would just sit around and drink and talk to our fellow Ravens in our living room/bar. A favorite topic of conversation was after action reports from recent absences from the site or plans for the next. At some point in the evening there was dinner around the big table. I recall one evening that I asked for someone to pass me the salt or something and they passed me the salt and the pepper and the butter and the mashed potatoes and the meat and someone's tableware – you get the picture. We all got a laugh but I never asked anyone to pass me anything again, nor did anyone else. If you couldn't reach it, you didn't get it. Finally, tired, well-fed, and a bit drunk, we made our way individually or in small groups down the long outside catwalk to our bunks.

There were always exceptions to this typical daily routine. A pilot might be asked to fly an airplane south to Udorn for maintenance. This was a chance to check mail and have some fun downtown in Vientiane and/or Udorn. I recall one occasion flying an O-1 with no door and multiple bullet holes down to Udorn. I taxied into the AIRA "Water Pump" apron, jumped out of the airplane, and asked the maintenance officer, Lt. Col. George Vogel, for the keys to his jeep. He was a crusty old guy (probably pushing 50) who worked miracles keeping our shot-up kites flying. He shook his head and griped as he surveyed his newest repair challenge but always came through with a timely repair – and his jeep keys. First stop was Base Finance to get paid. Some old guys will recall before the days of computers our pay records were on a big yellow sheet rolled up in a blue cardboard tube. Remember now? Anyway, since Ravens were in TDY (temporary duty) status we hand-carried these tubes and presented them to finance to get paid. One day I took the pay record out and studied it. I recently read one Raven's account saying that we got no extra pay in the Raven program. I certainly did. The way it was done was the finance people checked every single box so that whereas normal monthly pay would have been about $500, I got well over twice that. But I sure plowed it back into the local economy quickly. Next stop was the Holiday Inn for a Kobe beef and rubdown. My circuit included Ben's Jewelers and a browse at one or two tailor shops to replace wardrobe items. After a long night in the Udorn Club I'd finish up with a nightcap in the Air America Club, get a couple hours of sleep, and go pick up my freshly repaired airplane for the trip home. Later when I was flying the T-28 I would load about 25 cases of beer in the belly compartment before returning to 20A. The Jolly Greens would bring beer up when they sat alert at 20A, but we discovered they were getting rusty cans of Black Label for free and then selling it to us. So we cut out the middleman whenever we could.

About half the assigned pilots (we numbered about 10 pilots at 20A when I was there) were on leave at any one time. We all flew hard and at 10 or more hours a day it did not take long to hit the max allowable 135 hours for the month. This could happen by the middle of the month. (Some Ravens told me they did not recall this monthly flying hour limit but it is clear in my own memory.) Unless there was a critical op going, you had to stand down and usually you were allowed to go anywhere you wanted until the next month started your clock again. We would often sit around the Raven bar at night and talk about where we would go on our next leave. We mentioned exotic places like Sweden and Switzerland, and the alcohol-fueled plans could get pretty detailed and elaborate. We had a handy set of TDY orders that in effect gave us government transportation to destination of choice in civilian clothes.

Despite all the grandiose plans I only managed to get to the States for two weeks in Sept-October timeframe. When I returned I found out the nice folks at 56th SOW at NKP considered me AWOL since I had not processed a leave application with the wing. I was genuinely surprised since NKP was completely out of my crosscheck. I responded with the usual Raven attitude – "What are they going to do, send me to Vietnam?" No, but you can expect a pretty lousy Officer Evaluation Report (OER). That in fact happened, but I certainly did not lose any sleep over the threat of a lousy OER at that point in my life. At some point I also got away for an enjoyable seven-day R&R to Sydney. Most of the other times, despite my best intention to get to Geneva or Copenhagen, I would typically blow a couple days in Vientiane, a couple more in Udorn, and I might even get down to Bangkok once or twice before my time and money ran out and I would have to hitch a ride home on the nearest silver bird. Down range it seemed to be a constant party and reunion with fellow Ravens and other SEA warriors from various organizations all trying to live large and one-up each other. I clearly recall ordering a scotch at the Charoen Hotel's Yellow Bird Bar in Bangkok, drinking half of it and leaving my last $100 bill on the bar. Today I'd like to have that $100 back to buy a new fishing pole. But back then I felt I had to uphold the image of larger-than-life big-spender Ravens. And at that point in my life saving money for future needs was not a priority.

The other breaks in our daily routine were caused by weather. Fog and low cloud might keep us on the ground, although if the weather was OK in the target area and we expected to be able to get back on the ground later, we could take off in practically zero-zero conditions. We practiced this on good-weather days, hitting the stopwatch at brake release and noting the time to turn on course and the climb rate needed to clear the hills. But neither the O-1 nor the T-28 was equipped with sufficiently accurate navigation equipment, nor were there suitable navigation beacons or GCA (ground-controlled approach) for instrument recoveries at 20A. At one time or other we all landed after dark or in pretty marginal weather, but we had to make a visual approach or try to get to bases in Thailand.

Another weather phenomenon that had a big impact on us was the seasonal monsoon rains. I don't recall exactly when these occurred, but there are several unexplained breaks in my BDA book that suggest we had two or three of these severe rains that beat down for several days and kept us in the building. You had the impression if you went outside the rain would literally knock you down. Anyway, the first day of rain provided a welcome break from flying and we caught up on our rest. As the rain continued to pound on the tin roof we partied a bit harder than usual knowing we would not fly the next day. The dart game would heat up. Ed Lauffer's party trick was to catch darts with his hand before they hit the dart board. His arm soon looked like a heroin addicts but he didn't seem to notice. We set up the projector and watched whatever movie was on hand. I recall we had the "Ten Commandments" – but only the second reel. Oh well, we saw that about 10 times – and even played it backwards. By the third or fourth day, despite being pretty mellow I could detect impending disaster as I watched semi-naked men running around the house throwing darts at each other. We needed to get back in the air soon – where it was safe!

Periods of enforced downtime also allowed us to rub elbows with the other inhabitants of Alternate. The road from our house down to VP's was lined with little shacks where families of the local Hmong lived. There may have been little shops or local food sources but I don't recall this amounting to much. I think I recall kids playing in the road with homemade toys and wondering what future they and their parents would have. You saw few men or young boys – they were out on the remote hill sites – kids whose M-16 was as tall as they were and old men who had somehow managed to get old despite 10 years of constant war against Communist PL and NVA in Vang Pao's little guerrilla army.

At the top of the flight line near the famous karst "barrier" were the control tower, the offices for airfield operations, and quarters of the Hmong T-28 pilots (call sign "Chao Pha Khao" pronounced chop-a-cow) with their ground crews and the Air America contract maintenance crews. We did not spend a lot of time in this area of the site, but sometimes stopped to pick up backseaters on our way to the Raven parking ramp mid-field on the east side of the runway.

Maybe 100 feet up the hill from our house was the CIA complex where the case officers and contract aircrew lived – I suppose pretty much like we did. We did not spend a lot of time up there – I think you had to be more or less invited for a drink or a briefing. But on several occasions I found myself either in the CAS bar or their briefing room. That must have been when we learned some of the old Air America and Continental Air Service flying tips that would help us survive. Someone took time to explain how to crash-land on a forested mountainside. This always stuck with me because the technique was not intuitive. The recommended technique is to dive your doomed airplane right toward the face of the mountain, building up speed to enable you to pull out of the dive as you approach the mountain and fly up the slope skimming the trees until you stall, hopefully gently falling into the tops of the trees for your best chance of survival. On the ground ops side CIA case officers would describe the situations at their respective locations.

"Good Times" Aug-Oct 1969

Despite not keeping a journal I could construct a rough framework of my flying activities each month of my tour by comparing the computer printouts from AF flight records with my BDA book entries.

Day-to-Day Flight Ops at 20A

I can't recall if there was a formal flying schedule posted assigning pilots to tail numbers and takeoff times. There no doubt was. (Karl Polifka recalls they posted a schedule such that takeoffs were staggered about 45 minutes and provided between two and four Ravens airborne depending on level of activity). Certainly after the first wave it was a bit of a free-for-all and we went wherever the action was and stayed on station as long as needed.

From time to time there were defined air-ground operations with actual typed-out FRAGs (fragmentary orders) listing fighters and TOTs (time on target), but most of the time we seemed to be kind of on our own to grab an airplane for the day and go out and patrol our area – check in with ground troops and look for targets under workable weather. My BDA book indicates a pattern of working in a particular place for a day or two, then moving on. When the ground troops had no close targets we conducted VR (visual recce) along the main routes for enemy troop movements and supply convoys – occasionally hitting the jackpot. During the first month or two of my tour the ground situation was relatively benign. Good spring/summer weather enabled a lot of accurate bombing of enemy positions so the friendly forces were preparing for a seasonal offensive. We would soon have friendly troops on the PDJ and the various hilltops to the north and east of the PDJ would be manned with troops to observe and obstruct enemy forces attempting to approach on the main roads from Vietnam through the Ban Ban Valley.

Other sources cover the strategy and major shifts in battle lines over the pivotal year of 1969 in much more authoritative detail than I can since I was a bit player in this drama, but my overall impression was that our summer offensive ("About Face") was very successful, but the territorial gains could not be sustained against the influx of determined regular North Vietnamese reinforcements and reduced US airpower effectiveness as the fall and winter weather closed in. I saw by my BDA book that my strikes followed a general geographical pattern beginning in the PDJ area in August and September, then reaching further north and east in November, then retreating back toward the PDJ in December and January.

Ravens got airborne with a basic plan – usually to make the rounds of the sites to see how they fared overnight. This became critical after November when all sites were under increasing enemy pressure. Three or four Ravens would typically be flying around talking to FAGs at the various sites and looking for good targets and airstrike weather. We would share this information with each other on our discrete frequency or we would hear other Ravens talking to Cricket and know who was where and what action they had going on. This allowed us to self-coordinate and cover the area efficiently. If the weather was dodgy we also monitored and position-reported on Air America VHF common frequency to minimize potential for midair collision with the many fixed-wings and helicopters flying between the sites – often in the clouds. So there was a lot of radio chatter if all three of our radios were in use. Even if we could not provide fighter support, we tried to cover the area calling in to obtain situation reports and provide encouragement to the guys on the ground manning the remote sites.

LS-46 (UF 9591) "Edward M. Kennedy International"

When we had time we would fly out to some of the sites to spend a little time on the ground with case officers, and I was struck by the remoteness of some of these sites. One that comes to mind is LS-46, well south and east of the PDJ about 30 miles due south of the Fish's Mouth, kind of out there in the middle of nowhere. There must have been an infiltration route for enemy forces nearby to justify placing a case officer at the site. Early in my tour the case officers sometimes stayed on their sites for extended periods. Later as enemy pressure increased the case officers were usually flown home to Alternate to spend the night and then returned to the site the next morning. LS-46 (for reasons that will become apparent in this story we called it "Edward M. Kennedy International" in memory of the Chappaquiddick incident) required a pilot to make careful approach and landing in the O-1, which was not really a STOL aircraft. The relatively short dirt strip at LS-46 climbed up the slope of a mound of high ground in the midst of a beautiful little valley. The pilot had to set up a straight-in approach, milk a little flap to control speed, plunk the bird on the first few feet of the strip, and let the bird slow as it climbed up the fairly steep hill. From short final the pilot was committed to land and if too fast or too high, the bird would roll to the top of the hill and over the cliff at the top end of the strip. The departure was a little sporty too. The aircraft would roll down the short downhill strip gathering just enough speed to stagger off the end and descend into the valley where you could then accelerate to climb speed. It was a bit of a test of flying skill so several of us used to go there just to say we'd done it.One day one of our highly experienced number landed his O-1 at 46, but unexpectedly a huge water buffalo crossed right in front of him as he flared for landing, causing him to touch down too long to safely stop. The hapless Raven did the only thing he could do – locked one brake to ground loop before going over the cliff. However, his speed was still too high and the landing gear strut buckled. (I recently learned a CIA case officer, Jim Adkins, saw the whole thing and told me the pilot's action probably saved his life and that of his passenger, John Jennings, another case officer). Thus the designation Edward M. Kennedy International. A few days later I was amazed to circle the site and watch an Air America Caribou on the strip load up the broken Bird Dog and take off. Those guys knew how to fly.

I went in to LS-46 a number of times and spent some pleasant time with the friendly case officer whose call sign was Swamp Rat and whose name I could not recall when I first drafted this piece, but subsequently learned was John Jennings. More on him later. I have in my collection a photo he must have taken of me offering a snack to a curious water buffalo that hung around the site. These were the "good days" when we were succeeding militarily, the weather was pleasant, and the case officers were relaxed. We felt safe on the ground at the remote sites and had spare time to enjoy the stark beauty of the countryside. That would all change too soon.

Mike Cavanaugh's Farewell

I think it was early October, it was Mike Cavanaugh's farewell party and we still lived in the old house. I recall I was rooming with Bob Dunbar and as previously described our little bunk room was bristling with weapons against potential ground attack.

A going-away party was reason to hit the sauce harder and longer than usual, and certainly this would be especially true when we said good-bye to Mike Cavanaugh, who I considered the informal leader of our little dysfunctional family. My notes recall the evening featured a songfest of truck-driving ballads to the guitars of Mike Byers and Moose Carroll. I especially loved their rendition of "I turned 21 in prison doing life without parole …" I recall I had the dawn patrol next morning so I slipped out of the party a few hours before my scheduled takeoff, which I considered prudent and reasonable, and I was not the first to retire to bed. One of the quaint traditions of the Ravens was to creep into a party pooper's room and pour a cold drink on him as he slept. The idea being to encourage him to return to the party and deter others from committing this protocol violation in the future. On this occasion Mike apparently noticed I was MIA and decided to give me the remedial treatment. Since I felt I had performed my social duties adequately, I decided not to play the game. As I lay on my bunk (I can't recall if my roommate Bob Dunbar was in his bunk or not), I heard the telltale creak of someone approaching on the wooden catwalk. Whoever was on the catwalk was not observing our unwritten rule about whistling or singing an American tune after dark. I have previously described the extensive arsenal packed into our small hooch room.

My .45 hung in its holster on my bedpost. I quietly pulled it and cocked the hammer. The room was dark and the early morning was pitch-black. As the creaking stopped just outside the door I could hear rather than see the enforcer of party protocol (I did not yet know who) slowly open the door a crack. At that point I placed two rounds in the door frame about head high. I saw Mike's face in the muzzle flash – a very white face with huge white eyes. He quietly changed his mind about the drink and began to slowly back down the catwalk the way he came. His problems were not over. Karl Polifka in the next hooch was aroused from a sound sleep and appeared behind Mike prepared to cut him in half with his sawed-off shotgun. I never did hear any more about that from Mike although we've talked a few times over the years. I guess in his mind that was just another typical day of all kinds of people shooting at him and usually missing. As I look back on that incident today, I know that two pistol shots in the early-morning hours within 100 yards of the CIA sleeping quarters in one direction and VP's house in the other direction would not escape notice and concern. But I don't recall anyone – including Mike – saying anything to me about it.

"Dark Days" Nov 1969 – Jan 1970

During the second half of my tour the military situation began to turn around. The NVA poured into Laos in strength and the weather deteriorated with the approach of winter. The gains of "About Face" were increasingly threatened.

In early November I was checked out in the T-28 by "Water Pump" IPs at Udorn. My AF flight records reflect a lot more time and sorties in this checkout (five sorties and 8.7 hours) than I remember. My recollection is we did a pattern ride, an instrument ride in the back seat under the hood, and a range ride to show me the guns and rockets. I recall the ground school was a 30-minute chat with an IP over a glass of whisky and then we retired to the Holiday Inn for a rubdown. I guess it was adequate and I had a ball flying the T-28 for the next three months. Karl Polifka would soon leave in December, leaving me and Mike Byers the only T-28-qualified guys at the site to fly our two birds – sweet.

Jack Hudson's Rescue

Sometime in November on a crisp clear morning I took off on the dawn patrol in the T-28 and checked in with Cricket to be told an A-1 was flying south in the PDJ with prop failed to full decrease. I was given the Skyraider's frequency and established contact. I soon saw him to the north of me coming my way, slowly descending. He told me the airplane should have enough power to hold altitude at some point and asked the lowest he could descend and still get south to the Thai border. The PDJ was roughly 4,000 feet elevation and there was higher terrain to the south. It soon became apparent he would not get south of the PDJ, and I picked a suitable bailout location for him. This was a fairly large grass-topped hill near the southern tip of the PDJ. He was a little skeptical. "I was bombing here last week, Raven." But time was up and as I sat on his wing I watched the Yankee extraction system work perfectly. The pilotless Skyraider slowly rolled and descended into the terrain a few miles south.

Meanwhile I observed the pilot's chute carry him across the top of the hill and down the side where he hung up in the trees. He made radio contact on guard and reported he was OK. I had previously talked to a "Greenie" (H-34) heli pilot who was in the vicinity and by now standing by to come in and pick up the downed pilot. Trouble was they were ill-equipped to pull a pilot out of trees. By now we also had a Jolly Green on scene observing the effort and he insisted the H-34 disengage and "let the professionals handle it," or something to that effect, which I recall pissed me off. But we let the Jolly come in and he pulled the pilot out and flew him the short distance to 20A. I returned home to meet the rescued pilot and it turned out to be my old Academy cadet wing commander – Jackson L. Hudson. He awarded me his ("combat loss") .38 which was kind of a tradition in these circumstances and we had a nice chat before the Jolly hauled him home to NKP.

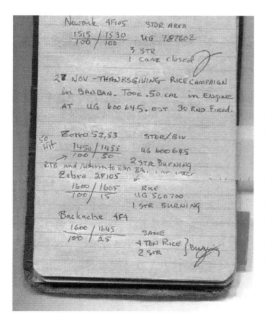

BDA Book Entry 27 Nov 1969

The Thanksgiving Rice Campaign

In late November we were trying to disrupt the enemy rice supply by attacking the harvested stacks of rice in the Ban Ban Valley and another smaller rice-growing area about 10 miles south of Ban Ban. We learned that rice was a difficult target. You could bomb the stacks and scatter the rice, but we learned they would collect the scattered undamaged grains. We considered some kind of poison but settled on napalm as the most practical means. The problem was the rice was in well-defended areas and finned napalm dropped from a dive just plopped in a small fire as opposed to the impressive splash you got when unfinned nape was dropped from a low-level pass.

So on Thanksgiving Day about 1430 in the afternoon I was directing a flight of Skyraiders (Zorro 52 and 53) with napalm against stacks of rice in about the center of the Ban Ban Valley. They were dive-bombing from fairly high altitude and the results were poor. I wanted them to try low-level delivery and decided to show them that there was no AAA in the area. I set up for a low pass from north to south trying to have a dramatic effect by having my shadow closely approach my airplane. I recall I even dropped a little flap. As I was about to transmit, "see, no problem," there was a problem.

About the time I heard the 12.7 open fire from about 300 yards east of me, the round entered the left side of the engine cowling, blew off part of a cylinder head, and continued out the right cowling, leaving an impressive exit wound. Oil immediately began siphoning along the side of the fuselage. I hope I didn't whimper over the radio but I probably did. I was about 10 miles east of Phu Nok Kok, Black Lion's hilltop stronghold, so my first instinct was to climb and head east. I asked the A-1s to tag along which they did, no doubt chuckling to themselves about my foolish stunt. I was not chuckling. But the Bird Dog was behaving very well considering the abuse she had suffered. I was intently scanning the few engine instruments for any sign of impending doom and saw none. I continued to climb and cruise southwest toward and then over the PDJ and finally to Skyline and home, the Skyraiders a reassuring presence throughout my anxious trip. (See picture of intrepid author and wounded Bird Dog).

My first reference to targeting rice was 22 November 1969 at UG5366 in the Ban Ban. I directed midmorning strikes by Firefly 22 (two A-1s) and Gator (two F-4s) and awarded BDA of four tons and two tons of rice respectively. I directed 15 sets of fighters on rice targets in the Ban Ban between 22 and 28 Nov. On 5 Dec I recorded a VR report "about 20 stacks rice in Ban Ban – pretty dispersed." That was my last reference to the rice campaign.

110

Some months earlier in anticipation I had secured a C-ration can of turkey from the storeroom and stuck it in my footlocker. On this day I carried it with me in the cockpit intending to celebrate with a turkey "feast" at some point during the day. Early that afternoon I had my foolish run in with the 12.7 but was back over the Ban Ban by 1530 when I put in Zebra, a flight of two F-105s, and then held Backache, a flight of four F-4s, high and dry while I opened and ate my can of turkey. They held somewhat impatiently while I relished my turkey dinner, then we struck at 1630 leaving four tons of rice and two structures burning.

The General's Aide

I can't recall exactly when the following events happened, but they coincided with a rare visit to 20A by a USAF general in the wake of congressional hearings on the expanded operations in Laos. That would make the timeframe late November or December 1969. Chris Robbins relates the story involves Maj. Gen. Robert L. Petit, 7/13 AF commander at Udorn, coincident with departure party for Polifka, Dunbar, and Daines. My own recollection was a little different than the Robbins account, but in view of convincing evidence I've adopted some but not all of the more commonly accepted version of events. Chris Robbins relates the incident as part of the evening farewell party, but my own pretty clear recollection is a little different. We were all aware of but not overly excited about the arrival of a USAF general at the site that day. It was afternoon and I had landed after buzzing the field in the T-28, which I heard later really impressed the general. I was drinking in the CAS bar with a case officer my notes refer to as "Big John." (This might have been John Jennings, the case officer usually at LS-46 – call sign "Swamp Rat," who I probably knew better than I knew other case officers). Robbins' account refers to the case officer as "Igor." So who knows for sure? I don't recall if anyone else was in the room except John and me but I've already proven how memory plays tricks so I could be mistaken. Karl Polifka told me he was present. Some old notes I scribbled down in the early 80s (10 years after the event) relate that Gen. Petit's aide appeared in the doorway looking a bit overawed and apparently not accustomed to traveling in civilian clothes. In an uncharacteristically friendly gesture, "Big John" asked the young man in for a beer. I winced as he drew himself up and replied stiffly, "I never drink on duty." I sensed rather than actually saw a huge hairy arm cross the room like a striking rattler, seize the startled martinet by the shirt collar, and propel him effortlessly across the room into and through the window. All this happened in the blink of an eye. I glanced out the window to see the dazed but apparently undamaged body sprawled on top of Floyd's bear cage with a surprised and delighted Floyd reaching up to explore his prize. As we turned quietly back to our beers we noticed General Petit standing in the doorway. Presumably he had witnessed the episode and a pregnant pause told him the ball was in his court. To his everlasting credit he cleared his throat, flashed us a nervous smile, and said, "I believe I'll have one of those beers!" That's the way I remember it. Subsequently word got around about the general observing, "You look like a bunch of Mexican bandits." So on a fine December morning those of us available posed for the famous "Mexican Banditos" photo out front of the Raven house. Hopefully someone sent the general a souvenir copy.

"Banditos" taken in front of Raven House at 20A in Dec 1969. (William E. Platt Collection)
Back: Jerry Greven, Hank Allen, Moose Carroll, Joe Bauer, Tom Palmer, Will Platt, Tom Harris. Kneeling: Bill Kozma,
Joe Potter, Smoky Greene. There are also four of our support troops in the photo I regret I cannot recall their names.

Moose goes MIA

I think it must have been sometime in early December when Terry "Moose" Carroll got very ill and had to be evacuated to Udorn. Here's how I remember that event. We were living in the new house by then so we had private bedrooms. Our dedicated cook Espi had DEROS'd some time earlier and the interim cook was either gone or unable to keep up with the job. For some time we had reverted to fending for ourselves individually and more often than not dinner after a long day of flying was a couple cans of beer. It was not a good situation and I'm surprised looking back now that something wasn't done by the adult supervision. I think we were too tired to complain. Another factor in this episode was that the Ravens did not have a rigid flying schedule or systematic personnel accountability. So one morning we finally missed Moose and started a search. We found Moose in his bed with pneumonia – near death. He was urgently carried to Udorn in a Porter, where he soon recovered and came back to fly with us as I recall. Moose can straighten me out if my memory is faulty as he is fortunately (and no thanks to his Raven buddies) still alive and kicking. One positive outcome was that Moose's condition focused attention on our lack of a dedicated cook and we soon had two excellent Thai cooks. I recall after they arrived I began to fly back to 20A to lunch on their excellent sandwiches rather than chance the roasted buffalo meat when we refueled and rearmed on the PDJ.

Another Moose and Me Story

New Year's morning 1970 I rose with the chickens – no doubt still a bit tipsy, and took off in an O-1 with backseater "Scar," a quiet but competent little guy – one of my favorites as I recall. I don't think we were aloft very long – somewhere over northern PDJ – when I suddenly felt ill and barfed out the left window. In an O-1 the backseater gets the full impact driven by a 60-knot slipstream. I looked back apologetically to see Scar peering scornfully over his splattered map, "Oh, Laven 42, you numbah ten!"

We soon landed at L-22 ("Lima Lima"), an old French strip in north-central PDJ where I tumbled out on the ground and rested my head against a main wheel. Scar wandered off to commiserate with other local troops and I assumed he would find his own way back home to 20A later in the day. Not 15 minutes after I landed, Moose Carroll's O-1 appeared on short final and he too landed and tumbled out on the ground for a combat nap. My BDA book shows I put in four sets of fighters between 0950 and 1040 at UG 6642, which is south of Fish's Mouth about eight miles northeast of LS-236. I have to assume this was after a period of recovery under the wing of my O-1.

Trucks!

Analyzing my BDA book I see only a few mentions of vehicles as targets. Ninety percent of our focus during my tour was on close support against troops and bunkers. But I recall an intel brief we got at some point from a very impressive gentleman on the CIA side, who we were later told was a colonel who had defected from the NVA. When we were told that, I recall thinking if they are all as sharp as this guy no wonder they are kicking our ass. Anyway, he made one point in his briefing that stuck with me. He said the road structure in the vicinity of the Fish's Mouth (far-eastern Ban Ban along Route 7) would support about 1,500 trucks. And that if we killed 1,500 trucks one day, there would be another 1,500 trucks using the same roads the next day. Encouraging. Anyway, I don't recall when we got that briefing or if it was factual. And I may have the 1,500 number wrong – I just recall it was a surprisingly big number. But for most of my tour Ravens did not find many of the alleged 1,500 trucks when we patrolled that area. Then in October we got a new guy, a former Nail FAC named Henry Allen. And as a Steel Tiger Nail, Henry was an expert truck finder and killer. I don't recall if he gave us any formal schooling on how to find trucks, but he began to find them and so for the first time we knew for sure they were really there. (After drafting this story I subsequently learned Moose Carroll was in the same category as Henry – an accomplished truck finder and killer from the Nails. Shows we either did not know or have forgotten things about each other from those days).

On 8 Dec my little green book lists three airstrikes on several trucks at UG 7367, which plots out at the Bird's Head in the Ban Ban Valley on Route 7. I seem to recall these trucks were in the open, and I suspected they were already destroyed or at least damaged from previous strikes or they would not have been exposed during daylight.

On 26 Dec my BDA book notes: "Found 3 trucks on [Route] 61. 12 actual found and 8 destroyed." This was about noon at UG647964, which is about 10 miles northwest of the Bird's Head. I think this was my breakthrough on finding and killing trucks. Just after lunchtime I was conducting VR from the O-1 north of the Ban Ban. My mental image is of a road running beside fairly thick trees on one side. I flew along the road looking across the road into the trees, using binoculars from some distance since this was a well-defended area. I thought I spotted something unnatural – a single truck tire. I took a closer look and sure enough I could make out the tire was attached to a well-camouflaged truck off the side of the road. I called Cricket for air and put Kingfish, four F-105s, on the truck. After lead dropped I checked and found his bombs had blown camouflage off several more trucks parked close by along the road under the trees. We had a convoy! The flight finished expending their bombs along the road and I awarded BDA of one truck destroyed and two damaged. I had to leave the area but reported the target to Cricket and on our Raven common frequency so another Raven could take over. Eventually eight trucks were confirmed destroyed at that location.

On 12 Jan I was conducting VR on Route 7 west of Ban Ban. I located a truck and called for air. I put in Mantis, two F-105s, at 1315. I saw what I reported as a "POL secondary" (POL means "petroleum, oil, and lubricants") in my BDA book and awarded BDA of one truck destroyed. I was low on fuel so I handed the target off to Raven 41 and returned home for fuel and rockets. I returned later in the afternoon and put three more sets of fighters on the same target area – killing several more trucks. This was my last attack on trucks. The remainder of the month we focused on enemy troop targets as all our forward sites came under heavy pressure from the enemy.

Dead Stick on the PDJ

In January my BDA book reveals I began putting in a lot of strikes near LS-184 about 80 nautical miles north of 20A. Rainbow was the call sign of the resident case officer. As you look at the map, Rainbow and Kingpin sat between some minor road arteries running generally south through the mountains toward the PDJ from the North Vietnam border. There was obviously a lot of NVA troop and supply movement around and past the position, and this intensified in December and January. Looking at the map, these sites were a long way north of the rest of the war focused around the PDJ and Ban Ban. Due to the distance I usually liked to have the T-28 to patrol in Rainbow's area, but one day I was in the O-1 and was putting in strikes late in the day. I can't pinpoint the precise day the following episode happened but it was one of two or three days in early January. As usual Rainbow had nearby enemy and I was putting in critically needed strikes. And I overstayed my welcome.

A word here about the range and endurance of the O-1. In Vietnam we generally were equipped with the O-1G with a fixed-pitch prop and we usually flew about 2.5-hour missions. Northern Laos presented a different challenge. Distances between base and target areas tended to be much greater and the need to loiter in the target areas to sustain friendly positions with air support was a priority. The elevations and altitudes we flew were generally much higher than in Vietnam and climbs ate more fuel. So we all soon learned tricks to extend the range and endurance of our Bird Dogs, probably from the Air America and CAS pros. At 20A we were equipped with more capable O-1Fs that featured variable-pitch props, although the engine and fuel capacity were essentially the same as the "A" models. Some claimed we applied the same technique as Charles Lindberg used to cross the Atlantic – that is, advancing full manifold pressure, increasing prop pitch, and then leaning mixture till the engine begins to run rough and then enriching the fuel mixture just a tad. If you do it right, you can almost see the prop turning out the front window and the bird will stay airborne well over four hours. We had to manually switch fuel flow from one wing to the other every half hour or so to keep the wings balanced. When you got a bit low you exhausted the fuel in one wing and switched to the other as the engine started to die. You knew then the remaining wing contained all the fuel you were going to have to get home. So if you have been following along and doing the math, the O-1 could fly about 4.5 hours at about 65 knots covering almost 300 miles. Of course you would use more fuel maneuvering and putting in airstrikes. Some Ravens reading this will claim they could get more out of the O-1 but most would agree that's about right. The thing is that a miscalculation on the short side could lead to a dire situation.

Arrowhead Lake, northeastern PDJ - Heading south for home

Anyway, back to LS-184 and hitting enemy troops near the site late on a January afternoon. As evening approached, if we had serious enemy activity we would hand off our targets and ground frequency to the arriving NKP Skyraiders who covered the night shift – call signs Zorro or Firefly. As I completed handoff to the A-1 flight my engine sputtered and I switched to my remaining wing fuel and pointed the bird south. After a short time I began to realize the remaining fuel was not going to get me the 75 miles I needed to reach home. I hoped I could make it another 40 miles to the PDJ before the engine quit. I came up on "company" frequency and broadcast my position and a request for any available assistance. Within minutes I was relieved to have a CAS Huey flying in loose formation off my right side. At least the weather was good, but the sun was getting low as the PDJ came in sight. Now at that time we still technically "owned" the PDJ but all bets were off after dark. I was at a few thousand feet above the ground and just entering the northeastern PDJ when the engine sputtered and quit. Fortunately, there are several old French airstrips in the northern and eastern PDJ. I lined up on one – not sure which exactly – and anyway I could no longer be too choosey. I recall the strip was near the eastern edge of the Plain. Even overloaded with radio equipment the O-1 glides pretty well, and I don't remember the landing being too rough. I did not have a backseater. I was understandably nervous about being on the ground in the eastern PDJ with night rapidly approaching.

The Huey did not land but hovered about 10 feet off the ground about 50 yards south of me. I gathered my weapon and map bag and began to move toward the helicopter. I assumed he would land and pick me up and we'd come back tomorrow for the bird. I briefly thought maybe I should torch the airplane to prevent it falling into enemy hands, but fortunately rejected the idea because I then saw someone kick a 50-gallon drum out the side door of the hovering Huey. A moment later I recognized the drum kicker as "Yellow Dog" (Burr Smith) standing in the door, and I could imagine him smiling as the pilot pulled collective and rapidly peeled off in a climbing turn to the south and home. I was somewhat astonished – and not smiling. All of a sudden I was alone (I hoped) on the PDJ in gathering twilight with an empty Bird Dog, a .30 cal carbine, and a 50-gallon drum full of AV gas. Could be worse, but could be a helluva lot better.

I rolled the drum over to the O-1 and then pondered how to transfer at least a gallon or so of gas into the top of the right wing. Time was getting to be a factor. I inventoried my available tools and pulled my .45 automatic and without a lot of thought put two holes in the top of the barrel. Looking back at that moment I imagine a lot of really bad things could have happened – but they didn't and a stream of fuel began pouring on the ground. The next challenge was how to capture the fuel and get it up and into the wing tank. I had a flying helmet and a canteen and I honestly don't recall which I used. But I somehow got enough gas into the bird to fire it up and fly 25 miles south to Skyline and home, landing in pretty dark conditions. I imagine I slunk quietly into the house, thoroughly embarrassed and hoping against hope that Burr Smith had kept the incident to himself. Since my BDA book does not refer to the incident I presume I kept it to myself, but I know better than to think the episode went unnoticed by the leadership. And it was yet another incident late in my tour that reinforced my conviction that I was running out of luck.

"Taking Hits"

Many war stories revolve around the interaction of airplanes and guns designed to shoot them down. People tend to be fascinated by this aspect of the business and certainly there was a fair amount of AAA, or more simply AA, on the ground in Laos. Despite numerous references in my BDA book to rounds fired and tracers observed there were a relatively few occasions when my airplane was actually hit. I think I probably took a below-average number of hits compared to other Ravens. Fred "Magnet Ass" Platt was off the chart. He could get hit walking to his airplane. I recall late in my tour (Robbins says it was 11 January) Fred flew into 20A one morning with a really beat-up old O-1G from Victor and jumped into our newest O-1F. I swear he wasn't gone 30 minutes before we heard he was shot down. Chris Robbins' book goes into a lot of detail about the incident and Fred's subsequent adventures as a renegade patient at the Udorn hospital. I seem to recall I visited him there and accompanied him on his infamous excursion to the Udorn O'Club in his neck brace and hospital PJs. But a lot of brain cells have been put out of their misery since then and I may have imagined it all.

Anyway, I felt like I saw a lot of AA during my tour but did not actually get hit much. Most of my hits occurred during the final two months of my tour. My experiences with AA tended to be concentrated along Route 7 from Ban Ban to the Fish's Mouth where Route 7 entered North Vietnam, at LS-184 north of Ban Ban, and up at Sam Neua. Of course you could encounter smaller 7.62 (AK-47) and 12.7 (.50 cal) weapons almost anywhere.

As FACs we were no doubt high-priority targets for AAA gunners, but we also believed that they would hold their fire to conceal their position unless they were pretty sure they could kill us before we were able to bring fighters in on them. Once the jig was up and the enemy realized we knew where they were, they would open up in a desperate attempt to prevent the coming airstrike. In my experience during the airstrike itself, the enemy seemed more inclined to fire at the attacking fighter bombers rather than the FAC directing the strike. During December I made several trips to Sam Neua where there were plenty of guns of all sizes very willing to open up but I never was actually hit while up there. My BDA book shows I did VR there on 6 Dec reporting that I saw rice, personnel, military supplies and POL, caves, and probable truck parks. I would visit this reputed PL HQ located near the North Vietnamese border some 100 miles northeast of home and put in strikes several times in December.

My BDA book notes I took hits on only four occasions. None of these hits brought the aircraft down before I was able to safely land at 20A:

27 Nov – "Thanksgiving rice campaign in Ban Ban. Took .50 Cal [12.7mm] in engine at UG600645. Est 30 rd fired."
28 Dec – "Took 2 hits small caliber" during F-4 airstrike on bulldozers in eastern Ban Ban Valley.
27 Jan – "Took 2 hits 12.7 [.50 cal] at UG670670" [Ban Ban Valley near the Bird's Head].
29 Jan – During the TIC at LS-184 (Rainbow) – "Took hit thru canopy before strike. Broke TIC. Friendly captured hill." [upon landing we found rear seat cushion shredded by 12.7 and several small-caliber hits on the wings and fuselage].

I took a hit on a fifth occasion on the T-28 prop not reported in my BDA book but described at the end of this segment.

There were a number of occasions I saw AA but was not hit. Reports of seeing AA guns firing showed up frequently in my BDA book during December and early January. There were about a dozen entries in my book, and I note the locations for every one were in a fairly compact area along Route 7 between Ban Ban and the Fish's Mouth.

The 23 mm AA piece was a spectacular weapon – the many white puffs of airburst reminded me of popcorn. These guns typically had twin barrels firing bursts of maybe 50 -100 rounds. Seems to me 23 mm was normally set to airburst about 4-6 thousand feet above the ground. The airburst pattern was awesome to see – especially at night. I recall after I returned the States and attended a fireworks display how certain fireworks were so similar to 23 mm that the sight and sound actually frightened me into a cold sweat. On the other hand 37 mm was fired in a five-round clip and was more of a gray airburst, and I think it airburst quite a bit higher. Because of the rate of fire and frag density we were more concerned about 23 than 37. Of course most of my personal problems resulted from the lowly 12.7 mm (50 cal), which seemed to be everywhere in great numbers.

I was hit most often when I was at low level relatively close to the AA weapon. Sometimes this was necessary, as in the case of the serious TIC at Rainbow, but sometimes I was just shining my ass, like on Thanksgiving Day on the floor of the Ban Ban when I richly deserved the death penalty and nearly got it. But I recall one day in the T-28, again over Ban Ban, I was at what I considered a very safe altitude – maybe 4,000 ft AGL (flying straight and level from A to B when a sharp CLANG knocked my boots off the rudder pedals. I started a belated jink and flew along for a few minutes intently studying the engine instruments and working on the old heartbeat. Everything seemed OK so I carried on with whatever I was doing, but upon landing we found a quarter-size dent in the prop blade – perhaps made by a 12.7 round. I was quite surprised to be hit just minding my own business at that altitude.

I Begin to Weigh the Odds

After my attention-getting introduction to flying in Laos shortly after I arrived in late July, things had settled into a relatively smooth pattern for me during August through October. I was busy learning the job, getting comfortable with the area, and enjoying the uniqueness of the country and the flying. And of course friendlies were doing well on the ground. From November through January I began to be more conscious of the constant risks. Perhaps the newness of everything and hard work to learn the job gave way to a little boredom and too much free time to think more deeply about what I was doing. I began to feel like the percentages were bound to catch up to me. My records show I had quite a few hits and close calls in the last couple months. Looking back, I don't think I changed my pattern of flying to try to reduce the risks because I think I was fatalistic about it – like there was nothing I could do to avoid it. I recall sitting on my bunk alone at night before sleep when I would briefly review the day and calmly say to myself, "This is simply not survivable." Then I would go to sleep. I don't recall nightmares or restlessness, and in the morning I rose raring to go down to the flight line and strap on an airplane. I never recall having black thoughts during the day. I enjoyed my flying and did plenty of it. I slept OK and certainly had a great appetite. But I'm sure it was there in the back of my mind. I was not afraid so much as *resigned* to what I came to believe was inevitable. I was not about to quit nor did I regret joining the program. It was all a kid could ask for – we were living very intensely. But there was just this little downside lurking in the background.

I suppose for a guy to be convinced for a lengthy period of time that he is likely to be killed any day is probably very unhealthy. The B-17 crews flying into Germany must have felt like that. And maybe the F-105 guys going for their 100 missions over the North. We used to joke that the definition of an optimist was a Thud pilot who quit smoking because he was afraid he would die of cancer. But B-17 and F-105 guys were seeing other airplanes explode and fall out of the sky all around them. On the other hand, my own concerns appear unjustified – we lost only one Raven during my time at 20A, my Academy classmate Dan Davis in August just after I arrived. He collided with one of his fighters. We would lose two more Ravens soon after I left. But it's not like we were experiencing heavy casualties – at least while I was there. Recently we did some research on casualties while designing a plaque to hang at the Air Force Academy to commemorate the Ravens. That research showed that there had been a total of 201 Ravens over six years. Of those, 23 were killed in action (KIA) in Laos. That's just over 11 percent loss rate. (In the special case of Ravens at 20A, Karl Polifka estimates there were about 90 Ravens between 1968 and 1971, and of these 18 were KIA for a 20 percent loss rate.) Doesn't sound so bad, but I guess the close calls I was experiencing from the AA, the hazardous weather, and my own carelessness made me feel like the next time I wouldn't get away with it. I haven't asked any of the other Ravens whether they had this same feeling – that's not what guys do, but I sometimes wonder.

After Laos I never felt this sense of impending doom again, although I occasionally recalled how I felt in those strange days. I don't think it affected my performance in future years – even in combat or other hazardous flying assignments. I just remember when Jerry Rhein told me I'd flown my last Raven sortie, I could not believe I had survived. I was relieved, I'm sure, but also a little confused. It's like I did not have a plan for life after Laos. I guess I somehow figured it out and would not today self-diagnose that I was emotionally crippled by my combat experience as I know some were, but I suppose I had some mild form of PTSD. I have not previously reflected on these very private admissions in such explicit detail, but I think it has been somewhat therapeutic to write them down.

Anyway, I haven't told others about this except my wife, who I met a few months after I returned from Laos. She told me years later she thought I was pretty messed up – a good project for her. She's still working on me 40 years later.

T-28 Attack Mode

We looked up to the old Special Ops heads like Joe Potter and Jerry Rhein. They didn't talk much about their exploits, at least not that I overheard, but we got the impression they had done cool things like flown Mustangs in little wars in Central and South America as "Yankee Air Pirates" opposing Commies wherever they were found. I remember flying to Udorn in a formation of two T-28s with Joe just before he left Alternate. When we reached cruising altitude he called to "synch props" and as briefed I slipped into trail and adjusted my RPMs till I could see his prop through mine making a stationary pattern. They don't teach that in UPT! This was just one of the many prop-fighter tricks of the trade, in this case to minimize the sound of the formation and delay warning of our approach to enemy forces.

Smoke with T-28D at LS-20A circa Dec 1969

Our two T-28D-5s were capable of carrying bombs and napalm, but Ravens were restricted by policy to 300 rounds .50 cal in two "suitcase" guns under the wings (or some newer models with guns fitted internal to the wings) and two to four under-wing seven-round rocket launchers.

119

Sometimes we carried only white phosphorous ("Willie Pete") for marking targets, but sometimes one pod was loaded with HE (high explosive), better against troops and light armor. Until my final action at LS-184, I do not recall using the T-28 weapons in an actual close air support strike. But I certainly practiced strafing – a lot. I seldom returned home with bullets. My self-taught technique was to roll in on my target and begin firing. As I saw the rounds hitting the ground I would adjust the airplane to move the hits up onto the intended target, pulling out at the last second. Experienced fighter pilots will recognize this technique as a recipe for disaster.

When I returned to the States I was assigned to the F-100, Pipeline SEA. I had to first attend AT-33 fighter lead-in at Myrtle Beach. (Yeah, I know, helluva deal). Anyway, when briefing prior to my first range ride my IP asked if I had ever strafed and I assured him I had strafed – a lot. So he skimped on that part of the briefing and we proceeded to the range. On my first strafe pass I rolled in and applied my personal combat-proven technique. As I was happily firing and adjusting the impacts up toward the canvas target the aircraft experienced a maximum-allowable "g" pullout initiated by the flabbergasted IP. "Greene, what the hell was that?!?" Once I recovered from a near blackout I replied, confused, "That's me strafing." We returned to base for a long lecture on proper strafe technique, emphasizing prevention of self-inflicted ricochet damage. On a serious note, my Raven experience did provide invaluable combat experience, but in some ways the independence that a FAC uniquely enjoys tended to complicate my transition to flying in the "real" Air Force in a regimented fighter squadron environment. In short, I was spoiled forever by the freedom of being a young and dumb "Yankee Air Pirate."

The Lure of Sam Neua

An exception to the general pattern of providing direct support to our manned sites late in my tour were some forays I made some 100 miles north and east to the traditional enemy stronghold at Sam Neua. As I recall the terrain there was unique and striking – flat open areas punctuated by huge steep karsts – and lots of natural caves that we knew housed lots of troops, equipment, and supplies. There were persistent rumors of American POWs held there by the PL. It was well defended by numerous guns of all calibers so it was a place to go and get shot at when you were bored or to throw some missiles and bombs into when you were pissed off. My BDA book shows I went up there and performed VR and put in fighters – usually F-105s with bombs or Bullpup missiles – about four times between 6 and 31 December. I recall one December morning at breakfast Joe Potter gently suggesting it wasn't wise or useful to go up there, but to his credit he wasn't usually dictatorial about things. But I respected Joe, and later Jerry Rhein, as the closest thing to adult supervision we had. So I think I went up there a few more times but was a bit more careful. I think I realized Sam Neua was a sideshow rather than central to our primary mission. But I also hated to think the enemy felt immune from strikes anywhere in our AOR (area of responsibility).

Adult Leadership – Lack Of

What? Greene complaining about too much ice cream? Not really complaining, but I think the command atmosphere was an important part of the Raven story and I should talk about it, though I suspect it's a sore subject with some. This is not so much a criticism of my fellow Ravens or our local leadership but just my observations that may help explain why things were the way they were.

At 20A during my time the command atmosphere (if you can dignify it with that term) was "relaxed." Since we were single-ship we could pretty much do what we liked in the air, not that we needed motivational leadership to urge us to perform the mission to the best of our abilities. But we certainly did things "our way" – which in retrospect may not have always been tactically sound or smart, but in fairness there was no Raven SOP (Standard Operating Procedures). So we were often making it up as we went along. You learned by doing and surviving – or not. The Raven program recruited people who were predisposed to independent action (a nice way of saying rebellious) – perhaps a necessary character attribute to carry out the mission in Laos. On the ground Raven behavior as a group tended toward the outrageous. It's as if we felt a responsibility to cultivate a devil-may-care reputation even though over-the-top behavior would not have been our normal personality as individuals. Although it would not have occurred to me at the time, looking back I think a case can be made that we young men occasionally needed a little closer and firmer supervision in the air and on the ground.

Distance from HQ and the lack of associated restrictions and regulations that constrained our pilot peers in the "real" Air Force was a big part of the allure of the Raven program. This was pretty well covered in Robbins' book. In retrospect I think it suited the ambassador to provide top cover to prevent too much command influence from 7/13th AF at Udorn. Regarding our local supervision, I am reluctant to voice any criticism of our on-scene leaders, who I respected and liked and I think did their best under trying conditions, or the 20A Ravens who actively resisted authority as a natural response by young men in the circumstances we found ourselves in. Our leaders at 20A certainly cut us a lot more slack than I would later cut the young pilots in my fighter squadron. For example, if Mr. (Capt. or Maj.) Smith suggested (i.e., ordered) Mr. (1st Lt.) Jones to do something a certain way, the likely result would be that Mr. (Lt.) Jones would tell Mr. (Capt. or Maj.) Smith that he could f --- off. And there would be no resulting disciplinary action.

Joe Potter and Jerry Rhein as site commanders tried in their gentle ways to give us the benefit of their long experience to keep us from killing ourselves. Ultimately Jerry Rhein cut my tour short by a couple weeks, which I have no doubt saved my life. But no question the "Terry and the Pirates" / civilian-clothes atmosphere led us to feel entitled to take with a grain of salt the military chain of command. We were very young – the tradition of military discipline was not yet ingrained. The 20A Ravens tended to be self-directed and on a very loose rein. The mission was to get up every morning and go look for trouble and when you found it – bomb it. There is no doubt in my mind that we Ravens had more pure freedom of action than any group of US military pilots since the Flying Tigers or Pappy Boyington's Black Sheep. Probably for the same reasons – we lived and flew in a remote, hostile environment demanding relaxed command structure to get the job done. We were actually disciplined in some ways. For example, we were very focused and self-motivated when it came to the mission of supporting Vang Pao's little army. But no question most of us took maximum advantage of our quasi-civilian status to rebel against military authority whenever the occasion presented. As a young guy having fun I certainly did not complain, but that does not mean I did not recognize a lack of normal military supervision which may have permitted, perhaps even encouraged us to take more risks, and no doubt added to my concerns about the odds against survival.

SEA FAC was my first assignment out of pilot training and it no doubt spoiled me for future "real" Air Force assignments. I was a young lieutenant seeing the Air Force through a very different set of eyes than a couple years before when I was at the Air Force Academy and then UPT. When I reported to my next base after the Raven tour I was soon reminded of the stark difference between an operational Air Force fighter squadron and the relaxed command atmosphere and air discipline of the 20A Ravens. It made for a difficult transition for me back into the "real" Air Force. I spent three years in the F-100 as an unruly captain struggling to become a USAF jet fighter pilot – behind my peers in fighter experience and often in trouble. But I survived to become a disciplined major. It was that or quit – or be fired – or killed.

Friendly Fire

During the month of January, Rainbow at LS-184 came under heavy enemy pressure. LS-184 is a relatively isolated site well north of our other friendly positions, 50 miles north of the PDJ and 80 miles north of 20A. I conducted strikes there for the first time on 4 January against bunkers and troops in the open and was credited with 20 killed by air (KBA) by Rainbow. My BDA book records that I "observed a body flying through the air" after an accurate bomb impact. I was back at Rainbow on 9 January directing seven sets of fighters between 1000 and 1730. As I study the BDA record I know I would have had to refuel around noon and I was back again by 1330. I was flying the T-28D according to AF flight records. I flew three sorties of about 2.5 to 3.0 duration for a total of 8.5 hours.

The afternoon brought disaster. Panda, four F-105s, checked in with Mk-82s at 1645. I gave them a strike briefing for a target near LS-184 and waited for them to arrive. I recall the weather as workable but with a low overcast, and it was getting late so it was rather gloomy. Panda lead reported me in sight so I fired a WP at my target and climbed to a position to observe the strike. Panda lead called overhead and that he had me in sight and had my smoke mark. I did not yet see him. So I waggled my wings and Panda lead acknowledged my waggle. He reported rolling in and asked for clearance. I then for the first and last time violated the FAC's cardinal rule and cleared him "hot" without visual. In retrospect I did this for a couple of reasons. There were no friendlies in the immediate vicinity of my target and I assumed the gloomy weather was masking the F-105 from me. Most importantly – I trusted F-105 pilots. F-105 pilots earned a great reputation with Ravens because of their bombing accuracy and willingness to work in very poor weather. The F-4 wings imposed strict minimum altitudes, which reduced their bombing accuracy compared to F-105s. Just two days before on 7 Jan an entry in my BDA book states: "WX D.S. THUDS ARE BEAUTIFUL." And Panda was so confident over the air that he had me in sight, even acknowledging my wing rock. So I cleared Panda lead while anxiously looking for him. The next thing I heard over the air was, "How are those hits, Raven?"

122

Oh s---! I saw no evidence of weapon impact anywhere near my mark. I directed "high and dry" and scanned the horizon for bomb smoke. There it was – about eight miles south. I flew in that direction and saw a CAS Pilatus bugging out. I called him on company freq and got a very terse "WTFO!" from an understandably shaken CAS pilot. He had been dropping rice to the village near LS-278 and the Thud pilot mistook the Pilatus for my T-28. He probably saw a cook fire in the village and assumed it was my smoke mark. What a classic blunder! My BDA book does not indicate damage or casualties, but a note says Rainbow will follow up and report. I don't recall what I said to Panda lead but it was my fault, not his – so I passed him some BDA and worked a waiting A-1 flight on Rainbow's target, then set course south for the very long ride to Alternate. I knew two Mk-82s had hit very near a village and there were bound to be innocent casualties. I was probably on my way out of the program in disgrace if not court-martial. And it occurred to me I had to go personally apologize to Vang Pao. I dreaded this. He had recently commended me for good work, but I also knew he did not hesitate to shoot people who screwed up. I spent a very long 30 minutes pondering my fate in the gathering twilight. I figured by the time I landed, the US and Hmong leadership would already know what I'd done, either from the CAS pilot or Rainbow's radio net. My only real clear memory of the evening was at VP's when I told him at dinner, "Today I bombed a village." I remember he gave a small shrug and said only, "C'est la guerre." I imagine he had been briefed and he and the US leadership had decided not to take action against me. Nevertheless, this incident still haunts me.

I guess I quickly shook off my funk after the friendly fire incident and I was back in the air in the morning of 11 Jan. At 0930 I put in two Skyraiders, Hobo 42 and 43, on troops at TH8650 (LS-196 call sign Kingpin), only about 10 miles west of Rainbow. My BDA book notes "Outstanding work – strafe and Rx BLO 50' ceiling. Made 8-10 passes. Friendlies 300-500m. 6 KBA [passed by] gnd." Obviously the reference to a 50-foot ceiling had to be quite an exaggeration, but no doubt the weather was pretty bad. The next entry shows I put in two A-1 flights 10 miles south of Ban Ban at 1710 that afternoon. This long gap in time and long distance between strikes that day illustrates that the weather could be very bad across the area, and despite the heavy enemy pressure on our sites we just couldn't always work airstrikes on some days in some places during this period.

"THUDS ARE BEAUTIFUL"

My Air Force flight records show I flew every day in January except 19, 20, and 22 Jan. This break in action was when I was given a few days off and ended up at the F-105 base at Tahkli where I sniveled a back-seat F-105G ride with my old Academy buddy Gary Fedel, who was flying with 333rd Tactical Fighter Squadron (TFS) Lancers. I was surprised how solid the Thud felt cruising at 600 knots calibrated and how much of a wallowing pig it was in the traffic pattern at 350. Sure made me appreciate all the times four F-105s would come snaking up a valley under low clouds calling for a quick smoke on the target.

I previously mentioned how much of an impression F-105 pilots made on me during my Raven tour. SEA FACs had a ringside seat to the greatest show on earth – tactical fighter bomber weapons delivery against an enemy target that often returned deadly fire. A quick count shows I watched with a critical eye 701 F-4s and 773 F-105s roll in and release bombs under my direction during my six months in Laos. Experienced FACs developed a feel for the professional skill of individual fighter pilots and their communities – I had an expectation when I heard a flight leader check in and report inbound to my rendezvous. I was tuned in to the confident tone of an experienced flight lead tested by trips over North Vietnam and the gun-infested Ho Chi Minh Trail. I could not help developing a bias, preferring to have a flight of F-105s to a flight of F-4s. While the occasional F-4 pilot would prove outstanding, it was more the rule that they abided by altitude and weather restrictions that precluded accurate bombing. The F-105 community did not seem to have, or at least the pilots did not observe such restrictions. Therefore, a Raven could expect more effective dive-bombing from an airplane designed for low-level, high-speed delivery of tactical nuclear weapons. To be fair, before the advent of accurate bombing computers and smart bombs, dive-bombing from jet fighters in a defended environment was never easy or very accurate. But in my experience F-105 pilots were a lot better at hitting targets in Laos than F-4 pilots. I recall one morning (my BDA book says it was 7 January 1970) I had gotten airborne out of a cloud-shrouded 20A and into northeastern PDJ. Black Lion was calling for help to repel a company of NVA attacking his overlook position from the direction of Ban Ban. (Break, break … quiet, unassuming Will Green, CIA case officer call sign "Black Lion," was actually black – and actually a lion. Would sure like to see him again, but according to Karl Polifka he died at Udorn some years after my tour.)

Resuming … Thick clouds covered the hilltops. It was marginal even for Skyraiders to work under the overcast and of course they would be at far greater risk from AAA guns. At 1000 Mallard, four F-105s, checked in. I briefed the target and weather conditions to the flight lead and I recall his words to this day: "Raven, if you are under there, we are coming under there. Give me a hold-down." A "hold-down" refers to me mashing my UHF transmit button for several seconds while an ADF (automatic direction finding) instrument in the fighter cockpit points to the source of my transmission. The key point here is that this ADF is by no means a precise navigation aid. On the strength of this flimsy evidence the F-105 flight leader was going to lead his three trusting pals down through the rock-filled clouds, hopefully seeing and missing the ground seconds before plowing into it. This was not an isolated case. Thud pilots penetrated clouds on FAC hold-downs frequently – but this was about the worst conditions I ever recall for this maneuver. Seconds after my hold-down the flight lead called that they were under the clouds and looking for smoke. I quickly sent a WP rocket into Black Lion's target coordinates and pulled to the side to observe four Thuds in loose trail weaving under the low deck, each in turn releasing accurate bombs and zooming up into the clouds to turn south to rejoin for their short flight home to Thailand.

Uncharacteristically, I editorialized in my BDA book, "WX DS [dog s---], THUDS ARE BEAUTIFUL."

Another F-105 story while we are at it. On the cloudy foggy morning of 21 October 1969, I was patrolling northeast PDJ talking to Lulu who was positioned on the southwestern side of the strategic Phou Nok Kok to overlook Route 7 connecting northern PDJ with the Ban Ban Valley. Lulu reported heavy fog but he could hear enemy on the road below. I imagined the enemy troops and vehicles as they moved along the road in the thick fog feeling safe from observation and attack. In lengthy spells of bad weather, I had been toying with the idea that I could direct strikes down through the cloud layer if I could pinpoint the target and distinguish friendly positions by triangulating the surrounding hilltops that stood in the clear above the clouds. I had to get the fighters on the right flight path and tell them when to release. This would involve a level release from above the clouds, so I had to estimate how far the bombs would travel after release. But I figured since this was a linear road target, as long as the bombs hit somewhere along the road they would probably do some good. I realized I would probably never know if the strike was successful unless friendly troops later found evidence. But I imagined at least the enemy troops' sense of invulnerability would suffer. So Bear, a flight of four F-105s, checked in at 0845 and readily agreed to arrange his flight in one-mile trail lined up to fly on a specific heading to cross under my Bird Dog and release their string of 32 Mk-82 500 lb. bombs on my command. It was an example of how Ravens tried to innovate to work around the weather conditions and the willingness of fighter pilots to try something unconventional to get the mission done.

Rainbow Rescue - 29 Jan 1970

I would go back to Rainbow (LS-184) again on 24, 26, and 29 Jan as the military situation on the ground deteriorated. When I arrived just after noon on the 29th I found the friendlies, including the American case officer himself, had been pushed off the site into the trees about 1 km to the west. "Rainbow" was the radio call sign of the Hmong FAG who accompanied the CIA case officer. The case officer actually came up on the radio himself, which was unusual and ominous. I don't think I had ever met the gentleman in person before but had talked to his FAG over the radio quite a bit recently. He had endured a tense month. As I circled the site I could see numerous uniformed NVA walking on the light-colored dirt mound that contained LS-184's several buildings and dirt strip. The light-colored dirt contrasted well with the enemy's dark-green uniforms. I was later told they were battalion strength with the mission to take the site. I'm still not sure of the strategic significance of these sites well to the north of the PDJ. Perhaps they sat astride important infiltration routes from North Vietnam. I was flying the T-28 that day, and after learning of Rainbow's dire circumstances I requested urgent air support from Cricket. Cricket reported there was no air available until Zorro, A-1 night fighters, were scheduled to arrive in about an hour. Meantime I was all that was standing between Rainbow and a battalion of NVA regulars. I was armed with 14 HE and 14 WP rockets and 300 rounds of .50 cal. I began to attack the enemy soldiers on the strip to distract them from their assault on the friendlies. Rainbow reported that I was taking fire, which was no surprise, but I was amazed that the NVA soldiers on the airstrip seemingly made no effort to take cover as I rolled in on the strip. It kind of pissed me off that they weren't taking me seriously. I pressed about 8 or 10 attacks until I expended my weapons, then made some very low passes thinking (absurdly) that I would get some enemy with my prop. Finally, Zorro 10, flight of two Skyraiders out of NKP, checked in at 1500 and gave me

50 minutes and lots of ordnance on target. Rainbow himself was providing corrections for their ordnance. I was worried for the case officer – a solitary round eye in the woods a hell of a long way from the safety of home. And it wasn't like these case officers were out there with Seal Team Six. The indigenous forces they advised were the elderly and very young remnants of a force whittled down over ten years of opposing the vicious communist PL and NVA. These case officers were cool customers with a serious amount of cojones. After the A-1s left, Newark, a flight of two F-105s, showed up with Mk-82s and delivered accurate hits. My little green book records Rainbow estimated 30 KBA (killed by air). I was now very low on gas and daylight so I said adios and pointed the T-28 south.

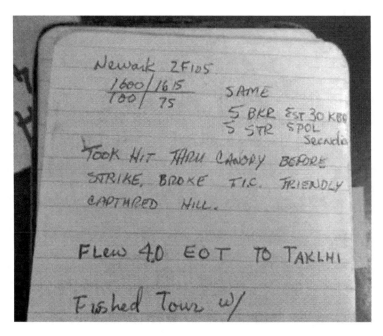

Page from my BDA book on my final airstrike - 29 Jan 70 at Rainbow

I hoped Rainbow had a ride home to 20A. He did. Later that evening he walked into the Raven bar carrying a dozen or so sets of bullet-riddled NVA uniforms and blood-soaked belts and canteens. Even though I was fairly inebriated by this time I clearly remember him in a dramatic gesture dropping this warrior-to-warrior tribute at my feet in the bar. It was really a huge pile of gear. I was astonished and speechless – as I think were the other Ravens present. As I think back on that moment today, I realize this guy had a very long and stressful (for me it would have been terrifying) day in a life-and-death struggle with a battalion of regular NVA determined to take his site. In fact, his site had been threatened for over a month. I imagine that after the NVA dispersed and the friendlies reoccupied the site that evening Rainbow must have climbed into an H-34 Greenie and flown for an hour back to Skyline. Once he arrived at the flight line he must have gathered up his bloody tribute and without passing go, grabbing a meal, or taking a shower, he marched directly to the Raven house and presented me these trophies. Over the years recalling his personal gesture meant more to me than the Silver Star I would later receive for that day's action. I very much regret I don't recall what we talked about in those few moments. I fear I shrugged off his thoughtful gesture in mock "no big deal" modesty. I would never even know his name other than Rainbow. I would like to have a beer with him now and catch up on old times, but he was in a very risky line of work so I doubt he is still around.

As for me, it turned out to be my last Raven mission. The T-28 had a number of holes in it, and one in particular that the Air Operations Center (AOC) ordered repaired immediately that night in the dark so none of our backseaters would find out about it. A 12.7 round had punched up through the floor right through the rear seat cushion and out the canopy. That shredded seat cushion was a sobering sight. I had felt some of the impacts during the strike but did not know until I landed exactly where I'd been hit. I was very grateful I did not have anyone in the back seat – and that the round did not come up through the floor a few feet closer to the nose. It kind of makes me wince to think about that. The crew chief also found a couple small-caliber rounds in the cockpit and I saved one in my little souvenir pouch.

At some point – probably the next morning when I was somewhat more coherent, Jerry Rhein took me aside and told me he was cutting my tour short by a couple weeks. He said something like he just couldn't afford to lose any more airplanes. I recall I accepted being relieved of duty early without protest. Over the years I've come to realize he had my best interests at heart. Bleak days were immediately ahead for 20A, and I would read about it on my way home to the warm welcome returning SEA warriors got from a grateful nation. (Sarcasm intended and I am adept at holding a grudge. But I am delighted that today's military is so widely and deeply appreciated by the average citizen. As a nation we seem to now understand you can hate an unpopular war, but the troops who are drafted or volunteer to fight should not be blamed).

Final Thoughts

Serious stuff now. What was the big deal about flying with the Ravens? A lot has been said and written about this. There is a hard core of men whose lives were so fundamentally affected by a six-month tour over 40 years ago that as senior citizens they still get together every year and relive the experience. The surprise is there are so many who feel so strongly that way. Why is that? I left Laos and went to a coveted F-100 assignment. I would fly and work in the "real" Air Force for another 27 years. I had a lot of plum flying jobs – all single-seat fighters, and single-engine till the A-10 (some say the A-10 was single-engine too – with half mounted on each side of the tail). I flew combat as an A-7 Sandy out of Korat in '73. I flew Harriers with the Brits in a NATO squadron in Northern Germany in the late 70's and later as an A-10 squadron commander when we were convinced (incorrectly) that the Sov's were 10 feet tall. It was a vital mission. I got to work with great people. But we don't have reunions every year. We don't spend money on party suits. Or write about our experiences for our grandkids. A surprisingly large percentage of the Ravens do all those things.

Upon reflection there was a fundamental difference between what I did in Laos and what I did subsequently. In Laos I experienced strong emotions I had not felt before or since. And I suppose many other Ravens to a greater or lesser extent feel the same. The flying was obviously great – maybe a little like the freedom of bush flying in the great wilderness with breathtaking scenery. But I think the most important difference was the mission. You weren't fighting for some vague political philosophy. You weren't just punching a combat tour ticket as a step in your Air Force career. (If so you were likely to be disappointed). It was very clear you were flying and fighting to preserve the way of life of people you lived in the midst of – some of whom you got to know intimately. Maybe a little like the Battle of Britain pilots felt. The Hmong had fought for years just to be left in peace, and by the time I was there they had lost all their brave young men resisting the most brutal of invaders. As a Raven you felt you could really make a difference with the weapons we could bring to bear. And it is heartbreaking to realize that we never had a chance in hell of success.

Visited Lloyd Duncan at NKP where he was Nail FACing
Soon to join the Ravens (as Raven 42) at Pakse

I suppose I suppressed my own feelings about my Raven experience for many years afterward for the reasons I outlined at the start of this piece. I was trying to have a successful Air Force career and live a "normal" life. While I was proud to have served as a Raven, instinct told me that it was better to keep my Raven experience to myself, like it was an aberration that would work against my career goals. In fact when I became a fighter pilot my first few years in the F-100 and later in the A-7 was a hard transition because my first 1,250 hours of operational flying was all single-ship combat calling my own shots. In some ways the young guys who started their Air Force careers as FACs in SEA would never again have the same degree of responsibility for the conduct of warfare as they had as lieutenants flying a 60-knot, high-wing, tail-dragging, prop-driven silver Cessna. Think about it. A 24-year-old first-assignment kid points at something on the ground and moments later it blows up or burns. You could have four colonels – maybe even generals – orbiting overhead in their magnificent F-4s or F-105s waiting for Lt. FAC to decide what target they would attack, with which ordnance, from which direction. And if the bombs weren't accurate enough – Lt. FAC would tell them to safe 'em up and take 'em home. Thinking about it now I wonder how the generals could have put so much power in the hands of young lieutenants. I was certainly happy to have the job, and I think most of us acquitted ourselves well despite being young and unruly. Nevertheless, after being the tactical on-scene commander for a year, I had to go through the process of becoming a lowly wingman in the formal and highly structured context of an operational fighter squadron. There were a lot of occasions when my experience as an independent scarf-in-the-wind bush pilot was exactly wrong in a post-war fighter squadron. In any case, despite

128

the great temptation to do so, I did not want to live in the past as a "professional Raven." Thus, despite enjoying the guys and being proud of my Raven experience, I tended to avoid the annual reunions during my working years. This may have been partly because of my experience at the first reunion at the Eglin Beach Club when PF (or someone) pulled a bowie knife on me five minutes after my arrival – and it went downhill from there. I joked for many years later that I was still paying my share of the damages to the Eglin Club. As evidenced by this narrative, I am finally willing after over 40 years to take a fresh look at my experiences as a Raven. And some of my closest lifelong friends, like Lloyd Duncan, happen to be Ravens. See you at the next reunion, and I may try to wrangle an invite to the next Sky reunion too. Let us not find ourselves saying regretfully, "I'd been a better friend, but I trusted time."

End (at last!)

Chapter 13

Gerald "Jerry" Greven, Raven 21
Long Tieng, July 1969 – Dec 1969

The Beginning

I was born in San Francisco in 1943. I was about seven years old when my dad took our family to an air show at Hamilton AFB. There was a C-47, with a ramp leading up to the belly of the beast so visitors could look inside, but I was too afraid to enter. Not an auspicious start for a future pilot. A few years later, we moved to Palo Alto, and once again my dad would take us to air shows at Moffett Naval Air Station in Mt. View. This was where my attraction for airplanes began.

By the time I graduated high school, my goal was to obtain a college degree and then enter the Air Force Pilot Training Program. I became a history major, concentrating on American history but with classes in Russian and Chinese history as well. I was accepted into the Air Force Pilot Training Program in 1966 and began reading history books about Vietnam.

As my pilot training ended, my instructor suggested I apply for an assignment as a forward air controller (FAC). They were the ones who "controlled" the choice of targets and the use of the fighters.

I was assigned to Hurlburt Field, Fort Walton Beach, Florida in the fall of 1968 for training in the Cessna O-1 "Bird Dog." The O-1 was a two-seater (fore and aft) high-wing monoplane, built in the 1950s. Its cockpit had a Plexiglas ceiling, with Plexiglas windows which gave the pilot great visibility, but no armament (which resulted in the pilot sitting in his flak vest). It flew at a speed of only 60 knots (70 mph). A week or two later I boarded a Braniff DC-8 for the Philippines and Jungle Survival School. We had a short layover in Guam, where I spotted the smallest car I had ever seen – a Honda. I knew they built motorcycles, but cars?!

Memories of Jungle Survival School

From Clark AFB we were loaded into trucks that took us on a mountainous dirt road into the jungle, occasionally passing a small native village where the children would come out and wave at us, shouting, "GI Joe!" When we arrived, our native guide taught us how to build hammocks to sleep on, so we would be off the jungle floor. That evening, as I was trying to sleep, I watched a rat, the size of a small house cat, scurry down a vine towards me. The next day I spotted a woman with a basket on her head and a man carrying a bow and arrow on the path behind her. When I asked our guide why the hunter wasn't in front of the woman, he replied, "There are many dangers in the jungle." (Maybe that's how a man opening a door for a woman began?)

Our last night there we were to hide and try not to be located. However, on the hillsides around our area I could see children watching us (no wonder the adults located us so quickly). While I hid and waited for our native searchers, there was little chance for sleep, as the sound of rats circling me (and my snack) continued throughout the evening. The native tribesmen were given a couple pounds of rice for tracking us down that evening.

After Survival School ended, I went to where our assignments and departure dates were posted, but my name was not listed. Undeterred, I visited the Clark's Officer Club nightly and took advantage of 25¢ drinks and enjoyed the company of stewardesses from the commercial flights that were transporting military personnel. The next day followed the same pattern as the day before, as did the next, until a week or more had passed. I finally mentioned to some administrative personnel that perhaps I had been overlooked for an assignment. I would never regret not getting to Vietnam on time.

Vietnam

My first visual memory of flying into Vietnam was of someone waterskiing on the Saigon River. We landed at Bien Hoa AFB, just north of Saigon, in January 1969. At the terminal I spotted a friend from pilot training, Bruce Scoggins, who was co-piloting a C-130 and heading to Da Nang that afternoon for a "quick turnaround." Since my check-in wasn't until the next day, I decided to take him up on his offer to "see some of the country."

After spending some time in Da Nang, we were ready to head back to Bien Hoa when the airplane hit a fire extinguisher that had not been removed from the tarmac. After a replacement pilot showed up, we finally flew to Bien Hoa the next morning, which caused me to be late for my first scheduled meeting. They were not happy, as they had been expecting me a week or more earlier. This resulted in my not going to Forward Air Controller School (FAC University, or FAC-U) just yet.

Vietnam - April 1969

The local commander put me to work for the next two weeks helping him analyze FAC accident reports and write conclusions. Fifteen hundred feet was the recommended operating altitude, and almost all the accidents were under five hundred feet and considered "pilot error." The knowledge I gained in those two weeks probably saved my life during my tour.

FAC-U was based at Phan Rang, just south of Cam Ranh Bay and along the beautiful South China Sea. I learned one very useful skill there – how to simultaneously turn and accurately hit a target with our phosphorous marking rockets. I also learned, while waiting in a movie line, how to tell "outgoing" from "incoming" after finding myself the only one lying on the ground!

My first assignment was at Lam Son Army base, a small base about five miles west of Bien Hoa and just east of Cu Chi. I immediately hit it off with my Army commander when I wore sandals to our weekly steak night dinner. The next day the commander requested my presence and informed me that sandals were not allowed at meals, as they represented a "health hazard." I reminded him that the Vietnamese kitchen help all wore sandals, and if it indeed were a health issue, perhaps sandals should be banned in the kitchen as well. He never brought up the issue of sandals at dinner again. I learned I could charm some of my commanders and, in fact, almost had a knack for it. Right!

Lam Son also taught me that sharing runways with Vietnamese pilots could be extremely dangerous. After receiving clearance to land from our tower, I was heading south and about to touch down when I noticed another plane (a Beaver) also attempting a landing, but from the opposite direction. Since he apparently was not on our radio frequency, it seemed best to let him have the right-of-way.

One day I was asked to provide cover for our troops as they were extracting their wounded with a medevac helicopter. I arrived to find a treeless landscape with knee-high grass and small cacti. After about 15-20 minutes of searching with binoculars, I cleared in the chopper. He had just touched down when he was hit with a mortar round. Under my watchful eyes the situation had deteriorated. I expected the enemy to be ghosts in the jungle, but not in this terrain. I was at a loss to explain what had occurred until weeks later, at Chu Chi. I was told about the Viet Cong's tunnel complexes surrounding the area. It turned out the tunnels were far more extensive than we ever imagined.

The Army guys I lived with at Lam Son were great guys, friendly and helpful. Some of their information, however, like the size of the rats that shared our base, I could have done without. It was helpful, though, to know that an exchange of a five-dollar bottle of bourbon with the hooch maid would result in a small bag of local pot.

One day I was asked to scout a particular set of coordinates when I spotted my first "enemy" troops under some trees. While the fighters waited, I started calling the different province headquarters and was told that "no friendly troops were in the area." These troops were not shooting at me or taking evasive action. Then I spotted what looked like a cardboard box. It didn't feel right, but finally three province headquarters informed me there "might be" friendlies in the area. In the meantime, the fighters were running low on fuel and wanted to drop their ordnance. I told them I was not able to put in their air strike, and they were not happy. It wasn't until over a month later that I received an article from Bien Hoa called "Short Bursts" and learned that the troops in question had indeed been friendly. It was not the last time someone using "military intelligence" would tell me to bomb a target, and I learned I had to live with the consequences of my actions, that I alone was responsible, so I alone would make that final decision.

While at Lam Son, I never saw the enemy, nor did I take any gunfire. I was never awakened at night by the sound of gunfire or shelling. I had bombed a lot of banana trees, but had not once seen an enemy target. To put it mildly, I was bored. That was about to change.

An Loc

My second assignment, at the end of March, was Hon Quan, located up Highway 13 to the north, in the province capital of An Loc, not far from the Cambodian border and the famous Fish Hook area. In less than 12 hours after my arrival at the town's Military Assistance Command Vietnam

(MACV) compound and being assigned a room, gun fire and artillery erupted all around me. I was sprawled out on the floor next to the door, with my AR-15 loaded, my helmet and flak vest on, waiting for what I expected to be a Viet Cong surprise attack, scaling the walls and attempting to overrun the compound. As it turned out, it was just another night of noise and was apparently quite common. I wished someone had briefed me ahead of time.

Within weeks we moved to the Special Forces compound south of town and across from a large rubber plantation. My first big decision was where to sleep. I was given a choice between a trailer (which my A.F. commander, Frank, favored), or the underground bunkers (which all the Special Forces preferred). I might not have picked the trailer if I had known the Special Forces, with their wicked sense of humor, had painted a red bulls-eye on the trailer's top. When I did a flyover and noticed it, I requested sandbagging all sides of the trailer, adding a fuel drum of sand to be placed in front of each of the two doors. The Special Forces placed the sand inside 55-gallon drums and stacked the barrels around the trailer, then added another level of barrels. They even sandbagged the roof of the trailer. Those barrels outside our doors would turn out to be a lifesaver.

Our airfield was located on the north side of town adjacent to an Army artillery base. Thus, we were provided jeeps and would travel through "downtown" An Loc to get to our airfield and planes. One of my part-time duties consisted of manning the Claymore mines at our front gates. I remember thinking there must be others more qualified. As a benefit, though, I was quickly beloved by the local native soldiers (Montagnards, Vietnamese, and Cambodians) that comprised the majority of our forces. They would follow me around, chanting "You number one" while we were in the trenches, and they gave me some comfort at a job I was very uncomfortable performing.

A normal day would consist of a morning briefing, where we listened to various intel and received coordinates for the day's flight, but like my first assignment, most of our targets seemed to be trees. Occasionally we would see some old bunkers. Unlike my first assignment, however, evenings were different. We could expect incoming mortars and rockets to greet us at night. Wearing a flak vest and a helmet to bed, as well as keeping my AR-15 and newly acquired M-79 grenade launcher within easy reach, made sleeping a bit difficult.

One evening a couple of weeks after arriving, all hell seemed to break loose as rockets, mortars, artillery, and gunfire erupted around the base. I exited the trailer, and with a lot of trepidation, moved to the center of our compound where I spotted a short, burly Special Forces sergeant standing atop a bunker and firing his M-16 into the surrounding jungle, without any apparent fear for his own safety. He asked me to join him up top, and I politely declined. We would spend some time together, and he became my best "new" friend – especially during firefights!

When our O-1s needed maintenance we would fly them down to Bien Hoa. During my first maintenance flight I had the chance to meet their commander. Actually, he requested my presence. I learned I had broken some serious rules while taxiing into the maintenance area, including not wearing gloves and my sleeves not being rolled down. I was going to comment about it being well over 100 degrees on the taxiway, but for some odd reason, I remained silent. He proceeded to explain the rules were for our safety, in case a fire was to break out inside the airplane. I also was tempted to mention that if safety was an issue, I would volunteer to go home today. He continued, pointing out I had also broken a rule for which he could have me "court-martialed."

Apparently no one knew that my placing orange and pink flower decals on the O-1's hubcap was "defacing of government property" – a serious crime! I remember thinking this was going to be a more difficult tour than I had imagined.

My first day off in Vietnam was spent taking photos of the artillery base next to our airfield. Their commander mentioned they had a helicopter that would be arriving soon to resupply a convoy on Hwy. 13, and if I wanted some action photos, I could catch a ride. By the time I returned to the commander's tent, the Huey had already departed. It turned out to be fortuitous, as minutes later calls on the radio indicated the helicopter had been hit by enemy fire and had crashed alongside the convoy, which was now stalled, under fire, and low on ammo.

Another chopper was called for, and the commander told me if I still wanted to go, he could use my help unloading ammo. I'm not sure why I thought volunteering would be a good idea – perhaps it appealed to some photojournalistic brain cell.

We were a couple miles out when I saw the smoke from the burning vehicles amid the convoy. It seemed to me the strategy of using Agent Orange to defoliate 200 yards of jungle alongside the road was working to the enemy's advantage, as he had a wider angle to attack. I quickly took a few photos before we banked and landed beside the convoy.

The difference in sound volume between flying an O-1 at 1,500 feet, with headphones on, and being on the ground while a firefight raged in all directions was incomprehensible. If there was a world record time for unloading ammo boxes from a Huey, I was sure we had set it. A few minutes later we were airborne, and the only noise was from our rotary blades. No one talked, and no one took photos. So much for my idea of a quiet day off!

A month would pass before I had another day off, and I vowed it would be different. I locked the trailer and stayed inside, listening to the new Jimi Hendricks and Cream albums. I was able to locate something to smoke for the occasion. I was rudely interrupted by a pounding on my door and was told I was needed in the air. The flight went surprisingly well, considering I had never seen so many shades of green before.

The rubber plantations were still owned by the French, and the rule about the trees was to not bomb them, or there would be economic consequences. One day the Special Forces radioed me and said they had made contact with the enemy, who were holed up in a rectangular-shaped rubber plantation. I provided air cover while the Army strategy was to send in some APCs (armored personnel carriers) lengthwise on both sides of the plantation, from one end to the other. Without a blocking force and with the noise of the vehicles, I was not surprised that no enemy were located, especially since no troops actually entered the plantation. I heard the Special Forces patrol say they had been "ambushed" and had two wounded, while they had killed a dozen enemy. We were still relying on "body count" at that time to determine who was winning the war!

The Special Forces were extremely resourceful. Like my previous Army base, we also had the occasional "steak night." I asked my favorite "Sarge" how this was logistically possible, since they theoretically were supposed to "live off the land." He explained there was a huge Army supply depot in Bien Hoa, and they would "now and again" commandeer Army supply items and then trade them back to the Army for what they really wanted. The steaks, however, were obtained by having one of the Special Forces jump into the back of an Army truck and throw boxes of steaks out, to be picked up by a trailing Special Forces jeep. I could tell from his smile that he enjoyed telling that story!

Early one evening we received a call from Loc Ninh, a town about 20 miles north of us. I had had a couple of night checkouts, and both times my instructors had become lost, relying on me for assistance, but this would be my first real night flight. Frank, our commander, gave Bill Angliss and me a couple of flares and some night-vision goggles. Off we flew into the night sky. When we arrived at the town, they were already being helped by "Spooky" (a C-47 gunship) that was already lighting up the sky with tracers. We were told the situation was "under control," which was great news, as the night-vision goggles were not quite ready for prime time.

Neither Bill nor I had ever used flares for landing before, so it came as no surprise that we were to have one small problem. We landed safely, but unfortunately, we had not considered that the parachute of one flare might not open, and we watched in horror as it burned down some of the shanties that surrounded the runway. In our defense, what could you expect from someone with no experience with flares? What did surprise us was that our commander did not want to take responsibility for the fire, and had all of us leave the scene of the crime! Two months later, both Bill and I left for Laos.

It was sometime in May, when a couple of our flight line personnel and I were enjoying my mom's "care package" of peanuts. We noticed three red rotating beacons trailing one another in the night sky. We thought we were watching a formation of B-52s heading directly west towards Cambodia. After seeing numerous large flashes on the horizon, and feeling the ground shake, we realized it had been a B-52 strike. We watched as two more B-52 strikes followed. What we didn't know was why we hadn't been informed and what the target had been.

The next morning, I woke earlier than usual and flew west to the Cambodian border area known as the Fish Hook. This area was separated from South Vietnam by a small river. I was impressed by the precision of the strike, as the craters started close to the river's edge and continued west.

I was used to seeing and giving bomb damage assessment (BDA), but this destruction was something altogether different. The bombed area spanned almost a square mile and was utterly devoid of life. Not just destroyed trees, but also trucks, equipment, clothes, and other materials scattered in the tree limbs. This had been a seriously large encampment or supply base, and I decided it would not be prudent to fly into a neutral country and take photos. This was a job for a fast moving F-4 recon flight, as anyone left alive on the ground would be decidedly angry today. No one at An Loc, including the Army Republic of Vietnam (ARVN), Army, Special Forces, or our Air Force contingent had any additional information about what had occurred the previous night.

I decided to fly to Bien Hoa and meet with an Air Force senior officer who assured me we were not bombing a neutral country (Cambodia), and with a slight smile suggested that "my maps were wrong." More bullshit. Much later I would find out they were purposely lying about the coordinates being in South Vietnam while actually directing the strikes into Cambodia, and also burning all paperwork evidence in 55gallon drums...at Bien Hoa! Now that was a court- martial offense!

One night, while eating dinner in An Loc, a nervous and excited waitress told me I should probably leave because "the Viet Cong were in town getting supplies." I jumped into my jeep and headed four miles back to our base. I arrived at the base to find the front gate closed and our native troops guarding it with rifles. Apparently they also knew the Viet Cong were in town! Since I had no success negotiating with them to open the gate, I decided to prop my feet on the hood, relax, and keep my headlights on them. They finally relented and let me in, but I was no longer their "Number One."

I had an unusual fear of being caught sitting on the toilet at night when the rocket and mortar attacks began. That fear became a reality one night. I was surprised the fear for my personal safety was greater than the fear of being embarrassed. After a short lull (and positional recovery time), I took off running to the nearest bunker. I was about halfway into this 50-yard dash when an incoming round hit about 20 feet to my right. The explosion was deafening, but I felt no pain. Just as I reached the bunker door, it opened, and I proceeded to bowl over our Special Forces commander. We were both relieved we had not fallen down the cement stairs to the bunker below. Luckily, someone had watered the grassy area where the round landed, and it was soft enough to cause the shrapnel to blow upward rather than outward.

One morning I was given our usual list of five or six target coordinates. I flew out to the area of the coordinates, looked for possible targets, found none, and relayed information to the fighters that one target was a "suspected hospital." I directed the fighters to bomb a group of nearby trees but found no indication of a bunker or structure, and passed that information along to the fighters. That evening, at our briefing, I mentioned this target and was later admonished by my commander for using the term "hospital" during the briefing. Apparently it was okay for intel to use the word "hospital" as a target coordinate, for pilots to use the term while bombing them, but not all right to use the term "hospital" during briefings. I suspected the admonishment was really a "CYA" (cover your ass) strategy.

One evening a couple of weeks after my first incoming close call, our base was hit hard again with over 100 mortars and rockets. I was inside my trailer and waited for a lull in the attack. I finally opened my "bulls-eye" trailer door and ducked behind the 55 gallon drums of sand that had been placed a few feet away. A loud whistle, followed by a large explosion, destroyed our medical building about 100 feet away. Another even louder whistle sounded, like an incoming round was going to land on my head, and I instantly became one with the drum. Following a deafening explosion and a cloud of thick dust, I was able to check my body parts. Surprisingly, they all seemed to be intact. I finally stood up and surveyed the scene. About 20 feet on the other side of the drum was a hole in the ground, and behind me was a trailer door with a shrapnel hole in its window. Through the dust I could see people headed in my direction to assist me. Other than my hearing, which improved over the next few days, I was unscathed. I will always be grateful to the Special Forces guys who placed and filled those 55 gallon used gas drums with sand!

My trailer surrounded by 55 gallon drums, and the shrapnel hole in the door window

It was now nearing the end of May. While flying north of An Loc, I noticed two Army helicopters – a Loch and Cobra team -- working together. I located their radio channel and listened in. Normally I flew at 1,500 feet and would occasionally spot a "bunker." This Loch, however, was flying about 100 feet off the ground and spotted not only a bunker, but in this case an actual spoon. Shortly after that, he saw a Viet Cong pointing a rifle from his bunker. Flying back to my base, I could visualize a Loch, a Cobra, and an O-1, with fighters overhead, all working together. Think of the real targets we could find and the firepower we would have at our disposal! I was pretty excited about this idea and expressed my enthusiasm to my commander. I'll never forget his reply. "I am not going to give our resources (fighters) to the Army!" It's no surprise we lost that war.

Shortly after that I spotted some mud huts and farmed fields along a river. I happened to mention this to my commander, and his reaction was to put in a flight of fighters with napalm. I suggested that perhaps the Special Forces or Army could check them out first. He replied, "If I tell you to bomb them, you will, or I will court-martial you." Really?! I mentioned to him how inaccurate bombs could be, and who knew where they would wind up landing. The subject thankfully was not brought up again. Between the increasingly dangerous life of mortar and nighttime rocket attacks at our camp, and my deteriorating relationship with my commander, I knew I needed options.

A large intelligence briefing was held, and we were told the Viet Cong and North Vietnamese Army (NVA) had plans to take a provincial capital. They believed it would be An Loc. Luckily, that attack and our use of B-52s to save the city would not happen for another three years, but the threat definitely reinforced my desire to find options.

I had heard about a highly classified operation code named the Steve Canyon Program, named after the comic strip pilot series in the 40s and 50s about a "real war" up country (Laos), so I decided to fly to Bien Hoa and obtain more information. It was now June, and for the first time in months, I dressed in my Air Force tans and headed for our bunker mess hall for breakfast. I had no sooner sat down than an incoming shell landed directly above us, which caused me to dive under the table. We had never been hit during daylight hours, and I was even more motivated as I left to change

138

into another clean pair of tans for my upcoming interview. I don't remember much about the actual Steve Canyon interview, but I do know they forgot to mention we would have a price on our heads and had suffered the highest casualty rate of the Indochinese war!

I was personally looking forward to a "gentleman's" war, where one could actually sleep without wearing a helmet and flak vest, and during the day one had the chance to spot real targets. Little did I know how real some of those targets would be.

I received news of my Steve Canyon Program acceptance in June, and was excited about leaving Vietnam for Laos and the remaining six months of my year's tour. I was not surprised my commander was also happy for my new assignment. I had almost a week before my arrival date in Udorn, Thailand, so I decided to make my tour a complete circle by visiting with my pilot-training friend, Bruce Scoggins, who I had met my first day in Vietnam.

Bruce Scoggins & Jerry Greven

Cam Ranh Bay - June 1969 Jerry with his octopus!

I hitched a flight to Cam Ranh Bay, where he was now stationed. We decided to go to the beach and do some snorkeling in the South China Sea, but we arrived to find "Off Limits - Dangerous Sea Life" signs. Apparently some military personnel had bumped into some local sea urchins, which caused their legs to swell up like balloons. The ocean was clear, with abundant sea life, including deadly sea snakes, stone fish, and an occasional shark, not to mention those pesky urchins. It turned out to be an exhilarating day!

After an hour long struggle, I was able to dislodge an octopus and bring it back to base. A Puerto Rican doctor was very pleased and prepared tender slices, with ink infused rice. I felt like I was on vacation.

Bangkok - a Buddhist Temple

Now I was off to Bangkok for another short adventure. My camera and I visited many of the local tourist sights. I was shocked that none of my friends had mentioned how friendly the local girls were.

My next stop was Udorn, Thailand and the Air America complex next to the runway. After the usual processing, I was told I was not expected in Vientiane for another two days, so I took the time to visit my best friend in pilot training, Steve Long, who was stationed in Nakhon Phanom.

Upon arriving at NKP and inquiring about Steve Long, I was devastated to learn his OV-10 was shot down over the Ho Chi Minh Trail the previous month, and he was presumed dead. It was the first time I realized being a FAC in Laos could actually be a very dangerous assignment. It wasn't until 1973 that I discovered Steve was among the POWs being released from North Vietnam. I wandered around the NKP runway, taking photos of their variety of airplanes, and was admiring an A-1 up close when a pilot approached me. He did not know Steve, but he had worked with the Ravens and was familiar with Laos (my new assignment, and Ravens was my call sign). He had a scheduled flight that afternoon and asked me if I would like to join him. Again, I volunteered on my day off!

My A-1 wingman from NKP on our way to a bombing mission in Ban Ban Valley

Within an hour I was briefed and sitting in the back seat of one of the four A-1s headed 200 miles north to Ban Ban Valley on a bombing mission. Luckily, all ended well that day. Little did I realize then how familiar I would become with that valley.

Before I few back to Udorn the next afternoon, my hooch maid asked me if I'd like to join her and her friends for lunch. The saying about "when in Rome..." occurred to me, so I said, "Yes." We had just sat down for a picnic-style lunch when I spotted the large beetles, which the girls proceeded to snap in half and then sucked out their interiors. At that moment I discovered my love of adventure had limits!

Back in Udorn I was given a room and roommate for the night. He insisted on showing me around. Our first stop was the Officer's Club, where he told some other pilots I was "a Raven" and was leaving for Laos the next day. I was not allowed to pay for a drink, and I concluded this "Raven" gig definitely had its benefits!

We then headed to the town of Udorn, which seemed like a town out of the Old West, with saloons of every imaginable type, each with musical bands and unusually friendly girls. A pedal-powered vehicle took us back to the base that evening. My new roommate was a very knowledgeable guide.

Laos - Vientiane

The next morning, I caught a flight to Vientiane, Laos and met my new Air Operations Center (AOC) commander, Jim Wall. He was straightforward, plain talking, honest, friendly, informative, and very different from my previous commander. I liked him immediately. He reminded me of Gary Cooper.

At the embassy I was given paperwork, briefings, and warm introductions, which I thought was very unmilitary (another Raven perk). From there I was taken to our lovely two-story "embassy house" and introduced to our staff. It was "nubie night," and I was the guest of honor. Memories of that evening were a little foggy, but I do remember the White Rose, where drinks were generously poured and there were dancing girls on top of our table, playing with ping-pong balls (but definitely not the ping-pong game I was familiar with). That evening was the most entertaining since arriving in Southeast Asia.

The next week or two was spent with the FAC that I was replacing. We would fly to various airfields, and I would be introduced to locals of importance, and to the surrounding terrain. I was stunned by the beauty of Laos, including the lush rice paddies surrounding Vientiane, and the karst mountains to the north, where waterfalls leaped over cliffs and plunged downward (sometimes over 1,000 feet), and the triple-canopy jungles that covered even the steep karst mountains.

One evening, after leaving the flight line, my AOC commander explained one of his duties was to keep track of the Laotian C-47 cargo airplanes based at Vientiane, and how impossible that was. It was not unusual, he said, for a couple of them to go "missing, usually flying off to Hong Kong and Saigon." He explained that was why there was so much 22 ct. gold jewelry in Vientiane. I didn't connect those dots until later in my tour.

Later that July, Jim and I were passing through Vientiane in our jeep when we saw a large crowd of Laotians outside of an electronics store. We stopped and noticed they were watching a TV in the display window and on the screen were images of men in spacesuits walking on the moon! It was a big deal, even in Laos!

I directed my first and only Agent Orange mission with four C-123s out of Vietnam. I am not sure whose idea it was, but we were to fly 30-40 miles north and target "crops" in what I thought was a relatively peaceful area. It didn't quite turn out that way, as each plane started reporting numerous hits from small caliber ground fire. With our first mission completed, the flight crews counted over 100 bullet holes in a couple of the C-123s. I never saw the planes again and have always wondered what "crops" were that valuable, and who they belonged to.

C-123 spraying Agent Orange herbicide (defoliant) north of Vientiane

I was asked to possibly talk to the villagers and explain Agent Orange was "not harmful." I didn't know how I was going to reach these villagers, as there were no runways nearby, let alone any villages to speak of. Next, I tried to explain they weren't very friendly the first time I was there, and if their once healthy and valuable crops were now dying, I doubted I could convince the natives the spraying was "not harmful." Needless to say, the idea was dropped, and so were further herbicide missions.

Mountain flying was new to me, but I soon learned not to get caught flying into canyons without a planned way out. Wind and weather could also create problems for the small O-1. My target was on top of a ridge about 3,500 feet in elevation. My plan was to meet a flight of Thai pilots flying T-28 fighters by flying below the rim and popping up and over the ridge to meet them. What I had not taken into consideration was the strength of the headwind on top of the rim. The result was, my airplane was not moving forward as I crested the ridge at treetop level and became an absolutely stationary target...never a good plan!

On another occasion, the mountains rose to about 5,500 feet as I headed south to Vientiane. As I climbed to 6,500 feet, I noticed a large weather system approaching quickly from the southwest. Within minutes I was in total darkness and pouring rain, with no radio communication. I kept heading due south for about 45 minutes before I began to descend. Luckily the headwinds were not as strong as they could have been. Sitting in the cockpit before I broke out of the clouds was the loudest silence I had ever heard.

My first flight with a Laotian "backseater" (they could speak to Laotian troops on the ground) began as a routine mission looking for possible targets. It stopped being routine when the sky filled with tracers coming from a group of trees directly in front of me. This was the first time I was the target! My backseater, who moments earlier could speak broken English now only seemed to remember his native language. I assumed this was his first time being shot at also. The only English he was able to say was, "Number 10, we go home!" For about five minutes he repeatedly pointed toward our left side and repeated his demand. I finally looked again in the direction he was pointing and realized he wasn't referring to the direction which the tracers had come from, but what I hadn't noticed — a large gaping hole near the leading edge of our left wing! He was relieved when I agreed with his "Number 10, we go home." To this day I still am not sure how close that round came to hitting the fuel tank (ours weren't self-sealing) or why I never felt that we had been hit.

Karst mountains of northern Laos

Shortly thereafter, I began thinking about the real possibility of being shot down and what items I could carry to improve my odds should such an unfortunate event occur. After some consultation with my commander, I switched rifles to an AK-47 and had six 30-round magazines duct-taped back to back, which equaled three 60-round magazines. I also picked up a half dozen or more hand grenades for my map bag. I bought some black jeans and black long-sleeved shirts. I hoped my choice of clothing would help me blend in, and using their rifle ammo (especially having the same colored tracers) might come in handy. What I hadn't considered was that I now had to lug around a map bag that weighed 40 pounds or more.

I was greeted at our flight shack in Vientiane by two unfamiliar older men in civilian clothes who noticed me carrying my heavy map bag. They commented that I must be "one of those forestry surveyors" they had heard about. I quickly sought out my commander and was informed they were not the press but rather senior AF officers.

A late-night call from a Laotian Army outpost outside of a small village reported they were under attack and needed support. Jim said we were not flying at night, but we could check it out the next day. We found out the next morning that a Communist Pathet Lao patrol had tried to sneak up on the outpost. They ended up being pounced upon by a tiger, which led to shots being fired by the patrol and then the outpost. The only casualty of this firefight had been the tiger!

While doing some reconnaissance, I spotted something large moving through the trees along a ridge line. I flew closer and spotted a trail. The object turned out to be my first and only wild elephant sighting.

One bombing strike I have remembered over the years occurred during my first month in Vientiane. I had been given a set of coordinates in a mountainous area about 40 miles north. A flight of four Thai T-28s

rendezvoused with me. It was a routine bombing mission, until a few days later when a Laotian military official congratulated me for "killing over 200 enemy." It was the first time I realized that my targets could also involve killing people, not just trees.

Most of the air strikes in the Vientiane area that I was involved in were conducted by Thai pilots flying T-28s out of Udorn. They were good pilots and would even follow me through cloud cover, but they had a few habits I had not had to deal with before. I would usually have them drop their bombs one at a time. It was not uncommon that one pilot would not drop his bomb for some reason, waiting instead to drop two on his next pass, or occasionally all at once.

One day, after telling the pilots "to hit my smoke," I watched with much amusement as the wind carried my white phosphorous plume down a road. For the next ten or fifteen minutes the Thai pilots continued to follow and bomb the smoke, rather than the original target. I called for a flight room briefing in Vientiane and, with the help of a large chalkboard, we reviewed what my "smoke" actually meant (where the target "is" or in this case *was*). The Thai pilots seemed to appreciate not being embarrassed over the radio and grateful that I had shown respect and humor during our private briefing. They invited me to join them for an upcoming party in Udorn. I was honored, and happily accepted.

Their party was held at a restaurant in Udorn, and I was introduced to about 30 or 40 Thai pilots as "their Raven." We sat at a couple of long tables and had a great dinner. Then the serious drinking began. There were numerous obligatory toasts, and by the end of the night they were standing on the tables throwing and breaking plates and glasses. I felt proud to be a part of them. I was also glad I didn't have to pay any of the bill that evening, as liquor and food costs were probably the least of its total!

Because of the presence of Air Force and Air America personnel, the town of Udorn had grown into a rural (Thai) Las Vegas, with every type of bar and dance hall. There were pop bands, country and western, soul/Motown, even a psychedelic underground bar with black lights. The bands would take turns, playing continuously throughout the night. Before you could order a drink, at least one strange but friendly girl would be sitting on your lap. It was, to say the least, much different from bars back home! About 30 miles north of Vientiane, a once royal hunting lodge was now being used as a Laotian Army training camp. Set at the base of the mountains and surrounded by pine trees, it was a surprisingly beautiful location. I received notice the local commander would appreciate it if I would visit and be his guest so that I could watch his troops perform some training exercises. I arrived and watched them fire machine guns, throw grenades, and fire mortars and artillery. The trainees were then assembled on bleachers, and their commander introduced me.

I was dressed in my black shirt, jeans, and boots and wore a western style holster with my trusty .38. As I was being introduced, the troops began shouting, "Ringo, Ringo, Ringo." I was confused and asked, "Who's Ringo?" Apparently, he was a Laotian cowboy TV or movie star I had never heard of. The next thing I knew, they were setting up beer bottles on a wood fence rail and wanted me to draw and shoot the bottles off!

Unbeknownst to the cheering crowd, I had never fired my .38 and was pretty sure this was going to be ugly. With the trainees still cheering and shouting "Ringo," I tried to do the next best thing...stalling. I tried to put on a show while warming up. I stretched my arms, my back, my legs, and finally my fingers, all the while getting ready to draw. The crowd went silent as I drew, fired six times, and left all the bottles still standing! I took a bow and told the commander to let the trainees know I'd be right back with my airplane.

I jumped in the O-1 and flew low over the grandstand before proceeding to gain some altitude. My target would be their mortar and artillery area, so I twisted and turned the plane and began firing all eight of my rockets. Even I was surprised by the sheer quantity of smoke they had created. I then flew back low over the grandstands, dipping my wings from side to side as the troops cheered and waved in appreciation. It seemed worth the cost of eight rockets!

Vientiane's Wattay Airport underwater after torrential rains

That summer we had some torrential rains that caused the Mekong to flood its banks. I flew out to the northeast in the morning and put in a couple of air strikes, then headed back to a small town close to the Mekong to refuel. I arrived to find the airfield under water. I radioed my predicament to Vientiane and was told there were a couple of small airfields on the Thai side of the Mekong, but these also turned out to be flooded. I estimated my gas supply to last about 30 minutes plus, but it was a 45-minute flight to Vientiane. I was advised to slowly gain altitude, lean the engine as much as possible, and that "Raven 1" (Andy Patten) would stay on the radio with me for the duration. Thanks Andy!

I considered my options: landing in the flooded Mekong, dodging telephone wires while landing on a local road, or the jungle. The only positive feeling I had while watching the fuel gauge and my watch was Andy's voice talking to me on the radio. Finally, the rice paddies around Vientiane were in sight, then the runway, and I was landing. Soon I was sitting inside our flight shack having a beer. Our mechanic reported he had "never seen an O-1 land with only a quart of fuel."

Jim Wall and Joe Potter, the AOC commander at Long Tieng, were close friends. One day, for some excitement I assume, they decided it was a good idea to take a T-28 and visit the Chinese road builders near the Burma border. When they returned to the flight line at Vientiane that afternoon they were unusually quiet and looked like they had seen a ghost. Jim reached into his desk, pulled out a bottle of whiskey, and proceeded to pour two generous drinks. They said they had received a very unwelcome reception. I was never told all the details, but they were shaken, as apparently the Chinese did not take kindly to prying eyes. You would think I had learned a lesson that day about "curiosity kills the pilot," but I did not. More on that later.

It was reported an Army airplane had crashed overnight in the mountains northeast of Vientiane, and I was sent out to try and locate it. I started searching early that morning until I needed to refuel. I went up and searched again that afternoon. I don't remember ever being taught to fly an O-1 without hands, but after a while, it became second nature, especially when you need two hands to steady the binoculars. That left our feet for steering!

It had been a long day, and I had dropped from my usual 1,500 feet above the terrain to about 1,000 feet to try to locate any sign of debris. I finally spotted a trail with empty foxholes on both sides. Next, there were some foxholes with people in them, and they were following me with AK-47s. I also spotted a few large structures hidden under the trees. About the same time, a lot of people on the ground began firing at me with small arms fire. I dropped my binoculars and realized I had lost altitude. I had inadvertently descended to only about 500 feet above the terrain, thereby giving a lot of people a juicy target. As the firing subsided, I felt a wave of anger for the first time and realized I was reacting to being shot at, and taking it personally! Flying at 60 knots seems dangerously slow, especially at 500 feet, yet they did not lead me enough, and their bullets passed behind me. Again, I was luckier than I deserved. All the way back to Vientiane I was pissed off. I had failed to locate the downed aircraft, and people had tried to kill me!

Jim's immediate reaction was to strike them the next day. I proposed we check out who they were first and then let them have a week before we returned; that way I would have time to plan my revenge, and possibly surprise them as well. The plan was to fly up to 10,000 feet and glide in, with fighters stacked up and waiting for me. About six flights of four fighters each bombed the area until there was barely a tree still standing. My BDA (bomb damage assessment) was that we had completely destroyed the target area.

Refueling - No gas station attendant available!

I received a call to pick up a high-ranking Laotian Army commander at an airfield near the Mekong who wanted to see this target area for himself. I was showing him around when I noticed sunlight reflecting off what I thought was still debris over the target. Then came the sound of pings from the O-1 being hit. The bullets started hitting the rear of the plane and were working their way forward before I was able to maneuver us out of range. The reflected sunlight that I thought was from debris turned out to be bullets, and there had been a lot of them. So much for a "completely destroyed" target! The general had been enjoying our flight up to then, but at least he understood it was an enemy target. Thankful to be alive, we headed home.

I met the Laotian commander again a few weeks later when I was refueling at the same airstrip I had picked him up at. One of his aides met me at the runway and asked if I was a Raven, I replied that I was, and he told me there was someone who wanted me to join him at his daughter's wedding ceremony, as he believed I had "saved his life." I accepted his invitation, and a few minutes later was sitting next to him at a very long table, with perhaps 60 other guests. He introduced me, and everyone rose and applauded. I was very flattered. The piece derésistance was a very large fish on the table in front of us. The fact that its head and tail were still attached was not troubling, but it had not been gutted! I watched everybody else dive in and place the fish on some lettuce-like leaves, add various other items and some locally made fish sauce. After one piece of the belly, I changed my tactics and ate the meat above the spine. The fish was great tasting, the intestines, not so much. It was a great afternoon and not something I could have imagined happening in South Vietnam.

I had coordinates to drop CBUs (Cluster Bomb Units are antipersonnel bombs containing metal fragments) into a hillside area above a village that was being harassed by the Pathet Lao. (The Pathet Lao was a communist political movement and organization in Laos, formed in the mid-20th century). When I returned to Vientiane, I heard that a CBU had been dropped long, landing in the village and resulting in a friendly death. I knew I was ultimately responsible for the direction in which the fighters had left the target area. I told Jim, who tried to console me, and told me there would be no repercussions, as the family would receive some money for their loss. It didn't make me feel any better.

Bill Angliss and Jerry looking at my "Where Are We" map

A few days later I was told by two other embassy house residents that a friend of theirs, the female owner of a bar and entertainment business, had been ill, and they were going to visit her. They insisted that I join them. We were going to the exotically named Les Rendezvous des Amis. I was given more information on the way over. The proprietor was named Lulu, and as the story went, she was from France and had brought the art of oral sex to Laos. I remember visiting Lulu in her room and wished her well. I also remember lovely ladies with exceptional skills in a loving environment. If my friends' plan was to cheer me up after the previous day's incident, it certainly worked.

After returning to the United States in 1970, I was reading my father's issue of *True* magazine. They had an article about the "Most Infamous Bars in the World," and among the top five were two that I had just visited in Vientiane: Lulu's and the White Rose (another perk of being a Raven).

Fellow Raven Bill Angliss, who I had been stationed with at An Loc in Vietnam, was transferring as a Raven from Luang Prabang, Laos, to Vientiane, I was headed to Long Tieng, but first I had to introduce him to the area: local landing strips and villages. One village chief even invited us to join him for lunch. On our plates were two small sparrows with their feet still on and pointing upward. At least the feathers had been removed.

Long Tieng (20 Alternate)

When I flew into Long Tieng that first day, I was stunned by the size of the complex and village area. Long Tieng was a Laotian military base located about 100 miles north of Vientiane. At the height of its significance in the late 1960s, the "secret city" of Long Tieng maintained a population of 40,000 inhabitants, making it the second largest city in Laos at the time. It had a single runway, with a large karst rock blocking the western end. It was an imposing sight, and the bustle of activity was overwhelming. It was said to be the busiest runway in the world in 1969. I was directed to the Raven hooch and was introduced to a Himalayan bear named Floyd, drinking a beer, who lived in a cage alongside and under the bar area of our hooch. I felt like I had just entered the Kingdom of Oz!

Our living quarters were not as luxurious as the "embassy house" in Vientiane, but there was good food, copious amounts of liquor, and occasional movies. My first dinner was at General Vang Pao's residence, followed by an intelligence briefing. General Vang Pao was the Laotian commander of Military Region II and the leader of the Meo (now known as Hmong), the indigenous mountain people of northern Laos.

My first day was spent flying around the area with another Raven, Craig Morrison, as my guide. We toured the Plain of Jars and its airfield with captured Russian tanks and artillery. We flew east over bombed-out villages and hundreds of craters from previous bombing strikes. We continued east to Ban Ban Valley along Route 7 (just a dirt road), and I saw an entire denuded hillside that had been bombed in order to stop truck traffic. Craig said the bombing of the hillside had not been successful, as the North Vietnamese had just backed bulldozers into the hillside and would come out at night and clear the road of rocks and debris. He warned me about the numerous antiaircraft guns east of Ban Ban and pointed out numerous destroyed trucks (real ex-targets) along the road. We returned to Long Tieng and I told him he didn't have to guide me the next day, as I felt I knew my way around the area. My "navigational" skills came in handy sometimes.

Jerry on anti-aircraft gun outside of Gen. Vang Pao's residence

Over the next few days I would locate a couple of unbombed trucks, which I had never seen in my previous nine months in Vietnam and Laos. I also noticed some flattened grass leading from the main road (Route 7) to a knoll that, unlike the surrounding terrain, was covered with what appeared to be some very large green vegetation. A closer inspection with binoculars raised the hair on my arms. There appeared to be a large log on the knoll that seemed to be pointed at me and following my flight path! I remembered the captured antiaircraft gun outside of Vang Pao's residence at Long Tieng and quickly realized it was no log.

I wondered how many other antiaircraft guns were along this road east of Ban Ban. I also decided to keep the airplane turning at all times. After about an hour of searching and relaying coordinates to "Cricket" (Cricket was our middleman C-130 coordinator that flew 12 hours each day over northern Laos), I had counted about six antiaircraft gun sites, which made me surprisingly popular. Soon another Raven, Hank Allen, was asking me to point them out to him. Shortly thereafter, an F-4 recon flight asked if he could take photos.

Hank and I took up positions north and south of the road. The F-4 flew east to west directly over the road at about 4,000 feet above the terrain, and at about 300 mph, with the plane's telltale plume of exhaust trailing him. He wiggled his wings a couple of times, and as he got between us we heard his mayday, "I've been hit!" Upon our return to Long Tieng, we discovered he had landed safely at Udorn.

A couple of days later I was flying in the same general area when who should contact me but the very same pilot. He was curious about why <u>we</u> were flying unmolested over those guns, and yet <u>he</u> was the one shot at. I, too, had given that thought much consideration over the past few days. I could picture some gunner watching an O-1 bounce around in the sky like a butterfly, with an understanding that if he shot at us, we would hear and see his location. The F-4 who was, however, flying straight down the road and couldn't see or hear an antiaircraft gun, was a better target. If an antiaircraft gun controller shot down an F-4 would he get a week of R&R rather than only an afternoon off? Or maybe the gunner was just bored, was tempted, and took a chance.

From that day forward, except for one incident, my policy would be to "not mess with guns" and perhaps they wouldn't mess with me – an unspoken gentleman's agreement. For a couple of months, it actually seemed to work. We lost only one pilot while I was in Laos, and it occurred within my first few days at Long Tieng. Dan Davis had just returned from R&R, visiting his family, and was putting in a strike with F-105s near Ban Ban when his "cleared in" flight ran over him. They found pieces of his O-1 embedded in the F-105 after it landed in Thailand. Neither he nor his plane was ever located.

[*Editors note: 1st Lt. Daniel Davis' remains were identified August 21, 1995 and returned to his family in the United States for burial in Ft. Bliss National Cemetary. He was awarded the Purple Heart and promoted to Captain posthumously.*]

That "except for one incident" (about not messing with guns) occurred when a flight commander asked me what type of targets were available. He was the only pilot who ever asked me that question during my entire year's tour. I should have given him my truck target, but instead I told him "trucks and guns." Unbelievably, this squadron commander chose guns!

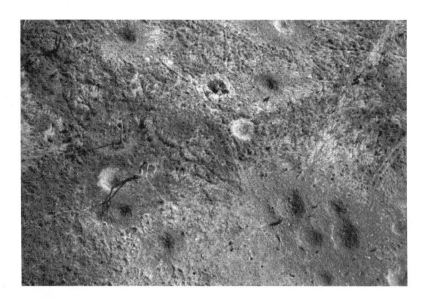

As he began his strike with his Number 2, his Number 3 shouted, "They're shooting at you!" They also shot at his Number 3 and 4. Luckily, no one was hit. The bombs dropped predictably long and short of the guns on the knoll. However, a number of shaken gunners emerged from hiding and ran from their green oasis to the nearby jungle. It was a good lesson for all concerned. I'm guessing the squadron had a relatively quiet trip home, and their leader had lost some of his wingmen's trust and friendship that day.

Remember an earlier story about my commander's taking a "peek" at the Chinese road-building project near Burma? I said I <u>should</u> have "learned a lesson." Nope. I was again on Route 7, heading east, looking for hidden trucks to bomb. I soon realized from my maps that the North Vietnamese border was not far from my location, and if you guessed I was thinking of taking a "peek," you would be correct. I approached the border area slowly, all the while flying circles, pretending to be interested in something else but with my binoculars and eyes glued to that area. I was still at least a mile away when my binoculars lit up with waves of red tracers. I made a quick right (it's amazing you remember those small details during a moment of "stress") and turned away from the border. But the streaking tracers still surrounded me. Putting distance between us finally achieved the desired results. I knew then how those gunners felt as they ran from their anti-aircraft gun. I still don't remember seeing anything at the border area. It was a valuable lesson I should have already learned.

A-1 (with shadow) dropping napalm on grain supplies in Ban Ban Valley

We had a flight of A-1s with napalm meet us in Ban Ban to destroy the large pyramid-shaped piles of grain. As I turned to fire one of my marking rockets, I noticed a farmer in a Buddhist prayer position kneeling in front of his grain. The fighters probably wondered what happened to their radios, as I fell silent. I couldn't bring myself to torch him and his grain. We went on to destroy the remaining grain supplies, and I felt good about my decision to spare that farmer and his grain.

In November and December of 1969, I concentrated more of my efforts north of Ban Ban on Route 6 as I started to locate more and more trucks there. We would fly along the road, like some airborne Sherlock Holmes, and try to locate areas that seemed likely truck parks, and the camouflaged trucks.

Once we had a target, we would call "Cricket" and be given a flight of fighters. Once in contact with a flight, we would give them our coordinates until they had us in sight. We would find out what ordnance they carried, explain what target we had, what ordnance to drop, and in which direction to approach the target. We would then fire a marking rocket and ask them if they could spot our plume of smoke. We would then explain how far the target was from our smoke, and in which direction. When they were ready, and we could see them, they were "cleared in" and we made sure we were out of the way.

At least one flight of F-4s lied. I couldn't locate them on their bombing approach (slight panic on my part), nor could I locate where their bombs had fallen. A minute or so passed before I saw the explosions above the treetops over a nearby ridge line a mile or more away! We had a little chat,

155

and they were a little better on their next pass. "BDA" was bomb damage assessment that they received and represented a percentage of bombs in the target area. Sometimes a good strike would receive 100 over 100. This flight received a 0/0, and I've always wondered what BDA numbers they actually reported when they landed!

The A-1s were slower, and often flew lower, which usually resulted in increased accuracy, but not always. I was flying north of Ban Ban on Route 6 when I spotted a truck parked on the side of the road under a solitary tree, on a hillside with a slope of about 30 degrees. I thought it would be a perfect target for a flight of four A-1s, each carrying eight canisters of napalm.

They first wanted to know how safe it was down there. I decided to take my plane lower in order (I hoped) to convince them. They were satisfied, and I was relieved when no one fired at me. I suggested they drop one canister at a time. Their first pass was up the hillside, as was the second pass. The canisters had landed below and above the truck. I asked them if we could try flying down the hillside, and two more passes again went long and short. The truck and the tree were located on a slight curve of the road, and they requested flying down the road from one direction. After two more passes, they tried flying from the opposite direction, trying twice again and using their last two canisters. Thirty-two canisters of napalm later, we still had a lonely, untouched truck under a now burning tree, and a scorched jungle in all directions!

The A-1 pilots and I were both disappointed. I thought we could all use some humor, so I told them about my backup target, a nearby bulldozer the enemy had backed into the hillside next to the road. I suspected it was a bulldozer, because all I could see was a very large metal blade tightly wedged into this hillside. The A-1 pilots were very enthusiastic and seemed to enjoy ricocheting their bullets off the blade. I think we all went home happier. Afterwards, I pondered the physics of bullets hitting a curved surface as the A-1s flew directly at it and then over it. As they say, "All's well that ends well!"

Jerry's photo of Craig Morrison flying back to Long Tieng

As November turned into December, I found more and more trucks. Even my friend, Craig Morrison, was probably beginning to wonder about the accuracy of my 6-12 "trucks destroyed" every day. One day he flew over to where I had spotted trucks and was preparing my fighters for their strike. I welcomed him, and he was happy to join me. That afternoon we destroyed almost 20 trucks and flew back to Long Tieng together, just as a beautiful sunset was unfolding. There was a disturbing question that lingered: Why were we spotting so many trucks all of a sudden? It was not a good omen!

I learned the definition of "destroyed" was not always accurate, even when the truck was burning when we departed. The next day I returned and found one of the aforementioned trucks, which was also blown off the side of the road and down a steep incline, had mysteriously disappeared!

I had received a letter from my mother that said she had seen Nixon on TV, and he was stating that our military was not involved in Laos. She had voted for the man and was inclined to believe him, so naturally she wanted to know where I "really" was.

One of the benefits of being a Raven was our non-military status. We were supposed to be civilians, so we took some liberties with our dress codes, especially our sideburns and haircuts. Now, don't get me wrong. We did not look like a rock band, as the "Bandito" photo in the book *The Ravens* proves, but enough that some military officers took serious exception. General Petit, the head of the 7/13th Air Force, was not the only one I encountered. My first R&R (rest and relaxation) was to Tan Son Nhut Air Base outside Saigon, be processed, and have our vaccines updated. An Army captain explained to me that I wouldn't be "leaving on a jet plane" (I guessed he liked folk music) until I received a proper haircut. I explained to him where I was based and my civilian status, but he didn't care about complications. I then requested to see his immediate superior. He was more than happy to take me to see his commander, an Army colonel. I waited in a reception room for half an hour and pondered why his rank was pronounced with an "r". He finally requested my presence. I explained what had happened and my situation. He hesitated before he spoke, and I can still remember his exact words. "Well, rules are made to be broken." Wow! I walked out of his room wondering why he wasn't in charge of the entire war.

In Australia, our maid at a Gold Coast hotel in Surfer's Paradise told us if we didn't want to return to Vietnam, she would be honored to hide us. It was a Friday night, and my roommate and I headed out to a local bar. As it filled up, we were astonished that the ladies outnumbered the guys about five to one. I've loved Australia ever since.

Surfer's Paradise

Once I got back to Vietnam, I had to catch a C-47 to Bangkok. I had just sat down when the co-pilot approached me, and if you guessed he wouldn't let me fly on "his" airplane without a haircut, you would be correct. I was gaining confidence in these situations and asked to talk to the pilot. I was escorted to the cockpit, but rather than talk about circumstances, I just told him I was a "Raven." The pilot seemed confused but said, "Okay," and then "Sorry." I went back to my seat, becoming more and more proud of being a Raven.

Another benefit of being a Raven was a second R&R. So while I was at Long Tieng, I caught a flight back home to San Francisco to visit my parents and a Braniff stewardess I had met while in the Philippines. She requested I wear my tans on my return. I actually felt some pride in wearing my uniform back to Vietnam.

Our flight stopped for an hour at Clark AFB in the Philippines. We had a chance to get off the airplane, and I sat in the terminal reading a book. It wasn't long before I noticed a pair of polished shoes and another tan uniform standing in front of me. An Air Force captain explained that I would have to get a haircut before I could get back on the airplane. Here we go again! I explained my circumstances and volunteered to change into civilian clothing if that would help him. No, he had his orders; if I was in the military, a change of my clothing would not matter. He had orders, and they were very strict.

After a short jeep ride I met the base commander. He listened intently to my circumstances then, with enthusiasm, asked me, "How's the war going up country?" We had a pleasant conversation. He called the captain back in and told him to take me to the flight line in his jeep and to make sure I didn't miss my flight. I had met another intelligent commander who should be running this war.

The accident reports of FACs I was assigned to work on during my first week or two in Vietnam resulted in my learning another valuable lesson: Flying low was dangerous to one's health. I think even Fred (another Raven whose nickname was Magnet Ass) might agree. Twice, while at Long Tieng, I had been asked to bomb villages. From my perspective, saving innocents was more important than killing the enemy. If I was going to be playing God (who lives and who dies), I was sure as hell not going to blindly follow orders.

My first and only village bombed while in Laos

The first village was located in the hills just east of the Plain of Jars. It appeared to be deserted, but I needed a closer look, which meant flying lower. I made numerous passes, each one lower than the previous, until I knew it was, in fact, abandoned. I still didn't understand why it was targeted.

The second village was located just a few miles south of Long Tieng atop a high plateau and under some large trees. It consisted of numerous large structures. I radioed in this information and was told no one knew it was there, nor who inhabited the village. I was also told it was "not considered friendly." Again, I had to fly lower until I concluded it was inhabited, and in my opinion, it was friendly. There would be no bombing strike.

Meo girls from village

Shortly after I had arrived in Long Tieng, Craig Morrison asked me if I wanted to join him and socialize with some Meo tribesmen that evening. We arrived at a house in their village, not far from the runway. There were about a dozen men present, and as we sat down, I noticed a bottle of clear liquid. I was told it was Lau Lao, a liquor fermented from rice. My memory to this day is a little fuzzy about the next few hours, but I think we passed this bottle around, drank from a small glass, then passed the bottle to the next person. I have no idea what our conversation was about, but I do remember there was laughter and smiles. I also remember there were casualties as time progressed, and that seemed to be one of the objectives.

Another evening in December the Ravens were invited to the annual Hmong beauty contest. The VIPs, Laotians and Americans, including our CIA associates, were given front-row seats facing a large stage. Behind us was a large crowd numbering in the hundreds, mostly Hmong men. There were also a variety of young Hmong girls dressed in their finest attire, accented with their silver jewelry. It was a rather chilly night, and Gen. Vang Pao distributed a few bottles of Whitehorse whiskey to the VIPs.

I thought a beauty pageant would be a rather quiet affair, with perhaps some murmurs and light applause for the favorites. This evening's event would be very different. When an attractive contestant was on stage, it was very quiet, and the audience was very respectful. However, when a much less attractive contestant was introduced, the crowd of Hmong men would howl, jeer, shout, and generally get very noisy. As one less attractive girl was introduced, the raucous crowd caused the fence railing on which they were sitting to collapse, along with the 50 or more Hmong men. I guessed Lau Lao had something to do with their behavior. It was a very entertaining and rare night out for me in Long Tieng.

Later that evening I found myself in a small wood building with a small room and two bunk beds, having a conversation with my "new" CIA friend. At some point his roommate started pounding on the door and was not happy he had been locked out. After much yelling, there was a short welcomed silence before a loud crash that shook the small room. My new friend's roommate, Igor, had literally dived headfirst through the wall and was lying on the floor with a Green Bay Packers knitted woolen beanie on his head. The cold draft created by his method of entry seemed like a good excuse for me to head home. It was probably just as well I didn't go out at night very often.

Sometime in late November I was asked if I wanted to extend my tour another three or six months. My going home date was January 1st, and I had not considered staying. But then, I hadn't been asked either. In the next few weeks, a couple of incidents occurred which would help me make up my mind.

Like any ordinary day, I awoke early, had breakfast, and headed out to the flight line. I was excited because I was locating more trucks each week. After takeoff, I contacted our friendly C-130 middleman, Cricket, and headed towards Ban Ban. Suddenly there was a voice on my radio, "Greven, is that you?" I couldn't answer, as I was totally unnerved. My mind raced through thoughts: I was the first plane off, so no other FACs were up; Cricket didn't know my name; could it be a North Vietnam trick? What the hell? I was afraid to say "yes," but finally asked, "Who is this?" Again the voice said, "Greven, is that you?" I was very confused but finally answered, "Yes. Who's this?" He answered, "Eric Jenson."

Eric Jenson had been a friend of mine in pilot training, and I had run into him at our embassy house in Vientiane about four months earlier when he stopped there overnight and informed me he was flying a Beaver out of NKP, dropping leaflets over Laos. We both now laughed at his call "from the blue," which he knew would unravel me. He had achieved the desired effect!

I was flying about seven hours a day, seven days a week, so our flying time added up quickly. Our commanders were under some pressure from the Air Force to keep us under 100 hours a month, as I recall, but 130-150 hours wasn't uncommon. At the end of November, I was already over 120 hours, so I was told to get my butt to Udorn for some R&R.

I hopped aboard an Air America cargo plane and headed for Vientiane. I found myself a comfortable spot and sprawled out on some burlap bags in the rear of the cargo hold when a Laotian soldier approached me with a rifle pointed at me and verbalized his displeasure. Thankfully there was a CIA guy in the cargo area also, and he stepped in to intervene. He told me to sit with him and explained they were very protective of their burlap bags, which contained opium. The Meo cash crop was being used to help pay for their war somehow, and Air America, a CIA-owned airline operating throughout Indochina, particularly Laos, was assisting them with transportation. That explained the volume of gold jewelry in Vientiane, and the missing C-47s in Vientiane, and the "mysterious flights" to Saigon and Hong Kong. The dots were finally connected.

I had been targeting trucks near Ban Ban. One day I decided not to follow my usual route home along Route 7, but to take a shortcut and fly directly to Long Tieng over some unknown terrain. I made the mistake of flying over unfamiliar terrain, with no roads, which I thought was safe, and flying in a straight line. An F-4 reconnaissance pilot radioed me and said, "Hey, Raven 21, do you know you're being shot at?" At first I thought it was another prank call, as I had not heard or seen anything. He told me to look up. Sure enough, there were seven puffs of black smoke above me – an antiaircraft gunner who did not know we had a "gentleman's agreement!"

I started looking around at my plane and my gauges for any problems. I spotted a small red light in my cockpit that was illuminated. It was the very first time in over a year of flying that I had even noticed the red light existed. I quickly called Long Tieng, explained my situation, and asked them about this light. I really did not want to hear, "It indicates you may have metal fragments in the engine." (It's amazing you can remember certain words years later.) Swell.

The F-4 pilot was also listening and was kind enough to volunteer to keep an eye on me for the next 30 or so minutes until I could land. He also instantly became my "new" best friend.

My mind drifted to the question I had been asked weeks earlier: Did I want to stay on an extra three or six months? Sometimes everything about a difficult decision can become illuminated (like my light) by a moment of clarity. Did I believe in this cause enough to possibly die for it? If we couldn't win the war in South Vietnam, we would have to leave Vietnam and Laos. Since I believed the war could not be won in South Vietnam, I knew this war in Laos was also lost. By the time Long Tieng's runway was in sight, I knew I would be leaving Laos in a few weeks. I thanked my new best friend for the heads up and for his escort home. You're probably wondering about that light. Well, I was told it was just an electrical problem – a serendipitous moment!

I had been to our Plain of Jars base and runway (Lima Site 22) numerous times. Once during the fall there had even been multiple unmarked planes parked, with a dozen or more Americans wearing civilian clothes, having some kind of official meeting. There were also Laotian paratroopers jumping out of planes overhead. I pulled out my camera and was told no pictures were allowed. As usual, that did not deter me from capturing the moment. I thought I might have made a good photojournalist.

Plain of Jars

A week before I was to depart Laos I flew into the Plain of Jars one last time. While flying on approach to the runway, I spotted what seemed to be 100 or more fuel drums hidden in a group of trees about two miles from the runway. When I landed, I asked about this hidden fuel dump, but no one was aware of it. An Air America chopper pilot overheard me and asked if I would show him where they were located. The concern was that they might not be old, but new fuel drums, and not ours!

Two previously camouflaged trucks that had been bombed

A small group of us were quickly assembled and told to bring our weapons "just in case." Stepping into the O-1 had always been comfortable and non-stressful, but stepping off that helicopter into head-high grass was a different story. We couldn't see anything around us except elephant grass and some trees 100 yards away. I remember telling myself this was the last time I was ever going to volunteer again. It definitely was the most stressful short walk of my life!

We arrived at the small group of trees and found over one hundred 55 gallon drums stacked up. After a quick check (the Air America guy put a few bullet holes in them), we realized they were indeed old, and I had confirmed I was no courageous photojournalist. I was extremely happy to step back into my O-1 before heading home

Bombed trucks, one on fire

Before I left I was invited to dinner at General Vang Pao's residence, where he hosted a baci (a Laotian ceremony celebrating the arrival or departure of friends or anything of social significance) that included a ceremonial presentation of a 22 carat gold ring that had a Laotian royal crest set into a blood red (symbolic, perhaps) enamel inlay, with a diamond at its center, and a Meo musket. I felt extremely honored and saddened that evening.

My last day was spent packing my meager belongings, my treasured Meo musket, and a Russian sniper rifle recovered from a cave complex we had bombed. At the last minute, Craig Morrison and another Raven decided to accompany me to Vientiane and celebrate my departure, and New Year's Eve. I was very grateful for their company, as I would have friends with me my last night in Laos. We decided to enjoy our last night together at the Third Eye, a mostly European patronized restaurant and bar. I was told many Europeans were in Vientiane because marijuana was legal in Laos. As midnight approached, I went outside onto the patio area. When I returned to our table I was asked by Craig, "Did you just go outside and smoke a joint?" Since it was my last night, I answered honestly. Craig's reply was, "Why didn't you invite us?" Pleasantly surprised by this turn of events, we all went back out to the deserted patio and watched the occasional fireworks in the sky, listening as firecrackers were set off. Suddenly, three or four Laotian Army trucks drove up and unloaded their cargo of Laotian troops, armed with M-16s. They surrounded the entire restaurant.

My last night, and this was going to be the way my tour ended?! After much confusion, the proprietors were able to convince the troops there were no firefights happening, just firecrackers.

It was New Year's Eve. Our celebration that evening, however, was definitely dampened. Thus, my Laotian experience ended, "not with a bang, but with a whimper."

Back in the United States

I returned to Fairfield, California and an assignment to C-141s at Travis AFB, a MAC Group Headquarters. My assignment was "still being processed" when I arrived. There was no warm welcome, like I had received in Laos, and no personal introductions, except for the squadron commander. Upon arriving back home, the only hostility I encountered was from some of the senior officers in the squadron, one of whom reprimanded me my first week back for being "out of uniform." He sent me home to change. I had been wearing my nylon jungle boots instead of the all-leather black boots, and as soon as I got home, I dyed the olive-colored nylon with some black liquid shoe polish. These "new" boots would go unnoticed for my entire assignment with C-141s — almost another three years.

I also reacted badly to loud noises at night (like an occasional backfire from a car), even going so far as to dive off my bed and break my nose on the nightstand beside my bed. There was also the occasional visceral reaction to something completely normal, like suburbia's neatly manicured lawns. More than anything, while in Laos, I had become an adrenaline junky, and not being able to start my C-141 training for another couple of months was a difficult adjustment and probably explains my purchase of a Porsche and a Honda 750 motorcycle.

I did realize, however, that leaving Long Tieng when I did was rather fortunate timing, as the North Vietnamese Army (NVA) was again on the offensive by January 1970. We began losing Ravens from ground fire. Some died, and some were badly injured. I was lucky to arrive home with no physical scars, but something had changed.

Then there was Nixon on TV in April 1970, explaining how the Cambodian invasion into the Fish Hook area (just west of An Loc) by some 30,000 U.S. forces was necessary, as the NVA was using Cambodia as a "sanctuary." He purposely did not mention our B-52 strikes of this area that had begun, and continued, since March 1969!

Because of our invasion of Cambodia, protests broke out on college campuses across the country, resulting in four student deaths and seven wounded at Kent State. Massive antiwar demonstrations occurred across the nation. The Ravens' motto was "Nevermore," so I joined the 100,000+ demonstrators in San Francisco's Golden Gate Park.

Our B-52 strikes of Cambodia, beginning in 1969, had probably delayed the NVA offensive in South Vietnam, which finally occurred in 1972. The question was: At what cost? The bombing caused the rise of the Khmer Rouge and the "killing fields" where one-third of the Cambodian population died (over a million people).

I had great affection for the Hmong people, and even as I write this many years later, I still feel tremendous sadness about their being abandoned when we left. I also know the Ravens did not start this war, yet we were pained by a sense of guilt. This guilt should be placed squarely on those who were responsible: the policy makers whose hubris ignored history and agreements.

As Chris Robbins (the author) pointed out in his book, *The Ravens*, the "Vietnamese were one of a few nations ever to defeat the Mongols on the field of battle, and routed Kublai Khan. . . in 1278." The Chinese also invaded Vietnam in the early 1400s. China at that time was perhaps the wealthiest country on earth, with the largest fleet of military and trading ships in the world, but their war with Vietnam almost bankrupted the Empire, and they were forced to withdraw. A new Emperor declared that all ships were to be sunk, and thus China moved into a self-imposed isolation that lasted almost 500 years. Our military and political leaders had not learned from Chinese history.

In 1941, in the Articles of the Atlantic Conference, FDR pledged to those countries who would assist us in fighting our enemies that they would be rewarded with self-governance. U.S. troops fought in WWII alongside of Ho Chi Minh who, after the war, wrote letters to Truman and requested assistance in obtaining independence. Truman did not respond. Instead, Ho looked elsewhere for help, while we allowed France to recolonize in Vietnam. We even went so far as to pay their military expenses. The French lost their battle at Dien Bien Phu in 1954, and it marked the end of the French in Indochina. As quoted in the book *The Ravens*, "The Meo were cruelly rewarded for their loyalty to the French," and America's attempt to stabilize Laos, by pouring money in, "actually helped the Pathet Lao."

Had free elections been held in South Vietnam (as they were in Northern Vietnam) in 1954, as was agreed to when Vietnam was divided, Ho Chi Minh probably would have been elected and there would have been no war. The Hmong would probably have been spared, as Laos would not have been a strategic piece on some military chess board. The losses of dead and wounded, on all sides (American, Laotian, Vietnamese, and Cambodian) were certainly in the millions. The policy makers are the ones who deserve the guilt, not the ones who were asked to fight.

I was adjusting to civilian life in 1973 and working as a pilot for Delta Airlines when I read an article in the *Miami Herald* in which the Pentagon was denying the use of B52s in Cambodia prior to our invasion in 1970. I was shocked they were still lying! I decided to call Senator Hughes, who was mentioned in the article, and managed to speak to his staff.

Soon after that conversation, I received a call from a *New York Times* reporter, Seymour Hersch. I was also contacted by the Air Force, who requested a meeting. Delta Airlines also wanted to meet, and I was told in no uncertain terms they (corporate office in Atlanta) expected me to be "patriotic and support the President," and "not to stick my neck out." I was also told not to go to Washington D.C. and testify, but if I did, I would "not be allowed to fly on Delta for that purpose." So much for southern hospitality!

To make a long story shorter, I testified anyway. I believe then, as I do now, that if the American public is not told the truth, they cannot make intelligent and informed decisions about their government's policies. I testified before the Committee on Armed Services United States Senate on the subject of "Bombing of Cambodia" on August 8, 1973. It was a long day, and I was assured they would protect a witness from retaliation. About a month or more passed before I received my pink slip. I never heard back from a single senator.

I attended my first Raven reunion in 1972 but did not return until after the release of *The Ravens*. My return was met with surprising animosity from Fred Platt, a fellow Raven. The following year Craig Morrison, our Raven president, was told by Fred that I had been voted out of the Ravens because of my testifying in the mid-70s. Craig decided to have me answer questions at the reunion. He then addressed the gathering and asked that the issue be resolved by a vote, adding, "If Greven goes, I go." We had liked each other before, but now there was a serious bond. I was voted back in, much to Fred's displeasure.

I put my *Ravens* and *Bombing in Cambodia* books away by the early 1990s, and they've gathered dust ever since. Then my December issue of *The Ravens* newsletter arrived with a request for more of us to write about how we got to Laos, impressions we had while we were there, and how it changed us. I decided to volunteer one last time.

What I thought would be a month-long project has turned into three. I had to dust off my books and maps and re-read them. I've spent more time with a dictionary than in the last 10 years combined. Removing my memories from some type of mental closet I had stored them in was more difficult than I had imagined.

I hope my effort will assist our *Ravens* book, as well as help my friends and family members understand why I am, at best, only "semi-normal." So these memories are for all of you, and especially in memory of those Ravens who are no longer with us.

To those of you I've talked to about this effort, like Craig, Will, Bill, Karl, and Ed, I thank you for your support. You made it easier to finish what at times became a difficult process. A woman I met at my 50th high school reunion a couple of years ago said, "The 20th reunion was sort of judgmental, while the 50th has been great because we're all just happy to be alive." I'm hoping our reunions have evolved as well.

Nevermore,

Gerald (Jerry) Greven Raven 21
Laos: July-December 1969
1st Lt., O-1, 'Bird Dog'

Chapter 14

Terry "Moose" Carroll, Raven 48, 23
Long Tieng, Oct 1969 – Feb 1970
Vientiane, Feb – Mar 1970

My full name is Terry Malone Carroll, Jr. Before you ask, I got the nickname Moose at the U.S. Air Force Academy because I was a fan of (or reminded a lot of people of) Bullwinkle the Moose on the cartoon show Rocky and Bullwinkle. I was born August 31, 1945 in Victoria, Texas. My father was a career Air Force chief warrant officer with a 27-year Air Force career in boats, from crash rescue boats, to drone recovery boats, to general officer pleasure boats on the Rhine River in Germany post-WWII. I grew up primarily in Florida with significant time in Japan and Germany.

I was Raven 48 at Lima Site 20A from October 1969 to near the end of February 1970; then was Raven 23 at Vientiane until the end of March 1970. My largest regret from my Raven tour is that I did not keep a journal or take very many pictures. In reading Christopher Robbins' book, The Ravens, and Karl Polifka's book, Meeting Steve Canyon, I realize I missed an opportunity to document and record a unique piece of my life. As Tom Harris (who was with me at Lima Site 20A) said, he and I just flew and flew until we fell over, then we flew some more. This narrative is almost exclusively from my memory, and if anyone wants to challenge me on names, dates, or other facts, I will immediately yield and acknowledge my errors.

I have always been lucky; although, not always good luck. I graduated from the U.S. Air Force Academy in 1967. Those of us in my class that were going to be (and were physically qualified to be) pilots were all herded into a large auditorium prior to graduation to select where we were to go to pilot training and when. On the stage was a large hopper with something on the order of 400 plus numbers in it, and we went up one at a time to pick a number. The person who drew number one got first choice of Undergraduate Pilot Training class and location. The most desired assignment was Williams AFB in Phoenix, Arizona, and other choice assignments included college towns like Reese AFB, Lubbock, Texas. I drew the very last number possible — bad luck and good luck, as will be seen. The last assignment left when my turn came was the "B class" at Laughlin AFB, Del Rio, Texas. That meant I would have 90 days leave (60 days everyone got plus my first year's 30 days) after graduation before I had to report to Laughlin.

So I took my new 1967 Chevelle and my new Suzuki 250 cc motorcycle and headed to my hometown of Port O'Connor, Texas. Port O'Connor is in the middle of the Texas coast and, at that time, had fewer than 1,000 residents. I proceeded to pass my leave time as a deck hand on my uncles' shrimp boats, playing cowboy, and mostly carousing with my male cousins near my age. I had developed a taste for alcohol (gross understatement) and that, plus my new motorcycle, gave me an early unhealthy disregard for danger that would carry on through my Southeast Asia tour. But my time in Port O'Connor brought another happening that has had a profound influence on my life and influenced my SEA tour.

Sometime in June 1967, my cousin Johnny was looking for a girl for me to date. In a town of 1,000, one had to look hard. Johnny had a friend from another town whose family had a summer house in Port O'Connor and that friend had a sister, Marie, who might be eligible. Marie was the steady girlfriend of our second cousin, but he was in the Navy in the Mediterranean. Marie's best friend was another second cousin of ours, Martha Hawes. One Saturday evening, Johnny and I waited outside the Catholic Church for Mass to end. When Martha came out, we asked if we could give her a ride home. Her father may have been a bit suspicious, since they only lived one block from the church, but he said okay and so did Martha. I did not know Martha other than she was a cousin, but in the slow one-block ride she agreed to ask Marie for me. A week or so later, the answer was "Yes," but only if Martha went with us as a threesome. Marie, Martha, and I spent the summer together — I had a flashy car, was comparatively rich by local standards, and was old enough to buy beer. What more could a local girl want? We rode around town partying with me driving, Marie in the middle (bench seat), and Martha on the right. In July, Marie went off to Colorado to be a camp counselor, and when she returned Martha was in the middle and Marie on the right. By the time I graduated from pilot training, Martha and I were not engaged, but I was hooked.

Our pilot training class got an assignment block that had very few fighters. There were two F-4's and two RF-4's that went higher than me in the class (assignments were chosen by class standing approximately two months prior to graduation). There were some F-111's, but that was a new aircraft with some problems and those assignments were not destined for the Southeast Asia war. When my turn to choose came, I took an O-2A forward air controller (FAC) assignment which was pipelined to Southeast Asia. After survival training at Fairchild AFB, Washington, I trained in the O-2A from December 1968 to January 1969 at Hurlburt AFB, Florida, and on February 19th at one o'clock in the morning flew out of San Francisco for the Philippines. After jungle survival training at Clark AFB, P.I., I arrived at Tan Son Nhut (Saigon) on February 27, 1969 to start my one-year wartime tour. The FACs on the plane all went to Bien Hoa the next day for in-processing and flew to Phan Rang for in-country orientation training on March 3rd. There were lots of FACs at Phan Rang with me, but only four of the O-2 pilots (me, 1st Lt Henry Allen, 1st Lt Phillip Mascari, and a captain whose name I do not remember) received assignments to the 23rd Tactical Air Support Squadron (TASS) at Nakhon Phanom (NKP) Royal Thai Air Force Base (RTAFB), Thailand. I left South Vietnam for Bangkok, Thailand on March 11th and began flying at NKP immediately. I said I was always lucky.

Flying with the 23rd TASS (call sign Nail) was very different from most of the FAC assignments in Vietnam. We were flying interdiction sorties over the eastern half of southern Laos trying to stop the North Vietnamese Army (NVA) supply traffic heading into South Vietnam. For one, there were no friendly troops in the areas where we flew and directed fighter bombing sorties. Also, there were big anti-aircraft guns, from the 14.5 mm ZPU and 23 mm ZSU-23 to the 37 mm, 57 mm, and 85 mm anti-aircraft guns. The 57 and 85 mm guns were mostly near the passes from North Vietnam into Laos and were often radar directed. Another difference was that we typically flew only one 4-to-5-hour mission per day. The Nails maintained FACs over three sectors of the Ho Chi Minh Trail in southern Laos 24 hours a day, 7 days a week. The big difference in flying with the 23rd TASS at NKP, as opposed to Vietnam, was that when we returned to base, there was no more war. We were in Thailand and the base was never attacked. I heard a rumor that NKP had mortars or rockets fired at it once, but I never saw any. The bunkers we had were used by the maids to cook and eat their lunches or were so overgrown that no one wanted to go in there.

170

At NKP, the O-2 was flying both day missions and night missions. The night missions flew with a pilot and a navigator. The navigator in the right seat spotted truck traffic by leaning out the open window with a handheld Starlight Scope (a night-vision telescope). On the night mission, the pilot primarily flew on instruments following directions from the navigator. The day missions were typically flown with just a pilot, and the Nail FAC was the boss within his assigned sector. Most of the mission was visual reconnaissance, but there were a lot of airstrikes to direct on a typical mission. The O-2 was a good airplane for this mission because it had decent speed, long endurance, and two engines. For day missions, we carried two pods with a total of 14 white phosphorous marking rockets. A few of the new OV-10's were at NKP flying day missions only and, as more arrived, they gradually took over most of the day missions from the O-2's. We did get shot at fairly often, especially by 37 mm guns, and we were taught to keep the nose of the airplane moving constantly while we were over Laos, a lesson I took with me to the Raven program.

I never took a hit as a Nail, and perhaps the most dangerous mission I had was an administrative flight from Ubon RTAFB back to NKP. I was being transferred from our detachment at Ubon and had all of my belongings and all my personnel records with me in the back of an OV-10 flown by a captain named Frank who had been grounded from flying combat missions due to recklessness. I was a little suspicious when I noted that the OV-10 had high-explosive rockets loaded in the pods. Frank and I took off right behind another OV-10 going out over Laos, and we joined him in formation so the radar sites would not see our aircraft going out over Laos. Then Frank peeled off and he and I attacked a spot just east of Tchepone "where he knew there was an anti-aircraft gun emplacement." We did not get shot at and made it to NKP. As I said, he was crazy (and I was always lucky).

When I first began flying with the 23rd TASS, morale was high and everyone was flying a lot. We typically flew 26 days straight and then got 4 days off. The squadron commander flew as much as anyone. Sometime in June 1969, the squadron commander left and morale took a dive under the new commander. He flew only the minimum to get his combat pay and was more concerned with safety and adherence to directives than with accomplishment of the mission. He was rumored to sneak into adjacent sectors to check if the other FACs were adhering to the minimum safe altitudes. Henry Allen and I decided we wanted out, especially since we would likely be flying more night missions if we stayed.

Sometime in mid-1969, a Raven in an O-1 landed at NKP and came to the Nail hooch (bar). I can't remember if it was Smoky Greene or Ed Gunter, both Air Force Academy and pilot training classmates of mine. Whomever it was told us some of what he did and where. Henry and I applied for Ravens immediately, but the word from the FAC headquarters at Bien Hoa was that the Raven program would only accept O-1-qualified pilots, since that was the primary airplane the Ravens flew. We were rejected and dejected. Less than two weeks later, a message came saying that, if Henry and I were still interested, we could apply for Ravens. Henry and I flew a couple of O-2's to Bien Hoa for maintenance and interviewed with the Mother FAC (the commander of all the FACs in Vietnam and Thailand). The colonel was very discouraging. He said they really needed pilots in the Raven program, but "They have no safety or standardization evaluation programs and they live like a bunch of wild Indians." While trying not to grin too much, Henry and I said we would like to give it a try. We both had to extend our tours to ensure that we had six months left before our return to the States. We were the first O-2 pilots accepted into the Raven program. I said I was always lucky.

I checked out in the O-1 in a couple of weeks at Phan Rang and was sent for ten days to fly with the FACs at Qui Nhon, South Vietnam to get a bit more time in the airplane. The FACs at Qui Nhon rarely put in airstrikes, but I did get to fly daily and assisted the local FACs in getting banned from the Officers' Club due to our drunken rowdy behavior. On September 24, 1969, I flew from Cam Ranh Bay, South Vietnam to Bangkok. I happened to meet Fred Platt (a departing Raven) in Bangkok in my one night there (yes, we drank a lot), then went to NKP to pack up and transfer to Detachment 1 of the 56th Special Operations Wing (SOW) at Udorn RTAFB. I was in the Raven program.

I really knew very little about the Ravens when I arrived at Udorn. I knew that, although I was assigned to Detachment 1, 56 SOW, I would be on temporary duty (TDY) with the air attaché in Laos "to provide operational support." TDY was a good thing (extra dollars) and our orders specified that we were to be in civilian clothes and got one round trip to Udorn per month. I left all my military uniforms and stuff in a CONEX (a large steel storage bin) at Detachment 1. I needed civilian clothes for my clandestine mission in Laos, so one of the Ravens who happened to be at Udorn took me to a tailor in Udorn town. The tailor took my measurements and my notes on where I wanted pockets, etc., and I ordered two suits to fly in. I remember the tailor remarking, "Oh, you want Raven suits." Some secret mission. I also bought some Levis and a Levi jacket, which became my favorite flying suit. The Raven then flew me to Vientiane, and I stayed overnight in the air attaché (AIRA) house. The AIRA house was a very nice French colonial-style house with offices and residences included. Whenever we stayed at the AIRA house, we were told not to drink excessively and certainly never bring female friends home from downtown. There was a big concern for maintaining the appearance that the air attaché and his staff were simply advisors to the Royal Laotian Air Force. Ravens, as Ravens, simply did not exist at the AIRA house.

The next day, Joe Potter (I think) flew me to Lima Site 20A in a T-28, and I began flying as Raven 48 that same day. Joe Potter was the American Air Force site commander, and 20A was a very busy airstrip. We had five to six Ravens. During my six-month tour I remember Mike Cavanaugh, Karl Polifka, Mike Byers, Henry Allen, Tom Harris, Smoky Greene, Al Daines, Bob Dunbar, and Bill Kozma were there with me at various times, but there were never more than six of us at any one time. We also had an intelligence officer and three or four maintenance personnel. In addition to the Raven O-1's and T-28's, there were Hmong T-28's (call sign "Chao Pha Khao") and all sorts of helicopters and fixed-wing transports flown by Air America and Continental Air Services in and out every day. Lima Site 20A was a 4,400–foot, 60-foot wide asphalt strip at 3,200 feet above sea level, surrounded by mountains, with a large karst formation at one end (the "vertical speed brake"). It had no lights and no approach aids, so everything was daytime flying and in good weather only. Potter was not supposed to fly other than administrative flights to other sites, including Vientiane and Udorn, but he loved to secretly fly with the Hmong T-28's on bombing missions. I remember hearing him disguise his voice trying to sound like a Hmong as he called in as "Chao Pha Khao Five" on his bombing runs. Once he went with the Hmong on a mission to the east not knowing where the actual target would be. When the leader rolled in, Joe realized they were bombing a bridge in North Vietnam! He was fearless. Potter went for dinner and a situation briefing with General Vang Pao every night and took one or more Ravens with him each time. These dinners were also fraught with danger, since the only beverage served was White Horse scotch. The Hmong New Year celebrations in December 1969 were especially hard on Joe Potter, and Karl Polifka would have to drag Potter back from Vang Pao's house late in the night. At that time, the air-to-ground war in northeastern Laos was very busy and was being run by one captain (Potter) and six 1st lieutenants (the Ravens and an intelligence officer). We controlled the air war in northeastern Laos, much to the chagrin of the USAF commanders in Vietnam and Thailand.

Lima Site 20 Alternate, or Long Tieng, was also a big secret airfield and the headquarters of the Hmong army led by General Vang Pao. It was called Lima Site 20 Alternate to disguise it from Lima Site 20 at Sam Thong, about five and one-half miles over the ridge to the northwest. Sam Thong was a busy supply airfield providing food and other aid to the Hmong. Whenever news reporters wanted to go "up country" to get nearer to the war, they were taken to Sam Thong — never to Long Tieng. Once a reporter somehow managed to get a guide and made it from Sam Thong to Long Tieng on foot. The local authorities wanted to kill him and dispose of his body, but the CIA personnel convinced them to simply return him to Sam Thong. We would sometimes send maintenance personnel to Sam Thong for supplies, but I never knew of any Ravens going there. The "Raven hooch" at 20A was fairly nice. We had bedrooms (two to a room), a kitchen, and a small bar. Unless the weather was bad, we were only there to brief in the morning, debrief in the evening, eat something, party at the bar, and sleep. I was rarely there in the daylight hours. We also tried to spend some time at the CIA hooch, because they had a nicer bar built over the top of a bear cage. The bears, Floyd and his mate, were kept by the CIA personnel (also referred to as "CAS" personnel for Controlled American Source), and Floyd had a penchant for beer, which we fed him through the windows of the bar.

Terry "Moose" Carroll

The CIA personnel at 20A were always a bit scary to me. They were serious military combat personnel who risked their lives almost daily. They were there to advise and assist the Hmong, and they accompanied the Hmong military units into the field to the numerous hilltop sites where the Hmong monitored the enemy activity and carried out attacks. These sites were frequently

173

attacked and overrun by the North Vietnamese Army units, and the Hmong and the CIA personnel had to defend and then abandon the sites and melt into the jungle. It was not uncommon during my Raven tour to have a site be overrun by the NVA, then have all the defenders appear uninjured at another site a week later. Support of these hilltop sites was one of the main missions for the Ravens of 20A.

I arrived at 20A at an auspicious time — General Vang Pao and the Hmong were just completing a very successful campaign that pushed the NVA and Pathet Lao troops out of the Plaine des Jarres (PDJ) and captured a lot of territory and equipment. Friendly aircraft began flying out of Lima Site 22 (also called "Lima Lima") in the northern PDJ, and it became one of the Ravens' main daytime refueling and rearming stops. I also flew into Lima Site 108 at Muong Soui just west of the PDJ. LS 108 had been lost to the NVA; then retaken by Vang Pao's forces in the late-summer offensive. The ground successes meant Hmong T-28's required extensive resupplies, and at one point USAF C-130's were tasked to bring 250-pound bombs into both Muong Soui and 20A. I directed the first USAF C-130 bringing 250-pound bombs into LS 108 for use by the T-28's for rearming during the day. At 20A I was sent to the airfield tower to talk to the USAF C-130's who had never been into 20A. The first USAF C-130 arrived overhead and expressed doubts upon seeing the airfield. He made a couple of low passes, then said he did not think the airfield was capable for a C-130. About that time, an Air America C-130 arrived and, without any fanfare, landed and began unloading his cargo. Needless to say, the USAF C-130 was suitably shamed and landed uneventfully.

Lima Site 22 AKA Lima Lima

Attacks on hilltop sites became fewer, and I often flew without a Hmong Army spotter in the back seat. Prior to my arrival at 20A, the Ravens had been very busy doing close air support for the Hmong, as the NVA pushed to the west and into the PDJ and were then pushed back. Interdiction of the NVA supply trucks and equipment along Route 7 from the North Vietnamese border at the "Fish's Mouth" to Ban Ban Valley northeast of the PDJ was not as high a Raven priority as close air support for the Hmong. We spent a couple of weeks in October 1969 burning rice with napalm

174

in Ban Ban Valley, since General Vang Pao thought it would reduce the NVA food supplies. The USAF brought in "fast FACs" consisting of F-4s with marking rockets and other armament to search the eastern end of Route 7. These fast FACs rarely reported seeing trucks or other equipment, but they put in some airstrikes on interdiction targets as directed by USAF.

Sometime in late 1969, with the ground situation looking calmer, USAF sent a request for either me or Henry Allen (presumably because of our interdiction experience) to take a look east along Route 7. I remember my first trip out Route 7 — I found trucks loaded with supplies parked on the road with just a minimum of camouflage. Once I followed truck tracks with my binoculars for several days before I found where they went into the jungle between karst formations just southwest of Ban Ban Valley. It was near the end of the day, so I reported it to our Intel officer, who sent it up the line. The entire truck park was obliterated by B-52's the next day. I killed more trucks as a Raven than I ever did as a Nail, despite the fact that this was the primary mission of the Nails. One day while I was way east near Route 7, a fast FAC contacted me and asked me to come look for a reported four-position 37 mm gun site near the North Vietnamese border at Nong Het (coincidentally the birthplace of General Vang Pao). The fast FAC was up at around seven or eight thousand feet as I came in the area at about 1,500 feet (as a Nail, our minimum altitude would have been 3,500 feet above the ground in this type of threat area) with my nose constantly moving, as I was taught as a Nail. Just as I got over Nong Het, the 37 mm site opened up. It was indeed at least a four-position site and all the guns had time to reload and fire again before I was able to exit to the south at 70 mph. Meanwhile, the fast FAC lit his afterburners and made a hasty retreat skyward. My experience was that the fast FACs were not very effective, given the altitudes and speeds they travelled.

We flew a lot — I logged 159 hours of flying time in my first twenty days at 20A. Considering that all of the time was daytime VFR (visual flight rules) and did not include the time we spent refueling, reloading, or even eating during the day, I was going all out. Our typical day would have two Ravens take off at daylight (remember, we had no runway lights or bad weather navigation aids), with the remainder following at hourly intervals. You flew until you were out of gas or rockets (or both), then dropped into a forward airstrip where crates of rockets and 55-gallon drums of gas were pre-positioned. You broke open the crates, put the rockets together, and reloaded your rocket tubes. Then you used a hand pump and pumped gas from the drums into the airplane's tanks. You took off again and repeated the cycle until sundown approached, when you had to be back on the ground at 20A. There was no instrument approach into 20A for use in bad weather. Once when I was still fairly new and had been working well east, I was trying to get back to 20A under a cloud cover and was having trouble finding a clear valley to get through the mountains. My back seater was asleep, but he then sat up, had a quick look around, pointed where to go, and went back to sleep. One of my best navigation aids was in the back seat.

Once we had several days of early morning fog that blanketed the whole valley and 20A. It would form just before daylight and stay thick for several hours. On the second day, Smoky Greene and I decided to beat the fog and take off in the dark. We had the maintenance personnel drive their jeep down the dark runway to make sure there were no pigs or people in the way; then we took off. We got off okay, but when I got airborne, my main UHF radio for talking to the fighters would not work, so I was worthless, and 20A was now covered in heavy fog. I could have flown on to Lima Lima in the PDJ and waited for 20A to clear, but I was frustrated and decided to use the emergency bad weather approach back into 20A. During my checkout, I was shown a narrow and steep-sided river valley leading from southwest of the PDJ to the west and south back towards 20A. The theory was to fly in the river valley under the clouds until you came to two burned-out tree stumps, then pull up into the clouds to the left and locate the road leading into the valley containing 20A. You then followed that road until you came to General Vang Pao's house, turned left then right (to get around the "vertical speed brake"), and you were then (in theory) over the runway, albeit heading the wrong way for landing. I located the river valley west of the PDJ (which was not foggy) and followed the procedure. While on the river, I was in an inverted pyramid with the clouds/fog covering the steep hills on both sides. I found the burned-out stumps and pulled up into the fog to find the road. By this time, I was flying by looking straight down from less than 100 feet. I followed the road, did the left-right turns, and landed opposite to the normal landing direction. By then, I was frustrated enough that I got in another airplane and took off again in the solid fog. I have always been lucky, and was pretty skillful that day.

Our main refueling and rearming site on the PDJ (Lima Site 22 aka Lima Lima) was a piece of cake for our O-1's compared to many of the sites where we landed. It was a PSP (pierced steel planking) runway and was busy with Air America ferrying troops and supplies into and out of it all day. The PDJ was grassland devoid of the jungle that covered the surrounding hills and mountains. It was also interesting, with the giant stone jars that gave it its name and the captured NVA equipment lying all around. I was able to climb all over Russian-made PT-76 light tanks and different types of antiaircraft guns. The PDJ was also the location of several herds of wild water buffalo, which the Air America helicopters would shoot for meat for the Hmong troops and villagers. The Hmong T-28 pilots were not supposed to fly into LS 22 except in an emergency, but one particular pilot announced he had an engine problem one day and landed there. Once he had his T-28 loaded with buffalo meat, his engine problem disappeared and he took off and returned to 20A. The second time he tried this "engine problem" routine, he forgot his flaps and ran off the end of the runway at Lima Lima. He was uninjured, but a few weeks later forgot his flaps at 20A and ran into a warehouse at the end of the runway. He announced he would go to Vientiane to a monastery "to get a new Buddha."

Lima Lima was also the location of the only time I ever got sick in an airplane. We had a rowdy drunken party at 20A one night that lasted well into the morning hours. Applying the Air Force guidance of "no smoking for 12 hours prior to flying and no drinking within 50 feet of the aircraft" (or maybe it was supposed to be the other way around), I took off with a very significant hangover. After my first mission, I refueled and rearmed at Lima Lima and my back seater took me to the local army unit to get something to eat. I seem to recall something like sticky rice and boiled water buffalo, which remained in my stomach only until just after takeoff. Fortunately, it was a relatively quiet day in the air war, and Smoky Greene (he was under the weather, too) and I returned to 20A early.

When we had slow times, we sometimes amused ourselves at 20A by going to the local firing range to shoot the many and varied weapons we had. I had a WWII .45 caliber submachine gun (a "grease gun"); someone had a Russian sniper rifle; and we all had some type of pistol and an AR-15 (our favorite personal weapon). We fired lots of rounds for several hours, although I only remember going there once or twice, so it was not a regular event. A couple of times when we were bored, we would take one of our rockets apart, exposing the solid rocket fuel open at both ends. We would then use gunpowder from a .50 caliber bullet to ignite the rocket fuel. It would make an awful racket with flames shooting out both ends of the tube until it eventually burned out. We were lucky we were not blown to kingdom come. Most of our entertainment at 20A was the nightly bash at the Raven bar. When I first arrived, we had a maintenance man named Les who could play guitar and sing country and western songs. After he left, I played some, but was never any good. Come to think of it, I got better as the night rolled on. I should have spent time in the local village getting to know the Hmong, but I saw my job as flying and concentrated on that. Once when USAF Major General Pettit (7/13 AF Commander at Udorn) visited 20A with his aide, the party got rowdy and the aide was thrown through a window at the CIA bar and onto Floyd the bear's cage. General Pettit's remark to Joe Potter was that the Ravens looked like a bunch of Mexican bandits. After the general left, we all donned our best Mexican bandit paraphernalia and posed for the now-famous group photo, which was sent to General Pettit. We were flying to exhaustion, getting shot at on every mission, and were in no mood to be lectured to about our appearance.

Getting shot at was not new to me as a Raven. As a Nail FAC over the Ho Chi Minh Trail in southeastern Laos, I had been shot at by all of the various types of high-caliber antiaircraft guns in Laos. I was even shot at once by a radar-guided 85 mm gun while I was flying in the weather on instruments near Ban Karai pass on the North Vietnamese border. As a Nail, however, I did not get shot at on most missions. The big guns sited along the Ho Chi Minh Trail did not routinely shoot at the FACs until the fighters showed up for fear of giving away their positions. Once in a while, they would try to get lucky with a FAC, but our higher altitude (3,500 feet above the ground or higher) made hits difficult. There were exceptions — Phil Mascari, who became a Nail with me, disappeared one day in his O-2 and was presumably shot down. As a Raven, it was a rare day that I was not shot at, with good reasons. For one, we were flying at much lower altitudes. I would fly anywhere from a few hundred feet up to 1,000 feet in the normal operating areas. Also, the O-1 was much slower than the O-2. We flew at 70 mph versus 125 in the O-2. Moreover, the people shooting at us were mobile and had no fear of giving away their positions. I took a total of 13 hits in my aircraft (none in my body) during my Raven tour. Almost all of my hits were while I was flying below 500 feet but none immediately disabled the aircraft. An aircraft flying really low and slow is a much more tempting target for the troops on the ground. Once in February 1970, when the NVA had pushed back into the northern PDJ, we had several Ravens working in the area. Hmong sites on the hilltops north of the PDJ were reporting taking fire and hearing enemy troops downhill from them. Unfortunately, there was a heavy layer of clouds at about 500 feet, and the friendly sites were in the clouds. I found a hole in the clouds and dropped underneath flying at a couple of hundred feet above ground. I began circling around one of the hilltop sites below the clouds. As I was leaning out the left side of the aircraft looking downhill, I heard a bullet hit the right window. The single small-arms round entered the cockpit about at my right shoulder and hit the gas gauge above my left ear. If the NVA soldier had an automatic weapon or if I had been sitting up straight, he would have had me for sure. It pays to be lucky.

Ravens were lost in record numbers compared to other USAF units in Southeast Asia during the war. In August 1969, two months prior to my arrival, Dan Davis was killed in a midair collision with an F-105 while working an airstrike. I heard about it while I was a Nail FAC. After that, no Ravens were lost until March 26, 1970, five days before I flew back to the States. That seven-month-plus-a-week period was the longest period without losing a Raven from the first (Sam

Deichelmann 9/6/1968) to the last (Skip Jackson 12/24/1972). During that seven-plus-month period and while I was a Raven, the Hmong had pushed the NVA and Pathet Lao out of the PDJ and back to Ban Ban Valley 25 miles to the northeast. There was not the intensity of ground operations during my Raven tour as there was both before and after. Plenty of Ravens were taking hits in their aircraft and some were wounded, but no deaths. As my tour was ending in March 1970, the NVA were on the attack. By the last week of March, the Ravens were not able to spend the night at 20A, and I remember leading a flight of over a dozen O-1's into Udorn.

March 26, 1970 was especially significant to me. On that day, I was at Udorn processing out for my return to the States. I was flying home from Saigon in five days and my combat flying was over. On that day, Henry Allen had only a few weeks left in his tour (he had extended longer than I did because he wanted more leave time between his Nail and Raven tours). He took Richard Elzinga, a new Raven, on an orientation flight in an O-1 from Vientiane up to the PDJ area. They checked in after takeoff but were never heard from again. Richard's remains were recovered many years later, but Henry's were not. Although I was processed out and was not supposed to fly, I got an O-1 and joined in the search for Henry and Richard. I searched for three days, then had to leave to catch my flight home. Henry Allen and I arrived in Vietnam together, went to NKP together as Nail FACs, and went to Ravens together (although Hank had taken a longer leave back in the States and his return date to the States was a few weeks after mine). Although occurring at the very end of my Raven tour, Henry's loss affected me more than anything. Henry was a bit older than me and was a steadying influence on me. He liked to party, too, but was not as reckless a party animal as I was. He was recognized for his serious approach to the mission and was checked out in the T-28 in addition to the O-1. Around December of 1969, Henry was wounded in the T-28 by a .51 caliber (12.7 mm) anti-aircraft round. He was hit in the left arm and lost a lot of blood before he was able to get the aircraft back to 20A. Henry Allen was a good friend and a great pilot. His loss is with me daily.

When Henry Allen was wounded in December, all the Ravens airborne at the time stopped what they were doing and tried to assist him, especially in case he had to bail out. When an aircraft was shot down, Ravens were known for being on the spot and providing assistance. Air America was also a workhorse for getting pilots picked up and brought back to the friendlies. I worked one search and rescue (SAR) as a Raven. A reconnaissance RF-4, call sign Bullwhip 12, was hit and had to bail out just west of Ban Ban Valley. A fast FAC was in the area. I heard the radio traffic and arrived within five minutes. The SAR site was just north of the main enemy infiltration road, Route 7, and at first there was a lot of confusion. The first thing I heard on Guard (the emergency frequency 243.0 MHz) was someone shouting "They're all around me. Strafe the chute!" Then another voice calmly saying "I'm okay. Don't strafe the chute." I found a parachute in tall grass in the open and flew over it at about 100 feet. I determined that one of the two-man crew was there, and he said he was okay and was staying put. I searched the area and finally located the second parachute in jungle about 200 meters southwest of the first chute. The second crewman had left his chute and evaded west in the jungle. He had seen military personnel near his location and was calling for us to strafe the area to prevent his capture. I put a smoke rocket on his chute from a very low altitude, and directed the fast FAC in strafe runs in the area. Another set of fighters were diverted to me from another target, and I used their leftover 20 mm ammunition to strafe the area, too. That downed pilot was reassured and was able to hide and stop evading. An Air America UH-1 helicopter came up on the radio, but I told him not to attempt a pickup because of the activity on the ground. Eventually, a USAF helicopter ("Jolly Green") came in with his A-1 fighter escort (the "Sandies"). The Sandy A-1s were pilots who specialized in SAR. They were a highly decorated and fearless bunch and their aircraft carried an enormous mix of various munitions that might be needed in a SAR. The Sandies would risk all to protect the pilot on the ground and "their" Jolly Green helicopters. I heard that in late 1969 some of the other A-1 pilots at NKP petitioned to be allowed to fly as Sandies, so they could get credit for these high-visibility missions. The Sandies on my SAR with Bullwhip 12 were of this later variety. The Sandy Low Lead, who directs the SAR and takes the most risks, never came below a 1,500-foot thin cloud layer in the area. At one point he directed the Jolly Green to the wrong site for the pilot in the jungle, and I had to come on the radio to tell the Jolly where to go. Nevertheless, the mission was a success and both crewmen were picked up safely and uninjured.

After my incident below the clouds in the northern PDJ in February 1970, I think Bob Foster (the Raven Mother FAC in Vientiane) got a little nervous about me and moved me to Vientiane for the last month of my tour. D. Craig Morrison had been the FAC flying out of Vientiane (there was only one Raven FAC in Vientiane.), and he was at the end of his tour. I became Raven 23. The Vientiane Raven supported the Royal Laotian Army (RLA) in Military Region 5 along the Mekong River east of Vientiane. Craig said the area was very tame and he never got shot at in MR 5. He showed me where to land (on a road at a nearby Laotian Army base) to pick up a back seater and gave me a tour of the flying area. He and I also flew low level along the Mekong River enroute back to Vientiane, which was great fun. I always enjoyed my return trips down on the river and only dipped my wheels in the water twice. On my second mission in MR 5, my back seater and I found a Pathet Lao soldier running across a field. I flew low and the RLA back seater fired his M-79 grenade launcher out the window. I don't think we hit the enemy soldier, but we must have scared him pretty badly before he was able to escape into the jungle. The next day we returned to the area and a local army unit reported engaging an NVA unit. I was able to get some fighters from up north and we bombed the NVA unit heavily. The Royal Laotian Army unit reported finding numerous wounded and killed NVA, and one prisoner reported that he was severely wounded next to an NVA general and thought the general had to have been killed. I took two hits from a .51 caliber machine gun in the wing root on the right side, puncturing the fuel tank. We made it back to Vientiane leaking fuel, and the maintenance personnel were amazed to see actual damage from ground fire. It was a new thing in that area at that time. Since I had put the only O-1 out of commission and could not fly the next day, and since Henry Allen had come down that day for a short break, I decided Henry and I could party hardy. We stayed out very late, and I was very hung over the next morning at daylight when Colonel Foster knocked on the door telling me I needed to fly back out to where I had bombed the NVA. I protested that the O-1 was inoperative, but he said there was a U-17. I protested that I had never been in a U-17, but he said "The crew chief will start it for you." That's what happened, and I became a U-17 pilot.

I did not like the U-17 as well as the O-1 because it was heavier and had a wheel instead of a stick for flying the aircraft. Also, the throttle was a knob that slid into and out of the instrument panel like most civilian light aircraft do, as opposed to the throttle levers on the left side of the O-1 cockpit. The nearest I ever came to crashing was in the U-17. I was sent to a dirt strip north of Vientiane to pick up three Royal Laotian Army officers and bring them back to Vientiane. I found the place okay, landed, and loaded the three officers and their gear. The officers had not seen each other in a while, and proceeded to converse animatedly in Lao while I taxied out for takeoff. I was still fairly new in the U-17, but I knew it felt much heavier on takeoff than I was used to in the O-1. As we picked up speed on takeoff, I put both hands on the wheel to pull the aircraft into the air. Suddenly I felt the aircraft slow and the stall warning horn sounded. I looked down and found that the throttle had backed out to near idle. I immediately pushed it to full forward and struggled to keep the aircraft flying. Fortunately, a farmer had cut down the trees for a field just south of the airstrip, and we went across that field between the trees with the stall warning horn blaring and the non-pilot Army officers continuing their conversations oblivious to the danger. I recovered and flew on to Vientiane. Lucky again.

Another word about my then-girlfriend, Martha Hawes, because she influenced my life and career, then and now. I went back to the States on leave in February 1970. During that leave, Martha and I became engaged. I wrote her often and even wrote her a letter on the back of one of my little-used maps of Laos. I returned to the States March 31, 1970 to fly T-38's as an instructor pilot at Laughlin AFB, Del Rio, Texas. Martha and I were married June 27, 1970 and are married still. I retired from the Air Force after 20 years, went to law school, then retired (for good) after 21 years as a lawyer.

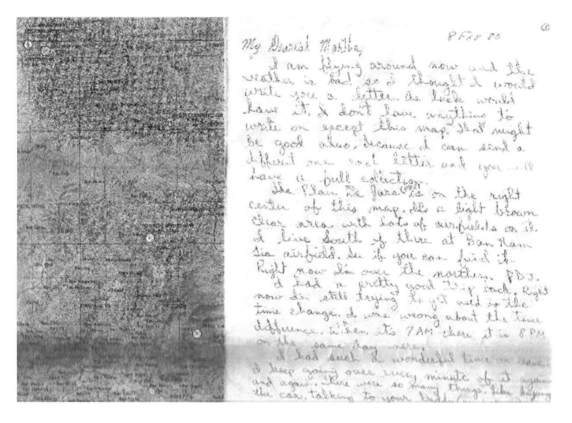

As I said, I regret not having kept records of my time as a Raven. I still remember a lot about that time. Joe Potter took me with him to dinner at General Vang Pao's house, and I met the General several other times. As with all the Ravens at 20A, he gave me a Meo ring which I cherish. I went to the first Raven reunion at Randolph AFB, Texas and have started going again after a many-year absence. I continue to miss my friends who were lost as Ravens, but I also look forward to a continuing camaraderie with the surviving Ravens. We did a special job under significantly difficult and dangerous conditions. I am lucky to be a Raven and will always be proud to be a Raven.

Chapter 15

William E. Platt, Raven 43
Long Tieng, Dec 1969 – Jun 1970

The Secret War
The first casualty when war comes is truth.
- H. Johnson

Call me "Tiny." I was a Raven forward air controller (FAC) at Long Tieng from December 1969 to June 1970. My call sign was Raven 43. I was a 24-year-old USAF first lieutenant pilot with six months of combat experience. In South Vietnam (SVN), I flew the O-1 Bird Dog, low and slow,

William E. Platt, September 1969 RVN

in support of the 5th Special Forces, "Montagnard" Mobile Strike Force operations along the Cambodian border. Bu Prang, A236, Duc Lop, A239, and their outlying firebases Kate, Martha, Annie, Susan, and Helen were my net responsibility. Under President Nixon's program of Vietnamization, the 23rd Division, Army of the Republic of Vietnam (ARVN), was replacing U.S. Special Forces units in my area of operation. I did not want to work for an ARVN General. After witnessing ARVN cowardly leadership and their anti-Montagnard bigotry I volunteered for a classified mission in the mountains of northern Laos. I now had extensive experience with close air support of hilltop firebases. The defense of Special Forces A-camps under siege by the People's Army of Vietnam (PAVN) was a skill requiring judgment gained by experience. We often controlled airstrikes on top of the enemy who closed to within 75 yards of friendly positions. I was fast-tracked into the Steve Canyon program. I was at the right place at the right time to go where my combat skills were needed.

American Embassy, Vientiane - 13 December 1969

I arrived at the U.S. Embassy in Vientiane, Laos. I was greeted by the Assistant Air Attaché, Lt. Col. John Garrity, who provided my initial Laos orientation briefings. John walked me around the embassy and introduced me to some of the staff. I met Ambassador Godley, the Air Attaché, Col. Tyrrell, and some the U.S. Air Attaché (AIRA) staff who supported Raven FAC operations at the five forward locations in Laos. Next we visited the Army Attaché, and I met a few of the U.S. Army Attaché (ARMA) staff, followed by United States Agency for International Development (USAID) refugee officers, and chief of station representatives.

In John's office, he began a series of briefings with the following topics: 7/13th AF fighter assets; General Vang Pao and his fight for Hmong freedom; SKY field officers; the USAID mission; Pop Buell and the LS20 hospital; Air America and Continental Air Service operations; Thai Army (RTA) (PARU) and Air Force units (RTAF) in Military Region II (MR II); the three-legged Laotian government status; the Royal Laotian Army (RLA) disunity; Royal Lao Armed Forces (FAR); Royal Lao Air Force (RLAF); Lao Neutralist Armed Forces (FAN); the Pathet Lao (PL), (LPF), (LPLA).

The briefings continued with a map of Pathet Lao and Peoples Army of Vietnam (PAVN) units locations, status and recent activity. John summarized the opium trade history, refugee evacuations, relocation centers, humanitarian food drops, and refugee medical services. He described our aerial re-supply of Special Guerrilla Units (SGUs) in the field and the overall expectations of Raven forward air controllers in Laos. The next morning I was on a Lao C-47 headed for Long Tieng.

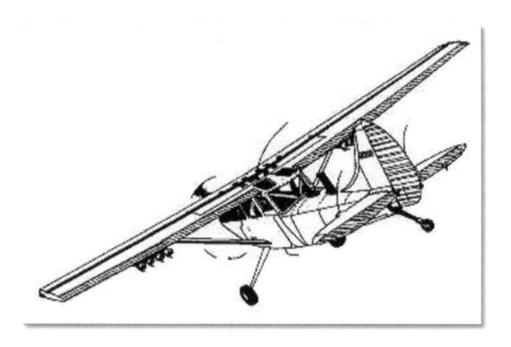

Raven 49, Craig Morrison 1969

Craig Morrison, was instrumental in recruiting me into the Raven program, met me with a brotherly smile. Craig introduced me to the departing Air Operations Center (AOC) commander Joe Potter, and his follow-on AOC Jerry Rhein. These men were veteran special operations commando professionals. Their leadership and expertise kept our O-1 and T-28 aircraft flying and fighting. The head Raven was Col. Bob Foster, call sign Raven 01. His job was to keep the young Ravens ready and able to fight. He was the buffer and absorbing shield between us and myriads of upper-echelon blame-game detractors. "Just do your job and stay healthy," he said, "I will keep the monkeys off your back." — and he did. Bob Foster lived in Vientiane and flew to each Air Operations Center to encourage our teamwork and evaluate out combat readiness, stress level and wellbeing. He read pilots well and grounded fatigued loose cannons when necessary.

Craig Morrison immediately began my Long Tieng orientation with detailed briefings and explanations of The Big Picture:

• *People*

Raven personnel rotations, Project 404 maintenance technicians, SKY team leader "Hog", Jerry Daniels. Refugees issues and conditions at LS20A, Hmong soldier attrition, Hmong women taboos, Thai and Lao artillery units in MR II, Special Guerrilla Units (SGUs) in MR II, Royalists (FAR) and Neutralists (FAN) units in MR II, Pathet Lao communists current strongholds, PAVN 312th Division dry season campaigns and strategies.

• *Places*

Long Tieng, Skyline Ridge, Sam Tong, Mong Soui, Plain of Jars (PDJ), Xieng Khouang City, Kang Khay, Chinese Cultural Center, rules of engagement, Ban Ban Valley dangers, Nong Het, Fish's Mouth, Barthelemy Pass, and Xam Neua.

• *Lima Sites*

LS20A, LS20, LS72, LS15, LS 108, LS22, LS32, LS36, LS50, LS85. Lessons learned from the battles of Phou Pha Thi and Dien Bien Phu.

• *PDJ roads and trails*

Rt. 4, 4z, 72, 4/7 split, 71/ 77 split, 7/ 6 split, 7/71 split, 71/74 split

• *Rivers*

Nam Ngum, Nam Phu, Nam Khaum, tributary streams,

• *Mountains and caves*

Phou Bai, Phou Nok Kok, Phou Pha Thi, Phou Gnouan, Phou Houat, Phou Nok, Phou Phaxai, Phou San, Phou Lat Tai.

• *Raven Survival Tactics*

Jink and yaw, one pass, no repeated orbits, random heading attacks, two-ship high-low formation when scouting low-and-slow, fuel reserves, Search and rescue procedures, Air America net, stories of life and death told by other Ravens.

• Radio frequencies UHF, VHF, HF, maps, navigation aids on Skyline Ridge, TACAN Ch. 98, ADF improvised approach to L20A. C130 Airborne Command, Control and Communication (ABCCC) call signs, Cricket and Alley-Cat. Anti Aircraft Artillery warnings and advisories. PAVN Pathet Lao (PL) strongholds Kang Khay, Nong Pet, Ban Ban, Nong Het, Xam Neua.

• *Things*

Personal weapons, ammunition, water, food, medical assistance.

Now I understood. Ravens in MR II were to be airborne, behind enemy lines and over the battlefield, eight to ten hours a day regardless of weather conditions and restrictions. We defended SGUs, Lima Sites, and fortified hilltop outposts from North Vietnamese Army (NVA) assault. Our mission was to fly and fight in support of the charismatic Hmong General Vang Pao. His leadership was the key to maintaining Laotian sovereignty and pro-American influence. If MR II fell to the communists, Laos, Cambodia, and South Vietnam could quickly fall, and Thailand would be next.

General Vang Pao loved his Hmong soldiers and pilots as sons. They in turn faithfully obeyed his every order. Ravens also were proud to call him our general. He led from the front lines and risked his life among his men. Everyone in Long Tieng honored and respected his cunning, and determined leadership. The Hmong soldiers were superior fighters and often able to defeat numerically superior PAVN units with quick reaction helicopter assault maneuvers and tactical surprise. U.S. air power provided air superiority over the Barrel Roll skies, allowing airdrop of food and materials to hundreds of Lima Sites, villages, and SGU locations in Military Region II. Covert U.S. FACs and tactical bombers became the blunt force instrument of attack since artillery support was limited to just a few MR II stronghold positions.

December 1969 and January 1970 brought frequent PAVN assaults on our remote mountaintop outpost on Phou Nok Kok.

Surviving the First Flight - 18 December 1969

My Plaines des Jarres (PDJ) orientation flight with Donald Craig Morrison, Raven 49, was an eye-opening first exposure to enemy anti-aircraft weapons. He showed me where the gunners were hiding and how to survive in this very hostile environment. Raven 49 was an extraordinary friend and warrior brother. His aerial skill, can-do-anything attitude, intellect, humor, and strength of character were life-saving for me.

After an aerial tour of the PDJ, we struck a mountainside bunker complex northeast of Ban Thak and Rt. 72. As we initiated the pull-up, a 12.7 machine gun opened up from an adjoining karst 200 yards south of our target. Tracers were flying by as I barked "Duck" into the microphone. Craig was crouched low in the T-28 front seat when a heavy round went through the cowl and slammed into the engine. "Tiny, are you OK?" "I am good," I replied.

Instantly the windscreen was covered in oil, and the engine vibration was violent. Time warped to slow motion. I took a deep breath and regained some semblance of composure.

The wounded motor fought to pull us through the shadows of a very dark valley. Time compressed. Just in case, I whispered, "Good-bye, I love you" to my wife and family. I was helpless to alter the course of events. Craig headed home as I prepared to eject. My ejection pins were pulled, the canopy was closed and locked, my straps and harness were cinched tight, my helmet strap snug, visor down, survival radio on. I was ready for Craig's "Bail out, bail out, bail Ooooo" command. The lead A-1 Sky raider we were controlling closed in to assess the damage to our T-28D. "We will escort you to Long Tieng in case you Ravens have to bail out." "Copy Firefly, Thanks."

A-1 battle damage assessment PDJ, 1969

The last ridgeline was still above us as Craig clawed for altitude at 100 feet per minute. The engine vibration was worsening. Our airspeed was bleeding off to near stall, and a rocky ridge remained a solid wall in our path. The foot pedal pre-stall vibration warning was constant and ominous. Craig nursed down 10 degrees of flaps. Our shattered T-28D cyclone motor made one last shuddering pull, and we cleared the last ridge to Long Tieng by at least 10 feet. Down into the valley we fell in a post-stall recovery. "Gear down, full stop." We glided to a safe landing, pulled off the runway, and shut down our valiant beast. That was my PDJ orientation flight, and just a mere sample of what was to come in the months ahead. During my time at Long Tieng, four Ravens were killed on initial orientation flights to the PDJ.

That night, NVA lead elements bypassed our Phou Nok Kok outpost and motored quickly down Rt. 7 to mount a diversionary tank assault on Xieng Khouang City. The ruse attack on this provincial crossroad center drew attention from their commando-style attack on LS22. The NVA objective was to destroy the captured heavy artillery and PT-76 tanks parked inside the perimeter wire of the LL (Lima Lima) airfield. The enemy sapper teams (commandos) were successful and sabotaged many of the long-range artillery and tanks they had abandoned to Vang Pao's forces during his Operation About Face rout across the PDJ.

Combat Operations over the PDJ

19 December 1969

I flew my next mission with an experienced Robin scout, Wa Ger Chang — we called him "Scar." On the way to the PDJ in our O-1 Bird Dog, Scar shared his personal story and his total loyalty to his leader General Vang Pao. His English was good, and he had been a Robin scout for three years. He was shot down and wounded twice. Scar pointed out his home village and shared a story about the atrocities of the Pathet Lao on his family. His fight was personal, and he expected to fight until

186

killed in action, a death defending his people. He would join the spirits of Hmong soldiers and ancestors who perished fighting the Communist thugs of MR II.

As we cruised toward the Plaine des Jarres, I began to see bomb craters and ruins from decades of modern conflict. For hundreds of years these awesomely beautiful high plateaus and mountain valleys had drawn bands of marauding soldiers to oppress the local tribes and control their opium trade. A mixed population of farmers, traders, and soldiers, from distant regions, colonized this wilderness. Ethnic minorities, tribes, and clans fled persecution and migrated south from China to unsettled, remote, mountain sanctuaries. Clear streams and shallow rivers poured from the mountains and meandered through the PDJ. The Nan Ngum River then re-entered the mountains and flowed south in route to the Mekong River 100-plus miles downstream.

Over thousands of years, Chinese, Khmer, Thai, Vietnamese, and Lao trade and military caravans traveled along ancient mountain footpaths to barter for the local cash crop, black tar opium. In a world of pain and suffering, opium was a treasured painkiller good for the body and mind in moderations. In their austere environment shaman practiced healing with ghost medicines and spiritual solutions from antiquity. More than 60 ethnically diverse, hill-tribe subculture settlements were spread across vast mountain and valleys of the Annamite Cordillera Luang Prabang range, and the Phi Pan Nam Mountains. Miao, Meo, White Hmong, Blue-green Hmong, Yao, Black Hmong, Tao, and Flower Hmong and others, maintained unique traditions, language, dress and customs. Many Hmong clans united under the leadership of General Vang Pao. Their mountain fortress strong hold in 1970 was Long Tieng. Ancient tribal disputes and long-standing animosities gave way to the need for mutual security. Freedom and independent self-rule was the common hope of these tribal warriors. They had a shared dream, a vision of a homeland of their own. A state of freedom, self-rule, sharing and equality.

Scar and I flew over a southern PDJ site of megalithic stone jars and made radio contact with a road watch team monitoring traffic on Rt. 7. They pinpointed a small Pathet Lao concentration guarding the road intersection of Rt. 7 and Rt. 4. We called for fighter aircraft and bombarded the enemy hideout with two flights of F-4 Phantoms from Udorn Thailand. When the day's work ended, we had located and destroyed three more small enemy outposts.

Jars and bunkers, PDJ, 1970

Thai fire base, 1970

21 December 1969

Northwest of the PDJ Hmong villages were threatened by menacing PAVN patrols, so a massive evacuation of women, children, and elderly was begun to remove them to safety before the enemy could muster a major attack on their settlements. We provided air cover for refugee evacuation corridors from distant Lima Site villages to secure refugee resettlement areas including Sam Tong and Long Tieng. USAF H-53s, Air America C-123Ks, Caribous', and C-130s bailed from combat re-supply of SGUs to USAID humanitarian evacuation missions. I estimate more than 8,000 refugees were gathered from villages north of Muong Soui and airlifted to safer areas of Laos during December 1969. It was a monumental airlift accomplishment, and we were proud to be part of the evacuation of war refugees.

Phou Nok Kok, January 1970

The People's Army of Vietnam (PAVN) soldiers needed a motivational victory after the humiliating retreat and defeat before Vang Pao's "About Face" campaign of 1969. I could envision the helicopter leapfrog assault on strategic PDJ hilltops by Royal Laotian paratroopers and Hmong Special Guerrilla Units (SGUs). Parachute assaults from RLAF C-47 aircraft by Hmong guerilla units and FAR paratroopers were made to re-occupy Xieng Khouang City and capture the nearby airfield dubbed LL or LS22. Operation About Face was an inexcusable defeat for the PAVN that must have infuriated General Vo Nguyen Giap. He doubled down with fresh soldiers and ordered two full divisions to retake and hold the entire Xieng Khouang Province. The PAVN plan was to siege and destroy Vang Pao's irregulars, the FAR army, Thai forces, and our strongholds throughout MR II.

Phou Nok Kok was a tall mountain with a commanding view of the surrounding terrain. Below and to the north of the outpost was Rt. 7 as it departed deep mountain passes into the Ban Ban Valley at Ban Lo. To the east in the Ban Ban were the PAVN storage depots, food stockpiles, troop concentrations, and equipment mobilized to advance. They were preparing to break through this critical choke point and storm back west along Rt. 7 to recapture the Plaines des Jarres.

Phon Nok Kok Rt.7 outpost airdrop, January 1970

The remote outpost on top of Phou Nok Kok (PNK) was comprised of two seasoned SGUs. One was Hmong, and the other was Lao Theung from MR IV. The SGU officers were advised by SKY field officers Will Green and Jim Atkins. Their radio call sign at that time was "Black Lion". Our outpost was pinned down by constant pressure from the PAVN. When conditions permitted our observers were often able to spot enemy concentrations in the valley below. Raven FACs located and directed airstrikes on many truck parks and hidden stores in the Ban Ban Valley. Scores of bombing sorties were made every day in defense of this precarious perimeter of trenches, bunkers, wire, and claymore mines. Three hundred vulnerable men on top of PNK temporarily choked off the advance of many thousand humiliated Communist soldiers.

The PAVN could not leave another functioning outpost behind their advancing columns. LS32 and LS36, to the north, and LS 02 were also under severe pressure.

The NVA planned to overpower our Phou Nok Kok (PNK) mountaintop outpost and speed west on Rt. 7 to re-assert their dominance of Military Region II. They were poised for a blitzkrieg sweep across the PDJ. They knew the terrain well and planned to re-occupy their old haunts that controlled the dirt roads of the northeast PDJ. They expected a crushing defeat of our PNK outpost that would demoralize the five remaining Hmong hilltop outposts still overlooking the Plaines des Jarres. The PAVN mobilized and re-equipped an overwhelming force of two divisions to conquer the PDJ plateau again.

The NVA patiently waited for low ceilings and reduced visibility to hinder the airpower defense of the PNK outpost. Smoke and haze from dry season agricultural slash and burn fires obscured flight visibility and target acquisition along Rt. 7.

Black Lion's outpost was the lonely keeper of the floodgate delaying the PAVN advance. A few hundred men in foxholes were a festering thorn in the side of the NVA logistics net and military pride. Jim Adkins, call sign "Swamp Rat" and Will Green, "Black Lion" were the U.S. flesh on the mountain. One SGU was Hmong and the others were Lao Theung from MR III. Tribal aversions, mistrust, and language variations were nonissues when cooperation was needed for survival. Diversity became working for a common good? Mortars, recoilless rifles, a French 76 canon, machine guns, grenades, Ravens, and airpower maintained the defense. The US and Lao Air Force C-47 gunships learned to guard the outposts at night.

Black Lion could occasionally monitor the north Ban Ban Valley up to Rt. 6 toward Sam Neua, or down Rt. 7 southeast toward the foul "Fish's Mouth" and Barthelemy Pass. Twenty-five miles east was the Laos/Vietnamese border. Russian truck convoys filled with NVA soldiers and supplies flowed down this upper tentacle of the Ho Chi Minh Trail. Flares lit up the night. A1 Sky raiders and Dragon gunships patrolled with mini-guns, lights out.

8 January 1970

Today, wounded soldiers could not be evacuated from Phou Nok Kok; medical supplies and body bags were in short supply. Water and ammunition were rationed due to meager supplies and the inability of resupply aircraft to reach the outpost for several days. The battered warriors were exhausted. They hunkered down under continuous bombardment by rockets, mortars, and sapper thrusts through the wire. Now a weakened fighting force, they made desperate calls for close air support.

A few Ravens were able to sneak under the low cloud deck, weave through mountain passes, and reach the Black Lion outpost. Just the sight and sound of our aircraft overhead may have dissuaded immediate enemy attack. Our airplane presence boosted our soldiers' morale for an instant. We would fire our rockets at tree lines and fire our AR-15 rifles out the window toward suspected sniper positions, trying to draw attention to ourselves and provide momentary respite for our battered soldiers. We patrolled and circled the camp below the overcast cloud layers. We evaded the enemy fusillade until our fuel was Bingo. Then we had to leave. Abandonment of our vulnerable soldiers to a vengeful enemy was a mental horror for all of us. We fought the best we were able. This time, it was not enough.

As the situation worsened, Ambassador Godley mandated that SKY officers return to Long Tieng at night. Reluctant, angry, and frustrated, Will Green complied and left his troops on the PNK precipice, maybe to die without him. Sturdy men agonize for brave friends left behind. Allies cornered, outnumbered, outgunned, and dying in the mud was a horrifying scenario for us to digest.

10 January 1970

American pilots, crews, support personnel, and SKY field officers shared the PNK soldiers' ordeal. By night, we had warm food, cold beer, a refreshing shower, and a soft bed. Our SGU brothers had been awake and fighting for their lives for days. There was little hope of rescue. I prayed for their safety and our courage. There were whispers in my dark room to my family back home, "I miss you!"

191

Now, out of resources, our exhausted fighters chose survival over death. They fought bravely as long as possible. On the night of Jan 10, 1970, they bolted off the high ground and down west into the forest. They escaped and evaded most enemy patrols on the 25-mile gantlet back to the momentary safe harbor of LS22. Many valiant soldiers did not survive that hostile trek. Good men were lost because evacuations were planned too late to execute during fair weather.

We each left a piece of our innocence on that blood-stained mountain. For me, Phou Nok Kok is a mountain shrine to the spirit of courage and a limestone marker to life's fragility. We awoke before dawn to fly, find, and defend the brave remnant.

11-30 January 1970

After the fall of Phou Nok Kok, NVA convoys rolled west to the 7/71 split under the cover of low cloud decks and the smoky haze of slash and burn agricultural fires. The PAVN re-occupied their old defensive positions along Rt. 7 and restocked their storage bunkers, ammo dumps, and POL (petroleum, oil, and lubricants) facilities as they advanced west to the PDJ.

25th Birthday - 13 January 1970

We flew north on Rt. 7 over Arrowhead Dam; we spotted a wisp of smoke rising from a hill near Nong Pet. My back-seat scout and chief of the Robin translators was the ferocious Maj. Yang Bee.

"Raven, go to the low. Enemy!" Yang Bee's arm rested on my shoulder as he pointed northeast, and glassed the valley trail 800 feet below with binoculars. "Many enemy, no friendlies here. Call fighters, many trucks, many NVA. We kill!"

My Hmong back-seater, Yang Bee,
had the eyes of an eagle to see,
His enemies run before his gun,
VP's chief "Robin" was he.

We separated from the target area to gain altitude. I took a deep breath and provided the strike briefing to inbound A-1 fighter aircraft.

"Copy Sandy21, CBU 24, Mark 84s, and strafe."

"You will be cleared random headings, multiple passes."

"The ceiling is 1,200 feet broken and clearing. Latest altimeter is 29.80. I will climb on top, rendezvous with you, and lead you to the target."

"Tally Ho!"

"You will see bunkers on both sides of the ridge line; a smoldering troop encampment is under the gray smoke on top. Looks like a breakfast gathering gone wrong. Hit my smoke on your first pass."

"In the ravine, under the low trees and bushes, are bunkers. Trucks are in the tree lines by the rice paddies to the north. I say again, small arms anticipated; no larger weapons observed but very possible. "

"Please save some 20 mm cannon to cover my post-strike bomb damage assessment (BDA). Tell me what you see on your run in. Good luck!"

"Raven, Sandy 21 lead, we have you and the smoke in sight."

"CLEARED HOT! Sandy, hit my smoke."

"Lead is in from the northeast…exit left."

"Small arms flash fifty yards south of the smoke, troops in the open."

"Sandy 21, number two is in from the south on the flash, west departure. FAC and Lead are in sight."

"Tally-Ho. CLEARED HOT!"

The Tank - 23 January 1970

PT 76 tanks Rt. 7, 1970

The NVA set a PT-76 tank carcass in the middle of Rt. 7. It was about four miles east of the entrance to the Ban Ban Valley. The tank was just north of our old forward position on Phou Nok Kok. What an excellent target. I made a low pass and snapped a photograph.

Somehow, this target did not look or feel right; too easy, too conspicuous. The engine cover was removed, and a track was off one side. The opportunity to direct an airstrike on a tank was exciting to say the least.

193

I first located it while scanning Rt. 7 with my field glasses. I reported my location to "Cricket" who began to find available fighters with the best ordnance to destroy the tank. I descended to about 700 feet out of sight of the tank and readied my 35 mm Asai Pentax camera to capture this handsome target. My windows were open, and my right hand held my camera. My left hand was on the stick as I kicked opposite rudder and adjusted the trim. I needed to see if there were any gunners defending that PT-76 tank. Threat information is a factor to the fighter pilot's risk/reward quotient.

I banked hard left, snapped this photograph out my left-side window, and there they were, in my face. Long-barreled anti-aircraft weapons protruded from several bunkers on each side of the road. Initially, they were all aimed east down Rt. 7 to my seven o'clock.

The NVA camouflaged nets over the guns were obvious and deep bunkers were plainly visible on both sides of the road. Maybe too late, I realized this was a dangerous target with bite.

Was a prolonged look at a damaged tank worth my life, or those of my fighter pilots? No, not today.

Two 12.7 or 14.5 anti-aircraft weapons were rotating my direction. They wanted to track and lead my progress through the gorge for an easy kill.

I was doing 130 KIAS and diving for speed. My eventual pull-up just about ripped the wings clean off my O-1 Bird Dog. I zoomed and only gained 600 feet of altitude and suffered a loss of airspeed back to L/D max. I kicked rudder and jinked for my life. Then I dove for speed again. This time, it was essential to be well uncoordinated and fly like a twisted purple martin.

White and green tracers flashed by both sides of my canopy. My windows were open, and the sound of popcorn made me get "TINY" in the cockpit. (Thus my nickname "Tiny.") Time stopped, and I was frozen in the mental slow motion of escape. It was like wanting to run and not being able to move my legs.

The tracers were passing further away now as I thanked God for deliverance. Then I composed my pucker. This flak trap almost got me. There would be several more.

I took a deep breath, the first one in 45 seconds. I reported the flack-trap guns to our Airborne Command Control and Communications aircraft 60 miles to the south. My voice was a few octaves higher, but my speech was "Cool Operator."

The C-130 mission commander confirmed that the weather was too poor for fighters to work effectively. They did not have A-1 fighters available. "Come back later Raven 43. We will find you some fighters when conditions in the target area improve."

"Roger, Raven 43 is RTB LS22. I will report LL in sight, over and out."

On departure, and from a standoff range of about two miles, I lobbed all eight of my Willy Pete rockets toward the NVA tank and headed for LS22. Now it was time to re-arm my bird, eat a Meal

Ready to Eat (MRE) for lunch, and drink a quart of water. I pondered the tactics of the hunter and the hunted as I ate.

Three days later, we finished off the tank and guns but it took 24 fighter sorties to destroy them all. We did not take small arms hits. It was a good fight with a good outcome. Everyone earned his keep, and the NVA got a well-deserved nose job. Was it worth the risk of jets to kill a nest of guns? Party Headquarters in downtown Hanoi was off limits now, so these guns were the best target available in our area.

18 February 1970

With the approval of the Laotian King, and Prime Minister, Ambassador Godley ordered up B-52 Arc light strikes on the southern PDJ. This was the first B52 bombardment in MRll. The carpet-bombing of enemy positions inflicted heavy losses but failed to stop the PAVN advance toward Sam Tong and Long Tieng. Enemy determination was evident as they absorbed their losses and replaced their casualties with fresh soldiers.

Each Raven averaged well over 120 hours of close air support missions each month. Every day a Raven controlled six or more flights of fighter-bombers in an attempt to halt the blitzkrieg advance of 12,000 PAVN regular army soldiers. Restlessly they swarmed the PDJ and quickly overran Laotian and Thai army positions.

27 February 1970

Thai Air Force T-28s flew combat sorties out of LS108, Muong Soui until the FAN security abandoned their posts. Muong Soui fell to PAVN pressure, and the RTAF moved their operations to LS15, Ban Na.

Soon the enemy would bypass General Vang Pao's Lima Site line of defense and breach the doorstep of our Long Tieng stronghold. LS20, Sam Tong was abandoned on March 17, 1970. Pop Buell and USAID personnel were evacuated just in time from LS20 as the PAVN shelled the refugee center. They burned the Sam Tong hospital as thousands of refugees scrambled down 19 miles of the freedom highway to the temporary refuge of Long Tieng. The siege of Long Tieng began as additional Royal Thai Army soldiers and artillery units moved into the Long Tieng valley to bolster our defenses.

The forward edge of the battle area became the towering Skyline Ridge overlooking the fortified valley below. The TACAN station and ADF navigational aids atop Skyline were destroyed while 122 mm rockets and mortar shells rained down on refugees, Hmong soldiers, Thai volunteers, FAR units, and American personnel.

The situation was dire so Ambassador Godley sent the Ravens south to Vientiane where the loss of FACs and aircraft would be less likely. We flew back to Long Tieng before first light each day when the weather permitted. We picked up our Hmong scouts and continued to engage the retreating enemy force.

With their supply lines now in disarray, and B52 Arc light missions bombarding their supplies and troop concentrations at the foot of the mountains, the PAVN advance faltered, and Vang Pao's soldiers pushed north to retake Sam Tong.

B52 Arc Light 18 February, 1970

Three camouflaged Pt 76 tanks, PDJ, Rt. 71, 1970

Anti-Aircraft Artillery, Rt. 71, 1970

26 March 1970

Raven FACs Henry Allen and Dick Elzinga disappeared en route from Vientiane to Long Tieng. We expected them to walk out of the mountains and greet us with great survival stories. They were not heard from again. We searched every mountain pass and riverbed for a sign of their crash site or survival markers. We found nothing. Our morale bottomed out for a week. The PAVN had secured the entire PDJ, and our airstrikes were now brutal payback for friends lost. The daily battles continued as new Ravens replaced the fallen FAC friends.

24 April 1970

On a rare fair-weather day, Jim Cross, an MR V Raven, loaded up a new first flight, Raven Dave Reese. It started out as a non-combat shuttle flight to LS20A; both pilots died in a 37 mm shoot-down of their U-17 near the Ban Ban Valley northwest wall. That was their first and last mission in MR II. Why they flew near the deadly Ban Ban, 40 miles east-northeast of LS20A, I could not imagine and do not speculate. Both men were experienced SVN FACs, but neither man was an experienced survivor in the deadly Ban Ban Valley. Decisions made were well intended and seemed reasonable to them at the time. It was not productive or necessary to second-guess dead men and senior warriors. We accepted that everyone did the best they could at the time. Then with a tear and prayer, we moved on with the dangers of the daily mission. Dwelling on the possible causes of the tragedy was fruitless. The lesson learned: never stop jinking in MR II. Never circle an area that looks suspicious. Big guns will track and kill the unsuspecting without warning.

The men I flew with as Ravens were warriors who understood the risks of war. We were all volunteers who relied on each other for survival and encouragement in the leaded MR II environment. We fought behind the enemy front lines and attacked his infrastructure with ferocity and derring-do. We believed that our Laotian and Thai allies deserved an opportunity for freedom from communist oppression. All gave some; some gave all. We will remember the tens of thousands of honorable men from many nations who fought and died for another man's freedom.

O-1, T-28, O-1 Formation, PDJ, 1970

These are the Raven FACs I called brothers in MR II. Every month, battle-weary men rotated home and replacements arrived to fly and fight low and slow in MR II. John Garrity, Joe Potter, Jerry Rhein, Tom Palmer, Ray de Arrigunaga, and Mark Diebolt were experienced senior leaders. We were a volunteer team generating O-1, T-28, and U-17B combat sorties for General Vang Pao's irregular army. Jerry Greven, Bob Dunbar, Al Daines, Karl Polifka, Fred Platt, and Mike Byres finished their Raven tour as I was entering the new Raven ranks at LS20A. Henry "Hank" Allen, Terry "Moose" Carroll, Bill "Koz" Kozma, Melvin "Smoky" Greene, Donald Craig Morrison, Tom "Tee" Harris, Jim "Tee-shirt" Strusaker, "Stanley" L. Erstad, "Weird" Harold Mesaris, "AD" Holt, Craig Duehring, Brian "Iron Bomb" Wages, John Fuller, Jeff Thompson, Park Bunker, Chuck Engle, Bob Foster, Jim Cross, Dave Reese, Dick Elzinga, Skip Jackson, and Joe Bauer, our intelligence officer, were men I respected as brothers in arms. Six of these men were killed by the enemy; many were wounded.

The brave Hmong Robin scouts I flew with included Yang Bee, Yia Kha, Wa Ger Chang, Francis Vang, and a Thai scout I called Boo. The Chao Pao Khou pilots I admired greatly were Yang Xiong, Vang Sue, Vang Cheng, and the phantom 4 Jerry Rhein.

Chao Pha Khao napalm airstrike, 1970

On our flight line were American, Thai, Lao, and Filipino technicians who kept our aircraft ready for combat. Our maintenance specialists, Clyde Barr, Dan, Pop, Bob, Glen, and others worked long nights keeping our aircraft flying and fighting. USAID leaders like Pop Buell, Mac Thompson, and staff provided medical services and food to war refugees numbering in the tens of thousands. Pop Buell established a nursing school at the Sam Tong hospital. I was just a small player in a cast of gallant giants. Hand salute. We did our best for a worthy cause.

SKY officers like Jerry Daniels and airlift contract professionals from Air America and Continental Air Service pilots like Lee Gossett and John Wiren, along with hundreds of cargo kickers, worked tirelessly to accomplish their humanitarian supply, evacuations and hard rice missions. They rescued downed Ravens and fighter pilots from enemy capture. The risks were high and the rewards mostly personal. We were the tip of the spear, and our support system included tens of thousands of Americans and Allies who contributed their all to freedom's cause.

I cannot finish without a shout out of appreciation to all of the aircrews who earned their keep in the Barrel Roll. Fighter pilots, bomber pilots, gunship crews, ABCCC crews, helicopter crews, photo analysts, and behind the scenes special operations personnel who worked so we could fly and fight. It was teamwork and fortitude.

Some 40,000 young Hmong soldiers paid the price to protect their people. They especially are my heroes.

Greater love hath no man than this, that a man lay down his life for his friends.

HD color images link: wep11345.com

Chapter 16

Clyde Barr, Crew Chief
Long Tieng, Dec 1969 – Aug 1970

In 1969 I was stationed at Washington National Airport in a detachment of the 89th Military Airlift Wing (MAW), the home of Air Force One. It was supposed to be a four-year tour of duty. I thought I would not have to worry about being transferred anywhere until my time was up. However, it seems we had pissed off Nixon some way and when he took office, his first act was to deactivate the detachment at National Airport and send everyone to Vietnam. So off we went. I went to the 19th Tactical Air Support Squadron (TASS) at Bien Hoa, Republic of Vietnam.

The time I had at the 89th MAW had been not only good, it had been great. Even though everyone knew their job, it didn't mean that promotions were any easier. One thing stands out in my memory of those days. I had nine years' time in grade and many others had more. Promotions had just been released and not one of us made Technical Sergeant. We were all disgusted.

On that same day, the Representative from South Carolina, L. Mendel Rivers, came by as he was frequently prone to do. He was the Enlisted Man's Friend! He came into the line shack and said, "Boys, what can I do for you?" Several of us spoke up and told him "We need a Navy type system for promotions, testing on both the job knowledge as well as military knowledge. It seems a sight fairer than what we have and in our opinion those who hang out with the 1st Sgt at the club seem to be the ones promoted." He said "Boys, I'm gonna look into it." We never heard a word for over a year and two more promotion opportunities came and went.

In the meantime, my family was getting older and my little girl was starting to go through a set of panty hose every day. I went into my commander's office and told him "Sir, I have over nine years' time in grade as a Staff Sergeant. I am in the top outfit in the Air Force where everyone is hand-picked and I still have not been promoted. He replied, "Sgt Barr you have been far more patient than I would have been and I think you are right. I am going to talk to the wing commander about you."

He did discuss my problem with Col Williams, the wing commander, who did not just call me over to his office but instead drove over from Andrews to meet with me. He told me he was going to bring my problem to the CBPO (Consolidated Base Personnel Office) and he wanted them to conduct a search of every person of my grade and AFSC (Air Force Service Code) and would get back with me, which he did several months later. He came back to see me and told me," Sgt Barr there is nothing in your records to indicate why you should not have been promoted a long time ago. I am going to see the president of the next promotion board to take an extra hard look at your records". He did and I made Technical Sgt the next cycle.

[Editor's Note: Congress was receiving so many complaints about enlisted promotions that Chairman L. Mendel Rivers (D-S.C.) of the House Armed Services Committee named a subcommittee to look into the matter. That panel held hearings on the promotion systems of all the services, but it clearly was most concerned about the Air Force. In fact, it seemed impressed by

Bien Hoa Air Base, Republic of Vietnam

Everyone in the 89th MAW had been hand-picked, their records reviewed for any indication of military problems and thoroughly researched to make sure of their knowledge and job performance. However, when I arrived at Bien Hoa I thought I had been thrown into a lion's den. Nothing to supervise but young airmen who, although good workers, had little real knowledge of the flight line. They required constant supervision, a thing I was not used to. Where I came from, when work came up it evaporated as each person knew and could perform each task the same as I could.

I began running the line truck on the OV-10 flight line, planes coming and going with me trying to keep up with what planes were there, which planes were to get preflight and which planes had squawks that had to be fixed and trying to get guys to fix them. Anyway, I got a call to immediately go over to the office. I went there as soon as I could and was asked if I had any objections on going to a classified location in Thailand and I said I had no objections.

I got my orders, which were mostly blank and really stated nothing. I forget how but I made my way to Saigon and caught a plane to Bangkok. When we got there the passenger service guy looked at my orders and told me these orders are worthless and he would have to contact my outfit for clarification as to our actual destination. He said with these I could go around the world. So the four other guys with me on the same orders and I spent a week waiting in Bangkok.

We wanted to go sightseeing and some Thai military man offered to guide us. He took us to the floating market and had a really good tour. The man who was to be our guide said he knew the owner of the boat we were on so it would not cost us anything. When the tour was over the boat owner/driver took us way out in deep water and told us we had to pay several hundred dollars to get back to shore. None of us has that kind of money but, one guy had just reenlisted and happened to have enough money on him could to get back us to shore. *Live and Learn.*

We finally made it to Udorn and checked in with the 56th Special Operations Wing (SOW), where we learned that our destination was "across the river". We went down and caught the daily shuttle to Vientiane. We didn't know where we were after landing and remained on the airplane when it deplaned passengers at the military side, nobody had briefed us on anything. When we finally were told to deplane, it was on the civilian side of the airport. I went inside and called the embassy which directed my call to the air attaches office. Transportation finally came and took us to the embassy. We were quartered in an embassy house and told to report to the Air Attache the following morning, Christmas Day, 1969. The air attaché asked who the tech sergeant was. When I answered that I was, he said I'm sending you to where the action is. I went back to the airport and soon wound up at Long Tieng, Lima Site 20 Alternate. Again, I wasn't sure where to go and started walking. A CAS (Consolidated American Sources) officer picked me up and told me that they were expecting the president to land any time and wanted all round-eyes off the flight line. I went to our office and met Lou the nine year old boy who came with my job. I realized I was also the house mother who had to shop for groceries. I quickly found the duty day to be from can't see to can't see. I believe we had eight O-1's at that point in time. Thus my time at 20A began.

Happy Valley

We maintenance guys used to call Long Tieng "Happy Valley". I was the crew chief assigned to maintain the O-1's but most of the maintenance was done by the Pilipino mechanics so we mostly loaded ordnance. It was only WP (white phosphorous) rockets for the O-1's. I do remember one time I had to scrounge up a bucket of grenades and the Raven, I forget who it was, was pulling pins on grenades and strafing with his M-16. It took me forever to get all the pins out of the cockpit and some even made it down to the control pulleys.

599 being fueled at Long Tieng March 1970   Photo Courtesy of Wayne Klucas

The T-28's and O-1s mechanics worked together. I remember John Johnson was the line chief. Things were hopping day to day. Ravens coming and going and recycling for rockets. Ravens occasionally putting down for rough engines at Lima Lima, Mong Soui or some other site. I had Hank Allen pick me up from some of these sites several times. He said he could get me sick in an O-1 but he never could.

I remember the time a sapper blew up one of my O-1's. I think we were watching *Gone With the Wind* (how I remember this stuff, I have no clue). One of the CAS guys said: "Oh it's just one of the guns we took up today. Another guy spoke up and said, "Yeah but we didn't take any ammo up." The room emptied fast when everyone split, movie still going on. Anyway, there is a copy of that movie somewhere in Laos or least it was left there.

I helped disassemble seven different airplanes while I was at Alternate. Udorn didn't like it though when we took a crash axe to get the landing gear off Fred Platt's bird when he sat down in a rice patty. I was one of the guys that policed up that airplane. We took it apart wings, engine off, landing gear off and tail off, loaded it on a Jolly Green and we were off the ground in 45 minutes. We had to roll the engine up a rice dike to get it aboard and it took a crash axe to get the landing gear off. Fred told me when I was at an Air Commando reunion he had the prop from that airplane hanging on the wall of his den. How he got that prop I have not a clue.

Sometimes I would send one of our birds to Udorn for excessive oil consumption when they started burning over a quart per hour. Their maintenance guys would send them back saying that the oil consumption wasn't excessive. I argued that the mission we had at Alternate was such that it was excessive. When the only place to sit down was back at the place you took off from, over one quart per hour <u>was</u> excessive.

Clyde and Doc Robinson at Long Tieng

I remember Doc Robinson once telling me to come over to the hospital as he had someone he wanted me to see, I went and he showed me a woman who was starving herself to death and it was too late to save her. She was a walking skeleton. He told me many times they sent patients home to die because the local witch doctors would tell them if they had not gone to the hospital they would be well. Seems like her husband told his wife and the daughter out in the bush and he told her to stay there until he returned and she stayed. Anything she found to eat was given to the daughter who was not nearly in the same shape as her mother. I think the mother died the day after I saw her.

One day I was sitting in that large tent by the O-1 area waiting on my planes to return. I forget who, it might have been me, started whistling a Christian hymn. The two locals who were also sitting in the tent also started singing the same hymn. I was shocked. We sat there for some time singing hymns, me singing in English and the locals singing in Lao or Thai.

Father Buchard, who walked the mountains in Laos spreading the gospel and the Christian faith, would come to the house whenever he was in our area and have a mass for those Ravens of the Catholic faith. I have often thought of him. A fine Christian man, sharing the gospel to people who would never have the opportunity to hear it but for him. What a guy.

Back to nine year old Lou. I was his caretaker and saw to it he had good clothes and generally behaved himself. The house paid for him to go to school. I remember listening to him do his multiplication tables in Thai or Lao. At one point, the enemy was getting so close, they decided to move us and the airplanes to Vientiane for a while. The day we split, Lou came down on the flightline where we were loading ordnance on the AT-28's. He was with the cook and said " me want go Thailand with cook" I had $5 with me and gave it to him. That day, the T-28's were flying 15 minute missions, dropping white phosphorous bombs right at end of the runway. Even VP (General Vang Pao) was down helping load bombs. I never saw Lou again, but would sure like to. I was going to try and bring him home with me but it's a moot point now.

I remember lots of the little things. It was one of the majors I think, we never knew their rank, who came back and parked an O-1. I noticed a hole in the bottom of the cowling and behold, a large hole in the top of the cowling. Looking at the engine, a dud AAA round had split the left magneto like a ripe watermelon. I think it was the same guy that ground looped and flipped an O-1 on landing at Alternate. When we went to the end of the runway he was leaning on the upside down aircraft with its landing gear straight up smoking cigarette. Unconcerned.

I tried to look out for the Ravens the best I could. There was pile of WP rockets down on the flightline behind where our birds were parked. I watched the locals who would use a WP warhead as a hammer to get at the wood of the box. They had buggered up the threads of the rocket head so badly they wouldn't fit in the rocket body. I took a file and filed down the threads until I could get them to fit the rocket body. I asked the pilots if they worked alright and they said yeah. So I got rid of about 50 or more warheads saving the taxpayers a little money. WPs are dangerous laying around in the sun, discarded as they were. Mr. Rhein was going to get EOD to come and blow them up but I saved them that job, and the money too.

I believe I was submitted for a medal back at the 19 TASS, since we were TDY from there. It was classified, they apparently didn't know what to do with it. and I never heard anything more about it. The recommendation was for my saving a T-28 that had gone down in Mong Soui. Air America took several of us mechanics to see if it could be fixed before dark. Air America told us we had 45 minutes and then they were leaving with us or without us. It seems a T-28 flown by one of the locals flew through his own bomb debris and his rudder cable was severed. Don't ask me how, but I managed somehow to cut the two ends from what looked like bird's nest in each end. I managed to use a large electrical lug connector, swedged the connector on with vise grips, put a bolt through the connectors. The other guys had to fix holes in the fuel tanks as it seems the pilot got hosed down by an AK-47 before he could land. It might have taken us a tad more than 45 minutes, but not much longer, and Mr. Rhein flew it back to Udorn.

The Chief of Maintenance in Udorn almost had a heart attack when he saw my fix and had the cable put on a machine that measures strength of cables. He couldn't get the swedges to break. and sent it back to us on a plaque. We put it on the wall, I think in the bar. I would like to have that plaque now. My grandchildren have heard the story, and I think they would like to have my medal also.

A Few Last Words for the Ravens

I remember when you guys would land late and cause us to either eat late or not at all. We would sing, "HIM, HIM, F--- HIM". Seems like another lifetime ago. I'm glad to have been associated with you guys and even though I was not a "Raven" I know I was in a small way responsible for much of the maintenance, launching and recovery of you guys and your planes. We had a really symbiotic relationship as I see it.

Chapter 17

John Fuller, Raven 28
Long Tieng, Mar 1970 – May 1970

It would be a bad two months for those flying near Long Tieng. The North Vietnamese and Pathet Lao had moved south to the other side of Skyline Ridge. Sam Thong and almost every site north had been overrun. Ground fire, weather, and the demands of flying long hours were as bad as ever. Maybe it was just that the bad phi, bad Hmong spirits, had been hiding and now showed up with a vengeance. At the end of March 1970, two Ravens took off from Vientiane, headed north for Long Tieng, and disappeared. That was the day before I showed up. Then an Air America C-130, making a routine descent through the weather into Long Tieng, crashed into Phou Bai mountain, killing all six onboard. They impacted just below the 9,250-foot peak. At the end of April, two more Ravens took a 37 mm round through the wing of their U-17, could not keep flying, and crashed just east of the Plaine des Jarres. They could not be recovered. One month later, I was shot down, picked up by an Air America Huey, and medevacked to the States. The only one lucky enough to make it home.

Prologue

I arrived for Project 404 at Udorn Air Base, Thailand, in March 1970. I had just completed eight months flying from Pleiku AB in Vietnam with the 20th Tactical Air Support Squadron (TASS), call sign Covey. We "crossed the fence" daily into southern Laos. Our primary mission was Steel Tiger, the southern part of the US interdiction program on the Ho Chi Minh Trail. The overall process seemed to be that the Soviets provided all the trucks in the world to the North Vietnamese, who then dispersed and sent them south through the many capillaries of the Trail. The USAF,

Navy, and Army would then wander purposefully through the night, trying every type of technology the US could think of, to find and blow up each individual truck, soldier, or local civilian pressed into service hauling material south to the fight.

I flew the O-2 on those nights, with a navigator in the right seat, hanging his head almost out the open window with an AN/PVS 2 Starlight scope. Most of the "navs" were senior to us young pilots; they deserved a medal for just strapping in with us. We droned through the night, searching for trucks, which were difficult to find even on a good night. The AAA (antiaircraft artillery) was pretty easy to see, however, as it tried to find us.

Bernard C. Nalty wrote at the end of his book, *The War Against Trucks: Aerial Interdiction in Southern Laos 1968-1972,* that "without precise knowledge of the carefully concealed network of roads and trails, pipelines and streams, the Air Force in Southeast Asia could not direct its weapons, many of them ill-suited for the job at hand, against North Vietnamese troops and supplies in southern Laos or assess accurately the damage that was done. In short, the airmen spent almost five years and billions of dollars trying with courage, determination, and ingenuity to do the impossible." He failed to mention the people who lost their lives in this pursuit, but I get his point. No source I am aware of estimates we ever stopped more than 15 percent of material flowing south.

In August of 1969, John LeHecka and I first flew into Pleiku in a Covey O-2 sent to get us at DaNang, the 20th TASS headquarters. We were each on our first operational assignment. My personal call sign became Covey 579; his became 580. John had a few years on me, as he had spent a tour in the Peace Corps near what is now Bangladesh. He was married, and was a bit more settled than most of us first lieutenants.

About five months after arrival, and after logging many night hours, we were selected at nearly the same time to fly the Prairie Fire (PF) mission, supporting long-range reconnaissance patrols (LRRPs) near the trail structure in Laos. It was Covey's most demanding mission; not everyone was asked to join the program or opted in when asked. I don't know how, but we had made the cut. It was very very Top Secret, since we would be putting American troops on the ground in Laos, which President Nixon adamantly denied. Maybe nobody told him.

Prairie Fire pilots would fly with an experienced "Covey Rider" in the right seat. He was typically an Army Special Forces NCO or junior officer who had several tours in Vietnam running the LRRPs into Laos, North Vietnam, and Cambodia. We controlled Army UH-1 Hueys and AH-1 Cobras, Vietnamese H-34s, call sign Kingbee, and USAF A-1s during insertion and extraction of these teams. Teams consisted of about three Americans and nine indigenous Montagnards or Vietnamese or covertly imported Chinese Nungs. These Americans were assigned to the Studies and Observation Group (SOG) and were some of the toughest, most resourceful, and highly decorated soldiers in the war; we respected them highly. Consequently, we engaged in some high-risk flying for them. The teams conducted reconnaissance along the trail, captured prisoners, and on occasion their Bright Light teams were inserted to find downed airmen or missing team members.

"Typical" Prairie Fire team. Fourth from left is Ken Bowra, with whom I served at JSOC in the mid-80s.
Ken retired in 2003 as a Major General. *Snake Eater Does Good*!

When the country is in danger, the military's mission is to wreak destruction upon the enemy. It's a harsh and bloody business, but that's what the military's for. **As George Orwell pointed out, people sleep peacefully in their beds at night only because rough men stand ready to do violence on their behalf.** — *Adrian Grenier*

Some of these special operators went on to found the Army's Tier One special operations counterterrorist unit. Others, like Ken, become "plank holders" at the Joint Special Operations Command (JSOC), serving in the initial four years of its existence. I'm a "plank holder" myself, but I'm not even in the same species as these guys. I'll carry their water any day.

John L. Plaster, a Prairie Fire veteran, has written several books describing the Prairie Fire program. One of his books, *Secret Commandos: Behind Enemy Lines with the Elite Warriors of SOG,* describes my friend John LeHecka's last mission.

On that day, January 10, 1970, John and I flew together to Kontum, a forward operating base for the teams. John was scheduled to fly a mission with Covey Rider "Haymaker." Years later I learned his name was James "Sam" Zumbrun, a sergeant first class, on his third tour. He had already received the Silver Star, three Bronze Stars, and three Purple Hearts. All the PF riders wore sterile fatigues, as did the troops we inserted. PF Coveys quickly learned their call signs, but little personal history, or even their real names.

I stayed at Kontum Ops that day and they flew in support of a company-sized Hatchet Force near the tri-border area, where Cambodia, Laos, and South Vietnam meet. I was in the Tactical Ops Center (TOC) when a team on the ground relayed that Covey 580 had crashed near their location. The Army put a small team into the crash site. It appeared that John had been shot and neither he nor Haymaker could recover the aircraft before crashing. The recovery team had difficulty removing them from the wreckage, but eventually returned John, and later Haymaker, to Kontum. I remember the body bags on the Ops Center concrete floor, while we tried to continue the necessary business of the moment. It's hard to even imagine in my comfortable life today. John's body was returned to Pleiku and properly processed before being flown home.

Flying in the war "across the fence," aircrews who crashed were rarely recovered. I doubt John's widow Charlotte and family took much comfort in John's rapid return. What none of us knew at the time was that some "recoveries," when they did happen, wouldn't happen until over 40 years later.

I went back to flying Prairie Fire in southern Laos and occasionally Cambodia. The best strafing I ever saw was from an F-4 out of Thailand. Our team was on the run and I got an F-4E, call sign Gunfighter, overhead within minutes thanks to Hillsborough, the Airborne Command and Control Center (ABCCC). It or its nighttime equivalent was airborne over southern Laos 24/7.

We couldn't see the team's exact location due to the triple-canopy jungle, and the team was running too hard to use a mirror. They did tell us their general direction of travel. The team leader threw a smoke can over his shoulder and kept on running. As soon as we saw his smoke, I cleared Gunfighter in, perpendicular to the team's reported direction of travel. It worked and they broke contact. BUT, given the vagaries of smoke rising through dense jungle, the possibility for miscommunication, and the physics of spewing 20 mm high explosive rounds at the rate of 100/second from treetop level at 450+ knots made the whole enterprise pretty sketchy – *For Emergency Use Only.*

Judging by the three helmets, and the attitude, I suspect I was headed on a routine administrative run to Danang. I never took two people on combat missions, two more was too much for the O-2.

A good many of us were on our first operational assignments, with no previous fighter time. The Air Force and Army had agreed that only previous-fighter-time forward air controllers (FACs), called Class A FACs, could be assigned to support Americans. The rest of us, Class B FACs, with no previous fighter time, were assigned to Korean units, South Vietnamese units, or the out-country mission "across the fence" in Laos. It seems a lot of Class B types wound up successfully supporting small American-led teams in high-threat areas throughout Laos. A simplistic policy met reality, and the reality of necessity prevailed.

Moving Up Country

Transitioning to the Ravens required transitioning to the O-1. By 1970, the USAF was getting out of the O-1 business, consequently running out of O-1 pilots in theater. I did my O-1 transition training at Bien Hoa. My first time in the airplane I was sent, solo, to taxi an O-1 to the wash rack. This was a regular source of entertainment for the assembled ground crews, since the O-1 was a bitch to taxi for a neophyte. I didn't let them down.

Next, I received an introduction to tail dragging, landing in dirt, running a few airstrikes in-country, then flying parts and people around Vietnam accumulating hours. It was an excellent checkout, especially compared to the minimal ones received by some other Ravens.

At the end of March, I hitched a ride to Udorn in the back seat of a Covey OV-10. We made a several-hour pit stop up on the Bolavens Plateau at Pakse Site 38 (PS 38). The runway, dirt of course, was near the eastern edge of the plateau, west of Attapeu, which was down on the Xe Kong

River. The OV-10 pilot was scheduled to fly a mission with a local Lao in the back seat, a part of the X-Ray program.

PS 38 was one hub of the Consolidated American Sources (CAS) road watch and guerrilla battalion operations in Military Region IV (MR IV). These operations were conducted generally west of the trail, just west from where we had been flying Prairie Fire. Sometimes their teams worked the more western parts of the trail that descended into Cambodia.

While I waited for the OV to return, I jumped in a Continental Air Services Inc. (CASI) Pilatus Porter at pilot Lee Gossett's invite. We flew around southern Laos kicking out rice and providing taxi service to miscellaneous Americans and locals. We landed and departed from incredibly short clearings and relatively rock-free fields, an introduction to the rugged beast perfectly suited to the mission.

Lee Gossett in front of his Pilatus Porter at Sam Thong, L-20

Lee had arrived in Laos in 1966 for the second time, this time as a pilot. The first time he arrived he was an experienced smokejumper and became a kicker, riding in the back of C-46s, C-47s, and C-123s, rigging and pushing various loads to the forward sites and villages (1). Lee recognized the obvious, that it would be more fun controlling where the airplane is going than watching where it's been, and of course, the money was much better. So he got some more experience back in the US of A and came back under contract to CASI. Like Air America, CASI was essentially owned and operated by CIA, it just had a lower public profile.

Lee had seen a lot. He flew the first sortie to find Hoss McBride's fatal crash site out of Savannakhet in 1968 (2). He must have aviated about everywhere possible in the Land of a Million Elephants. Lee seemed to have met many of the Ravens, and wished me good luck. He knew more than I how important luck would be to us relatively green pilots.

Jay Puckett walked up to me when we finally got to Udorn. "Get out of that damn uniform" were his first words. He was sent to quickly guide me through the Detachment 1, 56th Special Operations Wing (SOW) intake. The Ravens were short of people and they needed me, nothing personal. Jay was one of the former Pleiku Coveys I knew that had gravitated to the Ravens. Larry Ratts, a recent alum, was then up at Luang Prabang. Jeff Thompson, a drinking buddy from Pleiku, would follow me shortly. He would be escaping the wrath of some senior officers at Pleiku.

Lt. Colonel Bob Foster was the Head FAC. He picked me up in civilian clothes of course and flew us north in an O-1, across the Mekong to Vientiane. On the short ride, Mr. Foster informed me that he was assigning me to Military Region II. This area was called Barrel Roll by the rest of the Air Force. I would be operating out of Long Tieng, Gen. Vang Pao's base of operations and a major CIA operating base. It was reported later to be the busiest airport in the world. Its existence was not acknowledged by any government and it did not appear on any official aviation charts. It was the first time I had ever heard of it. It was just south of the Plaine des Jarres (PDJ) and about 60 miles from North Vietnam, a very rough neighborhood.

As I quickly discovered, I was being assigned there to fill a gap created less than 24 hours before. On March 26, Hank Allen, Raven 41, and Dick Elzinga, a newly minted Raven 23, had taken off from Vientiane, headed north to Long Tieng, made one radio call, and simply disappeared.

Hank Allen on T-28D-5 Tail No 599   Photo by Will Platt, Long Tieng, March 16, 1970

It's hard to pin down the feelings I encountered on arrival in Vientiane. Most folks seemed temporarily stunned. Ravens had not lost anyone in over seven months, before most of the current gang had even arrived.

Records show that the official search phase was ended after two days. Moose Carroll crossed my path as he returned from out- processing to help in the search. He returned on his own initiative, and probably without any approval. He and Hank had been Nail FACs at Nakhon Phanom (NKP) and had been close. At that moment, he was totally focused, hardly taking time to say hello. We had been squadron mates at the Zoo (nickname for the Air Force Academy). Many years later Moose reflected how important Hank had been to him, and how he had helped him survive at NKP and then as a Raven.

Hank was an old head, seasoned and respected by the crowd at Long Tieng, L-20A. I'm sure he was imparting what wisdom and tricks of the trade he could, before departing for home. The schedule worked out that he was to follow Moose home by a few days. He planned to get married when he hit the states. His disappearance would be one of the true enigmas in the war's aftermath.

The 40-Year Search for Ravens Allen and Elzinga

As described in Chris Robbins' *The Ravens*, traces of the two did not first appear until three years later. On March 10, 1973, a Pathet Lao (PL) agent was arrested while attempting to enter the Long Tieng complex. A search revealed he was carrying Thai, Lao, and U.S. currency, along with three traveler's checks issued to Richard Elzinga when he had been in Thailand on March 11, 1970, weeks before he entered Laos for the first time. During interrogation, which you don't want to think about too closely, the PL agent stated that the money and checks were turned over to him by a PL officer to purchase supplies.

The mystery of the traveler's checks dominated much of a Status Review Board hearing on May 10, 1978. The Board's review resulted in Dick finally being declared KIA. A transcript of the hearing, including many comments and questions presented by his mother, Mrs. Richard C. Elzinga, is an emotional read, and can be accessed using a link to the *Raven Chronicles Archives* found in the notes for this chapter.

Real and bogus traces of the two appeared over the subsequent years. The following is extracted from a declassified Joint POW/MIA Accounting Command (JPAC) summary:

More than fifteen dog tag reports associated with this case {Reference Number (Refno) 1579} have been received since 1988. The reporting follows a common pattern, using information gained from Lt Allen's military I.D. card, or photo copies of the I.D. card, (which is known to be in the hands of remains dealers) in an effort to trade this information for financial gain. In addition, in 1990, analysts began to see a different variation of this dog tag reporting. Sources began to associate Allen's I.D. card data with an 18 May 1990 letter purportedly written by Lt Allen to the American Ambassador. The letter, along with a true sample of Lt Allen's handwriting, was submitted to the FBI for analysis. The FBI responded that there were "significant handwriting differences" between the two documents and discounted it.

There were also purported live sightings of a Caucasian implied to be Hank, living with a native woman and several of their children. This was investigated as much as possible, remembering that communists controlled the whole country after 1975. The sightings were never substantiated.

The Joint Casualty Resolution Center (JCRC) wasn't allowed into the country until the early '80s. Laotian and Vietnamese politics were a major obstacle. Intelligence Teams and Recovery Teams gradually began operating throughout Laos. The teams collected what intelligence they could from interviews, walked the ground, and dug into it using archeological protocols. Detachment 3 of the Joint POW/MIA Accounting Command (JPAC), the successor to the JCRC, was established in Vientiane in January 1992. It has supported teams operating around the country ever since.

The following is an email sent by Bill Forsyth to Lee Gossett as he was helping me collect newly available information for this input to the Chronicles:

From: Bill Forsyth
Sent: Monday, May 19, 2014 6:08 PM
To: Lee Gossett
Subject: RE: Raven Question

Lee,
Good to hear from you, I am very familiar with the incident, 1Lt Henry Allen and Capt. Richard Elzinga, March 26, 1970, case 1579. In March 2008, just before I retired, I investigated the case and previously located crash site in Vientiane Province. We located an old lady and her son who had a piece of remains the lady's father had recovered at the crash site and finally talked them into turning it over to us, it was later identified as Richard Elzinga. The next day we tried to get to the crash site, but the upland rice field we had identified as the closed LZ the day before was on fire, so we had to fly to a secondary LZ 2.5 kilometers away. It was a rough hike to the first LZ, when we got there, it was late, so I sent the guide, a Lao Official and two of our fittest guys to try and reach the crash site, while the rest of us put out the fire so we could extract from the LZ. Our pilot finally made contact with the guys trying to get to the crash site, but they said they could not make it and were heading down the mountain to extract. We asked the Lao to come back the next day, but since we were scheduled to relocate to southern Laos the next day, they said no.

In March 2011, a team finally got to the crash site with a witness the Lao had found who had seen two bodies at the crash site out of the aircraft. They surveyed the crash site and put it on the excavation list. I have no idea when it will be excavated.

JFA 08-3LA Team in front of their transport, a Squirrel Eurocopter AS 350

Interviewing villagers

SFC Kathy Hall and Bill Forsyth with villagers

Traveling from the LZ

"The Old Lady" Mrs. Mai Veu whose father removed remains from the crash site

Keeping and honoring remains of predecessors is not exclusive to Catholics and their saints; the Hmong often did the same with remains from ancestors or other significant people in their history.

Va Veu, her son, who turned over the remains to Lao authorities

The next team, JFA 11-3A, ultimately got "eyes on" the crash site in March of 2011. Their guide pointed out where he had personally recovered some remains. This was near the base of Phou Khao (Phou or Phu means mountain in Lao). There was another witness, Mr. Sia Got, who claimed to have been out weeding his field, heard an aircraft crash, went to the crash site, and saw two dead Americans in black suits. One telling of that story included reports that the locals on the scene removed and hid the wing and other parts of the plane to avoid detection and subsequent action by the Americans.

Mrs. Veu's father took remains from the site at the time and kept them until his death. These were the remains ultimately turned over to Lao officials by Va Veu in February 2008 during JFA 08-3LA as shown in the previous pictures.

The JFA 11-3LA team investigated the site and were able to recover pieces of a survival vest, a portion of an M-16 rifle butt stock, and some O-1 aircraft parts. They never recovered any remains (3). Thus, the only remains JPAC retrieved and tested were provided indirectly by local witnesses. Those remains, however, were tested conclusively as belonging to Richard Elzinga.

Richard's remains were confirmed through mitochondrial DNA (mtDNA) testing. The mtDNA is inherited only from the mother's side; therefore, the match had to be with a relative from his mother's side of the family. After an extensive search for an appropriate relative, Richard's DNA was ultimately confirmed, in October 2010, by matching the remains with his mother's grandmother's sister's descendants.

In summary, JPAC never retrieved remains directly from the crash site. Richard Elzinga's remains had been removed, probably from the site, well prior to the JFA 11-3A on-site search. Hank Allen's remains have never been recovered.

Richard's parents, Reverend and Mrs. Richard C. Elzinga, were no longer alive by the time of the burial service. Cousins Joan Bergsteinsson and Alan Brink, although they had never been in touch or aware of that part of the family prior to the search to support DNA testing, were the only members of the family alive to attend the ceremony at Arlington Cemetery on July 8, 2011.

Plaine des Jarres April 1970

"But to live outside the law, you must be honest" – *Bob Dylan*

I eventually got my paperwork and in-briefings completed. Below are two of the "official cover" documents we were provided. These indicated that we were non-military embassy employees. In case we were shot down and captured, we carried a DOD ID card, and appropriate rank insignia on a USAF flight cap. Some folks wore gold linked bracelets for negotiating their way out of such a situation. I was in the camp that thought a gold bracelet didn't give you much leverage when facing a pissed-off communist with an AK-47. Maybe a non-aligned local, as unlikely as that may have been, could be bribed for assistance.

I had been flying about 80 hours per month at Pleiku. In checking my flight records, I flew over 80 hours in the first 10 days upcountry. I continued at a high pace like everyone else for the duration. The Air Force lost all my flight records for the month of May, so I'm not sure how many hours I flew then. Plus, I started cooking the books.

Whatever the 7th AF established as the limit for flying hours authorized in a quarter was rapidly approaching for me. My solution was to stop logging flight hours every other day in the AF Form 781, used to record AF flying time. Our aircraft maintenance records were maintained separately for Air America and I filled out those forms correctly. At the time I figured Combat Rules applied, and we were breaking so many rules anyways, why follow the ones that got in the way of the mission.

Some folks apparently asked about the issue, and were told to stop flying for a while. I hope they learned the lesson that you never ask your boss for permission to break the rules. Of course he will say no. I never asked. This might have been the precursor to, "It's easier to ask forgiveness than it is to get permission." The irascible Rear Admiral Grace Hopper provided us that guiding principle a few years later.

At the time, the Ravens were no longer living at Long Tieng at night due to the security situation. We lived in Silver City, and then the Ice House in Vientiane. In the latter, we lived well, had a maid and her daughter taking care of the house and preparing breakfast. It was a helluva way to fight a war. We rotated one man for overnight stays at Long Tieng. CIA and Vang Pao's troops were still there, so it wasn't too lonely.

One late afternoon, returning to the Ice House after landing at Wattay airport, four of us in a white embassy jeep decided to detour slightly and drive by the Pathet Lao Embassy downtown. We drove down a narrow street in front of a big white building and compound. We got to the end of the street and it was blocked, so we reversed course. By that time, the young PL soldier guard at our original entrance to the street had lowered a barrier, and stood in front of the gate at port arms with his AK-47. Being combat veterans, we calmly and coolly discussed our options. I think Weird Harold was with us, but I can't remember who else. Shortly, the guard's boss appeared and, diplomatically – after all it was the embassy – opened the gate for us. With a few nods to the guard's boss, we drove on out. I'm sure all of us thinking we'll see you later, back in the war, *AMF – Adios My Friends*. Much self-congratulatory drinking ensued after the not-so-great escape.

"Those who may think war is the ultimate obscenity obviously haven't run the bars in Vientiane with a crew of Ravens after a day at the same"- Escort

I thought it wise to try to fly out of or below the weather in the O-1. Occasionally, flying up from Vientiane in the T-28, I was a little more comfortable flying in the weather, but my rule of thumb was to get above 10K ASAP, because of Phu Bai at 9,250 feet southeast of Alternate. Air traffic control was based on the big sky theory. Navaids were mostly nonexistent. Descent into Alternate or the PDJ required visual flight rules (VFR) or a hole in the weather. Most of us probably went beak to beak with someone sharing the same hole coming in the other direction. My turn had been with an ascending Xianghouangville Airline C-46.

The Air America C-130 crash occurred on April 10, 1970. It was flying through that same unfriendly weather. Air America flew clean, silver-appearing C-130s and C-7s in and out of Alternate routinely. The C-130s had been bailed from the Air Force. This aircraft had been inbound from Takhli, Thailand, on what would appear to be a routine fuel and ammo resupply. It was a C-130A, tail number 56-0510, that had been "leased" from the 374 Tactical Airlift Wing (TAW), Naha, Okinawa, sanitized with a silver finish, given the Tail No 605 (pretty clever, eh?), and transferred to Air America on April 9, 1970, the day before the crash.

The captain was Kevin Cochrane, an experienced aviator retired from the USMC about five years earlier. Other crew members included First Officer Huey Rogers, Navigator Roger McKean, Flight Engineer Milton Smart, and Air Freight Specialists Gerald Long and Billy K Hester. They most assuredly were trying to pick their way down through that weather. They impacted about 500 feet below the 9,250-foot peak, on the northwestern slope. All remains were recovered and returned to the United States, each accompanied by another Air America crew member.

Ravens Cross and Reese, Shot Down, Not Recovered

Jim Cross and I got along well in the short one month or so that I knew him. Jim attended Ohio University, then entered law school at George Washington University prior to entering the Air Force in 1967. He regularly received copies of the Congressional Record, and actually enjoyed reading them. He had also served as an intern in Congress. He was headed for a political career;

perhaps he would have been one of the rare good ones. At least he would have known more about real bullets than the politicians whose only experience with bullets is on a briefing slide. There's way too many out there in decision-making positions, even in the military, that have more experience with the latter than the former.

Jim Cross had been flying the AC-47 "Puff the Magic Dragon" Gunships prior to joining the Ravens

Jim and Dave Reese's shoot down on April 26, 1970 is also described in *The Ravens.* I was up flying that day, but Mark Diebolt was much closer when the Mayday call went out. He met them as they tried to maintain altitude, headed south from Ban Ban, a most unfriendly place. Not a good place to go at any time, let alone on a new guy's dollar ride.

Gomer David Reese

The U-17 had a gaping hole in the wing, big enough to be caused by a 37 mm round. Try as they might, they could not keep it in the air, and they crashed into rising terrain. Mark determined that the crash was not survivable. Another Raven on scene advised Mark he was taking heavy fire when he went low to inspect the wreckage. To my knowledge, we did not have access to Bright Light teams or a local equivalent. Mark asked the CIA to put a team in, but the answer was no, the area was too hot. No one ever came up on the radio. Ultimately all he could do was just report the location.

It was a tough call. It reflected the exigencies of intense daily combat operations, and the lack of resources. The on-scene commander made the call and we all pressed ahead. Thirty-eight years later the decision was proven to be correct.

Jim and Dave were declared KIA by the Air Force in 1978. The preponderance of evidence, all circumstantial at that point, was that they were killed in the crash.

222

Starting in 1994 joint US/Lao Peoples Democratic Republic (LPDR) teams, led by JPAC, conducted several investigations to find the crash site. During a visit to Detachment 3, Vientiane, Craig Duehring made a recommendation to check the north side of a hill they were investigating. The flight was headed south, and probably hit rising terrain on the north slope. He was right and they eventually pinpointed the crash site.

Teams had interviewed Laotian citizens who claimed to witness the crash, and the citizens turned over human remains they said were associated with this incident. The remains were consistent with human bone, but were too small to yield meaningful biological characteristics.

In 2004, another joint team re-surveyed the crash site and recovered life-support equipment, including a seat belt buckle, consistent with that found in a U-17.

In 2007, Joint Field Activity JFA-07-3LA excavated the crash site and recovered human remains and crew-related items. In the spring of 2008, a team completed the final excavation and recovered more human remains and non-biological material. The Senior JPAC Analyst for Laos and Cambodia, Bill Forsyth, was on that trip also. He provided these photos as he did the previous ones, and also provided me with the PowerPoint slides he had created for briefing Darryl Whitcomb, who was making a visit to JPAC in 2007. (4)

JPAC Team with contracted local labor and families, and one turkey in front of a Lao military Mi-17 in the spring of 2008. (six JPAC members died in a crash of an Mi-17 in Vietnam years earlier, the only JPAC team members to die while involved in field investigations.)

JFA 07-3LA Team

Raven 50 and 29 Recovery
U-17B hit by 37MM AAA

Metal detector and pin flags

Pick and shovel

Bucket line

Screens

Upper site nearly complete

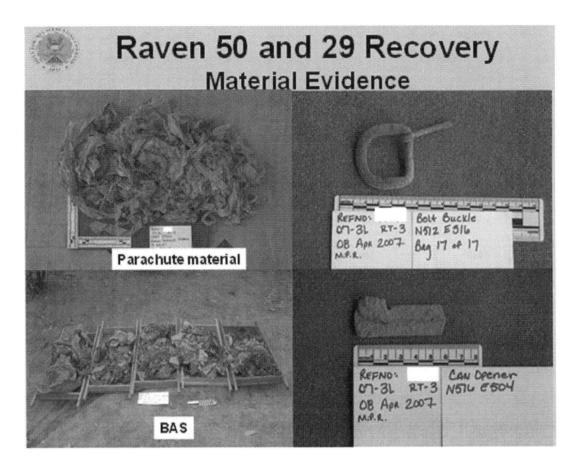

Raven 50 and 29 Recovery
Material Evidence

Parachute material

BAS

REFNO:
07-3L RT-3 N512 E516
08 Apr 2007 Bag 17 of 17
M.P.R.
Bolt Buckle

REFNO:
07-3L RT-3 N516 E504
08 Apr 2007
M.P.R.
Can Opener

The DNA science at the time confirmed Jim's remains, but could not positively identify other small samples. Analysis of prescription sunglasses found on the scene concluded they had the same prescription as Dave Reese's. This and all the corroborating evidence allowed them to conclude that in addition to Jim's remains, they also had Dave Reese's remains.

Jim was interred in Vienna, Ohio, near his home. Craig Duehring attended, as he did for Dave's ceremony later at Arlington National Cemetery. Dave's younger sister spoke at that service. "He's finally home resting peacefully; it's been a long journey but we're blessed that this day has come."

Craig Duehring with Jim's father and brother. The ceremony was conducted with full military honors at Crown Hill Burial Park, Vienna, Ohio, on October 10, 2008.

Gomer David Reese III was buried at Arlington with full military honors, April 24, 2009, almost 39 years to the day after he was shot down. Over 80 relatives, friends, and veterans attended the services.

We would like to acknowledge and thank the following for their generous efforts in making this day possible:

* The Air Force, for the part it played in helping David achieve his life long dream to fly.
* JPAC (Joint POW/MIA Accounting Command), they honor all life, do not forget, and do all they can to bring our fallen heroes home.
* The Air Force Mortuary Affairs, especially Mr. S. Todd Rose and Mr. Tim Nicholson, for their tireless efforts in assisting and guiding us through David's homecoming.
* Chaplain Charlie Stutts, who reverently celebrated and honored David's life with God's love.
* The Honorable Craig Duehring, Assistant Secretary of the Air Force and a Raven, who has been a kind and helpful liaison in countless ways.
* The Ravens, for their courage and daring. And, for holding David close as one of their own though he was with them for just one day.
* Ret. Colonel William A. Reese, for reading today and being such a large part of our journey over the last few years. Bill has been our "go-to-person" with various departments of the military as he helped us navigate through day-to-day questions.
* Eric David Bommer, for reading today. Eric is Betsy's son. He and his brother, Scott, are the only nephews/nieces David met in his lifetime.
* James Myers, for being so willing to share his talents with us by singing "Dream the Impossible Dream"*. James is the son of our cousin Barbara Reese Myers, which makes him David's 1st cousin, once removed!
* Sarah James and Whitney Palazzo, for being chief greeters today. Sarah is Betsy's daughter and Whitney is Nancy's daughter... and a special thanks to Mackay Bommer, Josie Bommer, Reese Bommer, Luca Palazzo and Oscar Owens for being fabulous greeter-assistants! (Betsy's and Nancy's grandchildren)
* And, a very special thank you to all our family and friends who have so fully shared our sorrow and our joy.

* This is the song that reminded our Mom of David. She chose to have it sung at his original Memorial Service, 39 years ago.

A CELEBRATION OF THANKSGIVING FOR THE LIFE AND HOMECOMING OF CAPTAIN GOMER DAVID REESE III – provided by David's friend, Raven Dick Welch.

Plaine des Jarres May 1970

On May 7, 1970, a fighter I was controlling was shot down. My log entry was "Tiger 06, Shot down Site 32, OK." Like everyone else in the FAC business, I had been in charge, but I had violated one of those "Rules of Three." This particular rule was:

"Never allow a fighter to make a third pass from the same run-in heading"

Tiger 06 was an F-4 Fast FAC from Korat Air Base in Thailand. Fast FACs would streak up and down the Trail in the highest-threat areas. They traveled very low, at the speed of heat, searching for and marking targets. On this day Tiger 06 was headed home, with ammo to use, but getting low on gas. Unlike us, the common man down low to the ground, the big jet could always pop up for a hit of gas off a holding KC-135 tanker.

I was working with Showboat, Site 32, and was about out of gas myself. Showboat had identified a DK-82 shooting at him from a nearby razor-backed crest. The DK-82 is a recoilless rifle that in this case was mounted on a tripod, Russian origin of course. The ridge crest ran north and south, west of Showboat's position. I could see two shooters in a pit with the DK 82.

I briefed the initial pass to be north to south, right break away from the friendlies, where I chose to orbit. The north-south crest itself curved downhill to the north, so the N-S run-in seemed like the best approach. Missing a pinpoint target on top of a sharp crest, however, meant missing by a mile, since the 20 mm would hit way down the hill.

I marked near the target; he had it and me in sight, and I cleared him. To neither one of our surprise, he missed quite a way downhill. I said I'll give you one more chance, make it a good one. He was close next time, but not in the hole. I said that's it, I gotta go.

Pilots occasionally recorded the radio communications during missions. The following is <u>not</u> from such a recording, but is an attempt to reconstruct the radio exchanges, and convey the gist of what happened:

Tiger 06: *Raven, give me one more pass, we can get it.*
Me: *Tiger, no more passes, we'll get it later.*
Tiger 06: *Give me one more pass, we'll get it.*
Me*: Cleared in.*

A nice shot group, dirt flies everywhere, but still no rounds in the hole. Next call, several octaves higher:

Tiger 06: *Raven, Raven, I'm hit!*
Me: *Tiger continue south, I've got you in sight, say status.*
Tiger 06: *We've been hit, lost hydraulics, we're bailing out.*
Me: *Cricket, Cricket, Raven 28, Tiger 06 is hit, bailing out, I have two chutes in sight, we are about 10 miles south of Showboat.*

228

At this point I was circling both chutes. One was descending faster than the other; his parachute was about 1/3 gone, apparently burned or ripped open in the high-speed bailout at about 90 degrees of bank and rolling fast. Fortunately, he hit in some trees; the other pilot hit in the open, and I got him headed towards the fast-falling guy once he was up on Guard.

Raven 24 {Stan Erstad}: *Raven 28, this is Raven 24, inbound to you, an F-4 just crashed in front of me, Jesus Christ!*
Me: *Roger Stan, it's empty. I'm about 10 miles south of Showboat, in a Tango, got both pilots in sight, and I'm out of gas.*
Raven 24: *Got you in sight, one Air America helo inbound, T-28 inbound.*
{*Jerry Rhein had diverted from an admin run with crew chief, Clyde Barr, in the back. As always we traveled with a full combat load if possible. Clyde's famous quote after this was "I've done everything but die and seen everything but the wind."*}

We coordinated on the location of the pilots; he had both in sight.

Me: *Stan, I gotta go, no more gas, you got it.*
Raven 24: *Roger, I got it.*

By the time I was overhead Alternate, Stan had both pilots and was headed home. Maybe I could have stayed to make the pickup. But time only moves one way, so no second thoughts. I landed; a quick post-flight revealed one bullet hole. I got a cold can of Coke and walked over to the Air America pad to greet the survivors.

Lo and behold, there was Dave Yates, my classmate from the Zoo, and a teammate on the USAFA rifle team back in the day. He looked like you'd expect someone to look who had just bailed out of an out-of-control jet, at high speed. It turns out his front seater, was the one in the rapid decent 2/3 parachute. He also looked like someone who had been snatched up almost immediately by an unmarked civilian helicopter, and put down at the busiest, but officially unacknowledged, airfield in the world. A cast of characters that looked like extras from a Terry and the Pirates movie were indifferently flowing around him and the other pilot, going about their daily business.

I congratulated him, gave him my Coke, and then humbly apologized for my part in the whole affair. I recall a rescue Jolly Green finally showing up, apparently assuming late was better than never, and taking the two south to Udorn and eventually Korat, their home base. Much joy and champagne probably ensued there. I'm sure Jolly would never claim credit for a rescue; that was just an urban myth.

I saddled up and headed back north to Showboat. Our DK-82 friends were gone, and I was sent to a new target way north, in no- man's land². I never found anything in the mountains of an area that was new to me. However, a six-level gunner reached out from my six o'clock (good tactic) and put a stream of tracers off my left wing. I got some F-105s inbound, and we dropped some bombs and strafed the area, since there were no friendlies nearby. The shooting stopped, but I couldn't confirm we got the shooters.

Later, my comrades-in-arms generally had a low opinion of my dueling with guns without a real urgent need. They were probably right. I think they also suggested I couldn't tell a DK-82 from a 12.7 machine gun which may have shot down Tiger 06. I think I was right on that score, it would have been a lucky shot, but who knows. I did store away a few new lessons, and an old one relearned:

- Three run-ins from the same heading, BAD. <u>Never</u> do that again!

- Don't start a fight, unless you have enough gas to finish it.

- If you're in a T-28, try to shoot the bastards yourself. 50 cal from 500 ft. and 160 knots on a small target has a better chance than 20 mm from 5,000 ft. and 450 knots.

The Team. I get 'em shot down, Stan brings 'em home

The preceding transpired shortly after my T-28 checkout at Udorn. For some reason, senior management had decided to get me checked out about a month after arrival. I'm sure this pissed off some of the older heads who had been waiting in line. Management apparently decided they didn't have enough time remaining on their tour to make a checkout cost effective, overlooking the fact that cost effective and fighting a war seldom occupy the same space at the same time. *Life is not fair!*

The checkout was a good deal, an early break from flying in the weather around Alternate and trying to find my way home more often than not. The pace had gotten a little more reasonable; I logged about 160 hours in the previous month. I got a thorough three-day, seven-ride checkout in the T-28D-5 model, modified for combat. My instructor was Don Morris, who had flown T-28

230

combat missions from NKP, then from Udorn. He seemed to be primarily an Instructor Pilot for us, Lao, Hmong, and Thai pilots. Later, I think I heard him leading some strike flights around the PDJ, more "student checkouts" I'm sure.

Don Morris

The early models of the T-28 had a reputation for losing their wings in high-g pull-ups. This was alleviated to a great extent in the T-28D-5, which included wing strengthening along with six weapons pylons, a 50 cal Browning in each wing and, progressively, additions of the Yankee Extraction System.

About two weeks after we flew together, Don was killed in a T-28 crash. I understand the wings came off in a pull-off from a dive. The wings folded up over the canopy and he couldn't get out; it was not a D model. Don had been flying in that theater as long as any Ravens, and had checked out some of us. His training pulled my bacon from the fire just a little further down the road. John Pratt wrote these words for Don – it spoke about, and for, us all (5).

The following poem was written for the funeral services of an AT-28 pilot at Udorn Afld, Thailand. The "little guys" in the title refer to the Meo, Laotian, and Thai pilots who flew the '28 and were never fully recognized for their bravery and sacrifice. Lt Col Pratt is presently assigned as an instructor at the Air Force Academy.

WORDS FOR DON MORRIS, DET 1, 56th SOW
(AND ALSO FOR ALL THE LITTLE GUYS)

HALF A CENTURY GONE, AN IMAGE PERSISTS, BORN
    WHEN SPADS AND FOKKERS DUELED
    (THEY RARELY REALLY FOUGHT):
MEN WITH TINY AIRPLANES, SHINED BOOTS, SMILES,
    AND SCARVES;
WHINE OF WOUND-UP ENGINES, TORQUE, SMELL AND
    CHATTER OF GUNS,
WATCHING FOR WHIMS OF WEATHER OR A BLOWN JUG.

NOW, TECHNOLOGY INTRUDES.
PILOTS IN THEIR AIRCONDITIONED WORLD SEEM
    FAR ABOVE ALL THAT.
SOMETIMES.

THERE ARE STILL A FEW WHO STRAP INTO SMALL BIRDS,
    CALL CLEAR, COUGH FROM BACKFIRE SMOKE, GROAN
    OFF THE GROUND AND SHUDDER SKYWARD,
BOMBS RIGGED WITH BALING WIRE AND WOOD BLOCKS,
    HANGING UPON A PROP.

THESE COULD CARE LESS ABOUT REFUELING TRACKS OR
    RADAR PLOTS.
THEIR NEED IS TO DODGE THUNDERSTORMS, SKIM PEAKS,
    KEEP LEAD IN SIGHT.
BOMB-LADEN TO CLIMB ABOVE THE CLOUDS IS TO STAGGER
    ON THE EDGE OF A STALL.
IT IS ENOUGH TO REACH THE TARGET, HIT IT, AND RETURN.

THEIR TEXTBOOK WRITTEN FOR AN OLDER WAR,
THESE PILOTS FIGHT, AND SOMETIMES DIE, IN THIS ONE.
IT IS GOOD TO KNOW THAT SOME MEN
    STILL FLY WITH SCARVES AND LAUGHTER
AS REAL PILOTS ALWAYS HAVE
    AND ALWAYS WILL.

By Lt Col John C. Pratt
from "The Laotian Fragments"

232

Back up country, I continued flying the O-1, but now could split my time with the Tango. It was a great aircraft for our mission. It had speed to the target, had enough smash to get outta there after going low, and of course could shoot, and carry a bunch of rockets, and not always the authorized white phosphorous kind. It wasn't quite flying a P-40 Curtis Warhawk, like my early heroes, the AVG (American Volunteer Group) Flying Tigers, who flew in 1940-41 against the Japanese. They had been only about 300 miles north of us. That was before we even entered the war, hence they were "off the American books" employees of the Chinese Army. But it was about as close as one could get to flying such a classic in 1970. Not too shabby.

John's Exit

May 25, 1970 was my last day in Laos. We were still flying the shuttle from Vientiane, and I was flying one of our two T-28s, Tail No 599, by myself. I continued the first mission alone, working my way through the weather into the PDJ. With not much to show for three hours or so, I landed at Alternate to get gas and pick up a backseater. I recall his call sign, Robin 06. I had no idea of his name then; we had only flown together a few times.

T-28 Tail No. 599 in unusual attitude – Wings Level

Preparing for the flight, we could not locate the Yankee seat lap belt for the back seat. Bad preflight on my part before leaving Victor. Since the belt was a necessary part of the parachute harness, which snapped into the extraction system, I elected not to take Robin 06 along. I recall his expression later. Probably thinking that was the luckiest thing that ever happened to him.

That second sortie of the day was fairly uneventful; it included the routine, for me, check-in with Showboat, north of the PDJ, successfully strafing a single target, and some visual recce. My strafing technique had much improved since my first near-suicidal attempt. My first-ever strafing target had been a soldier, with leafy camouflage, pushing his bike down a trail. When I finally broke my target fixation, and saw my own tracers bouncing above my head, I pulled out. That soldier lived to fight another day, as did I.

The ensuing events were covered pretty well in *The Ravens*, considering I had never responded to Chris Robbins' request for inputs to the book. My thanks to Mark Diebolt and whoever else for telling the story; I'll just buff up the details from my own perspective.

It was again time to refuel and rearm, so I headed south back to Alternate. I heard several muffled explosions in my aircraft, sounding like backfires. I was probably at about two thousand feet. I usually did random crazy eights while enroute, changing heading, altitude, and airspeed all the time.

I notified Cricket of my location and intentions to continue south. Shortly thereafter, I lost aileron control, and started getting smoke in the cockpit. A few years later Mark told me he had me in sight and the 50 caliber ammunition in the left wing was cooking off. To this day, I don't remember seeing that, my brain probably blocked it out.

The noises were getting louder, and the smoke was getting worse. It was time to go. I notified Cricket of my location and that I was bailing out, initiating the ejection sequence by pulling the fiber ring between my legs. The system did _not_ work as advertised. The permacord on the canopy did its job and blew a hole in the Plexiglas above my head, then the extraction rocket fired, but left on its own. After the fireworks, I was still sitting in a smoking hole.

At this point, one gets tunnel vision and presses forward hard, based on training and, hopefully, some forethought. My training had been good enough to automatically move my right hand to the manual release handle. I pulled it to release me from the Yankee system and leave me with the chute attached to me only. I stood in the seat to make sure I was separated from the system. By that time, I was halfway out of the hole in the canopy. So, pressing forward, I elected to continue out of the hole and pushed away from the aircraft to the right, trying to avoid the tail. A made-up maneuver that worked. So far so good.

After exiting, I had trouble finding the manual D-ring attached to the lap belt. At this point the harness appeared to be down around my ankles. Then, *Thank You Buddha*, I found the D-ring in some webbing, and pulled it, not knowing if I was still in the harness or not. It worked and all was quiet. Floating under canopy, I very briefly came up beeper on the survival radio and saw the aircraft crash. Years later, Mark informed me that the wing had separated from 599 before hitting the ground.

Drifting backwards, I impacted on a small hill, my butt and heels simultaneously. A less than great PLF (parachute landing fall). Later I learned I had a compression fracture in my back, noticeable but it did not slow me down much – adrenaline being your friend in such cases. I was able to collect my chute and move uphill and hide behind a few trees. Mark had contacted an Air America

UH-1. The Huey was inbound. I popped the night end of my flare, avoiding a huge "I am here" cloud of orange smoke for any bad guys in the area.

Mike Jarina, the Air America Huey pilot, touched down in a bomb crater just downhill from my hide site (6). I jumped aboard and we lifted off and got back to Alternate in just a few minutes. Air America was always there for us; we used to say they got us out before the Air Force completed their pre-takeoff check list. Not fair, since the Jollys were always too far away for an immediate pickup anyways.

I got a quick medical check on the ramp, and a shot of morphine. I remember Jerry Rhein coming over. He was the Air Operations Center (AOC) commander; he apparently wasn't in our chain of command, but who knew. For some reason I told him that this was a good example of why he should carry a survival radio. I didn't think he flew with one. About six months later, Jerry, a highly experienced leader in the propeller-driven, special operations business, flew an A-1 on the Son Tay raid.

Mark Diebolt, Will Platt, and a few others gathered around also. Robin 06 was there. I'm sure he was thanking his Hmong spirits and ancestors profusely for his good fortune. His luck wasn't perfect, however. Later he had to bail out of a T-28 piloted by Brian Wages. Both survived, but that's a story for another day.

Air America again provided me a ride, this time on a photo reconnaissance Volpar Beech. I was put on a stretcher next to the cameras on the center line of the cabin area, and then flown to Udorn for x-rays and treatment for burns to my left arm. I had been flying in my very "non" flame-retardant Banlon golf shirt, which was pretty crispy at that point.

I told the medical staff that I had been in a motorcycle accident, probably the wrong extemporaneous cover story, since I seemed to get a little more disdain than sympathy after that. An Air America pilot in the bed next to me helped me clean myself up. I also remember some downtowners showing up, asking why I didn't use trim to control the ailerons. Whatever I said is lost to the morphine and history, probably for the best.

I returned to the States via Clark Air Base in the Philippines. I was in a ward with a Marine who had lost both legs to a Viet Cong mine, and a local youth that had lost a leg to what turned out to be an only temporarily unexploded piece of ordnance at a local USAF live fire range. I have never forgotten the image of those two. I wish I had spent more time with them while I was there.

My luck continued, no traction required. I was poked and prodded for my burns, which did smart a bit. Bob Adams and Stan Wilusz, both from my pilot training class, now C-130 pilots at Clark AB, somehow found me and secreted me out of the hospital. I'm told we had a great time on the town.

The Air Force sent me back to Chelsea Naval Hospital in Boston, near my home, for recuperation leave. It lasted a few months. I tried to set up my next assignment from home. Four years at the Zoo, and I was totally naïve on working a new assignment with the Personnel Center at Randolph

AFB. Consequently, I got their first choice, a T-37 to Williams AFB, in Arizona. An OK assignment, but at a great location.

I returned to flying about six months after my exit from Laos. I remember the instructor on my first flight asking, "Fuller, don't you ever look inside the cockpit?"

Epilogue

I attended the 41st Raven Reunion in San Antonio, October 9-12, 2014. Ed Gunter had done his usual excellent job pulling it together. Craig Duehring had arranged for Yia Kha and his wife to be there. He had come down from Pennsylvania, where he is now living near his five kids and eight grandchildren. He is a fit and very engaging fellow. He had survived flying with the Ravens as Robin 09, became a Chao Pha Khao T-28 pilot, survived that, survived the communist takeover in 1975 by escaping to Thailand, then made it to the states in 1978. I asked him the inevitable question, "Did you know Robin 06, my lucky almost-backseater on May 25, 1970?" Why yes says he, we are good friends. He just had successful heart surgery and is doing quite well now in St Paul, Minnesota. His name is Francis Vang. Do you want his phone number? What!

Francis and I talked and I volunteered to present some Raven scholarships to Hmong high school graduates in that area in the spring of 2015. We got together, presented the scholarships, Jewell Lee and her father Koua Lee shown here, Francis Vang is on the right. I got to visit with a very strong and vibrant Hmong community in the Minneapolis area, one of the largest such communities in this country. Our small band of brothers has grown, and they had been out there all along.

Acknowledgements

I must first recognize my wife Barbara's tolerance of my procrastination and then the last-minute crash program trying to finish this minor yarn and then this book. That says nothing of the prior forty years of patience, love, and support. Lee Gossett was a gracious host years ago in Oregon and has been exceptionally helpful in gathering information. He connected me with the Air America people and Bill Forsyth, who despite an active retirement, found time to provide the up close and personal of the searches for our MIA and KIA. We should all recognize him, his fellow JPAC investigators, and the many active duty GIs who humped through the jungle in pursuit of *Bringing Them All Home.*"

Notes

1. Gayle Morrison's oral history, *Hog's Exit: Jerry Daniels, the Hmong, and the CIA*, is an excellent read about Jerry Daniels, a smokejumper and kicker who became a CIA case officer working out of Long Tieng for many years, including the time I was there.
2. Described on the Angelfire website by Thomas Lee, "The Day We Lost the Hoss," http://www.angelfire.com/home/laoslist/hoss/hoss1.html
3. JPAC ANNEX CAMP SMITH HI MSG 152132Z, SUBJECT: DETAILED REPORT OF INVESTIGATION OF CASE 1579 CONDUCTED DURING FIELD ACTIVITY 11-3A (118TH JFA) IN THE LAO PEOPLES DEMOCRATIC REPUBLIC. Declassified by DPMO 05-May-2011. Accessible at theravenchronicles.com.
4. The complete briefing, prepared by Bill Forsyth for Darryl Whitcomb in 2007, is accessible at theravenchronicles.com.
5. This image was copied from the back cover of a TAC Attack Magazine, an Air Force periodical. The background image of the O-1 and T-28 is from the Will Platt collection.
6. Lee Gossett helped me track down the pilot's name. According to Marius Burke, Air America Chief Pilot, and Dick Elder, who was in the area at the time, it was Mike who made the pickup. I can visualize the crew chief looking out at me, but we could not track down who he was. These pickups were so common for Air America that they were either not reported, or only peripherally mentioned in routine reports.

Chapter 18

Words for Chuck Engle

Charles E. Engle, Raven 26
Long Tieng, Jun 1970 – Feb 1971

"Sixth Tiger Aircraft Loss" by Rayford K. Brown

[Editor's Note:] *The Tiger FACs, by Don Bell, published in 2014 by Outskirts Press, contains first person stories about the Fast FACS who operated, at times, in Raven areas of operation. This short excerpt, pages 147-169, is from one rescued survivor's perspective of two Ravens at work.*

On January 2, 1971, Captain Harvey Wier, pilot, and 1st Lt. Rayford K. Brown, Weapon System Operator (WSO), crew of Tiger 02, an F4E from the 388th Tactical Fighter Wing, Korat AB, Thailand, were forced to eject from their aircraft in the Ban Ban Valley. This story, written by Rayford K. Brown, picks up after both pilots have successfully ejected and the SAR is beginning. Chuck Engle, Raven 26, was the first FAC on-scene and Grant Uhls, Raven 22, alternated with him during the approximately 20-hour rescue.

Concealed behind the vines and radio out of my survival vest, my next call was on 282.8 for any Air America helicopter. However, due to my location down near the bottom of the ridge my radio range sucked. I switched to Guard. Raven 26 immediately answered my call. I could hear his aircraft so I vectored him toward my position and he immediately gained a tally (visual) on my orange and white parachute. (Life Support had assured us that they were the required olive drab).

After Raven 26 had my parachute in sight I gave him my estimated 60-70 meter distance, NE and slightly uphill from the chute. He told me that he was going to mark my chute with a Willy Pete to confirm my position.

Did you know that Willy Pete comes in with a crack - a combination of supersonic travel and a super quick fuse to scatter the white phosphorus above the ground? This was an educational experience since I had not been on this end of a Willy Pete before.

I started sharing the direction and estimated distance to the ground fire from my position.

I had bailed out at almost exactly 1500 local time. This was the time on target - TOT, or station time, for the Sandys - the generic call sign for fixed wing dedicated SAR aircraft. These same aircraft and pilots sometimes flew under different call signs when not on dedicated SAR missions. Raven 26 was controlling the Sandys, call sign "Hobo", on a different frequency keeping Guard radio channel clear. For this reason and my location I did not hear many radio transmissions except for Raven 26. The Sandys arrived about 10 minutes after Raven 26. They began strafing and attacking enemy ground fire sites under his control. I continued to call out the ground fire to Raven 26. The ground fire was now timed to the arrival of the "Hobos" so I assumed that my importance had decreased a great deal. I was not jealous of the attention being lavished on the Hobos.

After several minutes of this I heard a single soldier, as in one and not his/her marital status, hunting through the jungle coming from my east to south and I estimated about 10 yards away. Why do I say hunting? The timing of the steps was crunch - peer, crunch - peer, rather than a normal 100 beat per minute walk. I was sitting in the back of my cover facing west and could not see anything moving. I whispered into my radio to Raven 26 and requested a strafe pass from my parachute up the hill. The crunching of the brush was getting much too loud.

The Hobos, A-1s, were configured with 7.62 mini-guns on one stub pylon just for such a situation. Suddenly I was spitting dirt out of my mouth as I heard the crack of supersonic rounds followed in a couple of seconds by the Whrrrrrrrrmth of the mini-gun. Another teachable moment, I hadn't considered that the bullets get there way before the sound of the gun. Inside my vines I could see three holes in the ground about a foot apart starting just short of my left foot and leading uphill to my right. My "up the hill" and the Hobo's "up the hill" had been about 45 degrees apart.

I told Raven what happened. He safed that Hobo up, meaning he had him secure his ordnance and not drop or shoot any more. I didn't hear the bad guy again. I was and remain grateful for that strafe pass even though it was very close.

I continued to hear voices to the south, down the valley, and they were joined by more voices coming from the NW up the valley toward where I had seen the fireball. They sounded like they were moving toward my position. Raven 26 obliged my request by having someone lay napalm up the valley just beyond my position. It turned out that this was also the approximate position of Harvey (Tiger 02A). Some of the napalm got really close to him. After about an hour and a half things began to slow down. I asked Raven 26 how much gas he had because three would make a crowd. He allowed that he had plenty of fuel left.

At about 1700 Raven 26 turned the On Scene Commander – OSC, job over to Raven 22, Grant Uhls. Grant was killed two months later.

There had now been almost two hours of continuous airstrikes by a variety of fast and slow movers. Air cover had begun within approximately 15 minutes of ejection/crash and this I think prevented an organized search for Harvey and me.

Those attacks had also largely suppressed the ground fire except for some random small arms bursts. The sun was low on the western rim of the valley and I had an "ear worm" running in my head. "My bags are packed, I'm ready to go. Taxi's waitin', outside my dooo…" Raven 22 called that they had started the last chance pickup attempt from the SW over Route 7.

Attempted Pickup at 1750

Just as I saw the first helicopter in the SAR force coming over the western valley rim he turned back and the sound receded into silence. Raven 22 said both Jolly's took fire and a Parachute Rescue Jumper –PJ, was hit.

By 1800L it was dark and the A-1s left. "King." the dedicated SAR ABCCC C-130, bedded us down for the night and promised a first light effort in the morning. The chill factor went down with the sun. I had been sitting on the damp almost muddy ground, plus I had been hot and sweaty in the backseat of our jet, and I was wet when I jumped. Miserably cold already, I was off to a good start for a long night. It was hungry out, too.

A Window Into The Mind

I felt strangely calm after the "King" kissed me goodnight. I had been the whole afternoon. I had accepted the fact that I was already dead and worrying would not change that. No previous aircrew had been recovered alive after spending the night in Laos.

At 2330, determined from my radio-active, glow-in-the-dark, radium filled navigator's watch, I heard dogs barking. I referred to my survival school training and came to the conclusion that the blood hounds had arrived. My heart dropped. I moved to a sitting position with my back against the wall, my knees drawn up, and my arms on my knees holding the .38 with both hands. I quietly cocked my .38 by holding the trigger down as I pulled the hammer all the way back then releasing the trigger. I was ready for one dog, one Gomer - slang for communist guerillas, and me as necessary. No more barking. Later I heard voices from my back right, NE of me, on the ridge but they seemed to go off to the south toward Rt 7. I still had my .38 out, but returned to lying on my left side with my back to the rock wall. After midnight the truck traffic stopped.

I kept the .38 out and my plan was to use cover until I was sure I could take out two of them should discovery be imminent or I was discovered. I planned to reload if possible. I fingered the rounds in elastic loops on the front of my survival vest, noting the direction to slide them out. I mentally rehearsed flipping the cylinder out, dumping the old rounds and reloading the new rounds one at a time so I wouldn't drop one in the dark.

Sunday 3 Jan 1971

At 0600 with first light I heard a fast mover fly over but was unable to make contact whispering into my radio. Then I heard a slow mover cross over and head to the southwest. I could hear him holding way to the southwest, maybe over the PDJ. I could just barely hear him. The weather was hazy clear and 40-ish Fahrenheit. It turned out this was Raven 26 (Chuck Engle). He said he came over and confirmed the parachute was still there. The fast mover had been Tiger 01 (Bob Jones and Jerry Sullivan) but they had been given a survivor location nearly five nautical miles east of our actual location.

As the first sunlight started to hit the far west hilltops I heard jets and ordnance far to the east. Scud clouds started to form as the sunlight hit the air. My bags were still packed and my radio was on.

I heard male Laotian voices coming up the valley from Route 7. The voices were accompanied by thrashing of the bushes. This was not the "first light pickup" effort that I wanted. I whispered into my radio and Raven 26 immediately answered. Minutes or hours passed and I could not tell the difference.

The Voices Moved Closer

The scud clouds had now formed a thin, solid layer at about 1,000 ft above ground level (AGL). I called again and made contact with Tiger 01 at about 0630. I expressed my concern to him with the bad guys in the valley about 20 to 30 yards away hacking my chute and survival kit down out of the tree, saying I might need some assistance. I lost contact as Tiger turned away from my position and headed east again above the overcast.

From the debrief I learned that there was a Nail FAC who flew an OV-10 out of NKP and King in the area but they were both new to the SAR and also had the incorrect coordinates passed out by intelligence.

By 0730 the bad guys had my chute down out of the tree, and not knowing their intentions, I tried to raise someone on GUARD. I again made contact with Raven 26 who had been there the previous afternoon and knew just where I was. Since my first contact he had been working in the background asking King to make him OSC, but King was trying to make the Nail FAC the OSC.

The Situation

When King and the Hobos bedded us down for the night they promised a first light effort. I expected a FAC to be orbiting overhead at sunlight with Sandys on his wing. I got nothing but a Gomer first light effort. I could not talk to the fast-FAC long enough to vector him back to my position because he was so far away. The afternoon before when King returned to base, the debriefing resulted in our position being mis-plotted by more than five-nautical miles. This had resulted in the jet noise and ordnance I had barely been able to hear over to the east. The next morning "King" could not hear me on the radio nor see my parachute, but he would not let Raven 26 be the OSC. Finally, Raven 26 got tired of listening to me whine and came up on Guard and said that if anybody wanted to play he was going to start another SAR. At this point "King" capitulated and made Raven 26 the OSC.

Two Korat F-4s, call sign "Miller" flight, with pilots Doug Henneman with Ron Akaka in back, and my roomy George Koch (pron. Cook) with Stan Hancock, from my Navigator School class, had been holding over the western PDJ. King weather aborted other flights from Korat and elsewhere, but Miller flight told Raven 26 they were ready to play, despite the weather and King.

Raven told the fighters to let down over the PDJ, an area of known terrain height, and head for Roadrunner Lake. Then they were to follow Route 7 until they saw smoke, turn left, then drop on the next smoke. Miller 1's Weapon Systems Officer (Ron Akaka) saw a thinning of the clouds where they could penetrate. George later told me they were able to hear my whining clearly while they were holding over the western PDJ and they really wanted to help.

Raven 26 told me to take cover, as he was going to mark the opening of the valley and the location the flight was to drop their ordnance. I was still lying on my left side peering out of my vines at the voices in the valley because with my chute cut down out of the tree I could no longer see any enemy activity. My left leg was completely numb from loss of blood circulation during the night and with the Gomers twenty yards away I was afraid of the noise I would make if I tried to sit up and pull it out from under me.

Raven 26 Marked The Play

Suddenly I was looking DOWN on the back of an F-4 with gleaming white Tiger teeth, doing the speed of heat as it passed into a little patch of orange sunlight. That image is still burned into my mind. I was only a couple of hundred feet above the floor of the valley. The F-4E was on the tree tops, banana tree tops. It rubbed off some cans of napalm and stood on its tail and disappeared into the clouds. The second F-4E laid his nape right beside lead's and disappeared vertically with at least a five-g pull-up.

There were no more voices coming from the valley. Instead the morning breeze brought the delightful aroma of napalm cooked bananas to me. It had now been 24 hours since I had eaten and bananas "a la nape" smelled really good.

Under the cover of Miller flight's noise I got my fingers into the left knee hole of my G-suit and dragged my floppy paralyzed leg out in front of me and leaned back against the rocks to watch the air show and take my mind off of it. Soon I started feeling a welcome tingling sensation.

After two more napalm runs Miller flight switched to snake eyes. Snake eyes are MK-82 500 pond general purpose bombs with eight-foot-span metal petals to create high drag to slow the bomb and give the fighter safe fragmentation clearance. I got a little more into the air show and raised up and peered out through my vines.

Did you know Snakes go off whooooomp and not boom like in the movies? Neither did I. About 15 seconds after the first explosions I heard this tinkle - tinkle coming down through the trees. Oh shit! That was pieces of the metal petals coming back down. Now I remembered that the casings of the MK-82s are propelled outward and upward as fragments traveling up to 6000 ft per second, twice as fast as a rifle bullet. I got my ass back in my cave and as low as I could get.

The SAR Had Started

There were continuous air strikes. After about an hour I heard a burst of small-arms fire from the west side of the valley that coincided with the arrival of a Sandy, and I relayed it to Raven 26. The Sandys covered the area with ordnance. I listened to chatter on the radio about ground fire along Route 7 to the southwest. In my humble unbiased opinion, the ground fire was pretty well suppressed by 0830.

However, while suppressing the ground fire on Route 7 they discovered the revetments that got me into this mess in the first place and started beating them up with CBUs and high-explosive rockets. Lots of missions went on beating up the area to suppress the enemy ground fire and they talked about using CS - tear gas, along the LOC using code words of course. The after-action report claimed six trucks damaged or destroyed.

About 0930 I overheard the Jollys talking about going in about 30 minutes. And then they would have to take a couple of hours to get out to the PDJ to aerial refuel off King. TWO hours!? Everyone said that it was still too hot for the helos to come in across Route 7 for the pickup.

We had been working the area for weeks as Tiger FACs. In fact, we had been beating up the caves on the backside of the hill northeast of where I was hiding. I was sure the enemy loved us over there. I also knew that there was nothing out to the northwest of our position. Route 7 ran off to the southwest. I came up on the radio to Raven 26 and suggested a pickup from the northwest, ignoring Route 7.

"My Bags Are Packed, I'm Ready To Go..."

Two hours? I was going to miss lunch and that had started to sound important to me. *"Taxi's waiting outside your door ...."* Also, Mother Nature was back violently waving the number-two card.

It turned out that Jan 2nd had been the first full day of operational capability for air-to-air refuelable HH-53, Super Jollys, at Da Nang in South Viet Nam. The Super Jollys had launched, on the way to the SAR area, refueled on, King ABCCC, on Friday afternoon. The local CH-3 Jollys from NKP in the northeast corner of Thailand would have had to land at a Lima Site, a small fortified landing site held by the Royal Laotian forces, and refuel in order to get deep enough to reach me and RTB. We were too far north of the border into Laos for a round trip with any hover time to pick us up. As a matter of fact, on January 3rd, Raven 22 and two CH-3 Jollys were deployed to Lima Site 32 only five miles north of the SAR, standing by if needed. The Super Jolly HH-53s were almost three times the size of the mere Jolly Green Giant CH-3s.

Slowly things began to get organized. Sandys 4 and 7 dragged down the run-in trolling for enemy ground fire. For those of you who do not fish, trolling is driving the boat at minnow swimming speed pulling bait or lures. It was clear from enemy fire. By my count I had not heard any ground fire for more than an hour. Two Jollys started in following one of the Sandys and another one S-turning above the formation, and the fast movers started bombing Route 7 again as a diversion.

All of this had been taking place under a 1,500 to 2,000 ft overcast. Raven 26 had been down at 1,000 feet AGL for two hours or more before being relieved by Raven 22 just before the pickup attempt.

Just as the A-1 leading the Jollys, crossed the western ridgeline, he told the Jollys to start slowing down. Then he told Harvey, who was closer to them, to pop his smoke. At about the same time the Raven put a smoke rocket where my chute used to be. I could hear the roar of the three mini-guns on the Jolly over the rotor noise. Orange smoke began to drift up from behind the low ridge to my northwest, and the nose of the Jolly pitched up to what seemed like a forty-five degree angle, and it pivoted around the axis of the rotor and put its tail rotor into the vegetation on the steep terrain east of Harvey. He hovered and hovered, the mini-gun on the left side was hosing out toward, but below, my position since I could see the top of the rotor. It turned out that a PJ from another chopper called the guy and told him to be careful for the survivor. I came out of my cover and was standing there watching the show again when I heard something in the grass in front of me. Fool.

I got back into my hole and peered out through the vines. Finally they dragged Harvey out of the jungle canopy trailing a vine. As the Jolly turned toward me, Raven 22 told me to pop my smoke.

While they were picking up Harvey, I prepared my smoke like they taught us at sea survival. I already had the seal broken and ripped the striker wire out of the flare. A tiny wisp of orange smoke about two inches long emitted from the flare…SHAKE IT SHAKE IT they had said. I shook the hell out of it and it began to spew a volcano of orange smoke.

The Jolly came to a hover about 50 yards in front of me in the slash and burn clearing with mini-guns still blazing. I waited for it to come to me. In jungle survival at Clark they had said to not try to move to the penetrator. At the debrief I learned that the trees beside my slash and burn area had been so tall, remember the falling helmet, they didn't think the cable would reach me. I had stowed my radio, gun, and camo-hat under my survival vest. At this point I threw the bullshit lag on survival school and came out of my hole, vaulting over large trees felled across the slash-and-burn area, racing and sliding for the Jolly, which was hovering at about the elevation of my hiding place with the penetrator downhill from me. At the SAR Debrief the left side PJ gunner told me that I had startled him when I came flying out of the bushes jumping over logs and racing toward him. He had started to swing his gun my way when he realized I was wearing a flight suit.

The terrain was quite steep and the penetrator slid further downhill from me. I grabbed the cable and started pulling it to me. They had left a couple of the petal seats down from the first pickup and they caught on some vegetation. NOT a problem.

I was still wearing my sunglasses but knocked them off putting the penetrator strap over my head instead of unhooking it. I picked them up with one hand while holding the penetrator against my butt with the other. Now I grabbed the cable above the penetrator and pulled up and give the PJ a thumbs-up.

They had cautioned us at survival school about getting the swivel at the top of the penetrator straight…I pulled up on the cable but failed. As the cable tightened I hugged the penetrator and put my bare head next to the swivel. I know you have this one figured out already. About half way up to the helo the swivel snapped up and bashed me in my left temple. I immediately knew what had happened as I dropped down an inch. I was still hugging the penetrator for dear life and didn't notice how much I was swinging back and forth. The technical term is oscillating, but just the same I was slammed into the bottom of the Jolly so hard that I was dazed a little. No way was I coming off this thing. I held on even tighter.

I was now beside the door and felt the PJ pulling the cable into the door way. He started letting out slack in the cable so my toes came back down to the floor as he pushed me over onto the cool anti-slip grit-coated aluminum floor of the helo. Boy did that feel good.

I looked across the helo and saw Harvey wrapped up in a blanket. After evaluating the odds of hitting something critical on the chopper if I shot him with my .38, I just reached over and shook hands. The helo was now climbing and moving forward toward the western ridgeline. I became aware of the roar of the three mini-guns hosing out the sides and back of the Jolly and the horrendous whine of all the gear boxes. There was an extra M-16 lying on the floor and I

244

considered picking it up but decided that an additional 20 rounds from me wouldn't be much compared to the 12,000 rounds per minute combined rate of fire from the three minis. The PJs were hand signaling me to see if I was alright. I gave another thumbs-up.

Stories about Chuck Engle from the personal notes of Craig W. Duehring

Chuck Engle was an easy guy to like. He was strikingly good-looking, raised on a farm in eastern Indiana, the first of four children. He was dignified in his approach and sincere in his speech, never flippant or verbose. And he was possibly the finest natural pilot I have ever known—but a man who was willing to take risks to get the job done.

He attended public schools in Lynn, Indiana, along with 28 other youngsters who went through all 12 grades together. He was extremely active in sports, a member of the National Honor Society for all four years of high school, vice president of his class twice, and drove a beautiful black 1957 Chevy Bel Air with red interior. His classmates describe him as very mature for his age, capable of deep feelings including a temper that he kept under tight control. He was a thinker and a dreamer who was deeply influenced by the book "The Prophet" by Kahlil Gibran.

After graduation, he became a physical education major at Purdue University, where he was commissioned through Air Force ROTC. He graduated from Undergraduate Pilot Training (UPT) in May 1969 and completed his O-1 Bird Dog checkout at Holley Field, Florida, before reporting in as a Forward Air Controller for the 26th Regiment of the "ROKs" – the Republic of Korea Army. There he flew under the call sign "Tum" for eight months before volunteering for the classified "Raven" program (Project 404) in Laos.

Chuck Engle (Raven 26) arrived in Laos during the month of May 1970, along with another new Raven and former Tum FAC, Bill Lutz (Raven 29). As instructed, both men ditched their uniforms in favor of civilian clothes and were eventually assigned to Long Tieng, the headquarters of the legendary Hmong leader, Maj. Gen. Vang Pao. There were seven or eight pilots assigned there at any given time with only two or three Ravens assigned at each of the other four locations. At that time, we at Long Tieng were experiencing most of the ground fighting that was going on in Laos, although the Ho Chi Minh Trail was a war of its own. We had lost four Ravens during the month of April so new faces were most welcome.

The Ravens flew the O-1 and the AT-28D interchangeably, sometimes with a Hmong interpreter, call sign Robin, in the back seat. We were incredibly independent by Air Force standards and did whatever was required to rain terror on the enemy. Cleverness, tenacity, adaptability, and solid judgment were of paramount importance to the Ravens and, while we may have consulted with our fellow Ravens for advice, we ultimately made the final decisions ourselves. This was fertile ground for a man of Chuck's abilities and he wasted no time in building a reputation that spread through the FAC/fighter community like fire.

Chuck's greatest challenge took place early in his tour—on June 20, 1970, the day he earned the Air Force Cross. I saw him do it from beginning to end. On that day, Chuck was flying back to Long Tieng from Vientiane when he heard King, the rescue C-130, say that an OV-10, Nail 42, had bailed out over the southern end of the Plaine des Jarres (PDJ). I took off immediately from

Long Tieng with a new Raven, Park Bunker (Raven 23), in my back seat and actually made radio contact with the downed pilot before my UHF radio receiver died. By this time, Ray DeArrigunaga (Raven 21) had spotted the parachute and vectored both Chuck and me toward the crash site. Chuck made radio contact with Nail 42 on guard channel and he and Ray took over the SAR while Park and I listened in on our hand-held survival radios. Chuck dropped down under some low clouds to about 25 feet over the PDJ while Ray coordinated the arrival of two sets of A-1s. Both Chuck and the Nail heard the sound of AK-47 fire as Chuck flew low around the area searching for the survivor. Chuck finally located the Nail hiding in a clump of bushes. Then he flew out over the PDJ to a clear area so that he could lead the fighters to the target area. The A-1s saturated the area with ordnance, all the while taking heavy ground fire. The first set of fighters withdrew and the second set dropped under the clouds just as Chuck began taking much heavier ground fire from another clump of trees only 25 meters north of the Nail. He marked the target and circled back over the downed pilot and cleared the fighters in hot.

When the second set of fighters silenced the machine gun, Chuck cleared an Air America H-34 in to attempt a pickup. The helicopter took numerous hits from fresh enemy positions that suddenly opened up south and west of the survivor. The helicopter was badly damaged and forced to head for Long Tieng. A second Air America helicopter attempted a pickup and got as far as a hover over the Nail. Yet another gun began firing and the helicopter took a serious hit in the fuel tank. Chuck spotted the gun and flew his aircraft between it and the badly damaged UH-1, surprising the enemy but taking a hit of his own from an AK-47. The bullet entered the left wing root and clipped the fuel line that ran above his head before it flew completely through the cockpit and out the roof. Immediately, fuel spewed down the outside of the fuselage as well as down the inside of the cockpit itself, drenching his clothes on the left side. The break was upstream of the fuel selector valve so it could not be turned off.

Knowing that the radios in the Bird Dog are bolted to the floor under the back seat, he wisely shut off the FM and VHF radios but retained the UHF radio until the end of the mission. He also only fired marking rockets from the right wing as sparks under the left wing could easily have ignited the fuel spray. He marked the new target and cleared the waiting fighters on a strafing run. Only at this point, when the Nail was safe, did he finally say he needed to head home while Ray continued to direct the SAR. Park and I fell in behind Chuck and I told him to simply shut down the last radio as I would clear the way for him.

As we cleared the very last ridge (Skyline Ridge) his engine died of fuel starvation but he spiraled down and landed perfectly, rolling to a halt on the runway. While waiting for the runway to clear, I watched him run out of his dead airplane and jump into the last remaining spare aircraft. In minutes he was airborne and returned to the SAR. After swapping radios, we followed suit. When I saw him again, he was back under the clouds at 25 feet pointing out troop formations as well as another .51 cal machine gun that had been set up on a hill to the south during his absence.

By this time, the Jolly Greens and Sandy forces had arrived on station and the SAR was handed over to them. Soon Nail 42 was safely on his way back to Thailand.

On October 24, 1970, Chuck and I were flying our own O-1s, searching for enemy soldiers near Xiangkhouangville on the PDJ and, finding none, decided to try a new tactic – high/low. Chuck dropped to a few yards above the ground along Route 4 while I flew in his high 6 o'clock position, covering his actions. As Chuck jinked his aircraft back and forth, he laughingly called out enemy positions where he could clearly see the startled look on the soldiers faces, while I dutifully noted the positions for an airstrike. But it wasn't long before a burst of AK-47 fire raked his aircraft, including a bullet that came through his left window, shattering the Plexiglas, and passing in front of his eyes. He actually saw the bullet go by. Simultaneously, he was hit in the leg by a second bullet, just above the left ankle with the AK-47 bullet passing completely through his leg and boot and then rolling loosely onto the floor. He pushed the throttle as far forward as he could and climbed while I fired a 2.75 white phosphorous rocket behind him. Then I struggled to catch him for a rejoin.

We spent the next 45 minutes in close formation with me trying to help him overcome the feelings of nausea that threatened to steal his conscious state. At first he said his leg was numb but bleeding. I asked if he had a tourniquet with him and he replied "no." Then I suggested that he retie his boot as tightly as he could and he did so. Eventually, the feeling returned to his leg and the pain was incredible. An Air America helicopter joined us for the last 15 minutes of the journey and, as we cleared the last ridge line over Long Tieng, I watched my friend circle toward the tiny runway below. As he touched down and dropped the tail wheel to the runway, Chuck saw that he was crooked and heading for the right-hand ditch. With tremendous resolve, he picked up the useless limb and smashed it onto the left rudder pedal, simultaneously pulling the mixture to the cut-off position. I saw the aircraft ground loop violently but it rolled to a stop on the tarmac. Within moments, our resident doctor and the crew chiefs had him out of his plane and onto a waiting Air America Volpar for a fast flight to Udorn. Chuck refused to tell his family of his injuries and, likewise, refused to return to the U.S., choosing instead to heal himself among his buddies first on crutches, then with the help of a cane until he finally returned to the air, flying combat missions.

I remember that a couple of us visited him in the hospital where we found him propped up in bed with bandages covering his outstretched leg. After a bit, he asked us "Hey, you want to see something neat"? "Sure," we replied. He unwrapped the bandage all the way to his ankle. The hole had a small piece of gauze sticking up out of it. He proceeded to gently pull the antibiotic-soaked gauze out of the hole further and further until our stomachs churned and we begged him to stop. It produced a good laugh – and a good memory for us all.

Amazingly, it took only a few short months before he was back in the air. Wounded warriors heal faster when they are among their buddies – something, it seems, that we have to relearn in each war.

By the time the dry (winter) season arrived, Chuck's reputation had begun to grow and spread throughout the fighter community in northern Thailand. At this point, he flew yet another remarkable mission. On December 30, 1970, Chuck was looking around the northern Plaine des Jarres when he spotted a PT-76 tank parked under a tree. He called for an airstrike but the A-1s were still a long way out and he was running low on gas. So he turned the mission over to Park Bunker and headed home. Tragically, the tank had been set out as a trap and Park was shot down by a ZPU-23. Although short of fuel, Chuck turned back to the scene but was unable to get there before the Raven and his Hmong backseater were executed by the NVA. We can only imagine what thoughts went through Chuck's mind as he heard his friend describe his final dying moments on his survival radio. He arrived scant moments later, as did Wally Krueger (Raven 20) with Yia Kha (Robin 06) in the back seat, and saw the enemy soldiers scatter when Wally fired a rocket near the downed O-1. At this point, it was critical to know if either man was possibly alive and Chuck characteristically volunteered to make a low pass over the one visible body while the A-1s covered his action. All aircraft received extremely heavy ground fire and one of the A-1s (flown by Hugh Place) was severely damaged but managed to make it home. Because of Chuck's visual assessment, we knew that our friend was dead. It was late in the afternoon and recovery of the body was impossible because of the intense ground fire. By the next day, the body had been removed.

Barely three days later, an F-4 Fast FAC (Tiger 02) was shot down just east of the Route 7/71 split and again it fell to Chuck, who was closest to the survivors, to begin the task of enemy ground fire suppression and recovery of the crewmembers. He flew under a 1000-foot overcast sky and found first the burning F-4 and then the two crewmembers. He first brought a set of two A-1s under the clouds but it was too tight so they dropped their bombs on the nearby road and returned with only their .20 mm strafe. Tiger 02B (Weapons System Operator/WSO Rayford Brown) heard an enemy soldier approach within a few yards and whispered on his survival radio that he needed strafe from his parachute up the hill. A moment later he was covered with dirt splattered by the impact of the bullets. The strafe impacted within three feet of the WSO but the enemy withdrew.

The next set of A-1s carried napalm, which Chuck directed against another enemy patrol that was nearly on top of Tiger 02A (pilot). Later, after the rescue, the pilot said that the nape had passed under his arm and past his ear setting his dead palmetto bush on fire. He moved and then returned after the fire went out. According to both survivors, Chuck and the fighters received heavy ground fire from 12.7 mm machine guns and AK-47s. Eventually, one of the A-1s, Sandy 03, took a hit in the engine which forced him to break off the attack and head for home. F-4s from Udorn continued the attack but Chuck had to turn the SAR over to another Raven and head home for gas. The Jolly Greens attempted a pickup at sunset, but pulled off when one of the pararescue men was hit by ground fire.

Well before sunrise, Chuck and Chad Swedberg (Raven 24) took off as a two-ship to get to the rescue site before dawn. Chad was forced to return to Long Tieng with a rough engine so Chuck continued on, alone, in the dark. He observed that the 1000-foot overcast deck was still covering the valley so he dove underneath and again made contact with the survivors. Heavy ground fire greeted him but three successive flights of F-4s silenced the guns including two .37 mm anti-aircraft guns. Again, he directed napalm drops within a few feet of the crew members. In the end, they were both recovered successfully.

Chuck flew to Thailand to celebrate their survival and was treated as the hero that he was. Chuck was later awarded the Silver Star for this mission.

Chuck was scheduled to return to the U.S. in late February so, as often happened, he moved his belongings to the Raven house in Vientiane so that he could begin the out-processing actions at the embassy and at Udorn. His flying was on an "as-needed" basis. For those of us who remained at Long Tieng, the battle was intensifying daily. Rocket attacks by the steadily approaching North Vietnamese Army (NVA) became a regular night-time event. During the day, we hit back at the enemy, often directing as many as eight sets of fighters in one sortie – a limit set by the number of rockets we carried. We anticipated moving the entire night recovery operation to Vientiane but the embassy was reluctant to make a decision that could be interpreted that we were abandoning our Hmong allies. As long as General Vang Pao remained, so did we.

In the very early morning hours of February 14, the NVA attacked our compound with six mortars and recoilless rifles while we fought back with two machine guns, M-16s, and hand grenades. The lengthy battle, known ever afterward as the St. Valentine's Day Massacre, is recorded in detail in Chris Robbins' book, "The Ravens." Suffice it to say, the sapper attack was halted at dawn when Killer flight, a flight of two F-4s from Ubon, accidentally dropped a full load of CBU 24/49 on the friendly position, tragically killing both friendly and enemy alike.

Chuck had been sleeping when he was notified of the attack at Long Tieng. He raced to Wattay Airport, cranked up an O-1 and took off in the early morning hours. When the F-4s left, we remained in our bunkers for 90 minutes waiting for the delayed fusing to set off the CBUs that littered our compound. I remember distinctly the race from door to door as we moved to the flight line to see if any of the aircraft remained in serviceable condition. At that point, the familiar drone of an O-1 pounded across the rooftops as Chuck arrived on scene, followed by a seemingly endless array of fighters that had been diverted from their night-time missions along the Ho Chi Minh Trail. I instinctively pulled my little plastic camera from my pocket and snapped a photo of his aircraft during his next pass. As usual, it was Chuck to the rescue.

Chuck could make the O-1 Bird Dog fly as no one else possibly could. He often ended his pre-strike fighter briefing by putting the aircraft into a spin, spiraling ever downward until he recovered at the altitude he wanted and then firing a marking rocket at the target before bringing the nose back to level flight. It was a real crowd-pleaser that suitably impressed the fighter guys. It was always a great lead-in to "hit my smoke." He was incredibly brave, more so than I could ever be. Whether he was setting an altitude record for the O-1 (19,720 feet) or making a dangerous low pass to help a friend in need, he flew his aircraft to the limits as though it was simply the only way to fly. We held him in the highest esteem.

On the day he crashed (Feb 22, 1971), I had driven out to the Wattay Airport at Vientiane to meet Chuck and to go over some awards and decorations write-ups with him. I sat on the ramp in the open jeep and waited what seemed an unusually long time. Finally, someone came out from the operations building and told me that Chuck's O-1 had crashed. I asked if Chuck had made it OK and was told he burned in the wreckage. I was in total shock. I walked in a daze across the flight line and stumbled against a revetment. Then in the privacy of my thoughts and the obscurity of the flight line, I fell over and cried, and cried, and cried until I had no more tears to shed. As I pulled myself up, I knew that I would never feel a loss as great as that again, and so I promised myself on the spot that I would never cry again like that for the rest of my life – and I never have.

"Bad Day," My Version of Chuck Engle's Death by Tom "Waldo" King

This is the only version with historical accuracy as I'm the only one who was present at the time and still alive, but who was never interviewed by the author for the book, *The Ravens*. The original book's version is total poppycock. Later versions have been modified, but this version is from the horse's mouth and, trust me, is permanently etched in my memory!

My warrior bud, Chuck, is going to be the first Raven to earn the Air Force Cross. As he is nearing the end of his tour, he is transferred from Military Region (MR)-2 to MR-5, a much lower-threat area. Occasionally bored, Chuck still comes up to the MR-2 area. At this time (Post Valentine Day attack on 20 Alternate), the 20A Ravens are overnighting at Vientiane, flying to MR-2 in the morning, operating out of 20A all day, but returning to Vientiane at day's end.

On the afternoon of February 22, 1970, I am at the end of my day and heading south toward Vientiane from the middle of the Plain of Jars (PDJ). Chuck calls me and asks where I am. I tell him. At intervals, he asks me again where I am. I keep replying, but looking out of my plane for Chuck as I have my suspicions that he is coming to bounce me for some of our occasional rat racing. As I get close to the southeast edge of the PDJ, Chuck appears at my rear quarter.

We engage in some of our standard dog fighting with Chuck stuck at my six o'clock. But since it is going to be late when we get to Vientiane and I'm sort of low on gas to continue this dog fighting, I head out south out of the PDJ at treetop level, jinking along with Chuck still at my six. I came across a river and follow it at very low level, just above the water. This river starts heading southeast, away from Vientiane, so I pull up and head southwest toward home base, once again at treetop level with Chuck in tow.

Up ahead, I see a fairly large cleared-out area among all these tall trees we are flying over. I'm tired of Chuck at my six and I come up with a quick plan to change the situation. At the edge of the trees, I ducked down, hoping to be out of his sight, and do a hard turn to the right along the tree line to hide from Chuck. I go along for a bit, and then pull up right out of the clearing and continue my turn, hoping to see Chuck out of my six o'clock position where he had been in all this time. Sure enough, I now got Chuck across the turn circle from me at my three o'clock, a neutral situation in a dog fight.

But my heart is dropping to my knees!! Once sighted, I see that after 90 degrees of turn, Chuck has started up vertically, about 45 degrees by now, in what appears to be the start of a loop.

I know for a fact that a loop in an O-1 is an altitude-gaining maneuver; that is, IF you have a good entry airspeed (in excess of our normal cruise airspeed). I had practiced it at altitude many times to confirm this, prior to doing it at ground level when entertaining our Hmong youngsters at their outposts and following it up with an aileron roll.

BUT, Chuck had just been flying basically level with no excess airspeed and had made a 90-degree turn to the right, which has most likely further depleted his airspeed. Not good! I did not think he could make it and there was nothing I could do. Continuing the loop was his only alternative and no calls could have been made to change the situation. I feared the outcome was not going to be a good one! By now, he is nose-up 90 degrees and could only recover by completing the loop. Oh, shit!! Amazingly, he comes out of the bottom of the loop just missing the ground by a few feet and didn't plow into the ground. But he runs into some tall elephant grass that explode around the plane. I'm elated!! He's made it!!! I think, we've got some explaining to do, but he made it and lives!!! A short-lived elation, as his plane ends up about 45 degrees nose high, stalls and falls off right into the tree line, explodes and burns. I am heartbroken and in deep despair!!!

I circle and make several calls to Chuck, even though in my heart, I know he's dead. It's getting dark and I'm low on gas. I return to Wattay Airport near Vientiane and report Chuck's downing.

One of, if not the, saddest days in my life!!!

The next day, the search party couldn't find the crash site. They returned, picked me up, and I guided them to his crash site, helped pull his charred body out of the wreck, and we placed him in a body bag.

Sorry, my friend! A more mature person might not have let us get into that situation. To this day, I have a heavy heart about the tragic end to the life of my favorite warrior (and to be categorized as a warrior is the highest of my accolades) Raven friends!! Our country and our USAF needed, and needs, warriors like Chuck!!!

Chapter 19

Tom "Waldo" King Raven 51/21 Aug 1970 – Mar 1971
Vientiane, Aug 1970 – Nov 1970
Long Tieng, Nov 1970 – Mar 1971

Nothing extraordinarily heroic about my Raven tour, hence my not coming forward to Chris Robbins when he was seeking information for his book, which told not only about our part in the "Secret War," but also about the sacrifices of our Hmong friends and allies. Here are some Waldo war stories and two of Chris's "The Ravens" book stories from my perspective.

I'm on my second Southeast Asia (SEA) tour in the F-105, the Thud, stationed with Tahkli Royal Thai Air Force Base (RTAFB), Thailand's 355th Tactical Fighter Wing, and have an approved six-month extension to my year tour in the Thud. I'm later told that they will be closing Tahkli and I should consider canceling my extension or plan on coming down to the 7th Air Force Headquarters and push some papers. Not being the paper-pushing type, and although I loved the Thud, I wanted to get into an airplane that I could go to the fighter pilot's master's program, the Fighter Weapons School (FWS), in some jet and the Thud FWS had been closed. One of the first Ravens, Jim Lemon, was on his second SEA tour in the Thud and was a squadron mate, so I knew about the Raven program, and had worked with them on many missions in northern Laos. Feeling that an experience as a forward air controller (FAC) would be a good one for my fighter pilot career, I requested that my extension be in the Ravens.

Since I was in Thailand, my interview process was different from most Ravens. I first went to Udorn and then on to Vientiane for my interview with Bob Foster. After the interview, Foster flew me on board an Air America plane up to Lima Site 20 Alternate, LS-20A (aka 20 Alternate or just Alternate), to observe the conditions under which I would be living. While there, a group of Raven pilots and maintenance guys were getting all garbed up with bandanas and various weapons to take a picture that they were going to send to some general. They asked me to come along, so my mug is in the right back row of the "Mexican Banditos" picture!!

I passed the interview, and much later in August '70, I went to Bien Hoa, got my checkout and FAC qualification in the O-1 Bird Dog, our primary Raven FAC airplane. The Bird Dog was a single-engine, tandem-seating, high-wing, taildragger plane with eight rocket tubes that carried the 2.75-inch rockets with white phosphorous rocket heads that we used to mark the targets where we wanted the fighters to drop their ordnance. It also had three radios: a VHF radio, which we primarily used to talk with the Airborne Command and Control Center, ABCCC (aka AB Triple C) to request fighter support and to communicate with other airborne Ravens; an FM radio that we used to talk to the ground troops; and a UHF radio, we used to talk to the fighters.

When I was in the Thud, I had worked a lot with Ravens in or near the Plain of Jars (PDJ). I knew it to be the action area, so I requested to be assigned there. Instead, I was assigned to Military Region 5 (MR-5) and flew as Raven 51 out of Wattay Airport located west of Vientiane, where I lived in the Raven house. I was initially a single-man operation, later to be joined by Flash Blackman. I cannot remember any significant intelligence support. I would fly over to a Royal

Laotian Army base, Chanimo, east of Vientiane, each morning and pick up a Royal Laotian troop as my back seater. Since I had no intelligence of the area and assumed my back seater did, we would go where he wanted, mostly to areas northwest and north of Vientiane. (Apparently these areas had no enemy troops as we discovered no targets and put in no strikes. But we were safe!). After a while, I decided I'd go where I wanted and proceeded to search the area to the northeast of Vientiane.

I didn't really find many troops in this area either, but did manage to pick up two hits. The first, an AK-47 round, was almost spent when it entered the baggage compartment area of my O-1 and ricocheted around inside the compartment before coming to rest there. Upon landing, I recovered the round. That night, I took it with me on my date with an Air America pilot's daughter, whose name now escapes me. We were at a popular nightspot in Vientiane having some drinks when one of her dad's fellow Air America pilots joined us at our table. Later, he asked someone to join us, who turned out to be the Vientiane Russian Embassy's Third Directorate. We started drinking shots of vodka and the Russian was making toasts saying "Na zdorovje," whatever that meant. (Ironically, it means "To your good health"). My thoughts: "Na zdorovje, my ass you f___ing Russian Communist, I'd like to show you what your country sent me today!!!!"

The second round came in and hit my back seater in the bottom of his thigh. I took him back to Chanimo for medical treatment, and I think he recovered OK.

Frustrated in not ever finding any significant military targets in these areas, I started flying further east out to Paksane located along the Mekong River, about 80 to 90 miles east of Vientiane and toward North Vietnam. There I teamed up with a real aggressive officer as a back seater. We flew together a lot and started finding and striking better targets.

First Truck Kill

On one of these flights well east of Paksane, I find a road under construction and my first truck—a dump truck! It is late in the day, but I am determined to kill this truck and request fighters from ABCCC. Since as Ravens we did not fly at night, or at least were not supposed to, most of the fighter support for Northern Laos had been used already. The only possible air support for me was two Sandy A-1s. The Sandy mission was to conduct search and rescue (SAR) missions to pick up any downed aircrews. ABCCC would not release the Sandys until their assigned orbit time had expired. This was going to make our strike really late in the day, just before dark. If I was going to use the Sandys to kill my first truck, I would have to land at night on the unlit dirt runway at Paksane, drop my back seater off, and refuel myself for my flight back to Vientiane.

I am determined to kill this truck!!! I needed to come up with a plan. I asked my back seater to call his folks in Paksane and have them come to the airport and place vehicles at each end of the runway, facing down the runway. When we called in, we would have them turn on their lights to highlight the runway, so I could not only find the runway, but also land there. He wanted this truck as much as me, so the plan was coordinated.

The Sandys were released. We killed the truck! We found the runway. I landed, refueled, and flew the 80-90 miles at night back to Vientiane. My first truck kill as a FAC!!! Mission accomplished!!!!

AO-1 Gunship

So, what road was this truck working on and where did it come from? I went back to the area with my Sierra Hotel (a politically correct term for shit hot, a term first used in Southeast Asia to express an extreme accolade) back seater and we followed the road to the east looking for more trucks, etc. We found an area with several caves. My back seater assured me that these were enemy positions. Since we were out of our Military Region 5 area, I did not think I could put in air in this area. Upon landing back at Vientiane, I reported these caves and suggested that the Ravens from MR-3 come up and attack them. In perfect 20/20 hindsight—; Number 1, these caves were out of their range and Number 2, I should have asked someone if I could put air in on them.

Some days later near the end of my time in MR-5 (I was finally going to be assigned to MR-2), my shit hot back seater and I returned to the caves and employed our AO-1 gunship tactics—well, my tactics, but like I said, he was gung ho!

Some background to set up the AO-1 capability. Since the enemy in Laos did not take prisoners, especially Ravens, if I went down, I was going to have a fight on my hands. Since I was destined to die, I was going to die taking as many of the little SOBs with me as I could. Never give up! In addition to the standard 38 revolver, I carried a CAR-15 (a short-barreled version of the standard M-16 carried by most ground troops) in the O-1 with me. I had two bandanas with loaded clips in each bandana with another half-clip of rounds stuffed beside each loaded clip. I had a third bandana with a boxed clip plus another half worth of rounds to load into any empty clips if needed. In my map case, I also carried about 15 clips loaded with tracer rounds that I used to shoot out my window if needed. My back seater was armed with his own M-16.

For our OA-1 attack, we both opened our left-side canopy windows and stuck our weapons out to the left side. The first set of cave openings were on the south side of a large karst hill. I flew along at about ten feet off the ground to be able to see the cave openings at close range while flying the plane with the stick between my knees to keep the plane level. As we passed the first cave opening, we opened fire in full automatic. I still remember seeing some guy hanging up his laundry. I emptied my clip, dropped the empty clip out, and loaded another in time to open up on the second cave a little further east, upon which I emptied another clip. My back seater was empting his clips also.

Two other caves were on the north side of this mountain, so I continued to fly east a bit and then climbed north up and over the mountain. We dropped back down to low level and proceeded to fly westbound and continued our attack in the same manner on these two caves. So far, so good!

There was another cave about a half mile or so to the north-northwest on the west side of a smaller, isolated hill. I turned north, flew to the east side of this hill and turned south to set up an attack on this cave opening. We were just about to open fire again when we started to take fire from the southern caves. Tink! Tink! With the sound of rounds hitting our plane, one hit on my right rudder pedal, we broke right and flew west-northwest out of their line of fire. We got out of range and as a departing gesture, I turned back on the northern cave, pulled up, and toss-fired all my rockets at it.

We ended up taking 10 hits in our OA-1, but no injuries and no major damage, so I flew the plane back to Vientiane. Later, a CIA radio intercept traffic indicated that a battalion of enemy troops had been fired on by an O-1. To this day, I wish I had been more informed or more persistent in obtaining knowledge on how to request permission to attack this target. What a missed opportunity!!!

On many of my trips to Paksane, I would join my back seater with the headquarters' staff at lunch. They would have a large table with various foods served family style. To not be considered a pansy-ass American by not eating with them, but also avoid getting sick, as we were warned about the dangers of eating local foods, I would eat sticky rice, fish, and vegetable-type foods, and never had any digestive problems.

On my last day in MR-5, sometime in the first part of November, I was in Paksane and the headquarters was having a farewell event for the U.S. Embassy's Army Attaché who had been in Laos for several years. I noticed he was eating some meatball-looking things that looked good. I figured, if he could eat them, so could I! They were delicious, but....WRONG!!

That night I had all kinds of vomiting fun. Our very nice Laotian cook and housekeeper, Susan, at the Raven house in Vientiane, was concerned and gave me some sort of medicinal patches to put on my temples to help me, but to no avail. The next day, the head Raven in MR-2, Wally Krueger, flew to Wattay to pick me up for my trip to my new assignment in MR-2 and 20A. He took me on a tour of the PDJ and pointed out various landmarks that I was familiar with from my Thud tour, while I was in the back seat puking my butt off. I'm sure he thought that I was overcome with fear and wondered how in the hell did this pansy ass, chicken sh..t guy made it in the Raven program! We landed at 20A and he showed me my room. That night I slept off my sickness.

At 20A, I started flying with back seaters, but found myself attacking points where the good guys thought they had seen where they had been fired upon by a mortar the night before; tree-busting and not effective, as undoubtedly the mortar had moved long ago.

Although I totally supported these brave young boys (and they were mostly boys), I felt I could better serve them by going to the PDJ and killing significant interdiction-type targets. This did not require the translating abilities of a back seater nor his strike approvals, so I didn't carry one on these missions. No use putting another person in harm's way.

On several of these sorties, Chuck Engle and I would work together along the northern Route 71 after the Route 7/71 split. One of us flew at treetop-ish level looking under the trees for trucks, etc., while the other guy flew higher looking out for antiaircraft artillery (AAA, Triple A) fire; switching roles back and forth. At other times at the end of the day, Chuck and I would join up and end the day to get in a little dog fighting. Chuck assuming, I guess, that as a fighter guy, I knew what I was doing (not knowing that we didn't do much of that type training in the Thud), but it was entertaining. No Internet or cell phones for entertainment back then.

Quick ABCCC story: One day I'm up flying and I call ABCCC. No answer. This goes on for an hour or more—calls to ABCCC with no replies. MIGs would sometimes enter Laos and bomb the friendlies. As later information surfaced, I guess on this day MIGs had crossed the border and ABCCC egressed the area, but didn't bother to tell us! Thanks guys!

Another ABCCC story: The Hmong/Laotian T-28's were awesome bombers and adhered to the fighter pilot bombing error minimization technique of releasing your weapons at minimum slant range to the target in order to minimize any release errors and generate better bombing accuracy (aka filling the forward windscreen of your plane with target before pickling off your bombs). If I had a point target, I'd prefer to use them to kill a target, even with their 250 pound bombs, rather than the generally less accurate F-4s with their 500 pounders.

At the time, these T-28's would come work with us without contacting or going through ABCCC's normal check-in procedures in which the fighters would check in with ABCCC and be told which FAC they'd be working with, where to find him (radial and distance off a TACAN station), and what UHF frequency to contact him on. The general in charge of Seventh/Thirteenth Air Force wanted to gain control over these assets. He demanded that they start checking in and out with ABCCC.

Now these Hmong/Laotian pilots flew using the call sign of Chao Pha Khao, usually with the addition of a color to denote which flight lead was leading the flight; i.e., Chao Pha Khao Red, Yellow, etc. Two of the flight leads had taken up with their American fighter pilot lingo and were known as Chao Pha Khao Shit Hot and Chao Pha Khao Fuck It. I couldn't wait until these guys checked in with ABCCC!

Another part to this tale is that the Asians had a hard (maybe impossible) time pronouncing English Rs and they came out as Ls. So Cricket came out Clicket and Raven came out Laven. Sure enough, on the first day of this new policy, I'm up flying and on my VHF radio I hear, "Clicket, Clicket, Chao Pha Khao Fuck It. Want to go wuk with Laven." Long pause and no answer from Cricket. So Fuck It repeated his call, "Clicket, Clicket, Chao Pha Khao Fuck it. Want to go wuk with Laven." I'm laughing my butt off, but Cricket finally responds and Fuck It flight goes on to work with a Laven.

A Chao Pha Khao Shit Hot story goes on about how he used to fly with a long scarf around his neck—World War 1 pilot image. One day, he's returning to Ubon RTAFB and can't get his gear in his T-28 down. The tower operator is watching him through binoculars and observes the 28's canopy coming aft, the pilot stands up, the gear comes down, the canopy closes and the T-28 lands uneventfully. The story goes on that Shit Hot wrapped his scarf around the stick, opened the canopy to stand up while flying the plane with his scarf and stomped on the gear handle to get it to come down.

My introduction to FACing opened up a new aspect of combat to me. Previously in fighters, I could only see the AAA fire. In the slow-moving O-1, I could now HEAR them shooting at me!! I could also tell what sort of weapon was shooting at me by the type of sound, usually AK-47 or 12.7 mm. Once after working a flight of four T-28s out of Udorn (the T-28 instructors who trained our Hmong/Laotian pilots) who had killed a tracked vehicle used to move AAA around (one jock

256

put a 250-pounder beside the revetment and the vehicle, which sent the vehicle twisting and turning up in the air before it returned to Mother Earth. AWESOME!!!), I was flying west from a point below Arrowhead Lake, a known 37 mm haven from there and to the north (and one we tried to stay away from as much as possible as 37s were a major threat to an O-1). I heard four or five distinctive deep-pitched sounds. Thinking 37s, I did my O-1 jink described below and sure enough, as I looked out my right window as I started my left turn, I saw a couple 37 rounds go by. Whew!!

In fighters, when fired on by AAA, we were taught to jink (move the jet in random flight axes), to reduce the chances of getting hit by aimed Triple A firings by destroying their lead of the jet. My experience in the O-1 was that the chicken-shit bastards would usually wait and shoot at me from my rear, my six o'clock-ish position. So I devised a tactic that when I heard AAA fire, I would push the O-1's nose over to both get out of that axis in the quickest manner as well as building air speed (to also possibly destroy the gunner's lead), while also turning, usually left, for another axis change. I would continue my turn to my previous six o'clock position, into the AAA fire's estimated direction while I looked for the proverbial "smoking gun." (As they fired, the bullets leaving the gun would generally produce smoke at the gun barrel's exit.) Once I found the gun site, I'd put a rocket on it and that would end their firing. Then I would get some fighters and strike the gun site. Bottom line, "Don't mess with me or I'll make you pay!" After several of these instances, I think they knew who was flying and where, because I was not fired on as much, even in the higher-threat areas on the PDJ, to the dismay of Jim Hix who, at a Raven Reunion, remarked that I did not take AAA fire.

My Version of Jim Hix's Shootdown and My Best Combat Mission Out of 988

This description is somewhat different than that related in the book, "The Ravens."

After the loss of both Park Bunker and Grant Uhls in the PDJ, it seemed like Chuck Engle and I were doing most of the flying in the J. The enemy was bringing in lots of 85 and 122 mm artillery guns to support their ground troops. During this time, I got to know the southern part of the J like the back of my hand. As they did most of their movement of supplies, trucks, etc. at night, the next morning I could tell when new truck tracks or new features appeared. With any new feature, I'd spend time viewing it from about 800 to 1000 feet above ground level, looking through my binoculars for straight lines that indicated a man-made object. Soon I'd see what was under the camouflaged feature and occasionally, I would swoop down to low altitude to confirm that I had found a specific kind of target. During this period, I found and struck at least eight to ten 85 and 122 mm artillery guns (as well as a truck carrying ammo and an ammo storage area which blew up for hours) that were brought into the J—especially in the southwest part where they could fire upon the Thai artillery base, Ban Na, situated some five to six miles south of the southwest corner of the PDJ.

After the bad guys' Valentine's Day (1971) night ground attack on Alternate, the Ravens had been moved out of Alternate as our overnight base and we stayed in a new and bigger Raven house in Vientiane. One morning as I returned to our region, there were calls from the Thai arty base that they were being fired upon. There was a low broken -to-overcast cloud deck over the J. I found a hole, got below the clouds, and found the enemy arty firing on the Thais. I put a smoke on it and their firing stopped. I directed the Thais in their return fire on this threat. Later, I even had a sky spot attack on it. Sky spots were radar-directed level-flight bombings on a target's coordinates when the fighters were prevented from visually attacking a target because of weather. This one was done from the coordinates I had given ABCCC. Came close, but no kill. Eventually, the clouds cleared and I put fighters on the gun.

One broken cloud deck day (2–3,000 feet above ground level (AGL) as I remember) in which the visibility was lousy due to the local farmers' slash burning of their fields in preparation for their growing season, I had found another artillery piece in the southwest corner of the PDJ and was working two F-4s on the target. Since the clouds were broken, the F-4s would have to circle the area to find a hole to see the target area. I had to wait and mark the target just as the fighters called in, so that they could see the mark due to the bad visibility. I ran out of marks (eight white phosphorus rockets on an O-1), but the F-4s still had bombs. I called on the VHF radio to see if any other Ravens were in the area that could mark the target for me so we could kill this target. Jim Hix was flying in the Ravens' lone remaining T-28 at 20 Alternate up around Muong Soui, northwest of our area. He answered and came over to our area. I talked him onto the target location. He began marking the target, as I still controlled the F-4s. On Jim's second or third pass, he took a hit and began trailing smoke. He said his cockpit was full of smoke and he could not see out of the plane. Somehow or other, either he was headed south when hit (as I remember) or when hit, he turned south (as Jim remembers) toward Ban Na, the Thai artillery base and the closest friendlies, four to six miles away. As he could not see out and where to fly, I gave him modified gyro out type directions and directed him to turn right, stop turn, nose down, level off, etc. to guide him toward Ban Na and safety.

All the while, fire and smoke continued to come out of his engine. In his faster T-28, Jim was getting ahead of me and to my right in my slower O-1. All of a sudden, there was a very large explosion from the left side of his engine. Fire was spreading back toward and close to his cockpit with flames coming around the cockpit area.

I was worried that fire would be entering the cockpit and burn Jim or that possibly the plane would explode before he got out. From my position well aft of Jim about 5-6,000 feet, I thought he was approaching the Ban Na outposts (hilltops manned by friendly troops) and therefore, close enough to friendlies and recoverable. I said something to the effect that IF he had fire in the cockpit, he might think about ejecting. No command! His decision! Seems like in the adrenaline-induced heat of the battle, he thought I told him to eject.

BOOM. Out he went.

As I caught up, I saw that he was coming down at the bottom of a very steep hill adjacent to one of the friendly outposts. I made the call to ABCCC that we had a Raven down. That call went to 20A and as I was later told, "Rooster," our 20 Alternate USAF base commander, rushed over to the Air America flight line restaurant and passed the word, "Raven down!!" Air America pilots scrambled to get airborne, as they would do for any American pilot downing.

Meanwhile, ABCCC was stacking up fighters for me to use to suppress enemy fire in the SAR (search and rescue; an operation to recover any downed airman). I was trying to contact Jim on his emergency radio with no luck. (As it turned out, he forgot to check his radio that day and his battery was dead.) Unbeknownst to me until I saw it, as he didn't call me, an Air America helicopter came in and did an outstanding job of picking up Jim by placing his rotors into the treetops due to the steepness of the hill, rescued Jim, and the SAR was successful!!

So why was this my best combat mission? I felt I saved Jim's life. When hit and unable to see out, to me he had four choices:

1. Ride the airplane in as he couldn't see out to fly it. Not good!
2. Bail out immediately. As the bad guys did not take prisoners, Jim could have joined Park Bunker or Grant Uhls in getting shot to death or possibly rescued in a SAR effort. Not good either!
3. I'm not a T-28 expert, but maybe he could have pulled the canopy back to see out, but that might have allowed fire into the cockpit. Additionally, I've read that if he ejected with the canopy open, he would most likely have been killed, as this opening exposed a metal bar through which he would have to pass. Doesn't seem like a good option either!
4. Listen to my directions and live to drink together at future Raven Reunions!

I like Option 4 the best!!

BTW, after Jim's pickup, I returned to 20A, reloaded with rockets, and flew back to the target. I finished killing the field artillery gun, found a 12.7 mm very near that gun (and one that most likely hit Hix), and killed it also.

I don't remember talking to Jim after this incident or about this incident until years later at a Raven Reunion.

Conclusion

Of all my combat experience, 988 combat missions as a mission ready pilot in five different fighters (F-4, F-105, A-7, F-16 and A/OA-10) as well as in the Ravens' O-1 and U-17, I am proudest of my Raven tour. Helping the Hmong (who were in a war of ethnic attrition) in their battle to defeat the communists in our country's support of the war in Southeast Asia, this defense of Laos (and thereby occupying several North Vietnamese Army divisions and keeping them from going to South Vietnam) was the most rewarding accomplishment of my almost 38-year military career!

What I am not proud of is how our country abandoned most of these loyal comrades, as well as others in South Vietnam and Cambodia, when our national will gave out in 1973, leaving them to continue to fight on their own for their survival. (The communists continued to hunt and kill the Hmong long after the 1973 peace treaty had been signed). Just another sad piece of evidence on the reliability of my beloved country as a partner in world affairs that continues to this day. Not good!

Chapter 20

Words for Park Bunker

Park Bunker, Raven 23
Long Tieng, Jun 1970 – Dec 1970

Sandy 3 Crash Incident Report by Park Bunker

EDITOR'S NOTE: *Below is a transcription of Park Bunker's report. A copy of the original, typewritten and signed, follows but is difficult to read. Considering it was undoubtedly written at the end of another very long day, we should respect the professionalism and quality. Park Bunker was KIA six days later, December 30, 1970, as described in the next two sections by Craig Duehring and Yia Kha.*

```
FROM:  AOC Long Tieng (Bunker)   24 December 1970
TO:  AIRA Vientiane – Operations
SUBJ:  Sandy 3 Crash, 24 December
```

1. The following is my eyewitness statement of the Sandy 3 crash on 24 December 1970. Please forward to the necessary agencies ASAP.

2. Early in the afternoon of 24 Dec the ground FAG Badman notified Gold 88 and the Raven FACs that the he had casualties, and was requesting a medevac. Badman's location was at approximately UQ6170, in the northeast corner of the extremely heavily defended Ban Ban valley. Although two other A1E flights had refused to work in this airspace 24 Dec, Sandy 3 volunteered his flight to fly CAP for the Air America helicopters making the pickup of the casualties. The mission was briefed with all aircraft circling LS-2 prior to entering the Ban Ban area. Raven 25 led the Sandies and the helicopters (Durax 30, 31, 32) across the Ban Ban valley, and then turned control of the mission over to Durax 39 who was to make the actual pickup. I was circling about 2 miles west of the HLZ in a T-28 watching for groundfire. And Raven 25 departed the area. Sandy 3 was to follow Durax 30 down, while Sandy 4 and Durax 31 and 32 held high. Shortly after Durax 30 called that he was starting down, I heard Sandy 3 state "I've got a rough engine." Then he said, "It's backfiring." Then someone, Sandy 4 I believe, said, "climb south, I'll pick you up." Sandy 3 then stated, "I can't, I've got to get out now." About a second later I saw the seat's rocket fire followed by a apparently normal chute deployment. I reached the chute while it was approximately 1000 feet in the air. Durax 31 and 32 were already circling the chute, and I heard someone state, "there's no one in the chute. I immediately began watching the slowly descending chute through my field glasses. I watched it until it impacted the ground. There appeared to be at least

```
```

part of the harness hanging below the chute, but there was no one in it. The aircraft was descending at a 30 to 45 degree angle, and it impacted just seconds after the seat rocket fired. Raven 25, Durax 31 and 32, Sandy 4 and I circled the crash site and the chute for approximately 30 minutes. There was absolutely no sign of a survivor, and no beeper was ever heard. The plane crashed at UG 645702 and the chute landed at UQ 656698. I am certain that there was no one in the chute harness from the time I started watching it. Someone aboard 592, an Air America C-7A in the area, reported that Sandy 3 was in his chute when it first opened. Neither I nor any crew members of the Durax aircraft can confirm this. In my opinion, the pilot could not have survived the crash if he remained with the aircraft, as it exploded on impact and was completely consumed by fire.

3. Badman stated that the friendlies were moving towards the chute and the crash site at nightfall. I will forward any additional information as soon as it is received.

4. I requested that the crewmembers of the Durax aircraft prepare statements. They will be forwarded as soon as received.

5. The above statement is true and correct to the best of my knowledge.

[SIGNED]
PARK G. BUNKER
Captain, USAF
Raven 23

FROM: AOC Long Tieng (Bunker)   24 December 1970

TO: AIRA Vientiane - Operations

SUBJ: Sandy 5 Crash, 24 December

1. The following is my eyewitness statement of the Sandy 5 crash on 24 December 1970. Please forward to the necessary agencies ASAP.

2. Early in the afternoon of 24 Dec the ground FAC Badman notified Gold 88 and the Raven FACs that he had casualties and was requesting a medevac. Badman's location was at aproximately UG6170, in the northeast corner of the extremely heavily defended Ban Ban valley. Although two other A1E flights had refused to work in this areaon 24 Dec, Sandy 5 volunteered his flight to fly CAP for the Air America helicopters making the pickup of the casualties. The mission was briefed with all aircraft circling LS-2 prior to entering the Ban Ban area. Raven 25 led the Sandies and helicopters (Durax 50, 51, and 52) across the Ban Ban valley, and then turned control of the mission over to Durax 50 who was to make the actual pickup. I was circling about 2 miles west of the HLZ in a T-28 watching for ground fire, and Raven 25 departed the area. Sandy 5 was to follow Durax 50 down, while Sandy 4 and Durax 51 and 52 held high. Shortly after Durax 50 called that he was starting down, I heard Sandy 5 state, "I've got a rough engine." Then he said, "It's backfiring." Then someone, Sandy 4 I believe, said, "climb south, I'll pick you up." Sandy 5 then stated, "I can't, I've got to get out now." About a second later I saw the seat rocket fire followed by a apparently normal chute deployment. I reached the chute while it was approximately 1000 feet in the air. Durax 51 and 52 were already circling the chute, and I heard someone state, "there's no one in the chute." I immediately began watching the slowly descending chute through my field glasses. I watched it until it impacted the ground. There appeared to be at least part of the harness hanging below the chute, but there was no one in it. The aircraft was descending at a 50 to 45 degree angle, and it impacted just seconds after the seat rocket fired. Raven 25, Durax 51 and 52, Sandy 4, and I circled the crash site and the chute for approximately 30 minutes. There was absolutely no sign of a survivor, and no beeper was ever heard. The plane crashed at UG645702 and the chute landed at UG656698. I am certain that there was no one in the chute harness from the time I started watching it. Someone aboard 592, an Air America C-7A in the area, reported that Sandy 5 was in his chute when it first opened. Neither I nor any crew members of the Durax aircraft can confirm that. In my opinion, the pilot could not have survived the crash if he

262

remained with the aircraft, as it exploded on impact and was completely consumed by fire.

3. Badman stated that the friendlies were moving toward the chute and the crash site at nightfall. I will forward any additional information as soon as it is received.

4. I requested that the crewmembers of the Durax aircraft prepare statements. They will be forwarded as soon as received.

5. The above statement is true and correct to the best of my knowledge.

PARK G DUNKER
Captain, USAF
Raven 25

Stories about Park Bunker from the personal notes of Craig W. Duehring

(This first note is an extract from my days at the little farming village of Duc Hoa, Vietnam, in Hậu Nghĩa Province, the home of the 25th ARVN Division, which was located about halfway between Saigon and the Cambodian border in III Corps. This took place in March 1970. I left for the Raven program in April.)

My log book indicates that a few days before going to Dion, I had flown a couple of rides with Capt. Park G. Bunker. Park was a breath of fresh air – a laid-back, quiet guy who was in charge of the pool of lieutenants assigned to cover Duc Hoa operations, and a filter of common sense between us and the unpredictable lieutenant colonel who happened to be collocated with us. Park was older than we were, probably pushing 30 years old. He was married (most of us were bachelors) and was an Air Force Academy graduate. There certainly weren't many of those folks around in the late 1960s. He was mature and easygoing and we all liked him instinctively. Little did I know at that time just how close he and I would become.

(Park's arrival at Long Tieng)

On June 19, I picked up a "new" Raven in Vientiane – my old friend from Duc Hoa, Park Bunker. We piled his belongings into the back end of a Birddog and headed north. Again, the weather was terrible and we diverted into L-272, where we met Father Bouchard O.M.I. once again. After waiting a bit, we took off and decided to try flying over the clouds, which we did, until the ADF needle swung and we knew we were over L-20A. By this time there were holes of varying sizes drifting through the valleys and the guys on the ground said there was sufficient room under the clouds to land safely, if you could get down. I waited and finally saw a portion of the runway come in view. "Hang on," I told Park. Then I pulled the throttle to idle, pulled the nose up to nearly stalling speed, and dropped full flaps. By watching the flap-limiting airspeed like a hawk, I was able to spiral down through the hole at a rapid rate of descent. We were pointed at the ground and there was no turning back. I suspect that Park was about to pee in his pants as this was all totally new to him and he might have been at the mercy of a madman. Down and down we spiraled, seeming to take forever as we followed the hole in its movement across the tiny runway. Then we popped out of the hole under the clouds and the excitement was over. I raised the flaps to something manageable, entered downwind and landed. "Welcome to Long Tieng," I said with a smile as we taxied clear of the runway.

(Various stories about Park Bunker)

On the very next day after Park arrived in Long Tieng, he and I were scheduled for his local area checkout when a call came from Cricket (the Airborne Command and Control Center or ABCCC) that Nail 42, an OV-1, had bailed out near Xiengkhouangville after having a mid-air collision with an RF-4C. Since we were on the flight line, I jumped into an O-1 with Park in the back and we flew as fast as we could out to the southern PDJ, followed by Ray DeArrigunaga. Chuck Engle was inbound from Vientiane but diverted himself to the SAR scene. I made initial contact with the downed pilot on the UHF Guard channel, but when I asked him to confirm his location, there was no answer. I tried several times until Ray called me on the FM radio to be quiet, that someone else was talking to the Nail FAC. My UHF receiver died at that critical moment. I learned that

264

the location that I had been given was in error and the pilot was near the western edge of the PDJ. We had overshot his location. So we turned around and watched Ray and Chuck conduct the most "classic" SAR I ever saw in theater. Park and I orbited while listening to the SAR unfold using our survival radios as UHF Guard receivers. The complete story is written under Chuck Engle's chapter, but this turned out to be Park's checkout ride. After those first two sorties he must have wondered what the hell he was getting into.

We had a great group of guys there at that time. Occasionally, someone would come into the program who wasn't really prepared or who had a "personality disorder" best summed up by referring to the part of the body you sit on. I'll try to be nice and concentrate on the good guys.

My log book has an entry for September 9, 1970, that mentions Park Bunker crashed but is OK. Years later, I heard the story from Yia Kha, Robin 09 (who later became a T-28 pilot), who was in the back seat. He and Park had been flying around the PDJ in some bad weather and decided to return to L-20A. The ridgeline in front of them had clouds obscuring the hilltops but a small saddle-shaped valley appeared to be open. The altitude required Park to climb just to get through. Yia said that he didn't think they were climbing fast enough and suggested to Park that he complete a climbing circle before attempting to shoot the gap. Park didn't agree and pressed forward. As they entered the gap, a gust of wind or a downdraft smashed them into the trees and the aircraft flipped forward until it was upside down. Yia was the first to drag himself out of the aircraft and then looked back to see Park stuck in his seat. The area around the door and window had collapsed and Park was simply too large to crawl out unassisted. Yia went back, got him released from his straps and dragged Park through the opening and onto the grass. Then he pulled the survival radio from Park's vest and made contact with the Air America folks. Eventually, Park took back the radio and directed the AAM helicopter in to pick them both up. I believe Park had some minor cuts but Yia was fine. In effect, Yia rescued Park from a very hazardous situation and should have been recognized officially for that action.

The other incident that I remember about my friend Park was the day several of us caught a ride on a flatbed ammo truck from the flight line to the compound. Rather than get inside, the guys just hung onto the sides of the truck while standing on the running boards. The truck stopped at the Raven hootch and we jumped off. Park was one of the few Ravens who were married, so he wore a wedding band. Unfortunately, the wedding ring got hung up on the side of the truck and he let out a shriek of pain. I saw that the ring had shredded the skin on his finger forward, exposing tendons, blood and heaven-knows-what-else. In an instant, he pushed the ring and skin back into place and ran into the hootch dripping blood all over the place. Someone called Dr. Jim Steinbeiser, our flight surgeon, who took one look at the bloody mess on Park's hand and said that the ring must come off. Of course, the finger was beginning to swell rapidly, causing the pain to increase. Soon, it was nearly impossible to even see the ring. Someone found needle-nose pliers and a tin snip or hack saw and the doctor went to work. It wasn't a pretty thing to watch. He finally sawed his way through the ring and pulled it off. It was at that point that he could begin dressing the wound. Park walked around with a bandaged hand for quite a while after that, but he would return to flying eventually.

In November 1970, Park went home on a 30-day R&R, which all of us earned if we signed up for a consecutive overseas tour (i.e., six additional months). He returned to complete another month or so of flying before he was to return home for good. That never happened.

(Park's final mission)

On December 30, 1970, I was flying my second sortie (of three that day) somewhere southeast of Long Tieng. Of course I was talking to Cricket, the C-130 Airborne Command and Control Center (ABCCC) that coordinated all flying activities in the Barrel Roll region (northern Laos), and talked occasionally with the other Ravens who were airborne. But because I was so far from the others, I had trouble hearing them most of the time. I recall that I was chatting with Cricket when he asked me to hold on a moment. When he returned, he said that Raven 23 was down on the PDJ. I knew that was Park. I was already low on gas so I continued home to refuel and then headed north to the crash site.

It seemed that Chuck Engle was looking around the northern PDJ when he saw a tank parked under a tree with only the rear portion exposed. We determined later that it was a trap set by the NVA. Since Chuck was low on gas also, he called Park and offered the target to him for destruction. A set of fighters, possibly A-1s, was on the way and I'm sure Park relished the idea of blowing up a PT-76. They swapped off and Park began briefing the fighters. However, at some point in the process a large caliber anti-aircraft gun, probably a ZSU-23-4, opened up on him and shot out the engine. He called out for help and then concentrated on crash landing the airplane.

He selected an open field that was surrounded on three sides by a tree-shrouded shallow stream, leaving the only open area to the north. Unfortunately, the stream bank was the hiding place for an estimated company of NVA soldiers who began shooting at him as soon as he got out of the aircraft. His backseater, Tow Hua Xiang or Robin 05, went down with him. I remember Tow Hua Xiang very well. He and Yia Kha were probably the two best backseaters but he seemed shy, possibly because he was very small. The pistol that he carried on his hip seemed to run from his waist halfway to the ground. But he had a lot of courage and flew anytime we needed him.

Wally Krueger was flying to the north of the PDJ and was actually the closest to Park when he went down. Chuck, although low on gas, turned around and raced back to the area, as well as the A-1s who finally came over the ridge. Wally talked to Park and asked him how he was. Park replied that he was lying in a shallow depression near the O-1 and that he was taking fire from three sides. Wally asked him about his backseater and Park replied that he had no idea what happened to him—he simply vanished. Wally suggested that Park try to surrender. Park said that he had tried but they kept shooting. Eventually, he said "I've been shot five times. I'm as good as dead." A few minutes later, Wally saw the airplane on the ground in front of him. Then he saw figures gathered around the aircraft so he lobbed a 2.75 Willy Pete rocket into the area, which caused the troops to run back under cover. Chad Swedberg (Raven 24) with Yia Kha in his back seat arrived shortly thereafter.

As I recall, all four aircraft arrived overhead about the same time. And, as Chris Robbins writes in his book, Chuck Engle made a low pass across Park's position and was shot up as a result. Chad said he clearly remembers seeing the ZPU 23-2/4 fire on Chuck as the sky seemed to be filled with tracers – a sure sign it was a "Zepe." The lead Sandy then made a low pass, receiving heavy ground fire and taking at least one round – possibly in the engine. This caused the A-1s to pull off and head toward Long Tieng for a possible emergency landing there. But the engine held together and they returned to Thailand. The A-1 pilot (Hugh Place) clearly saw a figure clad in brown (the chocolate-colored walking suit that so many of us wore) and a flack vest with part of his head blown away. Chuck flew home on fumes but Wally, in spite of what two people saw, refused to believe that Park was dead and would not put in any airstrikes. He believed Park was captured, so with the exception of the initial strike by the A-1's against the ZPU, there were no further airstrikes that day at that location. Again, it was becoming late in the day when I arrived overhead and there was no hope of trying to pick up Park's body before the sun set.

The next day, the body was gone and we blew the aircraft up. Strangely, I remember the tail number of that O-1. It was "603."

In 1994, when Terri and I returned to Laos, we met with the folks at the embassy who were trying to recover the remains of missing airmen and we discussed this event. They told me that they had located a former NV soldier or political advisor who was at the location of the crash that day. He said that they buried Park's body nearby. Our folks actually took him back to the PDJ but he said that his mind was not clear and that everything had changed. Thus, he could not tell our people where Park might be resting. We have never recovered Park's body, but there is a plaque commemorating his sacrifice at the U.S. Air Force Academy cemetery where so many other Ravens are buried.

Park Bunker on far right, Craig Duehring on far left. Long Tieng 1970 Photograph courtesy Craig W. Duehring

Rescue, Park Bunker December 1970
Story From My Memory by Yia Kha, Robin 09/Chao Pha Khao

Park and back seat Robin 05, Tou Houa Xiong were shot down by 37 mm PDJ. I was a back seater for a Raven, we had a mission close by when we heard the emergency radio saying that Raven 23 was shot down, the Raven flew to the location.

When we got there we saw the 01 Bird Dog was on the ground. We saw Park about 200 feet south of the 01 Bird Dog under the tree. I asked him about his back seat Robin 05, Park said he got out first and didn't know where he was and he said his leg got hurt badly. The Raven called cricket for air strike and they said they will send two F4 Phantom carry all CBU. It will take about 45 minutes until they get there. Then I saw two bad guys run towards Park, I called Park that I see two bad guys running towards him at south west front of him. He said to me, he will not let them arrest him alive, he will fight... about 5 minutes later I heard his gun fire about 16 rounds, shortly after, another 16 rounds, then I call him, "Park are you ok?"... No answer. The Raven also call him a couple of times... no answer, but his radio was still on. We know that when he shot the bad guys, they shot back and killed him right in front of our eyes. It was so sad to see.

Two F4 Phantom arrive, a Raven talk to them and told them where to drop CBU around Park. Each one made two passes. When they pulled up the bad guys shoot behind them. I can see 5 black smokes almost hitting them. After that F4 finished, and they went home. I said good bye to Raven 23. My tears came and I cried until we landed at LS 20A. That is the end of Park Rescue.

Chapter 21

J. Briggs Diuguid, Raven 26
Long Tieng, Feb 1971 – Oct 1971

Getting There

Hundreds, maybe thousands of stories have been told about the small group of forward air controllers (FACs) who flew in Laos with the call sign Raven. During the Viet Nam conflict, the stories were whispered among pilots in bars all over Asia. After the program was declassified in 1992, books were written, videos made and tales told in the open.

Some of the stories remain humorous, such as the one started by F-4 crews at Udorn Royal Thai Air Force Base which created the legend of the one-eyed Raven after Pepsi taxied by their arming area wearing his famous Volga Boatman hat and an unneeded black eye patch.

Unbelievable, yet accurate tales described events. Magnet Ass crashed ten airplanes due to a combination of ground fire, mechanical failure and lots of combat flying. His eleventh crash broke his back and took him out of combat flying and into extensive combat with doctors and rehabilitation.

Some of the tales have grown with the telling but most needed no embellishment. All Ravens dodged bullets every day, jinked around cloud-covered mountains which we called cumulogranite, and often landed on muddy, bumpy puddles in the wild hinterlands of Laos. Each individual's experience varied depending on which military region they operated in and the time of year. During the dry season, when the smoke from the slash-and-burn agriculture of the Hmong and Lao filled the air, the bad guys would go on the offensive, as they were able to move men and supplies over the dry dirt roads. When the monsoon rains started, the clouds would often reach from the high heavens to the ground. The Hmong would counterattack, knowing the enemy's mobility and resupply were limited. Despite the terrible weather and thick cloud, they knew we'd find a way to provide air support. We flew through it all without electronic navigation aids, using nothing more than a paper map, magnetic compass, and a clock to fly our self-designed routes through the mountains to find a spot where we could descend and work.

Luck and skill play a part in war. On his first solo ride as a Raven, my friend John experienced a ton of bad luck, getting shot flying over what was thought to be a low-threat area. When he finally got out of the hospital, he came back to the program stating, "I won't be known as the only Raven to fly just one mission."

Skill worked with luck to save lives. When Swanee's engine crapped out, he had the presence of mind and skill to land on a tiny sand island in the middle of a river. His airplane stood out sitting against the background of sand. It made him easy to find and easy for the SAR (search and rescue) force to pick him up, and the river provided a small moat of protection against the bad guys on the far shore who would have loved to have captured or killed him.

While all Ravens have unique individual stories and experiences, they all shared the hazards of the mission and, whether from a FAC or fighter background, had a single common experience. Each found his way to an assignment in an all-volunteer, highly-classified, clandestine program. Many paths led to the same end. This is simply my personal "getting there" story.

As I neared high school graduation, I wanted to be out in the world. To accomplish that, I enlisted in the Marine Corps. Since I was only 16, my parents managed to void the enlistment and begged me to go to college. They didn't complain very loudly when I selected a state university from Playboy's List of the Top Twenty American Party Schools.

I had only been aware of two presidents: Eisenhower and Kennedy. I respected both and believed America to be a moral nation. When I entered college, the war in Viet Nam was not a major issue, though anti-war demonstrations gained strength and garnered press as the years passed. That crowd had a lot of appeal, mostly girls and marijuana. I was a pseudo hippy, on the fringe, looking for benefits but not a true believer. In my mind, our government would not be involved in Viet Nam if it was not important and right. The "Domino Theory" sounded plausible.

I knew that I didn't know enough to make an informed decision about government policy so I studied the Annam Republic and the history of the Viet Nam conflict. Safe in academia, my study left me without passion or a sense of the right and wrong of the war. Long-haired young women and the summer of love attracted me. Burning my draft card and running to Canada didn't.

Kennedy was assassinated. American politics changed. I graduated; got married, and landed a job I wanted teaching handicapped kids and coaching junior varsity football. Many of my peers, who were facing the draft, envied my exempt status. The anti-war protests shifted into high gear, becoming a nightly news event. I remained confused and conflicted. Then I read a quote, I think it was Hemingway, which said, "War is the experience of a generation." Something clicked and I decided the best way to understand the noise and rhetoric was to support our government and participate.

My family had no ties to the military. My father was too old to serve during WWII and spent the war years using his engineering talents to design and build parts of Fort Knox. My favorite uncle Joe enlisted to serve in the cavalry. He had trained and bred horses all his life and thought he could contribute. When he finished basic training, the horse cavalry was dissolved. Joe, who had never driven a car or even a tractor, became a fuel truck driver. He ground gears and humped fuel across Europe chasing General Patton, emerging from the war as a PFC (private first class).

Two of my fraternity brothers had been in the Marine Corps but not the war. They did not have much insight. Ignorant but determined, I hit every recruiter's office and took tests for all the service branches. Looking at my test scores, every recruiter told me I needed to become a pilot. Honestly, I had never considered it. I liked mechanical things and had built motors, raced motorcycles, and played at racing sports cars, but flying was an exciting new idea.

Recruiters often get a bad rap. Mine were exceptional. The Marines said if I failed pilot training I'd be an infantry officer. The Army stretched a bit saying they would guarantee me a helicopter. The Navy sold the excitement of landing on an aircraft carrier, but being at sea for months at a time with a shipload of men was not appealing. The Air Force was all about flying. I signed on the dotted line, passed the physical, and received a date for Officer Training School (OTS).

In retrospect, I should have shaved and cut my hair before arriving at OTS. I was in a class with prior service enlisted men who looked military and knew the drill. I did not. Despite exceeding the required physical standards, I was ordered to perform remedial physical training (PT) every morning. OTS doesn't have much sleeping or preparation time in the schedule. It is one way to see how officer candidates handle stress. Getting up early every morning to run cut into the little time available, as did having Charge of Quarters duty every weekend while some of my fellow OTs got to go off-base and relax. I did not quit and graduated with my class. Just prior to graduation, those of us on the slate for Undergraduate Pilot Training (UPT) were asked our preference of training bases. I did not even know there was more than one UPT base so I answered, "Wherever the Air Force wants me, sir." I was assigned to Williams AFB in Phoenix, Arizona, which I later learned was the plum choice.

UPT was a huge challenge. College had been easy. OTS had been a bit of a pain, but UPT was flat hard, academically more difficult than college, and physically more demanding than OTS. Our initial flying was done in the Cessna 172, which the Air Force designated as T-41. Regardless of the name, it was a small civilian aircraft. All of us would get up in the middle of the night, drive to the base, and board a bus which took us to Eloy Airfield. Bouncing along in the bus, we would quiz each other on emergency procedures and aircraft operating limits because the moment the bus stopped we were to be in our seats waiting for the officer in charge. When he showed up, we snapped out of our chairs to stand at rigid attention: chest out, butt in, fingers aligned with nonexistent trouser seams. We were allowed to sit and then one at a time were called on to answer a question. Stress was part of the process. We had to stand in front of our peers and the instructors and answer the question verbatim or be told to sit and stand down for the day. Anyone who missed too many questions could not complete the curriculum on time and was dismissed from pilot training. As I remember, we lost about seven guys at Eloy.

My civilian instructor was topnotch. He was a grizzled old guy with some 14,000 hours of flight time. He loved flying and just wanted to share that love with his students. We had a ball. I got to solo a ride early and spent the rest of my Eloy time with him playing with the aircraft. We did every kind of stall, Lazy Eights, Chandelles, and some unapproved maneuvers. I sailed through my T-41 check rides with military evaluation pilots and looked forward to the next phase of training.

The T-37 (called the Tweet) was a small twin-engine jet. We flew from the Air Force base so the dreaded bus ride was gone. The Tweet had side-by-side seating. My instructor thought that the design was to allow him to hit students. After a few rides, my tablemates asked for a different instructor. I stayed and despite him, I managed to complete this phase. My instructor kept it from being fun, but I did run into him after my first tour as a Raven. He was still a captain and still an ass but that's another story.

The final phase of pilot training introduced us to the T-38, a sleek white afterburning supersonic airplane. My instructor, a lieutenant, believed in explaining and demonstrating rather than yelling and hitting. Waking up every day with a smile, eager to get to the flight line became the new norm. I flew a few rides with an instructor who had completed a Viet Nam tour in the F-105. We talked a lot about assignments. I let him know that I had joined to go to Viet Nam and that I'd been reading a lot about the Air Commandos and the first Special Operations Wing. He provided great insight into their various missions and aircraft, suggesting I might opt for either an A-1 or an assignment as a forward air controller (FAC). My assignment dream sheet was topped with an A-1 followed by an O-1 or OV-10 FAC aircraft. My assignment was an O-1. It made me a happy camper.

Fledgling forward air controllers trained at Hurlburt Field, home of the 1st Special Operations Wing. I flew most of my rides with two exceptional instructors. Both were brash and cocky, but had the obvious respect of their peers. They had "been there, done that, and survived." The classes at Hurlburt were about as simple as the aircraft. Flying the O-1 certainly was not difficult. I connected with my instructors and found the entire experience fun.

About halfway through training both instructors took me aside and mentioned a program they would only refer to as Steve Canyon. Both cautioned me not to mention it to my classmates but told me if I wanted some exciting combat flying after my 12-month tour in Viet Nam I needed to request a meeting with the commander of whichever Tactical Air Support Squadron (TASS) I was assigned to and tell him I was a Steve Canyon volunteer. They never would tell me exactly what I was volunteering for, saying only, "It's classified. Volunteer and you'll have a need to know."

Like most young males I knew I was indestructible. This felt like an exciting, enticing opportunity. I had read Milton Caniff's comic strips: "Terry and the Pirates" and "Steve Canyon." Both featured bold pilots flying around Asia doing the impossible. If this program lived up to its name, it had to be great.

The trip to Asia included a stint at winter survival school. I doubted I would be shot down over Siberia so did not take it too seriously. The enlisted instructors were excellent. The city boys probably learned a lot; those of us who grew up hunting and fishing, not so much. We bussed to the woods for our survival trek. The instructors asked for a volunteer to carry the extra parachute material. Ever cocky, I raised my hand. They loaded me up and directed us to don snowshoes. Standing on firm snow over a ploughed road, snowshoes seemed unnecessary. I said, "I'll carry this stuff but would rather not wear snowshoes."

The instructor said, "Fine." He directed us to walk across an open field dotted with small bushes. I took my first step and sank in snow which was well above my head. The *small bushes* were the tops of pine trees. As the instructors and my classmates laughed, they hauled me back up to solid ground. My ego flag flew at half-mast as I strapped on the snowshoes.

The prisoner of war (POW) camp portion of training did not go much better. We were taught the Code of the American Fighting Man and knew we had an obligation to attempt escape if captured. But we were told we had to coordinate escapes with the ranking POW who, in training, would grant or refuse an escape chit. The boss POW refused my request. In my mind, the man had been co-opted by the enemy (our instructors). I escaped and called in as we had been directed. Expecting an "atta boy," I got an "oh shit" for escaping without a chit. Another error, which bought me a lecture, extra time in the dust-covered black burlap hood, time in the compression box and the steel coffin, some extra roughhousing, and some anger on my part. I thought I had applied the lessons taught.

The next step saw me flying off to Clark AB in the Philippines for jungle survival. The class bussed from the base to our quarters in Angeles City. The bus's windows sported wire mesh to stop grenades. The motel's decorations included guard towers, a fence, barbed wire, and armed guards. It was my first exposure to a potentially hostile environment, in this case martial law in the Philippines. The instructors provided tons of potentially life-saving information. During the escape and evasion phase, my partner and I watched the contracted Negritos search for us from a parachute turned hammock high in the top of a tree. It felt very real.

Finally, we boarded a contract commercial jet bound for Viet Nam. On arrival, I expected to see scenes resembling the pictures in Life magazine: bunkers, soldiers, barbed wire, the sound of gunfire. That was not the case. We landed at Cam Ranh on one of the widest, longest runways I had ever seen. The base fronted the ocean and had a beautiful beach, WWII-style barracks, paved roads, an Officers' Club, and many of the amenities you would expect stateside. I roomed with Pinky, a great guy I knew from pilot training, and a former B-58 pilot who would later be my boss.

All new guys attended Theater Indoctrination School. Most of the classes were a repeat of lessons learned at Hurlburt with the addition of a list of things not to do and extensive coverage of the rules of engagement. I flew a couple of pointless rides with instructors from the 21st TASS, demonstrating mastery of emergency procedures, navigation and, on one ride, actually adjusting some artillery on a small patch of seemingly uninhabited jungle. Then, as if by magic, I was deemed combat ready.

The commander of the TASS held a pilots' meeting and asked, "Where do you guys want to go?" Hands went up all over the room; guys knew their desired destinations. After everyone had voiced their selection, the commander asked me what my choice might be.

I answered from a zero knowledge base saying, "Wherever you need me, but I'd prefer a small, remote location." Well, I couldn't have done better. They gave me an airplane, a survival vest, a parachute, a weapon, and orders to report to Bao Loc.

Once I found the place on a map and looked up what information was available, I realized I was off to an Army post which had a pierced steel planking runway, no tower, and no navigation aids. It looked like it would be about an hour-and-a-half flight. Since I had three hours of fuel, I took my first mini tour of Viet Nam, hoping to hell I didn't get lost and run out of gas. I would be lying if I denied the fear associated with that first "combat" flight. Flying along over rice paddies and then triple-canopy jungle it finally dawned on me that this was a war zone and I'd face whatever came up flying alone and on my own—a sobering experience.

The runway at Bao Loc had a hump in the middle that changed the elevation by about 40 feet. It does not sound like much but it meant you could not see another aircraft at the opposite end of the runway. When I flew over there were no people, aircraft, or vehicles in sight. The radios remained silent despite repeated calls on all listed frequencies. I flew over the Army post, wagged my wings and landed. My new boss, a B-52 pilot in his other life, met me accompanied by our radio operator, a tall blond airman on his first assignment. They explained that no one manned the radio unless there was a FAC in the air. My boss did not want to fly a lot but he gave me a tour of the area and sent me off to fly most of our assigned missions. That worked for me.

The Army guys assigned me as a bunker commander at one of the fortified positions on the camp's perimeter. I inspected our little battle station and met my first snake, a cobra. Thinking quickly, I found the ranking NCO in our little group and found out what to do if attacked and, by the way, how to dispatch a cobra without firing a shot. The good news in this was getting checked out on the .30 caliber machine gun and the M-79 grenade launcher. The Army folks also saw to it that I got a personal AR-15. Now fully armed, and dangerous in my ignorance, I'd really arrived.

We had a 175 mm artillery unit stationed with us. The guns were not too accurate but they made a big boom and a huge ground impact. I used them providing convoy security for the trucks traveling the highway through the mountainous part of our area of operations (AO). The downside of having them so close was that they blew the screens out of our tents when they fired over the camp.

Bao Loc provided a "soft" introduction to the war. The farmers in the flat, rice-producing section of our area seemed to appreciate being able to keep their crop rather than having to surrender it to the Viet Cong (VC). The patrols in the mountains often made contact with the enemy but had good artillery coverage. When they needed a bigger boom, the artillery impacts made it easy to spot the enemy and mark for fighters.

Most of my missions involved convoy escort. I would fly the convoy route at or above the regulation-dictated altitude of 1,500 feet above ground level (AGL) and use my eyes to look for changes in the surrounding jungle foliage. Then I'd climb a little higher and use binoculars to scan. Just before the convoy entered my area, I would bend the rules and fly down the road at a very low altitude, 20 to 50 feet, so I could look under the trees. When I found an ambush site, I would call the convoy commander on the FM radio. If they had assigned attack helicopters, I would mark the target and get out of the way. The Cobra choppers were low and slow enough to keep their own eyes on the target. If no Army air was available, I would use the UHF radio to request air from the Direct Air Support Center (DASC). I would usually get either F-100s or A-37s, both of which could put bombs on target. The F-100s were particularly effective when they had a load of "shake and bake," fin-retarded iron bombs and napalm. I read the articles and saw the pictures in the stateside magazines describing the horrors of napalm. The writers did not seem to realize that there is no "nice" way to kill another human being. Perhaps politicians should have to kill an armed, resisting human being before being allowed to send troops into battle. I also got to do a little work from the ground, accompanying a convoy in our unit's magic, radio-equipped jeep.

I learned to FAC Ranch Hand missions, which involved the low-altitude spray of defoliants by C-123 aircraft. My task involved locating and marking the spray-on and spray-off spots plus suppressing any enemy ground fire. The Ranch Hand flights would always be at least two aircraft and often more. After finding the desired spray location, I'd troll the area once watching and listening for ground fire. The Ranch Hand aircraft were usually accompanied by two F-100s who would hold high until needed. Since the O-1 would not go as fast as the C-123s, I would hold at a spot about halfway down the spray track. This allowed me to fire two smoke rockets, one at the spray-on and one at the spray-off spots. About the time the second smoke left the aircraft, the C-123s would be flying under me. I could then complete a split S to fall in behind them and listen for ground fire. If the Ranch Hand aircraft took fire, the F-100s came into play. If not, they'd go to a secondary target. Who knew it wasn't too healthy to soak yourself (flew windows-open to better hear ground fire) and your aircraft in defoliant (Agent Orange)?

I ran my first search and rescue (SAR) mission trying to locate a general officer whose helicopter had failed to reach its destination. The SAR force involved both Air Force FACs and Army helicopters. Between us, we found a lot of enemy soldiers and finally located the wreckage. A ground team went in and recovered the bodies. There were no survivors.

While my first SAR experience provided no elation, one of the high points in any FAC's career is running or participating in a successful SAR and recovering an aircrew or ground team. My second SAR involved another helicopter with four GIs on board. Unlike many SARs it was a relatively simple mission. The helicopter pilot knew about where he was, executed a textbook auto rotation and came down in an area covered by low trees and high grass. None of the survivors were seriously injured. Once I located the wreck, another Army helicopter came in and made the pickup. There were no enemy forces in the area.

Later, I had the honor of being involved in more difficult SAR missions. I am honestly unable to capture on paper the adrenaline rush or the difficulty of running a SAR. Finding the survivor presents a remarkable challenge. Most jet pilots know where they were when their aircraft was hit. Then they focus on coping with the emergency condition, radio a Mayday call, and try to keep the bird flying. It can be all "assholes and elbows" in the cockpit.

Of course, while they're doing this, they're whizzing along at five to ten miles a minute. If forced to eject, the parachute drifts. Most survivors on the ground have only a general idea of their location. You can often home on the signal from their survival radio and once close the survivor can often vector you to his position. But they can still be hard to see. You might think the big white parachute they used to get to the ground would be very visible. But the first thing an able-bodied survivor does is to hide his chute. The enemy can see that big white canopy as easily as another pilot. Even if deployed or stuck in the trees, a chute remains a difficult find: big jungle, small cloth. If the survivor lands in the jungle or a mountainous area, he becomes invisible under the foliage or just over the ridge. While flying, usually very low, and searching the FAC is on the UHF radio scrambling the SAR force. In Viet Nam that was usually A-1s accompanying Army choppers or the Air Force's Jolly Green Giant helicopters. Later it might involve those same forces with the possible addition of Air America.

With the survivor finally in sight, the FAC gets real busy keeping enemy soldiers away from the pickup area. The FAC talks to the survivor on one radio, to the attack aircraft on another, and quite often to ground forces on a third, while enemy soldiers try to down another aircraft. You learn to fly left-handed or with your knees on the stick as you twist radio dials and select rocket stations. Intense does not begin to describe the experience. There is no risk too great. At the same time, it requires restrained bravado. If you get shot down you've added to rather than reduced the difficulty of a pickup.

Para-rescue men (PJs) often have to ride the helicopter's hoist down into enemy territory to help injured survivors. Their courage has to be seen to be understood. When the survivor is riding the hoist to rescue, the PJ extracted, and the remaining enemy forces killed, the mission ends and you fly home. I was always flooded with relief not to have made a mistake which could have killed the man on the ground or prevented his rescue. Recognizing the raw courage of the A-1 drivers, helicopter pilots, and PJs made me both humble and grateful, knowing they would be there for me if needed. As the adrenaline faded, exhaustion would override emotion. Beer time started with landing.

After several months of flying and learning, I had to take an aircraft to Cam Ranh Bay for maintenance. While there the commander asked me if I would mind moving to Gia Nghia, which he described as an even smaller base. Not knowing anything about it, I said, "Sure, when?" I was told to pick up the fresh aircraft, stop by Bao Loc to pick up my gear and press on to the new location.

That required the same old drill, find the damn place on the map and figure out how to get there. The data said that Gia Nghia was a 1,000-foot-long dirt runway on top of a plateau. An interesting note read, "Only assigned pilots may use this runway." That sounded great as it meant less head-shed folks dropping in for inspections and check rides. Off I went and found a red clay runway that looked a lot less than 1,000 feet long, had two wrecked aircraft sitting alongside, and had steep drop-offs at either end. As I lined up to land, some fool fired a single round at me. Never could find the guy even though the single-shot final approaches continued off and on the entire time I was there.

My new boss was the B-58 pilot I had met at Cam Ranh. We flew one orientation ride and it turned out I had put in considerably more air strikes than he had and had more combat flying time. He seemed pleased to let me fly most of our allocated hours so I could "get experience." We lived in a converted stable which was a step up from tents. The Army unit focused on developing indigenous Regular/Popular Force units in the surrounding villages and seldom needed air support. We had a 105 mm artillery unit attached which proved a good thing—less noise than the 175s and a great deal more accuracy.

Our AO had two Army Special Forces camps, Bu Prang and Duc Lop. Duc Lop was fairly large and enjoyed good support from attached helicopters and FACs from Ban Me Thout. Bu Prang was far smaller but its location near the Cambodian border generated a lot of activity. On one of my early flights, I radioed the camp and asked if their dirt strip, which was well outside the perimeter, was secure enough for me to land so I could meet them. They responded, "It is today. Come on down."

The gentlemen I met were very special indeed. They explained that the original camp had been overrun and that they and their Montagnard allies patrolled aggressively and could often use support. Since I was a "B" FAC, one without prior fighter experience, I was not supposed to support U.S. troops. My Army friends at Bao Loc had not cared and neither did these guys. It was one of the many rules of engagement that did not seem appropriate to the time or place. Bu Prang provided a lot of business, most of which involved troops in contact under triple-canopy jungle. Flying over the sea of green treetops, trying to find the fight, locate the friendlies, and attack the enemy without causing friendly casualties remains the stuff of nightmares. Often the friendlies would have to fire a pen gun flare through the jungle canopy so I could find them.

On one occasion, I was flying with my boss in the back seat when we got an urgent call for help. The guys were in contact with a larger enemy force and had two wounded. We responded, found the fight, and called the DASC for air. The response we got was not helpful. The target was deemed too close to the border. I responded that I'd made a mistake sending the coordinates and revised my request only to hear that the first air available was 20 to 30 minutes out. We called two Army units and managed to get some helicopters on the way. In the meantime, I used our eight rockets as an attack weapon, firing a single rocket into the enemy position on each pass. Both my boss and I could hear the volume of fire on the ground; he said, "This is terrible. What can we do?" We had six grenades between us, so I dropped down to skim the trees while he pulled pins and dropped them. I am sure they were not effective, but they did divert some attention to us. We followed the grenades with multiple passes firing our AR-15s. Again, it was probably not effective but created a fine diversion. About the time we were winchester (out of) everything, the helicopters arrived, ended the firefight, and evacuated the wounded. I will admit that my boss both surprised and impressed me. He was a warrior.

The Special Forces troops recommended us for a Bronze Star for the day's events. When it got to our headquarters it was disapproved and we received a letter reminding us of minimum altitudes, B FACs supporting U.S. troops, actions close to the Cambodian border, and other trivia. I thought the letter and the attitude behind it peculiar for a war zone.

In retrospect, it reflected the politics of the time. We'd had one president who sat in the oval office picking targets in North Viet Nam like a second lieutenant target officer, seeming to worry more about angering the Chinese or Russians than winning the war. We had a Secretary of Defense who was determined to use gadgets to gain an advantage. The funniest or saddest depending on the mood of the moment was the sensor array dropped along the Ho Chi Minh Trail to "pinpoint" enemy traffic. The sensors sort of looked like banana plants but didn't match any indigenous jungle growth. I always wondered what the North Vietnamese Army (NVA) thought about that effort and why the powers in DC couldn't trust the eyeballs of the trail watchers on the ground.

Nixon seemed bound and determined to use his foreign-born and much-beloved-in-DC Secretary of State to negotiate a peace. He too limited the attacks in the north until he finally figured out that limiting damage to the enemy doesn't advance your cause.

While the anti-war forces demonstrated and most of the press wrote their stories from the safety of Saigon, we fought the war. The generals brought in more and more conventional ground forces. The Air Force decided that all pilots needed a tour in Asia before others would be forced into second tours, putting transport and bomber pilots with little inclination or experience in fighter assignments. The military got busy punching their "been in combat" tickets so they could get the next promotion. Our government welcomed Hanoi Jane back to the states and refused to charge her with treason, a real morale builder. Our Army in Asia ended up with a tooth-to-tail ratio of 15; translated that yields 15 support troops for one fighter. Even those of us in the Air Force do better than that and we are often accused of building Officers' Clubs before anything else.

I realized there were two different war perspectives in play when I was ordered to go to Saigon to brief a general officer on a strike I had put in close to the Cambodian border (of course others were under orders to put in "illegal" strikes at the same time). I figured I'd get chewed out for something even though my Special Forces guys seemed rather pleased with my efforts. I cut my own hair, shined my mud-red boots as well as I could, and wore the cleanest set of jungle fatigues I owned. I thought I was ready. Alas, the briefing site was off the air base and the air police wouldn't let you off the base with weapons. I didn't even bat an eye, just got fuel, jumped back in my little airplane, and left. My boss explained my absence as a maintenance issue.

I encountered my first antiaircraft site north of Bu Prang. It was a classic triangle with one 12.7 mm machine gun at each point, which probably had helicopters as a primary target. I could see the troops and the guns but continued straight and level, hoping they would think their camouflage had worked and hold fire. They did not shoot and I stayed well away while calling for air. Magpie, a flight of three Australian B-57s, checked in to work. I briefed them on the target and told them I had never worked B-57s before. Lead said, "We fly rather long final approaches as we bomb from level flight."

"Tell me when to mark," I radioed as I dropped well below the AF's mandated 1,500 feet AGL (didn't think they could shoot me through the trees).

"Mark now." came from Magpie lead.

"The target is 15 meters left of my smoke lead."

"Tally ho." The first bomb came off his plane and went right into the gun revetment.

"Shack lead. I'm in to mark the second gun." Here came number two, straight and level. "Magpie two, you're taking fire," I radioed, trying to be cool but very concerned.

He replied, "Negative mate, we're taking hits." His airplane never wavered and boom, the second gun was gone.

Magpie three repeated the performance and the guns and revetments were gone, nothing left but scrap metal. We used the rest of their ordnance to see if the guns had been protecting anything. No luck there. After watching some of our fighter aircraft fling bombs everywhere but on target, the Magpies were impressive. My boss let me fly over to their base to thank them and give them some enemy weapons we had on hand. The party that ensued was legendary in its own right. Awesome Aussies!

The Special Forces guys allowed me to accompany them on some "walkabouts." They also introduced me to the Mike Force at Ban Me Thout East. While I did not get to do a lot on the ground, I did get to watch the night FACs (call sign Covey) work a target. The aircraft could not be seen until the FAC dropped a flare for the fighters. Then the sheer amount of tracer accompanied by air bursts looked like a massive 4th of July celebration. Curled up under the bushes in my little hide I felt a lot safer than they must have.

After 11 months and some 700 combat hours, I still did not know if the war was right or wrong. While the cities and large towns had reasonable infrastructure (roads, sewers, running water), the villagers got little from the central government. On the other hand, the NVA and Viet Cong routinely committed atrocities to force villagers to provide intelligence or to give up the food they had worked hard to grow.

I decided that war fought for anything less than national survival simply reflects the foolishness of man. But the war had become very personal. Friends had been wounded and killed. My country had spent lives and treasure. The enemy, which had been sort of a faceless idea, had become real. I felt a nearly overwhelming enmity and animus toward them.

I flew to Cam Ranh and made an appointment to see the TASS commander. I walked into his office and reported in a proper military manner – tossing my very best salute while saying, "Sir, Lieutenant Diuguid reporting with a statement."

The boss returned my salute and asked, "What have you got?"

I told him exactly what my instructors at Hurlburt had briefed me to say. "Sir, I want to volunteer for the Steve Canyon program."

The Old Man went into aggressive question mode: "Where did you hear of this? Do you know where you'd be flying? Do you know you have to extend your tour for six months?" and on and on.

Once again my ignorance came to the rescue. "Sir, I don't know anything about it other than my IPs at Hurlburt said it was challenging combat flying." His office called the next morning and told me to keep flying at Gia Nghia until a replacement could be sent and then to return to Cam Ranh for assignment.

I did what I was told despite some last-minute reservations and *What have I gotten myself into?* thoughts. My replacement at Gia Nghia arrived. It was the same friend from pilot training that I'd met at Cam Ranh months ago. I left with a single duffle bag and my personal weapons: a 9 mm pistol, AR-15, and an M79 grenade launcher. The Cam Ranh head shed told me to go to a specific part of the aircraft parking ramp and to board the C-123 aircraft that would be parked there. Nice guys at the head shed, no offer of a ride to the aircraft, no explanation of where I was headed or what I was to do on arrival. But I did not have to deal with the passenger terminal so that was a plus. I humped my load through the heat and humidity and found a very strange black C-123. My name was on the passenger list so I got on and joined a rough-looking bunch of GIs and, I guess, allied soldiers.

Our first stop was Nakhom Phanom, a base in Thailand. I could guess the location because I saw a bunch of A-1s and OV-10s on the ramp. Most of my companions off-loaded. We took off, flew a short while, and landed. The ramp was lowered and I was told to get off. I thought *What the hell?* It was nearly dark and we were on the taxiway. On my left were F-4s being armed for takeoff. On my right was a red and white gate with an armed guard. A jeep appeared from the gate. The driver and passengers were from Detachment 1 of the 56th Special Operations Wing. They welcomed me to Udorn, Thailand and said we were going to their hootch for beer and food. The evening was fun but little was said about the detachment or the mission.

The next morning I learned that the red and white gate protected the entrance to the Air America ramp. On one side of the ramp were C-46 and C-47 transports, H-34 helicopters, and some short takeoff and landing (STOL) aircraft that I didn't recognize. They turned out to be Pilatus Porters. On the other side were O-1s, T-28s, and another multi-passenger STOL aircraft I had not seen before, a U-17. The national markings on the aircraft presented an interesting mix of nations.

I finally learned my destination and was directed to turn in my Air Force ID, dog tags, and personal identification cards. I got a red and white checked card, number 0038, which gave me access to the Air America ramp and club. The NCOs in life support asked me how I wanted my survival vest configured and did not bat an eye when I asked for two holsters, one for the AF issue .38 and one for my 9 mm, two survival radios, an extra radio battery, a pocket for 9 mm clips, a tourniquet, a survival knife, and a clip for three small "personal-sized" concussion grenades, sometimes called ping-pong balls by the GIs I had been around. They sent me off base to a Thai tailor for some "civilian" clothes.

The following morning Air America flew me to Vientiane, Laos. Some embassy guys picked me up at the Air Operations Center and took me to the Raven house. My briefings were scheduled for the next morning at the embassy. That evening, a couple of the guys came dragging in from the war. I learned Long Tieng, also called 20 Alternate, would be my new home. They informed me that we were supporting General Vang Pao and his army of Hmong soldiers against both Pathet Lao and North Vietnamese Army forces. We had a couple of beers and they hit the rack. They headed out at zero dark thirty to go fly. A fellow from the embassy picked me up and escorted me into a secure area of the embassy compound. All the embassy personnel were working feverishly sending messages and answering radios. They seemed far more interested in "administrating" than in providing the promised briefings. Instead they handed me a prepared map bag that included a 1:250,000-scale general navigation map which covered the area from Vientiane in the south to the northern border of Military Region II, which abutted China and ran to the area's eastern border next to North Viet Nam. A collection of 1:50,000-scale maps for precise target location finished the bag, which ended up being about 18 inches long, 12 inches wide, and 12 inches high. They told me the "old heads upcountry" would brief me. They did not bother to tell me that Alternate had nearly been overrun during the night with all hands engaged in a major firefight which included a short round of cluster bombs delivered by an F-4. One staffer suggested that he could give me a ride to the airport and I could catch a ride to Alternate with Air America. Air America ops put me in a Porter headed to Alternate. So my first real view of Laos was as a passenger. When we arrived, the Porter touched down, spun around on the runway, and went back to Vientiane. The pilot said it was too hot to stay on the ground.

I like to think I am self-reliant, self-assured, and maybe more than a little cocky. But as I stood in Air America ops trying to find a ride back to the Raven house (which I could not have found on a bet) I wondered, once again, exactly what I had volunteered for and where I might gain a little insight into what was happening. I hope I looked more confident than I felt.

All the Ravens from Alternate came stumbling in that night. They looked beat and sounded angry and depressed that they would not be flying out of Alternate at first light. Collectively they summoned up the energy to take me out on a new-guy night, which included tours of every bar and whorehouse in Vientiane. The next morning I got pulled out of the rack in the dark, jumped in a jeep, and was off to the airport. My checkout pilot, Craig, was a very quiet, very serious young man. I flew in his back seat and got a comprehensive tour of Military Region II, our AO. He received a request for support from a ground unit in contact and led me through requesting air from Cricket, the airborne command and control post. He controlled the fighters with ease and expertise, putting ordnance in very close proximity to the friendly force. While I certainly recognized his professional competence, not a wasted word or motion, he seemed overly cautious. At the time, I did not know the extent of the recent losses the Ravens had suffered or the number of aircraft that had been shot up. I did not realize I was a replacement for a man who had been killed in action. In the past, I had replaced men who had finished their tour and rotated back to the States. When reality caught up with my oh-so-feeble and uninformed mind, things made more sense.

After landing, he gave me a thorough briefing on flying with Hmong backseaters, cautioned me against flying over or attacking the Chinese Cultural Center, an area on the north end of the Plain of Jars (PDJ) close to Arrowhead Lake, and stressed the Ravens' self-imposed rules of engagement. The primary rules were: never claim any battle damage (BDA) results that you were not sure of; do not kill any friendly forces. I later learned that 7th Air Force doubted our effectiveness and sent random RF-4s to photograph recent targets, trying to catch us exaggerating. We flew another mission or maybe two with me in the front seat. I put in some F-4s while he observed. That evening we flew back to Vientiane.

The next morning I flew as Raven Two Six. It had been a long, convoluted journey.

My learning curve remained high for the next couple of months. I thought I had earned a doctorate in FAC operations at Gia Nghia but found there was much more to learn. My first "solo" combat mission provided a lot of insight into my own shortcomings. I took, as advised, a Hmong backseater with me. My task was to check in with three friendly positions to see if they needed support. If not, I could go hunting. After a lot of radio conversation, my backseater reported that none of the friendlies were in contact or in need of air. So I flew by the Chinese Cultural Center and entered the Ban Ban Valley. After a bit, a 37 mm antiaircraft gun fired a few half-hearted rounds at us. I could not find the gun but a little further down the valley I did find some trucks hidden under trees. I called Cricket for air and was fortunate to get a flight of F-105s that had been weathered off their target in North Viet Nam. While waiting for them, I heard rounds zipping past the aircraft but could not see any tracers. The noise was more of a whir than the pop pop pop of 12.7s. Fortunately, the gunner missed and even more fortunately I happened to see the light smoke from his gun. My wild jinks – fear and adrenaline – made the backseater sick. Miraculously, most of that discharge also missed me.

When the Thuds showed up, I briefed them, "The first target is what I believe is a 12.7 protecting some trucks. There's a 37 mm gun about a click west, so let's work this from SW to NE with a right break." That was fine with lead so I shot a rather long-range rocket which hit about 60 meters from the target. "Lead, that was a poor mark. If you'll notice the tree line is very straight except for a little pimple on the south side 60 meters east of my mark. That isn't a tree. It's a camouflage net. Hit it."

"Got it," said lead, "in hot."

"In sight, cleared hot," and the gun disappeared, emerging from the bomb smoke on its side in pieces. The rest of the flight took care of the trucks and got some secondary explosions.

I was pretty proud of me.

When I debriefed Intel, Craig, my mentor, listened quietly. When we were alone he explained just how foolish I had been without coming right out and calling me a dumb ass. "Ban Ban doesn't have any immediate effect on the enemy's offensive. It's a high-risk area better served by two aircraft. If you'd been shot down, we'd have diverted all the Ravens and our air to a SAR. That puts everyone at unneeded risk and, more importantly, takes us away from our primary mission, which is to support the Hmong and defend Alternate." He went on, "You have to think of the big picture. By the way, if you heard rounds and didn't see any tracer it was probably a ZPU. They often have green tracers and don't light immediately after leaving the gun." My ego took yet another major hit because everything he said was obviously right. It explained his effective, if seemingly cautions, flying. Once again, I found myself the rookie with a lot to learn.

That was okay by me. After a long journey, I was one – Raven Two Six.

Four decades later, memories still float around in my head. Many concern individuals or specific missions but most focus on things we did not do; things we did not see and the sheer difficulty presented by some targets.

We did not fly more than the 125 hours per month mandated – unless it was necessary. For about two months we operated short-handed. We had lost some pilots to combat, some to normal rotation, and had rejected a volunteer who lacked the experience and ability to fly the mission. The tempo of the war never slowed. Those of us left flew and flew and flew. I believe all of us logged the actual hours flown so that the maintenance men would have accurate numbers. Every so often, we would hear from flight records at Udorn, "There must be a mistake in your records. They indicate you flew 260 hours last month."

"I'm sure you're right. Just put me down for 125. Thanks for the call."

During this same period, the bad guys must have received a load of 122 mm rockets. At irregular intervals, rockets would come flying into our valley. Rockets are not precisely aimed; they target an area. Most of us tended to ignore them but they added to the tension and the crushing fatigue of continual high-risk flying. At one point, a Hmong patrol encountered a company of North Vietnamese about three kilometers from the runway at Alternate. That morning the routine became: take off, climb a little bit, turn left, fire eight rockets into the enemy force, land, get eight more rockets and do it again. Each sortie lasted perhaps 15 minutes. The Lao T-28s maintained the same routine until the enemy was routed. It is difficult for me to describe how wrung out we all were. Perhaps the phrase "bone weary" best captures it.

Air America pilots would often be asked to land at a Lima Site that had been re-occupied by friendly forces. If the runway was clear and the area was not too hot, they would make a call on the Air America common frequency that Lima Site XX was open. My friend Kayak and his company of Hmong troops took over a Lima Site on the southern end of the PDJ that had been occupied by the enemy during the monsoon season. I checked in to see if he needed any support and he told me the runway was clear of unexploded ordnance and ready for use and asked me to certify it open. I landed without incident, received no ground fire and got out and walked the runway. It was fine. So when I took off I went to Air America common frequency and noted that I had just landed at the site and that it should be open for traffic. Even before I landed my boss got a message from the desk-bound in Vientiane grounding me and ordering me to report to the embassy. Sandy, Raven Two Zero, was senior FAC and our immediate supervisor. He called the desk-bound twit and informed him that there was no rule against us landing at or opening a recently captured Lima Site. Further, he went on, now talking to the desk-bound's boss, I was ungrounded and would not be reporting to the embassy. Some days, life was good.

After that, those of us who sometimes landed at questionable sites for fuel simply failed to report it. Funny enough, the desk-bound never thought to ask how we flew some six-hour missions in an aircraft that only had fuel for three.

Later when it appeared General Vang Pao's forces might recapture the entire military region, our political betters established a Raven Box. We were informed that we could only provide support within that area. The plan was designed to contain General Vang Pao's forces and maintain some unseen political balance. We *never*, of course, bombed out of bounds.

When I had completed my six-month tour as a Raven I tried to extend for another six months as did my friend Growth. We were told that we could extend but we would have to transfer to another military region. Growth moved. I declined, seeing the decision as yet another arbitrary choice made by the desk-bound. Why force men who operated successfully in an area to go learn another? I was told, "Military Region II is simply too hazardous to allow anyone to fly there more than six months." The logic failed to impress.

Many years later I was thrilled to see that Generals Schwarzkopf and Horner demanded a clear political objective, used overwhelming force to achieve that objective, and did so with minimal loss of friendly lives. War will never be a nation-building exercise. It has one aim, the achievement of a political objective through destruction—would be nice if people better understood that.

Many things seen remain invisible. Four different Ravens, on different days, reported seeing a high-speed silver jet aircraft that looked like a MIG north of the PDJ. Intel told us there were no MIGs flying in Laos and that airborne radar would have seen them if they were there. Ergo, they were not seen. A few months later a MIG-21 flew over Alternate and was engaged by F-4s. I imagine it was then deemed possible to have MIGs in the area.

Redcoat, the CIA officer at Lima Site 32, passed me a target several miles northeast of his position. I found it and was working a flight of F-4s when the crew in the second aircraft reported activity on their radar warning gear. As two radioed lead, I was telling him that he had black airbursts just behind him. I do not know what F-4 Intel did with that report but I assume that I did not see any black airbursts because Intel said there were no radar-controlled guns and certainly no 57 mm weapons (which happened to make black airbursts) in MR II.

A couple of other Ravens and the fighters they were working reported seeing antiaircraft missiles fired. The SA-7 shoulder-launched missile had been developed by Russia. But there were none in Laos. Those became rocket-propelled grenades (RPGs) despite the fact that the guys said they tried to track the fighters and self-destructed well beyond normal RPG range.

Growth and I were flying two-ship reconnaissance over an area when we found a large metal frame, fat in the middle and tapered at both ends. It looked sort of like a canoe. Two uprights supported it and it was connected to a heavy electrical cord that terminated in a bunker. It looked like some kind of radar to us but neither of us had enough experience to positively identify it. We took a picture and described it to Intel. They did not identify it as anything in the enemy's order of battle. The next day, the thing was still there. So we blew it to pieces. The bunker contained a generator. Our battle damage assessment was: one large canoe frame and a generator destroyed. We did not see a radar.

Some targets were far more difficult than others. Many hidden targets required a lot of looking and some luck to locate. Terrain and sheer size made some very visible targets difficult to destroy.

The enemy's refueling station on the PDJ fit into the hard-to-find category. We knew it existed. Several of us had searched for it with no success. One day Waldo, Raven 21, noticed some bushes adjacent to the road out of the Ban Ban that looked dead. He explored more and found truck tracks under the bushes and a small vertical standpipe. As I remember, it took two sets of fighters to get bombs exactly where he wanted them but when he did there was a huge secondary explosion and fire. The next day fighters were still reporting a smoke plume above 20,000 feet.

Moose, one of our civilian intelligence partners, provided us exact coordinates for several enemy communications centers. When you arrived, you would find triple-canopy jungle but no visible target. If you dropped down to treetop level you could see one straight line just above the trees. The antennas looked like a two-inch water pipe. If you flew by, they would somehow tip or lower the whole thing and become invisible again. The technique that worked required pulling the pin on a smoke grenade and holding it out the window in one hand while you flew with the other. When you saw the antenna, you dropped the smoke can. Then it did not matter what they did with the antenna. Smoke in the trees provided a target reference. Bombs would thin out the trees so you could tell how well or poorly you had done.

One invisible target caused us a lot of grief at Alternate. The enemy must have expended near-superhuman effort to move 122 mm artillery pieces within range of the runway. They had a spotter hidden somewhere on the surrounding ridges to direct their fire. Unlike rockets, aimed artillery rounds do a lot of damage. We knew the range of the weapons and could look at the impact craters to derive a direction but that left a huge area. We all looked for the damn things using eyeballs, binoculars, and every trick we had. They had to have been towed into place but we could not find a truck track or dirt from a recently dug bunker. It was frustrating. If we had a Raven over the southern end of the PDJ they didn't fire, knowing he would probably see the smoke. That was not a long-term option. The guys all needed to be working immediate targets, not flying around in circles. The solution was to drop down just over the tall grass on the southern plain to look for the gun ports. I do not think anyone was thrilled with that challenge. I know I did not look forward to my turn in the barrel. Like the antennas mentioned, the gun ports showed as straight-edged rectangles, a form not found in nature, and like the antennas you could not see them from altitude. When they were finally destroyed, we found that the grass along the track to the bunkers had been dug up and replanted for nearly a kilometer. The dirt must have been hauled out on the trucks that put the guns in place. There were live plants covering the back entrance. It was an invisible, but not impossible target.

There really were not too many targets in the "difficult to destroy" category. But those few caused myriad problems. The NVA and Pathet Lao used a huge cave, about one mile in length, as a truck park and storage area. We found both entrances to the cave and a chimney at about the midpoint. But we could do little or no damage with conventional bombs in front of the entrances and the chimney did not go directly into the cave. After flying, several of us would drink a beer while we perused the Joint Munitions Effectiveness Manual, looking for ordnance that would do the job. A couple of the guys tried the Navy's Zuni rockets and found that even a perfect delivery did not get far enough into the cave to do substantial damage. Bombs with long delay fuses would not penetrate the rock. That is when we started thinking "outside the box" and looked for weapons that created killing overpressure. Initially fuel/air bombs sounded like the answer. But they simply were not big enough. Then we found the answer. There was what I remember as a 15,000-pound bomb listed. We put in a request for one and in a couple of days it appeared on the daily FRAG order.

For some reason, I was elected to FAC this new bit of ordnance. The delivery aircraft was a C-130, normally a transport. When they checked in, I had trouble finding them. The Herkey Bird was way up in the stratosphere, far higher than any fighters I had ever worked. I told the pilot that I had never seen this ordnance delivered and asked him what he wanted me to do. He told me to mark the target and that their first drop would be a dummy to confirm their offset. When he was ready, I put a rocket in the mouth of the cave. I saw a bundle come out of the 130 and shortly after that a parachute deployed. The practice bundle landed about 60 meters from the target. I relayed that information. After a bit, the 130 pilot said he was ready for my mark so I put in another good smoke. The bundle came out of the 130, the parachute deployed and it suddenly dawned on me that I needed to get away from the target area. I pushed everything in the throttle quadrant forward, traded altitude for airspeed and attempted to egress the place. I verbally encouraged my little airplane to get on with moving. Looking over my shoulder, I saw the bomb come down right in front of the cave and then it went off. I have only seen pictures of nuclear explosions but the shock waves traveling out from ground zero sure looked like the same thing. The blast wave flipped my little airplane inverted and when I recovered and turned around the cave looked pretty much the same except that all the surrounding vegetation was flattened. A CIA operator, Kayak, led a ground team in shortly after the strike and found boxes and boxes of weapons, trucks, artillery pieces and, of course, dead enemy soldiers. I noted that "stuff" came out of the other end of the cave and the chimney. We had found the way to put that area out of the war business.

Doc found an entire NVA regiment in an area called the jungle's mouth. We had lost one man in the area and several of us had been shot at but we failed to find the bad guys. Doc did and started putting in air strikes. It seemed that every time a bomb went off some jungle growth would blow away and another target would appear. A couple of other guys went to help Doc and it became apparent that there was not enough tactical air available to destroy all the targets coming into view. That night the guys went to work learning how to request an Arc Light, a B-52 strike. After passing many messages and pictures from our little handheld cameras plus photos from RF-4 reconnaissance aircraft, the mission was approved and flown. The results were remarkable in both destructive power and the number of additional targets exposed. We worked that target for three solid days. We later learned from radio intercepts that Doc and our communal efforts destroyed the entire NVA regiment, including its assigned trucks, artillery, supplies, and soldiers. The regiment remained out of action for the rest of my tour.

When I was back in the States an Air Force acquaintance whose only goal was his next promotion asked me, "Why did you volunteer for that? What did you get out of being a Raven?" I gave him a lightweight, unthinking answer. I never felt obligated to try to explain much to the "anything for the next promotion" crowd. But his question did make me think.

As a Raven, I had a front-row seat as an observer of our government in action. My civilian counterparts forget that the military does not start wars. Our political *betters* decide when and where war will be waged. When they articulate a clear political objective and get out of the way, our military will achieve their goal; remember the first Gulf War. When those same politicians try to micromanage war, the military does not function well. Presidents do not need to pick targets. The Secretary of Defense does not need to inject his "technology is the answer" views into the middle of a war. Most of the members of the Joint Chiefs of Staff remain more political animals than war fighters; too many belong to the "anything for the next promotion" crowd. Grunts and airmen take the fight to the enemy. The folks who believe you can use smart bombs and drones to avoid any collateral damage have not been to war. War is a messy business. There will be collateral damage. If that is not acceptable, do not send our forces to fight.

My favorite combat leader, General Aderholt, was not a particularly skilled pilot. He certainly was not a politician. He was retired as a colonel and only recalled and promoted when the Air Force leadership realized they had no clue about leading the special ops air effort in Asia. He articulated a mission and gave his troops the equipment and latitude to get the job done. Then he supported their actions against those who would "second guess" or "what if" a particular mission. That's combat leadership.

Having been grilled, insulted, and called a liar by a general officer at 7th Air Force, I can testify that the all-jet, supersonic Air Force hated what a few of us managed to accomplish with outdated equipment and an indigenous pilot force. It is true that we could not have been as effective without the support of modern tactical air. We all acknowledge that. It is a shame the accomplishments of the Air Commando force from first deployments in the early 60s to the last day of the war were so difficult for the "establishment" to recognize.

I got to stand shoulder-to-shoulder with General Vang Pao, to appreciate the Hmong culture, and to support some of the fiercest warriors on earth. I was fortunate to work with CIA ground combat leaders, a group that was uniformly brave and dedicated to the mission and their troops. I was privileged to fly with the most honorable group of men I've ever known. Men who know the ugly, horrible face of war but have responded to the call in Panama, Central America, Grenada, the Gulf Wars, and Afghanistan.

Finally, it saddens me to say that I also got to see how our government treats our allies. We deserted the Hmong and later the Cambodians, leading to persecution for one group and the Killing Fields for the other.

My hot-to-be-promoted acquaintance would not have understood that answer, but it reflects a large part of what I got out of being a Raven, and perhaps why I'm a bit of a cynic.

Chapter 22

Darrel Whitcomb, Raven 25
Long Tieng, Sep 1972 – Mar 1973

I was assigned to the 23rd TASS (Tactical Air Support Squadron) starting in February 1972 as an OV-10 forward air controller (FAC). We patrolled the Ho Chi Minh Trail and flew in Military Region (MR) I of South Viet Nam (SVN) during the Easter invasion in support of the 20th TASS, out of Da Nang Air Base, SVN.

In August, H. Ownby and I had a chance encounter with USAF Capt. "Jocko" Haden, an acquaintance from our Air Force Academy days. At the time, he was also on a FAC tour, but doing special duty at 7th Air Force, handling special assignments. He was the detailer for FACs to be assigned to Project 404, "Steve Canyon," the Raven program. We told Jocko that we were interested in the program. He told us that he had lots of volunteers, but, for the cost of dinner and drinks, he would "see what he could do." Done. I received my orders in September, and flew from Nakhon Phanom (NKP) to Udorn to report for in-processing with Detachment 1 of the 56th Special Operations Wing (SOW), "Waterpump." I turned in my personal gear, did all the necessary paperwork, and received my assignment to our detachment up in Vientiane, which worked primarily with the Hmong forces in MR II in north-central Laos. I also found out that originally, I was supposed to go to our southern detachment at Pakse. However, just before my arrival Rich Herold, an MR-II Raven, had been killed, and I was now his replacement, call sign Raven 25. I then flew on an Air America C-123 up to Vientiane. There I was met by US Embassy personnel and my Raven boss, Maj. Jim Coombes.

After more processing, I started flying on 18 September with Vinnie Pastori to become qualified on the O-1 and the U-17. Since I had never flown a tail-dragger aircraft, I had to perform 100 landings. That was a painful process, but that training saved my ass later on when I had to land the O-1 in some austere locations. When complete, I then started my operational flying with Spike Milam as my instructor. He flew me up to the Plaine des Jarres (PDJ), checked me out in our area of operations (AO), and introduced me to all of the key commanders with whom I would be working, including Gen. Vang Pao.

Interesting vignette. We used our VHF-FM radio to speak with ground forces, and generally monitored a common frequency in case they needed to contact us on short notice for support. On one of my missions with Spike, I heard a call that sounded like, "En-nee leven, hab bery bad situation." After several calls, Spike asked me if I was going to answer it. I told Spike, "I am Raven 25, not N eleven," thinking that somebody in the area probably had that specific call sign. He quickly corrected me by explaining, "What he is saying is: 'Any Raven, have very bad situation.'" He further explained, "These guys only know limited 'pidgin' English and he is calling for help." Ah ha. That was great gouge which served me well for the rest of my tour.

Then I started flying operational missions. At that time, the other MR-II Ravens were Jim Coombes, Ted Hanson, Steve Neal (see attached below), Lee McKinley, Pete Dang, Skip Jackson, and Spike Milam.

The days were long. We lived in a nice contract house in Vientiane. It was a bustling Asian city with a strong French colonialist influence which gave it a rich culture and nightlife. We made good use of the great restaurants and bars.

We would launch out of the main airport early and fly to the PDJ, usually logging about three hours. We would then turn the aircraft at Long Tieng twice before flying back down to Vientiane by sundown. At that time, we were not allowed to stay overnight at Long Tieng. Every mission was different. Some days, I would work directly with ground forces who were in contact with enemy Pathet Lao or North Vietnamese Army (NVA) forces. This was classic close air support. We would work USAF fighters – F-4s and A-7s, USAF AC-130s, Laotian T-28s, and contract gunship teams with UH-1s. Many of these were insertion or extraction missions with Air America providing the load helicopters, UH-1s and old H-34s with upgraded engines called "twin-packs." The enemy resisted these efforts, and we got into some pretty good fights. They were equipped with air defense weapons like 37 mm, 23 mm, 14.4 mm, and 127 mm guns, and we took lots of ground fire. My aircraft were hit several times.

In October, Jim Coombes went home and Maj. John Carroll reported in to be our boss. H. Ownby, Terry Pfaff, and Craig Dunn arrived up in MR-II after me. In early November, John Carroll was shot down over the mid PDJ. Terry Pfaff and Steve Neal covered his search and rescue (SAR). Two Air America helicopters tried to get in to him, but he had come down near an NVA bivouac area and the swarming enemy forces precluded any survivable landing. One of the helicopter crewmen reported that John had been shot to pieces and was clearly dead. That night intelligence reported that the NVA had found his remains and he was dead. They identified him by name. The next morning, I was the first FAC up and flew over his wreckage at sunrise. I saw the aircraft and surrounding enemy personnel, and placed a 2,000-pound laser-guided bomb on both. A few days later, Maj. Chuck Hines arrived to be our Raven boss in MR-II.

Note: Years later, a recovery team from Joint Task Force – Full Accounting found the crater in the recovery effort for John's remains.

On 10 December, I was supporting a Hmong element which had been ambushed east of Skyline Ridge. I spotted the enemy force and started directing airstrikes against them. My aircraft was hit by multiple AK-47 rounds. Some came though the cockpit and one missed me by just inches, penetrating the back seat at chest level. Several more hit my engine and it stopped running. Fortunately, I was high enough that I was able to "dead-stick" the aircraft back into Long Tieng.

I took some leave over Christmas and was back in Fort Walton Beach visiting a girlfriend when the Hanoi bombings occurred. It was hard to stay in the holiday spirit when my thoughts were with the many friends that I had who were participating in those missions. It was more difficult still, when H. Ownby called me from Laos to inform me that Hal Mischler (Pakse Raven and former Nail FAC buddy) and Skip Jackson had been killed and I was needed ASAP back in the fight.

When I returned, we continued to fly a heavy schedule. I flew missions all over the AO, close air support for friendly units, infil/exfils, and interdiction missions to find and destroy enemy troops, supplies, and trucks. We called the latter "truck busting," and we killed a lot of them. The enemy gunners always shot at us. We would stay at higher altitudes when away from the friendly forces as our only form of protection. However, I can still recall the heavy "whump-whump" sounds made by the 37 mm shells going by my aircraft. In fact, on one day in January, I was working a target up northeast of the PDJ when a 37 mm just kept firing at me. I requested a flight of F-4s to bomb it. While waiting for them, one of the Hmong FACs that we had trained, Xong Li Tu, heard my call and flew to my location. He saw the gun firing at me and attacked it from a different direction. Several of his rockets hit it and the gun stopped firing. I saw him when we both landed at Long Tieng and I told him that he saved my ass. His reply was classic. "Hey, no sweat Raven 25."

During January 1973, several of us were flown up to Lima Site (LS)-32 for a big celebration. That location was the northernmost position still held by Vang Pao's forces. It had been under siege for several months, and airpower and Air America had held the enemy forces at bay. We were flown in on Air America aircraft and had a smashing party. Lots of stories were told and we all got quite drunk. At one point, I fell out of an open window into a mud puddle. As I opened my eyes, I recall seeing Chuck Hines sitting on a tree trunk, also quite drunk. Sweet youth.

We flew until 22 February 1973, until ordered to cease missions as per the theater-wide cease-fire. As I flew back from my last mission, I could hear on my FM radio the plaintive call, "En-nee leven, en-lee leven, we hab bad situation, need help velly fast." Obviously, the enemy was not observing the cease-fire, but there was nothing more that we could do.

We sat around Vientiane for a few more weeks awaiting orders. I had requested to extend my tour in Southeast Asia (SEA) and return to FAC OV-10 duty with the 23rd TASS. I received my orders and rejoined my old unit at NKP. Subsequently, we flew combat in Cambodia until 15 August 1973, when the "cease-fire" there was directed by the US Congress. After that, I continued to fly the OV-10 at NKP until sent home in March 1974. I then reported to Moody AFB, Georgia to be a T-38 instructor pilot.

During my time as a Raven, we lost John Carroll, Hal Mischler, and Skip Jackson. Several more were wounded, and all of us were shot up and/or shot down. But we were young men at war and that was the deal.

Steve Neal Story
A Raven FAC story © Darrel Whitcomb 2003
Circa 1972, Somewhere Over The PDJ In Northern Laos

Seems there was this Raven named Steve. Now Steve was a Texas Tech boy - linebacker type, and no neck. Really. His body went from chin to shoulders nothing in between.

Anyway, he is out Ravening one day in his deadly O-1 with his trusty Hmong interpreter in the back seat when this ground team calls and asks for help. Seems the guys have gotten themselves in a bit of a scrap and needed a little airstrike to help out. "No problem," says Steve as Cricket – that trusty controller in the sky - tells him that a flight of God's finest Phantom-4s from Ubon Ratchitani are inbound and looking for a target or tanker. Steve thanks him and hears the bombers - sorry fighters - check in with a full load of enthusiasm and Mk-82s. Steve gives them all the briefing stuff and asks what they need. "Just a hold down," replies the steely flight lead. Steve admired such spunk and two minutes later, he looks up and there they are, entering the orbit just above his position. Great.

Steve rocks his wings and the bombers call tally on him. He checks with the ground team and things are getting tense and they are really ready for that airstrike like right NOW.

OK. So Steve rolls in to mark the target. Now he liked to use a real steep dive for his shot. Made for better accuracy. And this day was no exception. "Whoooosh," goes the rocket and splashes the enemy location. "Good mark," call the friendlies.

But as part of his expert rocket technique, Steve also liked to do a steep recovery to escape the pull of the earth and the enemy gunners. But as he got the nose up way high, God decided - at the exact moment - that the front bolts holding Steve's seat in the aircraft would release. And they did. Well gravity being what it is, Steve and his seat rotated back until Steve's head was in the lap of his backseater. To which the surprised Hmong replied, "Steve, what you do?"

Well unfortunately as Steve rotated into the back seat, he held on to the only thing that he had a hand on which was the stick. Now the throttle was full and the airplane was smart and knew that stick back meant go up. So it did. Except that the O-1 does not have a lot of smash for going up much. Well aerodynamics being what they are, the airspeed reduced.

Now Steve liked to fly with the windows open. As the airspeed got real low, all his maps went out the window. That happened just before the airplane stalled. But all that torque from that full throttle told the nose to go left and the aircraft started to spin. The ground team wanted to know what Steve was doing. He didn't answer. The enemy gunners all thought that it was real neat and they celebrated with lots of groundfire.

But Steve was cool. He grabbed hold of one of the side braces and got the seat back forward. Then he did some real neat pilot stuff and got his machine flying again - the guy puking in the back seat didn't faze him at all. Then he decided to take a few minutes to climb back to altitude because he knew that the most important thing for a FAC to do was to sound good on the radio and a few minutes might settle the voice.

Well, back to the airstrike. Steve checked with the ground team and yes, they were ready. He checked with the fighters and yes they were ready too. Just to be on the safe side, Steve asked them if they still had the target. Oh yes they replied. So Steve cleared them in hot.

But instead of rolling in, the flight lead asked for another mark. Steve was confused and asked what the problem was. "No problem the leader replied, "We've got you and we've got the target, we would just like to see that rocket pass again."

A true story dedicated to the memory of fellow RAVEN, Steve Neal. Even copyrighted.

Darrel Whitcomb, Nail/Raven 25

Chapter 23

Chuck Hines, Raven 20
Long Tieng, Nov 1972 – Mar 1973

I was serving my second forward air controller (FAC) tour in Vietnam, flying the OV-10 out of Da Nang, when I sent out my formal message volunteering for duty with Project 404 as a Raven FAC. Was accepted and placed in a waiting queue without a reporting date. Squadron commander, Lt. Col. Abe Kardong, was walking down the long hallway of the 20th Tactical Air Support Squadron (TASS) building one evening when he stopped me and said, "John Carroll has volunteered for the Raven program but will have to extend his current tour in Vietnam for six months in order to be accepted. If you will agree to switch your slot with his he'll still have six months remaining on the current tour and won't have to extend." John was our squadron executive officer. I immediately agreed to the slot switch. John departed Da Nang for Laos and was reported as killed in action (KIA) on the Plaine des Jarres (PDJ), 7 November 1972. I received orders directing me to report for duty as John's replacement on 10 November 1972. An easy-to-remember date. The tenth of November is celebrated annually. The birthday of the U.S. Marine Corps. I enlisted as a private, USMC in February 1952 during the Korean War.

Packed my bag and flew right seat in an O-2A from Da Nang to Udorn, Thailand. Demonstrated how to lean out the engines of an O-2A and explained that if one always flew their cruise legs in that bird with the mixture selector in Full Rich, the front engine would shut down all by itself when the throttles were retarded for descent. That was news. "Is that why my front engine has been shutting down and I've had to do an air-start to get it running again?" "Yup." Landed at Udorn early afternoon. Thanked the pilot for the ride. Picked up my bag and found a temporary bed in a bachelor officer quarters (BOQ) room, then reported for duty at the Special Operations Wing (SOW) inside an isolated, fenced-off area. "Somebody will pick you up in the next couple of days." H. Ownby was sitting on the floor inside the SOW, waiting, and provided his counsel. "Pay no attention to anything these SOW guys tell you – they don't know sierra about anything going on upcountry." It was a lovely day at Udorn air base. Bright sunshine. The scent of blossoms was in the air. Thai ladies were busy laundering clothing by rubbing wet garments against large rocks in a flowing stream. Smelled a lot better than the permanent rotting odor at Da Nang. Took a short nap. Then walked over to the Officers' Club to see if there were any Marines on base celebrating the birthday. Didn't find any.

Next morning Glenn Gemelli hauled me and my A-3 bag in the back seat of his O-1. A thirty-minute flight across northeast Thailand and the Mekong border to Vientiane, Laos. Glenn was an instructor pilot (IP) I had known while stationed at Da Nang. We talked over the interphone. Glenn provided his inflight overview of the Laotian flying regulations and the rules of engagement (ROE) upcountry.

"Laos is not a signatory to any International Civil Aviation Organization (ICAO) agreements so none of the ICAO rules apply in Laos. None of the U.S. FAA Federal Air Regulations (FAR) apply in Laos. Air Force Regulations 60-16, 60-1, and none of the Air Force 50- series of regulations are in effect within Laos. No flying regulations existed in Laos!" "Does a lack of flying rules create a problem for Ravens?" "No. They've been flying in accordance with all their familiar U.S. rules since pilot training – and just keep flying the same way in Laos without ever even thinking about it."

In Vietnam our ROE consisted of a huge printed volume of Top Secret rules, which was stored in a locked safe. FACs frequently sat down and read the ROE in order to pass periodic written tests on the contents. "Tell me about the Laos ROE, Glenn." "There are no ROE for Laos. There is only a single rule called The Ambassador's Rule." "The ambassador wants every Raven to have his ass on the ground somewhere by sundown. None of our aircraft are properly instrumented for either weather or night flying." Later it turned out that I had to intentionally violate the ambassador's single flying rule on three different occasions.

Prior to arrival in Laos I had logged more than 8,000 pilot hours flying military aircraft. But had only flown once before in the back seat of a tail-dragger while a young Marine. The O-1 is a tail-dragger, which means that it has only two non-retractable landing gear and has no direct means of controlling what the tail end of the airplane is doing while on the ground. I found learning to fly a tail-dragger bird to be a significant challenge while taxiing prior to takeoff and, again, when back on the ground after landing. Took me three hours with an instructor in the back seat to learn how to control a tail-dragging O-1 on the ground. The secret method was simple enough: pretend that there is a plow attached immediately under the aircraft's tail. While on the ground pretend you are plowing a furrow in a corn field under you. Doing that requires holding the stick deliberately in a full aft position while taxiing. The runway for learning all that was a short strip of dirt a bit wider than the wing span of the airplane. Weeds taller than the airplane grew on both sides of that strip. I managed to become totally immersed inside those weeds during a takeoff.

Normal-looking runways were rare in Laos. Most of the runways the Ravens flew from every day were concave slopes which began at the bottom of a steep ridge line, convex rock-filled strips which ran across ridge tops with tall trees on either side. Runways which terminated at the top edge of a steep cliff which then descended several hundred feet straight down. Or runways which terminated in the vertical face of a tall rock karst jutting upward out of the earth. Once committed to land no safe go-around procedure existed. Landings in Laos required a Raven to do everything absolutely right the first time.

Both the OV-10 and O-2A FAC airplanes had an illuminated gun sight mounted just above the instrument panel. These gun sights had mil-settings which FACs adjusted to provide a proper vertical angle for putting a white phosphorus smoke rocket on target in order to precisely identify, with a smoke plume, the fighter's target you wanted them to hit. None of the O-1 or U-17 (a six-passenger militarized version of the Cessna 185) aircraft which the Ravens flew in combat were equipped with a gun sight. FAC just eyeballed the target, visually adjusted delivery angle by experience, then pickled off a single rocket with a trigger button on the stick. Turned out that doing that worked just fine. Ravens could routinely put a rocket on, or very close to, any target they had selected.

By the Book

Steve Neal, Raven 24, aggressive, experienced, and getting close to his Date Eligible for Return from Overseas (DEROS), took me out in his back seat on my new guy dollar ride. Purpose of this 3.5-hour mission was to familiarize me with all the details of operations in Military Region II and the Plain of Jars (PDJ) in northern Laos. Departed from Twenty Alternate, Long Tieng, and climbed out to about 9,000 feet. Weather was clear, no clouds, and visibility was very good. Heard some 14.5 millimeter rounds go by the right side of the aircraft. Cyclic rate was quite high. Passing rounds made an identifiable sound similar to coal coming down the metal chute, back home, into the basement coal bin. With the side windows of the O-1 open, one could clearly hear and identify the kinds of rounds coming by the aircraft. Looking down at the ground below, I occasionally observed what looked to me to be a lot similar to large leaf Bright tobacco just growing randomly, not planted in rows in the usual fashion. "Steve, what's that long-leaf stuff growing below?" Steve said "Looks like tobacco to me." There were several dirt roads visible on the PDJ. Steve pointed out small dirt runways which the Ravens had previously used but which were now almost all occupied by enemy forces. There were large cave entrances, some with brass from expended 130 mm rounds lying on the ground about 80 meters from the cave entrance. Near Muong Soui we passed over a square, fenced-in area which looked like a county-size road maintenance facility. It contained a few parked road graders, some trucks with plows on their fronts, and a couple of D2 caterpillar tractors. "Don't waste bombs on that stuff – all that road maintenance stuff has been dead for years." Flew over Xieng Khouang. "A now dead city, pretty well totally destroyed after a long battle." Flew out to Arrowhead Lake. Nearby there was a pretty large area containing many kinds of trucks and armored vehicles – tanks and armored personnel carriers (APCs). "All that armor was destroyed long ago. Don't waste time discovering it again or putting still more bombs on any of it." Flew over Roadrunner Lake then up to LS-32. "That's friendly territory up inside the bowl on top – but don't try to land on that runway inside the top if you are flying a U-17. Damn thing will float forever and you won't be able to get it down on a short runway." Flew over Ban Ban. Place was totally quiet and peaceful that day. No one fired a single round at us. Turned around and flew west close to Highway 7 which ran along the north edge of the PDJ. Not far from LS-32 there were a large number of trucks, many more than 100, parked pretty much nose-to-tail along the north edge of the road. Windshields were shattered, engine compartment hoods were open and up, and a lot of dirt had been scattered across all these trucks, presumably from nearby bomb detonations. "Those are all dead trucks." Steve pointed out occasional 120 mm artillery pieces sitting out in the open, usually on tops of hills. "Dead guns." Most of the PDJ was littered with hundreds of empty fifty gallon fuel barrels lying on the ground everywhere one looked. Steve pointed out a few of the Jars the plain was named for, but I couldn't see what he was talking about. "Make sure you report your present location to ops about every fifteen minutes. Doing that will make it easier to find you if you get into trouble out here. If we can't get to you quickly, Air America will." Implicit: new Raven FACs weren't expected to last long in this business. Steve and I returned to Vientiane and landed at Wattay. My dollar ride and area checkout completed, I was now cleared to begin flying daily missions using my own call sign, Raven two-zero.

During my first solo mission over the PDJ my engine shut down all by itself. Notified ops of the problem. Another Raven recommended I head for the Jungle's Mouth if I had to make an emergency landing without power. I got a good air-start. Then landed at Long Tieng for maintenance. Each Raven flew a different tail-numbered O-1G model with adjustable props each day. No one had their own airplane. Took a while to figure out what was going on. Many of our pilots had graduated from an all-jet undergraduate pilot training program flying the T-37 and T-38. A FAC assignment was their first encounter flying airplanes using reciprocating engines with variable-pitch propellers. What went on inside a recip-engine remained something of a mystery for many. From initial engine start to engine shutdown at the end of a mission they flew with their fuel mixture selector in the Full Rich position. Result: engine exhaust valves would build up a heavy layer of deposited carbon then the engine would eventually shut down all by itself. Solution to that: during run-up repetitively burn out the engine carbon build-up by leaning mixture close to Best Power point while closely observing cylinder head temperature rise. Then repeat that process over again until you got an absolutely perfect mag check. I experienced no subsequent engine problem during the remainder of my tour in Laos.

An essential component, for any new guy moving into new turf and a new job, is to quickly learn what's going on and absorb current threat assessments shared by others you are working with. Had a brief introductory meeting with Vang Pao in his narrow, rather dark office and got insight into what he thought was going right, what was going wrong, and what he immediately needed most. Subsequent to that initial meeting Vang Pao and I briefly talked with one another almost every day while standing somewhere out on the flight line. There was uncontested, universal agreement among Vang Pao, CIA case officers, air attaché (AIRA) staff, and Intel troops that Long Tieng remained the primary offensive target of the North Vietnamese Army (NVA). And that we would soon see sappers and armor attacking us again, moving across Skyline Ridge. I had no reason to doubt their collective perspective about what was going on or was anticipated to happen. Daily flying activity at Alternate was consistently intense. Helicopters hauling troops, rice, and live pigs to remote locations. C-130 transport aircraft bringing in munitions and supplies. A very busy place.

On the first Sunday after completion of my checkout, I received a phone call at the Nong Bone hooch from our air attaché, Colonel Curry. "Can you take me up in an O-1 this afternoon?" "Of course, sir." "Let's meet out at Wattay then, about thirteen hundred." Took me three tries at putting in the rotating sequence of digits required to open the walk-in safe mounted inside a grey-painted mobile trailer located near the flight line. Finally got the safe open. First time he'd seen the inside of that room-sized safe. The colonel expressed surprise at the quantity of weapons and munitions lying around on the floor inside the safe next to the wall edges. Said he hadn't expected that Ravens used that many different kinds of grenades. Found him a survival vest to wear during the flight, two extra survival radio batteries, and a thirty-eight special. Picked up my gear and map bag including an M-16 and ammo, shut the door, closed the safe up again and carefully checked that it was locked. Then we walked out onto the parking ramp and I did a quick preflight of an O-1. Put the colonel in the back seat. Defined the radio/interphone selector switch options, explained how the emergency yellow handle could jettison the cockpit door, checked that he was strapped in properly, then strapped in and started the engine. Neither of us wore a parachute or harness. Called airborne to Dragon Control, then switched frequency and checked in with Cricket, which carried an airborne command and control team operating from a large module mounted inside the cargo compartment of a C-130. Cricket continuously orbited in vicinity of the channel 119 tactical air navigation (TACAN). We flew north from Vientiane, crossed above Vang Vieng, then turned to proceed direct to his destination, Sala Phou Khoun (TG303511), a hamlet located near the intersection of two major dirt roads – Route 7 (running east/west north of the PDJ) and Route 13 (running north/south between Vientiane and Luang Prabang). Trimmed up the aircraft, then turned over flight controls to Colonel Curry so he could maneuver the bird and see whatever he was looking for through his back-seat windows. I could see five doughnut-shaped 12.7 mm gun pits dug in near the road intersection. No troops visible. No armor. No trucks or other vehicles. We orbited the target area for about thirty minutes, received no fire from the ground, then returned and landed at Vientiane.

To provide near-constant FAC coverage over the PDJ the duty Raven scheduling officer posted a "go" list of FAC takeoff times by call sign. First "go" was shortly after sunrise. Second "go" an hour later, etc. Beyond that single departure schedule, no one ever told a Raven where to go or what to do. He just went out and did it. Even Vang Pao was indirect and circumspect, "Have report twelve bad man by TG256399. Maybe if have time go look see?" FACs responded immediately to ground troops-in-contact (TIC) with an enemy force, found their own targets and called in airstrikes to destroy them, and individually hunted the NVA on their own initiative wherever they chose to fly. Most of their days were spent deep over enemy territory with no other American within forty miles. After flying about a four-hour mission a Raven would land at Twenty Alternate (a synonym of Long Tieng), log his sortie flying time in the 781 form, get out of his O-1, then urinate on the ground. Verbally reported any write-ups to a crew chief then walked uphill alongside the runway and checked in with ops. Next, walked over to a small building about the size of a three-seat outhouse painted dark green and debriefed his mission, in detail from his notebook, to Air Force Intel troops. When that debrief was completed Ravens walked over to a different building and debriefed CIA Intel people, providing them the identical mission details. This absurd redundancy was part of our culture in Laos. Air Force and CIA Intel people did not routinely exchange information or confer with one another. Each group regarded themselves as being in direct service of some distant commander who used the information they gathered and reported to make decisions and issue orders, which then flowed downward for action through a hierarchical system. A top-down view of the world. Intel folks never noticed that most of the major decisions in Laos were being made daily by lieutenants and captains flying small, unarmed airplanes with propellers. Our last debriefing stop was indoors, the CIA weather office. Their weatherman lived, slept, and worked all alone inside a 2,000 square foot building constructed on a concrete slab. Socially isolated, Hmong children had given the weatherman a gift of an ocelot kitten about four inches long which they'd found in the jungle. He was keeping his kitten in a huge, steel wire cage – convinced that the kitten would grow into a tiger. Demonstrated that his kitten liked being held and purred while being stroked. Told him it would grow up to be the same size as any house cat. "Feed him cat food, provide fresh water, a box of litter, give him a toy, let him out of that cage and he'll sleep with you."

Each Raven put in several air strikes each day; the number depended on the tactical situation on the ground. Most of his time was spent doing visual reconnaissance (VR) – looking down at the ground through open aircraft windows to see what was new or what had changed. Before volunteering for duty in Laos he first had flown for six months as a FAC in Vietnam where he first learned to "see."

That statement requires a short explanation. Every Air Force, Navy, or Marine Corps fixed-wing pilot was medically checked annually to verify that his visual acuity was 20/20, corrected or uncorrected. Which meant that he had absolutely perfect vision. Which, in turn, implied that he could see anything on the ground perfectly. That last assumption turned out to be quite wrong. A staff officer in the Training Command read a master's thesis about human vision written by a graduate student at a Texas university. The essence of that thesis: an extraordinary amount of information entering human eyes is routinely filtered out by the brain as useless information. The eyes are seeing things which never arrive into conscious processing within a pilot's mind. That turned out to be true. New FACs arriving in Vietnam, after their training at Hurlburt, had to learn to "see" before being permitted to go out on their own and put in airstrikes in support of ground troops. Training required was essentially passive. An air liaison officer (ALO)/FAC had each new FAC fly about three hours a day. His instructions were to become familiar with the province border lines, roads, firebases, hamlets, villages, rivers, names of mountains, and locations of protected cultural features like statues of Buddha. Then to drop by and give the ALO a quick debrief after each mission. Map in hand, the new FAC just stayed at least 1,500 feet above the ground every day while looking at the ground below through the cockpit windows. Standard post-mission debriefs were short. "Nothing going on in the province, another really boring flight." After about three weeks of these boring missions the FAC would land and debrief his mission to the ALO. "Today there were Vietnamese ladies wearing conical hats hunkered down at the edge of a rice paddy while it rained. I flew over a house where a woman with two children playing in the yard was hanging out laundry on a line to dry. There were both ducks and geese in her yard." "You can tell the difference between ducks and geese from 1,500 feet?" "You bet!" "And there was about a nine-year-old boy riding on the back of a water buffalo and this lad was telling the buffalo which way to go by tapping him with a short stick." All this common kind of activity had been visibly happening on the ground during every one of his previous boring missions. This was the first day his brain had stopped filtering all that out and permitted him to consciously "see" this activity below. He was now cleared to put in airstrikes in support of troops. And his seeing ability continued to increase with every mission and grew to the point where, while debriefing Intel, he'd state that he knew the enemy had passed across a trail at this point because he could see a broken branch that they had stepped on. "Impossible," Intel would say. "No one could possibly see a tiny detail like that from your altitude!" He had, in fact, seen that broken branch and knew what that branch was telling him about enemy movement. What a Raven FAC could see on the ground below him remained incredible to the Intel people of both flavors at Long Tieng.

Shortly after departing Alternate and still climbing out for the afternoon mission, got a call on UHF from Cricket. "There's a Buffalo Hunter orbiting Lima Site 32. Looks like there may be a problem with the mission." Told Cricket I was proceeding direct to LS 32. Had never heard the term Buffalo Hunter before. Almost there, Cricket finally told me – using very indirect and creatively obscure language concerning rubber band models – that this thing was a friendly photo-recon drone. It orbited LS 32, then someone remotely shut down the Buffalo Hunter's engine. It ended up on the ground just outside the perimeter wire near the edge of the mountaintop bowl. Orbited and watched as someone went out through the wire to get the photo module. The NVA pulled a 130 mm gun from inside a cave about two klicks away so I called Cricket for fighters to strike the gun. An F-111 was diverted from another mission to my target. When he checked in I immediately recognized the F-111's pilot's voice. It was Major Johnson, Bow Saw, my gunnery school instructor at Cannon AFB three years earlier. Departed LS 32 and headed for Alternate flying along the row of dead trucks at the edge of Highway 7. Noticed a couple empty parking spots in that long row. One of the dead trucks normally parked at the east end of the row was missing. Flew almost to the far end of the PDJ and then saw a truck driving on a road below.

Definitely in enemy territory. Pretty unusual during daylight hours. The truck stopped. The driver got out of the cab and ran up the slope of a ridge. I made a low pass to see from the rear what was inside the truck's cargo compartment. It was empty. Then climbed and visually followed the running driver's progress as he passed behind the ridge line through a few large leaf tobacco plants then he disappeared into a tiny cave entrance. Called for air to take out the truck. No air available. Now late afternoon, deep shadows on the ground growing. Departed and landed at Wattay.

Had the first go the next morning. Paused just at the edge of the hill horizon overlooking the PDJ to check for any long visible scar in the dirt – the initial stage of an NVA hole being dug prior to installation of a 130 mm artillery piece. No scar. Then continued on to check status of the truck abandoned by its driver the previous afternoon. Truck was no longer there. Flew east to VR that long row of dead trucks parked on the north side of Route 7. Yesterday's empty dead truck parking spots were no longer empty. A dead truck was parked in each spot. Front wheels at the usual angle about an inch distant from the weeds which were about ten inches high. Hood up. Dirt thrown up across both hood and top of cargo compartment. Looked exactly like all the other dead trucks in that nose-to-tail line along the road. Obviously, the NVA had become quite competent masters of a simple technique: Hide your functioning stuff by placing it visibly out in the open, then making it look very much as though it had been damaged or destroyed in previous combat. Bombs were always in short supply so doing in each of the dead trucks parked in that long line to assure their destruction wasn't an option. Decided to do two things that morning. First was to closely VR construction equipment parked in the county road maintenance yard to see if I could detect movement and confirm repositioning after being used at night in road repair work on the switchback. Second was to check areas where large tobacco plants were growing to see if traces of light trails from foot traffic converged near cave entrances in the immediate vicinity. Told the other Ravens what I was doing and why.

Wild tobacco is a member of a nightshade family which includes tomato plants. Wild tobacco plants grow only to a height of about eight to ten inches tall, produce rather tiny leaves, and annually re-seed all by themselves, to produce the next generation of plants. Large leaf tobacco, such as Bright and Burley, is a result of years of careful genetic crossbreeding, selection, and constant care during growth. Large leaf tobacco does not re-seed itself and requires intervention by humans for germination, transplanting, and growth. Tomato hornworm caterpillars eat both tomato and tobacco plants and can totally denude either kind of plant of all its leaves during a single day. Inspection, removal, and destruction of caterpillars, by hand, remains an every-morning requirement of tobacco crop production. Since the NVA planted their tobacco randomly rather than in rows, it was their foot tracks left behind while removing hornworms that I was looking for. NVA on the PDJ would send Hanoi a short requisition for two wood pencils and a can of shrimp paste to provide basic dietary protein. Hanoi staff provided no comfort items to their troops in the field. If the NVA in Laos wanted to smoke they would have to grow their own.

Completed my PDJ survey of large leaf tobacco growing locations in one afternoon. Turned out that, in addition to tobacco, they all shared similar characteristics near the edges of the PDJ. Each was located on the backside of a hill providing good visibility of the PDJ. Faint foot tracks from tobacco plants converged like vectors to a cave entrance which was too small to provide for movement of an artillery piece into the cave. Put in three air strikes on other targets that afternoon and saved one bomb from the last strike. Moved the fighters to the new location, briefed, defined and marked their new target with a Willie Pete (WP). Then had lead put in his last bomb as close as he could get it to the cave entrance. Passed the bomb damage assessment (BDA) for both targets to Miller flight, a flight of two Marine F-4s working out of the Rose Garden in Thailand. They went home. I landed at Alternate, debriefed the afternoon missions to Intel, then departed and flew back to Vientiane.

There was a two-engine prop aircraft, call sign Baron, constantly in orbit over the PDJ. Boring job for the two pilots up front. The people in the back of that airplane consisted of electronic warfare specialist's quite busy reading the mail. They monitored enemy radio communication frequencies, mentally translated each intercept into English, and then sent messages about what they overheard to friendly Intel networks on the ground. In an aside comment during debriefing Intel said, "That cave you hit two days ago resulted in a report of several cases of 'the dread lung disease'." This was the NVA's term for ruptured lungs and internal bleeding resulting from instantaneous overpressure generated by a bomb detonating close to a cave entrance. No NVA surgical intervention capability for ruptured lungs existed out in the field. Cave residents usually slowly died from their dread disease after about three days. Each location on the PDJ growing their own tobacco turned out to be an enemy command and control node.

Took about eight days of occasionally flying over the county road equipment repair lot south of Moung Soui, without orbiting and appearing to a ground observer that I was just passing by. Used my binoculars while looking for fine details of how equipment was parked. A parked road grader verified what was going on. The angle of the front wheels of the grader changed to about a ten-degree different angle – and the distance between weeds which normally touched against the edges of the front wheels became about four inches of open space. Obviously this NVA maintenance equipment wasn't "dead" and was being used at night. Chapakao Red, flight of two T-28s, came by and asked if I had a target for him. Marked the road grader with a Willie Pete, the T-28s went to work. We both landed at Long Tieng at about the same time. T-28 pilot walked across the ramp and asked, "Why you have us bomb dead target?" Explained how I knew target wasn't dead and was repairing switchback road at night. "Ooooh!" It had taken me far too long to tumble to what was going on with all of those parked dead trucks and dead road repair equipment. The probability was quite low that a long row of trucks could have been individually destroyed in combat and retained sufficient steering capability to be parked on only one side of the road, nose to tail. Several trucks were doubtless dead – and remained there as a source of undamaged parts which could be cannibalized and then used to repair and maintain the operational status of other trucks. D2 diesel tracked Caterpillars continued to be used to dig 130 mm gun pits on the PDJ at night. Hiding things out in the open had worked very well for the NVA.

It took about three weeks of VR to conclude that Long Tieng was intentionally being bypassed in favor of NVA initiatives to take control of roads connecting Vientiane, Vang Vieng, and Luang Prabang. Harassment and Interdiction (H&I) artillery fire into Long Tieng continued daily as an effective diversion. At that time no Raven FACs were assigned to Military Region One, so occasionally flew up to Luang Prabang to keep an eye on what was happening on the ground to the north.

Offhand mention during a debriefing to Air Force Intel at Alternate – the Intel debriefer read aloud two intercepted messages which had been exchanged between the Hanoi staff and the NVA artillery commander in charge of all activity on the PDJ:

"How do enemy know where you place your 130 mm guns then come and destroy guns so quickly?"

"I don't know. I follow instructions and do everything just the way the book says to do it every time."

Nothing in combat is more wonderful than fighting an opponent who does everything "by the book." Makes what he does, and how he does it, almost totally predictable. Sometime during a previous assignment this NVA commander had made an original creative decision, been severely rebuked for doing so, then been transferred to Laos as punishment. He was not going to make that kind of career error again. His tactical assault plans and destinations became almost transparent as they slowly evolved in observable by-the-book stages. Ravens knew where the artillery commander lived, the precise location of his underground command bunker out on the PDJ. Through AIRA, I staffed a 600 meter no bomb ring around the entrance to his command bunker to preclude any injury happening to him which could lead to his being replaced by a competent NVA officer.

Late on Christmas Eve afternoon, 1972, Skip Jackson (Raven 21) died (BNR – body not recovered) as a result of an air-to-air collision with Chuck Reiss (Slam 04) flying a USAF A-7 aircraft during an airstrike on a large number of stacked boxes and supplies which were visible on the PDJ. The A-7 became uncontrollable. Captain Reiss ejected, got one good swing of his chute, then he landed within a few meters of the NVA command bunker. Enemy troops who were standing there watching the show helped him out of his parachute harness, took his wristwatch and boots. They stuck him in a hole until dark, then they walked him barefoot all the way to Hanoi over a period of several days. Reiss was returned to the U.S. in March 1973. One of very few POWs returned after being captured in Laos during the war.

A very common FAC technique during our war in Southeast Asia (SEA): FACs could easily recognize the difference between a triple-A gunner who was actually trying to hit his aircraft, and a gunner who was intentionally missing the FAC while attempting to keep his cadre convinced that he was trying but was a bit slow in learning. Intuitively, a FAC would begin to function as a perverse NVA personnel officer by killing off, with airstrikes, competent enemy gunners who were putting rounds in close to his bird. Then the FAC left those enemy gunners who were reticent, incompetent, and missing him by a substantial distance, quite unbothered. Over a rather short period of time the local enemy would become reduced to fighting FACs while manned with a residual force consisting of incompetent and unmotivated gunners.

Raven on first go would cross just above the perimeter hills, look down and see a deep, long, straight hole dug into the ground across the PDJ. He'd record the eight-digit Universal Transverse Mercator (UTM) coordinates on his map and knee pad notebook, then avoid flying anywhere near that excavation on the ground all day. Second day, FAC would cross the hills, see that a dirt berm had been constructed on both sides during the night, would again write down coordinates of the center of the hole – then remain flying well away from it all day. Third day, he would cross the hills. Hole had disappeared. Professionally swept and competently camouflaged. No visible tracks left by vehicles or construction equipment left anywhere on the ground. PDJ ground looked untouched, totally natural. Gun pit job had been performed with perfection and every tiny instructional detail of the process had been completed and double checked "by the book." Early afternoon four F-4s would check in over the PDJ, including an instructor pilot checking his new pilots and a laser illuminator to light up the target. New F-4 pilots had to first put in four strikes somewhere in Laos before being permitted to fly strike missions over North Vietnam. Had nothing to do with the threat environment. Had everything to do with becoming adapted to working targets over turf where Intel had briefed them they'd be skinned alive if captured by the enemy on the ground. Psychological adaptation to realities of combat. Explained that since I was flying lower and slower below them with only 12 gallons of fuel remaining, they'd make it home for supper again tonight. That usually calmed them down and dissipated anxiety. Raven would brief the strike, get out of the way, then a laser guided bomb (LGB) would destroy, or severely damage, the 130 mm artillery piece which was concealed inside that brand-new gun pit. It is difficult to totally destroy an almost 12 meter long artillery piece with a single 750 pound LGB. It is even more difficult to dig that long piece out of the ground to recover and examine it after a bomb detonation covers the remains under several tons of earth.

VR consistently revealed easterly enemy movement at night crossing along a dirt road north of Long Tieng. Little things like faint trails of armor tracks exiting dense bushes where armored vehicles had laagered-up during the daylight hours. Observed a crescent-shaped area near the edge of high terrain where the weeds had been compressed earlier and were now recovering. That crescent location provided a lovely, unobstructed view of lower terrain to the south, almost down to Vang Vieng. Debriefed Intel that an NVA force, size 80 to 120 men, had stopped there earlier, and been briefed on where they were going. "How do you know what time they were there?" "By the angle to which the grass had recovered since their departure." Intuitively knew where they were going. Waited a few days for them to arrive at their destination then did a late VR in late afternoon while on the way to Vientiane. Orbited the hills, which formed a steep canyon through which the road travelled between Vang Vieng and Muang Kassy. Heard a single AK round pass by the left side of my aircraft. Cricket passed me two sets of fighters, armed mostly with pyrotechnics and carrying a few cluster bomb units (CBUs) used in rescue missions, who were returning home after duty flying rescue combat air patrols (CAPs) over North Vietnam. Pretty well covered likely ambush sites up and along the southern canyon walls where banana trees were densely growing. Fighters' ordnance expended, sent them home with BDA RNO (bomb damage assessment results not observed). Then flew to Wattay. A couple days later a U.S. Air Force lieutenant colonel, accompanied by a Lao officer, was driving a jeep through that canyon and noticed a foul odor. They dismounted and walked the terrain while counting 82 dead NVA on the ground. Updated the fighters' BDA to 82 killed by air (KBA).

February 1973. Had spent the afternoon on a Bright Light mission performing VR over three areas where AIRA had received reports that U.S. POWs were currently being held in Laos. Found nothing visually. An F-4 photo recon bird checked in and I asked if he had infrared (IR) photo capability on board. He did. Had him do IR photography over one of these suspect areas to thermally reveal any well-camouflaged facilities existing on the ground. The war was winding down. While in the landing pattern at Wattay noticed that a Special Air Mission (SAM) bird out of Andrews AFB was in the process of parking over on our military ramp. Although we had zero prior notice, it was obvious a distinguished visitor (DV) had come to Vientiane to talk with the Lao government downtown about something. Stayed in the air and made a call on the ground control frequency, "SAM bird, come-up Company." Their DV got into a car and headed for downtown. Switched UHF frequency and waited. Heard "Up Company." I said, "Regards to the eighty-ninth. I'm overhead in an O-1 and will fly CAP cover for you while you are on the ground." Crew expressed appreciation of the service. Orbited Wattay. SAM bird was on ground at Vientiane for about forty minutes, then departed for an unknown destination with DV aboard.

Combat consistently turned out to be an intensive learning experience. What did I learn? The most valuable primary weapon system during any war is your own adaptable human brain. My most useful asset, day after day, was my intuition. Had to learn to recognize intuitive input and pay attention to it. Took a while. If you ever need to select pilots for some kind of high risk combat duty, don't bother doing record checks or performing individual, formal interviews of your list of volunteers. Doing so will just waste your time. Instead, just put a dozen or more candidates into one room, provide them with an arbitrary agenda, then quietly stand in the back of the room and observe the overall conduct of their meeting. The people you are after will be easy to identify. Your optimal choices will be those who delay, obstruct, tangentially divert, introduce specious topics, and drag out scheduled meeting lengths well beyond reason. Those who don't do meetings well will be precisely what you are looking for. They'll be extraordinary and wonderful in combat.

Sheep

In the 1930s I grew up on a farm in the lower-left corner of Minnesota near Slayton, Avoca, and Fulda, just about a mile from one of the smaller hamlets in the state, Wirock. A two-seater outhouse, never painted. A hand pump provided water for the kitchen sink. And a windmill squeaked all night while pumping water for the cattle. Candles illuminated the stairway to bed at night. Electricity was still years distant in the future. Grew corn, wheat, flax, barley, oats, and soybeans. Two draft horses pulled plows, harrows, rakes, wagons, and the manure spreader across fields. Each cob of corn was hand shucked in the field then thrown up against a tall green buckboard into a wagon. Fed cattle, hogs, and a few dairy cows. Work was called "doing chores." One of the daily chores was milking the cows into a bucket early morning before sunrise, then running the milk through a cream separator which had to be cranked to store rotational energy much like an old fashioned aircraft engine starter. A small herd of sheep were kept in pasture down a lane back of the red barn. While out walking fields one day I came across the remains of a sheep which had died a short time ago. What surprised me was that most of that sheep had so quickly melted away, disappeared including the bones. All that remained of this sheep was a flat layer of bad-smelling wool, less than half an inch thick, lying on the surface of the dirt.

While serving as a FAC supporting grunts in Vietnam I found it useful, after putting airstrikes on a target, to land, gather helmet and rifle from our tent, then get a ride in a Huey going that way. Walked the ground, now occupied by U.S. Army troops, where my bombs had impacted earlier that morning. Eighteen-inch-tall volcanic-shaped tunnels were erupting from the ground everywhere, castings left behind on the surface by Vietnam's huge night crawler worms. Directly observed and assessed weapons effects and BDA results. Learned that a 500 pound bomb doesn't do much damage to a bunker covered with rough logs, rocks, and wet dirt. Just dusts it. 20 mm cannon fire, delivered by fighter aircraft, turned out to be quite useful to ground assault troops moving through jungle terrain. Those 20 mm rounds really tore up foliage and brush. Troops could move forward much more quickly while no longer having to slowly hack a path through jungle terrain using a machete. Walking around and talking with grunts in the field was useful. Meeting up with the FAC who had put in an airstrike a few hours earlier helped build their confidence in what tactical air could do for them when they were in trouble. Occasionally went out in an APC on night recon missions with the 1/10 armored Cavalry. And noticed that one could walk the empty turf of a recent battle in relative safety. Both enemy and friendly forces tended to quickly abandon battle sites, then move on to other locations.

Landing and walking the ground after a battle became a much less frequent activity in Laos. After an enemy assault on Muang Kassy, where two tanks and fifty-two mixed NVA/Pathet Lao POWs from a single battalion had been captured there, several Ravens landed on the gravel runway and inspected the captured enemy tanks. With rifle and bandolier, I left the aircraft ramp and went up the road to the east to have a closer look at the battleground, which I'd previously seen only from the air while the NVA was firing 12.7 rounds at me. This was a dirt road consisting only of two broad tire tracks with weeds growing in between. Passed an unpainted house, with a sagging porch in front, on the south side of the road. House had been hosed by the tanks. Continued up the road a bit further, then found the remains of an NVA soldier who had been quite busy firing his rifle at me a couple weeks earlier. I had put a Willie Pete on him. A Willie Pete is just a smoke rocket which contains no explosive material – but it goes through the Mach after being launched and acquires substantial kinetic energy while descending on the way down to its target. Sheer luck, my smoke rocket had hit the green-uniformed NVA soldier who was standing there on the road shooting at me. Knocked him down. I stopped walking near that place in the road. No rifle, no munitions or canteen, nothing visible from that event still lying about nearby on either side of the road bed. No visible hat. Looked around for his rubber Ho Chi Minh shoes carved from used automobile tires and held on his feet with strips cut from inner tubes. No shoes. His entire skull, bones, and most all the flesh of his body had been consumed by some kind of very hungry and aggressive bacteria. Duplicated that dead sheep I'd seen back on the farm. All that remained out on the surface of the road was a thin, flat, putrid-scented layer shaped like a body, outlined by the edges of his green uniform fabric. I'd done in a lot of enemy troops during my FAC tours. This was the first one I'd personally dropped by and visited with afterward. Stood there for a few moments while conducting a brief memorial service on behalf of the late soldier thinly spread along the road surface just in front of me. Told him I hoped Buddha had graciously recycled him and that he was now on his way to still another existence, a new life during which he'd be a lot more reticent and restrained about shooting at FACs. No hard feelings. Walked back down the road and onto the ramp. Strapped on my O-1, cranked, ran-up, and departed for Vientiane. A short vesper quietly uttered each evening after completion of my final Intel debrief of the day downtown at AIRA. "I came home to supper tonight. My enemy did not." That's how you can tell if you had a good day at the war.

Vang Pao

The Raven FACs assigned duty in Laos performed in the field as civilians. There was no squadron. No flight structure. Ravens functioned without grade or rank while upcountry and were normally addressed either as Mister or by their personal tactical call sign, e.g., spoken as "Raven two five."

Each Raven remained, in fact, still continuously serving on active duty as an officer of the U.S. Air Force and was being paid his standard amount monthly by the U.S. government, usually by direct deposit to a U.S. bank account. No Raven FAC received any additional or augmenting pay of any kind from anyone in return for his service as a Raven. There were no U.S. military quarters or messing facilities in Laos. Every Raven was on per-diem status while in-country. Occasionally each Raven would fly down to Udorn air base and fill out a per-diem partial payment form in which the location where he was serving had to be entered on that form as "classified." He'd receive a check within a few days and use it to pay for his food and billeting arrangements in Laos. If he wrote down his real duty location on the form, instead of writing "classified," his partial payment per-diem form would be immediately destroyed by the Udorn finance officer and he'd receive no payment. Destruction served to protect formal U.S. policy that there existed no U.S. troops serving on the ground in Laos. No finance paper evidence was ever permitted to exist to confirm the contrary.

Ravens were not "sheep dipped." (Sheep dipping in a much earlier war consisted of formally honorably discharging a pilot from the USAF, sending him off for covert service somewhere, then later returning him back to active duty status with time credited to his military record covering the missing interval during which he'd been gone.) Civilian status in Laos provided a Raven with an extraordinary advantage: No one ever gave a Raven a direct order or told him where to go or what to do. He simply went where he was needed and did what he obviously needed to do using his experience and personal judgment. He was unconstrained by standard ICAO or U.S. military flying regulations, or rules of engagement (ROE), in Laos. All this worked out wonderfully without generation of discipline or behavioral problems.

With considerable financial and logistic assistance from the CIA, General Vang Pao (VP) was personally in charge of the war in Military Region Two (MR II) in Laos. VP lived and worked out of Long Tieng – a bowl-shaped valley with a 5,400 foot long macadam runway immediately surrounded by tall karst formations and steep mountains. VP was consistently socially engaged and actively companionable while working with his troops, the CIA, Thai forces, and the Raven FACs supporting his operations. He supported and maintained his several wives which were authorized by Buddhist tradition. Each wife was supplied with her own house for herself and her children. Hmong ladies, easily identified by the identical black and white knit pattern of the hats they wore, were well adapted to living in the mountains. They all complained of feeling ill when temporarily visiting down in the lower altitude of Vientiane.

Synonyms for Long Tieng are "Twenty Alternate" or just plain "Alternate." For security reasons, Long Tieng received no mention in the Defense Mapping Agency Aerospace Center (DMAAC) Pacific and South Asia Flight Information Publication (FLIP). U.S. maps and topographic charts of Laos intentionally displaced Long Tieng's actual map coordinates to remote, false ground locations for the same security reasons. The Long Tieng runway had close to a four-degree upslope while landing. Landings required a steep descent, at idle power, passing just a few feet above the surface of about a forty-degree mountain's downslope followed by a quick change of attitude to match the rising runway during round-out. The far end of the runway terminated in a tall, vertical karst. A fixed-wing go-around after becoming committed to land was physically precluded by that granite karst obstruction. Air America pilots operated C-130 and C-123 aircraft using that runway several times daily. An abundance of helicopters lifted people, cargo, rice, and live pigs while conducting daily resupply operations in all geographic quadrants. Flight operations at Alternate were consistently intensive during daylight hours. One of the busiest runways in the world. Terrain, lack of runway lighting, and nonexistence of instrument approach aids precluded nighttime operations into or out of Long Tieng.

Jerry Rhein introduced me to Vang Pao. VP had a small office up the hill from the runway, inside the lower level of a building constructed of rock. Office had an outdoor entrance. VP's office was about five feet wide and thirteen feet long with a continuous seat bench running the length of the left wall and a single desk placed at the intersection of the rear and right walls. His office was dark. Only a single bulb with lampshade illuminated VP's desk and office. As usual in Laos, conversation was conducted merging verbs, nouns, and syntax creatively assembled from at least four different languages, all crunched together and compressed into one single ad-hoc sentence. Jerry addressed Vang Pao as "Kim Sahb." Which sounded much like dialogue from an old *Lone Ranger* script to me – but turned out to be the Hmong term for "close friend." We both shook hands with VP. There was occasional nodding, pointing into space, a brief discussion about what the NVA was up to which mixed French, Japanese, and Vietnamese terms. Mostly I sat, watched, and listened. I had first seen Jerry about six months earlier at Hurlburt while I was getting checked out in the OV-10 for a second Vietnam tour. An elder pilot and obvious acquaintance had walked up to Jerry in the Hurlburt club one evening expressing surprise at seeing Jerry back home in the U.S. Jerry held up his hand with gold ring toward him and said, "They threw me out of the country and sent me back here to Florida." Who or why remained undefined. I had never inquired. Most of the continuing office discussion which followed remained between Jerry and VP. Jerry gratefully thanked VP for his personal efforts in getting him back into Laos from his exile to Hurlburt and assigned again to Long Tieng. A silent nod to me from VP indicated that my new guy welcome interview was completed. Jerry and I departed the office and walked back down to the flight line.

Two days later, without the slightest prior mention of any scheduled senior visitor, Jerry introduced me as the senior Raven to a USAF four-star general who was standing outdoors while waiting near the entrance to VP's briefing room. The general was wearing a two-piece, commercially tailored "walking suit" sewn up from a bolt of light gray colored fabric. Wear of U.S. military uniforms in Laos was prohibited, with exception of those few officers who were diplomatically accredited to the Lao government such as the U.S. Embassy air attaché (AIRA), Colonel Curry. Wearing a twelve-dollar walking suit became a generic apparel solution for U.S. military visitors to upcountry Laos. (One origin of the term "Purple Suiters" commonly used to describe case officers serving in-country with the CIA. One could immediately recognize CIA people by their attire – the curious bold colors and jolting patterns of neckties they wore consistently appeared to be discards they'd purchased at some Saturday morning garage sale in Dubuque, Iowa.) The general was obviously quite familiar with previous problems encountered by Raven FACs in Laos and immediately asked if aircraft parts were now flowing properly and if our engine problems on the O-1 had been resolved. I told him I had been in-country for only ten days and that aircraft maintenance was the first thing I'd looked at.

"NORS parts and regular replacement components are now flowing to us properly and without delay in transit, sir. We have a new, superb crew chief who identified and corrected our major engine problem. Turned out that there is a small, two-position selector switch at the base of the

O-1 carburetor. One switch position for sea-level flight. A second position for high-altitude flight operations. Switch position easily permanently changed manually using only a screwdriver. Our birds had all arrived in-country with their carburetor altitude switch selectors set to the sea-level position from depot. Ravens operate in mountainous terrain throughout Laos, high-altitude for an O-1. Our crew chief has checked all of our aircraft carburetors, has re-adjusted each to the high-altitude position, and we've encountered no further inflight engine failures since that action was completed." "Glad to hear that. Let me know right away if you have any more aircraft maintenance problems up here." "Yes, sir."

VP arrived to greet and brief the general. They entered the briefing room. The U.S. general dressed in his walking suit was seated on a firm, low white bench with no back. I watched and listened to VP's briefing from the rear of the room. VP's mastery of the English language was marginal but his body language and delivery were consistently enthusiastic. He used words and phrases from French, Thai, and English languages in merged, interwoven fashion, occasionally producing somewhat comic sentences. But managed to get his concepts across. As he neared the end of his briefing VP slowly began to move forward to close the physical distance between himself and the U.S. four-star general. VP completed his briefing with an identical statement repeated three times: "Our troops wait until they can see the whites of the enemy's eyes before firing." Briefing completed, the U.S general departed.

VP invited me to lunch on two occasions. I attended once. Combat activity in progress on the PDJ precluded a second participation. Lunch upstairs, one floor above his office inside VP's Long Tieng house, was a communal activity. Food was distributed along the entire length of a single long, narrow table. Huge heaps of sticky white rice were loaded onto several two-foot-diameter metal platters distributed along the center length of the table. There were smaller platters containing "lobster," which were actually unusually large, fresh-water crayfish or crawdads which had been captured earlier that morning in local mountain streams, then boiled. About twenty men sat in chairs along both sides of the table. No women. Ladies and children ate later. Chopsticks or cutlery were not required. Each guest at the table extended one arm over a common rice platter and fashioned a kind of one-handed snowball from one of the several heaps of still-warm sticky rice. Then he dunked each rice ball into a bowl of liquid salsa (Nam Pit) made from intensely pungent red Thai peppers. Then popped each sequential rice ball into his mouth and swallowed it down without chewing. A substantive and filling meal. This hot pepper salsa is consumed throughout Thailand and Laos. The capsaicin in those hot peppers survived digestion and was extruded as a component of their sweat. People of this geographical region radiated an attractive hot pepper scent. They smelled good. Social conversation, no speeches. By the end of the meal about half the sticky rice and crawdads on the table had been consumed. The remainder would be eaten by women and children. Children were especially fond of chewing on boiled chicken legs with feet still attached.

VP didn't conduct the kinds of daily staff meetings which were commonly employed by U.S. force commanders in the field to assess and discuss problems resulting from today's activity in the field and to plan tomorrow's actions. VP's senior staff people were all physically quite unavailable for meetings. They were spread out across several remote and distant sites for duty at different locations on or near the PDJ. A military leader, VP was also a political leader of his mountain people and spent a good deal of his time negotiating political issues with competing Lao military interests back in Vientiane. He frequently met with Ambassador Godley. Most of his interaction with the CIA was informally conducted with one or two case officers during which plans, logistic support, and financing issues were resolved. I would occasionally meet with VP, for a minute or two, when we were both on the ground at the same time and he was visibly standing outdoors and observing air activity from somewhere near the runway. His comments to me were always gracious. He expressed intense gratitude for all that the Ravens were doing in support of his troops. He never uttered a direct complaint to me. Under abundant daily stress from wives, children, the Lao Army hierarchy, and the constantly diminishing quantity of his troops, he'd walk out and stand on a spot of grass for a few minutes out in the open near the runway and quietly observe the intense aircraft activity which was always in progress during daylight hours. Observing relaxed and refreshed him. And gave him private time to be alone and think. One morning, as I was walking toward him, he assumed the position of attention and saluted me. I returned his salute. The only time I saluted anyone while in Laos. His guards observed that momentary personal interaction and subsequently treated me with implied deference.

VP was personally active and quite direct in daily problem solving. Early afternoon on a Thursday, an Air America helicopter pilot landed his routine resupply chopper at a remote site on the PDJ at which the NVA had initiated an assault during the early morning. Hmong troops stationed for duty at that site were in full panic mode. They boarded the rice resupply helicopter and demanded to be evacuated to safer ground. The Air America helicopter pilot was in no position to negotiate. The troops in his cargo compartment were all armed and insistent that they be airlifted to some better place. Pilot and kicker offloaded their rice, pigs, and other supplies onto the ground at the site. Then cranked and lifted the bird up into a hover about three feet above the ground to verify that he had sufficient rotor torque available to fly with the undefined weight and balance of his floor-loaded passengers already onboard sitting on the metal deck in the back of his helicopter. Torque checked as sufficient, he departed the site and flew the load of panicked troops to Twenty Alternate. Pilot notified ops by radio while enroute about what was going on while responding to ops inquiries about why he was returning to Twenty Alternate so early. "No, the helicopter doesn't have any maintenance write-ups."

VP met that helicopter as it landed. Wind, a brief flurry of dirt and dust generated by prop wash from the still slow-turning rotor blades flowed outward in all directions. After engine shutdown the troops disembarked and this dissenting group of his soldiers walked toward VP. Many were quite young. Looked to be about fourteen years old. A brief discussion with his troops followed. VP ordered them to get back in the helicopter and return to their duty site, now. The group's ringleader refused VP's order and began walking downhill toward the valley away from VP and that helicopter. VP drew his sidearm from its holster. VP fired a single round and blew away the noncompliant leader where he stood. Silence. Troop faces expressed total surprise. Unanticipated shock. Body of dead trooper lying face down on the ground in front of them. Thin filaments of fresh red blood searched out their separate paths while flowing downslope across a ramp littered with dust and dirt too dry to absorb moisture. Instantly attracted flies. VP asked if there were any others among them who didn't want to return immediately to their original duty site. No further dissent was uttered. Remaining troops turned back and voluntarily got into the same helicopter in which they had arrived. They were then returned to their original duty site out on the PDJ. The pilot offloaded the troops at their destination then reloaded those heavy jute bags filled with dry rice, box pens containing live pigs, and other essential supplies with the help of his kicker. Then the Air America helicopter pilot continued flying his daily resupply circuit over the PDJ.

VP's active interest was totally concentrated only on what was going on within his personal turf, Military Region Two. Whatever was happening in the rest of Laos was a matter of indifference to him. Through visual reconnaissance of residual evidence left behind by NVA night activity, truck movement, and installation of new doughnut-shaped gun pit positions, I slowly became certain that the NVA had decided to bypass Long Tieng as their immediate assault objective and had chosen to pursue a new and different target. Concluded that their immediate new objective was to take control of the existing Lao road communication structure, including a road which ran northwest through a steep canyon pass between Vang Vieng and Muang Kassy. An extended set of several connecting dirt roads included the single land route north up to Luang Prabang. Connecting with roads extending east, north of Long Tieng, all the way to Ban Ban. NVA occupation and control of these roads would competently divide the country and tactically threaten Vientiane. VP, CIA, Intel – the entire institutional memory of those who had long served at Long Tieng – remained certain that Long Tieng would continue to remain the primary target of the NVA and Pathet Lao forces.

This threatened road network was peripheral to VP's immediate interest because much of the structure joined together at a junction near Sulla Phou Khoun, mountain country within Military Region One. At that time, we had no Raven FACs or Lao FACs assigned duty in MR I. We had no spare Ravens. FAC manning had been winding down as the end of the war in SEA was obviously approaching from continued negotiation activity in Paris. I arranged my routes in the morning, flying from Vientiane to Twenty Alternate then back to Vientiane in late afternoon, so as to fly over the southern portion of MR I. My twice-daily visual road reconnaissance of that small portion of MR I revealed what the enemy was doing and where they were headed. Passing overhead during a morning flight up to Twenty Alternate I noticed a crescent-shaped area where the grass and weeds had quite recently been tromped down. Crescent was on high ground at the edge of a visibly descending trail to much lower valley ground. That location provided a panoramic view to the southeast for a distance of several kilometers. Debriefed Intel after landing at Alternate: "From the size and crescent shape an enemy force, of a size between 80 and 120 troops, had paused at the coordinates of the crescent and been briefed on the route to their target. Stomped area of the crescent defined number of troops. Enemy briefing at that location had been just after sunrise this morning – time defined by the angle at which tromped grass and weeds had recovered toward vertical later as I was passing overhead."

Waited a few days then orbited their likely target area while returning to Vientiane late in the afternoon of 5 January 1973. During my second orbit over the north ridge a single AK round fired from my six o'clock direction audibly passed by the left side of my O-1. (With cockpit window open, FACs could hear bullets passing by them and could identify the weapon caliber by the unique sounds each kind of projectile made.) That single AK round verified for me that the enemy force had arrived and were now in position somewhere close to the location I had anticipated as being their target destination. This canyon, normally a quite peaceful drive, with a road passing between the lengths of two long ridges, was a wonderful ambush site. That road connected Vang Vieng with Muang Kassy in MR I.

Cricket called me on UHF. Said that they had two sets of unexpended A-7s coming off Rescue CAP orbit over North Vietnam. "Do you have a target and can you expend them?" "You bet." In sequential order Hobo (12 CBU 52 plus 20 mm) and Sandy 6 (10 LAU 3 plus 2 CBU 38), each a flight of two A-7s, checked in on UHF, rendezvoused quickly using their onboard inertial navigational systems, received the required FAC target briefing. Then the fighters went to work on the inside slopes of the southern canyon walls. Munitions being delivered were somewhat unusual in that some were primarily designed to function only as pyrotechnic firework displays to keep enemy heads down during an integrated, overhead rescue effort and chopper pickup of a downed pilot. There weren't many places inside the canyon walls where NVA troops could hide out or dig in. Their limited choice was to conceal themselves beneath the heavy leaf growth of a large and extended banana orchard. Banana trees share botanical membership with the lily family of plants and provide little protection against any kind of munitions. The CBU dropped by the fighters did a job on the bananas. Two days later a USAF lieutenant colonel accompanied by a Lao lieutenant were driving that same road through the canyon on their way north to help a Lao ground commander at Muang Kassy fill out his supply requisitioning paperwork. They noticed an intense bad smell inside the canyon. Both dismounted from their jeep and carried their weapons while walking the walls of the canyon. They provided unusually accurate airstrike BDA, having personally counted a little over 80 KBA lying dead on the canyon ground.

12 January 1973. I had the first go of the day. A five-minute pit stop upstairs at downtown AIRA to pick up copies of today's Top Secret fighter frag order mission schedule and listen to the duty officer's brief rundown concerning the night's reported events out on the PDJ. Departed Vientiane's airport, Wattay, using the 9,700 foot long concrete runway well before the sun first appeared above the horizon. Flaps up. Fuel boost pump off. Climbed out to the northeast above the Mekong. Destination was Long Tieng. Still dark out and nighttime on the ground below. First light from a rising sun brightly illuminated the gilded tops of a huge thunderstorm to the north, which extended from ground level up to about 36,000 feet. Tried each of our several different routes to the PDJ but all were blocked by the thunderstorm. Landed on the short gravel runway at Muang Kassy to wait for the storm to dissipate. Topped off the O-1's fuel tanks then walked over to the Lao tactical operations center (TOC) tent to check their maps and get some idea what their ground forces were currently up to. Was taking notes of coordinates of their listening outposts and current observation positions when a Lao officer walked in and complained he had received no radio contact with any of his troops since two A.M. He wanted me to take him up in the O-1 so he could see what was happening with his troops. Language barrier precluded his understanding that he wouldn't be able to see anything from the airplane because the thunderstorm base was right on the ground surface. Solution: I put him in the back seat of the O-1 and climbed to just below the base of the clouds, a 700-foot AGL ceiling, so that he could begin to comprehend the reality imposed by the weather. Followed the dirt road east to the point where the rising road disappeared up into boiling and rolling fog. Coming down the road from the mountain pass two NVA troops carrying AK-47s at port arms emerged from the fog. These lead troops were immediately followed by two T-34 tanks, and an infantry battalion mix of NVA cadre and Pathet Lao troops descended the road after emerging from the base of the thunderstorm. We were quite close. I could see those two enemy's faces and the details of what each was wearing. Pulled up into the cloud base for cover, turned south, and flew instrument flight rules (IFR) with the only useful instruments the O-1G had, needle, ball, and airspeed. My battle with this enemy armor ground force lasted almost three hours. Will compress all that to a few sentences. Put a Willie Pete on their infantry, which

resulted in intense noise causing the infantry to abandon their armor and seek refuge in the jungle. Cricket had seven sets of fighters orbiting overhead but the solid cloud ceiling was too low and the mountains too high to put in an airstrike. Lao T-28s were willing and available at Vientiane – but their ordnance loads kept being changed by their honcho and they never got into the air to fly a strike mission. The two tanks stopped on the road, the crews got out and had a meeting out on the middle of the road between the tanks which involved a lot of hand waving. Put another Willie Pete on their communal gathering in the middle of the dirt road. Rocket didn't hit anything of interest – but both NVA crews climbed into the lead tank, abandoning the rear tank, and pressed on toward their destination, Muang Kassi. AIRA called me on VHF as the low ceiling clouds began to evaporate and said, "Don't use your fighters to destroy those tanks – we have people on the ground who will take care of them." I observed no friendlies existing anywhere on the ground. The Lao officer in my back seat remained mute even after I'd put in the FM frequency of his TOC and put his selector switch in the FM position so he could talk to his troops. The lead tank with doubled crew abandoned their tank and headed north into the woods. Ed Chun came by in his O-1 with a student in his front seat who needed to put in only one single airstrike to become fully qualified as a Lao FAC. Passed my targets off to Ed, then I headed for Vang Vieng to refuel. Landed. Ate a hot dog. Never saw that Lao officer in my backseat again. U.S. Army attaché people took control of the NVA tanks. One tank started right up. They fed it a jerry can of fuel and drove the lead tank to Vientiane. The rear tank wouldn't start. It was partially disassembled then towed to Vientiane. Both tanks were placed on static display next to the vertical runway as a public relations effort informing the Lao citizens of how well their war was going. The NVA and Pathet Lao infantry troops and their tank crews found the Lao jungle to be an inconvenient and uninviting environment. Fifty-two of them were scarfed up and became POWs the next day. The NVA commander's tactical plan to bypass Long Tieng and take command of the northern Laos road structure had just been defeated.

A cease fire being declared throughout Laos, each of the Ravens flew his last combat mission in-country and landed, as scheduled, at a predetermined time before noon that morning. After engine shutdown we were met with a variety of smoke grenades billowing red, purple, and orange smoke across the ramp at Wattay. Vang Pao scheduled a goodbye party up at Long Tieng, called a baci (pronounced bah-see). Air America flew all the Ravens up together to Alternate in a Pilatus Porter – a short field landing and takeoff aircraft – which had an interesting cockpit configuration. Just inside the front cockpit window, there was a twelve-inch deep horizontal board mounted just below the instrument panel, running across the cockpit. That board functioned as a desktop for writing notes. The flight and engine controls were concealed beneath that board, not visible. Before supper and the usual sticky rice balls dipped in salsa, we enjoyed Johnnie Walker Red scotch while listening to VP's congratulatory speech delivered sequentially in three different languages. VP presented each Raven with an ancient flintlock, muzzle-loading rifle to keep and take home with him as a souvenir of his service in Laos. Many short lengths of individual white strings were tied around each Raven's wrists by the local people. Strings on wrists were intended to protect us while travelling to each of our separate destinations. We moved to an auditorium-sized room with a stage where town people had gathered, including women and children. The band played. We sang and danced. And sang some more. Late in the evening I went outdoors to get some air. Climbed a tree. As ladies departed from the auditorium for return to their village, I spoke to them from up near the top of the tree. They then walked much more briskly, certain that bad Phi were speaking to them in the dark of night from the treetops.

Learned a lot of useful things about surviving in the air during combat. Short rules which sound somewhat like aphorisms:

Never fly in coordinated flight during combat – keep your ball in the needle-ball instrument off to one side or the other in the ball race. The enemy aims ahead of the bird in the apparent direction where the aircraft nose is pointed. In uncoordinated flight the aircraft is actually flying sideways, not where the nose is pointing. Munitions being fired at you will miss.

During a mission you'll have to get out different maps from your map bag several times as you move across the terrain. Pull back on the stick and up into a steep climb. Release all back pressure on the stick when your attitude is about twenty-five degrees up. While the aircraft slowly recovers on its own, you'll have time to paw through your map bag and find the map you are looking for. Fly the bird only with your feet and rudder pedals while all that is going on.

Occasionally, after recovering from a rocket pass, you'll need to get back on the target area quickly. Leave the power set as is. Release all back pressure on the stick as the airspeed drops off to zero. (An aircraft can't stall when there is no loading from the flight controls.) With zero airspeed showing on your instrument, your aircraft is now flying backwards. Apply a very light pressure to your right rudder. The aircraft will turn left. Release that rudder pressure when the nose has turned and is again pointing toward the ground. Now let the airspeed increase normally while descending. You are visually back on your target and ready to go to work.

Sometimes in flight your brain will speak to you as though it were a third person, saying something like, "Break Right, Now!" Even though there is absolutely no evidence that anyone is shooting at you, go ahead, believe it – and break right. Shortly after that change of heading you'll see a detonation at about the place and altitude where you would have been if you hadn't broken right. That's your intuition working for you. Pay attention to your intuition.

All combat takes place between or among two or more human brains. Your brain is, and will remain, your primary weapon in combat. Learn quickly. Combat is the most intensely Darwinian event you'll encounter during your lifetime. When you arrive at your first war you'll be reasonably certain that you have been properly trained and are fully prepared for combat. Turns out to be untrue. Combat is a totally experiential event in your life and, like most of life's experiences, is intensely personal and not at all teachable or communicable to others. Hostile emotions or personal feelings about your enemy are surprisingly rare in combat. Doing in an enemy who is doing his best to kill you is an impersonal activity. There is no satisfaction or sense of having won. At the end of the day I'd sit down, and quietly say to myself, "I came home to supper and you didn't."

Section Four

MR III, IV, V   Savannakhet, Pakse, Vientiane   War in the South

Lao village east of the Bolaven Plateau (Lee Gossett Collection)

Chapter 24

Jerome W. Klingaman
First Tour: AOC Commander
Vientiane, Sep 1966 – Feb 1967

Preamble

This narrative describes my life as an Air Operations Center (AOC) commander and air combat advisor in Laos during the late 1960s. The story actually involves two vastly different experiences in that country--one being my first tour as AOC commander at Vientiane, Laos, directing a third-country contingent of Royal Thai Air Force (RTAF) pilots flying AT-28s. The other story entails a second tour as AOC commander at Pakse, in southern Laos, supporting Royal Lao Air Force (RLAF) combat missions in the same type aircraft. These "in-country" activities, like many others performed by Air Force personnel augmenting the office of the air attaché in Laos, were carried out under code-name "Project 404."

My aim in telling this story is to add my testimony to a small body of literature describing covert operations carried out by a relatively small group of people who, over time, threw their combined efforts against a catastrophic intrusion by Communist forces in Laos. I also want to record the makeup and character of a small RLAF fighter unit that I flew with and advised at Pakse (Lima Site 11) during the war. That story, from the southern region of Laos, is missing from the literature. Finally, I want to cast some light on how our role in Project 404 played out against the overall conflict in Southeast Asia (SEA), for it was not simply a "Viet Nam" war.

There were actually several armed conflicts going on in Southeast Asia, involving Viet Nam, Cambodia, and Laos, each having their own internal dynamics, agendas, and goals. In fact, there were five distinct conflict arenas in Laos alone--one in each Lao military region, which provided the political and geographic context for actions carried out by AOC personnel, Butterfly FACs, and the Ravens. Perhaps least understood is why we operated covertly and how these covert actions contributed to the "grander" scheme of U.S. objectives in Viet Nam and the rest of Southeast Asia.

Over the years, a great mystique has wrapped itself around the conflict in Laos, especially the covert operations we conducted there. No one will ever remove that mystique from the Kingdom of Laos; it is too impenetrable, too enduring. At the same time, this mystique lends color to great stories, some true, some not so true, but there were, for sure, very real adventures among the participants that equal or exceed some of the best fiction. I think we all knew at the time that we were taking part in something so bizarre and improbable that people might tend to disbelieve our accounts of what happened.

As the years go by, time and the loss of living memory will eventually blur the details and move them even further out of focus, and the stories will take on the character of legend rather than fact. The best we can do now, as I have tried to do in this narrative--however inadequately--is preserve small bits and pieces of what happened during the last, fading days of the Lao Kingdom and hope that the story of that period of time does not disappear completely.

I want to emphasize that I speak for myself here; others among the various participants in Laos may have had vastly different experiences that shape their perceptions and understanding of that strange and tragic war. Also, the participants' professional backgrounds prior to entering the war varied a great deal, and that, too, colors their perceptions.

To that end, I beg the reader's indulgence in my beginning this story with a short account of what I experienced after joining the Air Commandos in 1965. That experience defines, at least in part, who I was at the time I entered Laos and what I had, and did not have, to bring to the fight. I won't claim that any of these special operations activities, including the Laos missions, constitute any "life-defining moments" for me, but going to war in a country that most people have never heard of, dressed in blue jeans and a denim jacket, possessing no personal identification, has a tendency to change your outlook considerably.

Special Operations: Learning the Trade

Time and chance have a way of sneaking up on you once in a while and dealing you in for the game of your life. Maybe that's why literal translations of the Homeric tales spell *Fate* with a capital F. The game of *my* life began when I returned from four years in Great Britain in June 1965 to fly with the Air Commandos (later the USAF Special Operations Force). Those people were very often the weapon of choice for missions in Southeast Asia and other places that were, well, different.

I started out in the 319th Air Commando Squadron, 1st Air Commando Wing, at Hurlburt Field, FL, and spent the first seven months easing into a special operations mindset. I also learned how to fly the C-47 "correctly." I had flown C-47s in Great Britain, but not the way they did it in the Air Commandos. My typical mission profile from Wethersfield, England, was a morning takeoff for Wiesbaden, Germany, wearing wool-blues with Eisenhower jacket and tie. If we didn't remain overnight (RON), the day would be spent waiting for senior staff-members to wind up their meeting and appear at base ops for the flight back to Wethersfield. The flight home was usually a quiet night flight across the English Channel.

Crossing the Channel with a C-47 in the dead of winter with sleet and freezing rain could be exciting, but at least the runways in Europe had lights, and no one was trying to blow up my airplane or kill me.

Flying C-47s at Hurlburt Field was somewhat more challenging. I spent part of my time training pilots for deployment to C-47 units in Viet Nam. The internal mission we trained for, however, was personnel insertion, extraction, and resupply of Army Special Forces (SF), SEALS, and Air Commando teams, flying low-level profiles, primarily at night under clandestine circumstances. That was very exciting; at least it was for me.

My night checkout, shortly after arriving at the squadron, started out with a basic qualification ride that quickly moved into the tactical mode. My instructor pilot (IP) told me that the next event would be a lights-out landing on a small clay strip some distance from, and parallel to, the main runway. As there were no runway or approach lights, the strip was just a black void, and there was no moon.

About the time I started wondering how I was going to pull this off, the IP told me I would probably not be able to see the ground on the final approach and flare, but not to worry; a Combat Control Team (CCT) would switch on their flashlights for 30 seconds on both sides of the approach end as I came in. *Oh, great, flashlights; just what I was hoping for.* "And then," he said, "As you come in over the end of the strip, just set up a 50-feet-per-minute rate of descent (the width of the vertical-speed needle) and let the bird settle in until you contact the ground. The aircraft will bounce a bit, but keep the controls well forward after contact, and the tail will come down on its own. After that, you taxi back, make a blacked-out takeoff, and bring the aircraft around for another landing."

We did the "clay pit" full-stop landings and takeoffs that night I don't know how many times. It wasn't exactly a piece of cake, but I learned how to do it; it just takes a bit of getting used to. Remember, we had no night-vision goggles (NVGs), no on-board radar, and no radio altimeters in those days, just a basic set of instrument flight rules (IFR) instruments. Those first seven months at Hurlburt were also spent learning how to arrive at an initial point (IP) at 250 feet above the ground at night and pop up to 500 feet to deliver resupply bundles or 1250 feet (800 feet for combat insertion) to jump a stick of Army Special Forces (SF) on a tiny drop zone in the woods. On my first solo night drop, the wind was 17 knots across the drop zone. I briefed the SF guys about the forecast winds prior to takeoff, and, later, relayed the 17-knot wind force to them just before the drop. They told me that these were the sort of adverse conditions they trained for, so "Let's press on."

So we pressed on, and they all went in the trees. I had offset the drop with the aircraft's nose angled into the wind to kill the drift, but it wasn't enough. That was a bit worrying—their leader on the jump was a tall, ramrod-straight SF full colonel—but no one was hurt, they got their training, and everyone was happy. That's what I mean about easing into a special operations mindset. During the day, low-level flight profiles for airdrop and personnel insertion were made at 50 feet above the ground. The minimum altitude at night was 250 feet. Did I say that we had no radar? That made your navigator a valuable and highly respected person. Back then, I don't think we even filed flight clearances for some of these low-level gigs.

Quite frankly, this kind of flying was great fun, and it does give one a feeling of possessing a few "special operations" skills. But later, when reading through some of the command's contingency plans, I realized that all this training would have been barely adequate to get ourselves through a real-world operation alive.

I saw some amazing things while I was at Hurlburt. We dropped a lot of flares on the Eglin range for night air strikes by A-1E Sky Raiders and A-26 Invaders. Those were more or less routine missions, but I remember one sortie that was not routine at all. A squadron colleague and friend, Captain Kit Carson, and I were out on the range one night dropping flares for A-26s. Everything was going fine until there was a brilliant white flash outside the aircraft to the left and rearward. Carson, who was flying left seat on this sortie, beat me to the question: "Loadmaster, what is going on back there?" His response was very reassuring: "Oh, one of the flares just exploded going out the door when it came to the end of the arming lanyard, but there wasn't much fragmentation against the aircraft."

Now it was my turn to ask a question: "Loadmaster, why did that happen, and will it happen again?" His response was equally reassuring: "I don't know for sure, Sir, maybe these old Mark 6 flares are defective." One flare going "bang" doesn't shut down a mission, so we continued dropping flares for the attack ships until another Mark 6 exploded going out the door, showering the side of the bird with aluminum particles. We went home, downloaded the Mark 6 flares, and uploaded a more recent type for the next sortie that night.

Now it was my turn in the left seat. We returned to the range and continued throwing out flares for some A1-E Sky Raiders until very late in the evening. When it was over and we called range control to check out, they asked us to stick around for one more flare drop, telling us, "Your customer should be over the target in about 30 minutes."

"OK, Control, what kind of aircraft is it?" They told us it was a "special-mission" aircraft, not very enlightening, but wasn't supposed to be. An hour and a half later, well past midnight, the "special-mission" aircraft showed up--a civilian, twin-engine Piper of some kind that made one pass over the target and covered it with napalm. No more questions; no more evasive answers. One minute you are training, and the next minute you're in the combat test business.

And speaking of the test business, on another mission, I was told to join up with a C-130 at an initial point (IP) south of the Eglin range at a designated time and altitude. The C-130's airspeed would be well within my speed range, so all I had to do was fly a loose formation on the C-130's left wing with an Air Force combat photographer capturing a film clip of the event out the right window of my bird. We met at the IP at the designated time and proceeded to the range flying a couple hundred feet above the ground. After arriving at a spot on the range with ditches and deep holes all over the place, a huge cargo chute emerged from the back of the C-130.

Of course, I thought, a bundle drop; I had done many of them. But the chute extracted an enormous aluminum canister that swung down into a vertical position and impacted the ground, spraying liquid chemical and heavy smoke-like vapor all over the place. Some little gizmos went flying out of the canister, landing around the edges of the vapor. The vaporous stuff flattened out, seeping down into the holes, and then--nothing. This all happened rather quickly, but time slows down when you're watching something like this, and it all looked like a big fizzle. Suddenly, the little gizmos ignited and the whole mess erupted in an enormous explosion that filled the holes and lifted a huge fireball into the air. I found out later that we had been part of a live test of the propane bomb that was subsequently used in Viet Nam to take out heavily dug-in North Vietnamese Army (NVA) troops. Squadron life was interesting then.

Pre-Launch

In the late summer of 1966, I was a C-47 instructor and flight examiner in the (re-designated) 319th Special Operations Squadron (319 SOS), but now at England AFB, Louisiana. The battle wing had moved from Hurlburt Field to England AFB in March 1966, leaving a pipe-line training unit at Hurlburt. The operational focus at England AFB was mainly on in-house training and preparing for contingency operations. Rather than training C-47 pilots on their way to Viet Nam, I spent most of my time training and upgrading our own copilots and aircraft commanders.

My assigned copilot, and a valued friend, was Tom Shera. Tom was extremely professional and just plain fun to fly with. In 1966, I had the privilege of upgrading him to aircraft commander in the C-47, neither of us knowing at the time that he would become a renowned Raven FAC who flew an enormous amount of combat over an extended length of time in northern Laos.

Another close friend of mine at England AFB was a combat controller named Bob Farmer. Bob did crazy things like jump out of perfectly good airplanes at high altitude and parachute to a little spot on the surface of the Earth—with equipment, at night. Bob had an infectious spirit that made me want to jump out of airplanes as well, but during the day with no equipment. I never did.

Riding around base in his Pontiac GTO hardtop one day, he told me quietly that he had drawn a temporary duty (TDY) deployment to Laos under a classified program. I don't think either of us knew much in the way of details at the time, but he told me some stories that another Air Commando officer had brought back from Laos. The stories sounded hairy and exciting.

It was the summer of 1966, and Bob was on his way to Laos to become a Butterfly FAC at Site 20 Alternate, the secret CIA base up north. That story, of course, is better told by Bob Farmer somewhere else in *The Raven Chronicles*. I envied Bob his forthcoming adventure almost as much as I envied him his 1966 Pontiac GTO, and wondered how I would eventually enter the Southeast Asia (SEA) arena. I was soon to find out.

We all had additional duties in the 319 SOS; mine was administrative officer and "exec" under the squadron commander, Lieutenant Colonel Russel (Russ) Uhlmann. The job was rewarding and it filled the hours between C-47 sorties. I enjoyed just being in special operations and flying by their rules and tactics, but the war in Southeast Asia was in full fury, and I had not served a SEA tour. Knowing that, Lt Col Uhlmann approached Colonel Hugh Fly, the 1st Special Operations Wing Commander, offering him my name to fill the wing's ongoing commitment to furnish a fighter pilot every six months to serve as Air Operations Center (AOC) commander at Vientiane, Laos. The job was traditionally offered to AT-28 drivers in the wing at Hurlburt Field, but I had flown F-84 Fs and F-100s in a previous life, so I was accepted. Later, looking back on it, I realized that this was Lt Col Uhlmann's way of giving me a boost and saying thanks for my work in the squadron. I will always be grateful for that gesture.

All this AOC-commander discussion with the wing transpired without me knowing anything about it. The mission was highly classified, and details were released only on a need-to-know basis; the proposed incumbent had to be a volunteer, and was only read into the assignment at the time it was offered. And it was offered:

Lt Col Uhlmann approached me outside the squadron building, laid out the general terms of what I would be getting into, and asked me if I wanted it. While listening to him describe the mission, I could see that a current, qualified AT-28 pilot would probably have been preferable, but I wasn't going to argue. I really wanted the mission, so I made it clear that I was a volunteer.

Then I got the details. The job entailed running an AT-28 combat launch facility using third-country aircrews from a remote corner of the international airport at Vientiane, the Laotian capital. The airport had a hard-surface runway, and was normally referred to as Wattay. The assignment would be for a maximum of 179 days temporary duty (TDY), which meant that I would return to the Air Commando Wing at England AFB when it was over. That was a huge plus, as I did not want to leave the command. The official assignment location was Detachment One of the 56th Special Operations Wing at Udorn, Thailand, code name *Water Pump*.

At the Water Pump compound, I would be stripped of my military identity and sent across the border into Laos. I would report to the office of the air attaché (AIRA), Vientiane and operate from then on in civilian clothes. Supposedly--and I know of nothing verifying this policy--the Air Force, at least at that time, would not directly acknowledge ownership of a "demilitarized" member who wound up in enemy hands. Whether or not that was true, no one had ever tested the policy. Actually, I don't think everyone understood the ground rules the same way, if at all. The guidance, both at home and in Laos, was essentially word of mouth; I don't remember seeing anything in writing at the time.

In whatever form it took, I was fine with the guidance, but there was one policy I did not feel comfortable with. After my discussion with Lt Col Uhlmann, I asked if I could have a checkout in the AT-28 at Hurlburt Field. That seemed reasonable. But the answer was *no*; there wasn't time; it wasn't scheduled, and the American Embassy (AMEMB) in Vientiane did not allow Air Force members to fly combat in the AT-28 in Laos.

This proscription was political. The 1964 Geneva Accords had affirmed the neutrality of Laos, forbidding the presence of foreign military personnel with the exception of the various military attachés and a legal 50-man French training contingent stationed there in uniform. U.S. combat operations originating from, and conducted within, Laos would have been in violation of the Accords and therefore (in a very specific and peculiar sense) deemed illegal.

This was essentially all I knew about the mission when I departed for Laos. The conflict in that country and the relationships among the various players were murky to begin with, and remain so today, becoming increasingly complicated as one advances into the depths of this odd, convoluted world of covert operations, unbelievably bizarre rules of engagement, and political intrigue. I think it is impossible to make sense out of this story apart from certain key events leading up to our involvement in Laos, including the interlocking and opposing agendas of the various players.

So, perhaps this is a good place to establish the political-historical context for AOC commanders, Butterfly FACs, Raven FACs, and other Air Force personnel operating in Laos under what was eventually designated as Project 404, Palace Dog, the code name referring to the covert augmentation of the office of the air attaché, Vientiane, Laos.

Departure for Laos

With departure for Water Pump only a few days off, I was told I would be taking an AOC assistant with me, a C-123 aircraft commander at England AFB named John Lee. We had not met, but when we did meet, I liked him immediately. I don't remember if John was a first lieutenant or a captain, but this would be his third deployment to Southeast Asia (SEA), so he was way ahead of me on that count. I was also pleased to have a colleague and accomplice. None of us deploying to Laos for the first time knew what we didn't know, a most unfortunate situation. There was no specialized training for combat aviation advisory personnel, not even in the Air Commandos. It would take almost 30 years to get that fixed.

Finally it was time to leave, taking one tropical suit with shirt and tie, per instructions, and one short-sleeve summer uniform that we would wear on the airplane going over. I also carried blue jeans and a Lee denim jacket. I still have the jacket. I also carried my classical guitar, a priority, but no weapon.

John and I flew commercial to San Francisco, spent a day in town, and left out of McClellan AFB on the Embassy Courier. The flight to Bangkok, Thailand, was long and uneventful. Before proceeding to Water Pump at Udorn Air Base, we were required to check in at the Bangkok "Requirements Office," which, among other things, managed the going and coming of Project 404 personnel.

As I remember, the office was located on the fourth floor of a building leased by the U.S. Government. John and I could stand on the fourth-floor balcony and look out over the tops of glistening palm trees that stretched out like a green sea covering the entire city. Today, it is a mega-metropolis. The great Chao Phria River, which ran right through town, kept the city continuously flushed out through a network of connecting klongs (canals) that were dug during the 19th century. The klongs also served as public transport. During the mid-20th century, western nations showed the Thais how to fill in the klongs to make roads that could be filled with new automobiles. After that, it no longer flushed out every day. During the early 1970s, I served two accompanied tours in Bangkok, and watched the old city change at a devastating pace.

I had intended to meet the officer I was replacing (Bill Keeler) either on site at the AOC in Vientiane or at Udorn Air Base, but there was a note at the Requirements Office asking me to contact him at the Tracadaro Hotel in Bangkok. According to the Army Project 404 officer, Bill and his team had been flooded out of the AOC at Vientiane when the Mekong River went over its banks a few days prior. The wet season had ended with a terrible inundation of the surrounding countryside.

I got Bill on the phone and arranged for John and me to meet him for dinner at his hotel. The Tracadaro probably doesn't even exist anymore; it was only two or three stories tall and was old then, but the atmosphere was fabulous. We had a couple of drinks and adjourned to the dining room, where I had my first water buffalo fillet steak. Not bad, but different. The flood precluded any overlap between Bill and me at Vientiane, but those things happen.

The Requirements Office had John and I booked on a C-130 to Udorn Air Base a day later. We made the flight, looking down on an open, mostly featureless landscape--trees and scrub, and a few tiny villages. Someone met us when we arrived and drove us over to the fenced-in Water Pump compound on the other side of the runway from the Air Force facilities. The Water Pump operations building shared this large compound with Air America and some other folks Air America called "the customer."

At the Water Pump ops desk, we were told that our insertion into Laos was delayed because of widespread flooding in Vientiane. The desk sergeant gave us the name of a hotel in Udorn City and told us to go there and check in. It is difficult to remember all this clearly after 48 years, but I think John and I parted company soon after our arrival at Udorn. The air attaché office in Vientiane was critically short of Butterfly FACs at Site 20 Alternate in the highlands of north Laos, so John was picked to fill that vacancy. So much for having an AOC assistant and accomplice. Anyway, I found myself billeted with another officer in civilian clothes whose function was never made known to me.

The hotel was made out of rough, locally-sawn timber, and it reeked of new wood, garlic, and cilantro—wonderful! Udorn had dirt streets in those days. I had been in the hotel a couple days when I was called out to the Water Pump. At the ops desk, I was given a white envelope containing $100 dollars and told to go into town and find a certain old woman named Mary, or something, at a particular stall in the local market. I was to give her the money, and she would know what to do. At this point, I want to make it clear that I am not making this up; it really went down like this. Following the directions I was given, I found "Mary" and gave her the envelope. She gave me her best betel-nut grin and brought out a tailor's tape measure. She measured me up and down and said, "You come back, two days; I give you clothes."

Two days later, I found her again, and she gave me a package tied up in string. Thinking how absolutely bizarre this was, I didn't even open the package, but just headed back to the hotel. In the room, I opened the package and found three sets of RLAF two-piece flying suits; not so bizarre after all. I've often wondered how many other Project 404 guys went through the *money-in-a-white-envelope* thing. Whatever the case, I loved my new flying suits, and things seemed to be off to a good start.

Waiting for the flood water to recede, however, was agonizingly slow. I certainly wasn't needed around Water Pump. In fact, no one in the detachment except the ops-desk NCO would even talk to me. So I made myself scarce and waited it out in the hotel. I read the Bangkok World, got my hair cut, had my laundry done, bought a switchblade knife, ate more water buffalo, and, finally, after an eternity--about one week--I was told to report to Water Pump with everything I owned. It was time to "cross the fence" into Laos.

At the ops desk, I turned in my uniform plus my military identification and Geneva Convention cards. They emptied my billfold of all other personal identification and stuffed everything into a big manila envelope. They sealed the envelope, and I signed my name across the flap. They told me I could have it back when I extracted from Laos at the end. From there, it was just a quick ride in the detachment jeep out to the flight line where some other folks were waiting beside an unmarked UH-1 helicopter; probably a Pony Express bird, but who knows? Being a 32-year-old captain with a line number for major when this happened might suggest I had some worldly experience, but I was about to learn something about being from special operations and fending for myself as an outsider in someone else's assumed bailiwick. An older person sitting next to me in the Huey was wearing a short-sleeve shirt and tie. That meant he was an officer and probably worked in the embassy. After lifting off and clearing the base perimeter to the north, he leaned over and asked me who I was. He knew perfectly well who I was; he just wanted to make sure I knew who he was.

He was an (augmentation) operations officer at AIRA, Vientiane, and a lieutenant colonel. When I told him who I was, he asked me if I had any fighter time. That seemed like an odd question, but maybe he knew I was not current in the AT-28. At first, I thought he was genuinely interested, but it became apparent from further questioning that the approach was hostile, as if he was challenging me to account for myself and establish my right to be there. I said: "Yes, I flew fighters. I flew the F-84F at Great Falls, Montana, and both the F-84F and F-100D at England AFB Louisiana; how about you?" He was quiet for a moment and then said, "I flew F-100s as well." That remark explained a lot to me; I didn't expect him to say "welcome to your new job," but here we were—two fighter guys looking at each other from opposite sides of a Luffberry, and I was a much lower-ranking new guy. *"So, ease up, Klingaman; turn off the arm switch and be quiet. You can't win this one."*

It turned out, of course, that he was my immediate boss, though he never rated me. We got along increasingly well after that, especially after I had a chance to "prove" myself. Funny, months later, I tried to check him out as a copilot in the embassy C-47. It didn't work.

Still, I learned something I never forgot over many subsequent SOF deployments— it's not that new guys have to be hassled; rather it's that people from the outside can be resented for performing in-country operational missions that are not given to the embassy home team. Such instances may be exceptions, but there is a rule, and it's simple: always be professional with the country team, take nothing for granted, and watch six o'clock every minute.

Arrival at Wattay Field, Vientiane

The Huey ride from Udorn Air Base to Wattay went quickly. Coming in across the fence, the scene outside the window was sobering. The Mekong was still over its banks, flowing across the landscape to the east and north of Vientiane; it looked like a water world. For some people outside the city, the devastation was lethal; whole villages were swept away or wiped out from cholera.

We headed for the AOC aircraft parking ramp across from the international airport, and touched down on a small crown of open macadam at the highest point on the ramp; the rest of the compound was buried in wet Mekong mud. The two main buildings, constructed by the Japanese military during the Second World War, had been flooded several feet up from the ground. The bomb dump, on lower ground, had probably been completely submerged. Everything, including the insides of the buildings, was inundated by at least one foot of heavy mud.

And there were snakes; many snakes, some dead and buried in the mud, and some alive, all venomous. A second Huey landed behind us carrying some of my enlisted AOC team members. One was a medic, the one-eyed Fitzpatrick. Actually he had two eyes, only one was made of glass. I occasionally found it looking up at me from the bottom of my drink when visiting the guys at their enlisted hooch. Fitz was old and skinny, a survivor from WWII, but worth his weight in gold.

Months later, Fitz saved me from what I thought was going to be a Lao firing squad. I was always grateful for that. He's gone now, damn it. The other guys were my line chief, a comm operator, and a couple weapons specialists. The rest of the AOC team arrived over a period of several days as they were located and brought back to Wattay from their home bases in Thailand.

Eventually, vehicles from the embassy arrived at the AOC to carry us to our quarters, and that required a drive through downtown Vientiane. The streets, normally compacted dirt, were virtually destroyed by the flood waters. There were holes big enough to swallow a Jeep and hummocks so tall that the Jeep had to climb over them at a very steep angle in four-wheel drive and the lowest-possible gear setting. We moved at a slow crawl, but finally made it "home."

Officer quarters were located in a single compound containing two buildings--Ice House 1 and 2, collectively known as "the Ice House." The name derived from the presence of an ancient, abandoned French ice-making plant made of weathered wood sitting just outside the compound wall. Ice House 1 was primarily for Project 404 types, the AOC commander, visiting Butterfly FACs, and eventually, the Ravens.

Ice House 2 was for more senior folks who worked downtown in the embassy, mostly operations supervisors, intelligence analysts, current ops guys, and such. The enlisted team members lived in a couple buildings at a place called Koon Compound, several blocks from the Ice House.

I was quartered in Ice House 1. I loved it from the first minute I walked in. The building was mid-century French masonry design and spacious. Main power generation in town was wiped out, so auxiliary-power lighting in the evening filled the rooms with a wonderful, dim yellow glow. It reminded me of staying with my aunt and uncle on their Iowa farm with only kerosene lamps for light. Miraculously, we had water for showers, but we didn't drink it.

My room was huge. I had a bed, a standing armoire for clothes, and a nightstand that came complete with an M1 frag grenade in the drawer. A second bed was reserved for John Lee, but he wasn't there, so I had the room to myself. When I arrived at Vientiane, Bob Farmer had moved down from 20 Alternate to sort out the AIRA command post, and he was living in Ice House 1 as well. It was great spending some time with him before he rotated back to the States.

There was no personal weapon for me, so I wrote home and asked my wife Alice to buy a very small hand gun with ammunition and mail it to me. A few weeks later, two heavy coffee tins of chocolate-chip cookies arrived in the mail. In the bottom of one tin was a Hi-Standard .22 cal over-and-under magnum derringer--perfect for what I needed. The other tin contained two boxes of ammo.

Later, I asked her where she bought the derringer. Her answer surprised me, but women operated differently back then. "I bought it at the jewelry store downtown," she informed me. In those days, women didn't go into gun shops to buy a personal weapon, so high-end jewelry stores kept a few undersized, small-caliber hand guns behind the counter for them. So now you know.

Later, I received an AK-47 assault rifle with ammo as a gift from General Vang Pao, Commander of Military Region 2 (MR 2).

Command and Control

Before we proceed too far into this narrative, it's probably best to describe the rather unconventional command and control structure created for U.S. operations in Laos. The ambassador was operational, as was the office of the air attaché (AIRA) in Vientiane; i.e., their authority extended into the military operational realm. This situation was not unique, but it was extraordinary.

In 1966, the ambassador was William H. Sullivan and he ran the show, which is to say that he supervised all U.S. military operations in Laos including bombing on the Ho Chi Minh trail. As one might expect, this kind of civilian control over military activities in Laos rankled the U.S. military.

The ambassador exercised supervision and control over Project 404 assets through the air attaché who, at that time, was Colonel Pappy Pettigrew. In the operational arena, the ambassador was the senior validating authority for U.S.-controlled strikes. This authority was delegated to the air attaché, who, in turn, exercised the responsibility directly through such assets as air advisors, AOC commanders, Butterfly FACs and, later, the Raven FACs. Butterfly FACs were replaced by the Ravens in late 1967.

Bombing by U.S. aircraft outside the trail and certain designated strike zones was strictly controlled from the air by the Butterfly and Raven FACs. Targets for bombing by the RTAF B-Team were validated by U.S. Agency ground teams at specific sites in North Laos. In some cases, a Butterfly FAC, or even a B-Team member, might acquire validation directly from a host-country resource on the ground close to the target. I actually witnessed a B-Team strike that was validated and directed by General Vang Pao from inside a Porter aircraft. A B-Team strike might or might not be directed by an airborne FAC.

Bombing by RLAF AT-28 fighters was another story. These strike assets supported the host-country Forces Army Royale (FAR) and provided a means to take out certain targets that were normally outside the scope of U.S. air operations. The regional FAR commander was senior validating authority for RLAF strikes in his military region, and exercised target validation directly through FAR ground assets positioned forward in the field. RLAF strikes were occasionally directed from the air by a Raven FAC.

The RLAF had no airborne FAC capabilities of their own, which was unfortunate. If they had possessed FAC assets, they could have deployed them forward to work with FAR ground positions and generate valid targets, thus removing some of the guesswork. As I will explain later, the AOC commander in Military Region 4 (MR 4), where I was located, was the direct link between the local FAR headquarters and the Lao fighter pilots for mission execution and control. That may have been true in other military regions as well.

The AOC commander was essentially a sterilized asset placed in position to direct B-Team or C-Team strike operations. Predictably, the Air Force had no interest in RTAF or RLAF fighter operations and even less in the advisory effort, which, in 1968, totaled no more than 50 people manning five AOC locations in Laos.

The AOC commander was operating outside the boundaries of conventional Air Force tactical air control and supervision, which, in itself, alienated senior Air Force leaders. The way we exercised autonomy under Project 404, however, resulted in quick response, often using AT-28s, to emergency situations on the ground outside the designated strike zones, and served to contain U.S. involvement and prevent widening the war for the United States.

Getting Started

Our first morning at the AIRA office went well. The air attaché, Colonel "Pappy" Pettigrew, gave us a warm welcome, and the ambassador, William H. Sullivan, personally greeted us and gave us an overview of U.S. objectives in the country and of how we fitted into the picture. I got to know Ambassador Sullivan much better over the years, and spoke with him later in the Philippines over a plan Colonel Heinie Aderholt and I had put together to establish a Joint US Military Assistance and Advisory Command at Clark AB, post war, to cover the whole Southeast Asia region. Such a "post-war" initiative would have, of course, required a favorable solution in Viet Nam. Again, that is another story.

The first order of business at Vientiane was reassembling the AOC team and getting the launch facility at Wattay back in operating condition. With the dry season starting up, Communist PL and NVA forces would soon be on the move. Some of the friendly sites up north were vulnerable to enemy attacks and overrun even during the wet season and now, air support from the AT-28 aircraft would be critical to the survival of any site. Air attack sorties would also be needed to support FAR ground offensives.

Recovering the launch facility at Wattay was like conducting an archeological dig, except there were no volunteers to do the job. Some of the FAR security personnel had taken up residence down in the bomb dump on top of the revetments and were living off rice, rats, and snakes. After a long translated conversation with these guys, none of them was interested in digging mud out of the buildings and pushing it off the ramp. We did, however, receive some initial help from the Agency. During our first day working at the site, an Air America U-10, a small, single-engine utility aircraft, flew over our position and dropped little parachute bundles containing simple medical supplies and antivenin serum for different kinds of snakes.

My AOC support team, totaling 18 individuals, eventually reconstituted itself, and was now working at Wattay. Most of them, now returning after several weeks' hiatus, had worked at the AOC prior to the flood. Some of them had crossed the Mekong into Vientiane with their motorcycles on the ferry from Nong Khai, Thailand. We all did what we could with the cleanup, but the task was beyond our physical capabilities. We needed a small army plus some earth-moving equipment.

I approached local representatives of the United States Agency for International Development (USAID) and asked for help. They weren't opposed to being involved in the recovery, but they had other, more pressing, things to do. They did hire some young men to come over to the facility to drag and push mud out of the buildings. USAID also gave me some bags of rice for paying locals to help out. That proved to be a loser; either it wasn't the right type of rice (sticky rice), or it was of a type available everywhere.

Two old Quonset-style buildings occupied the AOC site, one for ops and one for maintenance. There was no electricity at the time, so both buildings were dark inside. The days were very hot, and digging the rooms out by hand was hard work and just plain awful. You would reach down into the wet mud to pull out a buried object and feel something fleshy in your fingers. Did I mention there were snakes? Yes, many varieties—red-tail vipers, small cobras, Russell's vipers, kraits, etc. The locals classified each one by the number of steps you could take before you fell over dead. The Russell's viper was classified as a "two-step" variety.

After the buildings were cleaned out, USAID came over with a road grader and a front-end loader to clear the ramp. They made short work of it. A Chinese gecko, about a half-meter long, attacked the front-end loader, biting into the rubber tire; it wouldn't let go even while it was going round and round on the tire.

We had a terrible accident near the end of the cleanup. Going into excruciating detail about the accident serves no purpose now, but I won't treat it as a nonevent either. Next to the ops building, there was a large metal-covered pole shed intended for sheltered aircraft maintenance. It had been filled with light munitions, mostly 2.75-inch high-velocity rockets and pods brought up from the bomb dump weeks earlier to avoid rising flood water. The shed was inundated nevertheless. All the flooded munitions were condemned by the armament crew and prepared for salvage. There was one type of non-standard munitions that I had never seen before, and which may have been a holdover from the Korean War. All our bombs, for that matter, were left over from World War II. The non-standard item was a 3.5-inch diameter white-phosphorous rocket warhead mounted on a 2.75-inch motor. The standard configuration was a 2.75-inch warhead mounted on a 2.75-inch motor.

Several of the 3.5-inch versions were found lying on the floor of the pole shed with the safety pins pulled from the warheads. Pins were reinserted, but because of a design quirk in the warhead's antiquated firing mechanism--something unknown to the munitions crew--one of them exploded during disassembly, killing two of our munitions people. It is impossible to describe the emotional impact of losing those two people, and I won't even try.

Show Time and the B-Team

After all the mud was cleaned away and the condemned munitions destroyed, it was time to notify the "customer" up north that we were ready for business and to bring the B-Team and AT-28 aircraft up to Wattay for combat. The B-Team consisted of volunteer, strike-qualified RTAF pilots stationed at Udorn Air Base. The B-Team had been negotiated for and financed a couple of years earlier by the Agency (CIA) to support General Vang Pao's small army of Hmong (Meo) fighters headquartered up north at a place called Long Chen, or Site 20 Alternate. The Agency had previously created and financed Vang Pao's army because they knew the Meo would fight. Accordingly, the B-Team flew missions up north, and Vang Pao's needs took priority over other users in that region.

The B-Team pilots stayed at Udorn Air Base on the Air America-Water Pump side of the field with an RTAF lieutenant colonel commandant to look after their interests. They wore RLAF flying suits and all carried RLAF ID cards, something that would not have done me much good. As they were paid by the Agency, separate from their RTAF pay, they were often referred to as the "Mercenary Thai Strike Force," a term I had heard before, and which eventually fell out of use.

For obvious political reasons, the B-Team was not allowed to fly strike missions out of Thailand. Thailand was not an open participant in the war, so the birds had to launch from a base in Laos. Because of the sensitivity over Thai involvement, B-Team operations were necessarily covert. By "covert," I mean operations where you cannot hide the act (bombing raids are hard to hide), but you do attempt to hide--or maintain plausible deniability of--the identity of the actors. Vientiane was the closest base to Udorn and had the best, most secure, support facilities, so that was chosen as the launch site.

The AT-28 aircraft actually belonged to the Air Force at Water Pump for training RTAF and RLAF pilots, so the aircraft were allocated to the B-Team on a day-to-day basis, depending on how many aircraft were left over after building the daily training schedule the evening before. The aircraft would fly from Udorn to Wattay every morning, landing about 0800, fly their missions, and return to Udorn every evening before dark.

On average, we were allocated something like eight fighters per day. The number occasionally reached 15 aircraft because of extenuating circumstances and heavy demands up north. The B-Team operated seven days per week, but the aircraft did not remain overnight at Vientiane to avoid having them blown up by sappers.

The time finally came for the B-Team to mount up and fly to Wattay. I had targets already set up by the customer, so we knew where we were going. That was a real thrill watching two flights of four arriving over the field and pitching out for landing. Also, the thundering sound of eight of them taxiing into the parking area was very rewarding after all we had been through to get the site ready to launch combat sorties. We flew one turn-around for two sorties per bird that day. It was a great feeling to see it all come together at last. It was interesting to meet and eventually get to know the RTAF pilots.

The lead pilot was Captain Anant. He, like many of the other pilots, had been flying B-Team missions since before the flood, so these were not new guys. Their backgrounds were fascinating. Several had flown combat in round-engine AT-6s against guerrilla forces in their own country. At that time, the AT-6 was still on the line as an operational attack aircraft in Thailand. An older pilot with a razor-thin Hollywood mustache out of the 1930s had flown F8F Bearcats in the past. He told me that few of the RTAF Bearcat pilots survived the experience--too much torque for small people. Whether that was the case or not, the F8F was enormously powerful, very fast, and a real handful.

The B-Team was not a "come and go" outfit. They knew each other well, often as close friends, and they had great respect for each other. As a result, they functioned effectively as a fully-developed team. With very few exceptions, I ended my tour with the same B-Team flyers that I started out with. One of them, a new pilot, was shot down on his first mission with the team. They were notably a very reserved, mature group of guys. Not all of them were commissioned RTAF officers; some were warrant officers and sergeants. Getting the B-Team guys to fly was not a special trick; they all had careers in the RTAF, drawing RTAF salaries, and they were also given incentive pay by the Agency. Accordingly, they flew combat every day on a professional basis.

There was one very interesting young officer on the B-Team. His name was Prince Chao Vanthasawadee, and he was a Lao Neutralist. He was related to the Royal Family, but was not a pilot. He had been kept out of pilot training at Water Pump because he belonged to the Neutralist faction, and, as such, had no sponsorship by the senior RLAF staff. His function was to accompany the Thai pilots on raids and talk to Lao ground positions to coordinate "call for fire" and strikes. In many cases, he was there to validate targets. In that regard, he was very important to B-Team efforts, and I suspect he kept them out of trouble more than once by avoiding collateral damage. The B-Team pilots held him in highest regard. In the photo below, I am standing in the middle with Major Anant immediately to my left. Chao is kneeling, second from the left, in the bottom row.

Jerry Klingaman (standing center) with B-Team "The Hoodlums"
Wattay, Vientiane, Laos 1967

The AOC support team was made up of volunteer enlisted men who were serving in one-year permanent change of station (PCS) assignments at various bases in Thailand, mainly Nakhon Phanom. An assignment to the AOC at Vientiane was a real prize, but would have only appealed to the more adventuresome types, which is a gross understatement. The work was grueling-- working dark to dark, seven days per week, usually preparing, and loading two combat sorties every day. As with me, they had no identification and operated in civilian clothes. They were incredibly motivated (you would have to be) and enormously skilled. As they saw it, operating across the border in a covert mode carried a certain élan that made it a unique, once-in-a-lifetime opportunity.

Like the B-Team, they functioned extremely well as an integrated, compositely-structured, team. These were tough guys, and their presence in a sensitive place like Vientiane might have been a bit worrisome to some of the senior Air Force types temporarily augmenting the AMEMB staff. After all, Laos was declared a neutral country by the Geneva Accords, and Vientiane was legally open to all combatants plus those in support roles--Pathet Lao, Neutralists, East European countries, and the Chinese as well as U.S. friends and allies. What made it work for this team, however, was their way of policing themselves and meting out discipline internally.

The senior NCOs supervised their people intensely, but the team members clearly saw themselves as a privileged lot, and they went to great pains to ensure they never let anyone down. The worst thing that could happen to any one of them was to be sent back to their PCS home base in Thailand and denied membership on the team. I worked very closely with these airmen, and that, for me, was a great privilege.

Watching the AOC mission-support team in action was worth the price of admission. One doesn't usually get this close to actual aircraft preparation and conventional weapons loading in an Air Force fighter squadron, especially one whose principal mission is nuclear weapons delivery, as in my case. Weapons loading and maintenance was usually completed by the time I arrived at the aircraft for preflight. So I had never watched anything like this.

The mission-support team would arrive at the AOC just as it was breaking dawn and immediately drive down to the bomb dump to load up little flat-bed bomb dollies with bombs, rockets, and 50-cal ammo. Yellow tugs hauled the bomb dollies back to the revetment area and positioned them at the ends of the revetments. The revetments ran parallel to the aircraft parking row, so each aircraft was pointed into a revetment after engine shutdown.

Squat, self-propelled, MJ-1 bomb loaders were positioned along the revetments facing the aircraft. The driver controlled a hydraulically-operated arm with a bomb cradle mounted on the end. With this rig, he could drive a bomb under the wing of the aircraft and lift it up into the attachment latches of the bomb shackle. We attempted to keep a minimum of four MJ-1 bomb loaders on the line during operations. That was not easy. The MJ-1 cost as much as a Ferrari sports car and was about as easy to maintain. If there was ever a "special-purpose" vehicle, this was it.

When the AT-28s arrived from Udorn and taxied into the revetment area, the ground-support crews were waiting with the MJ-1s already holding bombs in the cradles. As soon as the props came to a stop and the pilot exited the aircraft, each MJ-1 drove into position, locating the bomb just under the bomb rack. The driver raised the boom until the bomb lugs clicked into position; the bomb was now hanging from the latches. Two people, crouched under the wing next to the bomb, would screw down the four sway-brace bolts on the bomb rack until they pressed against each side of the bomb, holding it in position.

Meanwhile people would be loading 50 cal ammo either into a gun pod under the wing or into the wing ammo bays, depending on the type of AT-28. Others would be doing post-flight inspections and minor maintenance and repair. All this happened quickly. The movement of the vehicles and people gave one the impression of it being choreographed, and in a sense it was, through procedure and endless practice. Everyone was engaged in a hands-on enterprise.

The most kinetic actions involved bomb handling and loading, making the MJ-1 the weakest link in the chain. After several days of max effort, when the bomb loaders started breaking one-by-one, I asked the armament chief what happens when all the loaders are down. "Load by hand," was his reply. I didn't know whether to believe him or not, but I watched it happen several times after recovering aircraft from strikes. A bomb dolly loaded with 500-pound bombs was pushed under the wing and two bombs rolled off on the ground directly under the pylons.

Next, round shipping rings were screwed into holes at the nose and tail of the bomb, with the ring positioned vertically. The guys would then push a burned-out .50 cal gun barrel through each ring, giving them something to hang onto. With one person at each end of a gun barrel, four of them would lift, and then press, the bomb up into the latches until the bomb attachment lugs clicked into place. That required a lot of strength; it was impressive, and they could do it all day long if necessary.

I am going into detail here to make a point: Because of the political sensitivity associated with the presence of U.S military personnel in Laos, Project 404 team sizes were held at the absolute minimum. Even now, one can expect a deploying team of this nature to be held to minimum size in a foreign country. At Vientiane, we had eight weapons loaders, one engine mechanic, one aircraft electrician, three AT-28 crew chiefs, one line chief, one senior munitions NCO, one maintainer for our 60 kv generator, one communications operator, and one enlisted physician assistant (PA). Those 18 people serviced anywhere from eight to 15 combat aircraft from a "non-improved" facility, often supporting two sorties per day. And they did it seven days per week without complaint. The maintenance effort included on-site engine changes.

Word eventually reached me that the AOC mission-support team was referred to by some embassy folks as "Klingaman's Hoodlums." I took that as a compliment, and was so proud of them I could bust. Every evening after the combat sorties were completed and the B-Team had departed for Udorn, I would stand outside the AOC ops building and brief them on what we knew about bombing results up north. Feedback and buy-in are critical to an operation like this. One evening, one of them said he had heard about the "Hoodlum" thing and asked it was true. I said, "Yes, it is, and you guys are the best bunch of Hoodlums I have ever known." They loved it. They called themselves the "Hoodlums" from then on, and I was "Chief Hoodlum."

To round out the team, I actually had a "batman" of sorts (using the English term) assigned to me. He was a Thai national named Vuet. He kept my vehicle washed (a jeep-like International Harvester with an ocean-liner turning radius), and worked at keeping the ops rooms tidied up. Keeping anything in and around the buildings clean was impossible. The dry season was upon us, and there was dust and dirt covering everything, especially with all the mud that had by now dried into a fine powder.

Vuet's most important function, however, was bringing lunch to the AOC for the B-Team. The food came in stacked enamel pots and tasted like the best home-cooked Thai cuisine. And in fact, it was—Vuet's wife prepared it every day. Vuet came to me one day and said that he was no longer being paid for the lunches. I asked how much he was owed, and I paid him that amount out of pocket. I mentioned it to the embassy, but continued paying for the lunches for several weeks until I was reimbursed in full with cash, hand-delivered in a white envelope.

The BC-47 Arc-Light Bomber

Just prior to restarting AOC operations, the embassy and the RLAF both approached me on the idea of turning a C-47 into a bomber. The RLAF C-47s operated extensively out of Savannakhet Air Base, and they wanted a night bombing capability. The C-47s were provided to them via security assistance "titles turned over," so the modification could be accomplished in-country with no questions asked. This sounded a bit bizarre, but I met with my munitions and maintenance people at our little AOC "conference table" to brainstorm ideas. What they came up with was amazing in its creativeness and ingenuity.

The first order of business was finding an appropriate airframe. A C-47 was just coming out of major phase inspection at the Thai-Am contract maintenance facility at Udorn, so we chose that one and had them paint the entire aircraft black. There was also some resource acquisition to be done, and that was apportioned out among various AOC members.

When the aircraft and all the bits and pieces were finally brought together at the AOC parking area, work began on the BC-47. Brass rods were cut, bent, and braised into large brass rings that were strung on a steel jump cable that was brought up tight inside the aircraft. Next, a set of roller conveyers was installed going all the way down the floor and turning right out the left cargo door. We also had a large aluminum box fabricated to hold illumination flares in a vertical position.

Mission prep consisted of placing wooden rice pallets (courtesy of USAID) on the roller conveyers. Three 100-pound, general-purpose (GP) bombs were placed on each rice pallet with a 100-pound plasticized white phosphorous (PWP) bomb placed on top and between the GP bombs. The three bombs and the pallet were then strapped together as a unit. Both GP bombs were fused and the arming wires brought up to the brass rings and secured. The PWP bombs didn't need fusing as they would explode sympathetically with the GP types. A heavy steel pin was inserted at the end of the roller conveyer to prevent the rice pallets from going out the door until it was time for "bombs away."

I worked out a tactic and flight pattern that I would later use in modified form on a project with the Korean Air Force to locate and attack high-speed boats at night. The BC-47 would approach the target coordinates at night on a given heading and toss out two flares 30 seconds prior to the designated coordinates. A second set of two flares went out 15 seconds after that, and every 15 seconds thereafter until 30 seconds past the target. At that time, the BC-47 would stop throwing out flares and execute a 90-270 degree turn coming back around to line up on the string of flares, flying in the opposite direction. If they had the right coordinates, and visual confirmation, the pilot would turn on the drop light in back, and the loadmaster would pull the steel retaining pin. The bomb pallets would rush down the roller conveyer and exit the aircraft one by one. The arming wires would be retained by the brass rings, setting up the first stage of the arming process.

The saving grace, if there was one, was that the little arming propellers on the nose of each fuse had to spin off before the bombs were really armed and ready. That guaranteed some time and distance separation from the aircraft before anything happened. I wasn't sure the little propellers would spin off, but they did.

When completed, the BC-47 flew to Savannakhet and immediately went operational. It was, by all accounts, very successful. A line of bombs and white phosphorous exploding across a line of enemy troops must have been quite a sight. I was afraid they would run into a mountaintop doing this at night. The RLAF C-47 crews had some instrument and night-flying capability, but it was minimal by most standards.

The RLAF BC-47 eventually came to an end when they burned it up on the ground through mishandling flares. Incidentally, burning up an RLAF C-47 with a flare accident was not an isolated incident. One of them burned up at Pakse, Laos, during my second tour when they taxied into a pallet loaded with crates of flares. The accident happened at night, and we could see the fire from our house several miles away. What they were doing with crated flares on the ramp at Pakse was something of a mystery.

AIRA's suspicion at the time was that RLAF C-47 flights into Pakse entailed a refueling stop prior to clandestine flights into Cambodia, possibly to Siem Reap, for smuggling gold and opium. My closest guess was that the flares were intended to illuminate the runway during an overhead pass at Siem Reap, or some other site, before coming around to land. There would have been no runway lights at fields outside Phnom Penh. Today, Siem Reap is an international airport.

As with most air force units in the developing world, such issues as safety, standardization, training, examinations, and check rides were only vague concepts in day-to-day operational settings. It may not have made a difference, but there was no dedicated Project 404 advisor to the C-47 unit at Savannakhet at that time. That is not meant as a criticism, only a statement of how it was.

Intelligence and Targeting

One of the most frequently-asked questions by visitors was "How do you get your targets for launching strikes?" That was certainly a fair question, and the only realistic answer was "Any way we can." That was hardly an exaggeration. Most of our targets were passed to us by Agency folks at 20 Alternate, and it was carried out in the clear. Given where we were and what we were doing, encryption was impossible, especially in those days.

The Agency possessed both controlled and uncontrolled targeting and intelligence sources, which, for the most part, were not revealed to us. Some of their sources were outlying sites, while others involved highly mobile teams or individuals. There were more sophisticated forms of intelligence operations in Southeast Asia, but the targeting information available to the AOC for AT-28 sorties was essentially human intelligence (HUMINT).

Our only wireless communication with anyone was via a Collins high-frequency KWM 2A single-side-band radio with a powerful linear amplifier to drive a ground wave out towards the first point of skip. That's as technical as I'm going to get with this description, but it was the only means we had to acquire targeting data from upcountry.

During critical close-air-support or interdiction activities, we would almost always be jammed by RF energy. We had no Have Quick-type frequency-hopping capability, so we worked up a set of prearranged frequencies with the people up north that allowed us to manually go up or down the frequency band to certain designated wavelengths.

The jammer would try to follow us, but by the time he found our frequency, we would have transmitted the critical data. During one particular operation, Bob Farmer, the embassy comm specialist, and I got a directional bearing on a radio-jamming source. We drove around town in an unmarked station wagon and found it--a highly directional "rifle" antenna on top of the Chinese Embassy.

We took a compass bearing on the antenna, and it pointed directly at the AOC. We assembled the equipment to generate a directional wave back at the radio antenna and burn it out, but we got caught by the attaché and had to quit. He thought we were doing unilateral jamming. It wasn't unilateral, but, admittedly, that kind of thing can get out of hand. The incident clearly indicated that there were other international players involved in this game at the local level.

On rare occasions, FAR would launch an offensive campaign up north supplementing, or conducted parallel to, General Vang Pao's activities. Requests for B-Team support would then come directly from the FAR liaison officer to the AOC. This FAR major would spend every day in the AOC while the campaign was underway, coordinating aircraft rendezvous frequencies, coordinates, and arrival times. Equally important, at least from my perspective, he provided intelligence and battlefield updates to keep me posted on current and planned campaign outcomes.

An initiative like that, aimed at capturing ground from the Pathet Lao, always drew the attention and interest of AIRA, Vientiane. During the offensive, I gave them periodic status briefings at the AOC, complete with maps and AT-28 sortie data. That would have been impossible without the FAR liaison officer. His usefulness extended into other areas. One afternoon, I had to call him on the phone from the Vientiane Police Station where I was being booked for driving the wrong way on a one-way street that had had its direction reversed during flood repair. The road-construction sign was in Lao, of course. Things were not going well, and it didn't help that I had no ID, only a Lao driver's license. They probably wanted money, but his appearance at the station changed all that.

There were also a few people who waged war on their own, acquiring their own targets and attacking them using the most extraordinary means imaginable. I heard of guys dropping rocks out of the low-altitude cargo delivery door in the belly of a Porter, but I never paid much attention to those stories. Rocks? Turns out, it was true. Not long after we dug the AOC out of the mud, my comm operator told me that someone outside the building wanted to see me but didn't want to come in.

I walked outside and found an American dressed in old, ragged pants and faded Hawaiian shirt and wearing rubber thongs. Turned out it was Al Zimmerman, Tony Poe's (Anthony Poshepny) Porter pilot. Tony Poe was the legendary Agency case officer at a very remote site up north. Al was terribly shy, making it almost impossible to make eye contact or get to the point. He obviously wanted something, but was afraid to ask since he didn't know me. After much rambling and irrelevant discussion, I finally asked: "Al, what can I do for you?"

Well, things had been bad since the flood, and they had nothing to drop from the Porter except rocks, and they wanted a few more 100-pound PWP bombs. I told him to taxi his bird into the AOC and the munitions specialists would load up what he needed. I asked him if he knew what would happen if he dinged the bird and one of the bomb casings split open. The question was perfunctory, but I had to ask it. Risk assessment takes different forms in this environment. If you have to fight using unconventional means and procedures, then you apply your risk assessment to those means and procedures. Yes, he knew what would happen, and I'm sure he did. Al was a professional.

General Tao Ma and the 1966 Vientiane Coup Attempt

About 0800 on the morning of 22 October 1966, the Hoodlums had positioned the munitions and equipment in front of the revetments across the parking area from the AOC ops building, and the B-Team had taxied in and shut down. I was standing in the front room of the ops building talking to my line chief, Mr. Wright, and watching my comm operator madly translating a coded message from AIRA, Vientiane. All coded messages were transmitted in voice, one letter at a time, via the Collins radio.

I could sense something was wrong, so I waited until he was finished. Finally, he said: "Mr. K, you need to read this." I grabbed up the scrap of paper and read it. All it said was, "Air attack imminent, take cover if necessary." That didn't make any sense. *Come on, who would attack the AOC from the air?* At the moment, it didn't really matter. I had to get airplanes and people off the ramp. The MJ-1 loaders were already driving 500-pound bombs under the aircraft, and the Thai pilots were walking in the front door.

I met their flight lead as he entered. "Anant, we may be under air attack in a few minutes; get out of here now!" Without hesitating, he asked, "Ma?" referring to B/Gen Tao Ma, RLAF commander. Just like that; he could put it all together because he was tied into a Thai information net that was apparently not readily available to AMEMB, Laos. The first indication that AIRA, Vientiane, had that Ma was going to do something crazy was when someone handed them a hand-written note from him saying: "The time had come to end the abuses of the General Staff." Those abuses were, among other things, rampant corruption, graft, smuggling of gold and opium, bribery, and criminal mismanagement of the Royal Lao Air Force.

I turned next to my line chief, telling him, "Mr. Wright, download now." Wright ran out the door, extended his arms, and jabbed his thumbs down. The munitions load chief, in turn, ordered "weapons jettison." The munitions loads that morning were 500 and 250 bombs, so the guys simply reached into the cockpits and pressed the red emergency jettison buttons. Everything fell to the ramp with a big thump. I don't remember if any of the bombs were fused or not; it wouldn't have mattered, and right then, I didn't care.

The B-Team pilots got the engines started in short order and taxied out for immediate takeoffs. We stood out on the ramp to watch as the RLAF C-Team appeared in the distance. The B-Team was climbing out like a string of bees for Udorn, almost crossing paths with the C-Team AT-28s as they approached Vientiane. I was concerned for a moment that the C-Team might interpret the encounter as a hostile intercept, but nothing like that happened. As I remember, there were ten of them. Their attack would have required a lot of passion and conviction, to say nothing of fierce, almost insane, loyalty to Tao Ma.

I had met a few of Tao Ma's C-Team when they came into the Wattay AOC to refuel their birds one morning. From the way they looked and carried themselves, they seemed very different from my Thai pilots, and of course, they were. From the stories their advisor Don Moody told me about missions they'd pulled off in the past, these C-Team pilots seemed like the stuff of Terry and the Pirates. I remember wishing then that I could be imbedded as advisor in a C-Team of my own. I had no way of knowing at the time that this would happen in a couple years.

But, right now, the C-team was about to make history in a very unfortunate and unforgettable way. They struck the Army Headquarters at Chinaimo and the military training base at Phong Keng. One of the aircraft made a rocket run on Chief of Staff General Kouprasith Abbay's house, trying to kill him. Only seconds prior, the air attaché, Pappy Pettigrew, was at Kouprasith's house beating on the door to wake him up and get him out of there.

Pappy said that Kouprasith came to the door just as he heard the AT-28's engine backfiring overhead when the throttle came back for the roll-in. Pappy grabbed Kouprasith and ran, both of them throwing themselves on the ground, and sliding along, as a rocket exploded taking off a corner of the house. One of the AT-28s even made an ineffectual, but apparently satisfying, strafe run on a French administrative building. Ma hated the French.

By now, we could see smoke rising from targets in the Vientiane area. At this point, the fighters headed towards our position at Wattay. Mr. Wright walked up and asked if we were going to fuel and arm them if they taxied into the AOC. "Only at gunpoint, because we're not part of this," I told him.

I was about to tell everyone to leave Wattay immediately and go home, but as the birds approached the field, they were far too high to enter initial for landing. It was apparent what they were going to do. I yelled, "Take cover, now!" The Hoodlums hunkered down at the base of the revetments, and I ran back to the AOC ops building to get my hands on the radio. I never made it to the radio. The first rounds of rocket fire started impacting as I entered the front room.

I ran out the back door and went down in a full squat close to the wall. About three feet away, squatted down in the same position, was a small Lao soldier, probably on routine security duty. Jagged, smoking-hot rocket shards were falling all around us. One of the shards, about the size of a sugar cube, was lying on the ground about two feet away with white wisps of smoke trailing off it. At the bottom of each pass, the attacking aircraft would come zooming over the building, quite low.

They were obviously not making high-angle attacks, and they weren't after the AOC. Otherwise, I would have been wiped out. Going after the AOC didn't make any sense anyway; Ma had nothing against me. In fact, we had met and talked in the AIRA current ops room just a couple weeks before the attack.

When the attack ended, I walked through the building and stood in the front doorway as Mr. Wright walked across the ramp with the rest of the Hoodlums following him. I asked for a battle damage report. His reply was a huge relief: "All present and accounted for, Sir."

About two rice paddies away, smoke and fire were rising from what had apparently been ground zero for the rocket attack. Secondary explosions were popping off, suggesting that the site was an ammo dump. I told the comm operator to call AIRA, Vientiane, and tell them we had been under an air strike, but everyone was OK. AIRA acknowledged our report and said that a coup was in progress. *No kidding.*

The secondaries became heavier, and finally the dump exploded with a horrendous roar. All kinds of stuff, including whole 105mm howitzer shells were flying through the air, tumbling end over end. Most spectacular were hundreds of colored smoke canisters making long red, white, and purple arcs across the sky. Every time there was a heavy ordnance explosion, our AOC building's frame shook as if it was going to come down. The noise and concussion were awful, shaking loose dust and dirt that rained down from the ceiling, covering our hair and clothes. We were pinned down by secondaries for almost two hours.

I really wanted something more substantive from AIRA on the security situation in the local area, but no one seemed to know anything. This didn't feel good. I ordered comms to unlock the file cabinet top drawer and prepare to issue weapons. He got the handguns out and quickly inserted preloaded clips. A moment later, looking through the back door of the AOC, I could see two FAR weapons carriers filled with armed soldiers. They disappeared down the road, but it was time to move and to do so as quickly and quietly as possible. At that point, I gave the order to issue weapons. One was not normally armed on base and downtown, but this was not a normal situation.

I got the Hoodlums in a clutch around me and told them to go directly to their quarters at Koon Compound and stay inside. "Do not stop on the way, and do not go out tonight. Wait for me to contact you." Comms called AIRA, Vientiane, and told them everyone was returning to quarters. This did not give me the best feeling I'd ever had, watching the Hoodlums motoring off across town on their motorcycles, all cannoned up with .45 cal Colt automatics, but it was the best we could do under the circumstances. Remember, we still didn't know what was going on in Vientiane.

I waited until they were all gone, and then I left. Just before I got off the airfield I was stopped by an armed FAR officer. I got out of the International Harvester and walked up to him. He angrily accused me of being behind the attack. "You are responsible for this; you are part of it," he kept insisting. I think he meant that U.S. authorities were supportive of Tao Ma and were complicit in the attack against the FAR. I simply told him that it was as much of a surprise to me as it was to him. At least that much was true.

Gen Ma was a friend to AMEMB, Vientiane, but I seriously doubt that any U.S. authorities would have encouraged something as daft as staging an air attack as the centerpiece of a grand coup with no ground backup. Ma may have expected support from certain FAR commanders to pull this off; I don't know. There are lots of stories about what actually happened, but who knows where the truth lies.

The Lao officer was acting very belligerent; he was clearly scared and full of adrenaline. I was standing there with my hands on my hips, a Colt .45 stuck in my front waistband, and my fingers about three inches from the grip. His weapon was holstered at his side. I wanted this to end in a good way, so I just stood there, quietly watching him, saying nothing. He finally backed off and walked over to his vehicle. Good thing; these people were notoriously inept with weapons.

I got into my vehicle and started off for the Ice House when Lee Webb, an assistant air attaché, intercepted me and asked me to meet him at the civilian terminal. When we got there, Lee told me that AMEMB, Vientiane, was going to evacuate American non-combatants who wanted out. He and I would fly them to (I believe) Udorn Air Base in the embassy C-47. Lee took names and made up a manifest, while I filed a flight clearance, something I rarely did in Laos. We made the delivery, and everybody was happy to get out of Laos.

On our return to Vientiane, we learned that it wasn't quite over; there might be another attack. Ma's birds had recovered at Savannakhet (their launch site) and reloaded for a follow-up strike. We waited outside the Ice House drinking beer until late in the evening. Nothing happened. Finally, Ma and his ten C-Team pilots jettisoned their ordnance on the ground and left for Thailand. Supposedly, American authorities talked him out of a follow-up raid, but maybe Ma simply changed his mind and bugged out. Whatever the case, they flew to Udorn Air Base, where they were arrested by the Thai authorities, and the aircraft confiscated. They were imprisoned, and eventually released.

The story of Ma's coup does not, of course, end there. In 1973, Ma assembled a small task force of trucks and headed back into Laos. I was living in Thailand at the time and heard about it almost immediately. After the convoy reached Vientiane, Ma and six of his pilots captured some AT-28's at Wattay Air Field to make another attack. A current Wikipedia article states that Ma and his six pilots carried out an air attack against FAR Headquarters, but the field was retaken by government forces while he was airborne.

An eye witness account by a Continental Air Services pilot (retired Air Force officer and pilot, Lt Col Howard Hartley) states that Ma's aircraft was damaged by ground fire while he was landing, and he was captured by FAR officers. Hartley's account is recorded in an official Air Force oral history interview conducted several years later. My understanding, going back to the time it happened, was that Ma was driven away in a car and shot.

There is another account of Ma's death by John Gunther Dean (Deputy Chief of Mission in Vientiane, Laos, 1972-1973). In this account, published by the Association for Diplomatic Studies and Training, Dean states that in personally stopping the coup, he blocked the Wattay runway to prevent General Ma from taking off in his aircraft:

"He fired up his plane and he tried to take off. Since I was about midway on the airstrip, he tried to avoid the car. He did not have enough height.. In the process of avoiding a collision with my car, he veered off to the right and crashed. He was killed instantly."

The enormous discrepancy between these two accounts causes one to suspect that two people may have been witnessing two separate events, each one thinking that General Ma was the pilot.

Anyway, there are more detailed accounts of what led Ma to such extremes, and the reader is recommended to investigate that body of literature.

One could say that Ma was emotionally and psychologically off balance during the last years of his life, and maybe he was; I am not qualified to say. One could also say that he lived and died as a defiant Lao patriot, something quite rare in that country. It's just sad that innocent people were killed because they were standing in the wrong place during the C-Team raid.

A Serious Infraction of RLAF Rules

After the 1966 coup attempt, Tao Ma was replaced by B/Gen Sourith, who immediately came out to the AOC to meet with me informally and establish a contact regarding the B-Team presence at Wattay. The next time I talked with him, however, the circumstances were tense and a lot more formal.

Shortly after Sourith assumed command, the B-Team approached me and asked that I try to get Chao Vanthasawadee into the pilot training at Water Pump. I agreed, because it sounded like the right thing to do. Chao had hundreds of back-seat combat missions in the AT-28 and knew better than anyone how to coordinate strikes with friendly ground forces. He also had a lot of back-seat stick time in the AT-28. Later, on a trip to Udorn, I talked with the Water Pump commander, Lt Col "Spider" Ramsey. I gave him Chao's credentials, and asked that he take Chao into the flying training program.

Spider Ramsey was a tough, no-nonsense officer from USAFSOF who wasn't afraid to make decisions and stick by them. He told me that he would consider Chao after an interview, but I would have to wait until Water Pump had a washout in the program. Chao would be starting late, but he had an experience advantage that would close the gap. Ramsey told me to bring Chao to Water Pump immediately on his call. A few weeks went by and I got a call from Ramsey's office through the AIRA command post. It was on, so I called AIRA to get the C-47 released the next morning to fly Chao to Udorn. Chao was airborne on a strike mission, but when he got back, I told him to put everything he owned in a bag and report to the flight line one hour prior to preflight time.

The next morning, I flew Chao down to Udorn with our C-47 crew chief, Sam Sapiri, on board. Sam was awesome; he was completely comfortable sitting in the right seat operating the landing gear lever and locking latch so I didn't have to put my head down in the cockpit and do it myself. After we landed and taxied into the Water Pump parking area, I took Chao into the building for his interview. I had an idea how this was going to go, so I walked into Ramsey's office with Chao, and we both saluted.

Ramsey, who was from the deep South, returned the salute and immediately said, "Boy, put your right hand on top of your head." Chao, who spoke excellent English, looked sideways at me with a puzzled look on his face. I nodded, giving him a reassuring slow blink, and he did as he was told. The next command was "Boy, put your hand down. Now put your left hand on top of your head." Chao did that, putting his hand down when Ramsey told him to.

Ramsey then looked at me and gave his assessment. "He'll do. At least he knows his left from his right hand." And that was it; Chao entered the flying training program and graduated along with everyone else. After I returned to the States, Water Pump sent me a big photograph of Chao receiving his USAF wings.

After Chao entered the Water Pump program, however, I was summoned to RLAF Headquarters by General Sourith and given a time to report to his office. There were apparently some hurt feelings over Chao's appointment. I put on a clean Lao flight suit and told the Hoodlums where I was going so they would know where to collect my body. Doc Fitz wanted to go along, and I let him. When we walked out to my International Harvester, I noticed that Fitz was carrying a small cardboard box.

I didn't have a good feeling about this, but we walked into General Sourith's office and I saluted him. Fitz quietly put the little box on the floor next to General Sourith's desk and sat down in the corner. The room was filled with angry senior RLAF officers. I stood at a loose parade rest while they ranted at me: "Did you know that Chao is a Neutralist? Did you know that there are other officers (*cousins, family friends, important political connections, brothers-in-law, etc.*) waiting for appointments to pilot training?" *Yes, I knew all that.*

I kept my reply short: "Chao is highly experienced in combat and can already fly an airplane. He is certain to be a valuable addition to the RLAF." Their rejoinder was a bit disappointing: "No, this is for you, Major Klingaman, not for us." I was only going to make one more statement, so I wanted to make it stick: "No, this is not for me; this is for Laos." That probably did not make much sense to them, but I said it anyway.

About that time General Sourith was looking down, poking around inside the little box on the floor. Suddenly, he straightened up and announced, "Alright, that's enough. No more arguing. Major Klingaman, we will allow Chao to stay in pilot training, but do not do that again." "No, Sir, I won't." Everyone got up and walked out. On the way out to the vehicle, I asked Fitz what was inside the box. "Penicillin and tetracycline," he replied. *Great, now we're on the books for bribery, but maybe distribution of antibiotic medicine in a place like this qualifies as humanitarian assistance.* Fitz was a real pro.

Chao did, indeed, make a great addition to the RLAF. I saw him a few years later at Luang Prabang when I accompanied B/Gen Joe Wilson, Air Force Special Operations Force Commander, on a visit to the LAO AOCs. Ed Gunter, the AOC commander at LP, had all his AT-28 drivers lined up for handshakes. When I came to Chao, I told him quietly, in whispers, how terribly proud I was of him. And I really was; he was a flight commander. It was wonderful to see him standing there, smiling broadly, next to the other C-Team guys.

I wish I could say that Chao survived the war, but I can't. Like so many other RLAF fighter pilots, he was shot down and killed. After all, there was no "end of tour" for them; they would simply fly combat until they were either killed or captured. I know of none who were captured.

A Trip up North

Just before Christmas, when the AOC was up and running, AMEMB hosted a big get-together for all officers under embassy control. At this event, I met two U.S. Army artillery advisors from the Neutralist camp at Moung Soui (site 108), Major Morton and Captain Harnley. Mort said that his Neutralist counterparts could use air support from attack aircraft, but no one had any idea how to request or direct strikes—could I come up to Moung Soui and help out? I said I would, and a couple weeks later, I hopped a ride to Moung Soui on an Air America C-46.

The C-46 was hauling live fish in lard cans filled with water, two adult fish per lard can. USAID had airlifted bulldozer components to Moung Soui, assembled them, and dug out a huge lake that filled with rain water. It would be a fish farm for Hmong tribal people who had been forced off the PDJ by the fighting. They were just now filling it with USAID fish. It must have been a fiendishly expensive project.

Moung Soui was the Neutralist faction's stronghold. Prior to my arrival, the Neutralists had crossed over from the Communist Pathet Lao side to fight with the Royalists. The Neutralists and Pathet Lao had gotten into a big scuffle on the PDJ a couple years earlier, and someone was killed. I think there was alcohol involved. The Neutralists stalked off, first moving to Vang Veng, and eventually to Moung Soui. I won't go into that story; it's too complicated and makes my head hurt.

I spent several days at Moung Soui with Mort and Harnley discussing procedures for requesting air support plus the capabilities and limitations of air strikes with various types of air-deliverable munitions.

I liked Moung Soui; this was wooded mountain country; the nights and mornings were cold and the sharp smell of wood smoke permeated everything, including your clothes. The place was extremely primitive. The buildings were all hillside huts made out of small bamboo poles and sticks interwoven with large leaves. I was struck by how few people actually made up the Neutralist force at that location, and I don't think many of them existed elsewhere. There wasn't actually a village that I could see, but there were a few huts in an open clearing that made do as a communal gathering place to drink lao-lao (firewater), beer, and Running Deer whiskey.

Mort asked me if I would like to see some artillery action and go out to the front. That sounded like something different, and I wasn't about to miss it. We drove his jeep a fair distance to a 155mm howitzer battery. I wasn't crazy about this piece. It used bagged powder, and the barrel had to be swabbed with water every time it fired. I understand its usefulness, but it entailed a lot of work and a lot of people, including a security force, and it looked way too permanent for fighting in a fluid situation like the highlands of Laos. We then drove on to one of the 105mm howitzer batteries, closer to the front, where Mort worked at teaching me how to load and fire the weapon. I liked the 105; after some instruction from Mort, I was able to load and fire it myself. That doesn't mean, of course, that I was safe with it, or that I could work out a firing solution on paper.

Our final stop was the observation post (OP 1) on top of a wooded promontory looking out across a small ravine towards dug-in PL positions on the opposite ridge. Now Mort set about trying to teach me how to call for, and adjust, fire. Not easy to do with precision. The guns were already surveyed in, so he went through the adjust-fire procedure and he gave me a point to shoot at with the 155mm howitzer. You first fire for effect, and then start walking the rounds into the target.

It was odd listening to the big round coming over your head like a fast freight train and watching it impact on the other side of the ravine, scattering hard rock all over the place. The occupied enemy positions were just on the other side of the ridge across the ravine—a good place to put in attack aircraft with 500 pound bombs, and I explained that. Anyway, I remember thinking: *Holy smoke, we're barely outside sniper-rifle range, and this is for real.* My other thought was--*If those were NVA forces on the other side of the ravine, we and OP-1 would already be overrun.* That eventually happened, but I wasn't there.

We explored around the countryside, although in a different direction, and crossed a large expanse of open, rolling terrain where the brush and dry grass were black and burning from artillery and mortar fire. Driving along, we came across an elderly USAID heavy-equipment operator, Penny, who was leaning on the counter of a tiny wooden stand talking to a young girl selling Running Deer whiskey. Penny was a little bit drunk.

I couldn't believe it. Here they were, standing in the middle of the open countryside with nothing in any direction--not one tree--and you could see for miles. Never mind Penny and how he got there; what was she doing out there alone, except for Penny, selling Running Deer whiskey from a little wooden stand? There was no one within miles. It was like a surrealist scene from a Kurt Vonnegut novel. We grabbed Penny, threw him in the jeep, and took off. That night, we made a foray into a large cave complex. We were armed like Mexican bandits, and it was exciting, but it was also crazy, considering we weren't there on a mission. The floor of the cave crunched underfoot like soft gravel, but it wasn't gravel. It was tens of thousands of little votive Buddhas cast out of dark-brown resin and strewn about the floor. Most were broken into pieces.

I had the privilege of attending the wedding reception of a Neutralist officer and a beautiful young Hmong girl. The reception was something to behold. The men shot a full-grown ox and hung it from a huge log tripod over a big fire for a couple of days before the event. At reception time, only the outside of the ox was cooked, but it didn't matter. You walked up to the carcass, carved off a piece with a knife or bayonet, and the meat continued cooking.

There were also vegetables laced with super-hot fish sauce that would make your scalp itch. It was very noisy and great fun. This reception was not, however, a place to be noticed too much. I felt accepted and welcome, but with most everyone else drinking heavily and shooting into the air, the trick was to hang back and remain as invisible as possible.

It was eventually time to leave. I hitchhiked back to Vientiane on an Air America Porter and resumed my AOC duties. I traveled up-country many times over the years after that--including Laos (to fly with the Butterfly FACs), Thailand, Burma, and Cambodia--but the Moung Soui trip was without equal for sheer, flat-out adventure.

I learned later that immediately after the USAID fish farm was completed and stocked, and everyone was instructed on how to run a fish farm, the local Hmong threw grenades into the water and killed all the fish, to be dried, smoked, and eaten. A fascinating case of differing world views; there were many such cases over the years in Southeast Asia. We never cease viewing other cultures through our own values and technology.

The Great Beaver Caper

I believe it was sometime after Christmas 1966 when assistant air attaché Andy Pearson got his hands on an L-20 Beaver for his personal war machine and had it assigned to AIRA, Vientiane. He then brought it over to my side of the field and asked me to modify the aircraft to communicate with U.S. fighters and to shoot 2.75-inch rockets. The L-20 is a tough old bird that still flies commercially in remote parts of the world, but one does not usually think of this aircraft as a forward-firing platform, particularly at high dive angles. Nevertheless, Andy's motives were well placed, and I certainly admired his pluck. This happened, of course, before the introduction of O-1 Bird Dogs and the Raven FACs.

The Butterfly technique of bringing in fighters, and then throwing a colored smoke canister out the vent window of the Porter to mark the target, left a bit to be desired. Depending on the Porter's altitude, the smoke canister could take a while reaching ground, and it could drift with the wind, making accuracy somewhat problematic. And then, the fighters had to be directed to a point offset from where the smoke canister actually landed. Still, it worked with considerable success, and Butterfly FACs often successfully directed fighters with reference to geographic features.

But none of this could match shooting a high-velocity rocket into a target and telling the fighters to "hit my smoke." Also, an O-1 maneuvering around sharply and firing rockets was more survivable than a Porter flying over a defended position. This is essentially why the FAC program in Laos moved from Butterflies to Ravens. At the same time, we must not forget that Butterfly FACs, flying on Air America and Continental Air Services turbo Porters, held the line for several years by directing thousands of strikes against enemy targets.

Back at the AOC conference table, I asked my maintenance guys about mounting rocket tubes and racks under the wing of the L-20. After some discussion, they said they would do it as long as they didn't have to drill into the main spar. That sounded reasonable, so we proceeded accordingly, and it worked. We also modified the antenna configuration, and Andy flew the L-20 up to 20 Alternate and prepared for war. By this time, John Lee was a very experienced Butterfly FAC at Alternate who knew the terrain cold, so Andy took him along on missions.

What happened next was related to me by John. On one mission in the L-20, they had a target not far from the Plain of Jars, so they called the orbiting C-130 Airborne Command and Control Center (ABCCC) and requested fighters. In due course, the fighters showed up and checked in. John read them the numbers, and everyone was set for the strike.

Andy armed one of the rockets and rolled into the dive. Everything looked good when, suddenly, there was a big explosion in the aircraft, and the cockpit filled with fumes. Andy aborted the pass and called the fighters, telling them he'd been hit. The next call went out to the ABCCC in case a search and rescue (SAR) effort had to be launched.

John said that after Andy tested the controls and found them OK, they anxiously flew home with grim faces, imagining their Distinguished Flying Crosses being awarded. After landing, they walked around the aircraft, checking for battle damage. One of the ground maintenance guys pointed out that the battery had exploded, probably because no one had cleaned the dirt out of its vent holes. It even blew the battery access panel open. Big letdown, but such are the fortunes of war.

AC-47 Tail Number 0-16364

The weeks and months rolled by, mostly taken up with launching B-Team strike sorties and surviving occasional catastrophes and disasters. There were lots of engaging things to do besides run the AOC. A problem apparently resident in AIRA for some time, maybe forever, was that there was no local C-47 checkout, requalification, and evaluation program in place. The legal attachés and I were qualified to fly the C-47 as aircraft commanders, but it was a crapshoot among the designated copilots. There were no written exams and no aircrew training and evaluation records, i.e., Form 8s. I couldn't maintain Form 8 files, and neither could AIRA, but I did prepare open and closed-book exams and established a checkout program. I could have made good use of a laptop computer and printer back then.

John Lee moved down to Vientiane from Alternate and took up a job in the AIRA command post, much as Bob Farmer had done previously. He also flew as copilot with me in the air attaché C-47, tail number 0-16364. John was an excellent pilot, primarily qualified in the C-123, so it was great having him with me on AMEMB missions. One such mission was to Ching Mai, Thailand for an overnight stay.

We left late the next day for the return flight to Vientiane, flying on into the night. As we approached Wattay, we received a call from the AIRA comm operator in an MRC-108 radio jeep, telling us that there were no runway lights at the field. He and the attaché pointed their headlights across the approach end of the runway to mark the threshold. The trick was to find the vehicle headlights and get the bird down low enough to illuminate the runway with the landing lights. And that worked out OK, which was great, because the back of the aircraft was filled with people.

On another occasion, I flew Ambassador Sullivan and a State Department dignitary to Louangphrabang (variant—Luang Prabang) so the dignitary could cut the ribbon at a ceremony commissioning a bridge that USAID had funded and built. The dignitary showed up at the aircraft wearing formal striped pants, black jacket, and top hat. Don Moody was AOC advisor at LP and, fortunately, knew we were coming. He called on the Collins radio to warn us about guns off the approach end of the runway. The way you deal with that, of course, is an assault-style landing. We came down final approach with full flaps and 15 inches of manifold pressure, almost standing on our nose. A quick round out and we were on the ground. Great fun. Ambassador Sullivan knew what was going on and told the dignitary that we were doing that to avoid mountains.

I saw something really bizarre towards the end of the tour. John Lee, our crew chief, Sam Sapiri, and I showed up at the airplane one morning to fly Ambassador Sullivan to Bangkok. He was on his way back to Boston to attend the funeral of a family member. We were sitting in the aircraft, parked in front of the AOC ops building, waiting for the ambassador to arrive when I heard John say, "Oh, my God, what is that." I looked up, and here was an old woman with henna-dyed hair, slowly wandering up to the airplane, wearing an ancient, scruffy-looking fur coat about the same color as her hair.

I looked out the left window at one of the Hoodlums stationed at the fire extinguisher. "Lulu," he said. I couldn't believe it--the most notorious madam in Laos, and she walked right past the guard and everyone else, and took a seat in the ambassador's aircraft. Of course, that had to be the very moment Ambassador Sullivan arrived in his Checker Limousine. When he got on board, a couple staff personnel were already trying, unsuccessfully, to get her off. She kept insisting that she was going to Boston. Ambassador Sullivan, always the gentleman, reached out to help her get up from the seat, and you never heard such foul language.

This was not a good scene. John got up to do something, but Sam beat him to it. Sam, no less the gentleman, ran back and got Lulu off the aircraft quickly. She then started meandering down the parking ramp until a Lao security guard grabbed her and escorted her away. What I found most intriguing was that this drug-addled relic from the French Indochina War knew when, and from what location, the C-47 was departing and where Ambassador Sullivan was going in the United States. The underground intelligence net was always up and running, but right then, it was time for engine start.

Final Approach

My replacement showed up a couple weeks early, because all AOC slots filled by USAFSOF personnel in Laos were being replaced by PACAF resources. That was a political decision initiated by the Commander, 7th Air Force. I think he wanted everyone performing in-country covert operations to be PACAF resources and clearly under Theater command and control. They already were, but he simply wanted USAFSOF out of it. I won't comment further on his attitude towards special operations; that's not the purpose of this account.

My replacement was Major Joe Holden, who just happened to be a special operations AT-28 pilot from Hurlburt Field assigned PCS to PACAF somewhere in the Pacific Theater. Joe wanted to fly, so he asked for a checkout in the C-47, and AIRA agreed. I had time to do some pattern work with him before I left, but I didn't take him all the way to checkout because of my time remaining in-country. Joe was a very good pilot and learned to fly the Goon quickly. Joe had a long career in Air Force Special Operations, including advising, so he eased into the AOC commander slot easily.

Finally, it was time to go. The AIRA folks and the Hoodlums threw a memorable going-away party for John and me the last evening. The next morning, the embassy C-47 flew us to Udorn to check out of Water Pump and retrieve our ID cards and uniforms. From there, we flew to Bangkok and met our scheduled departure time for the States. Nothing dramatic, but I knew I was going to miss the Hoodlums and the B-Team. Three days later, we were home at England AFB, and life took off in a different direction—at least momentarily.

Chapter 25

Tom Richards, Raven 01
Pakse, Feb 1968 – Jul 1968
Vientiane, Jul 1968 - Dec 1968

Pre-statement: *Accepting to do this interview has caused me to reflect back on some issues most of the people who served in Viet Nam had to wrestle with at some time in their tour. The issue was and still is for many, WHAT WERE WE DOING THERE? I personally spent many nights during my TDY tours and some during my early days in Viet Nam thinking about why we were there and why many of my fellow service members had given their lives. In 1967 it was obvious to many of us in uniform, our country in general did not support the war and the political leaders, and many of the military leaders were either incompetent or just afraid to speak out when things were going wrong.*

I finally accepted the fact I wasn't fighting for the President, our political leaders, or the military generals charged with executing the directions of Washington. I wasn't fighting for nation building, democracy for Viet Nam, or to stop the spread of communism.

I was fighting because I had sworn an oath to the Constitution of the United States and as an officer I had an obligation to honorably serve the country, the Air Force, and my fellow service members, especially those I was charged with leading. Once I had resolved these things in my mind I determined to ignore the politics and do my best to bring destruction to the enemy and hopefully bring the war to an end. Looking back that was probably a little naïve, but it provided me with the motivation to aggressively carry out the mission as I saw it.

Gen. (Ret.) Tom Richards interview by Darrel Whitcomb 13 Apr 2014

[Editorial insertions are enclosed in square brackets.]

DW: Today is 13 Apr 2014. I am Darrel Whitcomb. This interview is with Gen. (Ret.) Tom Richards concerning his experiences as a Raven FAC in Laos in 1967/68, for the Raven historical project. Before the Ravens, there are some interesting things that have kind of taken on a myth of their own. You enlisted in 1948. You did service in Korea as an infantryman.

TR: Yes. But before I respond to your questions let me tell you this is the first time in many years I have reflected back on the details of my early years in the Army. As I started thinking about our talk I realized over 60 exciting years have passed since I was in the Army and I'm afraid my memory has been fogged by time, a very busy life, and circumstances. I remember several events with great clarity but many details are missing.

In the summer of 1948 some friends of mine and I decided that it would be a great adventure to join the Army, get the GI Bill, and then return from the Army and be able to go to the college of our choice. At that time the Army was also offering young men in groups of three or more the opportunity to enlist for specific units or geographic locations. Our group enlisted for assignment to Japan with the 11th Airborne Division. We all ended up in Japan but not in the same unit. After a couple of very short assignments I ended up assigned to the 34th Infantry Regiment of the 24th Division stationed at Sasebo, Japan. This unit was a part of the occupation forces and as such we did a lot of ceremonial things and very little real combat training. The 24th Division, as well as the other occupation divisions, was about two-thirds manned and armed with leftover equipment from WWII. The divisions had two regiments rather than three. They had no tanks and the division artillery units only had 105 howitzers but none of the authorized 155 mm guns. We were equipped with old well-used equipment from WWII. No one thought we would ever go to war again so it was a great surprise when we were notified in June of 1950 that the North Koreans had invaded South Korea and we were going to be deployed to help. There was great excitement and speculation about how long it would take us to kick North Korea's ass. I was assigned to the Regimental Intelligence and Recon Platoon—a small unit whose mission was to patrol on the front lines and occasionally behind the lines gathering local intelligence.

We boarded old LSTs and departed for Pusan, Korea sometime in late June 1950. When we landed my unit tied our equipment down on Korean flatbed train cars and started the trip north. At that time none of us knew where we were going or what we were expected to do when we got there. On the trip north we saw some damaged trains and a lot of wounded and dead South Korean troops. The South Korean constabulary forces were in full retreat. We downloaded from the train as I recall in the small town of Suwon just about 20 miles south of Seoul.

My platoon was then ordered to head north on the best roads available and locate the enemy. The roads were crowed with Korean families fleeing south and travel was very difficult. At that time we were armed with one box of ammunition for our machine guns, 15 rounds for those armed with carbines, about 80 rounds for those with M-1s, and one grenade for every two men. We drove north and in about a half hour ran directly into a very large unit of troops taking a break along the road. At first we thought they might be South Koreans but they started shooting at us immediately. We took cover and beat a hasty retreat. We lost three members of our unit either killed or wounded.

From that point forward I was involved in the hasty retreat south into the Pusan perimeter. In July I was wounded and evacuated to the Tokyo General Hospital. During my stay in the hospital I had the great honor of having my Purple Heart pinned on by General Douglas MacArthur. I was out of action for about three weeks and then returned to Korea.

DW: You were actually under enemy control for a while?

TR: Yes. It happened in the first week I was in combat. We were dug in along a railroad track in a small village and under attack by T-34 tanks, infantry, and artillery. I was wounded by an artillery round, and the concussion knocked me unconscious. I woke up and saw troops walking around and I thought they were South Koreans. Then one walked up and kicked me and I realized they were not the good guys. They were screaming at me and poking me with their rifles. They had about 10 Americans bedded down in some houses and kept us there for about 2-3 hours. They made no effort to treat the wounded. Some of the men in the group had serious injuries. Later in the day they started to march us north but we came under attack by fighter aircraft with guns and bombs. They were P-51s, probably from Japan because I don't believe we had any aircraft stationed in Korea at that time. The guards drove us into the houses along the street. Two of us went into a very small building with one North Korean. We sat there and waited for the attack to end. Some strafing rounds or the concussion from a bomb caved in part of the thatched roof. When that happened, I jumped up in the smoke and grabbed the guard, killed him, and we escaped out the back. We got in a sewage drainage ditch and started moving south along the roads choked with fleeing refugees. We didn't encounter any more enemy troops and made contact with some American forces within about 30 minutes. They took me to an aid station where they took care of my wounds. I had a piece of shrapnel about the size of a quarter sticking out of my hip and several other small cuts. A funny thing happened during my treatment. The doctor was trying to get the shrapnel pulled out of my hip with his surgical instruments but it would not come out. After a few tries he instructed one of the corpsmen to go to his jeep and get a pair of pliers. I was watching all this as he assured me that it was OK to do whatever it takes in an emergency.

God was watching over me during this experience because many of our soldiers taken captive in those early days of the war were lined up along a railroad track and shot. Some were from my unit.

DW: Did you get a decoration for that?

TR: I don't know. After I returned from Korea I received the Bronze Star but I don't know what it was for. I either did not receive the citation or I lost it. It was posted to my DD-214 and Army records but that's all I know about it. Because of my wounds I was never returned to my unit. I went back by truck to the evacuation hospital in Pusan and then after a few days on to the Tokyo General Hospital in Japan. By this time I had a bad infection in my wounds and was heavily drugged for about a week. When I started to recover no one asked me to debrief them on how I was wounded or how I got to the aid station. That was understandable given the disorganization and disaster the Army was facing in the first month of the Korean War.

After I recovered I volunteered to return to my unit thinking most of my good friends would still be there. While I was in the hospital the 34th Regiment had continued to suffer severe casualties, and shortly after I rejoined the regiment it was disbanded and the colors retired. I was then assigned to the 19th Regiment where I remained until I was again wounded and returned to the States. The 24th Division had been thrown into battle first to try to brunt the North Korean attack. The plan was to slow the North Koreans until MacArthur could bring in the 25th, 7th, and 1st Cavalry Divisions from Japan. As a consequence, the division suffered exceptionally high losses, to include the loss of Major General William Dean at the battle of Taejon. The greatest tragedy of these early days was the loss of a great number of experienced officers and NCOs from WWII as they tried their best to lead inadequately trained and poorly equipped young soldiers.

DW: Great story. You went to VPI [Virginia Polytechnic Institute]; were you in the corps of cadets?

TR: Yes, I was in the corps of cadets, the last two years. I went to Virginia Tech on a football scholarship, and had the GI Bill from the Army. At that point I did not know if I wanted a military career or not. During my second year at Tech I talked to the ROTC unit and they told me I could join the corps and get a ROTC contract the start of my junior year. So, I stayed a civilian for the first two years, played football, and then joined the corps and ROTC the last two years. I was a cadet officer, distinguished ROTC graduate, and qualified for pilot training.

DW: Did you play for the Baltimore Colts for a year?

TR: No, I did not, but I am aware this story has existed for many years. When I graduated from Tech I had a problem that I had not anticipated. About the time I started college I was advised by one of our neighbors that I should be evaluated by the VA for a disability related to my wounds in Korea. I did that and was awarded a 10 percent disability. That amounted to about $60 per month, which came in handy since I was married during my junior year. I made the mistake of assuming that the disability would be terminated once I passed my Air Force flight physical. That was not the case. I took and passed my flight physical and then applied to the VA to terminate my disability. They refused and told me I would have to be reevaluated. This all happened just prior to graduation.

The Air Force told me I needed to have the disability terminated or not be commissioned. The VA was telling me it might take time, and I could not afford to be delayed because I was 26 years old and the cutoff for entering pilot training was 26 and a half.

While discussing my dilemma with some friends from the football team, one of them, who was at the time playing football for the Baltimore Colts, recommended that just in case I could not go to pilot training, I should try to make a pro team by walking on. I went to Baltimore, talked to some of the coaches, and met several of the players. I told the coaches about my problem and they agreed I could walk on with no commitments. Only four days into the walk-on practice I received word from the VA that they had dropped my disability. I then left not knowing if I might have qualified. I went on active duty on 25 Aug 1956.

DW: Instead, you went to pilot training.

TR: Yes. I went to pilot training at Bainbridge Air Station, Georgia and advanced training in B-25s at Goodfellow AFB, San Angelo, Texas. When I graduated from pilot training I wanted to fly fighters but at the time the Strategic Air Command [SAC] was growing rapidly and most of my class was assigned to SAC. I was given my choice of KC-135s, B-47s, or B-52s. I asked the personnel officer, "Which one flies the fastest?" At the time I didn't know much about bombers. The guy said, "I think the B-47 is the fastest." So I said, "I'll take the B-47." I went to B-47 training and ended up assigned to the 19th Bomb Wing, Homestead Air Force Base, Florida.

When I got to SAC I found a lot of disgruntled young officers. At that time SAC was growing and the other commands were shrinking. SAC had a lot of pilots out of TAC [Tactical Air Command] and ADC [Air Defense Command]—F-94s, F-89s pilots. They were assigned as copilots. Many of them had hundreds of hours of fighter time and as a result some ended up with very bad attitudes when they found themselves in the rear or right seat of a bomber. I didn't like my situation at the time but decided to give it my best. I started flying extra missions with other crews and ended up assigned to the Standardization and Evaluation team. When they broke up the wing in 1960, I had about 1,020 hours and the cutoff to go to aircraft commander school was 1,000 hours. I was sent to McConnell AFB, Wichita, Kansas for aircraft commander training and then to the 301st Bomb Wing at Lockbourne, Ohio as an aircraft commander. I got there and they didn't have a crew for me. So I flew with pick-up crews for a couple months.

They sent me back to training, this time to Little Rock AFB. The plan was for me to pick up a new crew. Having just recently completed aircraft commander school the training was very easy and redundant. As an example of being watched over, I reported for flying one morning and my instructor pilot [IP] told me I didn't need to fly because the copilot was scheduled for most of the training and I would be out of the seat most of the time. I went home and later that day learned the aircraft had crashed while shooting touch-and-go landings at Pine Bluff airport. The IP and the other two members of the crew were killed.

I returned to Lockbourne AFB and finally got a crew. I stayed assigned to the 301st BW for about two years until my wing was again broken up. I was then sent to Castle AFB for B-52 aircraft commander school with follow-on assignment to Barksdale AFB.

DW: Barksdale. Good base.

TR: It was a great base. The B-52 was a monster to fly but I had no real problems getting fully checked out and combat ready. I had a good crew that I trained with at Castle, which made my job a lot easier. Not long after we became combat ready my squadron, the 20th BS, was sent TDY [temporary duty] to Guam along with another squadron from Mather AFB. We were among the first B-52s deployed to Guam and ultimately the first to fly missions into Viet Nam.

DW: Did they call them Arc Lights then?

TR: I don't think so. I believe it was before Arc Light. During my two deployments to Guam while stationed at Barksdale we only flew missions into South Vietnam. They were long missions of 12-13 hours.

DW: Didn't you guys have a mid-air there?

TR: Yes, they did. Maj. Gen. Crumm, who was the division commander, was killed in a mid-air sometime after our first deployment. I don't remember all the details but as I recall it happened when a cell of bombers attempted to make a 360-degree timing turn and ran into a following cell.

DW: Do you remember what your targets were?

TR: No, however they were all in the south and consisted of boxed areas in the jungle. The boxes were reported to contain enemy troop concentrations.

After I came back from the second TDY, the 20th Bomb Squadron was transferred to the 7th BW at Carswell AFB, Fort Worth, Texas. Soon after that we deployed again to Guam. During this time I believe I spent 6-9 months TDY.

When I came back the last time I went to MPC [Military Personnel Center] and volunteered for a full SEA [Southeast Asia] tour and specifically asked for a fighter assignment They said they would accept my volunteer request but the party line at that time was, they wanted to send people who had not been to Viet Nam before they sent people back for a second tour. They told me to wait.

During this period I was also talking to people at the Air Force Academy about a job on the football coaching staff. I also talked to an old friend, Jim McCarthy, who was serving as an AOC [air officer commanding] and recommended that I interview for that job.

Note: This is the same McCarthy who went on to four stars and relieved me in Europe when I retired.

I went to the Academy on leave and talked to Jim about the AOC job. He explained the job and set up an appointment for me with the commandant's staff. The staff then set up an appointment for me with the Commandant of Cadets, Brig. Gen. Seith. During the interview the general told me he would work my assignment and I told him that I would like to complete a full combat tour before being assigned to the Academy. He agreed to that and said I would be hearing from MPC shortly. It wasn't long before I received orders to F-100 training at Luke AFB, with follow-on training in the O-1 aircraft and assignment to the 101st Airborne Division as a forward air controller [FAC].

DW: What time frame was that?

TR: It was early 1966.

DW: Were you jump qualified then?

TR: I was jump qualified from the Army but it had been almost 20 years since I had made a jump. After my training at Luke and Hurlburt I went to Fort Campbell where we spent a lot of wasted time watching the Army train. So rather than waste time I volunteered to go to jump school to get requalified. MPC approved the training and I went to Fort Benning and completed the course. It was interesting and tough. I was a major at the time and not in great shape, and the instructors took no pity on me. Going through airborne training a second time was very worthwhile because it gave me a lot of credibility with the troops when I returned to Fort Campbell.

DW: You know what? You might have been down there about the same time that my class went through. That was in the summer of '67. I went through airborne training that very summer. I remember that we had a few officers with us. You missed the best part.

TR: Let me tell you. I lived on the third floor of the BOQ [bachelor officer quarters]. The first couple of days when I got back from training I stopped at the little beer hall on the first floor of the BOQ, had a couple of beers, and sat down and rested. I then made it to the second floor and sat down and rested. I got up to the third floor and just conked out in my room. I didn't even have dinner. I wasn't in very good shape, but I got in good shape after that.

When I returned to Ft. Campbell, it wasn't long before they shipped the FACs to Viet Nam. That was well before the 3rd Brigade of the 101st Airborne shipped. When we arrived in country they sent us to the FAC in-country school and then farmed us out to other Army units for in-country orientation. I went to the Australian unit at Vung Tau. It was a very nice beach area where the Australian and Korean troops were stationed and doing a great job—highly professional. I believe there was also an informal agreement between the friendly forces stationed in the beach area and the Viet Cong not to attack each other in town. That made it a good R&R area for both forces to enjoy the good restaurants and the beaches. This was my first indication of how strange the war was.

DW: So you were assigned to the 19th Tactical Support Squadron?

TR: Yes, I think that's it. I stayed with the Australians until the 3rd Brigade of the 101st Airborne arrived in country. I then joined them over near the Cambodian border.

DW: Were you the brigade ALO [air liaison officer]?

TR: Yes, I was the brigade ALO.

DW: Were you qualified to fly something?

TR: An O-1. I went to Hurlburt for training. I was with the brigade for a couple of months pulling FAC duty near the Cambodian border. One night they called me and said, "One of our companies is in trouble. Can you get airborne and get out there to help them?" I got in my O-1 and went out and contacted the company commander. I knew the company commander and he told me his company was under heavy attack and about to be overrun. I told him I had a call in for fighter support and that it should arrive very soon. The brigade commander was airborne at the time in his helicopter talking to other helicopters and trying to talk to the company commander who was under attack. This was not unusual for Army commanders. I told them to get off the air because I was going to work some air for them. They didn't like it but they cleared the air. I got a flight of F-100s and talked them down. I located the company on the ground. I marked the target; the company commander said it was good marks but the enemy troops were very close and the fighter strike would have to be very accurate. The fighters dropped close and laid down napalm right on the bad guys. Long story short, it broke up the attack.

I was at the staff meeting the next morning, and after it broke up, the brigade commander said to his staff, "Gentlemen, we had a close call last night. We're not going to do that anymore. We could have had a short round last night and we could have lost a lot of guys." I couldn't believe what I was hearing. So I asked to see him after the meeting. I asked him, "Sir, did you mean what you said at the meeting, that we were not going to do that anymore? We were about to lose a company so we attacked to save them. We're not going to do that anymore?" He said, "I can't afford to lose any of my men to a short round from your airplanes."

I got in my plane and flew down to Saigon. General Seith was at Headquarters Seventh Air Force. I went to see him and told him the story. I said, "Sir, I've got to get out of there. I'll go anywhere where the war is. I'll do anything." He said, "Go back to your unit. We'll let you know." So I flew back to the unit. As soon as I had landed, they said, "Go back to Saigon, you have an assignment." I went back to Saigon and saw the personnel director. This guy told me General Seith said I had volunteered to do anything, go anywhere, where the war was. Then he explained the Raven FAC program to me and asked me if I wanted to volunteer. I said yes.

DW: What was the time frame?

TR: I'd have to look back at my records but I think it was the latter part of '67. I went off to the Ravens through NKP [Nakhon Phanom] and then on to Udorn. The embassy people picked me up there and told me to get rid of my uniforms, get some civilian clothes from a tailor they recommended, and then they took all my military things and packed them away. I then flew to Vientiane for a couple days of briefing and then on to Pakse.

DW: So you went to Vientiane, did all the in-processing and sheep-dipping. Did they explain to you their various command and control relationships and related matters?

TR: Vaguely.

DW: So your first duty station was Pakse. They needed you down south.
TR: That's right.

DW: So you were down in Military Region IV in the summer of '67.

TR: Yes. I have attached a certificate from the Commander of Military District IV that lists the time I was assigned to Pakse.

DW: What did you run into down there?

TR: It was a laid-back place. We had a nice house on the edge of town. We had very good enlisted people who took care of our airplanes and at first the CIA people were very accommodating and easy to work with initially. The town was good size for Laos and it was peaceful as long as you stayed in downtown. Outside of town the enemy owned all the real estate.

DW: Americans?

TR: I think we had three at that time. We also had a squadron or two of Lao T-28s. As I understood the mission, I was to work with them, show them how to plan and execute a mission using the best intelligence available. We had a big weapon-storage area with plenty of weapons to choose from. Anything they needed, they had. The only thing they had a shortage of was a willingness to commit to combat where there seemed to be a risk. Although, when one thinks about that situation, it's important to remember they were in the war for the duration and we were there for only a short time. However, this does not explain why they were not good combat pilots. The pilots up north with Gen. Vang Pao were good and courageous pilots. I think it was just the difference of leadership and discipline.

DW: When you got there, it sounds to me as though you are older than any of the other Ravens. Were you the head Raven at Pakse?

TR: I believe I was, although I can't remember the issue coming up. I don't know about O'Neal's date of rank. I think I may have been senior but it didn't matter because we all went about our jobs in our own way. All the Ravens had extraordinary freedom to operate in any way they chose. There were almost no rules. That was probably the most important and attractive part of being a Raven. Ravens were pretty much free to determine how they would accomplish their missions. In my case

I chose to fly low on almost every mission because from low altitude it was fairly easy to find good targets. Obviously there was more risk associated with this decision. Some Ravens flew much higher and in some cases used binoculars to look for targets. That is not to say they were not successful using this technique. It was taught at the FAC school at Hurlburt. Given where we were flying, regardless of the tactics, the Ravens could find targets.

DW: In tracking your history, going to pilot training later meant that you would have been about four years older than the others, and that would have held throughout. So you were older and more mature than most guys. When I was a Raven, I was 25 years old.

TR: I was definitely older at 37-38 but I'm not sure I would say more mature. I don't know about date of rank. I was a little early in rank but a little late in age. I believe that gave me added motivation to do well.

DW: Did you get any resistance from the guys who were already there?

TR: No. I had a good relationship with the CIA contingent there. I had a hard time with the Laotian pilots. I tried to work with them but was not very successful. I couldn't get them to fly into heavily defended areas. They would fly and hit soft targets and drop bombs where they wanted to. They delighted in dropping CBU-25s so they could bring back the empty canisters to sell. They were not a good bunch.

DW: Were they ripping off the system? I see you alluded to the CBU-25s. So they were all in this for themselves?

TR: Most of them, yes. I kind of gave up on them. But for the entire time I was there I kept trying to convince them there were great targets to strike if they would just plan and execute better. Most of my time was spent finding good targets. Getting U.S. air to strike them, or as a last resort striking them myself, with rockets and grenades from my O-1. I also started borrowing T-28s. This was not authorized and the Lao pilots did not like it. But after having a checkout ride in a T-28 with Jack Drummond who was a great pilot, I just decided I could not stand to see loaded T-28s not being used properly.

I decided if there was a good target to be struck and I couldn't get anyone else to do it, I would. So I continued to do that and no one complained. I devoted myself to finding the enemy and trying to disrupt or destroy him. It became a very serious game to me, more like a duel or personal vendetta. It was all on my own. No one authorized me to fly the T-28 and I didn't ask. It just evolved. I never flew the T-28 up north, just while at Pakse.

I enjoyed flying the T-28 but because I flew the O-1 so much, 6-8 hours per day, I felt like it was a part of me. I could make it do about anything I wanted it to do, including flying it in an extreme crab when being shot at. I always flew with the windows open so I could hear ground fire. I am convinced no other aircraft could have performed as well for me as the O-1 did. There is no doubt in my mind that the O-1 saved my life many times.

DW: Who was checking up on you?

TR: Nobody. I just used the T-28s. The Laotians didn't like it because I occasionally came back with holes in the plane. I only flew when there were targets I thought needed to be struck immediately. Just to the east of Pakse was a beautiful high area, the Bolevan Plateau. It was fairly safe and I occasionally landed at a small CIA camp to talk about enemy action in the area. The agency had agents and road-watch teams just to the east of the plateau along the Se Kong River. The river and all along its banks to the south toward Cambodia was a hotbed of enemy activity. The Lao pilots would never go there because the area was heavily defended. The enemy forces were also concentrated around Attapeu in support of the Ho Chi Minh Trail. When I flew over there I could almost always find good targets. I was under the impression the Air Force avoided the area because of its proximity to Cambodia. I felt like the area was my private hunting ground and I struck in that area many times with the O-1 and the T-28. The only drawback was the enemy gun emplacements were well camouflaged so you had to fly low to find them. The enemy gunners also held their fire until they knew you had found their position, then all hell would break loose. The Se Kong River was occasionally a great place to hunt. Several times I found boats traveling up the river from Cambodia. This was especially true during rainy days when the fast movers were not available. One day I spotted a very large boat coming upriver. It was flying a flag from the stern but I could not identify it. I circled around and started to approach from the stern. About the time I was getting close enough to ID the flag they opened up on me with two stern heavy machine guns. I broke hard away and down closer to the trees avoiding their fire. My next pass was from broadside with my guns. I made some good hits and the boat started smoking and turned into the river bank. About 8-10 troops exited the boat and ran for tree cover. I made another pass on the boat and it exploded. When I got back home I went by CIA headquarters to see if they had a picture of a Cambodian flag. They didn't so I just waited to see if we got a report about the incident. Nothing happened so I let it pass. It was one of the most unusual and interesting strikes of my tour.

DW: What was your mission while you were there? Were you there to support friendly forces with close air support or were you there as an interdiction force?

TR: I was there, as I understood, to provide reconnaissance, intel, advise the Lao Air Force, and serve as a FAC for U.S. strikes in Laos. Most of the intelligence reports were made directly to the CIA detachment. The CIA reports disappeared into the system and I rarely received any feedback. As far as supporting friendly forces, I never controlled air in support of Army units because they were never directly engaged with enemy forces the entire time I was stationed in Pakse. As I said earlier, it was a peaceful place as long as you stayed west of the Bolevan Plateau.

DW: Were they feeding information back to you to help you with your targeting?

TR: No. At Pakse it was a one-way street but at the northern stations there was greater cooperation between the Ravens and the CIA. This was especially true at 20 Alternate where the Ravens got direct guidance from Gen. Vang Pao and enjoyed a close relationship with the Agency. This is not to say we didn't have a good working relationship with the Pakse Agency people. I personally had a very good relationship with Dave Morales, the station chief. He was extremely supportive and provided about anything we needed to include personal weapons. The relationship was friendly but decidedly one-way. We provided them everything we had and they provided us good logistical support. I stayed there until I was called up to Vientiane. I have some pictures in the folder of some targets and Pakse.

DW: Would you guys respond to calls for close air support from Laotian troops in the area?

TR: We certainly would have. But there were no requests while I was there.

DW: Really?

TR: The whole time I was at Pakse the Laotians were never in a big fight.

DW: Really?

TR: There was no close air support. There was only interdiction. On a typical day we would go out and find a target, call Hillsboro–ABCCC [Airborne Command and Control Center], describe the target, and they would send flights of fighters when they had weather diverts. They liked the targets the Ravens provided because they were in many cases better than the targets they were getting in Viet Nam. The targets in southern Laos, except for the area south of Attapeu, were in most cases not as good as the targets in northern Laos. It was also extremely dangerous to take an O-1 over the Ho Chi Minh Trail. There were ZPUs, 37mm, and heavier guns along the trail. I have some pictures of the craters. The best targets in southern Laos were along the river—the river that I talked about—that ran south toward Cambodia.

I rarely took backseaters with me. Most of them didn't like to fly with me because they thought I took too many risks, but the real story was they were Army officers with little or no training and just not cut out for the flying mission.

DW: Would the Laotians come out and bomb for you?

TR: They wouldn't bomb if there was ground fire. One day I led them, marked the target, and said, "Strike my mark!" The lead pilot said, "One's in." And I'm looking. "Two's in." "Three's in." I'm looking but I don't see anything happening. I happened to look away from the target area and saw smoke from explosions about a mile away. The flight leader said, "We tried but couldn't hit your smoke." There were a couple of antiaircraft guns in the target area shooting at us but they were not very effective against aircraft at our altitude. The Lao pilots were just responding to the tracers. So I gave up trying to get them to attack serious targets and spent my time finding targets and working with ABCCC to direct U.S. fighters against good targets.

DW: Any gunships down there?

TR: No gunships.

DW: You were recorded during that time period as having said, "I ran the air war in southern Laos." Is that true?

TR: Yes. What I meant was:

American fighters could not strike in my area of operation without the control of a Raven FAC. So in the case of American air, we found the targets and controlled the strikes.

The Lao pilots were ineffective and would not strike worthwhile targets.

We, the Ravens, found and approved targets and if we could not get U.S. fighter support, we could choose to delay a strike until U.S. air was available or we could attack the target in any other way we thought appropriate.

We did not have to get approval from anyone to take these actions. I call that running the air war.

DW: But not a worthwhile portion of the tour. You didn't get a lot of support from our friendlies so it was almost you on your own. Do you remember the Ravens you had down there at that time?

TR: Howie O'Neal was with me during a part of my time at Pakse. We operated independent of each other and he left shortly after I arrived. Dale Richardson came in just before they pulled me in to Vientiane. I knew Dale and we went through F-100 training together at Luke. He and I communicated when he was in Vietnam; I told him about the Ravens and he ended up coming to Pakse. He and I were good friends and I took him on his first T-28 mission in Laos. I left shortly after Dale arrived and I don't know if he ever flew the T-28 again.

DW: Did you get any air support from the 56th Wing up at NKP with the A-1s and A-26s?

TR: No. As I recall they worked well north of our operational area. I believe they worked in the area of Savannakhet and Tchepone.

DW: Did you ever fly over to the Vietnamese border?

TR: No, I don't think so. However, it is possible I crossed over the Cambodian border on one or more of my trips south along the Se Kong River. I'm pretty sure I never crossed over into Viet Nam because to do so would have taken me over the main part of the Ho Chi Minh Trail. There was a minor part of the trail that ran fairly close to Attapeu and I probably crossed it but I normally operated not more than 25 miles east of Attapeu.

DW: Did you ever have any knowledge of or contact with the U.S. Army SOG [Studies and Observations Group] teams that were being inserted along the Trail?

TR: Not much. I had contact with them only from landing at some of their sites. They had a site up on the eastern side of the Bolevan Plateau. I would land there and talk to them every once in a while. They gave me a little intelligence about the area just west of the trail. But I never worked with them directly.

DW: Anything else about Pakse?

TR: Given there was a war going on all around us it was a good place to live. We often stopped downtown and drank beer at a local outside restaurant. And we occasionally took our enlisted men to the local clubs. The food at the house was good and we had plenty of fresh fruit from the market. We had a bar at the house and it got plenty of use. There was also a special treat that very few people knew about. There were airline stewardesses, I believe from Braniff or Continental

Airlines, doing voluntary work at the Dooley Foundation on Kong Island south of Pakse, very close to the Cambodian border. They had a landing strip—that's about all I want to say about that!

DW: So you get notified that they are taking you back up to Vientiane. When did that happen?

TR: I left Pakse sometime in July 1968.

DW: You get back up there and they are going to make you the head Raven for the whole program.

TR: I think they brought me up for two reasons. First was experience and the second was at that time I was one of the senior Ravens, both in rank and age. They needed somebody to tell them what was happening in the field. All the people assigned to the headquarters were known by the Ravens as the Downtowners. The officers assigned to the headquarters did not fly with the Ravens and spent little to no time in the field. I don't remember ever being visited by anyone from Vientiane while I was assigned to Pakse.

DW: They didn't have someone already serving as an Air Force liaison?

TR: That would be Colonel Eugene Sonnenburg who was either the Air Force air attaché or the deputy. He spent most of his time involved with embassy programs and little to no time with the Ravens. Colonel Joe Williams and Major Harold Kloberdanz were members of the staff and the ones who were most concerned about the Raven program. They also spent most of their time in Vientiane operating what some would call an ops center. They made reports and were responsible for any awards and decorations that went forward.

When I arrived I moved into one of the Ice Houses with some of the members of the administrative staff of the air attaché, to include the two officers mentioned above. The Ice Houses were old French chalets. Both were fairly nice houses, right in Vientiane. They were in a little compound, but not well protected.

They brought me up because it had become obvious to them that they could not do their job without a better understanding of field operations. I spent very little time in the headquarters and traveled to all the sites and in some cases to fill in when there was a shortage of FACS at a given location. I went to 20 Alternate as often as I could because it was the most challenging and exciting location we had. I also had the sad duty to fill in when we lost a FAC. For instance, when a great and daring FAC like Sam Deichelmann failed to return from a ferry mission to Viet Nam, I went up to temporarily replace him.

I served as an informal evaluator in the field because the people in the headquarters needed to know what was happening and they also needed information for the preparation of the OERs [officer evaluation reports] and decorations they wrote on the FACs.

DW: Still flying the Tango?

TR: No. I flew the O-1 and a few missions in the U-17 and the Cessna 180. I flew the majority of my time in the O-1.

DW: Did you have any particular issues to deal with when you were up flying with VP [Gen. Vang Pao] on the PDJ [Plaine des Jarres]?

TR: Gen. Vang Pao was a great warrior general and treated me very well. I will never forget the dinners we had when we would talk about what needed to be done the next day, the battlefield situation, and where we might want to employ U.S. fighters. I enjoyed working with him. He was the first Lao officer I met that was a real leader. Unlike most of the other Royal Laotian generals. I don't believe he was involved in the opium, gold, or air passengers business.

DW: Did you have Hmong backseaters with you?

TR: A couple of times, but that didn't work out very well. I had one try to jump out of the airplane on the runway when we landed. We were landing at LS 36 with bad guys all around. He didn't like that and lost control. After that I flew by myself.

DW: Do you remember any of the Ravens who were there then?

TR: Yes. I remember Sam Deichelmann and Art Cornelius well and had great respect for both. I had flown with Art in Viet Nam and got to know Sam in Laos.

DW: What do you think happened to him?

TR: I think he crashed in the jungle. He was ferrying an O-1 back from Viet Nam and no one knew his exact route of flight and no one heard from him. He could be anywhere. He just disappeared. We'll never know.

DW: Great stuff. You are there in Vientiane as head Raven. What kind of administrative or supervisory duties did you have?

TR: I did not have any defined supervisory duties and didn't think I needed them. As I said earlier, I evaluated the performance of each of the units and the people assigned and fed that back to the staff at headquarters. I thought my job was to do everything within my power to make it easier for the Ravens to do their job. To ensure they had the right kind of equipment, support personnel, and to be the Raven spokesman in Vientiane and at Air Force headquarters.

DW: Were you writing their OERs?

TR: I helped to write them, but did not write or sign the final product. Major Kloberdanz and Col. Joe Williams took care of producing the final product and I believe Col. Sonnenburg signed the OERs. They were the two officers I worked with and lived with when I was in town so we had many opportunities to discuss field operation in an informal setting. They were also responsible for awards and decorations, which was not a very good story when I arrived in the headquarters.

DW: That is unconscionable.

TR: I agree, and we got the program moving. I give Joe Williams a lot of credit for elevating the efforts to gain proper recognition.

DW: There in Vientiane, what was it like trying to work with the Department of State folks? Did you ever meet the ambassador?

TR: I attended a few embassy functions but avoided them when possible. I met Ambassador Sullivan the first week I was in country. We met in a bathroom. I was invited to an embassy party and I got dressed in my best clothes. I was in the bathroom and this gentleman asked if I was Richards. I said yes. He said, "I'm Sullivan," and we shook hands. He told me to come and see him the next day. I did and he told me, "I run the operations in Laos," and he meant it. "If you have any questions about your duties here, come to me direct." That is how he was. He ran that country. I had great respect for Ambassador Sullivan and very little for the State Department in general. By the way, that opinion never changed as I moved on to higher positions in the Air Force. Ambassador Sullivan was a great American. He left Laos during my tour and we got a new ambassador who I never got to know well.

DW: That was Ambassador Godley.

TR: Yes. Not as aggressive as Sullivan. A nice guy.

DW: How about the CIA?

TR: My contact with the CIA was mostly in Pakse and 20 Alt. The relationship with the CIA at the sites was generally very good. They lived right there with us. The unit at Pakse was much larger than the one at Alternate and some of the agents had their wives with them.

I got to know Joe Morales the station chief very well. As I said earlier, he was a good man and very supportive. He was well-known in CIA operations. When Che Guevara was killed, he was called back to the states to help ID the body because of his earlier clandestine relationship with Guevara. I personally had good relations with him. He had a Mexican cook and I had dinner at his house several times. Steaks, Mexican food – they were living well in the combat zone. The relationship with the CIA at 20A was really a frontline, wartime operation. It worked well; we practically lived together and the enemy was just on the other side of that hill.

DW: It was a coordination of necessity. You had to get it done.

TR: Exactly. We talked every day.

DW: When did you come home? Did you do an after action report?

TR: I came back in December 1968. No after action or debrief. Just packed up and came home. I tried to extend but they would not let me extend. I had a follow-on assignment at the Air Force Academy.

DW: OK. What have we missed?

TR: I don't know what else.

DW: That was a long time ago.

TR: It was a long time ago, and until now I haven't thought about it much. Although my thoughts and some of my memories of Viet Nam and Laos remained in my mind, they grew dimmer with the passing of time and as I took on jobs of increasing responsibility. I am convinced not making that experience in Laos the biggest thing in my life helped me get on with my career. Looking back on life's experiences can teach you a lot, but dwelling on them too much can cause adjustment problems. I know a lot of people whose combat experience was so great they could not put it behind them and it adversely affected them for the rest of their life.

DW: How about Air America, did you work closely with them?

TR: Most of them were superb guys. I knew quite a few of them and had confidence they would come and pick me up if I went down. They were very good people to work with, reliable and brave. They were getting big bucks and didn't mind spending some of it on their friends. Occasionally one of them would throw a $100,000 party—they were spectacular.

DW: Did you ever work any rescue missions, guys going down?

TR: No, not that I recall.

DW: When you got back to the Academy, I have to ask, did you tell these stories to the cadets? Did you expose them to these kinds of things? I was still there then, and seem to recall hearing some of this – maybe from you. It whetted my appetite for that kind of duty later on.

TR: I did share some of it with my squadron, Cadet Squadron 28, and later with members of 3rd group. They loved to hear combat stories and any time we had some personal time together they would ask me questions about Viet Nam. I had a close relationship with the 28th Squadron and enjoyed spending time with them, especially the Doolies [freshman-year cadets]. I was very proud of the way the upper classes took responsibility for the training of the 4th class—they were an exceptional group of young people. I still stay in touch with some of them. The upper-class cadets took a very personal interest in tough but positive training for the 4th class and we did not lose a single Doolie that year. One of those 4th classmen later returned to the Academy as the Superintendent (Lt. Gen. John Regni, 2005-09). As an example of how motivated the 4th class was, one night I was in the squadron talking to them and when I finished I told them my car had slipped off the side of the ramp by Mitchell Hall and I needed a few of them to come down and push me out of the snow and back on the ramp. The whole class put on their parkas and came down and pushed me out.

DW: Jack Drummond talked about how you flew into Thailand and got intercepted by F-102s.

TR: I was going on a self-approved R&R to Bangkok. I flew a T-28 and headed into Thailand. I tried to call Lion Control (radar) as I had done on other occasions when I flew to Ubon but I had radio problems and could not reach them. My radio was breaking up so I transmitted a blind call and continued on course. The weather was broken and I was in and out of the clouds. The first time I knew there was a problem was when I looked out and saw two Australian fighters on my wings. I believe they were trying to speak to me on the radio but I could not hear them. They signaled me to follow them but about that time we flew into some heavy cloud coverage and when I broke out I had lost them.

When I landed in Bangkok, I was met by Thai authorities. They wanted to take me to jail since I was in civilian clothes and flying an unmarked aircraft. I finally convinced them I was not the enemy and they let me call the embassy, which was very surprised but got me released.

DW: Art mentioned a trip to Chiang Mai. You, he, and Jim Casey got on a C-47 and flew there for a vacation.

TR: Yes. It was a nice place and they were great guys to be with. I'm afraid I don't recall what we did there but I'm sure it involved some alcohol consumption.

DW: Do you recall Fred Roth?

TR: Yes, in Pakse. He was a fine officer and a good FAC but we did not get to know each other very well.

DW: From the Robbins book, you said that when you arrived at Pakse, you found a very loose operation and were determined to tighten it up.

TR: That was true, but I did not mean it as a criticism of the individual FACs or of the Raven field operations. What I meant was the whole Raven program was not well organized. There wasn't a chain of command that was understood by all the players. For instance, I was never told who I reported to or who to contact if I had problems.

Describing the situation as loose was probably incorrect. It would have been more accurate to describe it as disorganized or dysfunctional because no formal relationship existed between the headquarters and the field. As I mentioned earlier, the Downtowners in the headquarters were not FACs and never spent much time in the field so could not understand the needs of the people they were charged with managing. I believe that is precisely why they brought me to the headquarters— to provide the operators' perspective.

I wanted to bring some organization to the program, improve the interface between the Ravens and the staff in Vientiane and the staff at higher Air Force headquarters. I also wanted to get more recognition for what the Ravens were doing, and get them the supplies they needed—better aircraft, weapons, survival radios, vests, etc. I worked those things ever mindful that what we did not need was a program like the over-controlling program that existed in Viet Nam. One reason many of the Ravens had volunteered for the program was to escape the way the war was being conducted in Viet Nam; what they did not need was a return to ridiculous rules of engagement.

TR: [Discussing a target on the PDJ.] This was one of the most interesting and satisfying missions I flew. One day when I was up at LS-20A filling in for Sam Deichelmann, I got a call from our

CIA contact, stating one of their Army units up on the southwest side of the PDJ was being shelled by NV [North Vietnamese] artillery located somewhere in the PDJ. (I believe the site was Lima Site 22.) When I landed at the site I was met and accompanied by an American Army sergeant and we inspected the area where most of the incoming rounds had hit. From the impact pattern we were able to determine a loose azimuth back to an area where the guns could be located. As we got ready to fly, the sergeant asked if he could come with me and I said yes since he was an experienced combat veteran. We knew the guns would be at least a couple of miles away and fairly close to the azimuth we had computed. I also knew they would be hidden on the edge of a tree line and would be camouflaged. In the PDJ there were not many areas with enough trees to conceal large guns, so our search was not long. We found a tree line that ran along a very small river or creek, and as I dropped down to about 500 feet I saw the gun emplacements along the tree line next to a grassy field. Cricket Control had no assets so I decided to try to strike the position myself. I fired some rockets into the target area and they started shooting back. I believe this was the first time the sergeant was in an aircraft being shot at but he seemed to take it OK and he was very excited about what was happening. My rockets started grass fires in the field in front of the gun positions and I could see a strong wind was carrying the fire toward the guns. As the fire spread toward the gun positions the gun crews ran out to try to put the fire out. As they came out I fired additional rockets at them and they would retreat back into the trees. I also had a couple of thermite grenades and I had the sergeant throw them out as we made additional passes over the position. By the time we had to leave because of low fuel the entire field was on fire and the fire was raging into the tree line and what I think was artillery rounds stacked within the gun positions started exploding. As we found out later, there were 4-5 large artillery guns and numerous trucks and ammunition in the target area. I mention this mission as one of the more interesting and satisfying missions I flew because in a short period of time I was able to destroy a sizable enemy target and eliminate a clear and present danger to one of our forward bases and to our friendly forces stationed there.

End

Chapter 26

Jerome W. Klingaman, Raven 50
Second Tour: AOC Commander
Pakse and the "C" Team, Oct 1968 – Apr 1969

Pre-launch

With PACAF assuming responsibility for manning Project 404 positions, USAFSOF turned its attention elsewhere. In late 1967, I took a 12-person composite team to the Philippines where I was air component commander for unconventional warfare exercise *Eagle's Nest*. I had Bob Farmer with me to run the tactical stuff along with several of his combat controllers, combat weather specialists, and combat Intel specialists. The tactical stuff consisted primarily of training SF guys from 1st Special Forces Group, Okinawa, on how to request air support, communicate with aircraft, mark drop zones, and report local weather.

There was no money to fund our deployment, so the 1st SOW flew us to Greenville, TX, and turned us loose to hitchhike with 1200 pounds of equipment across the Pacific to Clark AB. Other than going through a magnitude 6.2 earthquake in the Philippines, it was a great trip. I also deployed to Korea as ops officer on a mission aimed at creating a Republic of Korea Air Force (ROKAF) capability to intercept and destroy high-speed infiltrator boats. We started with an intense in-country threat assessment and moved to open-ocean live tests at night in the Gulf of Mexico using F-5 fighters, helicopters, and C-123 flareships against real unmanned boats. This is where I used a modified version of the flare-dispensing routine that I worked out for the BC-47 in Laos. ROCAF F-5s and C-123s used this flare-fighter combination under actual conditions in Korea.

Back at England AFB, I maintained instructor/flight examiner status in the squadron but worked full time at Wing Operations Plans. That was a perfect combination for me. I flew a lot and started learning how to plan a live operation. The planning part was a valuable education that I carried forward for the rest of my active-duty Air Force career and beyond into a second career as a civilian assigned to the Air Force.In the late summer of 1968, the 1st Special Operations Wing (SOW) was directed to go back into Laos to resume supporting Project 404. Whereas the wing only supported one AOC commander position during my first tour at Vientiane, there were now five AOC locations and five commander positions to be filled. The tasking included a maintenance line chief, an enlisted physician's assistant (PA), and a comm operator at each of the five locations. We were asked to immediately man three locations plus provide a C-47 advisor. Teams for the other two AOC locations would be tasked to the wing later. I was asked to volunteer for this first return engagement, and I agreed.

I again asked for an AT-28 checkout. This time it was granted, and I flew to Hurlburt Field for training with the 6th Special Operations Squadron. My instructor, Major Carl Leuchner, gave me as much instruction as he could in the little time remaining. It always seemed to go that way; always pressed for time. When it was time to return to England AFB for deployment, I only had one event to go--the solo flight. I would have had to stay over another day for that, and another day wasn't available. Carl said: "Don't worry, you fly the airplane fine, and you can do it when you get there." Things were very informal in those days.

So, no Form 8, but then, there weren't any Form 8s in Laos anyway. Most everything was done on a by-name basis in the command, which, incidentally, works very well overall in special operations-type activities.

Our deploying AOC commanders consisted of me, Wayne Landon, and Larry Harwood. Howard Hartley was the C-47 advisor. Dr. Gene Kirkley was deploying to take over as emergency flight surgeon and physician at Site 20 Alternate. The team also included several NCOs heading for duty as maintenance line chiefs, physician's assistants, and comm operators. When we left the States, we had no idea which AOCs we would be assigned to. I didn't really care, except that I wanted a Lao fighter unit, even if it was a small one. I had done the B-Team mission at Vientiane, and found Don Moody's lash-up with the C-Team at Louangphrabang absolutely fascinating. I really wanted to do that mission. Anyway, we left for Bangkok, and it felt good. One is in a completely different frame of mind going in for a second time. I had my RLAF flight suits, a switchblade, my denim jacket, and the .22 cal magnum derringer. I already knew what buffalo steaks tasted like, so how ready can you get?

After arrival in Bangkok, we proceeded directly to Vientiane; I don't remember even checking in with Water Pump. The next morning at AIRA, we were met by Colonel Robert L .F. Tyrrell, now serving his second tour in that position. We also learned our individual fates. Howard Hartley was the C-47 advisor, so he would stay in Vientiane and function as AIRA liaison officer to the Lao Joint Operations Center. Larry Harwood would also stay in Vientiane as AOC commander for the B-Team. Gene Kirkley would proceed to 20 Alternate as planned. Wayne Landon would be AOC commander at Savannakhet, and I would be AOC commander with the small fighter unit at Pakse. AOC commander positions at Louangphrabang and 20 Alternate would remain filled by PACAF officers until their tours ran out. After that all AOC positions would be transferred to USAFSOF.

An official explanation for this shift back to USAFSOF would not have been appropriate, and no explanation was given. In time, however, we learned that the PACAF manning scheme for Project 404 was not completely successful. Apparently, the Air Force leadership did not anticipate, or want to embrace, the fact that not everyone is suited to this type duty. You cannot simply pull someone's name from a list of Air Force specialty codes and plug him/her into a combat advisory position in a primitive, foreign environment where standardization and the "USAF way" are not only unknown, but also impossible to attain, and probably resented by the host military. USAFSOF specialized in advising foreign forces in host countries, and the ambassador knew it. Accordingly, he asked that the Air Commandos return to run the five AOC locations.

Arrival at Pakse

After another overnight stay in Vientiane, the attaché C-47 flew Wayne Landon and me to our respective bases. Just before departure, an AIRA representative told me there would be no overlap with the officer I was replacing. He would get on the airplane as I got off. OK, fair enough, but again, no explanation. Anyway, we got airborne. Wayne got off at Savannakhet, and I proceeded to Pakse. I had visited Pakse once during the B-Team tour when I flew the embassy C-47 down there to collect two American bodies imbedded in the wreckage of an RLAF C-47 that had crashed into a mountain at night just north of the base. The two Air Force members were catching a ride to Pakse when the accident happened. I had Fitz with me to help identify the Americans.

When we taxied into the AOC area at Pakse, I remember thinking that I had never seen a more barren, primitive site for continually maintaining and launching combat aircraft on a permanent basis. There was no engine shutdown at Pakse, and dust and dirt were blowing in every direction from the rotating props. When we lowered the steps, the previous AOC commander climbed on board, introduced himself, and made one comment about the Lao pilots that told me what I needed to know about the situation there.

I climbed down the steps and walked out onto the ramp with my AFSOF team--Line Chief McDaniel (Mac), comm operator (Stan), and Physician Assistant Francis (Frank) Dean. It doesn't bother me to say that we were literally dumped off in the dirt; it sort of lends an adventurous air to the whole thing. There were six unmarked AT-28s lined up on the ramp and behind them, an ordnance storage area, mostly empty. There were no revetments. Back and to the right was a small open shack that had the looks of a restaurant or hangout of some kind.

When the dust settled, a lot more of the base revealed itself. A USAID compound and an Air America facility were situated further back and a good distance to the east. In the immediate AOC area, there was a tiny shack for storing 2.75-inch rockets and the fire extinguisher for O-1 Raven birds. Enlisted AOC team members already serving there came up to greet us. There was an engine mechanic, an ordnance storage specialist, and a couple bomb loaders. Their status was the same, and they came from the same bases as my Hoodlums at Vientiane. There was also an O-1 crew chief. The Raven staying there at the time was Dale Richardson.

I was handed the keys to my jeep and a .38 cal Smith and Wesson Combat Masterpiece with a holster, web belt, and Marine bolt knife. The line chief had his jeep as well. We drove to the house, located three miles south of town. A small French concrete marker on the road by the house read "Saigon 608." It was, indeed, 608 kilometers to Saigon. The road going by our house was French Route 1, which originally started at Laung Prabang in northern Laos and terminated in Saigon, Viet Nam.

We got into our rooms, unpacked, and had supper prepared by our Vietnamese cook and his wife. The two of them, together with their cute little kids plus a mean, wretched monkey, lived in quarters in back of the house. There was also a dog named Tiger, who stayed wherever he found a flat spot to lie down. The house was nice, laid out like a miniature version of the Ice House in Vientiane, with very small bedrooms. The smallest bedroom functioned as the comm center, employing the ubiquitous Collins KWM 2A HF radio.

First Contact

The next day, it was time to find out what was going, or not going on, at the launch facility. From what I could gather, it was very quiet out there. Mac, Frank Dean, and I drove to the base and parked by the fighters. No one was there except a few Lao maintenance guys. I asked where the pilots were, and they pointed over to the open-front restaurant hangout. I walked over and found the pilots sitting inside, watching me.

I sat down and told them who I was. I did not sense any hostility, but they were sullen and loath to speak. This was the first time I had been this close to a bunch of Lao fighter pilots, and I had no idea where this was going to go. There was no briefing before I left Vientiane, and now there were no smiles or talk. This was going to be difficult, and I probably had one chance to get it right.

I waited. Finally, one of them, the oldest, introduced himself. "I am Lieutenant Pitsami." I asked him if he was the flight commander, and he said he was. Then he started asking questions. "Are you the new AOC commander?" I told him I was. The next question was interesting: "Do you want us to fly a mission?"

"No," I told him. "Why, do you have a mission to fly?" No, he didn't have one; the question was simply a test to see if I was there to kick butt and get the sortie rate up. And then "Do you fly test hops?" he asked. I told him I did, and would he like me to fly all the test hops? That was when I got the first glimmer of a smile. Now, it was my turn to ask a question: "Do you guys want a soft drink or beer?" Yes, they would like that, a soft drink please.

The test-hop question was not self-revealing until I got a clear picture of the AOC maintenance program at Pakse. And you cannot appreciate their point of view until you have watched an AT-28 engine change carried out in the dirt using an A-frame, forklift, and bomb dolly with a couple rubber tires on top. Test hops obviously spooked them. So my AT-28 solo ride a couple days later was a test hop for an engine change.

But today wasn't over. I asked for the rest of their names. There was Pong Pat, alias "Frenchy." He had a French dad and a Lao mother. Then there was a tall guy named Sohn, alias "Ringo." There was also Boun Toum (BT), and two Somdets—Somdet K and Somdet H. That made six pilots for six aircraft.

I noticed there was a black cowboy hat and guitar lying on the floor next to Ringo. I asked him if he played the guitar. Probably a silly question, but it was a way to get things started. Yes, he played the guitar. And did I play guitar, he asked? "Yes, I do," I replied. He asked me if I would teach him some American songs. "Yes, if you teach me some Lao songs." That seemed fair, and he agreed.

The drinks were delivered, and I paid. Ringo picked up the guitar and played a few licks, singing in Lao. He handed me the guitar, and I picked and sang a bit of the Wildwood Flower, "hammering on" like Mother Maybelle Carter. They all sat there grinning. I was grinning too; there was going to be a functioning strike team at Pakse, and I was going to be on it. I left them sitting there with their soda pops and walked over to the ramp to look at the birds with Mac. I had never seen such grungy, soot-covered airplanes.

Preliminary Actions

Dale Richardson was closing in on the end of his Raven tour, but he still had a couple weeks left before departure. I spent as much time with him as I could, learning my way around the base and across the road at FAR Headquarters. I flew in the back seat of the O-1 with Dale several times to get a feel for how he hunted and interfaced with military and intelligence sources on the ground. Dale had already made a good start encouraging the local FAR Headquarters to put together a Joint Tactical Operations Center (JTOC) for MR 4. Actually, it was a concept that Dale had been trying to bring into being for some time, and for good reason: Valid targeting in MR 4 was probably the most perplexing problem I experienced during my time there.

Incorporating good intelligence into a planning process that brought both air and surface forces into coordinated play was not something the FAR was good at, at least not in MR 4. The Army would validate an area for armed reconnaissance and attack by air, and then take it back when a strike produced friendly casualties and complaints. Towns and military sites already overrun and occupied by enemy forces were fair game, but they seemed to have little knowledge of enemy movements and locations elsewhere. The FAR G-2 lacked a physical presence in the countryside with trained, motivated intelligence resources.

As a consequence, almost all the targeting data I acted on came from the customer located in the USAID Annex or from forward sites occupied by special intelligence collection assets linked up with the customer. I attended a couple JTOC meetings with Dale, where I met the key FAR players, including the MR 4 commander, General Phasouk, and his Director of Operations.

Dale took me over to the USAID Annex to check in with the Agency. His routine included an almost daily check-in with them as they provided most of his targets for exploiting with U.S. Air. When I asked them if I could get targets from them for the Lao fighter pilots, they appeared dubious about our ability or willingness to follow up with strikes. I assured them that the RLAF guys would fly and deliver ordnance--just give us a try. They agreed to play ball with us. I should add here that our assigned area of MR 4 was not exactly a target-rich environment at the beginning of this dry-season tour. That would change soon and in a very bad way.

While all this was going on, Mac and the engine mechanic were going through the AT-28s with meticulous, detailed inspections while Frank Dean talked with the pilots individually. Frank was trying to get an idea of their physical and psychological health. Psychologically, they seemed to be OK. Physically, they were a mess. That part needed fixing.

Two or three days into the week, I dropped by the Annex and met with the ops officer. He gave me a target consisting of a PL troop concentration. I now had all but the last component in place to get this program together. I drove over to the ramp and gathered the pilots around me for the first briefing. "OK, guys, we have a real target from the Annex," I said. "Do you want to do this?" Yes, they did. Great! All six would make the strike, and the birds were already loaded with bombs and rockets. So, again, I heard the sound of AT-28s starting up and taxiing out for takeoff. A man would have to be stone dead to not get goose bumps watching this scene take place.

When the birds landed, I went up to the pilots and spoke to them. They seemed to be pumped up and happy. There was no bomb damage assessment (BDA) and there wouldn't be any because there was no one on the ground to physically inspect the site. I took them over to the hangout shack and bought them soda pops, and we started the Lao-English music lessons.

Work on the ground continued even while the birds were in the air. Munitions had to be brought up the loading area on bomb dollies and MJ-1s positioned for reloading. The 500-pound bombs we had at Pakse were the newer Mark 82 type instead of WWII vintage. There were RLAF maintenance and munitions people on the team, and Mac was working like crazy to bring them together as a viable capability. Their formal training was really minimal, so it was a tough row to hoe for him. But letting them do the work while providing instruction and coaching brought them to life.

Mac noticed an old fire truck parked in the FAR Headquarters compound across the road. I don't know who he talked to, but someone gave him the fire truck for our ramp, the only caveat being that we would respond if there was a fire in the army compound. The truck looked its age, but it ran fine and the pressure-pump worked. After buying some long-handled brushes, we now had the means to wash the airplanes and mount an emergency response in case of an aircraft fire. As with the other four AOCs in Laos, our flight line maintenance area had no electricity, running water, or overhead enclosure, but Mac and his multinational maintenance team soon had all six fighters looking spiffy and running reliably. That, on its own, raised the confidence factor among the pilots to a very high level. The pilots had enormous respect for Mac. I don't think they knew what rank he was, nor did they care. They trusted him explicitly, although I wasn't sure how he engendered that level of confidence. It took a while, but I finally found out. After a couple months of operations, they started jumping in the cockpits and starting engines without doing a preflight. That got my attention. "Whoa, guys, not so fast. You need to do a preflight inspection." They told me that if Mac said the airplane was OK, then it was OK. That had to be fixed, but lecturing them on *preflights being a pilot's responsibility* somehow fell short of what I wanted. I did get them back into the preflight mode, but something was going on, and I knew it.

One evening down at the Chinese restaurant, after supper and a little beer, the youngest one asked "Mac, you fly with me tomorrow?" What? *So, what is this "Mac, you fly with me tomorrow?"* Driving home in the jeep, I asked Mac what was going on. He admitted that he had been flying in the back seat when the pilots asked him to, and while I was up at Vientiane or out with one of the Ravens. I had my answer. I admired Mac's courage, but I had to bring it to an end. He had already gained the pilots' trust in the airplanes.

They knew that if Mac would fly with them any time, no notice, then he personally trusted the condition of the airplanes. I don't think they realized how severely they had tested Mac's commitment--he had a fear of flying. With Mac taking care of the airplanes and Frank Dean taking care of the pilots and their families, we were bridging the gap between advisors and flyers.

(Mac) McDaniel, Line Chief at Pakse, Laos, 1968

Sometimes it's just little things that help make it work. John Mansur bought a hand-crank ice cream maker, Frank found French baby milk powder at Charlie's downtown, and we bought white strawberries from an old French farmer who lived up on the Bolavens Plateau with his Lao wife. Why the Pathet Lao didn't kill him, I'll never know; maybe he paid them off with strawberries. The cook mixed it all together with sugar, vanilla, and eggs, and the cook's little girls turned the crank (in exchange for ice cream, of course). Then we would have the pilots over to the house for ice cream and 8mm cowboy movies in the evening. They loved it.

The targets kept coming, the pilots flew the sorties, and the munitions dump started dwindling. I was concerned about the remaining inventory of munitions running out completely. I had not previously been in a position to start an aggressive buildup of armaments, but I was now. I contacted the USAID officer across the ramp and requested more munitions. There was plenty of time for replenishment to flow in seamlessly, but it didn't happen.

I asked the USAID officer if there was a problem. And, yes, there was a problem: USAID, Vientiane didn't think the pilots would fly and use the munitions, so they didn't send any. I called AIRA on our Collins radio and told them they needed to lean hard on USAID and break things loose. USAID was really skeptical of our ambitions. The RLAF pilots had apparently been flying only one sortie per week each, and USAID didn't believe the situation was going to change. But the situation was already starting to change and it would change even more as the weeks went by. The trick was convincing the pilots that you had their best interests at heart and really wanted to keep them alive. In short, you had to sincerely care, and to make that apparent.

Frank Dean told me to bring the pilots and their wives and/or girlfriends over to the house for movies and snacks. Gonorrhea was almost endemic in that part of the world, and he believed they all had it. On the appointed evening, they showed up, but not with all the women. Only one was married--Pitsami--and he did bring his wife. We got the 8mm projector started with some kind of ancient movie and served the snacks.

Upstairs, Frank had a table covered with a white sheet and little stainless steel basins loaded with syringes, alcohol swabs, and boxes of pills. One couple, or person, at a time would be invited upstairs to drop their britches and get their penicillin shot and little bottle of tetracycline pills. He then showed them pictures in the book and briefed them on safe sex practices. They were also given vitamin pills. Suddenly, life for them started looking up.

At the time all this happened, there was no physician in southern Laos. Frank was all we had if we came back shot up. Local people simply lived without medical attention. So here was an opportunity. Frank located a vacant shed behind the flight line and turned it into a civic action "clinic" for local civilians. When he opened shop in the morning, the line of patients, mostly elderly, was at least 50 people deep. He would listen to complaints through an interpreter, and examine his patients for related symptoms.

After that, he would dispense pills and provide instructions. He only dispensed one pill per person, so they had to come back the next day for the second pill. That prevented them from taking the whole bottle of pills at once. He had a little list to keep track of things. Then he would ask them where they were from and if they had seen anybody they didn't know around their home or village. He periodically visited the local Catholic orphanage run by French nuns, where he treated children, saving the life of at least one abandoned baby. Through these medical actions, Frank eventually established a small HUMINT and early-warning net in the local area. Frank was a real professional; I will gladly credit him with a huge portion of our success at Pakse.

Taking Flight

After Dale left for the states, he was replaced by John Mansur and then PF Reinhart. They would come and go as the situation required, but John stayed with me a good length of time before he went back north. When he returned for a second stay, he got out of the aircraft and handed me a colored drawing he had made. It was a Raven sitting on top of a human skull, with the word "Ravens" written at the bottom of the image. It reminded me of the scene in *Snow White and the Seven Dwarfs* where the wicked witch is brewing poison in a kettle with a Raven weaving around on top of a skull behind her. John asked: "What do you think of this as a patch for Raven FACs?" I thought it was wonderful. John had the first patches made up from that drawing.

I flew quite a few back-seat missions with John in the O-1, mainly because it gave me eyes-on familiarization with the western MR 4 area, both in the air and on the ground at remote locations, and because I wanted to share his adventures and risk. The Raven FACs did not officially come under the AOC commander. I was often in a position to work the Ravens into an ongoing operation, or ask for support, but the command and control thing was never an issue. We simply had a shared understanding of what had to be done. On one such mission over Laongam, a site overrun by the enemy, we took a hit in the prop blade. Nothing serious, but shooting at a lone FAC was not good form and had to be punished.

I had an AT-28 already loaded up with .50 cal guns and 2.75-inch rockets. We took off in close trail and headed back to Laongam. I got up to 4500 feet for the roll-in while John circled around looking for movement on the ground. Nothing was moving, so he made a marking run in the middle of town with me following close behind firing rockets in close succession down the street and across the smoke. With the rockets gone, I armed up the guns and rolled in for a shallow strafing run.

Things were happening much slower than in an F-100 pass, and I stayed on the guns too long. I heard John call: "You're too low, Mr. K," and I was. I was not going to hit the ground, but I was shallow and shooting through the windows of the buildings, and when I pulled up, the air in front

of me was full of flying tracers. A strafing run in an F-100 lasts maybe a second and a half, so it was a new experience being able to hang in there so long in this prop-driven fighter. It's a bit sobering, however, to know that for every tracer you see in front of you, there are four others, as only one in five is a tracer round.

There was a good lesson in this, but luck had to be working overtime. As I pulled up steeply and turned left to jink and regain altitude, the overheated right gun cooked off a round, and, of course, it had to be a tracer,
and, of course, John had to be in front of me at that moment, and, of course, the round had to pass in front of his windshield so he could see it. He very calmly asked me if I was trying to shoot him down. Good thing we were friends.

John Mansur at Pakse, Laos, 1968

Later, there was another lesson waiting for me out there that did entail a huge difference between the AT-28 and a jet. John and I were hunting targets in the O-1 and AT-28. John knew about a large storage shed in an area that had been overrun by enemy forces and we were going to deny it to them. We found the warehouse and set it up for a strike. We played it by the book for my benefit. John rolled in and put down some smoke. I was in behind him with a pod of rockets. It somehow didn't feel right, but I pressed in and fired.

The rounds went right of target; very embarrassing. Then it dawned on me: prop-driven aircraft have adverse torque when you pull the throttle back, pulling the nose right. Jets don't have that problem, and I wouldn't have had trouble either if I had just rolled in some left trim before roll-in. Just to make me feel bad, John rolled in again and put a single rocket right through the roof, setting the whole place on fire. I later got even on that one.

The Lao pilots had tons of missions behind them, but their flying was founded on very little formal training. They graduated and received USAF wings after only six months of pilot training at Water

Pump. They were qualified for tactical, day, visual-flight-rules (VFR) conditions only. They could not fly at night or on instruments. They knew virtually nothing about simple physics or the theory of flight. Granted, they were not tasked to operate at night or in weather, but it can sometimes be hard to avoid. I had to watch their takeoff times during late afternoon launches to make sure they made it back in daylight.

I flew in the back seat with them to see how they managed tactical procedures. Their bombing procedures seemed safe enough, regarding spacing and roll-in and recovery altitudes. A Mark 82, however, can throw shards 2000 feet, so these parameters are important. One type of munitions delivery was a real thrill. I rode with one of them on a CBU (cluster-bomb-unit) attack. There were four birds in our flight, and we were using lay-down CBU; i.e., a level release close to the ground. It works well for one pass, but you are vulnerable to ground fire making multiple passes that close to the ground.

They had a procedure worked out, however, that "did away with the problem." They would set up a cloverleaf pattern with all four aircraft so that one bird would be on the run-in 90 degrees to the flight path of another bird delivering ordnance. You could actually see another bird streaking across in front of you, punching out CBU bombs. With all four performing like the USAF Thunderbird team, CBU bombs would be hitting the ground and exploding right in front of you as you were coming in on your run. One thing for certain was that no one at ground zero was going to raise their head with all this stuff going on. The procedure was effective, but dangerous, the way they did it. I did get them to loosen up the pattern so one of the aircraft would not run into another aircraft's CBU pellets.

Something else that used to drive me nuts was their habit of rolling in on a defended target and shooting one rocket per pod at a time during the pass. That would put them over the target at least seven times as the LAU-28 pod carried seven rockets. The larger rocket pod carried 19 rounds. Nothing I said so far had any effect on their procedure. Finally, I got them together for a serious discussion on this issue.

"Guys, don't shoot just one rocket at a time; if you keep making multiple passes like that, someone will eventually score a hit on you. They will simply point an automatic weapon at your anticipated flight path, keep the trigger down, and let you fly right through the rounds, and I don't want that to happen. Shoot the whole pod and jink out of the way." Their response floored me. "No, Mr. K, you can't shoot a whole pod of rockets at one time." I asked them why not. They said that I wouldn't understand. This was getting hard to deal with.

"Yes, guys, I will understand, I promise, try me."

After much embarrassed silence, finally: "Aircraft will stop." I couldn't believe what I was hearing, but remember, I was learning a new game with the RLAF. Finally, I just said,: "trust me, the bird won't stop; shoot the whole pod and come home. A few days later, while I was out with John, I fired a pair of inboard pods and glanced at the airspeed indicator. Sure enough, the airspeed flipped back to zero for a moment. The rocket motors obviously create a violently turbulent condition in front of the Pitot tube outside the aircraft, disrupting the airflow. There is also an enveloping mass of flame in front of the aircraft when the pod fires.

I explained this airflow thing to the guys and told them: "You know what stops? Your mind stops; it freezes up for a split second when you fire the whole pod. OK? So there's nothing to worry about." It took a while, but they finally came around.

Pitsami, Jerry Klingaman, Ringo, Frenchy at Pakse, Laos, 1968

One does not manage Lao fighter pilots, and an attempt to do so is not very rewarding. There were little things, like trying to get Frenchy to wear a shirt when flying combat. His normal dress was a pair of olive drab (OD) pants bloused over his boots and nothing above the waist but a survival vest. And there were more serious issues, like the same Frenchy returning from a mission and landing with a full load of napalm because he couldn't find his assigned target. With no radio communication with the aircraft from the ground, I couldn't wave him off and have him jettison the load in a safe area. I explained the hazards of landing and going off our narrow runway with a blown tire and having the whole load ignite, or simply having one can fall off when touching down. "Jettison the napalm in the target area, Frenchy, don't bring it home."

A week later, Frenchy overflew the field heading west with a full load of napalm. He jettisoned the load over the Mekong River and returned for landing. So, we went through the discussion again about jettisoning over the target area. A couple weeks later, I received a note from a fisherman who had lost his boat when it burned up from Frenchy's napalm drop. The note asked why we dropped on him--a fair question. Fortunately, the fisherman had swum out from under the fire and survived. When I brought this up to Frenchy, he told me rather heatedly that it was the fisherman's fault. I asked why that was so. Believe me, you would have to be born and raised in that world to understand the answer: "Because the fisherman was there and in the way."

In a case even more bizarre and startling, a few weeks later I received a letter from someone in Cambodia, demanding payment for the partial loss of a truck convoy that had been attacked by my fighters. I have absolutely no idea how the person in Cambodia knew who I was or that they were my fighters, but this was potentially very bad. Cambodia at that time was hostile and crossing the border was forbidden. I had a little trouble believing it at first, but who else had fighters operating in this area. I got my guys together, showed them the note, and asked them if they had shot up a road convoy. Well, yes, they saw the convoy across the border and went after it with guns.

I wish I could explain why they did this, but there is nothing I can say that contains any logic or makes much sense. They knew that crossing the Lao-Cambodian border was forbidden, but to them, it was a truck convoy in a hostile place and needed to be taken out. The border wasn't important to them; they simply weren't sensitive to such subtleties as sovereign territory, overflight rules, border violations, and diplomatic complaints. In the end, nothing came of it, but given where the attack occurred in Cambodia, it is most unlikely that the convoy had any military significance.

There was a significant commercial trade coming into Laos from Cambodia and China, even during the war years. Our cold beer at "Charlie's," the general store on Pakse's main street, for instance, was Chinese, as were the flashlight batteries, rubber boots, and a thousand other household items.

The logistics lifeline for Cambodia was via the Mekong River on barges from Saigon, with goods for Laos continuing on by truck to Pakse, and eventually Vientiane. Business goes on in Asia even in the middle of a war. I wish I had kept the letter from Cambodia. What a priceless souvenir it would be today.

Responsibilities, Command, and Control

General Phasouk S. Rassaphak exercised command over all Lao military forces in MR 4. Tall and thin, with a very outgoing personality, Phasouk engaged himself in every aspect of his command from detailed campaign planning and execution down to target validation and approval. He even took an active role in the welfare and morale of the Pakse community. There are others more qualified than I am to say how effective he was in all this, but I valued his respect for the RLAF fighter pilots and ground support personnel.

General Phasouk knew that I was an advisor, but he looked to me as organic to his command. How else would it work? There was no one else between the fighter pilots and himself. The RLAF base commander was only involved with housekeeping functions. I reported to Phasouk routinely on such matters as targeting, air tactics, and air integration in ground operations and campaign planning. Going directly to the four-star commander was not an option for any of the Lao fighter pilots.

Job descriptions and responsibilities of all SOF-provided AOC personnel are contained in a 28 January 1971 document entitled "Project 404: History of USAFSOF Participation in Project 404, Palace Dog" This document, now declassified, was prepared by the author for (then) B/Gen Joe Wilson, Commander, USAFSOF.

During the late 1960s, the AOC commander at Pakse was responsible for maintaining the combat readiness of all assigned RLAF AT-28s. At Savannakhet, AOC responsibility extended to assigned C-47 and AC-47 aircraft. USAFSOF understood AOC responsibilities in Laos as follows:

Through coordination with special staff agencies (the CIA) and with senior staff personnel of the Forces Army Royal (FAR) in his military region, the AOC Commander develops targets for strikes by both RLAF and U.S. air in his assigned Military Region and advises the country team and Lao military authorities on the correct employment of air resources. With the exception of certain designated strike zones and special activities areas, he is responsible to the Air Attaché for the employment of all U.S. and RLAF air in his military region. He exercises operational control over the USAF-piloted Raven FAC program at his location. In summary, it is his judgment and his initiative that ultimately insure adequate RLAF and USAF air support for the FAR and for special agency programs in the military region.

A few words are in order here. In MR 4, "designated strike zones" obviously included the trail network to the east of the Bolovens Plateau, and that comprised a huge section of MR 4. The Lao AT-28s never approached the trail; they would have been wiped out quickly if they had, and it was not their mission. Even if they were bulletproof, there was no way for them to tie into the 7th Air Force Command and Control net to maintain up-to-date intelligence and antiaircraft order of battle.

A second point is that the Raven FACs did not work for the AOC commander. They tied into the AOC-supported offense/defense game plan, but command and control, *per se*, was never an issue. If an area of MR 4 was declared off limits by AIRA, Vientiane, that direction would be given to the AOC commander and subsequently passed on to the local Ravens.

The Ravens took part in tactical planning and could easily see what was going on regarding campaign execution. They simply ensured that their own activities lined up with FAR campaign objectives. In that respect, they requested tactical air support, and carried out the final clearing and validation for U.S. airstrikes during the day. Only once did we have to exercise a night air attack option, and that was during the Battle of Thateng.

The Ravens had a senior Raven (Raven 01), but he worked as a circuit rider, going where he was needed for additional FAC coverage. During the Battle of Thateng, for instance, Mel Hart, Raven 01, came down to Pakse to pick up the additional workload. The senior Raven also provided a point of contact at AIRA, Vientiane, for policy and performance issues for all the Ravens.

Locally, there was no one to supervise my activities on a day-to-day basis. My reporting official, whoever he was, lived a long way off at AIRA, Vientiane, which was probably the case for other AOC launch sites. That meant that there was no one locally to report on, or record, what I was doing. Overall results eventually emerged at AIRA through AOC and Agency situation reports. The air attaché visited my location once during my stay at Pakse, and that was during the battle of Thateng.

Being somewhat isolated, with no immediate reporting official, had advantages. I flew the AT-28, and AIRA, Vientiane, knew it. Neither I, nor anyone else they knew, was going to get the RLAF fighter pilots to fly combat every day, and hold the status quo, by sitting in a jeep all day reading a book. So, how did that flying take place? Well, you flew, and didn't mention it to anyone, not because anyone on the American side was trying to catch you out of bounds, but, rather, because no one wanted to hear about it. It was not a matter of trusting or not trusting someone.

Trust had nothing to do with it. We were simply living in a culture of plausible deniability that is inherent to the nature of covert operations. Typically, that culture exists even among members of the covert operating community and extends down to the lowest player level. It permeates everything, like spilled iodine.

Learning about an AOC commander flying AT-28 strikes in 1968 would have generated a tidal wave of indifference within AIRA. The real problem was having it get out of AIRA where someone might have to admit responsibility for letting it happen. So far, no one had done a press-to-test on the issue. That event was several years away, but when it happened, it was bad news.

It is generally understood that surgical black ops are carried out under well-defined military lines of command and control. There are obvious risks associated with these adventures, but operators feel safe in knowing that they are functioning within sanctioned rules of engagement and mission parameters. The covert operator, on the other hand, is often loaned out to other agencies to live in a murky world of hidden identities, purposely vague mission guidelines, and officially disavowed actions--call it beyond the black, if you will. Whatever you call it, achieving mission objectives, i.e., making it happen, may put the operator in the position of making a personal decision not officially sanctioned, and which may be disavowed if compromised. That happened at least once in Project 404.

After six years of covert AOC operations in Laos, the press-to-test on flying combat in the AT-28 finally happened. In 1970, the AOC Commander at Luang Prabang, went down at Nam Bak when he caught his own bomb frag. The Air Attaché at Vientiane was out of town, and an assistant left in charge immediately issued a declamatory message stating that the pilot had been killed while flying an unauthorized combat mission. And there it was: a clear disavowal to distance AIRA, Vientiane, from the accident. I was Director of Operations Plans for USAFSOF at the time, supervising the Command's support of Project 404, so I was called to Langley AFB to report to General Momyer, Commander of Tactical Air Command. (Then) Lt Col Dick Secord flew me up there from Hurlburt Field in one of his squadron's A-37's.

When I walked into General Momyer's office, he started speaking to me before I even reached his desk. There was only one piece of paper on top of his desk—AIRA's message. "Have you seen this? Have you seen this message from AIRA, Vientiane?" He knew I had, but he found the exact wording so offensive that he read it out loud to make his point. And he asked the pertinent question: "How can a fighter pilot lead from the operations shack?" He then went on about Air Force people having to operate under the control of an Ambassador, under embassy constraints, etc. I told him I understood his concerns, and agreed with the need to fly, but the deceased officer left a family, and USAFSOF was concerned about "line-of-duty" status. He was very clear about his position: "Well, it will be line of duty; I promise you that."

And that was the end of our conversation. I flew back to Hurlburt Field with Dick and waited for the other shoe to drop. It did a few weeks later when AIRA, Vientiane, issued a message stating that AOC commanders would not fly AT-28 aircraft in combat and would sign a statement acknowledging the rule.

The proscription was directed at AOC commanders flying strikes; the Ravens were eventually cleared to fly FAC sorties in this aircraft.

The requirement to sign such a statement made the Project 404 AOC commander's position very undesirable and hard to fill. Not many officers in USAFOF were qualified for, or even wanted, this mission. Still, there was a small handful of qualified officers who wanted to do it. For such an individual, living and flying in a remote battle zone was akin to a breathing reflex. He would eventually pick up the pen and sign, greatly complicating his life and putting himself under the gun for the next six months.

Hard Times

Disaster struck hard one afternoon. The local FAR Headquarters chief of staff, several of his own staff members, and my RLAF base commander were visiting a site near Paksong traveling in an H-34 helicopter. On takeoff for return to Pakse, the H-34 failed to clear some power lines and crashed. The bird caught fire, killing everyone on board. The chief of staff's funeral service, held in a large tent in Pakse, was an odd experience. The wife, dressed in white, sat absolutely motionless with no expression on her face. The mistress, dressed in black, was shrieking and crying and throwing her arms around the coffin. She would probably not have been mentioned in the will.

The Pakse base commander was replaced in time by an officer from Vientiane. He had shot an Air America crew member in the face and killed him in an argument over a woman up in Vientiane. I suspect alcohol was involved. His assignment to Pakse was apparently punishment for the crime. He had nothing to do with flight-line operations, but he was in charge of housekeeping, and I needed his support. He had gone through pilot training in France, but had misplaced his wings. I had someone buy a set of Air Force wings at the Udorn Exchange and I pinned them on him informally in front of the base ops building. That act lifted him enormously, and from then on, he was nothing but cooperation.

One is occasionally reminded that personal loss can come suddenly and without warning. As I drove up to the flight line early one afternoon, BT and Ringo were standing by the nearest aircraft waiting for me. They walked up and told me that Pitsami was dead; he was killed riding on the back of Frenchy's motorcycle on the way to town for lunch. The front wheel caught in a deep rut, throwing Pitsami off the bike and into the front of an oncoming truck.

That was difficult news to take. Pitsami was a really good guy who I liked and respected. Also, the most mature, experienced pilot on the team had just been taken out. In the ensuing two days, I probably learned more about Lao culture than I had acquired up to that point. For reasons I cannot explain, Pitsami's death impacted the local military community far more than the chief of staff's. It may have involved his connection to the community, but I suspected it had more to do with the fact that Pitsami faced combat every day, something not very common among the military. He was married, and his parents lived in a village close to Pakse.

I was told there would be a Buddhist cremation if they could raise the money. I appealed to AIRA, Vientiane, via radio for help, and in a few hours, $200 dollars was handed to me in a white envelope. I told the pilots there was money for the cremation. That was good news to them; we could do it right.

Pitsami was taken to the morgue in our little town while a decision was being made on what to do with him. I was told that my turn to sit with the body would be 7:00 that evening. I went to the morgue at the appointed time and entered a small, closed-in room with painted walls and a cement floor. There was nothing in the dimly-lit room except Pitsami. He was lying on the floor in his flight suit. His face had been cleaned, but that was all. I sat down beside him and thought about how different this was from the regulated, sterile approach we take to death in the West. Pitsami had probably died instantly; there was a deep, sizable hole in his forehead where he impacted the truck.

I finished my vigil at 8:00 PM and left to drive home. On the way, General Phasouk and several others came barreling down the road in the opposite direction in a newly-built 1938 Dodge weapons carrier, apparently headed for the morgue. Phasouk was driving. One cannot help but do a double take on the vehicle. In the mid-1960s, Dodge had a large stock of major components and parts for these 1938 vehicles. Through a USAID contract, these components were assembled into complete vehicles for distribution to Laos through the security assistance program. I had one at the AOC in Vientiane.

About 10:00 that evening, Somdet K came to the house and told me to go immediately to the local wat (Buddhist temple) and wait for further orders. Mac wanted to go, so we grabbed a couple weapons and jumped into the jeep for the ride to the wat. When we got there, Pitsami was outside the building in a wood box. The elder bonzes (Buddhist priests) were inside determining what to do. Finally, they decided that we could not do a Buddhist cremation. Cremation was intended to keep bad spirits at bay while the body was being consumed by the flames. In this case, however, Pitsami's body had been breached by the hole in his head, so--given the current phase of the moon—the bad spirits had probably already entered. This was a very disappointing turn of events.

Pitsami had to be buried, but the cemetery was located a good distance northeast of town in an area that we didn't own. So, what to do? General Phasouk made the decision: We would build up an armed convoy and make our way to the cemetery to do the burial. By now, it was past midnight, but we got the convoy assembled with two vehicles carrying ground-mount .50 cal machine guns on pedestals. Pitsami's coffin was loaded on the weapons carrier near the front; Mac and I were located somewhere near the middle of the convoy.

We left Pakse in a cloud of dust with probably 20 vehicles tearing along at very high speed down an old dirt road, bouncing up and down in our seats. Any Pathet Lao in the local vicinity probably fled in terror thinking this was a major night assault. When we arrived, pointed to a spot on the ground and some soldiers started digging a grave.

About halfway down, our four-star general jumped into the hole and began digging furiously with a pickaxe. When the hole was deep enough, the box containing Pitsami was lowered down into it. Somdet K was standing next to Mac and me while all this was going on, and he offered his sad opinion: "Poor Pitsami has left us."

Mac, wanting to be comforting--but in a very Christian way—said, "You know what I think, Somdet? I think that Pitsami is here among us right now." That was not quite the right thing to say to someone steeped in animistic beliefs in an Asian country cemetery at 01:30 in the morning. Somdet's eyes widened dramatically and assumed a startled look. Mac realized the effect of his statement and changed the subject, asking Somdet what would happen next. According to Somdet, the bonzes would determine Pitsami's final disposition. It could be years from now, but someday, depending on the moon's phase and position, the body might be dug up and consigned to the flames in a final cremation ceremony. I have always wondered if that ever happened. I doubt it. Pitsami was never replaced during my tour. The remaining five pilots carried on without their lead pilot. It didn't seem to me that any one of them wanted to step forward to assume the lead position. I left that one alone, as each one could lead a flight, and they were doing just fine.

People deeply respected Pitsami. After all, he was a proven, steady warrior. The chief of staff might have had a fancier casket and a cremation, but a four-star flag officer didn't dig his grave with a pickaxe. There was a large reception for Pitsami a couple days later, with dozens of people in attendance, and I still had the white envelope, now sealed. I had a quick conference with the base commander and quietly briefed him. I told him to give the envelope to Pitsami's wife, and tell her it was from a grateful nation. I watched him every step of the way, and I saw him hand it over. She graciously accepted it, and was obviously pleased.

A Straight Line in the Jungle

General Phasouk's briefing room had a large map on the wall that he used for military discussions and planning. He used to lay his hand over the map near the middle of the Bolovens Plateau and say, "Pathet Lao headquarters for Military Region 4 is somewhere in here; I'm sure of it." One's handprint on a map does not, of course, constitute a target position; it's just something you file away in your mind for another day. Time and events, however, eventually proved him right. The revelation began with an observation made by an experienced, sharp-eyed Raven. PF Reinhart came in one afternoon after being out for a good part of the day. After he shut down and got out of the aircraft, he walked up to me with a puzzled look on his face. "So, what is it, PF?" I asked. He said he had just seen something really strange up on the Bolovens, but didn't know what to make of it. There were all kinds of astonishing sights up there on the Bolovens, so I asked him, "Like how strange; what did it look like?" He said he was flying over a broad expanse of woods on the Bolovens and had caught something out of the corner of his eye that looked like a straight line. When he went back to look, it was gone. Yes, that is strange; there are no straight lines in the jungle. We discussed the possibility of finding it if we went back and searched the area; it seemed to be worth a try. I had a Nikkormat camera with a 105mm lens, so away we went with me in the back seat.

We flew around for a while in an area that PF thought was close and then suddenly he yelled, "There, right there!" I didn't see it, so we circled around for another look. This time I did see it, but only for a moment, and then it was gone. I took some quick shots with the camera. How he found that place again, I will never know. There was a small opening in the canopy off to the side so PF quickly dipped the nose of the bird down into the open space. Looking off to the right, we could see a fairly large group of buildings hidden under the tree canopy with radio antennae strung around on thin poles. The straight line at the top of the jungle canopy was the ridge pole of a roof.

We left immediately and returned to Pakse. John Mansur and I stayed up late that night in the USAID Annex lab developing and printing the shots I took. The next day, I took the photos over to General Phasouk and showed them to him. The site fell in the middle of his hand print on the map. His response was immediate: "Yes, this is PL headquarters MR 4." I asked him what he wanted to do. He said he wanted the place bombed and he was validating the target. I called AIRA, Vientiane, on the Collins and told them that PF and I were going to fly the photos up there the next day and that I would be requesting a USAF strike.

I briefed the target at AIRA the next day and asked for USAF air support with the provision that my Pakse AT-28s lead the strike. AIRA agreed, and someone flew the photos to 7th Air Force Headquarters in Saigon the day after that. I made one huge mistake in that venture that I will always regret: I did not inform the guys in the USAID Annex. I used their lab to process the target film and didn't even tell them what we had found. It was not intentional, just thoughtless. After the target was finally briefed at 7/13th Air Force Headquarters at Udorn, just prior to their strike, the USAID Annex guys caught hell from the head Agency officer for not participating in the target's acquisition.

The 7th Air Force targeting shop gave us a mission date and set our time-on-target (TOT) at 0800 hours. I loaded up the AT-28s with wall-to-wall napalm and guns. During the pre-launch brief, I told the Lao pilots that they would go in first and lead the show. They were flabbergasted by this information; I had never seen them so excited over anything. I wanted the Lao fighter pilots to have the unheard-of privilege of leading an Air Force strike against a preplanned target. Equally important, I wanted them out of there before the F-4s came in at super-luminal speeds. We also laid on two Raven FACs with me in the back of one bird and another Raven in the back of the other.

The next morning, we did not approach the target until the first Raven flew over the target at the assigned TOT and put smoke down. The AT-28s were right in behind him with napalm for low-altitude releases. The napalm cans were smashing the buildings down even as the stuff was igniting. They each made one strafing pass and got out of there. The F-4s were in next, coming in very fast and steep from high altitude dropping some kind of CBU that formed a huge ring on the ground. The Raven bird had put down some more smoke for them but they couldn't get the CBU even close to the target. The stuff went all over the landscape, but it didn't matter; the AT-28s burned the place to the ground.

Learning to Say Goodbye

One day, I saw three AT-28s on initial for the pitch and landing. They were not my birds; mine were either on the ground or off on a strike. After they taxied in and shut down, the pilots walked over to me and just stood there for a few moments before one said, "Hoss is dead. He was shot down and killed." These pilots were from Savannakhet, Wayne Landon's guys, and Hoss was Edward McBride, the Raven FAC at Savannakhet. Hoss's Lao back-seater was also killed. Looking for somewhere to turn, they brought their grief to me.

I already knew that Hoss was a lot more than a FAC to these people. From long association, he had become their mentor, benefactor, and counselor, and now he was gone. They were heartbroken. "How can we go on without him?" they asked. This is the kind of question young men ask when they lose their principal source of direction, approval, praise, and encouragement, as in the death of a parent. Why they flew down to Pakse to ask me this question is something I will never know. I had never met Hoss McBride, and they had never met me until this moment.

Their grief was far deeper than anything I had ever seen in an Air Force fighter squadron when one of the guys was killed. They were standing in a clutch around me and looking straight at me with unshed tears. They wanted an answer, so coming up with the right words at that moment was a bit daunting. I asked them, "What would Hoss say if he could talk to you right now? What would he want you to do? Quit? Would that make him happy?" No, they didn't think that would make him happy at all. "So, what would make him happy?" I think that at least helped them visualize the answer to their own question. They knew what to do, at least in principle; they just had to hear it from someone else.

They would return to Savannakhet and continue flying, but it was far from over. At that moment, these young guys were having trouble adjusting to a life of never-ending combat without their principal source of protection. One would have to personally experience this to understand it, but someone like Hoss can be a truly magic protector, a god that wraps his arms around you and ensures you never come to harm. This is all bound up in an unshakable belief in certain people and things in which spirits live and roam, and which animate the world.

To them, Hoss was magic, pure and simple, and they believed in him, just as they believed in the power of the Buddha amulets they wore around their necks. I wore one as well, or my guys would have been far less willing to put their lives in my hands. Hoss had been more than a fellow warrior and friend. He bought them orange juice and vitamins, and coached them on how to survive. They stayed alive under his spiritual grace, and now they would have to learn how to live without him. That would not be easy; it would take time. They left Pakse, and I never saw them again.

The Battle of Thateng

Three of the Lao pilots returned from a strike one morning and taxied in quite hurriedly. When they got out of their aircraft, they were obviously excited, and asked for an immediate turnaround. On their way to a pre-planned target, they had intercepted a call "for anyone listening" from Hong Tong (Golden Swan), the ground controller's call sign at a major FAR site outside the town of Ban Thateng. The site was under attack, with enemy forces already on the perimeter wire. The FAR garrison was desperate for immediate help.

Fortunately, the AT-28s were only minutes away from the site, and they just happened to be carrying four cans of napalm each. Also, the enemy had chosen to make their attack in broad daylight, which put them at an extreme disadvantage. The pilots arrived in short order and put their napalm down on top of the attacking force. They followed up with strafing runs and beat it back home.

We reloaded the aircraft with more napalm and .50 cal rounds and sent them out again. By the time they returned to Thateng, the attack was over, so they put their munitions down on the surrounding tall grass and flew home. An unknown number of enemy personnel were killed that morning, but equally important, two of them were captured at the perimeter wire, and they were NVA soldiers, injured during the napalm run.

An RLAF H-34 helicopter from Pakse flew out to Thateng and brought the prisoners back. I was standing on the flight line when they arrived, both of them on stretchers. One raised himself up and looked over at me and at the AT-28s. I'm sure he realized that these were the attacking aircraft. The two were flown to Vientiane and put on show as evidence of an NVA combat presence in Laos. I don't think we realized at the time how much of a presence it would become, but one thing was clear: North Vietnamese regulars were in the game at Thateng.

Thateng guarded the northern entrance to the Bolovens Plateau. The Bolovens, abandoned by the French years earlier, was now mostly wild, lightly populated with small, very primitive tribal groups, and essentially undefended by FAR ground forces. I thought it was one of the most glorious places I had ever seen, with large expanses of open grasslands, jungle, mountainous terrain, and enormous waterfalls that ended in deep pools in rock caverns. The open fields now lay fallow and covered with tall wild grass. Two-story French farmhouses, now abandoned and practically buried in a sea of grass, stood vacant, the empty windows staring out into the void.

The plateau was also widely known as having some of the most fertile soil in all of Southeast Asia. Sharply-rising terrain surrounding the Bolovens made approaches from the east and south problematic, and an approach from the west was complicated by the presence of FAR forces. That left the pass at Ban Thateng. If the enemy captured Thateng and overran the Bolovens, they would have literally taken the high ground plus an enormous amount of real estate, making further incursions into MR 4 much easier and quicker.

This attack was particularly worrying to AIRA as well as to the Royal Lao Government. Combined Pathet Lao and NVA forces had overrun and captured at least one major town and its military enclave every dry season during previous years. Laongam fell in early 1967, and apparently it was now Thateng's turn. Previous losses were major setbacks, but the strategic implications of losing Thateng included giving PL /NVA forces a clear run across the top of the Bolovens and a position from where they could launch an attack down the west slope into Pakse on the Mekong River.

Adding to this worry was clear evidence that enemy preparations were underway to attack Attapeu, the largest town south of the Bolovens. Pakse, with its back against the Mekong, would then be open to attacks swinging around from the north and south ends of the Bolovens as well as from down the west slope. From my perspective, the loss of these sites was inevitable, but the immediate prospects did not bode well for a strategy of maintaining the status quo to buy time.

Follow-on attacks at Thateng seemed to be mostly probing actions, but they had the effect of wearing down the garrison and running it out of supplies. Knowing the vulnerability of the site, the FAR at Pakse attempted to resupply and bolster the garrison with supplies, munitions, and food. They mounted up a truck convoy at Paksong and drove it north along the main route across the Bolovens towards Thateng. Less than halfway along the route, the convoy was ambushed. Nothing else was known except that the convoy failed to reach Thateng. There was no word of its exact location or the number of casualties.

John Mansur and I took off in an O-1 for the Bolovens and flew down the road looking for the convoy. We finally came up on it and made a high-speed run (100 knots) along the stalled line of trucks flying about 50 feet in the air. No wrecks and no sign of life or casualties. It did not even appear to have been looted. Nothing exciting, but when John pulled the nose up, the engine quit. That was very exciting. A quick change of fuel tanks and things got going again. That was a good thing, since walking out of there was a poor option, but it left open the question of why we flamed out.

I was always curious about what happened to the FAR soldiers in the convoy. Tall native grass as high as the tops of the trucks grew right up to the edge of the narrow road. They may have escaped into the grass and made their way back on foot, but we never found out. Whatever the case, the Thateng enclave, comprising some 300 soldiers, did not get resupplied. The situation was complicated by the fact that the site was located across a small creek from the town of Ban Thateng, and the soldiers' families lived in the town.

With the site surrounded and pinned down by mortar fire, NVA and PL forces attacked and overran the town Ban Thateng. The town had no telephone or wireless communication with the outside world, so we never learned the fate of its citizens. Presumably, they fled before the attacking forces, but their losses and whereabouts were never reported.

After several weeks of fighting, the garrison called airstrikes on the town because the enemy had assembled forces and taken up mortar positions there. Ban Thateng was eventually destroyed, presenting a sad sight from the air. The houses were torn open, revealing bits and pieces of household goods, furniture, and personal clothing. The flattened town now glittered in the sunlight with the reflection of broken windows, bottles, and mirrors.

More attacks came from machine gun and mortar fire. The worst of it was from 13 to 18 December. At times, it seemed as if a frontal assault was only minutes away. We put everything we could get our hands on into an effort to defend the site from the air. I had my own AT-28s, and the Ravens could call in Air Force and Navy fighters. To exercise air control at night, we had a Nail FAC with a Lao validating and translating officer in the second seat orbiting the site. Ground control (Hong Tong) could talk to the Nail, requesting strikes by U.S. fighters, and the Nail FAC could relay this to the ABCCC. The ABCCC would call me at the house in Pakse (call sign—Berlin), passing on target description, attack-aircraft type, and ordnance loads, and I would reply with a "go" or "no-go." If it was a "go," the ABCCC would send fighters to the Nail. The Nail could carry flares, but we also had USAF C-47 flare assets come in at critical times to light the area for the fighters and the ground site.

Something very odd happened one night. The ABCCC called me to say that the Nail was reporting the presence of another light aircraft, a slow-mover of some kind, flying around the Thateng site. The Nail could not identify the aircraft type as it was moving in and out of the flare light on the other side of the illuminated circle. With the flare swinging back and forth under the chute casting large, dark shadows rocking around against the background darkness, the whole scene would have been somewhat disorienting.

I had the ABCCC confirm there were no other U.S. aircraft in the local area and then called the USAID Annex and asked if they had anything out there. They gave me a negative, so I told them they better be sure, because I intended to identify the target as hostile. Yes, they were sure. I gave the ABCCC a "go" for a shootdown, but there were no assets available to deal with it. Every time the Nail tried to move over to the other side of the circle, the target would melt away into the darkness. Someone with a lot of skill, and a lot of interest in Thateng, wanted to see what was going on there.

As the U.S. fighters were out there at night with dumb bombs, we did not attempt close-air-support on the perimeter wire. Still, we were able to keep things under control at night using eyes-on Nail FAC inputs against what we believed were enemy fallback positions. During daylight, we put bombs, CBU, and napalm right up to the wire. Given all the resources employed here, this constituted a major joint-combined, defensive air operation. We were told later that the counterattack inflicted "extremely heavy losses" on the attacking forces.

John Mansur spent hours over the site marking perimeter targets for strikes by U.S. air. The AT-28s could communicate directly in Lao with the ground controller, Hong Tong, but precise enemy positions were hard to determine. In my estimation, acquiring precise, valid locations of enemy forces was the most difficult, frustrating aspect of the whole mission. At one point, John Mansur left for 20 Alternate, and Ken Eli came down to replace him. Ken Eli, like John and PF, could fly the crate the thing came in and was fun to be around. I flew several FAC missions with Ken. PF Reinhart cycled in and out of Pakse to ensure that we always had two Ravens on station.

John returned from Alternate to pick up the FAC mission. After he taxied in and shut down, he handed me his helmet. There were two holes in the visor where an AK-47 round had passed through it. I put it on, pulled down the visor, and inserted a pencil through the holes. The pencil just brushed the bridge of my nose. I think he was marking targets for A-1Es over the PDJ when that happened. He was momentarily blinded from small shattered pieces of Plexiglas, but with the help of the A-1s, he was able to fly in an orbit long enough to clear his eyes and find a small field off the edge of the PDJ to land on. After that incident, AIRA sent him down to me at Pakse.

Shortly after his arrival, I was informed that Air Force fast movers were going to lay down a barrier of CBU mines sealing off the site. Some of the mines would detonate on contact with the ground. Others would throw out little pellets connected to the bomb by very fine green threads extending outward about three feet. Disturbing one of the threads caused the bomb to explode. In time, the remaining bombs would sterilize themselves by blowing up.

I was against this plan as it would trap the garrison, giving them no future options and preventing escape, although I suspected that was the reason AIRA was doing this in the first place. I asked that a space be left open between the site and the town so the garrison could have access to water from the creek. At least that much was granted.

Laying down the CBU barrier required extreme precision, as the mines would be placed right up to the perimeter wire. John worked out a way to get this degree of precision: He would mark a run-in IP and release point with WP smoke and give the fighter a heading to make the straight low-altitude bomb run. The procedure worked, and a little corridor was left open for water access.

After a couple weeks of doing close air support and reseeding the mine barrier, it was obvious that John needed some time off. One has to keep in mind that Ravens were flying five and six hours of combat every day, all of it below 1500 feet and within the small-arms envelope. It was an intense life for everyone. So John took off for Hawaii to meet his wife and decompress a bit. While he was gone, the mine barrier had sterilized itself and had to be reseeded.

Another FAC came in to mark the IP and release points. From a purely technical standpoint, this was the toughest mission a FAC could take on. During the run-in, the fighter is very low to the ground, maybe 50 feet, and moving at several hundred knots. I know what a 50-foot run-in at 500 knots looks like from the cockpit of an F-100, for an over-the-shoulder bomb release, and you don't see a great deal to the side. For whatever reason, something went wrong during the lay-down part of this mission. The fighter took up a heading just slightly off course and carried the CBU release line directly over the site, killing nine of the garrison soldiers outright.

Now, the CBU would start going off at preset times. The garrison soldiers had been briefed about the characteristics of these mines so they put together wooden barriers they could move forward and hide behind to shoot at the bombs. This was a desperate measure, but it worked. There were already casualties from machine gun and mortar fire, and most of the wounded were lying in depressions above ground. Nobody could get to them from the entrenchments because of enemy machine gun fire. People threw food and water to them from the entrenchments. It was time for an emergency helicopter evacuation.

Local H-34 helicopters tried several times to carry out an evacuation, but aborted each time because of enemy fire. Each time, before they went in, we would pound the surrounding area with bombs and rockets to suppress ground fire. It still didn't work. Finally, a couple H-34s actually went in and landed long enough to pack the birds full of wounded.

I met the H-34 pilots when they landed at Pakse to congratulate them. They were glassy-eyed with fright, but they did it. Fortunately, some white envelopes materialized at the last minute, and that's the way it works sometimes. I know this is hard to believe, but the surviving wounded had been lying in the open on top of the site for 21 days before their recovery. Most of the wounded died. It was gruesome and pathetic.

Frank Dean helping unload the Thateng wounded at Pakse, 1969

The air attaché, Colonel Robert L. F. Tyrrell, came down to Pakse during the worst of the siege to discuss the enemy's campaign and our defense options. Neither of us was under any illusions about this situation. The enemy could attack in force any time they chose, and our defenders stood at less than 300 people, all trapped inside a minefield. I gave him my opinion that Thateng was a serious, must-do objective for the enemy.

My first indication of the enemy's resolve was when I was over the site one day and could see communications lines strung from the tops of poles leading north into the woods. I had neither seen nor heard of anything like this before. The enemy was obviously exercising command and control and directing logistics from a command site located some distance from Thateng. Following this line through the woods to its source was hopeless, but it helped me understand who was orchestrating events in this combat; the Pathet Lao did not build hard-line communications to do anything.

The area around Thateng looked like the surface of the moon from heavy bombing. Tyrrell told me that the Agency estimated I had killed more than a thousand soldiers of the attacking force during the siege. Whatever it cost the Pathet Lao, or whoever was doing the main fighting, our people on the ground were in pitiful condition and becoming less viable as a defending force every day.

It seemed as if the siege would never end, but Thateng finally fell after two months of horrendous fighting, suffering, and survival. With the dry season coming to an end, and the rains coming, it probably occurred to the enemy that it was time to get it over with, and they did it Lao style. We simply woke up one morning and the garrison was gone. The site had been abandoned.

I will admit to knowing many mysteries and few facts about anything in Laos, and the abandonment of Thateng is no exception. How the plan was communicated to the garrison inside the wire, I'll never know, but, apparently, the enemy opened up a corridor to the north of the site and let the garrison leave. I don't think the barrier was mined at the time.

If this is what actually happened, then the enemy got what it wanted: ownership of the northern gateway to the Bolovens, and the garrison got what it wanted: freedom. If only PL force had been involved, I would have no trouble believing this story. With the NVA involved, I don't know.

The loss of Thateng was not the beginning of the end; that had already happened with the previous loss of other key sites in MR 4. Losing Thateng only accelerated things. Our strategic thinking in Washington, as focused as it was on winning in Vietnam, probably didn't include the loss of Thateng. For the Royal Lao Government and its forces, however, the loss was a catastrophe. It was also another example that air interdiction and close air support, no matter how cleverly applied, do not necessarily offset, or somehow balance out, the presence of a large, determined ground force. We have a tendency to overestimate the efficacy of airpower.

Raven 50

While Thateng was still under siege, the situation suddenly became desperate again with attacks closing in from all directions, and John Mansur was not back from leave. It was also time to reseed the CBU barrier. I had an O-1 aircraft sitting on the flight line at that moment, but no Raven FAC or O-1 crew chief. I had received a call from the USAID Annex telling me that John Mansur was at Ubon Air Base, Thailand, but had no transportation to Pakse. I asked him if he would please provide an aircraft to give John a lift. Unfortunately, there were no aircraft of any kind available. That was one of the problems of living so far off the beaten path. Flying a Lao AT-28 combat machine into Thailand and landing at Ubon AB was not an option, and I really needed John to get things sorted out at Thateng.

I called AIRA that evening and asked them to contact John through Ubon Base Operations and tell him that his ride would arrive at 1000 hours the next day. The next morning, I told Mac to grab his weapon and ride with me to the flight line. Of course, he wanted to know what was going on. I told him, "I'll show you when we get there." On arriving, I drove up to the O-1, got out of the jeep, and crawled into the O-1 cockpit. This should be easy, I thought, but I wanted to see it done right the first time. "Mac, show me how to start this thing."

"Sure," he said, and reached into the cockpit to set things up, and then—"No, I'm not going to do this; I'm not going to be a part of it." I reminded him, in good humor that just because he was in civilian clothes didn't mean I couldn't give him a direct order. He told me I could get the paper work ready for a summary court-martial, but he was not going to do it, period. So, I said: "OK, fine, I'll start it myself." Well, that changed everything. My trying to start that beautiful engine, and possibly blowing a cylinder head off, was apparently much worse than a court-martial, because he reached in and got it started. I taxied out to the end of the runway, did a mag check, and took off. You don't ask for clearance to take the active at Pakse, because there isn't anyone to talk to. It was a gorgeous day, and the flight to Ubon was extremely pleasant. I flew in very low so I wouldn't show up on radar and get waved off or wind up answering a lot of awkward questions. About a mile out, I popped up and called in: "Ubon, this is Eagle Black. I'm an O-1, about a mile out; request landing instructions." The Lao pilots used the call signs Eagle Red, White, or Blue, so it seemed appropriate that I take Eagle Black as my call sign in the AT-28. I was using it now in the O-1.

The come-back was predictable: "Eagle Black, please state base of departure." I told him I came from the east and didn't want to go into details. The tower operator, an American, said: "Roger, Eagle Black, you're clear for a straight-in approach and landing." That was easy; he got the idea.

I taxied up to base ops, and there was John standing outside, all smiles, with a ghetto-blaster and an enormous B-4 bag stuffed full of dirty clothes. I didn't shut down, because I didn't want to go through the engine-start thing again. An airman on the flight line helped John get into the back seat and then piled the ghetto-blaster and B-4 bag on top of him, with the control stick stowed.

I got takeoff clearance, and we were on our way. John hadn't said anything up to that point, but on the climb out, it finally dawned on him what was going on. I could feel the airplane jiggle around a little bit. It was John thrashing around in the back seat desperately trying to get the control stick into the floor socket. There was no way he could do that, not with the B-4 bag on his lap. He gave up and finally got the headset on. I waited for the inevitable question: "Mr. K, when did you solo this airplane?"

"About 15 minutes ago, John." Silence; and then, a low moaning sound. That was funny beyond words, and I could imagine poor Mac back at Pakse praying I wouldn't crash so he wouldn't have to answer questions about his involvement in this caper. There was nothing John could do, so we just talked about his R&R and the situation at Thateng. When we got into the Pakse traffic pattern, and I set the bird up to land, John started up with: "Now, keep the downwind leg out a bit more to allow some room to maneuver; etc., etc." I had to bring that stuff to an end, so: "John, please be quiet, you'll make me crash and kill both of us." That was great fun; and it was fun to have John back. He was a real friend to me in those days, and he remains so to this day.

I started flying the O-1 when a spare was available and not on standby for a Raven FAC mission. PF Reinhart even took me out in the bird to coach me on calling in fast movers. My radio operator had been cooped up in the tiny comm room at the house for weeks on end and needed to see something of the outside world. He wanted to go up in the O-1, so I took him with me on a reconnaissance flight to the north along the main road from Savannakhet to check out what John and I were convinced was a brand new truck park.

The new box-like, windowless buildings with thatched roofs were located about four miles from the main road. They were each about the size of a gravel truck and perfectly aligned in five rows of five buildings for a total of 25 truck hangars. There were no vehicle tracks around the area, as it had obviously been swept clean to eliminate all visual evidence.

Actually, the evidence was a couple acres of perfectly-swept ground. I wanted to take them out quietly with WP rockets, but the target was too close to a well-traveled road to simply take them out, and the ambassador wouldn't allow it. I'm sure those 25 hangars were set up in preparation for an offensive sometime in the future. The NVA always led with logistics; i.e., tail in first, and then the teeth.

Over time, other sites in Laos had O-1 engines quit and start up again. Fortunately, no one went down, but the reason was simple: contaminated fuel. We started filtering all the O-1 fuel through a chamois we bought locally, and contacted AIRA, Vientiane, requesting assistance through USAID's supply manager, but to no avail. The contract tankers from Thailand obviously needed to be cleaned out, but AIRA, for some reason, chose to ignore our warnings. Filtering fuel through chamois works, but it is a very slow, tedious process, so, after being told by AIRA, again, that there was nothing wrong, I drained some fuel out of the wing of an O-1 into a clear plastic bag. The bottom of the bag was filled with heavy mud sediment. AIRA was a bit miffed when I told them I was coming up to Vientiane to discuss the issue, but I went anyway. John and I flew up in the O-1 with me in the back seat holding the plastic bag.

After arriving, I entered the AIRA office and walked up to the Director of Operations holding the bag up in front of his eyes. He looked at it, and only then did he recognize how serious the problem really was. Apparently, he had never seen anything like this before--couldn't even imagine it. People don't realize what sheltered, protected lives they live in the United States Air Force. We finally got AIRA to call the right people and get it sorted out.

I stayed at the Ice House that evening. While we were having supper at the big round table, the senior command post officer came up, knelt down beside me, and asked: "Jerry, are you flying the O-1?" He wasn't smiling, and I had that little shiver go up my spine that told me I was in trouble. I just told him flat out that I was, indeed, flying the airplane. I wasn't expecting his response.

"OK, great, there is an O-1 coming out of phase maintenance at Udorn tomorrow, and since the bird is for Pakse, could you fly it down there?" I told him I could, trying to keep my face as expressionless as possible. Then he said: "Pakse has 50 series call signs, and since you are the AOC commander you will take zero as the second digit, so you will be Raven 50." And that is the reason why, today, I belong to the Edgar Allen Poe Literary Society.

As a side note, after Laos fell to the Communists almost six years later, I was visiting Udorn to help with the repatriation of Khmer military refugees and their families to Camp Pendleton, CA. While I was at Udorn, Al Galante took me out in an O-1 for a full Form-8 check ride. In fact, the last landing I ever made in an Air Force airplane was with Al. After all those years, Al finally made a legal O-1 pilot out of me. Thanks, Al.

Flying Boun Toum's Wing

About a month from the end of my tour, BT walked up one morning and asked me to go with him to hit a target about 80 miles to the northeast. He would lead, and I would fly number two position. That was perfect; I'm sure he wanted to show me how well he could fly lead, as if he had to, and for me it was a huge privilege flying his wing. On an earlier raid in this area, I had tied into a POL cache starting a fierce blaze with billowing black smoke, so maybe we would get lucky on this one. Taxiing out to the end of the runway for takeoff, I remember thinking that I was exactly where I wanted to be at that moment—imbedded in a Lao fighter unit, sharing their experiences.

BT spoke decent English, but it hardly mattered; he did everything with hand signals. It's hard to recall all this in detail, but I believe John Mansur met us at the target and put some smoke down for us. When we arrived at the target, I dropped back for spacing. BT rolled in, and I was in a few seconds behind him. We each made another pass, getting rid of our ordnance, and went home. John left in another direction hunting targets. BT and I stayed fairly low on the way back. When the field came into sight, BT pushed the nose over slightly and started picking up speed. We would be landing to the north.

I moved in close to him, tightening it up, so we would have a decent-looking formation for the pitch. As we came in from the southeast, gradually bending around to the north, BT reduced our altitude even more and took up the runway heading. It was clear what he was going to do, something outlawed in the Air Force since Korea. Getting ready for it, I pushed the mixture and prop levers forward and stacked up just a hair. By now we were booming along very low and very fast heading towards the end of the runway.

About halfway down the runway at, maybe, 30 feet, we pitched up off the deck to downwind leg like a couple P-51 pilots coming back from a brawl with ME 109s over Nazi Germany. Of course, our flight back wasn't all that dramatic, merely returning from a set of coordinates over the jungle, but it was our flight, and it was mine to remember forever, one of the prize moments of my life.

One might wonder how something like that can be so important to someone, and I'm at a loss to explain, but coming in from a raid on the wing of a Lao fighter pilot, and a friend, was much more than simply memorable. I believe it is in the cinema version of Faulkner's *The Reivers,* where it is revealed that such moments of glory come very rarely, but when they do, they are the best of all.

Jerry Klingaman with AT-28 at Pakse, Laos, 1968

It kills me now to think of BT spending years in a Communist "reeducation camp" somewhere in Laos, as I was told. Being a fighter pilot and warrior who had killed his fair share of PL and NVA troops, he probably had a hard time surviving, if he survived at all. I would like to think that he escaped, or was released, but who knows?

End of the Tour

Approaching the end of my tour, the security situation around Pakse had deteriorated considerably. The ammo dump at the base had come under mortar attack several times, and small PL units (probably reconnaissance probes) were maneuvering within a few miles of our house in the country, three miles south of town. Our attack warning system at the house, however, was probably as good as anything going at that time. Our German shepherd, Tiger, would suddenly run for the alcove at the top of the stairs, tuck his tail between his legs, and start whining. Sure enough, within seconds you could hear the first mortar rounds impacting near the ammo dump, and you could see the impact flashes from the corner window of the northeast bedroom.

General Phasouk was not happy with us being that far out in the country, so he assigned an armed security detail to patrol around the house during hours of darkness. That *was* dangerous. The security guys were tooled up with automatic weapons they really weren't trained to use, and they were skittish moving around in the dark. Phasouk made AIRA aware of the situation and someone leased a brand new house for us in town. More white envelopes.

The first night in a new Asian house is usually a nightmare, and this one was no exception. It was stinking hot, and we all woke up on the first morning with our eyes almost swollen shut from mosquito bites. It takes a while to get all holes plugged and the air conditioner sorted out.

My replacement, Carl Leuchner, arrived on our third day in the new house. Carl, as you might recall, was the pilot who gave me my initial checkout in the AT-28 at Hurlburt Field. Carl was excited to be there, and I was excited for him. The next day was to be my last full day in Laos; I had been notified by AIRA that I would be extracted by C-47 the day after that. The next morning, I asked Carl if he would like to go out to the field, have a look around, and fly a combat mission with me to get things started. Yes, he would like that very much.

We drove out to the field, where we found BT at the hangout shack. I introduced the two of them, and proposed we go out to the Laongam area as a flight of three for an armed recce sortie. BT was all for it, so we crawled into three birds that were already loaded with munitions and started engines. We taxied out as Eagle-Black lead, two, and three. I led this one, because it was new terrain to Carl. Most importantly, the mission got Carl off on a good start with the Lao pilots. That was crucial. After we came home from the mission and landed, I waited for everyone to roll out at the far end of the runway and assemble in the run-up area. We then taxied back to the ramp in close, staggered trail. It felt good, but it was the last time I would fly the AT-28.

Back at the house, Carl and I cracked open cold beers and went outside to talk. Carl was pumped up as he was already in the fray, and I felt good because I was still alive and had completed my mission. While I was there, the Pakse fighter pilots took the record for the largest number of AT-28 combat sorties flown from one site in a single month. They had come a long way since the days of one mission per week.

It had been drizzling while Carl and I were talking, and then it started coming down in torrents. It was the first rain I had seen during my tour at Pakse; the dry season had ended. Carl and I stood there in the down-pouring rain, still talking, with big grins on our faces. What an incredibly wonderful feeling.

The next morning a C-47 flew in and picked up my USAFSOF team. The pilot was Dick Pollard, a close friend and sailing companion from the old 319th Air Commando Squadron at Hurlburt Field. I don't know where he got the airplane, or who he was working for, and I didn't ask.

Mac, Frank, Stan, and I were the only ones on board except Dick Pollard and his copilot and flight engineer. I sat in back and watched Pakse recede into the distance as we crossed the border into Thailand and, this time, it was a bit emotional. It was like watching an unforgettable piece of your life break off and drift away. I don't know how you can leave something like that behind and not feel emotional about it.

Epilogue

Having to dig up and visualize the details of these events 45 years after they happened is probably part of the reason I avoided writing this account for so long. I'm glad that Craig Duehring made me do it, however, because I owe it to the Lao fighter pilots at Pakse. This is probably the last, and only, time someone records the existence of that small fighter unit in the south of Laos. Few people know what happened to us in that almost unknown place.

In bringing this chronicle to a close, the very least I can do is record the names of these RLAF pilots so they will be remembered in some kind of document. I wish I could see them again, but that will never happen. They are gone now, and they have been gone for a long time. Pitsami, as I told you, was killed in a motorcycle accident in 1968. Sometime after 1970, Pong Pat (Frenchy) hit a mountain and was killed. Somdet K and Somdet H were both shot down and killed, sometime after 1970. I was told that Sohn (Ringo) may have made it out before the end, but that was only hearsay. Boun Toum (BT), according to another source, was sent to a "reeducation" camp. As a fighter pilot, he probably didn't make it out of there alive.

These young warriors, who were principal instruments in our covert war in Laos, flew combat six or seven days per week on two dollars a day plus a morning meal. They had no operable parachutes or rescue beepers, and their survival vests had nothing of value in them. The AT-28 chutes were so old that the silk was worn down through several layers of canopy. Yet, these were the pilots who prevented the Pathet Lao and North Vietnamese from overrunning the most populous areas of MR 4 until the war in Viet Nam came to an end.

I still feel badly about this. These were the guys I advised and flew with. I played guitar and sang with them (in Lao) at the village festival, and I sent them to combat every day. I wore their flight suit and fought under their flag. These were the guys we used up to maintain the status quo.

I am well aware that an advisor can identify too closely with the people he is advising and flying with, but identifying was part of being a Project 404 AOC commander and advisor. Somewhere along that fine line between caring enough and caring too much, you had to convince them that you had an interest in keeping them alive and well, and you couldn't fake it. You and your advisory team were all they had for direction, encouragement, and praise for the risks they took. My risk of covertly leading this small combat force was nothing compared to theirs.

Having only a tenuous attachment to the Air Force while deployed in-country, AOC commanders typically cast their lot with the RLAF flyers. As they were subject to the same fate, no one should be surprised if the AOC commanders identified more closely with the Lao combat pilots than with their Air Force counterparts outside Laos. What an AOC commander did to make it work could have serious repercussions, and there were few rewards, but that was part of the mission in the late 1960s. For most of us, however, the mission was its own reward. It had to be. It certainly was for me.

So, I just want to throw a nickel on the grass for Pitsami, Ringo, BT, Somdet K, and Somdet H. They were a great team, and I will always be part of it, if only as the one who lived to tell this Raven's tale about the ones who were, and always will be—brave hearts, forever young.

Frenchy, Somdet K, Ringo, BT, and Somdet H at Pakse, Laos, January 1969

Chapter 27

Lloyd Duncan, Raven 42
Pakse, Nov 1970 – Jun 1971

I started my combat career in December 1969 flying OV-10s out of Nakhon Phanom (NKP), Thailand. My call sign was Nail 36. After two months I volunteered to go down to Ubon, Thailand, and flew missions over the southern half of the Ho Chi Minh Trail in Laos. Our mission was to find trucks and guns on or near the trail. The North Vietnamese Army (NVA) protected the trail with lots of antiaircraft artillery (AAA)—primarily 14.5 mm, 23 mm, and 37 mm. We flew four-hour missions at 4,500 feet above the ground in a random pattern and used binoculars to look for the enemy. At first, getting shot at scared me to death. The tracers were like streams of death coming up to get me. After a while, though, I got used to it and even welcomed it. It was difficult to find active guns—but once they shot at you it didn't take long to find them. Then you could use the rest of the time on station making sure they didn't have a nice day. I would direct fighters to the target with smoke rockets, they would drop their ordnance, usually bombs or cluster bomb units (CBUs), on the target (hopefully). Once the laser-guided bomb (LGB) was introduced things changed quickly. The enemy stopped shooting at us during the day, because the LGB was so accurate and so deadly.

The year went by quickly and I wasn't ready to leave. Four of us from Ubon—Frank Kricker, Eric Erickson, Jim Withers, and myself—all volunteered to extend our tour and become Raven FACs. Frank, Eric, and I were assigned to the southernmost base at Pakse, Laos. Pakse was a small town on the Mekong River about 100 miles due east of Ubon, Thailand. We flew small unmarked Cessna airplanes—the O-1 Bird Dog and the U-17 (Cessna 185). The base was also home to a squadron of Laotian T-28s. The CIA also worked out of Pakse and used Air America H-34 helicopters, C-46s, C-130s, C-123s, and Helio Couriers. Continental Air Service also flew Pilatus Porters in support of the CIA. Our main area of operation was about 50-100 miles east of Pakse on the Bolovens Plateau. We flew out of several small dirt strips but the main one was Pakse Site 22 (PS-22). The CIA was in charge of operations at PS-22. We flew there to get gas, rockets, and intel of enemy activity. If I had the first go of the day, I would plan to arrive a little after sunrise and log a 10-12 hour flying day. The O-1 could not fly very high so we flew it at treetop level most of the time. The enemy could only shoot you if you flew right over them. In the OV-10 we usually flew 80 hours a month and had four days off in Bangkok. In the O-1 we flew 150 hours a month and had five days off in Bangkok. More on that later.

At Pakse, we all flew the O-1 and the U-17. Both were taildraggers. The O-1 was a two-seater (front and back) and the U-17 was a four-seater (two and two). The U-17 was not as good a FAC plane as the O-1 so we used it more for a spare and to fly to Ubon to get our mail and haul beer. The cargo area could hold about 20 cases of beer and we went through a lot of beer for some reason. One day, I think it was Larry "Pepsi" Ratts, flew the U-17 over to Ubon to get the mail, etc. After landing he taxied to the parking area in front of Base Ops. He got out of the plane, walked to the tail, and pissed on the tail wheel. This was a common thing we all did in Laos and he didn't think twice about it. Well, the Ubon Base Ops officer (an Air Force lieutenant colonel) came running out of the building screaming at Pepsi—"Get your ass off my airfield and don't ever come back!!" We got no beer or mail that day.

Normally there were five Ravens assigned to Pakse. Frank and Eric were already there when I arrived in November 1970. Joe Smith and Larry Ratts were the other two. We stayed in a fairly nice house a couple of miles from Pakse and about a mile from the airfield. We had a cook, a maid, a gardener, and a night guard, who only had one leg. We all thought this was a big plus because he probably would not be able to "book" very easily if the bad guys showed up. We paid each of them about one dollar a day—500 Kip in Laotian money. I really liked our cook but also teased her a lot. After she cooked us a nice meal, she would always ask, "Sep Lai, boh?" (Very good, no?) I would reply, "Boh sep!" (No good!) Then she would scold me and say, "You number loy!" In Thailand and in Laos, if something was very good it was "Number One." If it was very bad it was "Number 10." Number Loy was number 100 in Lao and it sounded like my name—Lloyd.

I was in charge of ordering all the food for our group from the commissary in Vientiane. Once a week, an Air America C-130 would land and deliver the supplies that I had ordered. Our cook was really pretty good and we ate well. We also went downtown to a good Chinese restaurant on a regular basis. Each night after dinner, we would have a short meeting—about 30 seconds—and decide who had the early go the next day. Frank and I usually alternated every other day. I don't know what the other three did. Actually, usually one of us was on a CTO (combat time off) in Bangkok, one flew to Ubon to get our mail and buy beer, and the other three flew between 6 and 12 hours, getting after the bad guys. On the days I had the early go, I would leave the house a little before sunrise, pick up my favorite backseater Pantee, get in the O-1, and head east to the Bolavens Plateau. It took about an hour to get there flying at 90 miles an hour. The main outpost/airfield on the Bolovens was PS-22.

It had a 3000 foot runway and several wooden buildings that were used by several different groups. The CIA ran the outpost but there were also Lao Army, Lao mercenaries, Air America, Continental Air Service Incorporated (CASI), Ravens and sometimes USAF H-53s using it. Only the Lao Army and some mercenaries stayed there during the night. When I got there in the early morning, I would try calling them on the radio but often there was no answer. If I got no answer, I would make a low pass over the field to have a look and see if anyone shot at me. If all looked normal I'd land and park. Sometimes the CIA guys were circling overhead—very high—waiting to see if all was safe. I was their guinea pig. One day late in my tour, I made a low pass and NVA soldiers—who had taken the outpost during the night—hosed me down with their AK-47s as I went by. I escaped unharmed, but if they had just let me land I would have been toast.

Lloyd Duncan, Cambodian officer and backseater Pantee at PS-22

The "customers" at PS-22 were Dick Santos and Eli Chavez. They didn't like you to use the term CIA—so we used "customer" or "the company" and that seemed to make them feel better. They were both tough guys and great to work with. Dick and another "company" man—Tom Briggs— were instrumental in my rescue and in saving my life. More on that later. Getting back to the "normal" operation—I would land at PS-22 and talk to the customer for the latest intel on the enemy and any requests they had that day. They often had small teams of mercenaries out looking for the enemy and wanted us to contact them and confirm their location. Actually, these teams were usually doing their best to avoid any contact with the enemy and were almost never even close to where they were supposed to be. It became a real cat-and-mouse game to find their real location. Later, the customer would just have these guys dropped off behind the enemy and let them walk back to camp. When they started yelling they were getting shot, we knew where they were and also where the enemy was.

In the O-1, we had a similar tactic. We flew low over the trees and when the enemy shot at us, we knew where to tell the fighters to drop their bombs. Every day on the Bolovens was different and it usually didn't take us long to find the bad guys and start calling in airstrikes on them. One day, I was at PS-22 and USAF four-star general (commander of the Tactical Air Command) Gen. Momeyer was there—along with several colonels and another general. Gen. Momeyer asked to speak with a Raven FAC and I was the only one available. He asked me what I'd been doing and what I was about to do that day. I told him and then left to fly the mission. The next day we got word from our boss in Vientiane that Gen. Momeyer wanted to know if ALL the Ravens just "wander" around Laos looking for something to do. He also didn't like the fact that a bunch of lieutenants and captains were running the war in Laos. I probably didn't impress him with my long hair and sideburns either. Nothing was ever said to me again about that meeting.

One of my first missions as a Raven was on the Bolovens near another small strip/outpost—PS-38. The enemy had attacked during the night and were still in the area. I had a backseater named

Kontee. He was dressed all in black and wore a black ball cap that said—Kill All Them-Come Back Alone. I'm thinking—man, this guy really gets after the bad guys. It didn't take me long though, to realize that he was full of shit and a chicken-shit to boot. This day though, we had enemy and friendlies fairly close to each other and I was working troops in contact (TIC) with T-28 Lao pilots. I had a flight of two check in with CBU and rockets. The flight lead was the Lao commander Lt. Col. Khouang. I was new and didn't know he was a weak fighter pilot. He had been flying H-34 helicopters most of his career. I briefed the target and told them not to fly over the friendlies. I marked the target and cleared them in hot. Col. Khouang came in over the friendlies and dropped his CBU a mile short of the smoke. All of a sudden people were screaming over the radio (in Lao) but I knew it was bad. I asked Kontee what they were saying. He shook his head and said, "We kill many many friendlies." My heart stopped. I told the fighters to go home and landed at PS-38 to talk to the customer. It turned out that we didn't kill anyone and only two men were slightly wounded. After that, I told all the other Ravens not to let Col. Khouang drop CBU anywhere near friendlies.

I only remember that we had four backseaters/interpreters. They were paid a dollar a mission by the U.S. government. It was common to fly 8-10 missions a day. At the end of the day, the Raven had to sign his book and note the number of missions flown. The four that flew with us were Pantee, Kontee, Nukeo, and Sihok. Pantee was really the only good one. He was reliable, smart, brave, and never complained. He always carried an AK-47 and loved to shoot it out his back-seat window at the enemy. He was later killed, after I left. I've already said what I thought of Kontee. Nukeo was unreliable but he had very good eyes and could find the enemy—if he felt like it. Once we were flying along and I smelled something terrible behind me. I turned to see what it was and Nukeo was asleep with his boots off and his stinking feet resting on the back of MY seat. I can't remember what I did next but Nukeo never did it again. Later, he was with me when we were shot down and crashed in the trees. He saved my life for sure. Sihok was a great big guy—about 200 pounds I'd guess—and pretty worthless. We called him Shit Hook— which was not very nice but sort of fit. None of us wanted to fly with him because of all the short strips we flew out of and we weren't sure we'd be able to take off with him in the back seat. He did speak English though—which was something positive. One of the main reasons I liked the early go was because I got to pick Pantee as my backseater.

The Lao Pilots

The Lao T-28 pilots were an outstanding group of young men. Not only were they excellent fighter pilots—they were really good guys. All of them spoke four languages fluently—Lao, Thai, French, and English. The names or nicknames that I remember were Lt. Col. Khouang, Capt. Methane, T. C., Somnuck, Bira, Hollywood, Killerman, and Shit Hot. Some were better pilots than others but all were very good—except for the colonel (as already noted). For the record, the colonel was a very good man—just not a very good fighter pilot. Their call sign was Cobra followed by a color. All the flight leads kept the same color always, so you always knew who you were working with. They flew about 100 missions a month and were paid a dollar a mission by the U.S. government, in addition to their Laotian pay. They also sold the brass from the used CBU canisters and collected another 100 dollars or so a month. U.S. pilots, after dropping CBU, would always jettison the empty canisters before returning to base. The Lao pilots never jettisoned them because they were like money in their pocket. So every once in a while our runway at Pakse would be temporarily closed because someone landed with live CBU spilling out on the runway.

Of all the pilots at Pakse, Somnuck (Cobra Black) was by far the best. When I marked a target for him, he only wanted to hear "Hit my smoke." He would then roll in and hit your smoke. One day, I found an NVA truck stuck in the mud while trying to cross a river. It turned out it was full of explosives. Somnuck rolled in and dropped a 250 lb. bomb that went through the cab of the truck but didn't explode. He had pickled too low and the bomb didn't have time to arm. On his next pass, the bombs went off and pieces of the truck almost hit me orbiting overhead.

Most of the pilots had been trained in Thailand by USAF instructors, but only to fly in visual flight rules (VFR) conditions—good weather and visibility. When the clouds were low and visibility was bad they didn't fly. Fortunately, Pakse usually had good weather. One day, Somnuck came up to me and was very proud to tell me that he was going to Udorn, Thailand—"to learn how to fly in the cloud."

The biggest character by far, of all the pilots at Pakse, was a wingman who called himself Shit Hot. In my experience, these types who thought they were shit hot were usually more shit than hot. I'll have to say though—this Shit Hot was pretty good. He was a loose cannon though, and hard to control. He was never made a flight lead, even though he was a very experienced pilot. About a hundred miles from the target area he would start calling me—"Raven 42 this is Shit Hot calling you—how do you read?" I could hear him but because I was flying low he could never hear me from that distance. But he kept calling. Besides, this was a flight lead's job. A wingman is not supposed to talk on the radio—except to acknowledge the flight lead's calls to him. Shit Hot's main goal, though, was to get to the target ASAP, drop all the bombs on one pass, and get back to Pakse and get ready for another flight. For him it was a money issue. Another day, another 10 dollars. When they checked in, all I had to do was tell them the name of the nearest town—usually Ban, followed by a name. They would then fly direct to you, drop their bombs, and head back. You had to really "sweet talk" them to give you more than one pass. I eventually started bribing them with cases of beer—if they'd give me three or four passes. That's another reason we went through so much beer.

Well, I got tired of Shit Hot calling me right after he took off so I came up with a new plan. I'd give him a name of a town I was near, that he wouldn't know. I was having a beer with one of the other pilots one day and had a "brain fart." I asked him how to say "fur burger" in Lao. Once I explained the term, he laughed and said "Hemoy." So the next time Shit Hot called me and asked for my location, I told him, "I fly over Ban Hemoy." He keyed the mike and laughed. Then he said, "42, you are very funny guy—BUT where you REALLY fly?" Another time, I was giving his flight a briefing on the target and was about to mark the target with a rocket, and Shit Hot says, "Already drop bomb!" It almost blew me out of the sky. Usually, as he rolled in to make his pass, he called, "Shit Hot in hot." He didn't this time and I was lucky he didn't get me. Like I said—he was a loose cannon.

One more Shit Hot story. Every payday, he got paid about 200-300 dollars—which was a lot of money for him. Then about the 5th of the month, he'd ask me for a loan of 50 dollars. The next month he'd pay me back on payday and then hit me up on the 5th again for 50 dollars. I don't think he needed the money—he just figured he might not have to pay me back some day. For fun, I got a hold of a ONE Kip note—very rare even then. Fifty Kip was a dime so that would make the one Kip note worth about a fifth of a penny. Later, when Shit Hot came to me for a loan, I'd pull out the one Kip note and tell him not to worry about paying me back. I still carry that one Kip note in my billfold. Shit Hot was killed in action a few months after I left.

The Gold Rolex

When I was in Thailand flying OV-10s, some of the guys bought big gold chains to wear around their necks. One guy had a 24K chain with a big round medallion attached that said "Fuck Communism" on it. I never bought any gold while I was in Thailand. When I got to Pakse, both Kricker and Erickson had ordered gold Rolex watches from Geneva, Switzerland and big 18K gold ID bracelets made by a jeweler in Vientiane named Villy Phong. At that time, 1970-71, gold was selling for 35 dollars an ounce. I decided to buy a Rolex and an ID bracelet—not because it was a good investment but I wanted to be cool like all the other Ravens. I bought a gold Rolex Day-Date for 350 dollars with the leather band and Villy Phong made the gold band for 250 dollars. I thought paying 600 dollars for a watch was absolutely crazy. I had a perfectly good Seiko that cost 30 dollars. It turned out to be a fairly good buy though, as the watch and band today would cost over 20,000 dollars. When I returned to the states and started flying again, I always wore the ID bracelet whenever I flew. I was superstitious about it. One of my sons wears the Rolex.

The Ravens of Pakse

I always thought we had a bunch of very unique characters at Pakse. But after attending several Raven reunions and meeting many others, I'd say our group was pretty tame and fairly normal human beings. All of them were "tigers"—aggressive, tough, skilled, and brave. I was excited and proud to be one of them. Frank Kricker was Raven 40. He was the oldest of our group at 30 years old but acted about half that—sometimes. He was funny and had a very infectious laugh. You could not be around him long and not laugh. He was sort of our boss (being the senior officer)—but wasn't really. If he was our boss, we didn't know it or admit to it. I don't know where I had heard it first, but I started calling him Ass-Eyes. It just sounded funny and it WAS funny. Pretty soon though, he was calling ME Ass Eyes. He was always holding out his finger—asking you to pull it. One day, he and I were in downtown Pakse at our favorite bar, sitting at a table having a drink. The owner had several young girls working for him and had two of them go join us. They sat down, Kricker held out his little finger, I pulled it and he cut this huge fart. Those girls screamed, jumped up, and ran out the door. It was totally rude and crude—but one of the funniest things I'd ever seen (or heard). What's really bad though—after things settled back down, the owner made those girls come back and sit with us. We left soon after that, but had a memory forever.

Kricker liked the ladies. He had one sleeping with him on a regular basis. I had the room next to him, separated by a thin wall. Some nights I didn't get much sleep. He decided to teach one of his girlfriends a little English. One night as I was sleeping she knocked on my wall and woke me up. She said, "Hey Loy!" I said, "What?" She said, "Fuck you!" A little later she knocked again— "Hey Loy!" "What?" "Up Yours!"

Lloyd Duncan, Pepsi Ratts, Dick Defer and Frank Kricker at Pakse

Another time, Frank was out at PS-22 about to take off. He prided himself in making the quickest turnarounds—from landing to takeoff again. He could land, get gas and rockets, and take off again in about five minutes. It took most of us 15 or 20 minutes minimum. This day though, he forgot to safe the switches to the rockets after he loaded new ones in the tubes. He jumped into the O-1, started up, and accidentally hit the trigger on the control stick. Eight 2.75 inch rockets went over the top (about three feet) of a multimillion dollar USAF H-53 helicopter. An Air Force colonel came running out of the ops shack screaming, "I want your name! I am going to court-martial your ass." Not being stupid, Frank zoomed to the runway and took off, never looking back. He laid low for a few days—I think he went on R&R to Australia or something—and all was forgotten.

Time and space permits only one more Kricker story. He did go on R&R to Hong Kong, and soon after he returned, three large boxes arrived. Each of them had a Honda 100 motorcycle in it—unassembled. He had bought one for himself, one for me, and one for another Raven—Jim Hix. We hadn't asked him to buy them for us, but were thrilled to get them. Frank was a motorcycle guru and had them put together and running in no time. I don't remember what we paid for them, but it was a real bargain. We loved riding those Hondas.

Next there was David Erickson—but he only answered to Eric. There are too many Eric stories to tell also, but you'll get a good idea of what he's like and what he's made of. Eric and I were good friends at Ubon in the OV-10. He grew up in Wyoming and went to the University of Wyoming. He was a wrestler in college and a very tough dude. I know this because he told me so. I know this—you did not want to pick a fight with Eric—no way. As a Nail FAC he volunteered for the last go of the day because just before dark, the enemy guns would start shooting and the trucks would start driving down the Ho Chi Minh Trail out of North Vietnam. Eric was pretty much fearless. He loved getting shot at and then making the enemy pay. I gave him no chance of surviving his tour. One day he landed back at Ubon and the entire nose of the airplane was gone—hit by a 23 mm round. He had fighters refuse to bomb his targets because the AAA was too intense—even though he was down there much lower getting hosed. One day he did get shot down. He ejected at low altitude and landed in trees. The next day he was rescued and there was a big celebration.

At Ubon, Eric had already been accepted to the Raven program, but was still flying OV-10s for a couple more weeks. He started to let his hair grow and grew some awesome long sideburns—as Ravens we wore civilian clothes and were supposed to look like civilians. One night at the Ubon officers' club, the Director of Operations (DO), a colonel who was second in command of the F-4 wing there, came up to Eric and said, "Eric, when are you going to get a haircut?" Eric didn't hesitate when he said, "Sir, I'll cut my hair when you hit my smoke." We all thought, Oooo—he is in big trouble now. The DO thought for a second and then said, "Fair enough." That was a DO you could go to war with.

As a Raven, Eric didn't change his ways. He often came back with bullet holes in his plane. He was finally told by "upper management" in Vientiane that if he took any more hits, he would be sent home. So he told our maintenance guy in charge of patching bullet holes—Stan Wilson—to stop reporting hits on his plane. Eric prided himself in flying in and out of very small air strips, strips that none of us would even think of going into. One day he flew into a very short field near the town of Paksong. I'm not sure why he did this. There were many rows of barbed wire strung around the compound. As he tried to take off, his wheels hit the barbed wire and the plane flipped over. Eric got out and started to walk away but people were yelling at him to STOP! He was in a mine field. Eric was a very lucky man—and still is to this day.

One day he decided he would go up to see another Nail/Raven buddy—Jim Withers at Savannahket. They went to some bar and evidently an ex-U.S. Army Special Forces guy was there and he slapped a young bar girl. So Eric went up to the guy and asked him nicely (I'm sure) to stop slapping the girl. The guy stopped slapping the girl and began slapping Eric. He took Eric down to the floor and before anyone could pull him off he had almost gouged Eric's eyes out with his thumbs. Eric was grounded for weeks and was very lucky he didn't lose one or both eyes.

Larry "Pepsi" Ratts was different by most people's definition, I would guess. He was funny—very funny—but always sober. He drank no alcohol—only Pepsi Cola. He played the accordion. How many guys do you know that play the accordion? He played it well, too. He always wore a Forest Service uniform to fly in and had a whistle attached to a shirt pocket. I never asked why. He carried an eye patch with him and would sometimes taxi in to the parking ramp wearing his eye patch. Are you getting the picture? Most of us carried an AK-47 or AR-15 in our cockpit when we flew. Pepsi carried an M-79 grenade launcher. I would say he was a little goofy maybe, but when it came to doing the job—getting after bad guys— there was none better.

He was flying over me directing air strikes and keeping the enemy away from me when I got shot down. I would not have survived that day had he not been there. I watched him fly in tight circles just above the treetops with enemy tracers just going behind his tail. He shot his M-79 at the bad guys—keeping them away until the fighters arrived. He is my hero—for life. After the war, he went back to Laos (even though it was controlled by the communists) to help his Laotian friends.

He married a most wonderful Laotian woman, moved back to the U.S., and now works as a male nurse at a hospital in Tacoma, Washington.

Next, there was Joe Smith. That was his real name. Joe was different—just like we all were—but not the same. He was quiet and sort of a loner. He loved to disagree with you on any subject. If you said you thought the enemy were bad people and needed to be taught a lesson, he would argue the opposite. Because of this, some of the guys didn't like him. I liked him. He was an excellent FAC and really got after the enemy—just like the rest of us. He prided himself in being able to fly the O-1 longer than any of us. I'm not sure how he did it, but he could fly about 30 minutes longer than the rest of us. I didn't much care how long I could keep it in the air because I was usually out of rockets long before I was out of gas. One day, Joe was running on fumes and had to make a quick stop for gas at an outpost about 20 minutes north of Pakse. He called on the common frequency that he was on final and an Air America plane took the active and took off. Joe had to go around. During the go-around, the engine sputtered and then quit. He tried to bring it around and land the opposite direction but there was not enough runway. He came to a sudden stop when the trees at the approach end took both wings off his airplane. Joe was not hurt, but the incident gave the boss a reason to fire him. He was gone in a few days.

Joe was replaced by a guy who had been flying up north at Luang Prabang—Frank Birk. Frank was not just different—he was scary different. He was a fellow Air Force Academy (AFA) grad and if Eric Erickson was fearless, Frank was his "daddy." Frank flew where no others would fly. We even stopped asking him where he flew—we didn't want to know. The amazing thing was— he always came back. Usually he came back with a plane full of bullet holes. No backseater wanted to fly with him, and I didn't blame them.

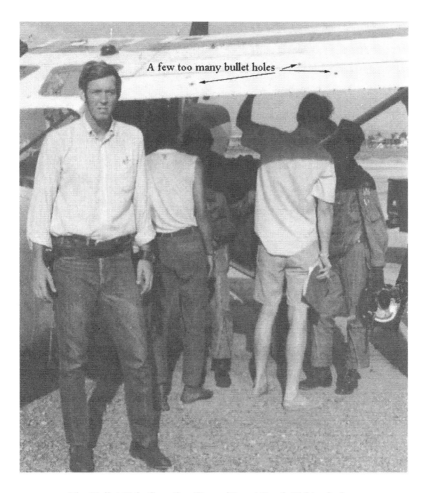

A few too many bullet holes

The Bullet Hole Counting Committee at Frank Birk's airplane

He was the calmest and coolest and most aggressive of all of us. He was a warrior's warrior and as far as I could tell he had no fear of death. He always sounded very calm and matter-of-fact on the radio. One day I heard him talking to "Hillsboro" (the C-130 ABCCC that controlled all the U.S. aircraft in the area). He asked them if they had any fighters (with ordnance) available. They said that they did and asked what the target was. Frank said, "Well, I've got a couple of tanks driving down this road and I'd really like to drop some bombs on them." I nearly died. None of us had ever seen tanks in our area—let alone going down the road. Hillsboro sent him a bunch of fighters but I don't remember if he killed them or not.

Another day, I was working some fighters just east of Frank. We usually let each other know where we were and what we were doing on our FM (Fox Mike) radio. All of a sudden I got a frantic call from Frank and I knew he was in big trouble. His call was, "Raven 42, 45 on Fox Mike!!" I replied, "What's wrong?" He said, "I'm on FIRE!!" I was about 10 minutes away from him and told him to head towards Pakse and I'd try to catch up to him. I caught up to him about five minutes out of Pakse, and checked him over. He had 12.7 mm bullet holes all over his plane. The "fire" turned out not to be a fire. He had taken a 12.7 round through the fire extinguisher (bottle) attached to the back of his seat. It had exploded and filled his cockpit with smoke. He made a good landing at Pakse but a little longer than normal as he had no brakes. There were 27 bullet holes in his plane but not one hit him. His backseater took a round through the leg, but was otherwise OK. Frank

403

completed his tour and became a test pilot at Edwards AFB. Sadly, he was killed testing a new airplane. The Air Force named a new test facility after him.

Eric Erickson got out of the Air Force when his tour was up but stayed right there in Laos. He was hired by CAS to fly Pilatus Porters. Soon after he left Pakse, we got a new boss—Major Dick Defer. Dick was much different from most of the majors I knew. He was a "light your hair on fire and go after 'em"-type guy. His problem at first, though, was he didn't know what he thought he knew and what he did know he didn't need to know. You know what I mean? We called him The Dufe, but not to his face. He was a super guy though and really stood up for us "Dufes" when we got in trouble. He always had our back and we liked him a lot. On one of his first missions with us, he took off in an O-1 and got lost. It was easy to do in the O-1 and in Laos. It took a while to get familiar with our area. Somehow he ended up flying over the Ho Chi Minh Trail at 500 feet and 90 knots. He survived that day—but just barely. He landed back at Pakse with a huge hole in the left wing of the O-1. Much of the wing was gone and I couldn't believe it could still fly. The O-1 was a very tough bird. He had taken a 23 mm round through the left wing. I don't think he ever talked about the incident after that.

One day, Pepsi was working north of Pakse near the river where some enemy trucks had stalled trying to cross. He had called me about it so I headed up there to help him blow up trucks. When I reached the target area, Pepsi was gone and not returning my calls. There were T-28s ready to go in so I put them in on the trucks. One of the T-28s was hit by a 12.7 mm gun and headed home. Soon after that I got stitched by the same gun. Four holes in the left wing. I thought, this guy is good and it might be smart to let him and us live to fight another day. It turned out Pepsi had taken a round in his radio and couldn't warn us about the gun. When I got back to Pakse, Dick jumped all over my ass for not staying and killing that gun. I told him that the gunner was having too good a day and would soon be an ace if we weren't careful. I told him that I decided we should all live to fight another day. Dick didn't like it, but later told me I had done the right thing. Just after I was shot down and left, Dick was moved up north to 20A to be their boss. After hearing some 20A war stories at reunions, they definitely needed some "adult" supervision up there. Dick wrote me several long letters while I was in the hospital in Denver, Colorado, telling me what was going on.

Then one day I learned that he was killed in action in northern Laos. He was a "leader by example"—and that's what I wanted to be someday.

The last Raven at Pakse (during my tour) was Jim Hix. He was another AFA grad and I would say he was a little more normal than the rest of us. He was an excellent FAC, totally dependable, and since he had been at 20A, he knew a lot about the guns that the enemy used on us. He was sometimes referred to as Honda 3 since he got the third Honda that Kricker brought back from Hong Kong. We often rode in formation down to the local bar for a "cold" Guinness Stout after flying. It was my good fortune that Jim Hix was flying the day I was shot down. The enemy was everywhere, lots of 12.7 mm guns were shooting at us, two T-76 tanks were in the area, and enemy mortars were pelting our troops. It was a "war."

The Rescue of Raven 42

In late May of 1971, things were heating up on the Bolovens. The NVA were getting ready to attack. A few days before the attack by hundreds of NVA, the CIA made a very important and smart decision. They secretly brought a large group of Thai Army troops into the outpost at Paksong. For days I watched the Thai troops string rows of barbed wire around the compound and dig trenches outside the wire. They put sharp punji sticks in the trenches and covered them up. The NVA attacked at night—expecting the Laotian troops to "get out of Dodge" as usual.

The next morning, as I was flying over the outpost, I saw huge piles of dead NVA bodies stacked outside the wire. The Thais lost two dead and a few wounded. Had the Thais not been there at Paksong, the NVA would have been in Pakse in a few hours.

Then, on the 7th of June, the enemy attacked again at Paksong. I had the early go and when I got overhead, the Thai commander called me and spoke to me in perfect English. I flew 12 hours that day and was shot down about an hour before sundown. Hix was in charge of killing the guns and Pepsi was trying to keep the enemy away from me. It took a while, but Hix got every gun in the area and no one else was shot down. It allowed the Air America helicopter (H-34)—flown by two Thai pilots—to hover over me and rescue both me and Nukeo. Had Jim Hix not been there that day to work his magic on those guns, I would not have been rescued. A full account of my rescue is written in a book by Tom Briggs—*Cash On Delivery*. It's a very accurate account as Tom got most of us who were involved to relate our memory of it.

Tom was one of the "company" guys at Pakse but I didn't know him very well. He worked with Laotian special teams that were sent out to gather intel on the enemy. I only knew him to say hi. He was on the ramp at PS-18 when word came that I'd been shot down. He was standing next to the H-34 when it started up to go get me. Tom can't explain why he did it—but he just jumped on that H-34 as it was about to lift off. After the pickup, Tom saw that I was in bad shape and had lost a lot of blood. He squeezed my left leg above the wound, which slowed the blood loss, and told the pilots to radio back to PS-18 to tell them I would need blood. When I arrived at the field hospital at PS-18, I had already lost three-fifths of my blood (according to the doctors). Several guys had lined up and given blood before I arrived and the two Filipino doctors stopped the bleeding and filled me back up. It looked like I was going to live—a miracle for sure.

The other man who played a major part in my rescue was my backseater, Nukeo. There would have not been a rescue without him. As I said earlier, I didn't think much of Nukeo, but he stuck with me that day. Some might say he didn't have a choice—but I think he did. First, we crashed through trees after the engine quit. He was not injured. The front of the plane was crushed around my legs and my left leg was broken. I was able to pull my right leg out but not my left. Nukeo pulled the metal away so I could reach down and pull my boot and free my leg. He then helped me out of the plane and tried dragging me away from it. After a short distance, I told him to stop. It was too painful. My survival vest—with the emergency radios—was hanging over my seat in the O-1. We were supposed to wear the vest but it was very hot and most of us hung it over the seat. Nukeo went back to the plane and got my vest and handed me the radio. I tried to call but it didn't work. I was not thinking clearly. Nukeo reached down and pulled out the antenna on the radio and it worked. I talked to Pepsi and told him the situation. He directed the H-34 to my location. Nukeo put the sling over my head and then rode it up with me.

There is one more guy who played an important part in my rescue—Dick Santos. Dick was the "customer" at PS-22 and we were friends. He heard that I was shot down, so he had a CAS pilot fly him to my location in a Pilatus Porter. He stayed high and out of the way, and observed. He kept quiet, but it was getting dark and he started worrying about it getting too dark to make the rescue. So he broke in on the briefing to the H-34 pilots and told them to go get me—NOW. They did—and the rest is history. So it turned out to be NOT my day to die. The Good Lord and a bunch of his "helpers" (who all did their parts perfectly) got me through that day.

Final Words

In the OV-10 (as a Nail FAC) most of the guys were "tigers," really aggressive and also great warriors. A few, however, disappointed me. Usually it was the higher-ranking pilots—majors and lieutenant colonels. Sometimes I was embarrassed at how poorly a few of them did their job—usually because they seldom flew a mission. As a Raven FAC, I was never embarrassed or disappointed by the way my fellow Ravens went about their duty and did the mission. In fact, I marveled at how most did their dangerous job on a daily basis. They were the bravest and craziest men I have ever met. Of all the things that I have done in my 70 years of life—I am proudest of what I did and who I did it with—when I was a Raven FAC in Laos in 1970-71.

Chapter 28

Tom Young, Raven 52/53
Vientiane, Jan – May 1971

Introduction

I have always wanted to document my experiences as a "Raven" forward air controller (FAC) who operated in Laos from January through April 1971. Raven was our radio call sign and became our identity to those we met only on the radio. Individual Ravens each had his own discrete two-digit number corresponding to the Lao military region that he was assigned to. I flew under the call signs Raven 52 and Raven 53.

I am writing this not from the perspective of a "story teller" but instead from the perspective of an instructor pilot attempting to pass hard-learned experience to his students. The intent is for them to use this knowledge to keep themselves alive and to be more effective.

I am also writing for the benefit of researchers to place these operations in historical perspective. Perhaps some experience can be gained by reading about Raven operations rather than having to be relearned the next time that we go to war.

The Raven program not only made a great deal of sense at the time, but continues to retain validity today. The program stands as a model for a nation to fight a covert war using mainly the host country's forces and augmenting those forces with additional specialized assistance, which in this case was airpower. The Ravens were there to direct and evaluate the use of this airpower. I will attempt to use the same language that we used when we were in Laos simply as a matter of historical accuracy and personal outlook.

I recently received an email from a fellow Raven who was in Laos when I was there. He indicated that some one-fourth of the Ravens have now passed on. He also asked me to share my experiences as a Raven. It didn't take any convincing on his part to get me to realize that now is the time to capture the history that we still can. I am also writing my story as a tribute to all of those that flew as a Raven. I apologize for those cases where my memory is not as vivid as when I first got home from Southeast Asia. I would dearly love to be able to still remember such things as radio call signs, but no such details come to mind. Hopefully, I can relate the events that were the most notable and significant without confusing the facts. I believe that one of the real values of this effort will be to get a substantial number of Ravens to write about their experiences. Hopefully, as these accounts are compared, not only will additional important information come to light but gross inaccuracies (e.g., bar stories) will be recognized and discarded as being untrue. I will also include at least some of the references that I have found helpful in providing information about the program which was not available until many years after we completed our Raven tours.

Who Were the Ravens?

Who were the Ravens and how did the Top Secret Steve Canyon Program, as it was officially called, come about? The United States was involved in Southeast Asia (SEA) as a matter of national interest since the end of World War II. When the French were defeated at Dien Bien Phu

407

in 1954, the U.S. picked up the burden of preventing North Viet Nam from overrunning South Viet Nam. The North Vietnamese had as their first priority the reunification of both North and South Viet Nam under communist rule. The Red Chinese and the USSR were only too happy to use the conflict as a proxy war between the superpowers. The South Vietnamese were supported by the U.S. and the North was supported by the Red Chinese and to a certain extent the USSR (Shultz, Richard H., Jr., *The Secret War Against Hanoi*).

Laos ended up getting dragged into the conflict because North Viet Nam was using Lao territory to operate the Ho Chi Minh Trail. The North Vietnamese were transporting supplies down the trail for their military activities in South Viet Nam. North Viet Nam also worked to have a friendly country on its western border. The U.S., under the Kennedy administration, sent Averell Harriman to negotiate the Geneva Accords of 1962. The intent was to guarantee the neutrality of Laos and prevent the loss of a strategic and friendly country. Unfortunately, the Geneva Accords guaranteeing the neutrality of Laos were not worth the paper they were written on. Under the accords, the U.S. pulled its military personnel out of Laos in 1962. North Viet Nam just ignored the agreement, kept its forces in Laos, and continued building the Ho Chi Minh Trail through Laos at an increased tempo.

North Viet Nam also had undue influence on the Lao government. This was because the government was headed by three half-brothers. One half-brother represented the Royalists, one the Neutralists, and one the Pathet Lao. The Pathet Lao (Communists) were supported by and heavily dependent on North Viet Nam. The situation for the U.S. in Laos continued to deteriorate during the next two years.

In 1964, at the request of Prince Souvanna Phouma, the Prime Minister of Laos, President Kennedy directed the U.S. Air Force to commence covert operations to counter the North Vietnamese aggression. The U.S. started providing combat air support for the Royalist and sometimes the Neutralist factions of the Lao government. The USAF would soon be providing air support for the CIA-organized Thai/Hmong army of General Vang Pao. With an increasing threat to the Lao government, and with substantial amounts of air support going into Laos, it soon became evident that the Lao military was not up to the task of directing where the air support was to be effectively placed, nor were they able to evaluate its effectiveness.

Thus in 1964, the U.S. Embassy requested that the USAF provide forward air controllers (FACs). Initially, the FACs were ad hoc and ground based with little formal training. In 1966, the Raven program came into being to solve this shortcoming. The Ravens were mostly young USAF pilots who had combat experience as forward air controllers and in some cases as fighter pilots. They flew the O-1, U-17, and eventually the T-28 aircraft to direct USAF, Thai, and Lao airstrikes. Both the O-1 and U-17 aircraft were light single-engine spotter-type airplanes. The T-28 was a slightly larger radial-engine two-seat trainer which was also used as a light attack aircraft by the Lao and Thai air forces.

While there were seldom more than 20 Ravens in the program at one time, some 161 served, of which 23 were killed in action (KIA) by the time the program ended in 1973. It was also reported that some 60 percent of the group were downed by enemy action at some point (Robbins, Christopher, *The Ravens: The Men Who Flew in America's Secret War in Laos*, pp. 335-336).

During the time that the Ravens were working in Laos, more bombs were dropped in Laos than the U.S. dropped during all of World War II (Bellamy, Alex, *Massacres and Morality*, Oxford University Press, 2012, pp. 160-222). The Ravens directed a substantial proportion of those bombs and likely more ordnance than all the rest of the U.S. FACs in Southeast Asia combined.

The Ravens flew during the day and operated in support of the forces friendly to the U.S. They did not have a responsibility to prevent the North Vietnamese from using the Ho Chi Minh Trail. The Ravens and their Lao allies did, however, tie up a significant number of North Vietnamese divisions in the Raven operating area that would have otherwise been available to transport goods down the trail or serve as fighting forces in South Viet Nam.

How I Was Selected to Be a Raven

I had an interest in Laos starting in the 1950s and had read extensively about the country and about Dr. Tom Dooley. Dr. Dooley was a former U.S. Navy doctor who established a number of hospitals in Laos to serve the local population. Some of these hospitals were still open when I was there in 1971.

When I was in college in the mid-1960s, I knew that I was most likely headed to an all-expenses-paid trip to Viet Nam upon graduation. There was just no decent way to avoid it. With guidance from friends and relatives, I decided that going as a pilot made the most sense. I chose the Air Force ROTC program and was commissioned a second lieutenant upon graduation from The University of Puget Sound in June of 1968. Nine days later I was in Del Rio, Texas starting pilot training.

I completed pilot training at Laughlin AFB, TX in June of 1969. I was assigned to the 12th Special Operations Squadron (SOS) (Ranch Hands) at Bien Hoa Air Base, Viet Nam. I arrived at Bien Hoa in October of 1969 to fly the C-123K tactical transport as copilot flying defoliant application. This was a controversial program in the U.S. and was being scaled back due to political pressure.

I had no moral issue with participating in this program because it denied the enemy cover to ambush our troops. One small, but probably the most effective, part of the Ranch Hand program was to spray the bad guys' rice each year just before harvest with a substance that made the rice look like it was not fit to eat. Each year, when this happened, hundreds, if not thousands of bad guys would rally back to our side to receive food. During the time I was there Senator Robert Kennedy made such a fuss about this rice-spraying program that Washington suspended the rice spraying. So at that point, a program designed to get the bad guys to give up because they were hungry turned into a situation where our side had to shoot them instead.

Life at Bien Hoa was really pretty dreadful since there was so very little to do. The mission was scaled back and the squadron was way overmanned with low-experience-level copilots. There is nothing worse than being idle and bored in a combat zone.

One day I was assigned to man the squadron office as duty officer and the phone rang. It was a major from our wing at Phan Rang. He asked for the operations officer. I told him that I was the only one there. He asked for the names of two lieutenant copilots for a 90-day temporary duty assignment to Nakhon Phanom (NKP), Thailand. I told him that I did not have the authority to make that decision. He demanded the two names, now! Not being a fool, and wanting out of Bien Hoa, I quickly gave him my name and that of a pilot-training classmate. The next day we were on our way to Thailand assigned to the 606th Special Operations Squadron. The 606th (Candlesticks) also flew the C-123K and served as night FACs on the Ho Chi Minh Trail. It also provided flare support both on the trail and for friendly forces in other areas of Laos.

Arriving in Thailand was like night and day compared to Viet Nam. We could fly nearly as much as we wanted and the flying was good. The base, our quarters, our food, and our morale were all excellent. I was also able to move up to aircraft commander, which I did as soon as I had the required hours. This upgrade also prompted me to extend my SEA tour by a couple of months to be able to stay in Thailand. Staying in Thailand, instead of going back to the 12th SOS Ranch Hands in Viet Nam, was not a difficult choice. Life was quite good at NKP and I enjoyed it. It would have been the greatest adventure of my life had this not been a war where folks were getting killed.

A troubling issue for me was the reality that unless I was able to shorten my remaining active duty commitment after returning to the U.S., I was most likely going to end up in Strategic Air Command (SAC) as a B-52 or KC-135 copilot. This was a fate that I was determined to avoid at nearly any cost. One way to avoid SAC was to stay in SEA as long as possible. This would cause my remaining time on active duty after returning to a new assignment in the U.S. to be as short as possible and SAC would not want me for this reason. I again extended my time in Southeast Asia to make this work, and it made me eligible for six months in the Ravens.

In so many ways it made sense for me to apply for the Steve Canyon Program. Not only was I working in the same areas as a night FAC, I was also working with the same clients that the Ravens were working with during the day. I was always very satisfied to hand off a client that I had flown over and protected most of the night to a Raven who was there to help him during the day. We knew on many occasions that our presence and support made the difference in their site still being secure in the morning. While I never had the chance as a Candle FAC to meet any of my customers on the ground, I got to know them on the radio. I was putting my all into seeing that they were still there in the morning. I knew if they were overrun, their families and likely many residents of the local villages also stood a good chance of being killed.

Welcome to the Ravens

I had a friend from pilot training who was selected for the Ravens and I contacted him. He told me who to contact and that he would vouch for me. I then talked to the O-2 squadron commander at NKP, who encouraged me to apply and flew me to Cam Rahn Bay to interview.

I was soon accepted in the program and shortly I was on the way to Cam Rahn Bay to check out in the O-1. My stay there lasted less than 10 days and I was then off to Udorn Royal Thai AFB in Thailand where the Raven program was based.

I checked into Detachment 1 of the 56th Special Operations Wing at Udorn, which the Ravens fell under, only to be made to feel absolutely unwelcome. The detachment commander treated me like something that had just arrived from the moon because I was not a day FAC and had not been through all the fancy day FAC schools in the States. I pointed out to him that I was familiar with the area and our clients and saw no valid reason for me to be excluded from the program. While he clearly had reservations about putting me in the program, he also badly needed pilots to meet operational needs. He indicated that he would give me a chance and to be ready to head to Vientiane later that day.

Prior to departing for Vientiane, I separated my USAF uniform items from the rest of my flying gear and had them secured at Udorn for my return. I was directed to keep my Air Force ID card and flight cap. While Ravens had been "sheep dipped"—that is, had their military identity sanitized—in the past while working in Laos, this was no longer the case when I served there. By this time, our cover story if were downed in Laos was that we were Air Force. This was actually a very hollow gesture since who we were and what we did was known to all of the parties in the conflict.

Since we were not wearing the standard flight suit it was up to us to come up with something suitable. Most of the Ravens wore blue jeans and jean jackets when it was cold. After a short time in the assignment most of the Ravens also had custom "walking suits" made at the local tailor shops. Most of these suits were sort of a cross between an Air Force flight suit and the "party" suit that most pilots had custom made during their SEA tours. It was more than interesting to see the looks that you received when you returned to USAF bases in Thailand. We would fly in using only a three-digit tail number as our call sign in our unmarked airplanes. Every place that we went on base we were somewhat of a curiosity in our walking suits. Every place we went we were given lots of space and most people were reluctant to engage us in conversation unless they already knew us. The walking suits were comfortable and worked quite well but had no real fire-protective qualities like we had in our Nomex flight suits. Note: I recently donated my walking suits to the Museum of the United States Air Force. I thought it was ironic that perhaps for the first time flight clothing that was worn on an actual clandestine mission could be preserved for the sake of history. Hopefully at some point the O-1 at the museum will be included in a static display that will honor the Ravens.

I was off to Vientiane and was met by Chuck Engle whom I was replacing. That evening, after moving into quarters in Vientiane, I was welcomed by a number of the other Ravens at the mandatory welcoming stops of the White Rose and Lulu's. Little did I realize at the time, this was one of ways that the Ravens had of evaluating how you would react to the pressures of the program by observing how you handled yourself out on the town.

The next morning, I was off on my one and only checkout ride with Chuck acting as my instructor. We checked out an O-l and headed straight for Lima Site 20A (Long Tieng). This site was the center of the U.S. effort in Laos during this time. Site 20A was located on the southern edge of the Plain of Jars (PDJ). The PDJ was in the hands of the Pathet Lao and their North Vietnamese sponsors during this period. Due to the number of hostile guns, the PDJ was not the place that you wanted to hang out in an O-1 during the day. Given my night combat background and my knowledge of the reputation of the area, flying over the PDJ in daylight in an unarmed O-1 was terrifying to me. However, since Chuck was familiar with the area during the day he obviously was less concerned. Chuck showed me a bad guy .51 caliber site that was open for business and greeted us by hosing off a few rounds in our direction. Chuck chose to return the gesture by firing an AR-15 from the back seat. Since we were at 1,500 feet above the ground and quite close to the .51 caliber, I soon convinced Chuck that there were other things that I really wanted to see. So we moved on to visit most of the important sites in Military Region (MR II).

Upon landing at Lima Site 20A for lunch and fuel, we learned there was an O-1 that needed to be ferried back to Vientiane. Chuck took the ferry flight and I stayed in the same O-1. We were headed for home by midafternoon. Soon after takeoff, we were joined by a third O-1 also headed south. It was pretty hazy and I had trouble keeping both of them in sight. After several minutes of heading south, I saw the sun flash off of Chuck's O-1 as it pulled straight up and entered a hammerhead stall at a low altitude. As the O-1 completed the hammerhead stall, it crashed straight into the ground, exploded, and burned. Clearly there was no way anyone could have survived. This was confirmed by a search and rescue (SAR) later that day.

A couple of days later I happened to be at Udorn and was approached by the detachment commander. He announced that I was out of the program because I was not qualified. I indicated as forcefully as I could that I was already checked out in my area of operations and saw no reason why I could not perform the job. He said that I could stay and keep flying until my replacement arrived. This did not happen for another four and a half months (out of a six-month tour).

Wow! What an introduction to the Ravens. Within 24 hours of my arrival my instructor gets killed and the detachment commander is trying to pitch me out of the program. Welcome to Laos and the Ravens!

Why I Fought

Those few people that were aware that I was a Raven have asked me, "Why would I put it all on the line for a bunch of folks that I didn't even know halfway around the world?"

Perhaps I was naively patriotic when I arrived in Viet Nam. At the time, I bought into the domino theory. The domino theory, which governed U.S. foreign policy in the 1950s and 1960s, held that a communist victory in one nation would quickly lead to a chain reaction of communist victories in neighboring states.

It is interesting to note that history has shown us that all of Viet Nam is now communist, as well as Laos. However, Thailand is still a constitutional monarchy and Cambodia has reemerged as a constitutional monarchy. Viet Nam is probably more dependent on the U.S. today than was South Viet Nam during the war. This is because Viet Nam is now dependent on the U.S. as a massive market for its goods, as witnessed by Nike and many other giant corporations doing business there. According to the website infoplease.com the U.S. is Viet Nam's largest trading partner, doing some seven billion dollars per year in trade.

The major reason that I was willing to engage in Laos was that I cared about the Lao people and particularly the Hmong. The following facts still stand out today:

Over 40 percent of the Hmong army was under 14 or over 40.

Over 40 percent of the Hmong between 14 and 40 had been killed in the fighting.

Those that were still fighting were being forced below the malaria line (elevation) and were dying in record numbers because they were a people who were adapted to living above the malaria line where they were effectively immune from malaria. When they were forced out of their traditional homes above the malaria line to lower ground they became vulnerable.

It was just the right thing to do. I certainly had no love for the North Vietnamese or the Pathet Lao and I got really tired of seeing them kicking the Hmong when they were down. I had the resources to try in my own small way to stand up for the Hmong. I chose to do so.

In short, I was there and it was a mission that I wholeheartedly believed in. So many times we knew that if we could not take care of and protect our clients, they might well not be there in the morning.

A Day in the Life of a Raven

If there was any sort of day that we could point out as being a typical "day in the life of a Raven FAC," it went like this. We would normally get up by six and jump into our Jeep and head for the Air America cafeteria for breakfast and a sack lunch. It was pretty decent and we knew that we were unlikely to get food poisoning during our flying day. It was also pleasant to see other American air crews and compare notes.

After breakfast we headed to the U.S. Embassy for our daily briefing from the U.S. air attaché. This is where we would get the latest intelligence (Intel) briefing and the big picture of what was going on in all of Laos. We also got the status of all of our customers and if any of them were in a critical situation.

From here it was back to the airport to grab our gear, which included firearms, survival gear, and navigation charts. Many of the Ravens carried Kalashnikov AK-47s as their preferred weapon for a number of reasons. Not only were AKs, including ammunition, readily available to us, AK ammunition in the field was potentially easier to get and you could use both AK and AR-15 ammo in the AK. The AK-47 ammo was not interchangeable to work in the U.S.-issue AR-15. While the last thing you wanted to do was to get in a firefight on the ground with the bad guys, should you end up doing so, and if you were shooting the same weapon as your pursuers, all the muzzle sounds were the same. This would likely be a serious advantage in your favor. In addition, the AK had a much better reputation for not jamming in the dirt and mud as did the U.S. AR-15.

From Vientiane we headed off to where we were to pick up our backseater. Our backseater was a Lao army officer that knew the area and provided authorization to use air support. It was not infrequently that we simply transported our backseater to a forward air strip and came back for him at the end of the day. This depended on how comfortable he was with your knowledge of the area and how much he didn't want to fly that day. Leaving your backseater there also gave him a chance to talk to his clients that we were working for. We would then proceed to check out the activities that the air attaché wanted us to look at. If you found worthwhile targets you asked the airborne command post (ABCCC) for an air strike to neutralize the threat. If they had air available you put in and evaluated from there. From the attaché requests you proceeded to those areas that you knew might have some enemy targets or activity. If you found worthwhile targets you again requested air and if available you put those air strikes in. It was not unusual for me to put in multiple sets of air a day.

There were also times when it was necessary to proceed to the closest friendly airstrip to fuel and to rearm with smoke-marking rockets. We fueled from 55-gallon drums with hand pumps at the remote sites in Laos. We also had to be very careful not to get water or contaminated fuel from the barrels. We would not fuel from a barrel that had been left overnight without a seal due to security concerns.

We also built and loaded our own 2.75-inch white phosphorus smoke-marking rockets in the field. We would get the rocket motor in one wooden box and the white phosphorous smoke heads in another. We removed the motors and heads from the boxes and screwed the head on the rocket motor and slipped the combined unit in the launching tube. We made sure that the rocket was seated in the tube and held in by a spring clip at the bottom of the tube.

Being in a different geographic area than some of the Ravens assigned to the north of me in MR V, I sometimes had better weather in MR II. This meant that sometimes I was requested to use up strike sorties that were pledged to MR V but they could not use. If I did not have a hot area to utilize the air strike we would go "prospecting" with it in areas that looked promising and sometimes it was very worthwhile. It was not unusual to set off secondary explosions of fuel, ordnance, or even parked trucks which had been hidden for future use.

It was always necessary to plan to be home before dark. This was always a challenge since it seemed inevitable that just when it was time to go home you would get troops in contact, find some really good fleeing target, or have some sort of operational issue that made it difficult to get home by dark. Once we arrived in Vientiane we wrote up any aircraft issues, secured our weapons, and debriefed with Intel. Then it was off to town to have dinner, usually at a French restaurant since that was about all there was. After dinner it was time to jump in the Jeep and head past the vertical runway (that I talk about in "Theatre of the Absurd") to our house.

Staying Alive

While "Staying Alive" (in the combat zone) was never taught as an actual flying course while I was in the theater, it was certainly one of the primary concerns on every pilot's mind. We started with our Air Force Undergraduate Pilot Training (where you learned the skill to be an Air Force pilot), which was absolutely topnotch. Many of our instructors had been combat fighter pilots and were only too willing to provide the solid foundation of flying skills that we needed.

We then progressed to the school for our particular aircraft, which for me was in Florida. Again, we had the battle-tested combat veterans who just did everything they could to give us the knowledge and skill to see that we had the best chances of survival.

When I made the transition from a night FAC to a day FAC I had to transition to the O-1. I was sent to Cam Rahn Bay, South Viet Nam to get my checkout. Again, my instructor was a combat veteran who designed a transition course specifically for my experience level and got me ready to head to Laos. He even took me to Bien Hoa AB where we found airstrikes to put in to the west in Cambodia. This was the first time that I had worked directly with the Army. It was an interesting learning experience and included a SAR (search and rescue) mission for two downed helicopters. Both helicopters were shot down as we were working with them.

I suppose that the best advice that I could give any FAC on staying alive in the combat zone is to never be predictable and to never be satisfied that no one is trying to shoot you down each and every moment. The minute that you get "comfortable" you are potentially in trouble. You also need to not only "have eyes in the back of your head," but also have all of your senses constantly engaged so that you do not get surprised.

One technique that we learned in flying the O-1 was to fly the airplane with our feet and to use our hands for other things such as looking at maps, setting up switches, and holding field glasses. This had the added benefit of ensuring that the flight path of the airplane was uncoordinated and unpredictable, which made it more difficult for gunners to track you.

When I returned to the U.S., one of the first things that I did was to go out to the local airport and check out in a Cessna 172. The instructor, a graybeard who had hung out at airports for the previous 40 years, had some interesting comments. He tactfully pointed out that he had no concerns about me being able to successfully fly the airplane. He also indicated that I should be aware that I would most likely terrify any passenger who chose to fly with me. I was more than a bit taken back as I thought that he was aware that I was simply attempting to minimize the flying time to accomplish the checkout by flying tight patterns and a very brisk style. I then realized that I had flown more like a FAC than like a smooth civilian pilot. I was still applying the "never fly in a predictable manner" method. Okay, so locations change and you just have to adjust.

Exciting Missions

There are days when I still feel that maybe I wasn't a real Raven. This was because in the area that I was assigned to there wasn't much going on as far as major threats and sustained large-scale battles. Many of my fellow Ravens had a lot more exposure and action when they were constantly putting in air strikes to prevent their customers from being overrun. While I put in a lot of air strikes as a Raven, the area that I was in was pretty minor league as far as there being much there or any serious threats. There were a limited number of roads and other important strategic sites that were ever contested. In looking back on it I was okay with leaving the really difficult work to Ravens that were better qualified and more eager to fly the really tough missions. Someone had to fly the missions in the less exciting areas. I did what I was asked to do, didn't endanger anyone else except bad guys, didn't have any major screw-ups, and came home alive. With this in mind, there were still some noteworthy (at least to me) events while I was there.

Art Dulaney, Tom Young and two unidentified Lao

Bad Day with the Phantoms

Perhaps the only combat air strike that really got my attention was a "troops in contact" event where my USAF F-4 fighters nearly dropped on the friendly forces. I had received a request through my backseater to provide an air strike to prevent an outpost from being overrun. It was a routine request in an easy area to work. I soon made contact with the customer on the ground, who fortunately spoke excellent English. I was able to quickly establish the location of the friendlies and of the advancing bad guys. The setup was almost funny-paper simple. I placed a single white phosphorous marker within a few meters of the advancing enemy. They soon halted and took cover. I went up on the airborne command post (ABCCC) frequency and requested fighters for troops in contact. Great, I had marked the bad guys and got them to back off- at least for a few minutes. For ABCCC this was a high-priority mission and I soon had a pair of Air Force F-4 fighters. They each carried 500 lb. Mark 82 bombs. When they came up on the frequency I checked them in and briefed them on the mission. The fighters acknowledged and indicated that they would meet me at the TACAN (tactical air navigation system) radial and DME (distance measuring equipment) location that I had previously provided. The F-4s were soon on station and after some difficulty we got a visual on each other. I then put another marking rocket within 20 meters of my previous smoke. I briefed the F-4s to run from south to north and to drop on my smoke. The friendlies were some 500 meters to the west and they were well away from the bad guys and my smoke. I made the F-4s acknowledge where my friendlies were and to not fly over them. I then cleared the lead aircraft in hot on the target. I was just astounded when lead dropped over a mile from my smoke to the west. I quickly told the number two F-4 not to drop even though I had not previously cleared him in hot. I did not get an acknowledgement from the number two F-4 until after he had dropped on the lead's bomb. I was just amazed and upset. How could they have dropped over a mile from where I told them on the other side of my friendlies? I quickly told the fighters to safe their bombs and to return to the ABCCC for reassignment.

It was then that the extreme whining began. Oh, we can't do that because we don't have enough fuel—even though they had just come from the tanker. So, needing to get rid of them quickly in order to get some air that I could trust not to destroy my friendlies, I said, "Okay, fine. I am just about to fire a couple of rockets up toward the PDJ." (The PDJ belonged to the other side at the time and was a free-fire zone.) I pulled the nose of the O-1 up about 15 degrees and lobbed a couple of Willie Petes (white phosphorus smoke-marking rockets) up toward the PDJ. I told the F-4s to hit my smoke. They acknowledged and I hoped that I would not hear from them again. No such luck. Just as I was getting another set of fighters set up to help my troops in contact they were back on the frequency asking for their bomb damage assessment (BDA). I told them that I was unable to provide BDA since I could not see where they dropped. They persisted that they had to have BDA or they were going to have to go back to the bombing range and requalify. I indicated that I thought that would be a very good idea, but if they really had to have something I would provide the BDA of "one hundred per cent on the ground." They finally caught the measure of my anger with them and departed. Fortunately, my client on the ground forgave me as the second set of fighters were four Lao T-28s who did a great job and took care of the bad guys.

While many of the F-4s were adequate when flown by competent pilots, by the time I got there, the F-4 pilot ranks were infested with far too many retreads, senior wannabees, and folks that were only interested in doing the minimum to get their flight and combat pay. The F-4 was just not the correct airplane for the job nor was it flown to its best advantage in the theater when I was there.

Blocked in a Box Canyon

I had an occasion where I was working with troops in contact on a ridgeline. This ridgeline continued on to run into a canyon with a narrow valley with steep walls and no exit to the north, only higher mountains. To the south of the friendlies the ground fell away fairly rapidly to the elevation of the Mekong River. As I continued to put in air strikes, I noticed that a couple of pretty good cumulonimbus rain clouds had begun to build to the south side of the friendlies' position. I was heavily occupied with my troops in contact (TIC) and getting my Lao T-28s in and out safely. After my client on the ground indicated that the airstrike had been successful, I directed the T-28s out through a hole to the west toward their home base. I then returned to the area around where the airstrike had been put in to scout for additional bad guys and I found some. Needless to say, they seemed to be less than thrilled with me and opened up with a .51 cal from further up the ridgeline. With the ceiling lowering in the entire area and deciding that I had better things to do than hang out with the .51 cal, I turned south to make my exit. I then realized that the rain clouds to the south had merged into a solid thunderstorm. I couldn't stay visual and exit to the north because of the rising terrain, the box canyon, and the lowering ceiling. To the south there was a thunderstorm. Thunderstorms are dangerous. It was time for a choice with neither option being desirable.

To me, the clouds to the south seemed to be considerably softer and more inviting than the rocks to the north. I turned south, shoved the power all the way forward and began a maximum-rate climb toward the lightest-colored portion of the clouds. I soon entered the clouds and attempted to transition to instruments. It is always a difficult transition, even for experienced instrument pilots, to suddenly be popped into instrument conditions when you are not expecting it and you have not flown instruments for the past 18 months. The O-1 also had the finest instruments that the army could buy in the early 1950s and I wasn't sure that they had had much care since then. Things seemed to go well for a minute or so and then the climb rate settled down to about 100 feet per minute. At this point I was feeling much better about the .51 cal not knowing where to aim to get me, but I was still very concerned about clearing all the rocks that might be on my route. I tried to calm down, concentrate on flying instruments, and figure out why the climb rate seemed to be so sluggish. By now, I was not only getting bounced around pretty good but I was also starting to get very wet from the rain and the leaks around the windshield. Nearly every spot in front of the pilot that had previously provided the entrance for a nice breeze in flight became a mini shower head. I still had considerable fuel on board and six rockets. While I had no way to dump the fuel, I could jettison the rockets and gain the lift from losing a couple of hundred pounds. I was continuing to push myself to calm down and concentrate on instrument flying and why the airplane seemed to be reluctant to climb.

I then had one of those "eureka light bulb" moments. I was working on my instrument cross check and a not-so-minor detail suddenly became apparent. Okay, Ding Dong, step on the damn ball and quit going through the air sideways. (For non-aviation folks, this means to use the rudder to coordinate all three axes of flight to get maximum performance out of the airplane.) With the airplane once again in coordinated flight, it actually started climbing at an acceptable rate. I was soon out of the thunderstorm and got the Mekong River in view. It was a happy sight and I was soon back at Vientiane and home for the night.

No Way Home for the Night

It was near the end of the flying day and I landed for fuel at the remote location that I normally worked out of. As I was entering the parking area, I noticed that my flaps were stuck in the full down position and would not respond to the control. This prevented me from using this aircraft to get back home. This was bad news as the site was subject to frequent attacks at night. Shortly after I discovered my flaps stuck full down I noticed an Air America H-34 helicopter arriving at the field. I quickly approached the helicopter, told them of my situation, and asked if I could get a ride back to Vientiane. Before I knew it the AA flight mechanic grabbed his tool bag, took out a pair of small vise grips, climbed into my O-1, disconnected the flap cable from the flap motor, clamped the vise grips on to the cable, took several turns on the cable and presto—the flaps were now in the up position. The aircraft was now okay to fly home with the flaps in the up position. I profusely thanked the Air America crew, jumped into the O-1, and departed for Vientiane. I was one much-relieved pilot. This was just one of the routine tasks that Air America did so well every day.

A Water Buffalo on Each Strut

One of the primary remote strips that I routinely worked out of was Paksane. There were a number of residents living in the local area who owned livestock. While I frequently saw this stock around the airport, I had never seen any on the runway, mainly because there was nothing to eat there. I frequently came back to the airport to refuel and rearm. I landed uneventfully and even had a piece of watermelon brought to me by this very nice woman who would nearly always show up within a couple of minutes after I landed. This airfield had but a single ramshackle hut and I never spotted a structure where I figured that she could make it to the parking area that fast. I quickly fueled, rearmed, gulped my watermelon, and jumped into the aircraft. I started up and headed for the end of the runway, all the while checking for kids, dogs, water buffalo, or anything that could interfere with my takeoff. It was hot and humid and the airplane was heavy with fuel and rockets. One last check for anything that was not supposed to be there and I turned onto the runway and pushed up the power. Suddenly out of the corner of my eye I caught sight of a water buffalo calf who had decided to check out the runway. I wasn't terribly worried about this until the mother water buffalo decided it was time to join her calf. At that point I had few options left. I was too fast to abort and stay on the runway and I was not about to risk a crash by steering off the runway to avoid the pair. Clearly I had but one choice and that was to stay on the runway, continue my takeoff and hope that I could either take off over the buffalo or go between them. As it turned out there was enough room between the tail of the calf and the nose of the cow to allow for the prop arc. However, the left strut of the O-1 bumped the hind quarter of the calf and the right strut contacted the nose of the cow and I was still flying. Not only was I particularly pleased that I had avoided a serious collision, but I am sure that both the cow and calf were also pleased. I had lived to fight another day. Imagine the Air Force casualty officer explaining to my mother that I had been lost in a collision with a water buffalo.

A Young Lieutenant and Not Much Supervision

As the years have progressed since my time in Laos I have read many accounts about the U.S. involvement in Laos and the rest of Southeast Asia. What emerges is a picture of a conflict that was incompetently micromanaged from Washington and in many cases from the desk of the President of the United States. What stands out to me is how the Raven program was allowed to exist and how little direct supervision I had as a young junior Air Force pilot in this environment.

According to Richard H Shultz writing in his definitive book *The Secret War Against Hanoi*, the vast majority of the U.S. role in Laos was directly controlled by the U.S. ambassador to Laos. Ambassador William Sullivan was on Averell Harriman's staff during the negotiation of the Geneva Accords of 1962 and thus knew the situation and all of its players. When Sullivan became ambassador in 1964, he chose to use the CIA and covert elements of the Air Force (including the Ravens) to the exclusion of the U.S. Army operating through Military Assistance Command Vietnam Studies and Observations Group (MACV-SOG). It was only much later in the war that SOG was allowed onto southern portions of the Ho Chi Minh Trail in Laos, and essentially only in an intelligence-gathering role. This is reported to be in large measure because of the U.S. fears of being seen to violate the Geneva Accords of 1962 pledging Laos to be neutral, and not wanting to offend China and risk China entering the war as it did in Korea in 1951. This perceptual need to appear neutral was being balanced against the potential loss of Laos to the Communist threat and the danger of allowing the North Vietnamese the use of Laotian territory to operate the Ho Chi Minh Trail to infiltrate men and arms into South Viet Nam.

In this case, Sullivan clearly protected the Ravens from 7/13 Air Force to get them what they needed to carry out their mission and to cause minimum interference from the Air Force. It absolutely drove the higher Air Force commanders crazy that a group of young pilots could decide on their own where the air strikes would be placed in their area in Laos. In order to be effective, this ordnance could not be allocated to one specific target three weeks ahead of time and missions shared up and down the chain of command with each level having a chance to further interfere with the mission. Sullivan liked the fact that the Ravens could put the ordnance on the spot that it was needed when it was needed instead of hoping that an enemy force would stay in the same place on a road for three weeks while the entire Air Force could decide exactly where the air was going to go and exactly how it was going to get there.

When I arrived, Ambassador Sullivan had been replaced by Ambassador Godley, who pretty much operated in the same manner. While I never really spoke with Ambassador Godley, he was well regarded by the Ravens and I was never aware that he interfered with the Raven program in any way. We felt that he would likely not interfere with us as long as we were in Laos and operating in a reasonable manner.

Sidebar for Godley

However, it should be noted that Ambassador Godley and Henry Kissinger may share considerable blame for their haste to declare that all U.S. POWs were indeed out of Laos in March of 1973. It appears that up to 60 U.S. POWs may have never even been negotiated for in America's haste to leave Southeast Asia. An excellent source for this information is Roger Hall, who wrote the "POW/MIA FOIA Litigation Account." This item may be found at www.powfoia.org/laos.htm.

Theatre of the Absurd

The war itself can hardly be considered rational or well-ordered during my time in the Ravens. It led me to a number of situations which I could only label as "The Theatre of the Absurd." There were times when these events became distracting, annoying, and sometimes humorous. It was not infrequently that I was sure that Joseph Heller's book *Catch 22* was the script. Even though *Catch 22* was supposed to be a spoof, I remain convinced that given enough time I could have identified nearly every event in the book with an actual equivalent event in Laos.

One of the first absurdities that struck me was due to the shared power in the Lao government. Each faction had their own compound and quarters in Vientiane. So if you didn't see any bad guys during the day you could always go back to your base at Vientiane and see Pathet Lao and North Vietnamese soldiers at night. You could also see the Red Chinese at their embassy as well as Aeroflot (the airline of the USSR) airliners at the same airport that you flew out of with rockets on your O-1.

I also need to mention that most of the time the war in Laos was conducted at a pretty relaxed pace, as was witnessed by all the sides taking Sundays off. I suppose that after you have fought for many years there is just something comforting about taking one day a week off.

Then there was the Laotian army draft in which I was nearly an unwilling player. I was returning from dinner one night when I was stopped by a Lao soldier on the street who pointed an M-16 at my chest and motioned for me to follow him. Since I doubted if he spoke English, I was somewhat uncertain how to convince him that we were both on the same side and that I really did not wish to be drafted into the Lao army. Eventually, I managed to slip my embassy card out of my pocket and show it to him. He immediately began apologizing in Lao and showing huge signs of embarrassment. This happened at a time when the Lao army was very short of soldiers and were even finding bar girls and other women of the night to draft into the medical corps.

Our living quarters in Vientiane were very nice by war-zone standards. I shared a two-bedroom French Colonial house (and a Jeep) with the other Military Region V FAC. We also had a local that lived on site with her two children and took care of the house and our laundry. As we traveled to and from our house each day, we had the opportunity to drive past this amazing monument which was built out of concrete and was huge and very tall. Shortly after arriving in Laos, I asked another FAC what the story on the monument was. It seems that this monument was dubbed by the Americans as the "vertical runway." Several years earlier, the U.S. had given the Lao government sufficient funds to build a significant military runway. For a number of years the runway did not get built and the embassy was always asking when the runway was to be finished. Several years later, a Lao government official took the appropriate U.S. Embassy officer to an elaborate new shrine in Vientiane and showed him the new vertical runway that the U.S. funds had built.

When I was first learning the military region that I was assigned to, I was encouraged to fly around my area and familiarize myself with its airfields and those military commanders who I might likely be working with. Fortunately, I had a Lao "backseater" who was a Lao army officer who was familiar with the area, provided coordination with the forces on the ground, and provided authority for conducting air strikes. He was with me to make the introductions and to translate if necessary. One day we landed at this small remote airstrip. It was far from anything and was hacked out of the jungle. Next to the airstrip was a heavily fortified jungle military camp which looked like it could have been a movie set for a John Wayne Green Beret movie. It had all the classic features of such a camp including bunkers, gun emplacements, sandbags, and punji stakes. We were introduced to the camp commander, who invited us into a small general-purpose building on the high ground of the camp. We were shown to seats of bamboo at a modest bamboo table. We talked for a bit and then were asked if we wanted a Pepsi. Sure, we would both like a Pepsi. Something was said in Lao followed shortly by us hearing a refrigerator door open and each of us was presented with a cold Pepsi. Really? In the middle of a long jungle war someone had gone to all the work to drag a refrigerator and generator to this remote jungle site so that they could have cold Pepsis? Really? Really absurd!

I will write about the rules of engagement (ROE) later in this chapter, I do want to point out one particularly absurd bit about ROE. I was just amazed to learn one day that not only were there benefits to living in Vientiane with all the bad guys, but there were also some definite downsides. It seems that the U.S. Embassy in Vientiane received a complaint from the Red Chinese Embassy (which was also in Vientiane), which was passed on from the North Vietnamese. The North Vietnamese were complaining that the Ravens were violating U.S. ROE standards. The complaint was passed on via the Red Chinese because they had diplomatic relations with the U.S. and the North Vietnamese did not. Really? Really absurd!

Without a doubt the top player in my Theatre of the Absurd was that toward the end of my tour at one location I was the only one on the same side at the end of the week. Every day that I flew in

Laos my day always started with my briefing at the U.S. Embassy with the air attaché and his staff. For several days the attaché had shown great concern that a certain strategic location was in danger of being overrun. Every day I would take note and make it my first order of business to fly up to this site and offer air support. Every day the forward air guide on the radio would assure me that all was quiet around his location and to please go away. After about a week of this, I showed up at my morning briefing to be met by a very agitated air attaché. He indicated the site had been overrun and that it was considered to be lost to "our side." I launched posthaste and, with some difficulty getting around some weather, finally made it to the site. The site appeared to be abandoned and all of the buildings were burned down.

Within the next week, I was to find out some amazing facts. First, the soldiers holding the fort had an agreement with the forces outside the fences that, if the forces inside the camp did not shoot at the forces outside the camp, the forces outside the camp would not attack the camp. At some point the forces outside the camp saw fit to renege on that agreement and attacked the camp. They made sufficient noise coming into the front gate of the camp that the soldiers in the camp were able to wake up and retreat out the back gate. There were no losses to either side except for a couple of soldiers who missed their wake-up call and had buildings burn down on them. Okay, so now the camp is in the hands of the Pathet Lao and the Neutralist forces are long gone out the back gate. But wait—there is more! It seems that the Pathet Lao forces that took the camp were actually Neutralist forces which had been previously captured and were looking for a way to rally back to the Neutralists. Within a day or two the folks holding the camp decided to rally back to the Neutralists and thus the Neutralists got the site back. And what about the folks that had previously been holding the site for the Neutralists? It was reported that they had rallied back to the Pathet Lao from which they had been captured a couple of years earlier.

Wow! This whole thing was really bending my mind. Both groups had switched sides and I was the only one left on the same side at the end of the week. This was just too much for me. By this time my replacement had arrived and been checked out, and the rainy season was on and would prevent any significant air operations for the next 60 days. I had been in Southeast Asia for over 20 months and I had really lost my ambition to pursue this absolutely absurd effort. It was really, really time to go home.

Rules of Engagement

For me the rules of engagement that I had to operate under in my area were never a significant burden in getting my job done. I knew that many of my fellow Ravens chafed under some ROE rules, but for me, by the time that I got there the rules had been modified to the point that ROE wasn't an issue. What I do say is that, particularly as a Raven, I would have not thought twice about violating ROE if it was essential to protecting my clients. If indeed the military is to be an element of national policy to achieve specific goals, we do have to understand just what we can and can't do to achieve those goals.

Stupid Raven Tricks

While I was in the Ravens I did a number of things that, looking back, I really wonder why I did. This brings up a whole topic that I have discussed with a number of other Ravens, and I can only wonder why my actions were so tame as compared to some of the other Ravens. For my entire time as a pilot I have occasionally looked with disbelief at the actions of fellow pilots and wondered "why did he do that?" As a disclaimer I have to say that it is really necessary to get all the facts straight before one even starts to examine the actions of other pilots and how they may have done some really irrational things. I believe that these types of actions should be broken down into a number of categories.

First there is the issue of Really Bad Judgment. This can perhaps fall under the category of "you did what?" I see bad judgment as operating way outside the norm, e.g., using the FAC airplane as a fighter, putting yourself at great risk because your guys are losing, and you are out of options, etc.

Events caused by fatigue also can fall into the bad judgment category. It was well known that when Ravens had clients that were in severe danger of being overrun, the Ravens were there for them and flight-time restrictions were simply disregarded. It was commonly accepted that some individual Ravens may have flown over 150 hours in a couple of weeks. While this may not sound like many hours, it is probably twice the number of hours that can be flown safely. You are likely to be on duty two to four times the amount of time that you are flying by the time that you have completed your duties. Frequently you didn't even have time to go to the bathroom or eat. The entire effort frequently produced a cumulative fatigue that at times clearly interfered with the pilot's performance and judgment.

At times we were just overwhelmed by too many events in too little time. The one thing that a FAC really needed to be able to do was to multitask and deal with multiple sources of information all coming at you at once. This was while you maintained situational awareness and flew the airplane. Four radios talking continuously, folks shooting at you, troops in contact on the ground, and trying to keep your fighters from running into you or dropping on your friendlies was at times an overwhelming task. One's sensory system can get overloaded and inputs may get screened out. For communication to take place not only must the message be sent, it must also be received and understood by the recipient.

Failing to follow some safety procedures was clearly one of our occasional serious shortcomings. One aspect of a lower level of supervision is that you only deal with what you perceive to be the most pressing of problems and let the less-important items take care of themselves. Two specific events are great examples of this situation. As time goes by and you see little need to continue to follow certain safety practices (or perhaps it's just because you can) the reasons for these practices may again become apparent.

During the time that I was in Vientiane an O-1 pilot picked up his airplane in the morning only to notice that there were no safety pins installed in the eight rocket tubes holding his white phosphorus marking rockets. Thinking that this would save him time getting airborne, the pilot simply chose to disregard their absence, even though it was long-established Air Force practice to have these safety pins installed while on the ground. When the pilot turned on the battery switch to do the preflight inspection all eight rockets promptly launched themselves across the Mekong River into a rice paddy in Thailand. Fortunately, no one was hurt but it certainly got the attention of the controllers in the tower. Okay, maybe we should be more careful and maybe those safety rules do have practical merit.

You Have Mail

Another example of safety lapses was a Raven who had flown a FAC mission and recovered into a Thai base where USAF fighters were also stationed. I have to admit that I do not have first-hand knowledge of this event, so names and geographic references are left out to protect what I perceive to be the guilty. It is required at those launch and recovery bases where aircraft carry droppable ordnance to have an arm/disarm area at the end of each runway. It is here where safety pins are installed or removed to prevent dropping ordnance on the taxiways. It is also where bomb fuses can be armed and disarmed prior to takeoff or after landing. This is a more than reasonable practice and has undoubtedly saved many lives over the years.

The Raven in question landed long, turned off at the end of the runway, and taxied past the disarm area. His excuse was that the disarm area was full so he taxied to transient parking without installing any safety pins. The Raven parked the airplane and headed for the post office. When he got back with the mail he noticed there was a crowd of vehicles and personnel around his O-1. They were all pointing to the single 2.75 inch rocket still in the tube without the proper safety pin. Being the practical person that he was, being familiar with building up this ordnance as we all were, and not wanting to be further delayed, he simply took out his nail clippers, used them to open the safety clip and slipped the rocket out of the tube. He then unscrewed the warhead off of the rocket motor and placed both of them in the back seat and headed for the Base Exchange. The Raven might have been in a limited amount of trouble with his first two breaches of safety rules but his final actions were sufficient to make the Air Force really crazy. I never heard the outcome and we all got a lot of laughs from the story, but it truly has to go down as a "stupid Raven trick."

Flying Acrobatics on Maintenance Test Flights

When I initially flew these flights, the idea of doing some acrobatics after the test card was complete never came into my thoughts. However, once I was shown this it seemed a bit unusual and then I found that it made a lot of sense. Occasionally, I found items that otherwise might have been missed. This could have caused a problem on operational flights had they not been found and corrected at the end of the test flight. This included items such as foreign objects in the cockpit and improper rigging of flight controls.

T-28 Caper

I checked in at the airport one morning to find that I could most likely not reach my normal areas of operation due to low clouds and rain. I was then asked to take an O-1 to Udorn for maintenance and return in the back seat of a Lao T-28. Sure! I got into the O-1 with the Lao T-28 pilot who was to bring the T-28 back to Vientiane and off we went to Udorn. Once we arrived, I delivered the O-1 and the Lao pilot signed for the T-28. We walked out to the T-28 and the Lao pilot asked me if I wanted to fly the front seat of the T-28 back to Vientiane. I replied that he might have to help me a bit since I did not have a checklist with me. I wasn't going to turn down the opportunity to fly the airplane.

At the T-28, we did a walk-around inspection and climbed in with me in the front seat and the Lao pilot in the back seat. Since I was familiar with starting big radial engines, I fired the engine up and taxied out without a hitch. I did an engine run up and checked to make sure the airplane was in the proper configuration. I asked the Lao pilot if he agreed that we were ready to fly. He agreed and we got tower clearance and off we went to Vientiane. I really had a nice landing in Vientiane and taxied into the T-28 parking area, parked, and shut down. As I was walking back to operations, the Lao pilot complemented me on my landing, told me that I was a "number one T-28 pilot," and asked how many times I had flown the T-28. I held up one finger and had a huge grin on my face. He also grinned and exclaimed "you get me put in monkey house." We both laughed and that was my entire career as a T-28 pilot.

It was also an opportunity to blow off some steam, which was something that all of us really needed to do given the pressures that we were working under. It was one of the small rewards that we took for ourselves because we were in the program, we were frequently hanging out in the danger zone, and just because we could. For me, after my one day as a T-28 pilot and a couple of other lesser events I slid back into my comfort zone and refrained from any more of this type behavior.

The bottom line is that while there was some of this type of behavior, proportionately there was very little of this behavior. In a situation where we had little direct supervision other than peer pressure, we soon learned that we needed to observe the important practical rules and norms if we were going to be around for the next day's missions and eventually go home.

Air America

I can't write about my time as a Raven without writing about Air America. Air America was a CIA peripheral company that provided air services for the U.S. government during the Southeast Asian conflict. Air America's principal customers were USAID and the CIA. They also provided our maintenance at Vientiane and did an excellent job.

While I was in the combat zone, I had nothing but admiration for Air America and its employees. They were a most professional group who did everything asked of them and more in their support of U.S. policy. In fact, I believe that they were much more effective than utilizing uniformed military personnel. The Air America folks wanted to be there, and they had much longer contracts so they brought important experience and did not require frequent extensive training to know their jobs. It seemed as if there was a constant stream of military personnel who came for six months or a year and were always just arriving or were just about to rotate. In addition, Air America could and did pose as just another American company providing contract services, which gave them cover. This simply was more efficient and effective.

There was another reason why the Ravens respected, admired, and appreciated Air America. We knew and history showed that if a Raven got shot down or ended up on the ground in hostile territory the one and only source of immediate rescue was Air America. Air America was usually working within a short distance of where the Ravens were working so they could be on scene very rapidly.

There were many Air America aircrews who were lost while carrying out their assignments. The best evidence of this is to look on the Ravens website, http://www.ravens.org/, under Air America aircraft. When one starts reading the individual history of each of the Air America aircraft you can only begin to understand the terrible losses the Air America folks sustained.

Another excellent source of information about Air America is the book *Air America* by Christopher Robbins. Unfortunately, this book was the basis of a Mel Gibson movie about Air America which was absolutely abhorrent to everyone who had ever known the real Air America. In a subsequent discussion with Chris Robbins he expressed his sincere apologies about how Hollywood had used his book to discredit the integrity and accomplishments of this fine group.

I was also appalled in some cases by how the senior military commanders treated the Air America flight crews. While there was not usually much direct contact between the uniformed military and Air America there were notable exceptions. I witnessed a very loud and raucous celebration at Nakhon Phanom (NKP), Thailand where an Air America helicopter crew had rescued a downed A-1 Skyraider pilot from certain capture in a very unfriendly Lao village. The Air America crew flew the downed airman to NKP. They were also invited to the officers club to celebrate. The party was really going good when Col. William Morris, the vice wing commander of the 56th Special Operations Wing based at NKP, entered the room, spotted the Air America helicopter crew, and promptly threw them out of the club because their civilian haircuts did meet the standard for Air Force personnel.

Christopher Robbins wrote in his book *Air America: the Story Of The CIA's Secret Airlines* (pg. 293) that during the evacuation of Saigon, Air America helicopter crews picked up the last evacuees and delivered them to carriers offshore. Once onboard the carriers with no place to go, the U.S. Marine Guards went out of their way to hassle the Air America Pilots and to treat them very poorly on the ship. I can only say how appalled that I have been ever since for these stupid actions by stupid people.

Returning Home

Returning to the United States and readjusting was a very difficult experience. I was pretty worn out physically and emotionally after twenty one months of combat and 900 hours of combat flying when I left Laos and Thailand. One of the few real perks of being a Raven was that you were supposed to receive preference in your next assignment. By this time, I knew that this preference had not been honored. I was headed back to the C-123 as an instructor pilot even though I was no longer qualified in the airplane. I felt that all my efforts and sacrifices had been ignored by the pencil pushers. At least I was going to be with friends that I had known from previous C-123 flying.

My pay situation was a disaster and no one was interested in resolving it. I had not been paid for the previous six months. I was getting by on my Temporary Duty Pay and my savings account. Since I had friends in Denver where the AF Pay Center also was located, I routed myself through there on my way to my next duty assignment. In Denver, as I entered a very large open room of desks I inquired at each desk as to who in the room was assigned to manage my pay records. I was finally directed to an E-9 at the head of the room. I asked him if he took care of my pay records and he responded "Yes Sir, I Do." At that time, I inquired in a loud booming voice that could be heard from one end of the room to the other, "Then I want to know why I haven't been paid for six months." Needless to say it was like a bomb had gone off in the place. It was just so sweet taking out six months of frustration about my pay mismanagement on someone who was actually responsible for the problem. It was also a symbolic blow for everyone who has ever been treated poorly by the military pay system. I later found out that I had got the E-9's attention to the point that he overpaid me by eight thousand dollars.

To get to my next duty assignment in Louisiana it was necessary to fly through San Antonio and Houston. How convenient! It gave me a chance to visit the AF Military Personnel Assignment Center at Randolph AFB. I went to the pilot section for assignments and actually found a squadron mate from my Ranch Hand days working there. I outlined my disappointment to him and he agreed that I had really been screwed. Unfortunately, there was nothing meaningful that he could do. Okay, that was it. The absolute final straw. I had made my decision to get out of the Air Force!

I was now off to Houston to connect to Texas International Airlines to Alexandria and my new duty station. I thought that something might be up when seat assignments were not being given out and it looked like there must be about 70 passengers for a 50-passenger Convair. They soon started giving out seats and allowing passengers with seats to board. When they had about 20 passengers remaining they announced that the flight was full and the airplane left. I noticed that a man in a suit was looking over the shoulders of all the remaining passengers to see their tickets. I started following him and noticed that all those remaining had reserved seats on the flight and all were enlisted military. The gate agent then made an announcement that the flight was full and that perhaps the passengers could contact Delta Airlines to see if Delta might have a seat. I then confronted the man in the suit and asked him if he worked for Texas International. He indicated that he did as station manager. I asked him why the flight was so oversold and why the military passengers had not been accommodated when they all had guaranteed reservations. I could just see the air drain out of him. He knew he was caught and he agreed to vouchers for food and motels and reservations on the first morning flight. Welcome home—it was just another example of the shabby treatment that so many of us received when we got home and were wearing a uniform.

When I arrived in Alexandria the next morning, Texas International had lost my bag with all of my uniforms. I did have a flight suit in a small carry-on bag. It was early on a Saturday morning and I wanted to sign into my new squadron to get off of leave. I decided to just put my flight suit on and go sign in. Bad idea! As I approached the squadron I was met by a lieutenant colonel (he turned out to be the squadron commander) who was departing the squadron headquarters. I saluted him which he did not return. I introduced myself and indicated that I was inbound to the squadron. He then proceeded to inspect me from top to bottom, stick his finger in my face and inform me that if I was going to be in "his squadron" that "you get rid of that black (camouflaged) rank and zip up that flight suit!" I was just dumbfounded at his boorish behavior. We got along almost that well for the remainder of the time that I was in the squadron. Welcome home! Thank you for your service as a Raven!

The next few days were busy as I was meeting new members of the squadron and catching up with friends that I had previously known from C-123s, pilot training, and Southeast Asia. I was soon informed by the squadron executive officer that I was not to be allowed to fly until I had completed all of my recurrent training items. This included many items that had been waived because of my extended stay in the combat zone. Welcome home! We are here to help you! It soon became obvious that I was not going to get any help getting this training done and it might be weeks before I could fly. I decided to take the direct approach with this absolute loser lieutenant-colonel-navigator-executive Officer who was last promoted in 1944 (this was now 1971). NOTE: My editor thinks that I should not use the previous sentence. I gave him a list of other training requirements that I also needed and highlighted many that could not be accomplished until others had been completed. I also pointed out the regulations which indicated the squadron would need waivers on certain items until they could get me into compliance. In less than a day I tied him in such a giant ball of red tape for which he was responsible that he never bothered me again. Okay-now maybe I will get to start flying again.

No, it was not to be. Just before the time that I was to start my checkout as an instructor, a by name request came down for me from TAC (Tactical Air Command) Headquarters to report to a classified, armed, single engine turboprop evaluation program. Great! Now I can start flying again in a fun program! At this point my friendly squadron commander jumped into the fray and blocked my assignment on the basis that I was considered essential to the training squadron. Really? I wasn't even qualified or current! This process repeated itself three more times and I was really getting upset. I wasn't getting to fly and saw no quick way out of the situation. I was getting hassled to move back on base and I really did not like Louisiana. Okay, time for decisive action! Desperate times required desperate measures. I went back to personnel and volunteered to go back to South East Asia and sent for an application to work for Air America. I knew that this would get me out of my remaining two year Air Force commitment and get me enough flying time to qualify for an airline job. Off goes my resume to Air America and three days later I had an Air America employment application in hand. I happened to be in the squadron building working on my Air America Application when the Ops Officer Lt. Colonel John Silva asked me to come into his office. He closed the door, sat down in his chair, and indicated that he had heard that I had volunteered to go back to SEA and was going to apply to fly for Air America. I said that I had because I was at a dead end in this squadron. I had been blocked by the squadron commander four separate times from going to the evaluation program and that I was not being allowed to fly at the training squadron because I might be going to the evaluation program. Lt. Colonel Silva then did the decent thing and indicated that my instructor checkout would commence the next day. I checked out as an instructor and withdrew my Air America Application.

I flew students for the next few months and with the exception of our universally despised squadron commander life was again pretty decent. In the spring of 1971, the Air Force was involved in a Reduction in Force to adjust to the end of US participation in South East Asia. Many of us were offered the opportunity to separate early if we were willing to sign up for the AF Reserve. By this time we were aware that our training squadron was closing and the airplanes were headed to Lockborne AFB and Pittsburgh. The choice that I was offered was to go to one of these reserve units and to get a year knocked off of my remaining active duty commitment. I jumped at the offer without hesitation and applied for the program. Very shortly after turning in my paperwork, I was summoned into my squadron commander's office. I saluted which he did not return. He left me standing even though he was seated. He informed me that in his left hand he had my regular commission. In his right hand he had my request for the early out. He indicated that he thought I should take the regular commission because "I do not think that you can make it on the outside."

I never missed a beat! I replied that I would take the early out and "Sir, with all due respect, please throw me in that Briar Patch." I saluted and left. As I departed, the world's most incompetent Lt. Colonel Executive Officer asked me what the squadron commander had said. I indicated that he offered me an early out or a regular commission. He then asked me what my choice was. I said that I had told the Colonel that "I was going to get out and get a job sucking c… and get my self-respect back." That was a short conversation. Welcome Home! Thank You For Your Service!

It was more than shameful that The Air Force as a whole could just care less about their member's combat service or being of any assistance in helping them readjust when we came home. In many cases those support offices on base and higher levels were openly antagonistic toward those of that came home from combat. The only help came from the personal relationships that we had built during our service. Help did not start at the squadron level until we got into the flight ops portion of the squadron.

The Continuing Need for a FAC

Do we still need the trusty FAC? It appears that the "big" Air Force thinks not. The idea is routinely dismissed by planners as being so "Last War" and a thing of the past. I believe that even in the current drone era there is still a need for a FAC in those areas where the threat level is low enough to allow a reasonable chance of survival. Drones can now observe battle fields half way around the world and carry out air strikes without any friendly forces being present. The fact that these drones can be placed so far away from a human with eyesight and a brain shows that they are not a complete solution by themselves. I am led to this position not out of nostalgia but out of the current situation in Afghanistan and previously in Iraq. One only has to look at the number of friendly fire incidents where wedding parties and other friendlies get shot up to conclude that a FAC who knew his area would have known that these folks were not legitimate targets. It is possible that with a modern nearly silent aircraft FACs could operate at night with little chance of detection from the ground from less sophisticated opposition. A FAC that is regularly working an area quickly comes to know what is routine and what is not. He knows who belongs there and who does not.

My perception of most of the drone surveillance is that you do not have a continuous full time 360 degree view of what is happening. The drone sensor may be aimed in such a way that it does not see the bad guys emerging from hiding as the drone passes by or many of the subtle changes that a drone camera may miss and that a human eye and brain would think to be significant. How does a drone coordinate with the local militia and intelligence sources when the drone operator is thousands of miles away?

The Legacy of the Raven Program and Why the Concept Should Still Be Used

I believe that the Raven program will long be recognized as an effective and efficient method to achieve a military objective in a minimum of expense and time. The program was effective because the FACs were on scene where they could gather the current information and use this information to protect their clients. They did not have to make a request to Washington and wait three weeks for an airstrike to be planned. It could be done in real time while the threat was still present. When the stated objective is to neutralize a single soldier riding down the road on a water buffalo or a motor bike, it is hardly effective or efficient to coordinate such attacks all the way to Washington through every level of the military, the State Department and to the President. Command should be on the lowest level possible where the operators have all the facts as well as a complete understanding of the objectives. Possibly the most glaring example of this was President Johnson's boast about no one being able to blow up even an outhouse without his permission. It seems that the US Military has always had a difficult time understanding the concept of letting the individual operator or his small group made the important tactical decision on the spot where he has the information to make this correct choice. A recent example of this was told to be by my nephew, who was a Navy Pilot flying FA-18s flying into Iraq. He indicated that during an entire six month tour he never dropped any ordinance the whole time he was there because every strike had to be approved by higher levels of command in Doha or Tampa. This command always took twenty five to forty minutes to approve the strike request. By the time the strike was approved the individuals planting the IEDs had and long since departed. Instead, the pilots had to land on the carrier with their laser guided bombs still attached.

The Ravens were truly an outstanding group of individuals who understood the situation, were given the authority and the resources, and did a near impossible task. It should be noted that the Ravens were able to protect their clients until they were withdrawn under the Paris Accords of 1973. I will forever be proud to have been associated with them.

Epilogue

Raven 49 Craig Morrison, Hmong diaspora at Long Tieng, 1970 (William E. Platt Collection)

I feel I speak for all the Ravens in expressing my deep admiration and respect for the Hmong people and the difficult struggle they endured during and after this war.

Raven 41/49 Jim Lemon

The Ravens were truly an outstanding group of individuals who understood the situation, were given the authority and the resources, and did a near impossible task. I will forever be proud to have been associated with them.

Raven 52/53 Tom Young

Abbreviations

AAA	Anti-Aircraft Artillery
ABCCC	Airborne Battlefield Command and Control Center
AIRA	U.S. Air Force Attaché
AO, AOR	Area of Operations or Area of Operational Responsibility
ARMA	U.S. Army Attaché
AWOL	Absent Without Leave
BDA	Bomb Damage Assessment
CAS	Close Air Support
CAS	Controlled American Source (CIA)
CASI	Continental Air Service, Inc.
CIA	Central Intelligence Agency
CONEX	Shipping Container
DASC	Direct Air Support Center
DEPCHIEF	Deputy Chief. Joint U.S. Military Assistance Advisory Group, Thailand
DEROS	Date of Return from Overseas
DME	Distance Measuring Equipment
FAC	Forward Air Controller
FAG	Forward Air Guide
FAN	Lao Neutralist Armed Forces
FAR	Royal Armed Forces
FM	Frequency Modulation
FRAG	Fragmentary
G's	Gravity Forces
HQ	Headquarters
ICC	International Control Commission
IP	Instructor Pilot
JPAC	Joint POW/MIA Accounting Command
JSOC	Joint Special Operations Command
JUSMAG	Joint U.S. Military Advisory Group
KBA	Killed by Air
LPF	Lao Patriotic Front
LPLA	Lao People's Liberation Army
LRRP	Long Range Reconaissance Patrol
MACV	Military Assistance Command - Vietnam
MAP	Military Assistance Program
MIA	Missing in Action
MR	Geographical Military Region of Laos
NCO	Non-commissioned Officer

NFSF, SF	Shorthand BDA: Nothing Further, Smoke and Foliage. Shortened to Smoke and Foliage
NKP	Nakhon Phanom Royal Thai Air Base
NVA	North Vietnamese Army
NVR	No Visual Results
OSC	On Scene Commander
PARU	Police Aerial Reinforcement Units
PDJ	Plain of Jars
PEO	Program Evaluations Office
PL	Pathet Lao. Communist insurgents operating in Laos
POL	Petroleum, Oil and Lubricants (target category)
PTSD	Post Traunatic Stress Disorder
REMF	Rear Echelon Mother F…..
RLA, RLAF	Royal Lao Army, Royal Lao Air Force
RLG	Royal Lao Government
RO	Requirements Office
RPM	Revolutions per Minute
RTA, RTAF	Royal Thai Army, Royal Thai Air force
RTG	Royal Thai Government
SAC	Strategic Air Command
SEA	South East Asia
SGU	Special Guerrilla Unit
SKY	CIA
SOG	Studies and Observation Group
SOW	Special Operations Wing
STOL	Short Takeoff and Landing
TACAN	Tactical Air Navigation
Tango	Shorthand for T-28
TASGp	Tactical Air Support Group
TASS	Tactical Air Support Squadron
TIC	Troops in Contact
UHF	Ultra-High Frequency
UPT	USAF Undergraduate Pilot Training
USAID	United States Agency of International Development
UTM	Universal Transverse Mercator map coordinates
VHF	Very high Frequency
VP	Major General Vang Pao
VR	Visual Reconnaissance
WP	White Phospherous
WTFO	What the F…, Over?

About the Editors

At the Table of Knowledge 2014 Raven Reunion

John Fuller retired from the Air Force in 1993, as a Command Pilot and Colonel. After return from SEA he was a T-37 instructor at Williams AFB, and later flew several models of the C-130, including the AC-130H from Hurlburt Field, FL. He is a "plank holder" in the Joint Special Operations Command, serving there from 1983 to 1986, as J3 Air Operations, and later helped stand up the Air Force Special Operations Command at Hurlburt Field. His last assignment in the Air Force was at Wright Patterson AFB, Ohio as Director of Big Safari, supporting multiple classified aircraft programs. After retirement, he worked as a Program Director for Link Simulation and Training, L3 Communications, and later formed Night Readiness LLC, which produces night vision goggle training systems for military, civilian and foreign customers.

He is currently retired in Mesa, AZ, splitting his time between the Arizona high country, family life with dogs, and volunteering in the Phoenix Veterans Court, the largest such court in the country. He is state coordinator for volunteer mentors supporting veterans in the court system.

Helen Murphy is the founder and director of the T-28 Trojan Foundation which promotes the North American T-28 aircraft as living history. She has compiled her extensive worldwide research of the T-28 into a website, t28trojanfoundation.com, as a central public reference. While researching its warbird status in the SE Asia conflict, she came to know the Ravens who flew the T-28 during their covert operations in Laos. She is honored and humbled to help publish this unique collection, believing "Raven stories are best told by the Ravens themselves." This is her second Raven publication, having recently assisted Craig Duehring publish his memoir, "The Lair of Raven." Helen works for a major airline and holds CFI-II, MEL & ATP ratings. She has served as one of the founding board members of the Arizona Pilots Association and has received state recognition for her efforts in promoting general aviation in Arizona.

Made in the USA
Lexington, KY
17 June 2016

52980833R00257